DR. PITCAIRN'S
COMPLETE GUIDE TO
NATURAL HEALTH
FOR DOGS & CATS

D1260120

SF
427
.P63
2017

DR. PITCAIRN'S
COMPLETE GUIDE TO
NATURAL HEALTH
FOR DOGS & CATS

RICHARD H. PITCAIRN, DVM, PhD
AND SUSAN HUBBLE PITCAIRN

RODALE.

Kalamazoo Valley
Community College Libraries
Kalamazoo, MI 49003-4070

WITHDRAWN

MAY 2 6 2017

RODALE
wellness

Live happy. Be healthy. Get inspired.

Sign up today to get exclusive access to our authors,
exclusive bonuses, and the most authoritative, useful, and cutting-edge information
on health, wellness, fitness, and living your life to the fullest.

Visit us online at RodaleWellness.com
Join us at RodaleWellness.com/Join

Mention of specific companies, organizations, or authorities in this book does not imply endorsement by the author or publisher, nor does mention of specific companies, organizations, or authorities imply that they endorse this book, its author, or the publisher.

Internet addresses and telephone numbers given in this book were accurate at the time it went to press.

This is fourth revised edition published by Rodale Inc. First published in 1982 by Rodale Inc.

© 1982, 1995, 2005, 2017 by Richard H. Pitcairn and Susan H. Pitcairn

All rights reserved. No part of this publication may be reproduced or transmitted in any form or by any means, electronic or mechanical, including photocopying, recording, or any other information storage and retrieval system, without the written permission of the publisher.

Rodale books may be purchased for business or promotional use or for special sales. For information, please write to: Special Markets Department, Rodale Inc., 733 Third Avenue, New York, NY 10017

Printed in the United States of America

Rodale Inc. makes every effort to use acid-free ∞, recycled paper ♻.

Illustrations by Susan H. Pitcairn, with appreciation to the following people who supplied their photos as chapter opening illustration references: James Peden (Chapters 2, 9, 13), Marybeth Minter and Jack Scalia (Chapters 15, 18), Colleen Patrick Goudreau (Chapter 4), Phil Brazell (Chapter 14), Samantha Clarke (Chapter 5), Shutterstock: Clari Massimiliano (Chapter 6), Shutterstock: Tompet (Chapter 7), Shutterstock: MyImages-Micha (Chapter 11), Shutterstock: Happy Monkey (Chapter 12), Shutterstock: Fly_Dragonfly (Chapter 16).

Illustrations on the following pages by Lizzie Harper: 311, 312, 462, 465, 467.

Book design by Tara Long

Library of Congress Cataloging-in-Publication Data is on file with the publisher.

ISBN 978–1–62336–755–8 trade paperback
Distributed to the trade by Macmillan

2 4 6 8 10 9 7 5 3 1 trade paperback

RODALE.

Follow us @RodaleBooks on

We inspire health, healing, happiness, and love in the world.
Starting with you.

M-17255 5.1.17 $24.99

We dedicate and offer this to the animals of the earth, who have
given us friendship and companionship, and have in many ways been our teachers.
We journey together. It is our deepest hope that what we contribute here will have
lasting benefit both to those special dogs and cats that are part of our
human family and to the much larger circle of animals with whom
we share this beautiful and precious planet.

We also acknowledge and deeply appreciate the countless teachers,
students, writers, colleagues, clients, editors, friends, family, readers, and
loving supporters who have made all the difference in our lives and our work.
You know who you are and you live in our hearts always.

CONTENTS

A DEEPER LOOK AT "NATURAL" AND "HOLISTIC"

Starting with the first edition of this now-classic book in 1981, we have been fortunate to help pioneer the holistic veterinary movement and its more natural approach to animal care, a full-fledged movement with associations, conferences, journals, websites, books, magazines, and products.

Looking back, we feel blessed to have known so many outstanding, dedicated individuals in this movement, people who truly seek to do their very best for their animals.

Looking ahead into the coming decades, we sense a shift in the wind, one that beckons all who value the natural and holistic approach to expand the scope of our vision to embrace *all* animals, including billions of disappearing wild animals and those suffering daily in hidden factory farms. All urgently need our thoughtful and loving attention. Widening our view still further, we see a very large patient in the waiting room upon whom all others depend: Earth herself.

There is no better group of people to help heal our ailing planet than those who value a natural, holistic approach to living and healing. But to live up to our full potential, it is wise that we reexamine the assumptions beneath our defining ideas: holistic and natural. Such a reexamination is necessary to understand fully all the benefits and reasons for the rather groundbreaking changes to the diets of dogs and cats that we recommend in this edition, changes that we see as exciting and appropriate for all species.

HOLISTIC AND NATURAL—
A DEEPER LOOK

Holistic derives from the word *whole*. In medicine, we have tended to interpret a holistic approach as a *comprehensive* approach, one that skillfully addresses the many factors that impact an individual's health, including diet, exercise, stress, toxins, pathogens, endocrine function, and even unseen energy fields encompassed within, or expressing as, that individual.

Important as these factors are, there is another, more profound meaning to "wholeness." In that view, we recognize a supreme, guiding intelligence that is more than the sum of the parts, an unseen force that both transcends and orchestrates all of life. Physicist David Bohm called this the "implicate order," which brings cohesion not only to the microcosm and the macrocosm but to the immensely complex patterns of evolution and ecosystems that we call life. In its wholeness, it seems to generate solutions and adaptations that are optimal for *all* life as it unfolds, seeking balance and order.

It's important to bear this view of holism in mind. Otherwise, we tend to restrict our understanding of another tenet: the "natural."

While we rightly take our cues from nature in attempting to provide the most "natural" diet, lifestyle, home, and relationships for our companion animals, we too often limit our considerations of what is natural to the patterns of the past, to nature as it *was*.

In so doing, we easily overlook the infinitely creative potential of the holistic intelligence within nature, which has helped all life-forms adapt to changing conditions throughout millions of years, often in relatively rapid evolutionary leaps. Genes can and do change. They have the power to express in entirely different ways, and something else controls that, not just DNA. Unless we see that clearly, some of our arguments for what is "natural" become arguments for the *limits* of nature, animals, and ourselves.

This is a key point in openly considering the groundbreaking recommendations in this edition to feed our pets and ourselves lower on the food chain, for the good of all. Under the banner of the "natural," many readers may acknowledge that a plant-centered diet fits us as primates. But by the same token, many will object that meat is the only proper diet for animals who have evolved as carnivores as recommended by the SARF (Species Appropriate Raw Food) model, which usually means not only muscle meats, but also bones and a variety of organs—as much like prey as possible.

Here is our concern. Without considering that the greater *holistic* intelligence within nature may be seeking solutions appropriate to *all life today,* many of us can easily lock ourselves and our animals into meat-heavy diets that not only harm other animals and the health of our planet, but perhaps our dogs and cats as well. That's because the vast majority of environmental toxins enter our bodies from the fatty tissues of animal products, along with residues of antibiotics, hormones, and herbicides.

Likewise, an overly limited view of nature could cause us to deny reports that many pets have thrived on plant-based diets for decades (see Chapter 5), ignore gene studies that show that dogs adapted to eating grains at the dawn of civilization, and repeat the myth that dogs and cats can't digest grains, even when studies show they can and that the greatest number of pet allergies are actually to meat.

By the same token, would it not be reasonable to ask ourselves if it is "natural" to feed a deep-sea tuna to a cat? To feed a cow to a Chihuahua? To give them plastic toys? To confine, breed, or even feed another species at all?

From one perspective, almost everything about modern life is unnatural. But a wider view is that *everything is natural*, because it all came from nature.

We can quibble about such ideas, but what is *not* subject to question is this: Every form of life as we know it depends utterly upon the health and preservation of our small blue planet's endangered soils, waters, air, climates, forests, and oceans. And in the last 60 years (within many of our lifetimes), we humans have destroyed half of Earth's forests, depleted a third of her aquifers, set her on a course toward dangerous climate change, depleted much of her bounty of fossil fuels and minerals, and exhausted most major fisheries. Without question, our chil-

dren will pay a very steep price in the coming decades.

Though all this may seem out of our personal control, the future is in our hands. That's because the chief cause of all this destruction lies not just in decisions made in offices of industry or government, but ultimately in the collective impact of one simple choice we each make daily: our unexamined purchases of meat, eggs, dairy, and seafood, including that fed to our dogs and cats. Animal agriculture, as we will see, is arguably the most destructive industry on the planet.

Nature is really simply the wholeness of life. And life is asking all who are alive today to shift our course of destruction by listening to that holistic consciousness that seeks the good of the whole. Nature is especially asking all who love animals to extend that caring to embrace all animals and all life.

This deeper understanding of nature is not only the true foundation of all natural and holistic healing, it is also a journey to discover our own true nature.

We know you, our readers, to be exceptionally caring human beings, people whose compassion for animals knows few bounds. So we invite you now to join us on a journey of exploration as we all expand our minds, our vision, and our love for the animals by our sides and for all animals everywhere.

Richard H. Pitcairn, DVM, PhD
Susan Hubble Pitcairn, MS

CHAPTER 1

A TINY DOG, A BIG SHIFT

The year was about 1976, long before I became a pioneer of holistic veterinary medicine. Back then, though I was already somewhat disillusioned with standard practice, I nevertheless made my living working in a typical suburban clinic in Oregon.

"Why don't you take care of this one?" my colleague asked me with a slight smile, the unmistakable look of someone about to unload an unwelcome problem. He pointed through the door to a little middle-aged Chihuahua sitting forlornly on the exam table. If Tiny's coat had ever been sleek, soft, and healthy, it no longer was. Obviously, his hair had been falling out for some time, revealing large greasy patches reeking with an unpleasant odor. Even his spirits were low.

Unfortunately, I'd seen cases like his all too often.

Sitting nearby were his equally dejected guardians, an aging couple who had "tried it all." Yet, Elaine and Tom Wilson still cared enough about their little friend to try again. The dog's hospital record showed a long history of treatments—cortisone shots, medicated soaps, ointments, more shots, more salves—none of which had brought any noticeable improvement.

"The poor little guy is just so miserable, doctor," Elaine pleaded. "We would do anything if we thought it would help." She looked helpless, frustrated, sad, and worried, all rolled into one.

I looked at Tiny, peering right into his searching brown eyes, where some mysterious Being dwelt behind all this suffering. I knew that finally the time had come to step off the beaten path. Here was the perfect opportunity to test out a fresh approach that had been brewing in my mind for years. We were clearly at a medical dead end and there was nothing to lose. But more importantly, I knew there was a good chance it would work.

And so it all began. As I carefully examined the little dog, I explained to the Wilsons why I thought the key to his recovery was not the right *drug*, but the right *diet*.

"Skin problems like Tiny's are probably the most common and frustrating of the conditions we try to deal with," I explained. "Because the skin is such a visible area of the body, it can show the first signs of underlying problems, particularly those caused by inadequate diet. The skin grows really rapidly. It makes a whole new crop of cells about

every 3 weeks. That takes a lot of nourishment, so when the diet lacks what's really needed, the skin is one of the first tissues to break down and show abnormalities like the kind we see here in Tiny.

"And you might not believe what's really in pretty much all commercial pet food," I ventured. We continued talking about the importance of nutrition and the toxic aspects of highly processed kibbles and canned foods brewed from unsavory food industry by-products. Soon Elaine and Tom were on board. This focus on diet made total sense to them, and together we marveled that it was not taught in vet school.

So we worked out a suitable feeding program for Tiny based on fresh whole meats, grains, and vegetables, also known as "people food," at least the better versions of it (minus the chips, fries, white bread, cookies, sodas, and ice cream!). In addition, they would offer him several supplements rich in nutrients important to the health of the skin as well as to the rest of the body—brewer's yeast, vegetable oil, cod-liver oil, kelp, bonemeal, vitamin E, and zinc. The Wilsons could hardly wait to begin.

"And it's also good to bathe Tiny occasionally with a mild, nonmedicated natural shampoo," I said, smiling as they scooped up the little dog in preparation to leave. "This will help remove irritating, toxic secretions from his skin without burdening him with harsh chemicals."

During the next weeks, my thoughts often went to Tiny, wondering how he was doing.

A month later, the Wilsons proudly returned to show the results of our treatment.

Tiny was like a new dog, full of life, jumping around excitedly on the examining table. His coat was much healthier, and hair was rapidly filling in the previously bare spots.

"You wouldn't believe the difference!" Elaine exclaimed. "He runs around and plays like he's a puppy again. Thank you so much, Dr. Pitcairn."

Tiny's transformation was very rewarding for all of us, but most of all for him. For the Wilsons, the added benefit was realizing that their dog's health was now in their control, and that keeping him well did not require monthly injections of cortisone or other medications with all their unsavory side effects.

Tiny's case was one of my first clinical attempts to apply the results of a long learning process about the vital role of nutrition in health, something I'd been exploring for years, especially as a researcher and lecturer in a doctoral immunology program at Washington State in the early 1970s.

Countless more such miracles followed, not to mention glowing testimonials from readers of earlier editions of this book and veterinarians I have trained and known through the years. We are indeed what we eat.

Fast-forward to the early 21st century. After decades of witnessing such clinical successes, the importance of nutrition in restoring health has never seemed more important. As we gaze upon the dietary landscape of today, any astute observer will agree: Our food supply has never been so compromised.

And yet, there is hope.

In this fourth edition of *Dr. Pitcairn's Complete Guide to Natural Health for Dogs & Cats*, in continuous print since 1981, my wife and coauthor Susan and I will take you deeper into the journey of food and its connection to health: the health not only of the dog or cat you care for, but also of your family, your friends, future generations, the oceans, the rivers, and wild animals—that is to say, all life on Earth.

Before we embark on a discussion of what's wrong with food today and how to address the issue, allow me to share a little more about how I came to the simple but profound insight about the role of diet in health. Countless health practitioners of every stripe, as well as millions of other people, have reached a similar conclusion, each in his or her own way, some in modern times, some even in ancient history.

> *As we gaze upon the dietary landscape of today, any astute observer will agree: Our food supply has never been so compromised.*

MY STORY

I graduated from a highly rated veterinary school (University of California, Davis) in 1965, eager to heal ailing animals. Yet my official training in the nutrition of dogs and cats had included little more than the admonition: "Tell your clients to feed their animals a good commercial pet food and to avoid table scraps." Beyond that, nutrition just wasn't considered an important part of our education. It was all about drugs and surgery.

In light of the growing awareness of the importance of nutrition today, it seems odd that I or anyone accepted this attitude at face value, and yet we did, assuming our predecessors and teachers knew best. And so, after graduation I confidently set out to conquer disease, armed with the usual arsenal of the latest pharmaceuticals and surgical techniques gleaned from years of schooling.

Soon reality hit. Faced with the day-to-day challenges of my first job in a busy mixed practice in Southern California where we treated cats, dogs, pigs, cattle, horses, and wildlife, I soon learned to my dismay that many diseases simply did not respond to treatments as we'd been told they would.

Try as I might, in fact it often seemed that what I did made very little difference. Mostly, I felt like a bystander at the battle for recovery—doing a lot of cheering and occasionally making a contribution of sorts, but often feeling ineffectual.

But I am a curious guy, often seen with a book tucked under my arm, and I am also endowed with a certain persistence, and so I tried to make sense of what I saw. I really wanted to understand what disease and healing were all about, a journey that continues to this day. Gradually, several basic questions arose; for example:

- Why do some animals recover easily, while others never seem to do well, regardless of which drugs are used?
- Why do some animals in a group seem to have all the fleas and catch all the diseases going around, while others are never affected?
- Why does it seem like there are more and more chronic illnesses in animals (and people)?

I knew there must be answers to these questions. There must be some basic understanding that I just didn't grasp about the body's ability to defend and heal itself.

To the Halls of Academia

When you ask a question long enough and deeply enough, life seems to provide the opportunity to find an answer. Soon a job offer as an instructor at the veterinary school at Washington State University literally dropped into my lap when a friend called out of the blue and told me the job was coming up. Eager to be, once again, in a climate of learning, I immediately applied and was accepted, giving notice at my first job. In spite of my prior education and decent grades, there must be something I did not yet understand. Perhaps this was the chance to remedy that!

During the next year I worked as an assistant professor, teaching epidemiology and public health, making farm calls, and working in the large animal reception barn. The position also offered me the chance to take some classes in the study of viruses, which I found fascinating. I did well in these classes, and one day I asked the professor if I might take some more.

"Let me check," he said, which I thought was an odd thing to say. Didn't he *know* whether they were offering more classes? A few days later the department head strode up to me and happily announced, "You're in!"

"In what?" I asked, not sure if this was a betting pool or a faculty clique.

"Why, graduate school, of course," he smiled, congratulating me with a handshake.

Those were the days, I have to say: no formal application, no letters of reference. Higher education was well funded, especially the sciences, and soon I was to be a full-time PhD student in veterinary microbiology, complete with a generous government fellowship.

"How wonderful," I thought as I began my new studies in the temples of science the following semester. "Now I can learn the real secrets of the body's defense systems."

And thus I set about studying and researching various problems, particularly the body's immune response, how it was stimulated to become active, how it "knew" that something foreign or counterproductive did not belong—such as cancerous cells. It seemed like the ideal way to learn to truly cure disease. Yet, some 5 years and a PhD degree later, I found that satisfactory answers to my questions still eluded me. Though I had acquired an even greater wealth of factual information about the mechanisms of immunology and metabolism, I still did not feel a sense of real insight about the issue that concerned me, how to promote greater health.

However, toward the end of my graduate studies, I finally came across a truly fascinating report. Doctors working with famished, starving children in Africa had determined that the immune system was very much dependent upon the presence of certain nutritional factors. By simply adding in certain missing substances, these children's resistance to disease was greatly enhanced.

Words cannot convey how extraordinarily exciting this now rather "of course" discovery was to me then. In years of studying the detailed workings of the immune system, I had never come across any findings about how the immune system could be made to work better, which was really all I was after.

A Personal Experiment

Here at last was the clue I'd been seeking, and so I decided to put it to the test, starting with myself. My then-wife and I changed our family's diet from the SAD (the Standard American Diet of processed foods, sugars, animal products, white bread, fried foods, and very little produce) to plates loaded with whole wheat bread, brown rice, beans and fresh vegetables, and much less meat. We took the superfood supplements of the day, such as nutritional yeast, wheat germ, and various vitamins. I also started jogging regularly, using herbs, and exploring my inner life with meditation and spiritual reading.

Before long I was feeling better than I had in years. It wasn't that I was particularly sick, but all these measures eventually played a part in removing things from my life that I didn't need—like the potbelly I was developing, plus my colitis, ear infections, excess tension, susceptibility to colds and flu, and a number of negative psychological habits.

Although this experiment was not statistically significant, controlled, or "double blind" (though I did have a little trouble seeing things clearly), it was tremendously valuable to me. Nothing convinces you that a treatment has virtue more than feeling better after using it. You don't need the interpretation or opinion of any authority to acknowledge positive changes in your own body and mind. We may not always know for sure the exact aspect that really made a difference, because we changed a number of variables and, of course, we had some confidence in what we were doing—and that positive outlook is nothing to be discounted—but I felt I was at last on the right track.

SPARROW, THE FERAL KITTEN

Back when I was still working on my PhD and unable to experiment with nutrition on clients, we adopted a fluffy stray kitten, half-starved and ragged from life in the woods. We named her Sparrow because she looked like a small bird made up mostly of feathers and fluff. At first, I fed her a conventional kibble and she did all right.

But when she became pregnant a year or two later, I decided to boost her strength. I faithfully added fresh, raw beef liver, raw eggs, bonemeal, fresh chicken, brewer's yeast, and other nutritious foods to her daily fare.

Unlike many cats I'd seen, she never lost any weight or hair during pregnancy, and her delivery was exceptionally fast, easy, and calm. She always had plenty of milk to nurse her three large, thriving kittens, who all grew up to be much larger than their mother.

We kept one of these kittens, and I continued adding supplements to the diets of both Sparrow and Genie, who became very chubby and happy. I was always amazed at how remarkably healthy they were. I never needed to use any flea control on them. And if one of these cats got scratched or bitten in a fight, the injury healed quickly and never developed into an infection or abscess. After a number of years, Genie was hit by a car, sadly, but Sparrow lived to the ripe old age of 18 years and never needed veterinary care for any of the common cat problems.

BACK TO PRACTICE, WITH DIET AND HOMEOPATHY

These early successes gave me the impetus to want to research nutrition and animal health in academia, but I concluded that there was not likely any financial backing for such research. So I decided to reenter practice and put the theory to the clinical test.

At first my use of nutrition with patients was tentative and limited. The veterinarians I worked for would let me talk about nutrition with clients but would not stock any supplements in the clinic itself. In spite of this, I encouraged my clients to add in certain vitamins or minerals, often in the form of unprocessed foods such as yeast, kelp, yogurt, eggs, etc.

Then for a few years I worked at a spay-neuter clinic every other week, which gave me ample time to study and learn more about nutrition as well as a new discovery, homeopathy. I started a small house-call practice in Santa Cruz, California, emphasizing these two approaches. In 1985 we moved to Oregon and opened The Animal Natural Health Center in downtown Eugene, based solely on nutrition, homeopathy, and use of a few herbs. I and several colleagues had astounding results over a period of 20 years—but I am getting ahead of myself.

Looking back, it's clear that my use and understanding of nutrition were part of a gradual process. At first I learned that particular nutrients were essential for the healthy function of the immune system. Yet I had no idea of the value of diet beyond that. What really spurred me on was seeing the rich array of clinical results as patients became so much healthier after suffering a variety of maladies when they were fed a truly healthy diet.

HEALTHY FOOD AND A SHRINKING WAITING LIST

It was as simple as this—someone would call our front desk at the Eugene clinic and ask for an appointment for a chronically sick animal. However, the practice was usually booked up, so the would-be client was put on a waiting list and given a recipe handout, the same as in previous editions of this book. We suggested they go ahead and start working with these healthy home-prepared recipes, as that would help their animal become stronger and respond better when, later, we could work up the animal's case with homeopathy.

Here's the kicker. Very often when the staff would call the person a month or so later to set up an appointment, they would tell us there was no need for a consultation because their animal was now healthy! And so we would cross the client off the waiting list (of course, there would always be more new callers the next day, as there is no shortage of sick animals).

"How could that be?" I mused at first. How could such a simple thing as fresh food lead to the outcome I had sought for so many years? Do you see why I continued to pursue the study of nutrition?

And if there is such a significant improvement in health simply from using well-planned fresh food recipes, then what is it about processed commercial pet foods that fails to do the same thing? Sure, most of them are not derived from the same fresh, nutritious sources my clients used, and this was a big part of the puzzle. But one also has to wonder, what *is* in those kibbles and canned foods?

What's in most pet foods is pretty unsavory,

as we will see in the next chapter, but nowadays I believe the problem with pet food goes much further than I ever anticipated decades ago. The same is true for what we feed our livestock and what we feed ourselves. Today we are experiencing a decline in the quality of our entire food supply due to our agricultural approach and what we choose to eat, as well as the spread of toxins in our world. These topics will be the subject of Chapter 3.

In addition, if we keep going the way we are now, experts warn that we humans will surely face serious freshwater and food shortages in the not-so-distant future, within the lifetimes of many readers. Chapter 4 will explore this increasingly concerning "big picture" of our planet and all its beings, which is the ultimate health question for all of us.

We cannot change the whole system, but we can each impact it through our daily choices. And that matters, affecting lives far beyond our households. Our choices can destroy the soils, aquifers, oceans, and forests we all depend upon. Or they can conserve and even help restore them. They can deplete fossil fuels, add to greenhouse gases, and cause suffering to countless humans and animals, driving thousands of species extinct. They can undermine the health of our societies and future generations of humans and other animals, both domestic and wild.

Or, they can create the conditions for all to thrive and to live in harmony, giving nature a chance to exercise its great resilience.

We have faith that, once people understand what is at stake, enough of us will make the compassionate and wise choices that will make a difference and create the kind of world any of us would be happy to be born into.

Welcome to what is most likely the final edition of what we are happy to say has become a leading book in its field, thanks to many who now hold this version in their hands. We will boldly explore important food issues of the 21st century as they pertain to pets, to us, to all living beings, and to our precious planet. They are inseparably linked.

And we will also offer some good news about some very simple yet profound things we each can do to better the situation and help undo much of the damage for the sake of all who live on planet Earth now or will in the future. We offer a special thanks to you, our readers, for looking at this new material with open minds and for anything and everything you may do to become part of the solution.

CHAPTER 2

WHAT'S REALLY IN PET FOOD

As I shared when discussing my early journey in the last chapter, I was both surprised and impressed how much difference it made for dogs and cats to be given food that was fresh and relatively unprocessed, basically the same healthy "people" food we would buy for ourselves at the market, not so much in the center aisles full of processed packaged food, but in the bulk, produce, and meat sections.

Often this change was dramatic. So, if it made this much difference, then what was it about pet food that did *not* provide this same level of health?

As we look into the rather unsavory ingredients that go into much commercial pet food, you could just become discouraged and depressed about the whole challenge of feeding your pet properly. I don't want that to happen. I think it's necessary to detail what is in pet food and the lack of quality control typical of the industry so that you can understand how important this issue is. The advertising for these products is so widespread and so convincing, it is not enough to just say "Don't use them."

Some of what you learn here about what you may have been feeding to your four-legged friends may surprise, sadden, or shock you. The same is true for the chapters that follow, looking at larger issues even with whole, fresh "people" foods today.

But do not despair. After that, we will show you easy and workable nutritional solutions to all these issues and try to anticipate and answer your concerns. We will show you several ways to prepare food yourself with simple recipes that are superior to most of what is out there.

The encouraging news is that these recipes have been used for more than 30 years by my clients and by readers of the previous editions of this book with great success. Some of the longest-lived and healthiest pets in the world have thrived on these approaches. You may find yourself amazed at what you will read, particularly in Chapter 5, our gallery of success stories. And when you are too busy to fix a meal or you are traveling, we will tell you how to identify the healthiest commercial products available.

I and many others find that animals respond very quickly and positively to a nutritious diet. In fact, it is *the major tool* you need to eliminate many of the chronic diseases your animal could experience in these times. If you follow the guidelines in this book, it is my opinion that it is almost certain that your animal will become healthier. I assure you that it is entirely possible to overcome the effects of prior feeding of poor-quality foods, even if such a feeding practice spans years.

Life is resilient. It is actually surprising how quickly health will improve, thanks to such a simple change. So screw up your courage and come with me into the little-explored world of pet foods. I will try to keep it brief.

INTO THE PET FOOD DUMPSTER

There may be exceptions among some of the higher-quality brands, but the source for most pet foods boils down to this: animal and plant wastes that cannot be used for human consumption.

Ann Martin, author of *Foods Pets Die For* and *Protect Your Pet,* has probably done more research into what makes up pet food than anyone else, making every effort to contact companies and inspectors and track down the truth of what we are feeding our pets. She concludes, "In all my years of research into this industry I have found little, if any, ingredients that are used in most commercial pet foods that would be considered anything but garbage."[1]

How can this be? Well, in a way it makes

perfect sense. Let's start with the meat and meat by-products that are usually featured in pet food.

MEAT INSPECTORS: ON THE HUNT FOR . . . WHAT?

The slaughter and processing of animals for human consumption must follow health standards set up by government agencies to protect the public, to keep disease-causing or harmful substances out of the food supply. Does this system work very well? Not really, but that is another story.

In any case, the evaluation of carcasses by meat inspectors results in an accumulation of rejected material that cannot be used. Something has to be done with it, and the thinking was, why waste it? So it became a standard practice that this rejected material could be processed into food for pets and even fed back to livestock who normally do not eat meat. This is entirely legal and seems an efficient way to use material that otherwise would have to be buried.

"So what's wrong with that?" you might ask. After all, doglike creatures in the wild will eat animals killed days ago, even ones that are partially rotted. (This is not the case for cats in the wild, however, who will never eat anything other than freshly killed animals.)

But the rejected material from meat-processing facilities is nothing like what you'll find in nature. Wild animals killed by wolves are generally not diseased or contaminated. They may be weakened from a lack of food, injured from fighting, or too young or too old to run fast—but they will generally be relatively healthy from having lived outdoors and eaten a natural, fresh diet. Yes, it's possible that a prey animal might have been sick, but that is the exception. Watch videos of predation on YouTube or television and you will see an apparently healthy, able-bodied antelope, deer, or moose running madly, trying to escape, and caught only because it was in the wrong place at the wrong time.

By contrast, the person who is in effect doing the predation for your dog or cat is the meat inspector. He or she is hunting for flesh with signs of disease—abscesses, tumors, cancers, abnormal organs, infected tissues, as well as parasites such as liver flukes, tapeworms—whatever does not look right. Inspectors only have a few seconds to look at each carcass, so they must decide quickly.

You might assume that livestock with cancer or obvious infection would be rejected for all consumption. Not so. The part considered diseased (such as the abscess or tumor) is cut out, but the rest of the sick animal goes right on into human food.

Guess where the abscess or tumor goes? Into pet food.

Prevention magazine once published a letter from a reader who offered an inside glimpse into the pet food industry.

I once worked in a chicken-butchering factory in Maine. Our average daily output was 100,000 chickens. . . . Directly ahead of me on the conveyor line were the USDA inspectors and their trimmers. The trimmers cut the damaged and diseased parts off the chickens and dropped them in garbage cans, which were emptied periodically. These parts were sent to a pet food factory.

So the next time you hear a pet food commercial talk about the fine ingredients they use in their product, don't you believe it.

That's bad enough. But, in addition to diseased tissues, the remains of "4-D animals" are added to the piles that go into pet and livestock food. These are the unfortunate cows, chickens, pigs, and others who arrive at the slaughterhouse already dead, dying, disabled, or diseased—too far gone to be used for human food. As well, the uteruses and fetuses of pregnant animals are removed and added to the pile.

Note that this material will be full of dangerous bacteria. It will be cooked, yes, but it will still contain endotoxins, which are not good for your pet. Endotoxins are substances that bacteria make in the unrefrigerated (often for a day or two) meat and animal tissues waiting for processing. They can persist and be carried over into pet food. One study of commercial pet foods found that all of them contained endotoxins, some in very large amounts.[2]

On to the Rendering Plant

This unsavory pile of diseased and unhealthy animal tissues from slaughterhouses then goes to rendering plants to be further pro-cessed. There it is mixed with a variety of other meaty discards. As Martin explains, "The product the plants render comes from various sources: garbage from grocery stores; grease and spoiled food from restaurants; roadkill too large to be buried at the side of the road; sick farm animals who have died for reasons other than slaughter; food substances condemned for human consumption; and euthanized dogs and cats from shelters, pounds, and veterinary clinics.

"All this material is dumped into huge containers at the rendering plants, cooked at temperatures between 220°F and 270°F (104.4°C to 132.2°C) for twenty minutes to one hour. The cooked material is centrifuged to separate the grease and tallow from the raw material. This material is finely ground and the end product is meat meal."[3]

There are many reports that the above materials can even include the packaging on expired meats and the collars of the euthanized pets, complete with residues of the euthanasia solution. Not my idea of wholesome food.

Meat By-Products

What we have just described is often labeled as "meat meal" or "meat by-products." Most people don't realize that terms like "meat by-products" or "poultry by-products" can actually include poultry feather meal, connective tissues (gristle), leather meal (yes, leather, like that used to make belts or shoes), fecal waste from poultry and other animals, and horse and cattle hair. Robert

Abady, founder of the Robert Abady Dog Food Company, describes meat meal and bonemeal as "generally comprised of ground bone, gristle, and tendons," and says they are "the cheapest and least nutritious of the by-product meals." Lamb meal, poultry or chicken meal, and fish meal are similar.

Meat meal, bonemeal, and other by-products are widely used in pet foods. Such ingredients would certainly boost the crude protein content, but they provide relatively little nourishment. (It's surely not my idea of a good meal for an animal.)

Because of the addition of tough, fibrous ingredients, dogs are typically able to utilize only about 75 percent of the protein in meat meal. And all meat meal is made even less digestible by the high cooking temperatures required to sterilize it. Dried blood meal, another cheap ingredient, contains even less usable protein.

What Else Is in Pet Food?

It can be upsetting to look at what goes into pet food, particularly if this is new to you, but that is often what it takes for people to realize that they need to take significant action to change their pet's diet. For more details, I refer you to Ann Martin's excellent books, but let's list just some of the other ingredients typically in pet food besides slaughterhouse wastes and artificial additives.

• **Remnants of food processed for human use,** such as potato or sweet potato peelings, beet pulp, and corn glu-ten meal (dried residue from corn after the removal of its starch, germ, and bran).

• **Rancid or moldy grains,** those rejected for human use.

• **Rice flour,** finely powdered, usually the end process of milling and of very low nutritional value.

• **Brewer's rice,** discards from the manufacturing of beer, which contain pulverized, dried, spent hops. Little, if any, nutritional value.

• **Fiber,** which may simply come from whole grains and vegetables (a good thing) or things like peanut hulls, feathers, or newspapers.

• **Hydrolyzed hair, dehydrated garbage, manure** (from swine, ruminants, poultry). These are realities according to the AAFCO "Ingredient Definitions."[4] AAFCO, the Association of American Feed Control Officials, sets feeding guidelines and standards, such as how much protein is recommended for a species, but does not regulate pet food manufacture per se.

• **Euthanized pets.** Pet food manufacturers don't officially acknowledge using the millions of dogs and cats euthanized in veterinary hospitals and humane societies, but there have been reports that some do. For example, a study at the University of Minnesota published in a veterinary journal demonstrated that the euthanasia solution, pentobarbital, came through the rendering process and was still an active drug.[5]

- **Antibiotics,** which are used continually on factory-farmed animals (some 99 percent of the meat produced in the United States). The conditions that most farmed chickens, turkeys, pigs, cows, fish, and other animals live in today are so unhealthy and stressful that the animals could not survive to profitable slaughter age without the steady use of antibiotics. Many of these antibiotics remain in animal-based foods, resulting in drug effects and development of bacterial resistances.

- **Growth-promoting drugs and hormones.** Farm animals are routinely given drugs (antibiotics) and hormones to hasten growth or to prevent health issues from the conditions in which they live. "Today, there are six anabolic steroids given, in various combinations, to nearly all animals entering conventional beef feedlots in the U.S. and Canada: three natural steroids (estradiol, testosterone, and progesterone), and three synthetic hormones (the estrogen compound zeranol, the androgen trenbolone acetate, and the progestin melengestrol acetate). Anabolic steroids are typically used in combinations. Measurable levels of all the above growth-promoting hormones are found at slaughter in the muscle, fat, liver, kidneys and other organ meats. The Food and Drug Administration has set 'acceptable daily intakes' (ADIs) for these animal drugs."[6] It is very likely these are affecting dogs and cats as well as people.

- **Pesticides and insecticides** that have been sprayed on livestock to control flies and other insects. These drugs can persist for months.

- **Radiation.** After the worst ecological disaster in human history, the 2011 meltdown of the Fukushima nuclear reactors in Japan, the oceans have become ever more filled with highly radioactive material, which is accumulating in marine fish and plants. This is especially worrisome for cats, who typically eat about 30 times the amount of seafood that we do, per pound of their body weight.[7]

- **Toxic heavy metals,** such as lead, mercury, cadmium, and arsenic, from a variety of processes and products, not to mention the collars and leg bands that can get carelessly tossed into the pet food bin, it is said. (We once found some visible metal pieces in a can of premium cat food.) Heavy metals bioaccumulate up the food chain. Consider that the sickest livestock that end up in pet food are also likely those with the greatest levels of toxins. So it's no surprise to learn that tests of commercial pet foods have found as much as 120 times the upper safe range for humans of mercury, plus dangerous levels of other heavy metals. Kibbles were worse than wet foods. Pet treats from industrial China have also tested very high in lead, and the FDA has received thousands of reports of pets sickened or killed by heavy metals in pet foods.[8]

Additives

Unfortunately, the story of pet food does not stop with unsavory sources from the food industry. Other ingredients can also significantly impact the health of pets on commercial kibbles and canned foods. Additives are of particular concern, in my view.

For example, pet food makers may add artificial food coloring to make their concoctions more attractive. To the dog or cat who does not see colors? No, to the person who buys these products, who feels more comfortable with a meatlike reddish or warm brown color than a gray mishmash.

It is also a standard and probably necessary practice to add preservatives to keep the dry food from spoiling for a long time while it sits on the grocery shelf or in your pantry. Not surprisingly, there are reports of health problems from some of these chemicals. Butylated hydroxyanisole (BHA), butylated hydroxytoluene (BHT), and ethoxyquin are three examples. BHA and BHT are added to oils (fats) as preservatives in pet foods and treats. According to California's Office of Environmental Health Hazard Assessment, BHA is on the list of known carcinogens and reproductive toxicants and BHT is also a carcinogen and causes kidney and liver damage in rats.[9]

Ethoxyquin is a chemical developed in the 1950s by Monsanto that was first used as an insecticide and pesticide. It began to be added to pet foods, and the Food and Drug Administration, Center for Veterinary Medicine (FDA/CVM) began receiving reports of adverse effects from those buying and using it. A consumer booklet produced by these agencies stated that "the reported effects include allergic reactions, skin problems, major organ failure, behavior problems, and cancer."[10] The report goes on to say there is no scientific evidence to support these claims, so the use of the product will not be changed. There was a later 3-year feeding trial done in beagles, commissioned by Monsanto, and the results were published in 1996. The report describes changes in liver color and liver enzyme levels but no effects on overall health.

You can see how it becomes difficult to know how to assess these substances added to food. It is certainly possible that they are harmless, but it could also be that there are differences between breeds of dogs, or between dogs of different ages and stages of development. It may even be that a substance like ethoxyquin is only a problem if there is already something wrong with an animal's health, so that perhaps the usual means of processing or discharging this chemical is compromised and it accumulates abnormally. To really thoroughly test all scenarios would be almost impossible. Even more to the point, a test in beagles may not tell us much about what happens when other breeds, young or old animals, or cats eat the same substance.

Another example is the use of propylene glycol, a humectant that was used in semimoist pet food for about 15 years. Propylene glycol, a second cousin to antifreeze, has been proven to be a major contributor to feline cardiac disease, according to research accepted by the FDA. The FDA publication "Understanding Pet Food Labels" states: "It [propylene glycol] was known to cause overt anemia or other clinical effects. However, recent reports of scientifically sound studies show that propylene glycol reduces red blood cell survival time, renders red blood cells more susceptible to oxidative damage, and has other adverse effects in cats consuming the substance at levels found in semi-moist food."[11] In January 2001 the FDA/CVM prohibited the use of propylene glycol in semi-moist cat food. It is, however, used in soft-moist dog foods.[12]

Here is what we need to understand more fully about this situation. It is satisfying to hear that a harmful substance was identified and its use halted. But we can ask how it got there in the first place. It is important that we realize that the various additives so readily put into pet food have not been tested for safety on dogs or cats. Safety tests for additives in human food are not very reassuring either. On January 1, 1958, the FDA established the Food Additives Amendment of 1958, with a list of 700 food substances that were exempt from any further evaluation and have been used without question ever since. The term used for this special group is GRAS, meaning "Generally Recognized As Safe."

Worse yet, today there are some 80,000 industrial or man-made chemicals in our environment—in the air, water, soil. These are taken up by both plants and animals,

but especially concentrate in the tissues of livestock fed industrially raised feeds, and then accumulate up the food chain to their highest levels in those who eat the livestock. That includes both humans and our pets, who get the dregs of the meat industry. We will devote an entire chapter to this (Chapter 3, What's Happening to All Our Food?) because we believe that it is a major factor in the chronic illnesses we are seeing now in animals, as well as people.

Ethics of Using Discards

All these ingredients are concerning. In prior editions of this book, we especially emphasized not feeding food industry waste to your pet, to use human-grade fresh ingredients.

But, as we increasingly tax the resources of our planet, some might argue that using commercial pet food makes sense from an economic, environmental, and even humane point of view. After all, it is a way of not wasting material that otherwise would have to be, at some cost, thrown away, or just used, as some is, for other products including cosmetics or fertilizers. It could even be considered a more humane approach, requiring fewer animals to be raised and slaughtered, often under brutal conditions.

But the question remains for anyone who cares about the health and well-being of the pets who are fed these diseased, spoiled, and contaminated materials: If they are not good for people to eat, why would they be good for dogs or cats? Are dogs and cats somehow more resilient? Stronger? Less prone to getting sick from spoiled, diseased, and overprocessed food? I don't think so.

Then why do we feed them this way? The answer that comes to me is that it is an expression of a cultural judgment. Our belief, when it comes down to it, is that other animals—in this case dogs and cats—are not as important as human beings. We must protect people, but dogs and cats? Ah, not quite as much.

Most readers of this book, of course, take special care of and want nothing more than to do the best for the animals they love and nurture. What I am describing is a larger cultural perspective, one that is not usually examined. Really, it is a spiritual and ethical issue, in our view, and the same exact objection applies to livestock who are also fed this waste—many of whom are forced, as are pets, to cannibalize their own kind, even when they are natural herbivores.

CHRONIC DISEASE IN PETS: "ALARMING INCREASES"

In any case, in our view, the poor state of most pet food is a serious health issue for companion animals, who have been suffering from a rise in chronic diseases, according to a 2015 study of 2.4 million dogs and 480,000 cats by Banfield Veterinary Hospitals.[13]

Overweight and obesity, which can actually be signs of malnutrition (see Chapter 3), are skyrocketing, now affecting 1 in 4 dogs and 1 in 3 cats. Excess weight is often linked with arthritis, diabetes, heart disease, and many other afflictions.

Food allergies are also a big problem for many dogs and cats. Given what we have seen so far, is it any wonder that most food allergies in pets are to animal products? The top 10 allergens for dogs, for example, are beef, dairy, wheat, egg, chicken, lamb, soy, pork, rabbit, and fish.[14] This may surprise some people who adhere to the grain-free trend of recent years and might expect to see mostly grains on that list.

Chapter 3 explores controversies about even fresh meat and grains, but just consider for a moment the two main plant food allergies for dogs: soy and wheat. Soy is highly processed and from GMO (genetically modified) sources in nearly all cases, and wheat is also likely to come from moldy, stale, infested, or low-nutrient discards from the food industry. These hardly compare to the whole, freshly prepared grains and legumes (ideally from organic sources) on which dogs and cats can and do thrive.

Killing Wildlife for Pets: Is This the Answer?

In response to allergies to common meats (which have developed from use of meat by-products), some higher-end manufacturers have been offering "alternative" meat sources that seem more natural or wild: buffalo, kangaroos, ostriches, elk, salmon, and deer. Lamb and rabbit were once recommended for pets allergic to beef, chicken, or pork, but now they are also problematic. So it seems likely that pets will develop allergies to each new class of less common meats, particularly if they are subject to the issues discussed above.

Some of these newer "wild" alternatives may be wildlife culled by agencies at the bequest of ranchers or farmers, or even roadkill. A story appeared in our local paper revealing that dead animals found on the highway are sent to rendering plants, where they are used in pet food. The reporter actually talked to the Road Department, which led him to Animal Control, which then led him to Eugene Chemical & Rendering Works, where he was told the rendered material was sold to companies that make pet (and livestock) feed. Similar reports have surfaced elsewhere, so I don't think this is just a local phenomenon.

It's hard to know the sources of these "wild" materials. But however they are obtained, we need to be vigilant about the environmental, humane, and health issues involved. Whether or not they are processed in a more wholesome way (which is hard to know), we must especially ask ourselves: How many wild animals can be sustainably killed for the many millions of pets that people keep?

FOOD: MORE IMPORTANT THAN EVER

Whether you are first learning about what's in pet food or just reviewing it, it's easy to see why I saw such health improvements when clients and readers would feed fresh, less-processed, and higher-quality foods to their animals. In fact, it's really a bit amazing that many animals do as well as they do, considering what they eat.

With time, I have come to place ever greater importance on the role of food in health. Human health researchers and professionals ascribe as much as 80 percent of chronic disease to preventable factors, particularly our poor diet: too much meat, too little produce, too many processed and refined "foodlike substances."[15]

The same is undoubtedly true of our pets. I saw the importance of what dogs and cats are fed early in my career. We have brought it up as a serious consideration ever since the first edition of our book in 1981. But I did not anticipate how food would become an even more serious problem with time.

From my more than 40 years of treating animals with all sorts of health problems, my understanding has steadily moved from what I was taught in veterinary school—that the major issues were infections, with an emphasis on use of antibiotics. I now believe that the great bulk of the chronic diseases we see in dogs and cats are due to toxic accumulations of harmful substances in their bodies, as well as a general decline in the nutrient value of food, which we will explore next. In addition, we are facing serious environmental limitations that are a fundamental threat to the health of every living being.

That's the bad news. The good news is that there *are* solutions—ways to achieve healthy, sustainable, and humane eating, for our pets and for ourselves, which we will outline in Chapter 5.

CHAPTER 3

WHAT'S HAPPENING TO ALL OUR FOOD?

Today we enjoyed a colorful, beautiful lunch out on our sunny patio: lush red cabbage and a tasty potato salad with fresh dill atop a nest of sunflower seed sprouts just harvested from the windowsill, all ringed by rich red tomato slices. Wish you could have joined us!

We have always made it a priority to prepare and enjoy good, healthy food. That's why, early in my career, it was really not that difficult to break away from the standard advice and realize that switching animals from highly processed pet foods to quality fresh foods could make a big difference in their health. And, indeed, time and time again, problems would resolve, their coats would get shiny, and they would get a new lease on life.

Many people understand the value of good nutrition today and do their best to feed high-quality diets to their animal friends, as well as themselves. Even commercial pet foods often use human-grade, organic ingredients and some small companies sell fresh or frozen pet foods of good quality.

GROWING CONCERNS

However, in recent years I've had growing concerns about what's happening to *all* food, even many of the foods we consider good and healthy. As we all become more informed, I think it will be common knowledge that most of the rise in chronic disease has come from unfortunate changes in our food, as well as what we choose to eat.

The pet food business is piggybacked onto the agricultural system that produces food for human beings. The way it is set up, dogs and cats are getting the same food that we humans will eat, just more in the form of by-products—what can't be sold for a higher price for people to eat. There is not a significant difference in food quality between human food and pet food in this sense. Yes, some of what goes into pet food is lower quality in terms of some spoilage or coming from animals that died on their way to the slaughterhouse. But if we focus on just this aspect, we lose the whole picture. Food in general, for humans and animals, has undergone very significant changes in the last couple of decades, and we need to

understand this as part of planning how to provide the very best for our animal friends.

In this chapter we will look at two worrisome changes in food quality today. The first is a notable decline in nutrients, especially in conventionally grown food. The second is an insidious increase in toxins. Pollutants accumulate the most in seafood, meat, and dairy, and especially in the animal products and by-products that we feed our dogs and cats.

We might prefer to turn away from these issues, thinking that our objections or concerns can't possibly change something as monolithic as Big Food. But the good news is that each of us can make a big difference in the world, starting now, this week, right in our own kitchens. It will be good for us as well as the whole of life. Last but not least, our dogs and cats can join us on this journey of hope.

So take a deep breath and let us explore each issue in turn, starting with what has happened to our food.

NUTRIENTS: A DISAPPEARING ACT

It is not just your imagination that foods often don't taste the way you remember. Many are missing some vital nutrients. According to University of Texas biochemist Donald Davis, there has been a *significant decline* in levels of protein, calcium, phosphorus, iron, riboflavin, and vitamin C in conventionally raised fruits, vegetables, meats, eggs, dairy products, and modern corn varieties since the mid-20th century. Davis attributes this mainly to the constant push for fast growth with modern fertilizers and breeding.[1]

Why does this matter? When plants or animals don't get the nutrients they need, their health is bound to be compromised. Another biochemist, the prominent researcher Dr. Bruce Ames, has warned that the health consequences of these dietary deficiencies, including increased cancer and accelerated aging, are actually far more serious than those due to pesticide residues in food, a more common concern.[2]

Though we may buy or even grow organic food to avoid such residues, it turns out that organic choices do double duty when it comes to nutrition as well. A 2004 meta-analysis of many studies established conclusively that organic foods do indeed have more nutrients, particularly vitamin C, iron, magnesium, and phosphorus, along with fewer heavy metals and nitrates.[3]

One such study, published in the *Journal of Applied Nutrition*, found that organic foods had a whopping 390 percent more selenium (a key to fighting cancer), plus 138 percent more magnesium, 125 percent more potassium, 78 percent more chromium, 73 percent more iodine, 63 percent more calcium, 60 percent more zinc, and 59 percent more iron compared with conventional foods.[4]

So why are conventional foods "losing it"? I see several reasons for this.

• **High-nitrogen artificial fertilizers.** Manufactured from petrochemicals, these make plants grow really fast, and that has given us an abundance of food for as long as we have fossil fuels available. However, quick growth gives plants less time to absorb important nutrients, including minerals crucial to their health and resistance to disease and pests. That spells less phytonutrient content, less color, less aroma, and less taste.

• **Sterile versus living soils.** By contrast, native or organic soils provide nitrogen through the slow breakdown of plant and animal wastes, plus nitrogen fixation on the roots of legumes. Healthy soil is a living superorganism. It fosters millions of kinds of bacteria, fungi, earthworms, and countless tiny organisms that team up to make minerals more available to plants. Unfortunately, many are killed by artificial fertilizers and the compaction and heavy plowing typical of industrial farming, and that makes it harder for plants to absorb minerals. For that reason, some growers now use no-till or raised bed approaches.

• **Genetically modified (GM) crops.** A more recent cause of nutrient reduction is what is called "genetic modification," usually abbreviated GM. When scientists create genetically modified foods, they introduce a new piece of DNA with a "gene gun," and that process can cause collateral damage to nearby genes. A way to understand this is to imagine the DNA sequence being like sentences in text that gives instructions (in this case, for how the body grows and is maintained). When you shoot a new "sentence" into the "text," it can end up anywhere and in the process make a "paragraph" no longer understandable. There is evidence that adding the new instructions comes at a cost, which is the loss of other instructions that are also important. This explains reports of fewer nutrients in GM crops. A 2012 nutritional analysis made a shocking finding—that compared to the usual non-modified corn, GM corn had 437 times *less* calcium, as well as 56 times *less* magnesium and 7 times *less* manganese.[5] One of the most interesting observations about these modified foods is that, given a choice, animals will not eat them. They can apparently smell or taste the difference and don't want these foods. One report I heard from a veterinarian was that free-range chickens would not eat the genetically modified corn that spilled from trucks on a farm as they were parked. The corn was left to rot.

• **Glyphosate usage.** Soil minerals can also get locked up by chelators (molecules that bind minerals, making them unavailable). Glyphosate, the main ingredient in the weed killer Roundup, was actually first used as a chelator. Since the introduction of Roundup-resistant GM crops in the mid-1990s, glyphosate use has greatly increased.[6] (And, due to superweeds that have become glyphosate resistant as well,

more potent herbicides are now in the pipeline.)

• **Growth hormones.** Livestock are also pushed to grow faster or produce more eggs through the standard practice of using growth hormones (this is not allowed in certified organic foods). These hormones are like the ones that athletes use to gain muscle and weight and are used to make the animals grow very large, very fast. There are six such hormones now in use in cattle. As with plants, fast growth means less time to take in nutrients, and much of the animals' weight gain is in the form of fat. Fat lacks other nutrients but is a great place to store toxins. Residues of growth hormones remain in animal-based foods. Because they are biologically close to our own, they will affect us more than the phytoestrogens in soybeans that concern some people. Women who eat no animal foods (vegans) have twins only 20 percent as often as omnivores, most likely because they are *not* receiving all these unsought hormones.[7]

OTHER WAYS NUTRIENTS GET LOST

Whether conventional or organic methods are used, other grower issues decrease nutrient density.

• **Breeding for fast growth.** For thousands of years, farmers have selected for the plants and animals that grew faster, bigger, or tasted best. We enjoy the results, and yet the price is this: Modern foods are remarkably lower in fiber, minerals, and protein and higher in sugar and fat than their wild ancestors, the ones early humans munched on.[8]

Modern knowledge of breeding and husbandry has really accelerated this process, and most farmers now push animals far beyond what is healthy or humane. Did you know, for instance, that chickens and cows produce far more eggs and milk than in the 1950s? Chickens now lay some 300 eggs a year in contrast to only 10 to 15 for their wild ancestors still in the jungles of southeastern Asia. This causes calcium deficiencies and painful reproductive conditions, whereas those bred for meat get so large that some cannot walk to the feeder.

• **Feeding grain to animals in feedlots and sheds** also reduces the healthy omega-3 fatty acids they used to get in abundance from pastures, reducing the omega-3 content of meat, eggs, and milk. Some doctors believe this is a major factor in the excess inflammation in our population that is widely seen as a breeding ground for chronic disease, including cancer. This applies to our pets as well—they have the same requirements that we do.

• **Premature harvesting** also reduces nutrients, whether it's done to grow more crops, beat bad weather, or make crops less perishable. Just compare the flavor of a rich, ripe tomato to a hard, pale one. It's not just pleasure that is lost, but also many of the vitamins, minerals, and thousands of phytonutrients that are the "keys to the kingdom" in plant foods.

• **Lengthy shipping and storage times.** Most food today is shipped long distances or stored to meet demand for year-round produce. This also will cause some loss of nutrition and flavor, not to mention the environmental costs of transport and storage. Much of the emphasis on crop development has been on this ability to ship produce without its being (or appearing to be) damaged. Making this the important factor puts flavor or high nutritional value in second place.

Convenience at a Price

As we get busier in modern life, many people frequent fast-food chains or rely almost entirely on packaged convenience foods, including those for pets. They are easy, tasty, and even addictive, but the jury is no longer out: They compromise our health, making us and our companion animals "overfed but undernourished."[9] Some 70 percent of Americans are now overweight to some degree,[10] with all its attendant illnesses. Likewise, a very large 2015 veterinary study found that 25 percent of our dogs and 33 percent of our cats are overweight or obese.[11] That was rare when I started practice in 1965.

While food manufacturers often fortify their products with certain vitamins and minerals, can this really make up for what is lost? There are thousands of little-understood nutrients in whole natural foods, especially in plants. When we or our animals eat too much "junk food," our bodies signal us to keep eating to try to get what we need. Yet, we turn again to processed foods, which are masterfully flavored with salt, sugar, fats, and other flavors that appeal to our evolutionary instincts to gorge on rich flavors that were relatively scarce in the wild.

Pet food makers excel at making their products appealing and even addictive to dogs and cats. The rendering plants that supply them must cook animal wastes at high temperatures to kill pathogens. Unfortunately, prolonged high heat denatures proteins and destroys crucial vitamins and amino acids, including taurine, which is essential for cats. Pet food makers add taurine (usually synthetic) and other nutrients back to the surface of kibbles before packaging to presumably compensate for this.

NUTRIENT-DENSE FOODS THAT HEAL

Both humans and animals pay a price for these nutrient losses. Dr. Joel Fuhrman (author of *Eat to Live: The Amazing Nutrient-Rich Program for Fast and Sustained Weight Loss*) and Dr. Garth Davis (who wrote *Proteinaholic: How Our Obsession with Meat Is Killing Us and What We Can Do About It*) have tested thousands of their unhealthy and obese patients on standard American diets. Even though many thought they were eating well and were often on high-protein/low-carb

fad diets, most tested surprisingly deficient in many important vitamins and minerals.

Americans eat very few colorful vegetables and fruits and greens, yet they are the most nutrient-packed foods anywhere, and most are suitable for pets as well, especially dogs. They—particularly leafy greens—contain thousands of nutrients we are only beginning to discover. Dr. Fuhrman has created a way to rank foods for nutrient value per calorie, the "Aggregate Nutrient Density Index" (ANDI). Amazingly, even iceberg lettuce turns out to have more nutrients *per calorie* than animal foods, which are nearly all at the bottom of the list.

The good news is that when the patients of these and many other nutrition-based MDs replace processed foods and animal foods (typically high in fat) with more nutrient-dense plant foods, they enjoy permanent weight loss and amazing reversals of all kinds of chronic diseases.[12, 13]

Likewise, even though dogs are descended from predators, people report remarkable health and longevity when their dogs are fed fresh organic veggies on a daily basis (see Chapter 5). I find that really intriguing.

WHAT ABOUT VITAMIN SUPPLEMENTS?

Vitamin supplements used to seem like the answer to nutrient deficiencies like these. At the least, it seemed wise to take them "just in case." But some studies indicate certain vitamin supplements can create imbalances and thereby do more harm than good. This seems to be the result of isolating nutrients from the complex matrix of nutrients in whole food. For that reason, many now look to superfoods or food-derived vitamins that include related bio-complexes, instead of strictly synthetic ones.

Many cutting-edge, nutrition-focused doctors who prescribe nutrient-dense, plant-based diets say that B$_{12}$ is about the only vitamin supplement they really recommend. Likewise, our new plant-based recipe options for dogs and cats (Chapter 6) do include special supplements with B$_{12}$ and other nutrients crucial for their special needs. Please do not leave them out.

The bottom line, however, is that no pills or powders can make up for a junk food diet. Nutrient-dense "food as grown" is the key to optimal health.

TOXIC SECRETS

Now let's address the second major issue undermining our food and our health. We're talking toxins—the 85,000 or so man-made chemicals making their way into our food and our bodies in the last few decades.

While most people, even health professionals, tend to overlook this issue, for anyone paying attention it is clear that the panoply of industrial and household chemicals loose in our world is an important cause of our health problems, which are getting worse with each generation. As a veterinarian with more than 50 years of experience, I think environmental toxins particularly impact our dogs and cats, as I will explain.

Food of today is *very heavily contaminated* with these chemicals. Some of this is deliberate. There are more than 3,000 chemical additives alone in US foods, including preservatives, colorings, flavors, and other substances.

On top of that, however, thousands of industrial chemicals have found their way from the air, water, and soil into the food that we and our animals eat—chemicals that have nothing to do with food, chemicals conjured up in modern times that were never intended to find a home in food or in our bodies.

It is an odd cultural blindness that we allow companies to make countless products to use in homes, lawns, yards, fields, pastures, forests—most containing substances usually toxic to some form of life. We do this even though we should easily realize that, after we are done with them, they are not going to stay put, but will ooze and blow into other areas, streams, lakes, etc., and diffuse throughout our biosphere—the place where we all live.

Imagine a neighbor spraying some nasty substance that blows into your yard or garden or drifts into your open windows, sending you into an asthma attack. Imagine your outrage. Now expand this, to millions of neighbors, farmers, and ranchers doing this with all sorts of chemicals, products, pesticides, herbicides, antibiotics, hormones, who knows what?

Paula Baillie-Hamilton, a physician and leading authority on toxins in food, laments: "An effect of this contamination is that we are now one of the most polluted species on the face of the planet. Indeed, if we were cannibals our meat would be banned from human consumption."[14]

In the largest study ever done on humans, the US Centers for Disease Control and Prevention reported in 2005 that most Americans carry more than 100 pesticides and toxic compounds in their tissues, especially compounds used in consumer products, many linked to potential health threats.[15] Unfortunately, the highest levels are found in children, showing us the problem is increasing, rather than diminishing, with each generation.

Consider this: There are now more than 30,000 prescription drugs and at least 200,000 brands of nonprescription drugs. Many eventually go down the toilet, into the watershed, and from there into the food chain. It's not as though these chemicals are all nicely removed from the water, even in the best sewage treatment plants. They remain in sewage sludge, which is just about the most toxic material you will find anywhere. But it has to go somewhere and, unbelievably, it is put on our food crops, those raised conventionally (certified organic farmers must not use it).

PRESUMED INNOCENT UNTIL PROVEN GUILTY

You might ask "But can't our bodies get rid of these toxins?" The short answer is no.

They are synthetic newcomers that our bodies don't know how to handle. The usual means of detoxing is for the liver to recognize undesirable substances and then add a biochemical marker that the kidneys recognize, causing them to filter the substance out of the blood and into the urine for a quick exit. The critical word here is *recognize*, and that is the core of the toxin problem. The unseen toxins within us and all animals are like a host of strangers our bodies don't recognize and just store away, out of mind, out of sight.

Also, some of these chemicals, such as DDT, as well as dioxin and other POPs (persistent organic pollutants), are not water soluble, so they can't be eliminated through the kidneys in any case. Instead, they dissolve in lipids (fats) and accumulate in our fat cells *and* in those of the fish, meat, eggs, and milk we and our pets consume. Though many equate these foods with "protein," most contain a higher amount of fat. And fat spells toxins.

"Well, okay," you may say, "but is it really so bad? We're still alive and kicking. Maybe most of these toxins are accumulating inside us in such tiny amounts that they are harmless." A reasonable question until you realize how much concentration of these substances occurs. Later in this chapter we discuss how these substances greatly increase as you move up the food chain. This results in rather significant doses, especially when we don't really know what the effects will be in dogs and cats.

In 1998, the Environmental Protection Agency (EPA) acknowledged that only 7 percent of chemicals produced in significant amounts had ever undergone the full slate of basic toxicity studies. Many were grandfathered in at the time the EPA was established. They were presumed innocent until proven guilty, and that has made them very difficult to regulate.

However, some *have* been tested, such as DDT, dioxin, polychlorinated biphenyls (PCBs), and various hormones, herbicides, and heavy metals suspected or known to cause health problems, including cancer, reproductive problems, birth defects, nervous system disorders, and many more. Some have been banned or restricted, yet they break down slowly, remaining in the environment, in food, and in our bodies even decades afterward.

So let's meet a few members of this cast of suspects.

• **Heavy metals,** widespread and persistent, accumulating in animal tissues: These include *lead* in bones and bonemeal, soil, dust, pipes, toys, cosmetics, ceramics, pre-1978 paint, and leaded gasoline; *mercury* in seafood, from gold mining, in vaccines (linked to autism: watch the documentary *Trace Amounts*), from coal-fired power plants, waste incineration, oil refining, cement production; *arsenic* in chicken products and manure and white rice and from additives, mining, smelting, former farm use; and *cadmium* in refined grains, from

phosphate fertilizers, mining, smelting, sewage sludge, batteries, paints, and plastics. The advice we are giving in this book regarding food preparation is directed at minimizing heavy metal exposure. (Also see Chapter 10, Creating a Healthy Home.)

• **Pesticides and agricultural chemicals and drugs:** especially herbicides, insecticides, and fungicides, including tick, flea, and heartworm products. Some pesticides, like DDT, are long banned (since 1977) but still found in fatty tissues worldwide. This category also includes nitrates as well as arsenic, hormones, antibiotics, and other drugs routinely used on farm animals. Choose organic, or better yet, veganic (no manure, which accumulates toxins). For an overview of the impacts of corporate food production, watch *Food, Inc.*

• **Chemicals in tap or even bottled water:** chlorine, trihalomethanes, and other disinfection by-products (produced by organic debris in presence of chlorine), fluoride, various contaminants from industry, agriculture, and fracking. Bottled water can also be full of contaminants. Use reverse osmosis or carbon filters and store water in glass or stainless steel containers. Watch the documentary *Tapped.*

• **Genetically modified foods** containing herbicides (insecticidal genes are built right into GM corn): Choose organic or non-GM soy, corn, canola, sugar, and other products. Watch the documentary *Genetic Roulette*.

• **Plastics and food packaging:** BPA, an endocrine disruptor linked with infertility, obesity, diabetes, and reproductive problems, is in 60 percent of US cans. Replacement liners may not be any better. Plastics are everywhere—in toys, bowls, plastic bags, containers, and countless household products (in the form of phthalates, BPA, and many unlisted proprietary ingredients). Watch the documentary *Plastic Planet*. Minimize purchase of canned foods. Avoid the use of plastic containers and bowls for either feeding or food storage.

• **Radioactive toxins from nuclear accidents** such as Fukushima and former weapons testing: linked with tumors, cancers, and various degenerative diseases. Avoid seafood, especially tuna other large fish, and products containing fish meal.

• **Natural toxins:** Molds and aflatoxins can develop in foods that are becoming old or have been on store shelves a long time. Try to buy and use fresh foods and store products carefully. You can even buy vacuum containers to minimize oxygen degradation so that foods can be kept safely for much longer.

• **Household cleaners,** air fresheners, fire retardants (in furniture and bedding), stain removers, solvents, paints, cosmetics, perfumes, lawn care products, cigarette smoke: Watch the documentary *Chemerical*. Use nontoxic, natural products (see below).

• **And thousands of other industrial chemicals** dispersed in air, water, and soil, mostly untested and bioaccumulating up the food chain: Of special concern are dioxin (from pulp mills, fires, incineration) and other persistent organic pollutants (POPs). For a good overview, watch *The Human Experiment*.

DO PETS HAVE MORE TOXINS THAN WE DO?

I think it very likely that many of the chronic diseases that both veterinarians and human health professionals alike must face today stem from the burden of these chemicals and metals building up in our patients. The difficulty for diagnosis is that there is not just *one* clear toxin or factor to point a finger at, but many. Their combined interactions no doubt work in concert to create degenerative conditions that are so resistant to treatment.

Pondering the issues of toxins for years, I now think our companion animals most likely get an extra big hit of these unseen strangers within us all. That's for at least three reasons.

• **Bioaccumulation in animal products:** As Dr. John McDougall reports, "Estimates are that 89 percent to 99 percent of the chemical intake into our body is from our food, and most of this is from foods high on the food chain: meat, poultry, eggs, fish, and dairy products."[16] These are the very foods most consumed by dogs and cats, as well as by people who are into the "more protein" and "fewer carbs" fads (see Chapter 5). Why do these foods have the largest amounts of pollutants? We will get to that in a moment (see discussion of the food chain below).

- **Exposure to the worst cuts:** Furthermore, the sad truth is that our pets usually get the lowest-quality slaughterhouse and rendering plant scraps, those wastes and rejects not approved for humans. That includes higher amounts of organs, bone scraps, and fat trimmings: all tissues that store more toxins than the muscle meats preferred by people.

- **Toxins in dust:** On top of that, dogs and cats live closer to the ground and floor, where toxins from lead to flame retardants in fabrics will settle into dust and get on their paws and coats. Then they proceed to lick themselves clean (see Chapter 10). Dogs are known for eating garbage and drinking dirty water from puddles, and more than one pet has lapped up antifreeze and other poisons.

Indeed, the few studies done on this topic support this idea. In 2008 the Environmental Working Group tested blood and urine samples from 35 dogs and 37 cats near Washington, DC. They found high levels of numerous chemicals, including many used in the making of furniture, fabrics, and electronics. Mercury was also very high, likely from fish used in pet food.[17]

In another test, dogs and cats had *five times the amount of mercury per pound* as human beings. A variety of heavy metals including lead, cadmium, mercury, arsenic, and even uranium has been found in pet foods and treats at amounts exceeding levels considered safe. The FDA does not set limits on heavy metals in pet foods. Even the USDA sets no limits on heavy metals in certified organic pet foods and treats.[18] We will look at heavy metal issues in depth shortly.

Taking this perspective a step further, I strongly suspect that their extra burden of toxins is likely *the number one cause of the rise in chronic disease in pets*, which has been reaching alarming rates in recent years.

> *"Estimates are that 89 percent to 99 percent of the chemical intake into our body is from our food, and most of this is from foods high on the food chain: meat, poultry, eggs, fish, and dairy products."*—John McDougall, MD

MORE ANIMAL PRODUCTS, MORE TOXINS

The high concentration of toxins up the food chain has especially raised questions in my mind about a practice popular since the mid-1990s among holistic animal lovers and veterinarians alike: feeding pets a "species-appropriate" diet consisting mostly of raw meat, bones, and organs and a few raw vegetables or berries. Some even go so far as to offer live prey.

This is far more meat than most dogs eat. It is also far more than most have received in previous centuries (see Chapter 5), when bread and barley with bits of whey, milk, or scraps of meat and fat were their main fare. Some dogs even lived on bread soaked in bean juice. Somehow they produced healthy offspring that made it to our era. (Cats seemed to live mostly by hunting, supplemented with porridge, milk, and meat scraps.)

No doubt many dogs and cats enjoy eating lots of meat, as do many humans, but what is the long-term cost? We now live in a very polluted world where widespread toxins accumulate in these very foods, even those from premium organic, grass-fed, and wild sources.

For example, the tissues of wild animals can contain as much as 70,000 times the level of POPs in the surrounding environment. This includes the heavy hitter dioxin, as well as DDT, aldrin, dieldrin, endrin, chlordane, heptachlor, polychlorinated biphenyls, and more.[19] Fish concentrate toxins even more, sometimes to millions of times the level in water.

I strongly suspect that their extra burden of toxins is likely *the number one cause of the rise in chronic disease in pets*, which has been reaching alarming rates in recent years.

While most (not all) pets seem to do well on such meat-rich diets, especially compared with standard kibbles, I truly wonder how this practice impacts their risk of getting cancer or other environmentally caused diseases over time. I don't know the answer to this question, nor do I know of any studies on this topic to date, but I do know this: Cancer is very much on the rise in pets, with half of dogs expected to suffer from it, whereas it was uncommon when I began practice in the 1960s. Thyroid issues, allergies, kidney disease, and skin problems are rampant in dogs and cats, all of which can be linked with toxins. Clearly, something is going on here.

This is an important issue for those who truly believe that their animals can only thrive on a diet natural for carnivores. So, before we go further, let's understand the food chain and why toxins accumulate at the top of it.

UNDERSTANDING THE FOOD CHAIN

• **Soil microorganisms, algae, and plankton** are at the bottom of the food chain. They absorb nutrients and toxins that drift and wash into the soil, air, and water from farms, industry, household products, litter, and sewage.

• **Plants** are next. They draw in somewhat higher levels of toxins in addition to the nutrients they absorb from this complex web of microbial life.

• **Herbivorous animals** (and most wildlife), whether insects, rabbits, or cattle, eat these plants and gradually concentrate toxins further, especially fat-soluble toxins that get stored in their fatty tissues. Other toxins are stored in their livers, while still others, such as lead, may displace calcium in their bones. The widespread practice of feeding fish meal and animal wastes to livestock to make them grow faster causes even further concentration of toxins in their tissues.

• **Predators** eat these herbivores, such as when a coyote eats a rabbit or a bird eats a worm, and concentrate an even greater load of toxins over time.

• **Top predators** eat smaller predators, such as when large ocean fish like tuna and sharks eat smaller fish, who eat even smaller fish, who eat still smaller fish or plankton. Toxins concentrate at each step, so big fish can concentrate toxins at *thousands or even millions of times* the levels in the water. When we or our pets eat seafood (or the meat of livestock), we have placed ourselves at the top of the food chain.

• In addition, **the young of each species,** especially those who nurse, accumulate more toxins than their parents. Breastfed babies take in a shocking *242 times more dioxin per pound of body weight* than do adults, and during a critical time in development.[20] You can now see why pregnant and nursing women are especially told not to eat tuna, which subjects vulnerable babies to dangerous levels of mercury and puts human infants at the very top of the food chain, along with the kittens and puppies of seafood-eating cats and dogs.

So, if you remember nothing else from this chapter, remember this: *the more seafood,* *meat, milk, and eggs, the more toxins.* Plants don't get a free pass, but toxic chemicals concentrate by far the most in animal products.

Looking at the Numbers

Decades ago, John Robbins warned in the bestseller *Diet for a New America* that meat contained 14 times more pesticides than conventionally grown crops. Dairy products had 5.5 times more. In the same book, he cited a study in the *New England Journal of Medicine* showing that vegetarian women had only *1 to 2 percent the levels of pesticides* in their breast milk as average American women![21] In his recent book, *The Food Revolution*, Robbins focuses on dioxin, considered by far the most toxic known chemical. Dioxin is thought to cause up to 12 percent of cancers and is also a prime suspect in genetic and reproductive defects, as well as learning disabilities. It's not made intentionally, but is a by-product of manufacturing and municipal and medical waste incineration and accumulates in fatty tissues.

The EPA estimates that 95 percent of human dioxin exposure comes from red meat, fish, and dairy products. It is obvious that eating diets with less, or no, meat or dairy will give less exposure to these chemicals. A shocking 1999 test found Ben & Jerry's rich ice cream from idyllic Vermont farms had 200 times the EPA's "virtually safe" dose. A year later, another sample of this ice cream featured 2,200 times more dioxin than the wastewater of a San Francisco gasoline refinery.[22]

More recently, Dr. Michael Greger cited 2009 USDA findings pinpointing that dioxin was, by far, highest in fish, followed by eggs, then cheese, with levels in human tissues exceeding EPA hazard levels in every age group. He also examined research on organochlorines, persistent pesticides that were banned in most countries in the 1970s. They continue to be high in breast milk, fish, meat, and dairy. Testing these banned organochlorines and a wide range of other industrial toxins, an international team of researchers found that vegans were significantly less polluted than omnivores. Yet, even the vegans had surprising levels, which the scientists attributed to the fact that most ate omnivorous diets during childhood.[23]

HEAVY METALS IN PET FOODS

So how is this impacting dogs and cats particularly? Heavy metals are one of the known bad guys that accumulate up the food chain, reaching unacceptable levels in pet foods in particular. *Spectroscopy* magazine (January 2011) reported an investigation of 58 pet foods (31 dry, 27 wet, about half dog and half cat foods). The researchers found that pets take in far more heavy metals on a body-weight basis than considered safe in people.

• **A 10-pound cat** eating a cup a day of dry food or 1 small can of wet food would take in *30 times more mercury, 20 times more arsenic, 2 times more cadmium, and 3 times more uranium* than the level considered safe in humans. (Is there really an "allowance" for this stuff?)

• **A 50-pound dog** eating 5 cups a day of dry food or 1 large can of wet food would consume *120 times more mercury, 20 times more arsenic, 2 times more cadmium, and 5 times more uranium* than considered acceptable for us.[24]

That's amazing, isn't it? Notice that mercury and arsenic are particularly high. Deva Khalsa, VMD, reports that the tissues of dogs and cats have had *five times the amount of mercury per pound* found in humans.[25]

RECOGNIZING HEAVY METAL DAMAGE

With such differences, we can expect to see health effects in animals, and they are important to consider. Yet few veterinarians would consider heavy metals as the cause of symptoms your cat or dog may show, and most likely would treat her with antibiotics and steroids as if she had an infection or an inflammation in need of suppression. How much better it would be to find the underlying cause and try to reduce or eliminate it.

How might heavy metal poisoning from mercury or arsenic appear? What might alert us to test for heavy metals and treat accordingly, with a change of diet and a program to support detoxification?

First let's look at mercury, which gets into the atmosphere from volcanoes or forest fires, but mostly from coal-burning power plants as well as gold mining, where it has long been used to help extract gold. Eventually it is rained or washed into the seas. Unfortunately, once there, the mercury is converted by the microorganisms living in the water into a much more toxic form, methyl mercury. From there it accumulates in fish. The bigger the fish, the more it accumulates, which is why we—especially pregnant and breastfeeding women—are advised against eating tuna more than once a month. Mercury, in this form, especially affects the young. It is *extremely* toxic and causes both acute and chronic illness.

Pet foods are loaded with fish meal and other wastes from fishing trawlers. As we noted earlier, it is estimated that an average-size cat eats 30 pounds of seafood per year, twice what an average American eats. If the cat weighs 10 pounds and the average person 150 pounds, that means cats get about *30 times more seafood per pound of body weight than we do.* I now advise against feeding seafood (or eating it yourself), also because fishing is devastating our oceans. Mercury is found in other foods, too, but not in as high concentrations as in fish.

A Picture of Mercury Poisoning

What would mercury poisoning in a seafood-stuffed cat look like? Reports from both toxicological and homeopathic literature on effects of mercury describe symptoms likely to appear.

Mouth problems: The mouth is especially affected, with inflammation of the gums, redness, bad smell, loose teeth, decayed teeth, and excessive production of saliva. I find that especially intriguing and have come to suspect that the accumulation of mercury in cats' bodies is a major cause of how much trouble they often have with their mouths—the inflamed gums and decaying, loose, and abscessed teeth I often saw first-hand, just as described for mercury poisoning. When I started practice in 1965, cats had none of this mouth trouble; it is something that has developed in the last decades—clearly from something in the environment.

Enlarged thyroid: The literature also mentions the development of an enlarged thyroid with goiter. Could mercury be a factor in the many thyroid problems we see in practice?

Other signs of mercury poisoning can include weakness and tremors; mental slowness; ulcers; inflammation of the eye (especially the cornea and the iris); a thick, yellow, bloody, and bad-smelling ear discharge; chronic inflammation of the nose and the bones of the nose, with a discharge of green, bad-smelling material; diarrhea characterized by frequent bowel movements, but after passing the stool, a continued straining and effort as if more remained; and finally, stomach disorders, with the odd combination of weak digestion and yet continuous hunger.

Arsenic: Another Suspect

The other heavy metal of special concern is arsenic. It has been reported that some 88 percent of chickens raised for consumption have been fed organic forms of arsenic (as a parasite treatment) and that it is detectable in cooked samples.[26] Looking both at standard symptoms listed online, as well as detailed findings in centuries of homeopathic provings of *Arsenicum album*, here are typical signs that might come from arsenic poisoning.

- In either dogs or cats, you might see a gradually developing body weakness, exhaustion from slight exertion, being cold all the time, trouble digesting food, weight loss, and even cancer, as well as an unusual timidity or fear of strangers.
- In dogs, I would suspect high arsenic levels in those with a fear of being alone, red and raw nostrils and corners of the mouth, epilepsy, or paralysis of the esophagus. Arsenic could also underlie severe chronic skin diseases such as allergies and mange, with the hair falling out in circular patches and the skin looking rough and dirty.
- In cats, high arsenic levels might express more as chronic mouth inflammation with bleeding gums, ulcers, and thick, stringy, copious amounts of saliva—somewhat like you see with mercury, but more toward ulceration. You might also see chronic asthma, chronic cystitis with urine sediment (calculus), kidney disease, and uremia. Fluid may accumulate in the chest, and blood clots might form in vessels leading to the rear leg.

There are several websites focused on heavy metal issues for pets that you might want to explore. One is www.arsenic-dog-food.com.

GMOS: TODAY'S BIG FOOD CHALLENGE

And then there's farming, and it's not what it used to be.

Some of our grandparents were born before cars were even invented, when most people were organic family farmers. It was just the way things were. Yet, in just two generations we have seen huge changes: Most people live in cities, drive cars, surf the net, eat fast food, and fly all over the place. There are still some family farmers, but most farming is done by big corporations with heavy use of agricultural chemicals.

Toxic chemicals are particularly dangerous to developing infants and toddlers, and our postwar generation of boomers was the first raised on persistent pesticides designed to kill insects, including DDT and Dieldrin. Who knows what damage they caused us or our childhood pets? Dieldrin has been linked with Parkinson's, breast cancer, and damage to immune, reproductive, neurological, and endocrine systems, issues common among us.

By the time our generation came of age in the 1970s and we learned that it had not been a good idea to run behind the trucks spraying DDT everywhere when we were kids, we were more than ready to found the environmental movement and help ban a number of such pesticides. Even so, while tissue assays show levels are slowly going down, they are true to their name, and still persist in the tissues of most Americans.[27]

Since that time, each generation has had to grapple with other agricultural chemicals that come and go. One of the most concerning ones today is glyphosate, used in such high levels on the genetically modified crops that have come to dominate American agriculture since the 1990s, particularly the soy and corn raised to feed livestock, as well as canola and sugar beets.

Glyphosate: A Prime Suspect

Here's what happened. After discovering a bacterium that was resistant to the herbicide glyphosate (used in Monsanto's Roundup), biotech researchers got the bright idea to insert its DNA into major crops. That led to "Roundup Ready" corn, soy, canola, and sugar beets. Now farmers could spray Monsanto's flagship herbicide right onto those crops without harming them, while killing competing weeds.

It seemed like a good idea at the time. We remember doing a little research on glyphosate for the first edition of this book, in 1981, when it was commonly used to control weeds around homes. Animal tests showed that it had a low toxicity, so it was given the green light. When genetically modified organisms (GMOs) came along, authorities assured us their use would be safe and we would actually see reduced use of herbicides on farms.

But neither GM crops nor glyphosate has lived up to that promise, with many downsides predicted by the FDA's own scientists before GM crops got fast-track government approval and were rolled out in 1996.[28]

As predicted by geneticists, weeds eventually picked up the same DNA in Roundup-resistant GM crops, and so farmers have needed to use more and more of the herbicide. (Stronger herbicides are also on the way, a combination of glyphosate and 2-4-d, which was in Agent Orange, and this is not good news.) Meanwhile, most wheat farmers have also been using glyphosate for decades to dry out wheat and barley crops shortly before harvest.

As a result of both trends, glyphosate use on US crops has greatly increased since the mid-1990s. In 2014, Swanson, Leu, Abrahamson, and Wallet compared this with a dramatic increase in serious illnesses and decrease in life expectancy in the United States from 2009 to 2014. Using government data and statistical analysis, they found strong correlations with cancers of the liver, kidney, bladder, and thyroid; IBS (inflammatory bowel disease); autism in children; and deaths due to hypertension, diabetes, obesity, kidney disease, Parkinson's, Alzheimer's, and senile dementia. Correlation does not necessarily mean causality, but this is clearly an extremely important issue to consider today. Supporting their concern, they also note that German scientists found glyphosate accumulating in animal and human tissues, with significantly higher levels in chronically ill people, and they cite studies finding that it disrupts metabolic and endocrine functions, enhances damaging effects of other toxins in food, is toxic to liver cells, damages DNA, and kills beneficial gut bacteria and has led to a steep rise in intestinal diseases, particularly in farm animals.[29] More than ever, it's wise to choose organic foods.

Bt Corn

Another concern with GMOs is genetically engineered Bt corn. It all started with *Bacillus thuringiensis*, a smart little soil bacteria that long ago learned to make a natural toxin that kills insects by damaging their stomachs. Not good for insects, and not bad for us, and so it was approved for use in organic farming.

When biotech scientists identified the gene that creates this insecticide, they had another great idea that seemed good at the time: insert it into corn! "Bt corn" does kill insects, but the trouble is that the toxin in the corn is thousands of times more concentrated than any residues from those organic Bt sprays. There is no washing it off, either, because it is "built in" to every cell. Hmmm.

Well, despite warnings by scientists, Bt corn was approved and took off like wildfire. It's now in nearly all US corn products, including chips, tortillas, corn syrup, cornmeal (and thus many pet kibbles)—not to mention every manner of corn derivative in processed foods beloved by so many people.

There is some concern that eating GM corn could transfer the Bt gene to gut bacteria, contributing further to GI problems, including autoimmune diseases, food allergies, and childhood learning disorders. Government-sponsored Italian scientists have found that mice fed Bt corn showed a wide range of immune responses, such as elevated IgE and IgG antibodies, as well as cytokines. These are markers typically associated with allergies, infections, arthritis, inflammatory bowel disease, multiple sclerosis, and cancer. They also found elevated T cells, also high in people with asthma and children with food allergies, juvenile arthritis, and connective tissue diseases. There were also signs of liver and kidney toxicity.[30]

That's quite a bellyful. Makes us think twice about all those corn chips we gobbled down while waiting for meals at Mexican restaurants and makes us envy Europeans, who rejected GM foods early on.

Leaky Gut and Declining Health

What are glyphosate and GMOs doing to us? It's hard to separate out the effects as, for example, GM corn sprayed with glyphosate has both factors in the corn itself. If it is fed to animals and causes some health issues, how do we know which factor caused the harm? In any case, the government has not required GM crops to be tested for health effects, so we don't have very much information either way. A few animal studies found increased inflammation in the stomachs of pigs on GM versus non-GM feed, and the intestines of most US pigs are too thin now to be used in making sausage casings.[31]

There have also been very concerning studies about increased tumors and cancers in rats on a diet of GM food, with researchers reporting it difficult to be heard due to industry influence.

Glyphosate, meanwhile, has recently become a prime suspect in *leaky gut syndrome* and thus many autoimmune and inflammatory diseases. What in the world is this syndrome?

It has been found that our intestines, and those of other animals including dogs and cats, are home to a very large and significant group of bacteria and other organisms. This is normal and in fact *essential* to our health. They are involved in processing food, keeping out pathogens, even producing some nutrients we can absorb. To give you some idea of how many there are, the actual number of these little guys outnumbers all the cells in our bodies.

What is being called "leaky gut syndrome" is not fully understood yet, but scientists at the Massachusetts Institute of Technology have found that since bacteria (and some other essential organisms like fungi) are actually plants, they are being killed by the glyphosate in food. This alters conditions in the intestines, even to the point of their being colonized by other, unusual bacteria. The intestinal lining is affected, becoming "leaky" and allowing in things it is not supposed to. Some suggest this as an important factor in the rise in celiac disease, gluten intolerance, food allergies and autoimmune diseases, and even

autism, all on the increase since the 1990s.[32] For excellent overviews of this issue, see the April 23, 2013, edition of *Rodale's Organic Life* online[33] and the bestseller *Gut: The Inside Story of Our Body's Most Underrated Organ*, by Giulia Enders.

We did not anticipate this outcome but probably should have thought it through before making all these changes in our food crops. I mean, after all, if they lower nutritional quality, and create foods animals won't eat and that make you sick, what is the advantage?

Who's Minding the Store?

We would like to think that our government and the scientific establishment were really looking out for our best interests when it comes to GMOs, as well as other potentially harmful new technologies. But these issues are not at the forefront of US research, as the USDA and FDA are usually led by individuals with one foot in the industries they regulate. That's why these high-tech suspects are most often presumed innocent until proven guilty. Not good. Just look at the history of the tobacco industry.

But things are different abroad. Many, if not most, other countries have declared themselves "GMO free." They will not grow the crops or allow imports of the GM foods.

Think how several generations of US dogs and cats raised on kibbles full of GM corn and soy, plus by-products of farm animals fed the same way, have been inadvertent test animals.

Ponder where most American snack foods, corn chips, cornstarch, corn syrup, foods fried in vegetable oils (soy, corn, canola), tofu, soy milk, and such come from. Unless you know they are organic, you can pretty much bank on them being genetically engineered and sprayed with glyphosate on the farm. In North America, more than 80 percent of our food contains GMOs.[34] Most Americans want products containing GMOs to be labeled. While the industry has blocked such efforts, many large food companies now see the handwriting on the wall and are voluntarily labeling their products, seeking "verified non-GM" or "certified organic" status, so this is a good sign.

In spite of all these concerns, much research on the subject is suppressed and excluded from industry-controlled journals, it is said, and the momentum toward genetic modification of organisms is increasing rather than diminishing. What is in the pipeline is rather shocking. Cats that glow in the dark, carrying DNA from a jellyfish that turns them green under certain blue lights, have already been "made." There is also a company that says it has produced an "allergy-free" cat by modifying it so it cannot make certain proteins. The cats' initial price tag was about $4,000. Since then, it has been bumped up to almost $6,000, with a Siamese variation going for $10,900 and an exotic "wildcat" version that costs $35,000. It is not clear if this has really been done, but gives you some idea where things are going. It could get pretty crazy.

GM-Free Diets: Remarkable Recoveries

Most of us know someone who can't eat this or that. Sometimes it seems more common than not. Makes it hard to eat out or have folks over for dinner. Yet, such people often say they are okay when they travel in Europe, where countries refuse to use these modified foods.

It *is* possible to avoid GMs here, however, by eating only organic or non-GM-verified foods containing soy, corn, or canola; sugar beets or their many derivatives; vegetable oils; high fructose corn syrup; soy protein isolates; and more. It's easiest and healthiest to just generally avoid packaged and processed foods, since most contain these ingredients.

GM activist Jeffrey Smith reported in a recent lecture we attended that the American Academy of Environmental Medicine recommends doctors prescribe non-GM diets to all their patients. A study of 3,600 subjects confirmed that GM-free diets help patients across the board: First they report gastrointestinal improvements, followed by increased energy, better memory, better moods, and clearer thinking, with less mucus, inflammation, yeast infections, eczema, need for sleep, and fewer headaches. Plus they are able to lose weight. Most results happen in a fairly short time.

A quick survey of the audience showed similar results among those who had tried non-GM diets.[35] We wholeheartedly recom-

- **The main GM food crops** to date have been **corn, soy, canola, and sugar beets**. Their oils and derivatives are in most processed foods, some 80 percent of US supermarket foods.

- **Most corn and soy is GM and is fed to livestock.** Unless labeled "organic" or "non-GM," figure that meat, dairy, and eggs are from animals fed these GM foods.

- **Corn, soy, and their derivatives are often top ingredients in supermarket pet foods.** Unless labeled "organic" or "non-GM," as of this writing, assume they are GM.

- **GM alfalfa, potatoes, zucchini, and papayas** are also in production and many more GM crops are in the approval pipeline. Even grass-fed beef is now suspect, with release of GM alfalfa.

- **GM-free diets** have been reported to reverse many chronic conditions, according to doctors and patients.

mend that you try this out for yourself, your family, and your animals. I would give it at least 2 months before evaluating. After that, it might even be that a pet or a person who has had trouble handling soy, corn, or wheat may be better able to digest their organic versions.

WHAT TO DO?

What can we do about all this? How can we bring back those disappearing nutrients and shuttle out those toxins we never asked for? In a nutshell, here's what we suggest, probably in order of importance. These guidelines apply to us, of course, as well as our companion animals. In fact, there are many meals you and your pets can share (see Pets plus People recipes in Chapter 6).

Other Steps to Take

Beyond diet, these practices will help your animal (and you) safely eliminate toxins that have accumulated through time and reduce nondietary sources of new ones.

- Drink plenty of pure, filtered, chlorine-free water.

- Get proper rest and daily exercise and grooming (Chapter 11).

- Drink gentle detox tea blends made from dandelion root, etc. (Chapter 18).

- Fast occasionally.

- Use safe glass, steel, or Pyrex food containers and bowls instead of plastics.

- Use nontoxic options for flea control, body care, and other household products (Chapters 10 and 11).

• Vacuum, sweep, and mop regularly (without chemicals!).

• Try to lower your stress levels, maximize your positive feelings, and play (Chapters 12 and 13).

We can blame industry, but in the end it is up to us to stop purchasing products that carry a burden of toxins and to find better alternatives. There are many things we can do without or we can reuse an existing item instead, reducing the need for more manufacturing. We can also look for simple solutions—often the tried-and-true ones of our ancestors. Coconut or olive oil makes a fine face cream. Vinegar and water clean most anything around the house. Bar soap is a good shampoo that eliminates the need for plastics. Organic cotton makes fine clothing, towels, and bedding, as do bamboo sheets. Baking soda is a superior deodorant and tooth powder. We can also support social action groups, laws, and politicians that address these issues more effectively. (See Chapters 10 and 11 for more on natural products for your home and for grooming animals.)

THE BIG PICTURE: PRESSURES ON THE FOOD SUPPLY

This update to our dietary recommendations has been quite a journey, chasing after a shifting world. Long ago, we realized how

DIETARY GUIDELINES FOR MORE NUTRIENTS AND FEWER TOXINS

• *Reduce or eliminate animal products*, especially fatty ones and seafood (applies to dogs and people particularly).*

• *Eliminate all GMOs* (any soy, corn, canola unless labeled "non-GMO" or "organic").

• Use *whole foods* rather than packaged, processed, or refined ones.

• Choose *organic* when possible.

• Include ample *nutrient-dense plant foods*** (especially applies to dogs and people).

• The more *local, fresh, and in season,* the better.

• Maintain a *lean weight* (see Chapter 8 for weight-loss suggestions).

* See our ample-protein low-meat or no-meat recipes in Chapter 6.
** Joel Fuhrman has an acronym for these for humans: GBOMBS (greens, beans, onions, mushrooms, berries, and seeds). For pets, we must eliminate onions, which are said to be toxic to them in large quantities. Focus on greens and beans, plus colorful veggies or veggie sauces from carrots, winter squash, tomatoes, corn, peas, and the like. Dogs enjoy berries as well.

the second-rate ingredients and overprocessing of conventional packaged pet foods can undermine health. As the years have passed, we have come to see how much even the ingredients you might use in a freshly prepared home diet are also increasingly loaded with toxins and lower in nutrients. We can help reduce the load by buying, eating, and feeding organic and non-GM foods, but we also have come to realize there is a bigger picture we need to understand.

Modern agricultural practices stem from one central and pressing concern: the need to produce more and more food for our growing population. That need is what really spawned new chemicals, engineering, and breeding to speed up plant growth, kill insects, and kill off competing weeds. It triggered the shift from small family farms to larger, more efficient and mechanized operations. It led to crowding animals into small enclosures, feeding them unnatural foods, and continuous use of hormones and antibiotics.

This pressure on the food system is also why most pet foods are made from the leftovers of the food industry. It also is increasingly pricing organic food—let alone luxuries like grass-fed beef for the dog—out of many people's budgets.

Then, as we explored food production

issues further, we came across some rather shocking concerns about food quantity that override those about food quality: The global demand for food, most particularly for animal products, is placing dangerous pressures on the world's resources and ecosystems, far more than we realized.

Eating lower on the food chain is more than just a good way to reduce toxins or increase most nutrients, as we have seen in this chapter. It looks to be the most important thing we can do to save our food supply and our world. And that is the ultimate health issue.

Furthermore, if we are to continue to feed and enjoy the bright-eyed dogs and cats who have long walked beside humankind, we must begin to reach out and gently beckon them to join us on this plant-based journey.

There is challenge in all this, but also opportunity. Making such a shift, with our animals beside us, will bring us to a kinder relationship with all our fellow creatures, and with Earth's forests, seas, grasslands, deserts, and farms: a partnership that is loving and respectful to all.

We were born to create such a world. It is never too late to learn from our mistakes as a species or as individuals, to make amends and to become the change we wish to see.

CHAPTER 4

LOVING THE EARTH . . .
AND *ALL* ANIMALS

Author and speaker Colleen Patrick Goudreau has loved animals all her life, with many dear dogs and cats in her home. Yet it was that very connection that helped her see that all animals are lovable, not the least of them the large, gentle cows she also loves to touch these days as she fulfills her life's mission: to help us extend our natural compassion to *all* species, including those countless unseen farmed and fished animals who end up on our plates (and, as we all know, in the bowls of our pets).

Like Colleen, most of us love dogs, we love cats, and we love nature, but true love knows no boundaries. So there comes a point at which our hearts speak up and we ask ourselves, "Don't we care about *all* animals? About all life?" The answer for us is a resounding yes.

We suspect that is your answer as well, and so we invite you into this part of our journey into food with an open heart, an open mind, and the joy that arises when we become part of the solution. Look over at that cat or dog you love and perhaps invite her to sit beside you. It is her world as well.

Our world is changing quickly, and that often requires us to change as well. As we saw in the last chapter, eating lower on the food chain is a real key to reducing the many toxins accumulating in our animals' bodies, as well as in our own. For us humans, that is not difficult. We are primates, after all, and there is much evidence that plant-based diets suit our physiology and do us good.

But dogs and cats? Our bent has always been to follow nature's way, and what could be more natural than feeding the popular raw meat diet that many advocate today to animals whose evolution and physiology are perfectly designed to eat other animals? So, when I first realized the impact of the environmental toxins accumulating in all meat today on the health of our dogs and cats, it was a conundrum, believe me. Yet, as I looked further, I saw other, even more compelling reasons to rethink what we feed our animals and ourselves in our changing world.

Raising and killing billions and billions of animals for food has now become the single most significant cause of the destruction of our planet's ecosystems. We have pushed past the natural limit of what our Earth can produce, and that threatens everyone's future and everyone's well-being.

More immediately, the consumption of meat, dairy, and eggs has a huge and appalling impact on farmed animals themselves. What we feed our companions and ourselves is a direct cause of prolonged and severe suffering for other animals who are just as conscious, sensitive, and emotional as that dog or cat sitting by our side, and we contribute to that suffering with every meal that is made at their expense.

It's a new century and a changing world, and we are being informed from many directions that we cannot continue our present dietary habits much longer if we are to have the kind of world we want to live in. Fortunately, as we will see in the next chapter, there is a healthy, humane, and sustainable alternative for our animals as well as for ourselves.

For now, though, let's look at some numbers and some facts, so you will understand just why we are so concerned about the impact that eating animal products has on our planet and on the animals whose lives are devastated by it.

EARTH IN CRISIS

One evening in late 2014 we watched a film with our monthly potluck group that changed our lives overnight. It is rare that a film is so powerful, but *Cowspiracy: The Sustainability Secret* was. Since then, we have shared many copies of this masterful documentary, now on Netflix, and it has changed the lives of many others as well.

First off, we learned that our beautiful blue-green Earth is in far more trouble than most of us realize. It's not just the climate change issue we hear so much about.

Experts from many fields warn of almost unthinkable consequences if we continue on our present course.

We have all heard about the destruction of nature, as well as threats to resources like water, fisheries, and forests. But until recently few of us have heard that there is *one key cause* of all our leading environmental problems: our high consumption of meat, dairy, eggs, and seafood.

As one sustainability expert summed it up, "Animal agriculture is an environmental disaster." Here's what we learned that night, and from continued research of our own.

THE HIGH COST OF ANIMAL-BASED DIETS[1]

EXPERTS WARN IF WE CONTINUE ON OUR PRESENT COURSE, THE FOLLOWING WILL HAPPEN.	IMPACTS OF ANIMAL FOODS
Forest and species loss: By 2025 we could lose the Amazon, the "lungs of the earth." Rain forests are the most biodiverse habitats on Earth. We are losing about 137 wild species a day. At this rate half the world's species will vanish by midcentury.	Ninety-one percent of Amazon destruction is due to grazing cattle or growing feed, mostly for export to the United States, Europe, and China, depleting soils in a few short years.
Disappearing waters: No one knows for sure, but it is possible that the Ogallala Aquifer beneath America's most productive cropland in the Great Plains *could go dry as soon as 2030.* To be sustainable, we must reduce its water draw by 80%, about the amount for crops fed to livestock. California is also in trouble, and some 25% of global aquifers are being depleted. Wells are going dry in India, and glacial loss in the Himalayas threatens major rivers throughout Asia. Meanwhile, climate change will bring more drought. Our desperate search for energy has brought us "fracking," a way of injecting huge amounts of freshwater into drilled holes to force natural gas and oil to the surface. It takes a whopping 100 billion gallons of precious freshwater per year in the United States.	Most US corn, soy, and oats is fed to livestock. It takes about 100 times more water to produce the same amount of protein from animals as from plants. One pound of beef can use 2,500 to 8,000 gallons. A pound of potatoes takes just 34 gallons. People protest fracking, yet animal agriculture uses more than 34 trillion gallons of good water, some 340 times more.
Fishless seas? By 2050, the oceans may be all fished out. Trawlers gather fish and other sea life by dragging nets along the ocean floor, destroying ecosystems. Seventy-five percent of global fisheries are already depleted or in decline. Despite a questionable industry rating system, experts say there is no such thing as sustainable fishing.	Half the catch goes to livestock, fish farms, and pets. Eighty percent is "by-kill," sea creatures not wanted, such as dolphins or sharks, which are basically thrown away.

EXPERTS WARN IF WE CONTINUE ON OUR PRESENT COURSE, THE FOLLOWING WILL HAPPEN.	IMPACTS OF ANIMAL FOODS
Ocean dead zones: Over 400 oxygen-depleted dead zones near inhabited coastlines are killing the richest concentrations of marine life. These are increasing in size and number.	The main cause of dead zones is massive runoff of fertilizers and manure from factory farms and croplands supplying them.
Climate change: Climate change is real, increasing, and human caused, according to 97% of climate scientists. It is expected to increase in severity in the coming decades, drowning hundreds of coastal cities and causing extreme weather and storms and large droughts that will lead to large migrations and increasing difficulties, threatening us all.	Some 51% of greenhouse gases may be due to livestock production, more than all transport. Cattle produce large amounts of methane, far more potent than carbon dioxide.
Soil loss: We may run out of topsoil by 2070 at current rates of degradation. Some 40% of global farm soils are already either "degraded" or "seriously degraded" (70% of topsoil gone). Soil is being lost 10 to 40 times faster than it can be naturally replenished, even on idyllic-looking farms in Europe.	It takes about 18 times more land to produce an omnivorous standard American diet than a plant-based vegan diet.
Mass starvation: One billion humans are underfed and malnourished, unable to afford grains, used mostly to feed livestock for wealthier people. Many die, including children. Yet, the world's population could double by midcentury. Another billion are overfed but malnourished on diets too high in animal products, and demand keeps increasing.	We could feed 12 billion to 15 billion vegans on current farmlands and actually re-wild much of the earth, allowing nature to heal.
Fossil fuel depletion: We are using up our finite fossil fuels, on which we depend for almost everything: transportation, heating and cooling, electricity, fertilizers, the pumping of water and sewage, medicines, plastics, and much more.	Each person who goes plant based saves enough fuel to drive 16,000 miles a year.

Wow. Now consider some of the impacts of feeding meat to your dog or cat, even if you yourself eat little or none.

• Feeding one dog just 4 ounces of beef (*one* burger) uses some 600 gallons of freshwater! That's 6 days' worth of entire household use in our area.

• One cat eating a couple of ounces of meat a day doesn't seem like much. But feed that amount to some 94 million cats in the United States and it is almost 12 million pounds daily, the equivalent of 3 million chickens that must be fed, watered, and housed for months, and then killed, processed, and packaged, each and every day.[2]

• As the world eats today, we are using up the resources of about 1.6 Earths. If everyone consumed as many animal products as most Americans, it would take 3 Earths. If everyone consumed as much as people on the popular low-carb, high-meat Paleo diet, it could take 10 Earths. *Feeding pets, especially large dogs, the "raw diet" is the equivalent of the totally unsustainable Paleo diet.*

A GAME CHANGER

Unless we cut way back on animal products, we will likely see widespread shortages of food and water, perhaps within our own lifetimes. In short, disaster. No one knows the future for certain. Some of these scary predictions may go too far.

Yet, what if even half are spot on? What would that mean for our children and grandchildren, and even us during the remainder of our lifetimes? What would it mean for all life on Earth? Is consuming meat ourselves or feeding it to our pets just a matter of personal choice and preference when it has such impact?

More importantly, is another future still possible? What if we can change the course of this *Titanic*? That's where *Cowspiracy* really inspired us, along with many books, films,

lectures, and blogs we have explored since. All agree that there is one simple but profound choice we can each make that will create a much brighter future: *to shift to a plant-based diet.*

The impact is immediate and significant. Let's start with us two-leggeds and work it from there.

EACH DAY A PERSON EATS PLANT BASED SAVES ABOUT:

• 1,100 gallons of freshwater
• 45 pounds of grain
• 30 square feet of forest
• 20 pounds of carbon dioxide (CO_2) equivalents going into the atmosphere
• Enough fossil fuel to drive 46 miles
• One animal's life

For us it was a no-brainer. We made the plant-based shift overnight, along with a number of friends, and we love our new diet. We are all eating a lot more fresh veggies and fruits and beans and whole grains, while losing excess pounds and experiencing reversals of thyroid, kidney, and arthritis problems. Our cholesterol is going down and our hearts are in good shape.

It's not just our physical hearts either. Eating plant based feels really good inside. It allows us to live by our values of compassion and caring for all animals. That gives us a deeper sense of purpose.

At the same time, many people we know,

including veterinarians, have also switched their animals to plant-based foods. For dogs, it's a breeze. They adapted long ago to eating plant-based human foods and often do remarkably *better* on such diets, as we will see in the next chapter.

YOU AND YOUR DOG, SAVING THE WORLD TOGETHER

So what would be the environmental benefits of switching your dog? Let's say you have a 70-pound Golden Retriever you have been feeding meat. An online pet food calculator at www.merrickpetcare.com/how-to-switch/food-calculator shows he normally needs about 1,472 calories a day, close to the needs of an average woman (1,500 calories). If he eats about the same percentage of meat as the average American (and some eat more), that means he could save the earth just as much as you. In just 1 day, the two of you teamed up together could save some 2,200 gallons of water, 90 pounds of feed grain, 60 square feet of rain forest, and two animals' lives. Not bad for a day's accomplishments.

Do it together for the next critical 5 years, and you are *really* cooking. You can share a lot of the same meals, improve your health, and at the end celebrate that you and your buddy saved:

- More than 4 million gallons of water
- 82 tons of grain to feed the hungry
- 109,500 square feet of rain forest, and its countless inhabitants
- 73,000 pounds of CO_2 equivalents

- Enough gas to drive 167,900 miles (around the world more than seven times)
- 3,650 other animals' lives

You might want to sit down with him after you finish this chapter and have a little chat about all this! If he could really understand the stakes, I bet it's what he'd choose. In fact, compared to a lot of humans, dogs can be downright accommodating.

Taking it further, what if you have been feeding a raw diet to several large dogs, each wolfing down more meat than most people eat? Shifting them to a healthy plant-based diet would be a huge environmental, as well as humane, contribution, probably more than anything else you could ever hope to do.

Imagine the possibilities. What if all 77.9 million dogs in the United States alone went plant based? What if millions of felines agreed to meet us halfway? What if every human in the world returned to our plant-eating primate origins?

What a different and more beautiful world it would be.

BYPASSING THE "MIDDLE ANIMAL"

As you can see, learning what a difference we could make just by changing our food choices was an exciting discovery for us for many reasons, including the huge difference it makes for all kinds of animals: wildlife, cows, pigs, chickens, lambs, rabbits, turkeys, and more.

But first, let's look at a few more numbers so we can better understand just *why* plant foods hold such promise for a better future.

The bottom line is this: Going to plants is going right to the source, and that's far more efficient. Instead of growing crops for livestock, watering them, housing them, transporting them, slaughtering them, and refrigerating their products, we can simply bypass the "middle animals" and get our nutrients the same way they do, from plants.

In spite of popular misunderstandings, whole natural plant foods have all the protein we and our pets need, plus they are richer in most vitamins and minerals, as we will detail in the next chapter.

To make this efficiency concept more real, let's say we have some land. We could raise beef, either turning it out to pasture, or growing corn and soy on it to feed them as most producers do today. Or, we could grow some crops directly for ourselves. How much food could we produce?

We did a little homework[3] and here is about the most we could get from each acre to feed our families, our working dog, and the cats out in our hypothetical barn (who would probably eat mice).

ON 1 ACRE	POUNDS OF YIELD	CALORIES OF YIELD	CALORIES COMPARED TO GRASS-FED BEEF
Grass-fed beef	22	19,140	1x
Grain-fed beef	250	376,500	20x
Beans	12,178	3,595,878	188x
Wheat	2,614	3,889,632	189x
Corn	7,841	12,984,696	678x
Potatoes	39,000	14,191,120	741x

Amazing, isn't it? I don't know about you, but we're planting potatoes, corn, soybeans, and pintos! You can see clearly see why those staple crops were the key to our past, and why they will also be the key to our future.

Despite the brainwashing we've all received about protein, *even potatoes have more than enough protein to meet human needs* (long established by the World Health Organization as just 5 to 7 percent of calories), and legumes have plenty for dogs and cats. We can also see why the United Nations declared 2008 the "International Year of the Potato," honoring the humble potato as crucial to food security and ending poverty.[4] Besides, potatoes are easy to grow, even in pots.

SUSTAINABLE MEAT?

Back to beef: Now we can see just why *97 percent* of cattle go to those big, smelly, fly-infested feedlots. Idyllic as it is to see animals grazing peacefully out in pastures, the reality is that we can only produce a very small amount of meat that way. Grass-fed beef requires some 20 times more land than grain fed, which *in itself* takes 9 to 37 times more land than the staple crops shown. As shown in colorful graphics in *Cowspiracy*, to grass-feed all the animals we Americans and our pets now consume would require the entire US landmass, plus much of Canada and South America![5] On top of that absurdity, pastured animals drink even more water and emit even more methane than feedlot cows because it takes them longer to reach market weight.

Nevertheless, there are lands better suited for grazing than farming. It's a much better life for the animals and much less disturbing to ecosystems than growing crops (although millions of predators are killed to protect livestock). Some small traditional mixed farms with rotational pastures will probably always be viable, especially in lush zones. Backyard poultry flocks or goats may be sustainable, depending on how much of their food comes from foraging or, for example, expired vegetable wastes from local markets.

People can and do debate the place of livestock and poultry, if any, in sustainable agriculture and if you do feel the need to use some meat, say, for your cat, pastured sources are your best choice. But to put it in perspective, how much meat might actually be sustainable? When asked this question, food writer Michael Pollan says it is difficult to know for sure, but he would guess "on the order of 2 ounces a week"[6] (and he eats meat himself).

In other words, once a week we and our pets could share about half a quarter-pounder (Sundays?). Right now we Americans consume about 32 times that much meat (62 ounces a week)—five times more than most people in the world—and many advocate that we and our pets eat even more.

As you can see, something's got to give. Fortunately, in 2016, China, which now consumes 28 percent of the world's meat, announced a plan to cut consumption by half, to combat global warming and stem its rising tide of diabetes.[7]

Finally, what about the impact that this choice might have on the animals that become part of our pets' meals? Besides feeling good about reducing our impact on the planet by choosing plant-based foods for ourselves and our pets, we can also, it turns out, feel even better about what that means for countless other animals we will never know, but who can also find a very large home in our hearts.

LOVING *ALL* ANIMALS

"There comes a time when we must take a position that is neither safe, nor politic, nor popular, but one must take it because it is right."—Martin Luther King Jr.

It was a warm spring day near Davis, California. The year was 1963, and I worked weekends at an egg production operation to pay my way through the University of California Veterinary School where I was enrolled. As I opened the door at the end of the long, windowless steel shed, my ears were assaulted as usual with angry, insane shrieks from the hundreds of hens screaming at me from every direction.

My job was twofold: to ride a cart down the aisle, dispensing feed into long rows of hoppers in front of the crowded wire cages, and to collect the eggs that rolled into a lower trough. Until then, my main experience with chickens had been with a small backyard flock my dad tended in Los Angeles. This was a new world to me, and it opened my eyes to the methods that corporate-run facilities use to create products at the lowest possible price.

As I reached out to pour the feed into the hoppers, the chickens would try to attack me, pecking with the fury of their pent-up frustrations. These hens were not like those we used to have. These hens never saw the light of day, never walked on the earth, and never pecked at a single blade of grass.

Beneath them was a pile of their manure, now several feet high. They were packed three or four into cages not much larger than a placemat, unable to even open their wings. It was not uncommon to see a dead bird oddly flattened to a feathery white carpet beneath some hens' feet, left to rot and dry up until the cages were turned over at the time of slaughter. For an egg layer, that comes just a year or two into her life, once her production begins to drop off.

Years later, when I was telling this story to my wife, Susan, she said, "That sounds terrible. Didn't it make you think twice about what you ate?"

The truth is, it didn't. No one I knew then was even a vegetarian, I had never even heard of the word *vegan*, and most of us just do not question things that are widely accepted. In the mid-1970s I met Susan, and we both became vegetarians, as did many others at that time, giving up meat but still eating eggs and milk products and eventually making exceptions for fish when vegetarianism became too inconvenient when eating out. So I understand the tendency to just go along with general trends.

Through the years we read books and saw films that offered plenty of reasons to adopt an all-plant-based diet and we would sometimes try it for a little while, always making compromises, mostly for taste and convenience. It was not until 2014, when we really understood the compelling environmental reasons to eat plant based, that I had my last piece of salmon, my last egg, and my last piece of cheese—not that they were really ever "mine," of course. The flesh, the eggs, and the milk all belonged to the animals themselves.

Seeing *Cowspiracy* pushed us over the edge and we decided to go vegan. But what has kept us vegan since then, and will keep us vegan for life, was what we learned next. With our new Internet-connected television, we began to spend many evenings exploring YouTube lectures on veganism, or reading books or blogs.

Only then did we really understand the true price that animals had paid all those years for our seemingly innocuous diet. We thought we were sparing animals' lives by not eating meat and did not realize how producing dairy products and eggs also resulted in early deaths for them. We may as well have eaten meat all those years instead of the many omelets, cheese sandwiches, and yogurts we had downed without a second thought.

Why? First, all dairy cows and egg-laying chickens are eventually slaughtered, if they have not already died of stress, disease, or injury. But meanwhile, they usually undergo even greater suffering and stress, often even if the word "organic" or "cage-free" was on their product packages.

THE STORY OF EGGS

Eggs, for example, come from chickens, and chickens come from hatcheries where fertilized eggs are incubated in stacks of drawers. Shortly after the chicks hatch, no mother in sight, they are tossed en masse onto a conveyor belt where they are sorted by gender. Since males have no use either as layers or as meat (on traditional farms, they were likely raised for meat), they are thrown into an auger that grinds them up alive, or else slowly suffocated in plastic bags or dumpsters. Sometimes they are plowed into fields while alive. These hatcheries supply small

organic farmers and backyard hobbyists, as well as the industry.

The girl chicks have it even worse. While still young, their beaks are painfully snipped short to minimize pecking damage in egg batteries much like the one I worked in. They are bred and otherwise forced with lights, feed, and other techniques to lay far more eggs than their ancestors. (Even in backyard coops, they typically die after a few years from reproductive tract problems owing to this stress.) Come slaughter time, they are pretty scrawny and pecked over. Some are too spent to bother with. All who are sent to slaughter, especially fattened "broilers," are stacked in hundreds of cages in trucks, deprived of food or water, sometimes for days.

Those that arrive alive often have broken wings. They are then stunned in electric baths and shackled upside down to have their throats cut. The trouble is, they are not necessarily unconscious as they are plunged into a scalding tank before their feathers are plucked out.

MILK: IT TAKES A BABY

Even though we all know better, were we to think about it (and who should know better than a veterinarian?), dairy cows do not just "give milk." They must have a baby first, like all mammals. So every year they are inseminated (artificially and somewhat uncomfortably). I was taught how to do this in vet school but was never involved enough with dairy farms to see the realities that happen after that.

Calves are inconvenient and use up too much product, so shortly after a modern dairy cow gives birth, her baby is dragged away, to her deep anguish. Both can bellow for days, a sound that we are told is more heartrending than anything heard in a slaughterhouse. We recently saw a video about a rescued cow who had lost several calves; she shed tears even years later when meeting a new calf on a farm sanctuary.[8] Male calves are then killed or chained by themselves in veal crates, where they are lonely and fed milk replacers to make them anemic (which makes their flesh pale and tender), or just raised briefly before slaughter. About half the female calves are also killed young as they are not needed to replace members of the dairy herd, with the other half headed for production. Most live indoors these days, or in pens. Pasturing them is, once again, inefficient. Like chickens, they are forced to produce far more milk than cows did just 50 years ago, often suffering from painful mastitis, uterine issues, calcium loss, and more.

There is much more we could delve into, stories that would break your heart. Stories about pigs crammed into tiny metal pens too small for them to even turn around in. Stories about abuse and routine mutilations, filth, flies, and ammonia in the air. Affidavits of slaughterhouse workers forced by large companies pushing the stunning process too fast to skin as many as 25 percent of cows while still alive and conscious. Stories of pigs thrashing for minutes in scalding water. Such atrocities are beyond unacceptable, and they are common.[9]

This information is everywhere, and easily found online. The question is whether we are willing to look at it and to act on what our hearts tell us. I'm pretty sure that most of us would not ourselves do the things we pay others to do out of sight.

And we would never, ever, not for a second, tolerate these things being done to the animals for whom we care.

So, when some people say it is cruel to deprive a dog or cat of meat, their natural food, I always think, at least to myself, "There are far greater cruelties involved in producing that meat." If a cat catches a rat or wolves down an elk, yes, that is natural. The lives of their prey are a far cry from those of trillions of animals treated as meat, milk, and egg machines, and not the feeling, sentient creatures they are—every bit as much as the ones in our homes.

A CHANGE OF HEART

As you can see, I have spent most of my life going along with a lot of the ways we were all raised to think about animals farmed for food. But nowadays, in my midseventies, my choice is to reconcile my actions with my heart and my deepest values. Factory farming has created such incredible suffering for animals. They have such pitiable lives, many never seeing the sun or touching the earth, kept alive by constant drug administration, subject to painful mutilations and crowding and killed young.

This is not a concern for everyone, but as a veterinarian, I ask myself why I would care for, study, and work hard to help certain kinds of animals but, at the same time, not care for others. I cannot. My heart will not allow me to support most of what we do to animals for food and other purposes. Since I would not kill and eat a dog just because he might make a tasty dinner, or pay someone else to do that for me, why would I do that to a cow, a pig, a sheep, or a chicken?

As a person who has devoted his life to healing and caring for animals, that sits really well with me. And it feels good to get to know more and more other people who feel the same way. I think our culture is undergoing a sea change when it comes to our treatment of animals, and as we do, we will surely come to treat each other much better as well.

Whether we are 4 years old or 80, it is natural for us to love and care for all kinds of animals, including those we never meet. When we do meet them, even if just in videos, it is obvious that cows, pigs, chickens, sheep, goats, and their kin are just as lovable as dogs and cats. They are intelligent, sensitive, curious, resourceful, nurturing, and remarkably patient with human beings.

We both hope that one day, all such animals will still be with us, but living peacefully on the growing numbers of farm sanctuaries, where they are treated with kindness and affection and serve to remind us that they are little different from ourselves in the ways that matter most.

One of our heroes in our new way of living is Howard Lyman, a former rancher who used modern production methods to rework his Montana farm into a large enterprise. One day, while recovering from a near-fatal disease, he had a change of heart and got out of the business. He became a vegan and has spent many years traveling and speaking to others about why he did that.

Gently stroking a cow in his beautiful online documentary, *Mad Cowboy,* Lyman tells us as only one with his experience can, "Cows don't have a bad bone in them." Turning, he whispers to her to please, when she gets to heaven, tell her friends that he is doing all he can for them.

It's a touching moment, in a touching film.

Lyman is not alone. These days, when most family farms have become corporate "operations" where 99 percent of animal agriculture takes place, many just cannot find it in their hearts to continue. That includes former factory farmers, such as described in the "Pig Farmer," a report by John Robbins (search this online), as well as small "humane farmers" who treat their animals better, but still perform many standard mutilations such as dehorning, tail docking, flesh notches, nose rings, ear tags, castrations, teeth removal, and more, without benefit of anesthesia, and still find they have to shut off part of themselves to send their animals to their deaths.

It is good to care, and to choose more humane products, but labels can be misleading. "Free range" or "cage-free" usually means thousands of birds crammed into a filthy shed with small concrete runs. "Pastured" can mean the animals are just kept in a dusty corral.

Some particularly beautiful films that might make you want to adopt a pig, chicken, lamb, or goat next time you are looking for a companion animal are *The Last Pig* (2016) and *Peaceable Kingdom* (2009).

As you have read this chapter, you may have wondered why most of us don't know these things, and why they are not headline news (so far). When we first learned about the true impacts of our casual food choices on others and on our future, we wondered that ourselves.

Maybe we are just too far removed from the realities of where our food comes from. Certainly, many companies don't want us to know those realities and stop buying their products, even creating "ag gag" laws with strict consequences for activists exposing truths about animal agriculture.

We also fear stepping out of the crowd, and sometimes it's just uncomfortable to change our habits, so we look the other way. Plus, there is much that keeps us busy and distracted.

But mostly, I think it's that we see no rea-

son to change. We still have it pretty good, much like the first-class passengers on the *Titanic,* dining in luxury and unaware of what soon awaits us. That is, unless we change our course.

In closing this important chapter, we very much want to acknowledge and appreciate you and all our readers for your love for animals and your desire to care for them naturally. A lifetime of work in this field has shown us that nurturing companion animals is an important way that many people maintain a connection with our disappearing natural world.

Even more importantly, it can also teach us about love and about being present. Animals and babies often teach us the joy of simply being, freed of thoughts about the past or future, relatively unencumbered by images that often stand between us and another.

So we invite you to take a moment and let that reservoir of the love and joy that you have ever felt for any animal simply expand. Let it expand now toward *all* animals, *all* people, *all* places where life lives. This expanded kind of love is not only lovely to experience in itself, but it is essential for opening your heart and mind to the more beautiful world we can all create.

A PRAYER TO THE ANIMALS

Richard Pitcairn

I am with you, brothers and sisters
of fur, feather, beak, and hoof,
for we share one life
and are one in the heart.
To all those caged and confined,
may you soon be free.
To those that have never seen the sun,
may light fill your being.
To those that have never touched the earth
your mother will embrace you soon.
To those that have lost their child,
no solace will suffice.
To the child taken from your mother
may you yet know love.
To those forced to eat each other,
may love become your only nutrient.
To our wild cousins
that have lost their homes
and are leaving this earth,
may you find the life you have sought.
To those to whom we have intentionally
transferred our diseases,
we beg forgiveness and pray
that we will now
keep our problems to ourselves.
To those we have killed and eaten
in worship to the god of taste,
may your sacrifice be seen
as our final learning
that the greatest pleasure
is truly
the love we have for each other.
May we travel together
brothers and sisters
in peace and harmony
paw in hand
wing on shoulder
tail on arm
to the world of oneness
the Garden of Eden
that we have always known.

CHAPTER 5

HEALTHY, HUMANE, AND SUSTAINABLE: NEW DIETS FOR A NEW ERA

In the 21st century, choosing what to feed dogs and cats has become a unique challenge. It's no longer as simple as being concerned about the poor ingredients and overprocessing of most pet foods. We are witnessing a growing decline in the health of dogs and cats that is connected with the decreasing nutrients and increasing toxins in all foods, but especially the bioaccumulation of toxins in animal products and seafoods today. On top of that, there is a very high cost to eating high on the food chain—for our planet and our children and no less for the countless factory-farmed animals and disappearing wildlife who pay the ultimate price each and every day, each an animal as eager to live and to have a good life as those we know and love.

So, while our classic diets for dogs and cats included meat, we knew we had to take a fresh look at food in this major update. With the destructive impacts of animal agriculture on our diminishing resources, we knew we were looking at an inevitable game changer for all of us, dogs and cats included. If we want to leave this an inhabitable world, we simply cannot continue consuming the amount of meat and other animal products that we have in recent decades. Frankly, it appears that we will soon have little choice.

And so the question has occurred to us and to many others: If we are to continue with dogs and cats as our companions, can they somehow join us on this needed journey? If so, to what degree? Should we not at least see what is possible?

To take that fresh look at feeding pets requires looking outside the box, beyond the common view in the holistic animal care world lately that the "raw," "species-appropriate" diet so centered on fresh meat is the only healthy way to feed dogs and cats. After all, the story goes, their ancestors were predators and they share that physiology, so therefore they need meat. Some will say that it is absurd or even cruel to suggest otherwise even though there are many reports of both dogs and cats doing fine on well-planned meatless diets that meet their nutritional requirements.

So, walk down the aisle of any pet food store, or browse the natural dog and cat journals and websites. Foods made of wild species and alternative meats are all the rage. In addition, the grains that sustained dogs and people for eons have now become the enemy. I have seen clients who successfully used our diet for years switch their pet to a raw, mostly meat diet because of this trend or because another veterinarian recommended it. Just yesterday, I heard from an old client who did this and now her dog's teeth are getting loose: The diet was not supplying adequate calcium. That is, in fact, a common story when people feed high-meat diets to pets. It takes some knowledge.

In any case, the story of the wild predator who needs its meat is a popular one, with parallels in the Paleo and low-carb trends for people in recent years. Put it together, however, and somehow both we and our pets are eating more meat than ever, all heading the opposite direction from what our planet and our conscience now ask of us.

A BREAKTHROUGH: WANTED AND NEEDED

So, when we decided to see if dogs and cats could be healthy eating less meat rather than more, we knew it would not be easy to go against the grain of current attitudes, especially when they are so "against grains" and so pro-meat.

Yet we felt that a breakthrough was both wanted and needed.

The funny thing is, when you thoughtfully seek an answer to a complex, controversial, and urgent issue, you never know what you might find. You might find an unsolvable dilemma. What we found, rather quickly and easily, was an elegant answer: At the very same time that this meaty trend was developing, many other people had been quietly and patiently exploring other ways to feed animals. What they now report, based on decades of experience, is nothing short of amazing.

- **Dogs:** For dogs, it is not only possible to eat much lower on the food chain, it's a good idea. There are countless examples indicating that dogs universally do fine on well-balanced, nutritionally complete plant-based diets. Many even thrive and live to extraordinary ages, especially if the diet is abundant in fresh, organic foods. So, based on what we found, along with corroborative studies in canine nutrition, we encourage you to try it out and offer many recipes as well as simple guidelines in Chapter 6.

- **Cats:** Surprisingly, even our "obligate carnivore" friends, the cats, can also be healthy on nutritionally complete plant-based diets, so long as they are carefully planned and include synthetic sources of taurine, preformed vitamin A, arachidonic acid, and other nutrients found only in animal foods. There are both vegan commercial foods and supplements for this purpose, both in use for decades. Most who have tried these diets report that 60 percent to 85 percent of cats can do well on them, and we heard of vegan cats who outlived meat-eating littermates. Others believe it is safer to feed cats some meat, especially males and those prone to chronic urinary issues.

Put it all together and it means that, in most cases, we have a choice.

It is a choice that will be wonderful news for many, allowing you to care for all animals and for the earth at the same time that you do your best by your own dogs or cats.

It is a choice, however, and it is up to you. For that reason we offer both meat-based and plant-based choices in our fully revised recipe section (see the next chapter). The program with meat is now simpler and easier, and the plant-based recipes are both nutritionally complete for your pets and completely suited to people as well, making it easy to team up and try them together.

INNOVATORS OF PLANT-BASED FEEDING FOR DOGS AND CATS

The choice is yours, but to help you make it in an informed way, we would like to first share results that courageous innovators have gotten feeding animals meat-free diets, then discuss common concerns about protein, grains, soy allergies, and more—all good to know regardless of where you land with these issues.

One of the most shining examples of a vegan dog pioneer is Anne Heritage of England, whose Welsh Border Collie, Bramble, is listed as one of the world's longest-lived dogs. She thrived to age 25 on a simple diet of brown rice, lentils, textured soy protein, nutritional yeast, and fresh garden veggies, sometimes including mint, turmeric, and the like.[1] Lentil Stew (page 88) is inspired by Bramble's diet.

It's a healthy, economical, and easy diet to prepare as well. But lest you think you have just been handed the keys to the kingdom of longevity, Anne emphasized to us and in her book (*Bramble: The Dog Who Wanted to Live Forever*) that it was not diet alone that fostered such health. Bramble and the other long-lived canines in her family all got plenty of daily exercise, were treated with exceptional respect and kindness, were never made to do pointless tricks, and enjoyed rich connections with animals, people, and nature. In a fascinating parallel, these are precisely the same practices that Dan Buettner identified among the longest-lived "Blue Zone" people in the world as well: simple foods, lots of fresh veggies, little meat, daily walks, a strong sense of community and purpose, and taking the time every day to "smell the roses."[2]

Another such innovator is James Peden, who meticulously researched companion animals' unique nutritional needs and ran the numbers for over a year in the 1980s, all to devise the world's first supplements designed to allow people to feed home-prepared, plant-based diets to cats (Vegecat) and later creating a supplement for dogs as well (Vegedog).

He even approached us for an endorsement when he first got started, but we were not sure it could work, especially since his cats at the time also hunted. But since then, thousands have used these products with success. So we are now pleased to endorse his program for all who wish to try it. Vegepet's new owners were updating the formulas just as we were devising our own new recipes, so we even collaborated and consulted together on the changes. We are both very pleased with the results.

One of Vegepet's longtime customers told us she has fed her cats plant based since 1989, when she attended a workshop showing it was possible. Her first vegan cats liked Vegepet's chickpea recipe, as well as Loma Linda's Worthington wheat gluten–based Veggie Burgers (canned), topped with Vegecat, VegeYeast, and 2 tablespoons of pureed veggies a day, including pumpkin, winter squash, peas, or baby food. They also loved corn on the cob, asparagus, zucchini, and sometimes lettuce. Both lived to the respectable feline ages of 17, while one cat's sibling on meat-based cat food only made it to 10.

And then there's Jan Allegretti, animal consultant, animal rights advocate, and author of *The Complete Holistic Dog Care Book*, who has raised two rescued Great Danes in excellent health and to exceptional ages (the first to 13, the second going strong at 11) with a broad variety of all-vegan, fresh whole foods. Jan was another generous collaborator, readily sharing her experience and expertise with this new approach to feeding and contributing her "Fresh and Flexible" program (see Chapter 6). She has seen dozens of animals enjoy greater energy, glossier coats, better digestion, and a new lease on life from switching to her program, all without animal products.

Jan believes that fresh foods are by far the best, a philosophy we share. Even so, many Amazon reviewers report both dogs and cats thriving on plant-based packaged pet foods as well: V-Dog, Natural Balance Vegetarian Formula (for dogs), Evolution (for both species), and Ami and Benevo (for cats).

In addition to such companies, whose products are easily purchased online and sometimes locally, several smaller pet food businesses offer healthy plant-based choices. DOGG in Vancouver, British Columbia, is producing an all-vegan fresh food for local canines, with excellent results from feeding trials.

Shina DeGucci of New York City's Malibu Dog Kitchen, with whom we collaborated on Pitcairn's Malibu Special (page 96), is excited about how well the dogs are accepting the new recipe. Shina told us that Dr. Andrew Kaplan, who won *New York Magazine*'s Best Vet of the Year award, is also thrilled by their new vegan option for his two dogs. As you can see, it's a team effort. The plant-based movement is full of good and generous people.

VEGAN VETERINARIANS

Professionals who dedicate their lives to helping animals are often quick to see how meat-free diets fit with their values of compassion and kindness. At the same time that we have gotten on board with plant-based eating, so have many other veterinarians in our circle, who are having good results with vegan foods and recipes with their own animals and interested clients. Tanya Holonko, DVM, for instance, discovered that tofu and yeast were a real hit with her cats. When our calculations showed that this combo contains a perfect balance of protein and fat, comparable to levels in wild feline diets, it became Wild Tofu (page 106).

Marybeth Minter, DVM, has been feeding her dog a combination of vegan kibbles and her own vegan meals, supplemented with Vegedog—and recommending the diet to clients.

Others, meanwhile—especially younger veterinarians—have been at it for years.

Armati May, DVM, founder of the Veterinary Association for the Protection of Animals (vapavets.org), is a leading professional voice in this growing movement, with a number of informative lectures on YouTube about feeding animals plant-based diets. We spoke with her and she confirmed that such diets often help dogs, especially with skin, coat, GI, and allergy issues. She feeds her own cats a vegan diet and suggests a protocol for monitoring urinary pH for cats going meat-free (see Chapter 7), similar to that recommended by Dr. Andrew Knight, an Australian veterinarian. She also finds digestive enzymes and probiotics very helpful.

Lorelei Wakefield, VMD (wakefieldvet

.com), consults by phone or Skype with people who want to transition their pet to a vegan or vegetarian diet because it's currently so controversial that most vets are not really open to that. She states, "Not only am I open to it, I'm also supportive of it, especially in the case of dogs on vegan diets. I know what to recommend for follow-up care as far as regular blood tests and urine tests. Dogs on vegan diets do extraordinarily well. They have shiny coats, fitter body conditions, less allergies and seem to heal faster. If possible, offer properly formulated home-cooked recipes such as those included with Vegepet supplements."

She also coauthored a professionally published survey study comparing cats on vegan and conventional diets for several years. Caregivers in each group equally reported their cats as "healthy or generally healthy" (97 percent and 96 percent). More vegan cats were reported as being in "ideal body condition" (82 percent compared to 65 percent).

Dr. Wakefield told us, "Ethically, it would be wonderful if we could save farm animals by feeding cats vegan food. The vast majority of vegan cats I have seen appear just as healthy as cats eating a conventional meat-based diet." And, for those who are not fully confident in a vegan diet for cats, she suggests a diet that is half plant-based and half conventional beef-based, in order to minimize the number of animals impacted and because cows usually live in better conditions. Another alternative would be to add ethically sourced eggs to a plant-based diet.

For those who want to try but don't have time to cook, one of her favorite prepared foods for cats is Amicat, and V-Dog for dogs.

She recommends a blood test for taurine and vitamin B_{12} a month into a plant-based diet for cats, as well as a urinalysis, noting, "Most cats fare well on a vegan diet, but those tests help the vet determine if any dietary adjustments are needed."

While some veterinarians openly support clients who want to feed their pets vegan diets, many may not. Sometimes simply listening to clients can reveal amazing things. Our friend Allen M. Schoen, DVM, a well-known practitioner, speaker, and author in holistic veterinary care, shares the following inspiring example.

JOY: THE 21-YEAR-OLD VEGAN DOG

"Some years ago a new client walked into my exam room with her glowing, rusty brown, youthful-looking, midsize, all-breed dog cheerfully prancing behind her. I immediately noticed how healthy both appeared. After introductions, I asked her how I could be of service. She responded that her 20-year-old dog, Joy, had never been to a veterinarian before. She had heard that I had a holistic, compassionate approach and thought at her age, perhaps it was a good idea to have Joy evaluated. My jaw dropped open. I was stunned that not only was this the oldest dog I had ever met, but she looked so healthy and happy!

"When I begin initial examination histories, I typically ask about what diet the animal is on. She responded that both she and Joy had been vegan for 20 years. Again, I was pleasantly stunned. She shared how she made both their foods from purely organic sources, as local as possible. It was quite a healthy, varied diet with a reasonable balance of protein and carbohydrate sources, rich in essential fatty acids and everything healthy.

"As I examined this 20-year-old tail-wagging bundle of joy, I found every parameter not only within completely normal limits, but in peak condition. Her heart and lungs were completely clear and her coat glowed with a shine that was incomparable. All organs palpated within normal range without any sensitivity or pain. There was absolutely no 'doggy odor' or dry, flaky skin. Matter of fact, her skin was radiant. Likewise, her gums and teeth were as healthy as a puppy's.

"After completing the examination and reflecting back to Joy's conscientious caretaker how healthy her dog was, I asked if she had any questions or wanted any diagnostic tests that might offer more insights into her dog's condition. She approved basic blood tests.

"When she returned for results, all were within normal limits. She was grateful that I had found her dog not only in great condition for her age, but for any age. Joy was one of the happiest and healthiest dogs I had ever met. We discussed the healthful impact their vegan, organic diets most likely had on both of them. She again was grateful that I was not only open to discussing vegan diets, but that I also wholeheartedly supported such a diet. She then confided that she had hesitated to take her dog to a veterinarian for so long out of concern there might be a lack of support or openness to her health care choices. She, Joy, and I were all in sync and appreciative of our meeting.

"Both were great teachers for me on the benefits of a vegan, organic diet."

See Dr. Schoen's books, *Kindred Spirits; Love, Miracles, and Animal Healing; The Compassionate Equestrian;* and *Complementary and Alternative Veterinary Medicine* (www.drschoen.com).

BOOKS AND SUPPORT GROUPS

Much of the impetus for feeding dogs and cats plant based comes from a growing grassroots movement of people who love companion animals but don't want to cause suffering to other animals in order to feed them healthfully.

They share what they are learning together on Facebook's Vegan-Dogs-Thriving, Vegan-Cats, Veterinary Vegan Network, and Vegan-Vets. YouTube hosts many videos of people preparing homemade vegan pet foods, and you can find excellent guidelines for home feeding at sites like gentleworld.org/good-nutrition-for-healthy-vegan-dogs, and some excellent success stories at "100 Vegan-Eating Dogs: An Encyclopedia of Vegan Dog Nutrition" at vegantruth.blogspot.com (January 22, 2013).

Many of these folks have now written books, especially about healthy diets for vegan dogs, including *Healthy Happy Pooch: Wisdom and Homemade Recipes to Give Your Dog a Healthy, Happy Life* by Sanae Suzuki (2015); *The Simple Little Vegan Dog Book: Cruelty-Free Recipes for Canines* by Michelle A. Rivera (Summertown, TN: Book Publishing Co., 2009); and *Plant Based Recipes for Dogs: Feed Your Dog for Health and Longevity* by Heather Coster (2015). See also the earlier books *Vegetarian Dogs: Toward a World Without Exploitation* by Verona ReBow and Jonathan Dune (Live Art: 1998–2007) and *Vegetarian Cats and Dogs* by James A. Peden (Harbingers of a New Age, 1995).

WHAT WE RECOMMEND

So, how do we put it all together? Based on these successes and all the issues we explored in the last few chapters, here are our updated recommendations for feeding your dog or cat today. It's a new diet for a new century, one that is healthy, humane, and sustainable.

Fresh diet: In a nutshell, we recommend you feed a fresh, organic diet with the least amount of animal products needed, using recipes with recommended supplements, together designed to match or exceed the latest standards of AAFCO, the American Association of Feed Control Officials. For those able to make home-prepared diets, we offer some great choices in the next chapter. You can use carefully calculated recipes or broad-brush guidelines. You can feed all plant based or you can use meat and eggs. (We advise against all seafood now.)

Plus, most are people-friendly foods to share with your animals and simplify kitchen time. We think you will like these changes!

For backup, or if you don't have the time, use commercial products with quality ingredients (page 64).

GMO-free: Please avoid genetically engineered or unlabeled soy, corn, canola, or their derivatives. Taking this step is likely to improve or eliminate many gastrointestinal and other symptoms.

SUPPLEMENTS

Modern nutritional calculators have enabled us to analyze and cover a much wider range of nutrients than in the past. Instead of our earlier Healthy Powder (nutritional yeast, lecithin, kelp, and a calcium source), we now advise using Vegepet's line of supplements designed for fresh vegan pet diets (compassioncircle.com). They are simpler, more complete, and have been updated by the company in collaboration with our new recipes (no financial ties). Our new recipes are all calculated with these supplements included. If unavailable, see supplement substitutions (page 78).

HEALTHY, HUMANE, AND SUSTAINABLE DIETS
FOR DOGS AND CATS

Richard H. Pitcairn, DVM, PhD, and Susan H. Pitcairn, MS

	BEST FOR HEALTH: A FRESH HOME-PREPARED DIET	HELPFUL FOR BACKUP OR TRAVEL: COMMERCIAL KIBBLE OR WET FOOD
BOTH SPECIES	• Use whole, unprocessed foods as grown. • Feed as plant based as possible (fewer toxins, sustainable, humane). • Feed as organic as possible. • Use no GMO soy, corn, etc. Grains are okay otherwise, unless known allergies exist. • Minimize meat and eggs, emphasizing pastured beef or bison (fewer individuals, usually with better lives), sustainable game meats, or pastured birds with forage. • Use no seafood (toxins, depletion) or dairy, except orphan milk substitutes. • Use digestive enzymes and probiotics to improve assimilation, especially of plant foods.	• Choose foods labeled "balanced, nutritionally complete." • Compare online reviews. • Buy foods that are as organic as possible. • Select foods without GMO soy, corn, etc. Grains are okay otherwise, unless known allergies exist. • Choose foods without seafood (toxins, depletion), meat meals, or vague by-products, grain millings. • Minimize foods with meat and eggs (see opposite column). • Supplement with fresh fruits and vegetables. With kibble, add healthy fats (ground flaxseeds or other seeds, hemp hearts, lecithin). • Seal dry foods to keep them free of moisture to prevent mold and spoilage. • Use digestive enzymes and probiotics to improve assimilation, especially of plant foods.
DOGS	• Feed about half well-cooked, mashed legumes, tofu, tempeh, eggs, or lean meat. The other half should be mostly grains or starchy veggies, with some steamed crucifers or greens, lettuce, fruits, healthy fats, nut and seed butters. Use a variety of balanced and complete recipes (see next chapter). • Supplement with Vegedog.*	• Vegan or 100% plant-based dry, canned, fresh, or frozen products are optimal for most dogs (fewest toxins and allergens), especially if you follow the suggestions above. • Otherwise, use minimal amounts of meat-based foods to reduce toxins and eco and humane issues. Breeds from less agricultural societies may adapt less well to grains. • Supplementation with L-carnitine and taurine may be helpful.

	BEST FOR HEALTH: A FRESH HOME-PREPARED DIET	HELPFUL FOR BACKUP OR TRAVEL: COMMERCIAL KIBBLE OR WET FOOD
CATS	• *Only* use carefully formulated recipes or programs designed specifically for cats. Try half meat-based and half plant-based, or else mostly vegan if accepted and animal is healthy. With low-meat home-prepared diets always *supplement* with Vegecat* as advised or you risk serious health issues. Otherwise, use commercial foods, preferably fresh or frozen "raw" foods for cats. • Offer fresh melons, cucumbers, corn on the cob, asparagus, peas, as desired.	• Only use fresh, dry, canned, or frozen products labeled "balanced and complete for cats." Dog food is too low in protein and other nutrients. • Consider half meat-based and half plant-based products. Monitor urinary pH (see Chapter 7) or try a 100% plant-based diet if accepted and animal is healthy. Do not feed raw pet mixes without adding a calcium source. • Moisten kibbles with sauces and broths to help prevent urinary blockage. • Enhance palatability with nutritional yeast and other condiments (page 117). • Offer fresh melons, cucumbers, corn on the cob, asparagus, peas, etc.

* Vegedog and Vegecat are available online at compassioncircle.com and elsewhere.

That's about it, with specific recipes and how-tos laid out in the next two chapters.

But first, let's address some common concerns about reducing or eliminating animal products. Even though you have just read that countless animals succeed on such diets, you probably have some lingering doubts.

The wild predator story clearly has an appeal to many people, as marketers well know. Sometimes I wonder if it simply speaks to the part of us that longs to return to nature, even though today's lap dogs and pussycats could not take down a cow or a tuna any more than a toddler could.

So let's look at some of the questions that may concern you and see if we can shed light on common misinformation about pets and pet food.

QUESTIONS AND CONCERNS

"BUT THEY'RE *PREDATORS*! AND GRAINS ARE BAD FOR PETS!"

There's no denying that dogs and cats are designed to eat meat, far more than we primates are. Their teeth, claws, strong gastric acids, and short intestines are perfectly adapted to hunt and digest prey, whereas our opposable digits, color vision, long intestines, and chewing molars are optimal for picking and eating leaves, fruit, shoots, and the like, plus eating an occasional egg, grub, or small creature, as our ancestors did before the invention of tools.

Yet, nature is surprisingly adaptable. Despite their primate nature, early humans learned to hunt and include meat in their diets, a useful skill during the ice ages. Likewise, much later on, both dogs and cats learned to eat our starchy plant foods, also a useful adaptation for living with early farmers.

But didn't the ancients feed them meat? Contrary to what you might guess, we have never lavished meat upon pets as we now do. Throughout the entire 10,000 years since we first learned to farm crops and domesticate animals, meat was a luxury for most people, treated more as a condiment or reserved for feast days, not something to eat three times a day and certainly not something to feed freely to pets. Read the fascinating articles on "Dog Food" and "Cat Food" on Wikipedia, and you will see that until recently, dogs were mostly fed bread, barley and other grains, plus whey or a few scraps from stew pots. Some historical writers went so far as to say that meat and animal fats were bad for them, especially house dogs.

Despite claims (even from some veterinarians) that "dogs can't digest grains," they actually adapted very well to our grains and tubers a long time ago. In spite of their abilities as predators, dogs and wolves are from an order that includes bears and other omnivores who can live on a wide range of foods. And compared to wolves, today's domestic dogs have evolved several times more genes to make amylase, an enzyme that digests the starchy carbohydrates that are such a rich source of energy in grains, tubers, and other plant foods.

Likewise, most humans have *also* developed more amylase genes than other primates or than humans whose ancestors never farmed. Together, we and humankind's oldest and best friends adapted beautifully to digest a new and abundant source of food: the cultivated grains and other starches that enabled the development of all major civilizations.[3]

So don't argue for your dog's limitations, or your own. In fact, the more we learn about genes, the more we realize that they are really rather mysterious patterns of potential, whose expression can be turned on or turned off by a little-understood intelligence, depending on circumstances and need.

"Aren't Cats Obligate Carnivores?"

It's true that cats, unlike dogs, are widely considered "obligate carnivores." They have not lived with us as long as dogs, and throughout history largely fended for themselves on the rodents and snakes attracted to our crops and granaries. So they have not really needed to adapt. For starters, cats have higher protein and fat needs than dogs. Their obligate carnivore status was underscored by studies published in the 1970s and 1980s indicating that cats, unlike dogs, will use protein to maintain blood glucose levels even when protein is low and carbohydrates are available.[4]

However, later studies found that cats can adapt to different protein and carbohydrate intakes so long as their minimum requirement for protein is met.[5] For example, it was found that "when properly processed starches and carbohydrates from whole grains are provided as a major component of balanced diets, cats are able to digest and use them, with an average apparent digestibility exceeding 90 percent. Thus, while cats may metabolize carbohydrates differently than dogs and other species, healthy cats are easily able to digest and metabolize dietary carbohydrate."[6]

In addition, cats cannot use plant foods to obtain enough vitamin A (as preformed retinol), taurine, arachidonic acid, and vitamin B_{12}. All of these, as well as choline, methionine, calcium, and other nutrients are typically added to commercial cat foods to ensure a complete and balanced food. That's because some of these nutrients can be destroyed by high-temperature processing and commercial foods are often mixed with grains or other plant starches. Similarly, home-prepared diets with little or no meat especially require careful attention to these nutrients. Vegecat is designed to meet all these needs to official standards, as discussed.

In summary, it appears that so long as their needs for various nutrients are met, as we currently understand them, most cats appear quite capable of living with little or no meat as the source of those nutrients.

Ultimately, the proof is in the pudding. If cats could not utilize grains and other carbohydrates for much of their energy needs, they would not be able to live on typical supermarket pet foods, which are largely just that. And if cats could not be healthy on high-protein, high-fat, plant-based diets supplemented to meet their needs for particular vitamins, amino acids, and minerals, then there would not be thousands of examples of healthy vegan cats. By the same token, there are certainly stories of unhealthy vegan cats, so it is important to do it right. The same is true of any diet; all-meat diets for both cats and dogs can be dangerous as well, particularly if calcium needs are neglected.

"BUT WHAT ABOUT ALLERGIES TO CORN, WHEAT, AND SOY?"

When pets eat lower on the food chain it often means eating more corn, wheat, or soy or their derivatives, to which some animals may be sensitive. If it is really an issue, there are options, including sweet potatoes, winter squash, and other legumes besides soybeans, such as pintos, lentils, or kidney beans.

But are these sensitivities really that big of an issue?

Though you might think otherwise, *pet food allergies are mostly to meat.* Puzzled by the grain-free trend in pet food, Lorie Huston, DVM, has noted that beef, dairy, and fish are far more common allergens than corn and suggested that this fad has arisen from consumer demand rather than science (search "What Is Grain-Free Pet Food, Really?").[7] Dr. Donna Solomon of Animal Medical Center in Chicago concurs in her blog post, "Grain-Free Pet Food Trend a Hoax?" and notes that dogs are especially well equipped to digest and even benefit from the fiber in grains.[8]

Do a search for "top food allergens in dogs and cats" to see this pattern yourself. A recent list for dogs is beef, dairy, eggs, chicken, lamb, pork, rabbit, fish, soy, and wheat. For cats, it's beef, lamb, seafood, corn, soy, and wheat gluten.

I can confirm this in my own practice. In the early 1990s many clients would report that their animals consistently vomited or had diarrhea or severe itching and skin problems when they would feed them the most common meats in pet food then, beef or chicken. So we'd switch them to lamb or rabbit and they would get better, at least for a while.

Yet, what has happened over time is that many now react to lamb or rabbit as well, so people turn to buffalo, kangaroo, and the like. Although there are allergies to plant foods (especially to the common ones that have been genetically tampered with, such as corn, soy, and wheat), dogs in particular have found real relief on plant-based diets, as you can see in customer reviews of V-Dog, Natural Balance Vegetarian Kibble, and others on Amazon.

My PhD studies were in veterinary immunology, so I have studied and thought a lot about how the immune system works and how it can go haywire. Food allergies and oversensitivities are a good example of a disturbed immune response, and in my view they are likely the product of several things.

• **Damage to the intestinal walls and gut biome:** In recent years we are learning that the number of microscopic species in a healthy gut is amazingly vast, and also vastly important. Many health professionals believe that a variety of things in modern life—antibiotics, chlorine in tap water, and herbicides like glyphosate—are killing off the variety and number of beneficial gut bacteria, making way for damaging species like candida, which are in turn fed by excess dietary sugar. The "bad guys" then damage the intestinal lining, which allows large, undigested foreign protein molecules directly into the tissues surrounding the intestines. Direct damage from various chemicals could also come into play. Either way, the immune system overreacts to the undigested foreign proteins from common foods as though an invasion were taking place. Commonly called "leaky gut syndrome," this is thought to trigger or worsen many autoimmune conditions, from allergies to arthritis to thyroid issues to diabetes.

• **A paired association between toxins and frequently eaten foods that contain those toxins:** Another line of thinking among some allergy specialists is that the body links common foods with common toxins that they may contain. It then begins to treat that food as a toxin itself, even when the toxin is absent. This could explain all the common food allergens listed above, all subject to the toxic loads in modern, nonorganic agriculture.

• **Reactions to overvaccination:** To put it briefly, vaccines unnaturally insert foreign proteins from pathogens directly into the bloodstream. This bypasses the layered tier of normal body defenses, triggering an inflammatory overreaction that becomes chronic. Throughout my veterinary career I would often see cases in which a chronic inflammatory problem began shortly after a multiple vaccination of a young animal. It doesn't happen all the time, of course, so it's likely that other stressors, toxin exposures, or issues occurred at the same time that the immune system was being unnaturally challenged. Consider how puppies and kittens are especially subject to stress. This includes being taken from their mother and littermates and adapting to a new home, a new diet, a training regimen, and much more. If your animal has chronic inflammatory issues or allergies, it may help to look back at the circumstances of his or her early vaccines. Homeopathy can help the immune system reset such an imbalance using remedies known to counteract these effects.

• **Inheritance:** Some true food allergies tend to run in families. Current thinking is that it's more the tendency toward food allergies than a specific allergy that gets passed on. Many food allergies in human beings occur more often in children and are eventually outgrown.

For treatment and more information, see the topics Allergies on page 326 and Diarrhea and Dysentery on page 366, as well as the discussion of vaccines in Chapter 16.

Is It Really an Issue?

Before we leave the topic of food sensitivities and reactions, I believe that we often make a mistaken association between a food and chronic symptoms without clear evidence, whether in our animals or ourselves. When someone says their animal can't tolerate such and such, I always try to get her to be specific, asking why she thinks that and what exactly she has observed.

Some believe that extra intestinal gas signals food intolerance, when it is just a normal process in the digestion of the high levels of fermentable fibers in certain foods. (See the tips on better digestion of beans and other foods on page 128 in Chapter 7).

Opinions about foods can be very strongly held and difficult to change. Just yesterday I heard someone insisting that all soy foods were very bad for the thyroid, remaining unconvinced when a registered dietician patiently pointed out that countless studies disprove that. Likewise, many oppose the use of soy in pet foods across the board, although most animals do not have soy allergies.

Certainly I have never seen one in my practice.

Soy: just a bean. For an excellent discussion about the origins and biases of the soy controversy, search the online blog "Is Soy Safe?" by Brenda Davis, RD, and the July 1, 2010, *Guardian* article by Justine Butler, "Ignore the Anti-Soya Scaremongers." They and others concur that the largest body of objective evidence clearly shows that soy is beneficial, especially in forms that have been consumed for hundreds of years. Yet, a few vocal organizations with an agenda to promote animal products have launched a vigorous campaign against it, using studies that do not pass muster on examination. Concerns about it interfering with the thyroid, for example, are only valid if there is a lack of iodine in the diet. Other studies have involved massive doses, and so on. Phytoestrogens in soy are a nonissue when compared to the high levels of biologically potent mammalian estrogens in animal products, especially dairy.

Davis is concerned that these myths have unnecessarily removed a healthy, high-protein food with an excellent array of amino acids from the plates of vegetarians and vegans. We share that concern, particularly because soy is one of the best plant-based proteins for cats, as well as dogs. It is easily digested in the form of tofu, tempeh, or soy milk, and we would not want a needless concern to stop you from using it, whether for your animals or yourself.

My view is that to the extent that there are issues with this humble bean today, the likely culprit is overuse of soy products or soy-fed animal products that have been genetically engineered and sprayed with herbicides. Many people and animals improve, especially regarding GI symptoms, on GMO-free diets. So unless your animal is clearly allergic, go ahead and use corn and soy products like tofu, tempeh, and even textured soy protein, as long as they are organic or certified GMO-free.

Gluten: just a protein. Another fad now demonizes gluten, the most commonly consumed protein in the world for ages. Some restaurants don't even offer breads or grains as options, and yet only a small percentage of humans, for example, seem to truly have reactions to gluten. As we discussed above, the "grain-free" trend in pet food has few legs to stand on.

Exploring the roots of the anti-gluten trend, which people generalize to pets as well as themselves, Michael Specter writes in the November 3, 2014, *New Yorker*, "Fad dieting is nothing new in America; it's what we do instead of eating balanced, nutritiously wholesome meals," adding "while there are no scientific data to demonstrate that millions of people have become allergic or intolerant to gluten (or to other wheat proteins), there is convincing and repeated evidence that dietary self-diagnoses are almost always wrong, particularly when the diagnosis extends to most of society." The article goes on to explore studies done on gluten.

We have a good friend who was once diagnosed with celiac disease and ate a strict gluten-free diet with a Paleo bent for years. At one point she went vegan and, partly to make life easier, she began eating bread again. To her delight, she found that she was fine, and she no longer argues for that limitation.

Accurately diagnosing food sensitivities can be a challenge, apart from obvious intense reactions to certain foods within an hour or two of eating. Though blood tests are often used to diagnose them, many believe that the only way to be sure is with a stringent elimination diet in which suspect foods are reintroduced slowly, one at a time.

The very concept of being "unable" to eat a certain food is limited and limiting. I do not deny that some people or animals have true demonstrable allergies, but often the problem is not so much with *particular* foods as a general weakness or imbalance that needs to be addressed in a holistic way, using homeopathy, acupuncture, or perhaps a careful detox program. Or it could be as simple as backing off the food for a while and then reintroducing it, organic only.

For sure, needless worry about particular foods can definitely set up a self-fulfilling climate of anxiety that could weaken your own health and impact your animal as well (see Chapter 12, Living Together: Responsible Pet Management).

My intent in raising issues about toxins and poor ingredients in food is not to make you afraid of food. Nor do I think we should ignore real concerns. Rather, I'd just like to nudge you gently along a wise course that considers all the factors as much as possible.

In spite of all these issues, the body can be quite resilient, and many pets and people alike are just fine on a healthy diet including a wide variety of whole, healthy, organic foods, as low on the food chain as possible, coupled with a good dose of exercise, love, and meaningful activity.

"BUT HOW CAN THEY GET ENOUGH PROTEIN?"

Even though some of the largest, strongest animals in the world live on plants alone, it's a common myth that plants lack adequate protein or that you must balance them carefully at the same meal to get enough (long since disproven).

Protein is not only overrated as the king of nutrients, but protein myths are now such that many even equate the words *protein* and *meat*, as when a parent hands a child a stick of chicken, saying "Now, eat your protein first!" It's not really that parent's fault. Most people are too busy to really look into these issues, so they are easily influenced by meat and dairy marketers and fad diet writers.

But don't underestimate plants. Many offer plenty of protein to meet dogs' and cats' needs and most provide far more than we need. Look at the chart on page 72, comparing protein and fat as percentages of total calories in various food with the needs of dogs and cats. (Fat has more than twice as many calories per unit of weight as protein or carbohydrates, so many nutritionists now compare foods as a percentage of total calories rather than by dry weight, used more in the past.) Also see the section "Half Protein, Half Fat, That Cat" in Chapter 7 for some new discoveries about why cats like what they like.

PROTEIN AND FAT IN COMMON FOODS

FOOD	% PROTEIN	% FAT
Pea protein	86%	14%
Seitan (vital wheat gluten)	81%	4%
Rabbit, composite of cuts	63%	37%
Textured soy protein	60%	0%
Deer, ground, raw	59%	41%
Nutritional yeast	53%	12%
Turkey, ground, raw	50%	50%
*WILD FELINE DIET, AVERAGE	46%	33%
Tofu	41%	49%
Beef, composite of cuts, 1/8" fat	39%	61%
Mushrooms, cremini	37%	3%
Bison, ground, raw	36%	64%
Egg, whole raw	35%	63%
Spinach, raw	30%	14%
*MINIMUM NEED, KITTENS AND MOMS	30%	20%
Lentils	27%	3%
Asparagus	27%	3%
Cheese, Cheddar	26%	72%
*MINIMUM NEED, ADULT CAT	26%	20%
Yogurt (cow's milk)	24%	47%
Kidney beans	24%	3%

FOOD	% PROTEIN	% FAT
Peas, frozen	24%	4%
Beef, ground, 75% lean hamburger	23%	77%
Black beans	23%	3%
*MINIMUM NEED, PUPPIES AND MOMS	22.5%	19%
Pinto beans	22%	4%
Hemp hearts	22%	73%
Broccoli	20%	9%
Cucumber, peeled	20%	12%
Chicken, back, meat, skin, raw	19%	81%
Garbanzo beans	19%	13%
Lettuce, romaine	18%	15%
*MINIMUM NEED, ADULT DOG	18%	12.4%
Kale	17%	12%
Quinoa	15%	15%
Whole wheat pastas	15%	3%
Peanut butter	15%	72%
Oats, steel cut	14%	14%
Buckwheat	13%	8%
Tomato sauce, canned	13%	6%
Flaxseeds, ground	12%	66%
Millet	11%	9%

FOOD	% PROTEIN	% FAT
Cashews	11%	66%
Sesame seeds/Tahini	11%	10%
Corn, fresh or frozen	8%	7%
Sweet potato	8%	1%
Butternut squash	8%	2%
Almonds	8%	78%
Melon and cantaloupe	8%	5%
Rice, brown	7%	6%
Watermelon	7%	4%
Potato, baking	7%	1%
MINIMUM NEED, HUMAN BABIES AND MOMS (WHO)	7%	
Carrots	6%	4%
Papaya	5%	3%
MINIMUM NEED, ADULT HUMAN	5%	
LEVEL CONSUMED by longest-lived, healthiest "Blue Zone"** humans	5%	
Bananas	4%	3%
Blueberries	4%	5%
Apples	2%	3%

*AAFCO guidelines, 2016, for dogs and cats, as a percentage of 1,000 calories.

**Dan Buettner, The Blue Zones (Washington, DC: National Geographic, 2008).

First, notice how plant protein powders like pea protein and vital wheat gluten top the list at 86 percent and 81 percent protein.

It's also clear why soy is a serious contender with meat and dairy. But who would guess that mushrooms, spinach, and asparagus have more protein per calorie than hamburger or most chicken?

Now compare each food with the official minimum protein needs of dogs, cats, and people, both as adults and while still growing. While a cat clearly can't thrive on a diet of spinach (too low in calories) or even pinto beans (too low in protein), if you center her meals around tofu, protein products, and lentils (or higher-protein meats, of course), she can still enjoy lower-protein favorites like corn or even melons. So, in the right proportions, each species can have some of everything on the list, though cats are unlikely to kill for an apple. Dogs, however, love them.

Also note that we primates have no risk of inadequate protein intake, so long as we eat a sufficient amount of calories from whole, real food. The World Health Organization stated this a long time ago, by the way. The greater risk for us is too *much* protein, as Garth Davis, MD, details in *Proteinaholic: How Our Obsession with Meat Is Killing Us and What We Can Do about It* (2015).

However, it does take some knowledge to get the protein and even the fat content right for cats, and sometimes even for dogs, which is why we have done it for you in our recipes and guidelines. It also helps that the supplements we now recommend have a few added amino acids that tend to be in lower supply in plant foods, boosting their amino acid scores to excellent levels.

So, please follow the recipes and supplement levels, especially for the kitties, and don't make the mistake of thinking that if it works for you it will work for them, or if it works for dogs it will work for cats.

On the other hand, don't make the mistake of thinking that an all-meat diet automatically meets feline needs. Some meats (hamburger, chicken backs with skin) are so fatty that the protein level is really too low for a cat's ongoing needs. Furthermore, in the wild, a cat would also get bone, organs, fur, ligaments, and more from a variety of small prey that would all balance out to meet their known requirements in a way that one simple muscle meat from a large animal can not.

On that topic, notice how most animal products contain more fat than protein on a caloric basis. Fat, unfortunately, is short on other nutrients but a little too full of stored toxins from today's world. This also explains why most plant foods, especially those with the least fat, pack far more vitamins and minerals per calorie than most animal foods, as explained by Joel Furhman, MD, in his YouTube talks and in his bestseller *Eat to Live*.

Plus they are full of valuable phytonutrients that fight cancer, inflammation, and aging. That's why greater consumption of produce is one of the best predictors of health and longevity in humans. We have also noticed that long-lived dogs seem to get ample amounts of fresh fruits and veggies—interesting. Lettuce and broccoli are also high in protein and fiber but low in fat and calories, filling the stomach while allowing healthy weight loss.

Most cats don't seem to want or need many veggies, and they can alkalize their urine a bit too much for some. We did use some mushrooms, asparagus, peas, and greens in our recipes; and let your cat gnaw on corn on the cob, melon, or cukes if that is her desire, so long as the bulk of the diet meets her protein needs.

Nearly all cats love nutritional yeast, a yummy superfood that is 53 percent protein and is in many of our recipes. Many also love it with tofu, which is 41 percent protein and 49 percent fat. Together with a complete cat supplement they make an easy meal pleasingly close to the diet of wild felines (see Wild Tofu on page 106).

"What about Calcium? B$_{12}$? Iron? Zinc? Iodine?"

As for common concerns about getting enough vitamins and minerals, the key in our diet is to use the supplements, tailored to supply nutrients a bit low in plant foods or recommended in extra-high levels for pets, such as calcium. Vegepet uses minimal synthetic sources and levels, so as not to create imbalances.

If you decide to eat more plant-based as well, vegan vitamins can ensure that you get enough vitamin B$_{12}$, zinc, and iodine, which you might otherwise not. The consensus among the experts is to take B$_{12}$, if nothing else.

In the past, we got a lot more B$_{12}$ from the

same place that grazing animals get it: contact with natural soil and surface waters, where it is manufactured by certain bacteria.

I suspect that pets get a lot of it that way as well, by licking their paws after spending time outdoors. Many, of course, don't have contact with natural soil anymore either.

Otherwise, a healthy plant-based diet is generally *higher* in most vitamins and minerals than the average omnivore diet. For an insightful analysis by a registered dietician, watch the YouTube video *Paleo Diet: Myths and Realities by* Brenda Davis, RD. Since we have gone plant based and upped our intake of nutrient-rich foods, we take fewer vitamins (mostly B_{12} and D) and are doing fine.

"WHAT IF THEY DON'T EAT IT OR CAN'T DIGEST IT?"

Many pets, especially dogs, should have little trouble adapting to the diets and recipes in the next chapter. Sometimes there are temporary adjustments, or you need to help fussy cats gradually shift to new foods. Monitor urinary pH if you are transitioning a cat toward a low-meat or no-meat diet. (See Chapter 7.)

RECOMMENDED FOODS FOR DOGS AND CATS

| HIGH-PROTEIN CONCENTRATES AND SUPERFOODS | **Vital wheat gluten:** used for centuries by Asian Buddhists to make seitan mock meats, now in many plant-based meat alternatives. See our New Day Roast for cats (page 110). Find it online or in natural food stores, organic if possible. Refrigerate.
TSP (textured soy protein): a chewy, low-fat, high-protein meaty crumble fed to Bramble, who lived to 25 (see options in Lentil Stew for dogs, page 88). Also in our very tasty Yum Burgers for Cats (page 109) and vegetarian bacon bits. Buy organic only, online or locally. Refrigerate.
Nutritional yeast: loved by most pets, high in glutamic acid, giving a rich "umame" flavor like chicken broth or cheese. Grown on molasses, safely deactivated by heat. High in protein, B vitamins and minerals, often fortified with B_{12} and extra B vitamins. We like Red Star, used in our calculations. Sold online or in natural food stores, often in bulk. For cats, consider VegeYeast, a more bitter brewer's yeast that acidifies the urine (online).
Nori and dulse flakes are excellent seaweed sprinkles, high in protein, vitamins, and minerals. Spirulina helps with detoxing, but is perhaps too alkalizing for feline urinary issues. Kelp is very high in iodine; avoid it for hyperthyroid pets.
Cranberries (fresh, dried, powdered, found in Cranimals supplement) help acidify urine on alkaline diets, especially for male cats or those at risk for FUS. |

(continued)

LEGUMES	Rich in protein, magnesium, potassium, copper, and vitamin B$_6$, and low in fat. Except for tofu or garbanzo beans, add supplemental fat to meet pets' needs (higher than ours). **Tofu and tempeh:** (get organic only) are easy to use and digest, high in protein and fat, comparable to meat, and accept many added flavors. Plain or flavored tempeh is a tasty treat or condiment. TIP: Use the firmest types to make sure you get ample protein. Even firm types vary in density, and thus protein levels. For example, 10 oz of Wildwood SprouTofu Hi-Protein Super Firm Tofu = 14-oz tub of many "extra firm" brands. **Lentils and split peas:** After soy, these are the highest-protein legumes, good for soy-free needs, easily digested and mashed. **Beans:** Black, red, white, spotted, and pinto beans, as well as garbanzos are all good mainstays for dogs as well as us. TIP: To reduce gas from larger varieties, soak the beans well, rinse three times, and discard the water. Cook until very soft, with potato or a piece of kombu (discard when done). Mash well by hand or in a food processor to improve digestion, along with digestive enzymes, until the gut flora adapt. A one-touch digital pressure cooker such as an Instant Pot saves time, money. Freeze extras in wide-mouthed jars (leave room at top) and thaw as needed. Cooked beans expand $2\frac{1}{2}$ to 3 times.
MEATS AND EGGS	**Local, backyard, or pastured** eggs, poultry, or beef are good choices. Game meat (deer, elk, rabbit) is optimal, if sustainably caught, or raw meat pet mixes. Avoid GM-fed cheap, fatty meats, pork, and all seafood. Vegan ("faux") meats are good treats, but, being processed, are not best for daily use.
WHOLE GRAINS AND STARCHY VEGETABLES	**Whole grains:** brown rice, quinoa, amaranth, barley, oats (especially steel cut), millet, buckwheat, whole wheat pasta, and bread. The finer and more cooked or ground, the easier for animals to digest. Soak to remove phytic acid, which binds calcium, magnesium, and zinc and improves digestion. High in protein, magnesium, and selenium. Important source of sustained energy. Avoid white flour, rice. **Starchy veggies:** Baked yams, carrots, sweet potatoes, all winter squashes and potatoes, are lower in protein and total calories than grains, but higher in a variety of nutrients. Orange ones are especially high in beta-carotene, good for dogs.

COLORFUL VEGGIES	**Colorful vegetables** are the best superfoods, rich in vitamins, minerals, and thousands of beneficial compounds. Increase amounts for weight loss, better health. Serve raw, or else bake or steam, and puree to increase digestion, palatability. **Favorites:** asparagus, zucchini, broccoli, cucumbers, carrots, corn (on cob or frozen). Also try kale, lettuce, tomatoes or tomato sauces, beets, cabbage, sprouts, mushrooms. TIP: Many dogs will chew on carrots, broccoli stalks, or corn cobs.
FRUITS	**Berries, apples, watermelon, cantaloupe, and bananas** are all liked by pets, especially dogs. Rich in antioxidants, vitamins, magnesium, potassium. TIP: Papayas help bloating, gas, and indigestion for dogs (remove seeds), as do pineapples. **Cranberries** (or the product Cranimals) can help acidify urine and prevent formation of urinary crystals on more alkalizing diets. **NO grapes or raisins.** Considered toxic to pets.
NUTS, SEEDS, HEALTHY FATS	**Ground flaxseeds** are very high in omega-3s, plus vitamins A, C, E, K, and B vitamins. Helpful for urinary and other issues. Grind flaxseeds weekly (necessary for assimilation) and then store in fridge, or purchase already ground. Soak in warm water to replace eggs in baking. **Hemp** hearts, seeds, and oil are tasty and rich in omega-3s and omega-6s, and linolenic acid, with vitamins A, D, E, and B vitamins. **Butters** made from peanuts, almonds, sesame seeds (high in methionine), cashews, or sunflower seeds. Whole nuts are fine if digested. **NO macadamias or walnuts.** **Lecithin** (sunflower or organic soy) is tasty instead of butter in many dishes and very high in choline, which the brain converts to acetylcholine with major benefit to memory. Eliminating eggs from the diet can reduce it by one-third, so it's a good boost in a plant-based diet. **Coconut oil** increases palatability and improves coats. Rub some on fur and your pet will groom with it. **DHA:** Senior pets benefit from an algae-based, vegan docosahexaenoic acid (DHA) supplement. With age, they are less able to convert omega-3 to DHA. Also good to use if diet is high in omega-6s (vegetable oils or processed foods), which trigger inflammation and compete with omega-3s, limiting manufacture of DHA. Follow label instructions and scale from human to animal size.

(*continued*)

HERBS, SEASONINGS, MUSHROOMS	Fresh mint and basil are good to add to dog meals. Helpful: alfalfa, carob, turmeric, dill, garlic, Italian herbs, parsley, cremini and shiitake mushrooms. **Salt** if bland, but not in excess, optimally no more than 1 mg sodium per calorie (1 tsp salt = 2,336 mg sodium; 1 tsp tamari soy sauce = 335 mg and provides amino acids as well). TIP: Black Himalayan salt is high in sulfur, which is low in many diets today and helpful for skin and coat. Gives rich, eggy flavor to tofu, potatoes, and other foods.
IMPORTANT PET SUPPLEMENTS AND SUBSTITUTES	**DOGS: Use Vegedog or Vegedog Growth as recommended in recipes.** Available online from manufacturer, compassioncircle.com, or elsewhere. **Substitute:** If unavailable, for each teaspoon Vegedog recommended, provide 1,000 mg calcium, plus a dog vitamin or complete human multiple scaled to the dog's size. Carnitine and taurine (human grade, scaled to dog's size) can be helpful as well. Animal Essentials Calcium, from algae, is a good powdered supplement for substitution (1 tsp = 1,000 mg) or else open powdered capsules of calcium sold for human use. We no longer recommend bonemeal (due to heavy metals, humane and eco reasons, plus it changes the calcium-to-phosphorus ratios worked into these recipes).
	CATS: Always and only use Vegecat, Vegekit, or Vegecat phi with low-meat or no-meat recipes, which contain all known nutrients needed for vegan cat recipes. Get it online. **Substitute:** If unavailable, either feed a complete commercial food or a fresh diet with some meat and a complete cat vitamin, meeting daily requirements for taurine, arachidonic acid, vitamin A, B_{12}, iodine, zinc, and copper, plus 1,000 mg calcium per teaspoon of Vegecat in the recipe.
PROBIOTICS AND DIGESTIVE ENZYMES	Helpful for animals with digestive issues or during dietary transitions. Gut biota tend to adapt as a diet changes. FortiFlora from Purina is well liked by cats. Prozyme Plus is a vegan formula, available from Compassion Circle, along with their Green Mush, a healthy mix of spirulina and other greens, with probiotics and digestive enzymes. Many other good products are also available.
PACKAGED PET FOODS	Best as backups, for treats, or travel. Moisten kibbles for cats to avoid urinary sand and blockage. To try meatless options, consider (for dogs) V-Dog, Natural Balance Vegetarian Dog Kibble, Nature's Recipe Healthy Skin Vegetarian Recipe, Evolution, Veganpet, and AvoDerm. **For cats,** Ami and Benevo, Evolution and Veganpet. Some are wheat-, corn-, or soy-free, some are not. Try a variety.

HOW MUCH SHOULD YOU FEED?

Cats are more uniformly sized and typically eat 280 to 300 calories a day, so we give you pretty clear guidelines in our next chapter.

Dogs vary so much in size and activity level that it gets complex. Just feed them in a commonsense way, as much as they like, taking up the food after 20 minutes or so. Watch their weight, and adjust accordingly. We also list the caloric content of each recipe, so you can use an online or other calculator, or your veterinarian's advice, based on that. Generally, dogs eat about 30 calories per pound of body weight each day, more if they are smaller or active, less if big or inactive. So, an 1,800-calorie recipe is good for a 60-pound dog each day, or 3 days for a 20-pound pooch.

The following are commonly considered foods to avoid feeding to dogs and cats. For another view, see www.drbasko.com/site/tomatoes-toxic-myth/ for a veterinarian's debunking of myths about tomatoes, avocados, and mushrooms being bad for pets. His view is that problems come from eating the wrong parts of the plant or poisonous varieties, with some rare cases of allergies, indicated by itchiness, rashes, licking the feet, and hot, red ears.

FOODS TO AVOID OR MINIMIZE FOR PETS

FOOD	RISKS, SYMPTOMS
Additives in pet food, etc.	Cancer, damage to liver and kidneys (from BHA and BHT). Hypersensitivity, allergies, behavior issues (due to food dyes).
Alcohol	Vomiting, diarrhea, decreased coordination, central nervous system depression, difficulty breathing, tremors, abnormal blood acidity, coma, possible death.
Chocolate (especially dark)	Vomiting and diarrhea, panting, excess thirst and urination, hyperactivity, abnormal heartbeat, tremors, seizures, possible death.
Citrus (in excess)	Citric acid and essential oils are irritating, may depress central nervous system. Small bits of fruit are fine.
Coconut flesh and milk (in excess)	Stomach upset, loose stools, diarrhea. Small amounts unlikely a problem.
Coffee and tea (in excess, no antidote)	Restlessness, rapid breathing and heart rate, tremors, fits, bleeding, possible death.
Dairy products	Some adults lack the enzyme to break down lactose in milk. Diarrhea, GI upset, can trigger food allergies, itchiness.

(continued)

FOOD	RISKS, SYMPTOMS
GMO corn, soy, canola products, derivatives	Nonindustry studies link GMOs and/or glyphosate with inflammation, intestinal damage, tumors, infertility (see Chapter 3). Only use organic or "non GMO" corn, soy, canola, and other known genetically engineered foods.
Grapes and raisins	Unknown substance can cause kidney failure. Avoid.
Hot, spicy foods	Indigestion, diarrhea, irritable bowels.
Mold and spoilage	Vomiting, diarrhea, and more. Seal bags of kibble to keep out moisture; avoid cheap brands.
Nuts (in excess), macadamias and walnuts especially	Possible vomiting, diarrhea, tremors, high body temperature, rapid heart rate, weak hindquarters in dogs, usually within 12 hours.
Onions, garlic (in excess)	GI irritation, possible red blood cell damage, especially in cats. Note: Studies of garlic used very high levels intubated into dogs. Garlic has been used for decades in some pet products. In small amounts, we are not concerned.
Raw eggs (in excess)	Avidin in raw egg whites can decrease biotin absorption and trigger skin and coat problems.
Raw or undercooked meat	Risk of food poisoning from bacteria. Some fish parasites can be fatal within 2 weeks. HPP (high-pressure pasteurization) best.
Salty foods and snacks (in excess)	Excess thirst and urination. Vomiting, diarrhea, depression, tremors, elevated body temperature, seizures, and even death.
Small raw bones	Small bones from poultry or fish may splinter, causing choking or punctures.
Spinach, Swiss chard (in excess)	Excess oxalates are linked with kidney problems or bladder stones. Cook lightly, discard the water, also advisable to decrease goitrogens in kale.
Sugary snacks	Obesity, dental disease, diabetes.
Xylitol (sweetener)	Insulin release and low blood sugar, causing vomiting, lethargy, and loss of coordination. Possible seizures and liver failure.
Yeasted dough (raw)	Painful stomach bloat, possible life-threatening gastric torsion.

RECIPES FOR TODAY

So now let's roll out our new recipes and feeding guidelines. They are a complete update of our earlier recipes, which still work fine. But we are especially pleased with what we are about to present to you. Developed in collaboration with colleagues and experts, these approaches will inspire you to fix some tasty foods for your animals and yourself at the same time. Together, you and your animal family can team up for better health and a better world.

For more information about why we recommend this program and about the foods and supplements they include, review Chapter 5.

WHAT'S NEW IN THIS EDITION

Your Choice: Plant Based or Meat: We offer nutritionally balanced plant-based recipes for pets, along with meat-based options. Meatless choices will offer relief to the many animals today who are suffering from (often multiple) meat and dairy allergies and/or the bioaccumulation of toxins in animal products. But, if you have access to relatively humane, sustainable sources of meat from wild game, backyard poultry, or local farms, we offer easy and flexible ways to feed it to both dogs and cats.

Pets plus People: These are tasty human-friendly recipes that you can serve the whole family. With the specified supplement, they also meet the nutritional standards for dogs and cats as determined by AAFCO (the Association of American Feed Control Officials). They will simplify your kitchen time and make meal prep fun as you and your animals team up for a healthier, kinder diet.

More Comprehensive Nutrient Analysis. With the aid of modern nutritional software, we can now analyze the whole panoply of vitamins, minerals, and amino acids, which makes us confident that all recipes meet animals' needs. See the analysis chart at the end of each species' section for details.

Recipes, as Well as Broad Principles: For the first time, we offer the option of broad guidelines, such as Fresh and Flexible or Dog Day, not just recipes. Particularly for dogs, there is wiggle room. Many thrive simply on a variety of fresh, whole foods, much as we eat, without watching all the numbers, especially when it's a really healthy approach with lots of fresh garden veggies. For cats, we prefer you to follow the recipes and guidelines as shown. Err on the side of caution, as cats have a number of dietary limitations compared to dogs.

Collaboration and Synthesis is another new feature. We've drawn upon the collective expertise and experience of many experts, recipe contributors, and fresh food feeders. All had something valuable to share and we will all benefit.

Go for the Veggies: We also now emphasize a rich variety of colorful veggies, fruits, and superfood treats, especially for dogs. They appear to be a major factor in why some animals are so much healthier than others, which has long been clear for humans.

New Supplements (Vegepet): The supplements that replace our "Healthy Powder" and calcium are now simpler, yet more complete. All recipes use updates of the Vegepet products originally created by James Peden in the 1980s. Ashley Bass at Compassion Circle, the new manufacturer, worked back and forth with us as we looked at ways to improve them further. We usually do not recommend specific products, but these are unique in their meticulous fit with vegan fresh food diets and they also work well with recipes including meat. Please use them or else follow the guidelines for substitutions in the "Recommended Foods for Dogs and Cats" chart at the end of the previous chapter.

Note: In a Pets plus People recipe, you can mix in the supplement and benefit from it as well, or just feed your pet the daily Vegedog or Vegecat label amounts.

Vegepet supplements are available direct from compassioncircle.com, 800-370-PETS (7387) or in various online outlets. They enclose additional recipes with the supplements.

IMPORTANT TIPS

Substitutions: Vary amounts and types of nonstarchy veggies like greens, broccoli, tomatoes, mushrooms, and bell peppers and condiments, but please use the main ingredients as shown, or the same amounts of similar grains, beans, meats, etc. This will ensure enough proteins and fats to meet your animal's needs.

Fats: When an oil or other fatty ingredient is in a recipe, it is usually to meet AAFCO standards. We prefer whole foods over refined oils. They are more stable and contain beneficial cofactors.

Salt: Feel free to increase or reduce salt or tamari to taste—just don't overdo it or underdo it. Some recipes need it to meet the minimum official standards established for dogs and cats.

Variety: We offer a variety of recipes to suit your time and budget, with options for food sensitivities and finicky felines. Even if there is a favorite, offer variety to provide an array of nutrients and minimize development of potential allergies.

Digestive Enzymes and Aids: Good digestion is crucial for optimal assimilation of nutrients. Reduce stress at mealtime and give each animal its own bowl and space. Most beans need to be soaked, cooked until tender, and well mashed. Read bean tips, page 128.

If you find undigested matter in your animal's stool, use a digestive enzyme product made for pets, plus probiotics. They can be very helpful with some animals. Follow label directions.

Water: Always provide plenty of fresh, pure filtered or spring water. For cats, it's a good idea to moisten any dry food. Their nature is to get all their water needs from food alone, so they lack the drive to drink as much as they need on dry food.

FRESH AND FLEXIBLE

Maintenance, Dogs or Cats

Pets Plus People

Courtesy, Jan Allegretti, D.Vet.Hom

We introduce our new recipes and guidelines with "Fresh and Flexible," an easy, varied approach you can use for both dogs and cats, generously shared by Jan Allegretti, animal consultant and author of *The Complete Holistic Dog Book: Home Health Care for Our Canine Companions.* It can be 100 percent plant based or include meat.

Rather than using fixed recipes that can lead people to repeat the same ingredients day after day, Jan likes a flexible, proportionate approach drawn from a rich array of fresh, whole organic foods. "It's important to emphasize that this diet is all about *variety*," she explains. "Feed something different every day, or every few days, so the animal has a variety of foods from which to draw whatever nutrients he or she needs."

Switching her clients' animals from packaged foods to this approach often leads to improvement or recovery from a broad range of symptoms, including skin, digestive, behavioral, and lameness problems. She herself has raised rescued Great Danes in glowing health to ages well beyond the usual, entirely with healthy plant-based whole foods. See Jan's YouTube video, "Can Dogs and Cats Go Vegan, Too?"

A great advantage of this program is that you can cook for dogs, cats, and yourself at the same time. When you cook beans or rice, make a salad, or steam some veggies, make extras for your animals. Serve in the following proportions:

MAIN INGREDIENTS

- **30–60% Proteins (Legumes or Meats):** (*60% for cats and for growth, and as little as 30% only for larger adult dogs*). Well-cooked, mashed legumes: especially red lentils, split peas, organic soy products (tofu, tempeh), garbanzos, pintos. Cooked lean meats. Seitan products.

- **30–60% Carbohydrates** (*higher levels for adult dogs only*). Well-cooked whole grains (brown rice, quinoa, buckwheat, barley, amaranth, millet), whole grain bread or pasta. Winter squash, sweet potatoes, yams, potatoes.

- **10–30% Vegetables and Fruits.** Raw or steamed kale, spinach, chard, collards, broccoli, cauliflower, zucchini, carrots, green beans. Raw berries, apples, bananas, melons, stone fruits with pits removed. *No grapes or raisins, no onions for cats, and no more than a small amount of onion for dogs.*

SUPPLEMENT WITH

- **Dog Supplements:** Use a human multiple vitamin and mineral supplement (with vitamins B_{12} and D, iodine, and calcium), scaled to dog's size. For vegan dogs, add L-carnitine and taurine, scaled to their size. Or simply use Vegedog, per label.

- **Cat Supplements:** *Always use daily label amount of Vegecat from compassioncircle.com* to ensure adequate taurine, arachidonic acid, preformed vitamin A, B_{12}, calcium, choline, and other nutrients cats need, or you risk serious health issues if little or no meat is fed.

- **Fats:** Feed ½ to 3 teaspoons per day (depending on size) of flax, olive, coconut, or hemp oil, or ground flaxseeds, hemp hearts, or nut butters.

- **Nutrition Boosters:** Rotate through a variety of probiotics and superfoods like spirulina, blue-green algae, nutritional yeast, or lecithin.

- **Condiments (optional):** Top with sauces, such as baby food squash or pumpkin, or corn pureed with nori, as well as nutritional yeast, dulse flakes, or oil, to improve palatability (especially for cats) as well as nutrition.

- **Treats:** Offer apples, tomatoes, berries, citrus fruits, peaches, cantaloupe, corn on the cob, carrot sticks, cucumbers, if liked. Make your own biscuits or kibble treats. *No chocolate, grapes, or raisins.*

- **Digestive Aids?** Monitor the stool. Do undigested pieces come through? If so, sprinkle a pet enzyme formula on food before serving. It can really help some animals digest plant foods, especially cats. Also, their digestion often improves as their bodies adapt to new foods. Probiotics are also helpful as they transition.

Jan provided us a typical day's menu, comparable to what she feeds her Dane.

SAMPLE BREAKFAST, LARGE DOG

¾ cup uncooked rolled oats (40% carbohydrates)

¾ cup (5 ounces) super firm tofu (35% protein)

½ cup fresh strawberries (25% fruits or vegetables)

½ teaspoon spirulina

1 tablespoon ground flaxseeds

½ cup fortified soy milk

1 tablespoon coconut oil

SAMPLE MIDDAY SNACK (LIGHT SALAD OR SANDWICH)

½ cup chopped spinach

½ cup brown rice (or ½ cup mashed garbanzos)

1 teaspoon flax oil

Option: A peanut butter sandwich is handy away from home (2 slices whole grain bread with 2 tablespoons pure organic peanut butter).

SAMPLE DOG DINNER

1½ cups cooked red lentils, from ½ cup dry (45% protein)

1 cup cooked quinoa, from ⅓ cup dry (30% carbohydrates)

¾ cup raw or lightly steamed broccoli (25% vegetable)

1 tablespoon nutritional yeast

⅛ teaspoon salt

½ teaspoon olive oil

1¾ teaspoons Vegedog

Yield: 1,459 calories (20% protein, 25% fat). High in healthy omega-3 fats, excellent for skin and bladder problems, inflammatory conditions, and general health.

DOG DAY

Dog Maintenance or Growth

Pets plus People

Adapted, Courtesy Dee Blanco, DVM

Our programs and recipes just for dogs feature another broad, flexible approach in collaboration with Dee Blanco, DVM, a longtime friend and colleague who has seen remarkable health improvements with raw meat, bone, and veggie diets.

"But they don't need as much meat as people often feed," she notes, aware of the environmental and humane issues in its production. She suggests a middle path, an easy and simple *two-part plan:* hot cereal and fruit for breakfast, with meat and veggies for dinner. It's ideal for those with access to quality meat or local-made raw meat mixes for pets.

This program nicely replaces the classic meat and grain recipes of our first three editions. It's comparable in nutritional analysis, but offers more variety and greater compatibility with how people often eat. We suggest using daily label amounts of Vegedog (compassioncircle.com) for calcium as well as other nutrients. Dee, on the other hand, likes Animal Essentials' algae-based calcium (per label amounts). We no longer recommend bonemeal due to heavy metal contamination.

DOG DAY BREAKFAST: A HEARTY CEREAL

Hot cereal (buckwheat, quinoa, amaranth, teff, oats or millet, or a mixture)

Fruit (apple, banana, or berries)

Milk (either plant or animal based)

Ground flaxseeds, hemp hearts, or coconut oil

Half the daily amount of Vegedog for your dog's size

One of Dee's favorite porridges, well loved by people as well as dogs, consists of half buckwheat, with the other half either quinoa or amaranth. We love steel-cut oats.

She recommends the Irish tradition of soaking and slow cooking grains to activate and then remove the protective phytate enzymes on their surface, which otherwise can block mineral absorption. Here's how.

Soak the grains in water for at least 7 hours, then drain and discard the water. Add at least 3 cups fresh water for each cup of grain. Cook overnight on very low heat, such as the low setting on a slow cooker. Add more water if needed. By morning you will have a soft, digestible porridge. Top with other ingredients and serve. Dee suggests making this about a quarter of the diet for dogs (or 15 percent for cats).

DOG DAY DINNER: MEAT AND VEGGIES

50% raw or cooked meat or "raw" pet mixes

50% winter squash, pumpkin, or sweet potatoes (plus lettuce or greens as desired)

1 teaspoon Animal Essentials Seaweed Calcium (or Vegedog) per pound of meat (= 1,000 milligrams of calcium)

Mix and top with the supplement. Coconut or flax oil can be added to lean meats. Because you served a lower-protein breakfast, you balance it with a higher-protein dinner.

Meatless Option: For dinner you could use any of our dog recipes with at least 22% protein, such as Savory Stew, Tofu Meat Loaf, V-Burgers, or Country Scramble, plus low-carb veggies like lettuce, asparagus, zucchini, kale, and broccoli to ensure enough total protein.

Growth Option (mom and puppies): Add an egg, some tofu, or a bit of meat to breakfast. Use the daily "Growth Measure" amounts of Vegepup (compassioncircle.com), as stated on the label.

Analysis: *We have analyzed several of the many combos possible in this program and all met AAFCO standards, as long as you use Vegedog or its equivalent. Here are two examples.*

Chicken and Butternut Squash

Breakfast: 1 cup amaranth and 1 cup quinoa (cooked), 1 cup fortified soy milk, 1 banana, 1 tablespoon ground flaxseeds, 1½ teaspoons Vegedog

Dinner: 1 cup chicken backs (meat, skin) or fatty meats and 1 cup butternut squash

Yield: *1,209 calories, 22% protein, and 32% fat*

Venison and Pumpkin

Breakfast: 1 cup amaranth and 1 cup quinoa (cooked), 1 cup fortified soy milk, 1 apple, 1 tablespoon coconut oil, 1½ teaspoons Vegedog

Dinner: 6 ounces venison (or lean meat or tofu), 1 cup canned pumpkin

Yield: *1,089 calories, 24% protein, and 31% fat*

LENTIL STEW

Dog Maintenance

Inspired by the work of Anne Heritage

This easy, healthy, economical, and Earth-friendly stew is ideal if you have several dogs or a large one. Lentils and soy are the two highest-protein legumes around. This stew is similar to what Anne Heritage reports that she fed Bramble, a collie who lived to age 25, as well as other long-lived, active, well-loved dogs in her family. Based on our analysis, we also added a couple of healthy fats, salt, and enough Vegedog to meet the full range of AAFCO standards. In *Bramble: The Dog Who Wanted to Live Forever,* Anne reports she also would often add fresh mint from the garden or, as Bramble aged, some turmeric for arthritis.

5 cups water

2 cups dried lentils

2 cups dry brown rice

1 cup or more fresh veggies (spinach, peas, greens, broccoli, cabbage, carrots, chard, etc.)

1 block (10 ounces) super firm Wildwood SprouTofu or 1 tub (14 ounces) Westsoy or Nasoya extra firm organic tofu

3 tablespoons nutritional yeast

1 tablespoon ground flaxseeds or fresh flax oil

1¹⁄₂ tablespoons tahini (sesame butter)

1 tablespoon organic tamari soy sauce or ¹⁄₂ teaspoon salt

1¹⁄₂ tablespoons Vegedog supplement (or daily label amount)

In a large saucepan over medium-high heat, bring the water to a boil. Add the lentils, rice, and veggies and simmer, covered, for about 45 minutes. Cool to serving temperature and add the tofu, nutritional yeast, flaxseeds, tahini, tamari, and Vegedog. Vary the veggies and be creative. You can also serve this over shredded lettuce.

Options: Instead of tofu, substitute ¹⁄₄ cup organic textured soy protein, which Anne used. Increase the flaxseeds and tahini to 3 tablespoons each, to meet AAFCO minimum fat requirements. If there are soy allergies, omit the tofu and use 4 tablespoons nutritional yeast, 3 tablespoons ground flaxseeds, and 3 tablespoons tahini.

Yield: 3,443 calories (22% protein, 13% fat). Freeze extras for small dogs.

SKILLET SUPPER

Dog Maintenance

Pets plus People

This quick, easy meal is a good use for leftover quinoa, brown rice, buckwheat, or millet. Nice on chopped lettuce.

1 carrot, grated

$1/2$ cup minced spinach or other greens (parsley, etc.)

1+ teaspoon organic tamari soy sauce or $1/8$ teaspoon salt

2 cups cooked quinoa, rice, or other whole grain

2 cups well-cooked kidney beans or 1 can (15 ounces)

$1/4$ cup frozen corn kernels or peas

1 tablespoon nutritional yeast

2 teaspoons hemp hearts, ground flaxseeds, coconut oil, lecithin, tahini, or peanut butter

$1^1/2$ teaspoons Vegedog supplement (or daily label amount)

Warm a large skillet over medium-high heat. Add a few tablespoons of water or broth and cook the grated carrot briefly, stirring, then add the spinach and sprinkle in the tamari. When the greens soften, add the quinoa, kidney beans, corn, and nutritional yeast. Heat up to serving temperature. Mash the beans with a fork for your dog's serving, then top with the hemp hearts and Vegedog. Excellent topped with salsa for people, but not for Rover (unless very light on onions).

Options: Substitute leftover sweet potatoes or winter squash for all or part of the grain for a filling and nutritious option with fewer calories (good for weight loss). If you substitute a lower-protein legume for the kidney beans, such as garbanzos, then also reduce the starches (quinoa, corn, etc.).

Yield: 1,123 calories, about a day's worth for a midsize dog (20% protein, 15% fat)

TOFU MEAT LOAF FOR DOGS

Dog Maintenance or Growth

Pets plus People

Adapted from a tasty recipe we picked up at a potluck, this is a favorite of our friend's dog Grace and a hearty entrée for people, along with a side of veggies or salad and some mashed potatoes.

10 ounces super firm Wildwood SprouTofu or 1 tub (14 ounces) Westsoy or Nasoya extra firm organic tofu

2 slices whole grain organic wheat bread, finely crumbled

1²/₃ cups quick oats

1¹/₂ cups water + additional, as needed

3 tablespoons organic tamari soy sauce or 1¹/₂ teaspoons salt (or less)

2 tablespoons nutritional yeast

2 tablespoons Dijon mustard

1 teaspoon Italian herbs

¹/₄ teaspoon garlic powder (optional)

¹/₄ teaspoon ground black pepper (optional)

1¹/₂ teaspoons Vegedog supplement (or daily label amount)

¹/₂ cup low-sodium ketchup (see Gravy Option)

Preheat the oven to 350°F. In a large bowl, combine the tofu, bread, oats, water, tamari, nutritional yeast, mustard, herbs, and garlic powder and black pepper (if using). You can either mix in the Vegedog at this point or just top the dog's share with their daily label amount. Knead everything together. Press into a lightly oiled 9" x 5" glass loaf pan. Top with the ketchup and bake for 30 to 40 minutes. Serve with as many greens as your dog would like, such as shredded romaine or steamed asparagus or broccoli. You can also add winter squash (baked and mashed), minced kale, spinach, or steamed broccoli to the loaf itself.

Gravy Option: Omit the ketchup. Add a cup of sliced cremini mushrooms to the loaf before baking and/or top with Tahini Gravy (page 124).

Growth Option (mom and puppies): Instead of Vegedog, use a scant 2 tablespoons Vegepup. Or give mom and pups the amounts on the label each day.

Yield: 1,335 calories, about 1 day's worth for a 44-pound dog (24% protein, 24% fat)

V-BURGERS

Dog Maintenance or Growth

Pets plus People

A delicious, super-nutritious plant burger for both dogs and people, full of healthy greens and seeds and a great use for leftover sweet potatoes or yams, which help bind the burger. Double or triple the batch and freeze some; later, you can put some in the toaster oven for an easy, tasty meal for you and your pooch, sure to be greeted with a wagging tail. Also see Yum Burgers (page 109), a very tasty, higher-protein burger for cats that is also fine for dogs if you use Vegedog.

3 cups cooked black beans (from 1 cup raw) or 2½ cups cooked lentils (1 cup raw)

2 slices whole wheat bread, crumbled

1 tablespoon nutritional yeast (can increase for more protein)

2 tablespoons ground flaxseeds

2 tablespoons sunflower seeds

2 tablespoons pumpkin seeds or almond butter

2 cups spinach or kale

1 baked sweet potato or yam

1⅔ teaspoons Vegedog supplement (or daily label amount)

In a food processor, Vitamix, or blender, combine everything. Puree, adding only as much water as needed. Chill a bit to make it easier to shape into patties. Then preheat the oven to 375°F. Form 3" patties, line them up on parchment paper, and bake for 10 minutes on each side. Cut up the parchment paper to stack extra patties to freeze or chill in containers. Before serving, we like to sear our own burgers a bit in a skillet and tuck them in toasted whole wheat English muffins with the usual condiments (mayo, mustard, pickles, onion, tomato, lettuce). All are fine for your dog too, except the pickles and onions.

Yield: *1,314 calories (8 or 9 burgers), about a day's worth for a midsize adult dog (18% protein, 22% fat). With lentils, it's 22% protein and 22% fat.*

Growth Option (mom and puppies): Use 1¼ cups raw lentils and, instead of Vegedog, use 5 teaspoons Vegepup (compassioncircle.com). Or give mom and pups the amounts on the label each day.

SAVORY STEW

Dog Maintenance or Growth

Pets plus People

Easy to prep (about 10 minutes), this hearty, minestrone-inspired, veggie- and protein-rich soup is delicious and satisfying! Some dogs don't care for tomatoes. If you omit them, add a bit of lemon juice and miso paste or salt to taste.

5 cups water or vegetable broth

2 cups dried brown lentils

½ cup organic textured soy protein
(Bob's Red Mill, available online, is good)

1 can (15 ounces) stewed tomatoes (optional)

1 cup minced kale or broccoli, zucchini, bell pepper, collards, or cabbage or a mix

1 cup sliced cremini mushrooms

1 cup corn kernels (frozen is easiest)

1 rib celery, diced

1 medium carrot, diced

2 tablespoons olive oil or coconut oil, divided

1 teaspoon Italian herbs, or more

½ teaspoon salt, preferably black Himalayan

3½ teaspoons Vegedog supplement
(or daily label amount)

2 tablespoons nutritional yeast

4 slices whole wheat bread

Combine all the ingredients except the last three and 1 tablespoon of the olive oil or coconut oil in a large pot. Bring to a boil, cover, reduce the heat, and simmer for 50 minutes. Or use a digital pressure cooker on the "Bean" button. Let the stew cool a bit, then stir in the Vegedog and yeast (or sprinkle it on top like Parmesan). Spread the remaining 1 tablespoon of oil on the bread and serve that alongside the stew (tear it up for your dog).

Options: Instead of serving with bread, pour the stew like a sauce over 2 large baked or mashed potatoes or folded in a tortilla and heated in a skillet. Serve with finely chopped lettuce.

Yield: 2,538 calories with the bread, about 3 days' worth for a midsize dog (23% protein, 15% fat)

Growth Option (mom and puppies): Reduce the bread to 2 slices. Add 1 tablespoon lecithin, 1 tablespoon hemp hearts. Instead of Vegedog, use a scant 3 tablespoons of Vegepup (compassioncircle.com) or the daily label amounts (23% protein, 19% fat).

TOFU NOODLES

Dog Maintenance or Growth

Pets plus People

Susan created this quick and easy dish years ago, inspired by her grandmother's chicken and dumplings. Whole grain pasta is well digested by dogs. Freshly made pasta really enhances this dish, as does a really firm tofu. Mushrooms are high in protein, full of good nutrients, and safe for dogs (poisonous types cause trouble!).

1 package (16 ounces) whole wheat or gluten-free fettuccine noodles

1 cup sliced mushrooms

1 block (10 ounces) super firm Wildwood SprouTofu or 1 tub (14 ounces) Westsoy or Nasoya extra firm organic tofu, or more

¼ teaspoon garlic (optional)

2 tablespoons or more organic tamari soy sauce

¼ cup nutritional yeast, divided

1 tablespoon organic soy or sunflower lecithin granules (optional)

1 cup soy milk or other plant milk

1 zucchini, sliced

2¾ teaspoons Vegedog supplement (or daily label amount)

Cook the noodles per package instructions. Drain and set aside. Meanwhile, in a medium skillet, cook the mushrooms with a bit of water and soy sauce or broth, stirring frequently, for 3 to 4 minutes. Then crumble in the tofu, garlic (if using), soy sauce, and most of the nutritional yeast. Toss it all together and cook just short of really browning it. Mix the tofu-mushroom sauté into the noodles, adding the lecithin (if using), soy milk, and remaining nutritional yeast (as much as you like). Boil or steam the zucchini to serve on the side (or add it to the noodle pot).

Add the Vegedog plus the zucchini for your pooch. Excellent topped with Healthy Sprinkle (page 122). Ground black pepper and a vegan Parmesan are nice on the people part.

Yield: *2,268 calories, about 2 days' worth for an adult dog (23% protein, 13% fat)*

Growth Option (mom and puppies): Add 3 tablespoons tahini (sesame butter). Instead of Vegedog, use 2 slightly rounded tablespoons Vegepup or the daily label amount.

CHEF'S BEAN 'N' CORN DELIGHT

Dog Maintenance

Pets plus People

This economical but delicious dinner was inspired by a scrumptious Southwest dish we enjoyed at a catered art event. It is just as the chef described it, except we omitted the onions and added Vegedog for the canine crowd. The chef routinely uses nutritional yeast for extra flavor. He also fire-roasted the corn fresh off the cob, but frozen corn kernels work fine.

2 cups cooked black beans or 1 can (15 ounces)

2 cups cooked pinto beans or 1 can (15 ounces)

1 cup fresh or frozen corn kernels

1 fire-roasted red bell pepper, diced (sold in jars)

2–3 tablespoons lime juice

2 tablespoons nutritional yeast

1 tablespoon olive oil

1/2 teaspoon salt

1/2 teaspoon ground cumin (optional)

1 clove garlic, minced (optional)

1 2/3 teaspoons Vegedog supplement (or 1/2 daily label amount)

1 cup shredded romaine lettuce

In a large pot over medium heat, combine the beans, corn, bell pepper, lime juice, nutritional yeast, oil, salt, cumin and garlic (if using), and Vegedog. Mix it all together until heated through. You may need to mash or even food-process your dog's part to aid digestion. Serve over the lettuce. If you feed this often to your dog, go easy on the garlic.

Option: Serve with a cup of cooked zucchini squash. Protein is a bit less, but still meets maintenance needs.

Yield: *1,316 calories, about a day's worth for a midsize dog (21% protein, 13% fat)*

COUNTRY SCRAMBLE

Dog Maintenance or Growth

Pets plus People

This has often been our Sunday breakfast, something you will definitely want to share! The black Himalayan salt (available online) is an invaluable aid to plant-based cooking, supplying the sulfur that is low in many diets and giving tofu the flavor of eggs, as does the nutritional yeast.

2–3 potatoes (red or Yukon is best), diced or thinly sliced

1 teaspoon chopped dill weed

Dash of tamari soy sauce

1 tablespoon olive oil or vegetable broth + additional if needed

5 mushrooms (cremini, if available), sliced

1 block (10 ounces) super firm Wildwood SprouTofu or 1 tub (14 ounces) Westsoy or Nasoya extra firm organic tofu

3 tablespoons nutritional yeast

¼ teaspoon garlic powder (optional)

Dash of ground turmeric (optional)

½ teaspoon salt, preferably black Himalayan

1 cup chopped spinach, kale, or zucchini

1½ teaspoons Vegedog (or ½ daily label amount)

1 tablespoon or several sprigs minced parsley

Warm a skillet over medium-high heat and coat it lightly with oil. Stir-fry the potatoes and dill for a minute or two. Add a bit of water or broth and a dash of tamari, cover, and steam over low heat until soft (8 minutes or so). Add more water if needed.

Meanwhile, heat another skillet over medium-high heat for the scramble. Add the oil or broth and briefly sauté the mushrooms. Crumble in the tofu, sprinkling with the yeast, garlic powder and turmeric (if using), and salt as you stir-fry, adding a bit of oil or water as needed. When well heated, add the spinach, heating enough to wilt it. Add additional tamari, if needed, to taste.

Serve, mixing the potatoes and scramble country-style, if you like. Sprinkle Vegedog on your dog's share. Garnish with parsley or other fresh herbs.

Options: Use pastured eggs instead of tofu. Add zucchini, tomatoes, diced bell pepper, or sweet potatoes. Serve with toast, Tofu Sour Cream (page 123), vegan cheese, bacon bits, or sausage.

Yield: *1,238 calories (23% protein, 27% fat)*

Growth Option (mom and puppies): Instead of Vegedog, use 2¼ teaspoons Vegepup (compassion circle.com).

PITCAIRN'S MALIBU SPECIAL

Dog Maintenance

Pets plus People

Courtesy, Malibu Dog Kitchen

This colorful, nutrient-dense recipe was a fun collaboration with Shina Degucci, owner of New York City's new Malibu Dog Kitchen, which is introducing fresh vegan as well as non-vegan foods for the lucky dogs of the Big Apple. A vegan herself, she was thrilled to add this to her line of first-class foods and tested it on the staff's seven canines, advising that you mash the beans very well for optimum digestion. Multiply for larger amounts. Pintos are excellent in elimination diets for dogs with food allergies.

1 cup whole dried pinto beans or 2 cups canned or reconstituted

1 cup dry brown rice, rinsed 3 times

1/2 cup finely minced or grated red or green cabbage (about half a head)

2 large carrots, finely minced or grated

1 1/2 cups coarsely chopped baby kale

16 ounces firm tofu, crumbled

1 tablespoon ground flaxseeds

2 teaspoons nutritional yeast

1 teaspoon black Himalayan or other salt

1 tablespoon coconut oil

1 tablespoon Vegedog supplement (or daily label amount)

Soak the beans overnight (if using dried). Discard the soaking water, place the beans in a large pot, and cover with about an inch of fresh water. Add a piece of potato or kombu seaweed to the cooking pot to help digestion. Bring to a boil, spooning off the foam that rises to the top. Cover and simmer for 1 hour or more, until very soft. Discard the potato or kombu.

Meanwhile, cook the rice according to package instructions.

Steam the cabbage over low heat for 10 minutes. Separately, steam the carrots on low for 12 minutes. Blanch the kale for 2 minutes, then strain, cool, and mince it as well.

Rinse the beans well, mash thoroughly, and stir in the rice, veggies, tofu, flaxseeds, yeast, salt, oil, and Vegedog. Fluff together gently and thoroughly. Serve warm but not hot.

Yield: 2,965 calories, about 3 days' worth for a midsize dog (21% protein, 16% fat)

DOG GARBANZOS

Dog Maintenance

Courtesy, Compassion Circle (Vegepet supplements)

One of the favorite canine recipes from Vegepet that has sustained many a vegan dog over several decades, including founder James Peden's beautiful, vibrant Border Collie, the model for the illustrations for Chapters 9 and 13. Add fresh veggies and condiments as your dog desires. Simple and tasty.

4¾ cups raw garbanzos (or use about 10 cups cooked or canned and skip the soaking step)

3½ tablespoons VegeYeast or nutritional yeast

2¾ teaspoons coconut oil (or hemp hearts, flaxseeds, tahini, etc.)

1⅓ teaspoons salt (black Himalayan is very tasty with garbanzos)

1 tablespoon + 1 teaspoon Vegedog supplement (or daily label amount)

Soak the raw garbanzos in water until doubled in size, changing the water to keep them from fermenting. Drain. In a large pot over medium-high heat, place the garbanzos. Cover with water to about an inch above the beans, bring to a boil, and cook until tender. Drain thoroughly and crush with a potato masher. Add the yeast, oil, salt, and Vegedog. Feel free to add basil, a tad of garlic, and a variety of fresh veggies in moderate amounts. Refrigerate extras in small covered containers.

Yield: *2,903 calories, about 2 days' worth for a 48-pound dog (19% protein, 16% fat)*

POOCH PAELLA

Dog Maintenance

Pets plus People

Not authentic Spanish paella, but inspired by one from long ago. Perhaps *pilaf* would be a better term. In any case, this richly flavored rice dish with chunks of real or vegan meat is one you and your pooch could eat often, varying ingredients and side dishes. Try it with chunks of commercial vegan sausages, chicken, or crab nuggets and the like.

1 cup dry brown rice

2½ cups water

6 cremini mushrooms

½ teaspoon salt or tamari soy sauce to taste

1 tablespoon olive oil

3 tablespoons nutritional yeast

1 teaspoon poultry seasoning

1 cup frozen or fresh peas

½ cup sliced zucchini

5 ounces New Day Roast (page 110) or any vegan or lean animal meat (about 1 burger patty's worth)

1 tablespoon hemp hearts

2¾ teaspoons Vegedog (or daily label amount)

In a large saucepan, bring the rice to a boil in the water. Add the mushrooms, salt, oil, yeast, and poultry seasoning. Cover and simmer for about 35 minutes. Then add the peas, zucchini, and New Day Roast. Continue cooking for another 10 to 15 minutes. Top with the hemp hearts and Vegedog. Serve with a baked sweet potato or winter squash. For weight loss or fewer carbs, serve alongside broccoli, Brussels sprouts, or a salad instead.

Yield: *1,821 calories, 2 days' worth for a 30-pound dog (24% protein, 22% fat)*

WOLF BURRITO

Dog Maintenance

Pets plus People

An easy, quick, tasty meal for a midsize dog. Watch him "wolf" it down! Make an extra for you.

1 can (15 ounces) refried beans (or 2 cups cooked)

1 teaspoon coconut oil (or add hemp hearts to the salad)

$^1/_{16}$ teaspoon salt (optional)

$^3/_4$ teaspoon Vegedog supplement (or $^1/_2$ daily label amount)

2 organic whole wheat tortillas

Dash of mild salsa (optional—minimize onions)

4–5 leaves romaine lettuce, thinly sliced

1 slice tomato, diced

2–3 tablespoons Tofu Sour Cream (page 123)

In a saucepan over medium heat, warm the beans. Add the coconut oil, salt, and Vegedog. Roll into the 2 tortillas with the salsa (if using). Heat the burritos in a toaster oven until slightly crisped. Serve over a bed of lettuce and tomatoes and top with the sour cream. You can make a large batch, roll them up in aluminum foil (minus the lettuce and tomatoes), and freeze. Thaw and bake as needed.

Yield: *499 calories (20% protein, 16% fat)*

Use this chart to see the nutrients in and special features of or uses for each dog recipe, indicated in the CODES row. For some health conditions, a minor adjustment is suggested in the key. Veterinarians may suggest further uses based on nutrient listings. Note that vitamin C is not an AAFCO requirement, as dogs make their own. The Fresh and Flexible option is not listed due to the wide variations and uses possible.

DOG MAINTENANCE RECIPES: APPROXIMATE NUTRIENTS PER 1,000 CALORIES

Calculated with tools at nutritiondata.com and custom entries.

NUTRIENTS PER 1,000 CALORIES	AAFCO ADULT DOG MINIMUM	CHEF'S BEAN 'N' CORN DELIGHT	COUNTRY SCRAMBLE	DOG DAY CHICKEN AND SQUASH	DOG GARBANZOS	LENTIL STEW	
CODES*		A, E, K, P, V, W	G, P, V	C, G, K, M, P, V	A, C, D, E, K, V	A, C, D, E, K, V, W	
Protein (g)	45.0	59.4	60.7	54.6	54.0	59.4	
Fat (g)	13.8	15.4	29.8	36.5	19.2	15.4	
Protein as % of calories	18	21	23	22	19	22	
Fat as % of calories	12.4	13	27	32	16	13	
Methionine + Cysteine (mg) (1, 2)	1,630	1,645	1,733	2,065	1,559	1,647	
Taurine (mg) (1, 2)		198	213	376	199	207	
Omega 6:3 ratio (low best)		2.6	1.22	2.9	26.2	5.4	
VITAMINS							
A (IU)	1,250	5,942	4,015	10,121	1,319	2,131	
D (IU)	125	128	138	253	129	134	
E (IU)	12.5	17.2	23.1	25.0	14.2	16.3	
K (mcg)		55	192	7	22	51	
Thiamin (mg)	0.56	9.84	16.2	0.5	5.3	7.3	

(1) Generally, must be supplemented in home diets to meet AAFCO standards

(2) Includes amino acids added with Vegedog: methionine, taurine

*Features: C = Convenience; **E** = Economy; **M** = Meat (or can be); **P** = Pets plus People; **V** = Vegan (or can be)

Best choices for: A = Allergies, GI, skin issues (no beef, dairy, wheat, egg, chicken, lamb, soy, pork, rabbit, fish—use options that don't include them and choose organic foods); **D** = Diabetes (increase complex carbohydrates, fiber); **G** = Growth or recovery from injuries, follow directions under the "Growth Option"; **K** = Kidney disease (reduce proteins, phosphorus, salt; increase potassium); **W** = Weight loss (increase vegetables, fiber)

	PITCAIRN'S MALIBU SPECIAL	POOCH PAELLA	SAVORY STEW	SKILLET SUPPER	TOFU MEAT LOAF	TOFU NOODLES	V-BURGERS	WOLF BURRITO
	D, K, P, V, W	A, C, D, E, K, M, P, V, W	C, D, E, G, K, P, V	A, C, D, K, P, V, W	G, P, V	C, E, G, P, V	E, G, P, V	C, D, E, P, W
	54.2	62.0	60.3	55.7	62.9	62.2	52.7	55.0
	17.8	24.7	15	17.3	27.6	14.6	26.5	18.8
	21	24	23	20	24	23	18	20
	16	22	18	15	24	13	22	16
	1,547	1,858	1,684	1,638	2,164	1,996	1,984	1,792
	235	243	218	211	210	192	308	119
	3.2	5.5	7.1	2.1	4.2	8.1	4.0	1.0
	13,844	16,557	13,793	11,641	2,266	2,301	15,866	7,116
	152	367	141	542	136	124	215	154
	19.1	25.9	23.6	17.5	22.2	16.1	21.4	20.0
	441	57	446	110	17	8	238	84.0
	3.0	19.9	6.9	7.8	10.6	12.4	6.8	1.2

(continued)

NUTRIENTS PER 1,000 CALORIES	AAFCO ADULT DOG MINIMUM	CHEF'S BEAN 'N' CORN DELIGHT	COUNTRY SCRAMBLE	DOG DAY CHICKEN AND SQUASH	DOG GARBANZOS	LENTIL STEW	
CODES*		A, E, K, P, V, W	G, P, V	C, G, K, M, P, V	A, C, D, E, K, V	A, C, D, E, K, V, W	
Riboflavin (mg)	1.3	11.2	17.4	2.8	1.3	7.0	
Niacin (mg)	3.4	61.5	102.6	8.6	11.8	41.0	
B$_6$ (mg)	0.38	10.9	17.0	1.2	3.7	7.0	
Folate (mcg)	54	1,190	642	192	968	742	
B$_{12}$ (mcg)	7.0	17.4	23.0	12.0	9.3	14.4	
Pantothenic acid (mg)	3.0	2.8	6.2	1.6	5.1	5.2	
Choline (mg) (1)	340	350	368	525	435	318	
MINERALS							
Calcium (mg) (1)	1,250	1,628	1,939	3,343	1,584	1,640	
Calcium: Phosphorus	1.0–1.8	1.18	1.22	1.69	1.24	1.12	
Iron (mg)	10.0	16.7	16.6	24.1	21.6	17.2	
Iodine (mcg)	250	723.5	752	687	702	733	
Magnesium (mg)	150	369	370	350	278	390	
Phosphorus (mg)	1,000	1,382	1,583	1,983	1,273	1,464	
Potassium (mg)	1,500	2,528	3,577	1,637	1,672	1,617	
Sodium (mg)	200	1,809	1,078	1,177	172	336	
Zinc (mg)	20.0	19.4	22.3	26.8	24.8	21.6	
Copper (mg)	1.25	1.6	2.0	2.4	2.6	1.6	
Manganese (mg)	1.25	2.7	4.1	3.5	5.7	6.8	
Selenium (mcg)	80	102	164	166	79	99	

(1) Generally, must be supplemented in home diets to meet AAFCO standards

(2) Includes amino acids added with Vegedog: methionine, taurine

Features: C = *Convenience;* **E** = *Economy;* **M** = *Meat (or can be);* **P** = *Pets plus People;* **V** = *Vegan (or can be)*

Best choices for: A = *Allergies, GI, skin issues (no beef, dairy, wheat, egg, chicken, lamb, soy, pork, rabbit, fish—use options that don't include them and choose organic foods);* **D** = *Diabetes (increase complex carbohydrates, fiber);* **G** = *Growth or recovery from injuries, follow directions under the "Growth Option";* **K** = *Kidney disease (reduce proteins, phosphorus, salt; increase potassium);* **W** = *Weight loss (increase vegetables, fiber)*

	PITCAIRN'S MALIBU SPECIAL	POOCH PAELLA	SAVORY STEW	SKILLET SUPPER	TOFU MEAT LOAF	TOFU NOODLES	V-BURGERS	WOLF BURRITO
	D, K, P, V, W	A, C, D, E, K, M, P, V, W	C, D, E, G, K, P, V	A, C, D, K, P, V, W	G, P, V	C, E, G, P, V	E, G, P, V	C, D, E, P, W
	3.1	21.0	6.9	8.3	11.3	13.1	7.1	1.8
	14.7	120.8	39.8	43.0	63.2	78.9	35.8	5.4
	2.8	20.0	6.6	7.5	10.3	12.0	5.3	0.8
	849	632	986	832	370	455	969	610
	12.3	20.0	14.4	16.4	17.9	19.7	19.6	11.2
	3.2	6.1	5.4	1.8	4.0	4.5	4.7	1.6
	298	609	381	366	312	250	647	392
	1,902	1,902	1,746	1,854	1,840	1,739	3,155	1,974
	1.39	1.51	1.19	1.14	1.18	1.25	1.16	1.44
	16.5	15.4	21.8	18.2	17.1	15.3	29.7	21.0
	846	1,384	780	753	745	677	703	840
	460	295	333	384	406	442	544	316
	1,367	1,600	1,473	1,451	1,564	1,391	2,715	1.374
	2,642	1,615	2,877	2,189	1,352	1,165	3,133	2,654
	923	956	965	987	2,805	982	1,236	2,668
	19.0	25.6	21.9	19.7	22.1	20.9	27.4	19.6
	2.2	1.9	2.4	1.8	1.7	1.9	4.3	2.0
	5.8	5.2	3.8	3.8	7.2	7.8	4.2	3.2
	133	175	108	89	172	261	130	151

RECIPES FOR CATS

Our updated cat recipes include options with or without meat and eggs. If in doubt, use a mix including animal products, but we do recommend you avoid fish and seafood at this point, due to toxins and overfishing.

That said, even though cats are classed as obligate carnivores, there are thousands of cats reported to be healthy on well-planned, high-protein, high-fat, plant-based diets *if supplemented* with special nutrients they usually get from meat: taurine, arachidonic acid, vitamin A (retinol), vitamin B_{12}, and others. For this purpose you *must* use Vegecat (or Vegecat phi for those at risk of FUS, or Vegekit for mamas and kitties), from compassioncircle.com, 800-370-7387. If unavailable, see advice in "Recommended Foods for Dogs and Cats" in Chapter 5. Before trying a vegan diet for cats, read Chapter 7 to see how to best monitor your animal safely, especially if male or prone to FUS (urinary crystals and blockage).

Whatever you choose, it's best to rotate recipes and offer a variety of choices if your cat agrees: See the next chapter for ways to deal with picky cats. Transition slowly, offering nutritional yeast and other "condiments" and focus on recipes using similar levels of protein and fats, which studies show to be a feline preference. Tofu and turkey both fill that bill nicely.

Always provide plenty of fresh, pure, filtered or spring water and moisten any kibbles.

You might also try using a vegan digestive enzyme product, such as Prozyme Plus, to increase the absorption of nutrients in recipes with cooked foods.

CAT DAY

Cat Maintenance or Growth

Cat Day is a two-part plan, similar to the Dog Day program inspired by Dr. Dee Blanco. It largely replaces our classic meat and grain recipes for cats, such as Turkey Fest (page 115).

It's a very easy, broad-brush way to include the raw meat so natural to cats, but with the option of vegan or vegetarian food at breakfast: a middle path that can offer the best of both worlds. We encourage variety, as much as your cat will accept.

BREAKFAST: CHOOSE ONE OR ROTATE

- Any quality, complete, balanced cat food, with meat or vegan[1]
- Any of our cat recipes (pages 106–117)
- Kitty Omelet (page 112), perhaps with a bit of buttered toast[2]
- Or, the same as dinner

DINNER: MEAT AND VEGGIES

Mix and serve with a sprinkle of nutritional yeast:

- 80% or more raw or cooked meat[3]
- 20% or less baked squash or sweet potato, well-cooked whole grain, or cat veggies[4]
- ½ the daily serving of Vegecat[5]

Growth Option: Use the daily label amount of Vegekit, a growth supplement for moms and kittens from compassioncircle.com. When using commercial foods, make sure they are intended for growth or all stages of life.

Mix 'Em Option: Finicky eaters might do better if you mix their current food with any of the other options. Each is balanced within itself. You could, for example, mix one of our vegan recipes with the dinner plan, commercial food, or an omelet.

---

[1] Kibble or canned food, with quality meat (preferably organic) or vegan (Ami, Benevo, or Evolution). Add moisture to kibbles, especially if your cat has urinary issues, is male, or is a senior. Avoid seafood and GMO corn, soy, or their derivatives.

[2] Eggs are a great cat option if from well-raised local chickens.

[3] Chicken, quail, rabbit, deer, beef—no seafood. If using a raw pet mix with bones ground in, you can reduce the Vegecat, but we caution you against eliminating it without knowing how much calcium a mix contains.

[4] Canned pumpkin, sweet potato, winter squash, creamed corn, nori, asparagus, or a chew on some corn on the cob, cucumber, or melon (cat favorites), wheat or barley grass.

[5] Or, half of any complete cat daily vitamin plus 250 milligrams of calcium per cat.

WILD TOFU

Cat Maintenance or Growth

This was inspired when our friend Tanya Holonko, DVM, discovered that her cats love the combination of mashed tofu and nutritional yeast. What could be simpler?

So, we added some Vegecat, a bit of pumpkin, ran the numbers, and the results are remarkably close in protein and fat percentages to the diet of wild felines (46% protein, 33% fat), hence the name! The protein in soy also offers a great amino acid profile, as do amino acid boosters now in Vegecat. Nutritional yeast is 53 percent protein (more than most meat) and rich in B vitamins, and cats almost universally love it on top of any food.

1 block (10 ounces) super firm Wildwood SprouTofu or 1 tub (14 ounces) Nasoya or WestSoy extra firm organic tofu

$\frac{1}{4}$ cup nutritional yeast or VegeYeast

$\frac{1}{8}$ teaspoon salt or 1 teaspoon tamari soy sauce, or to taste

$2\frac{1}{2}$ teaspoons Vegecat (or enough for 2 days per current label)

2 tablespoons canned or baked pumpkin or pureed veggie, such as asparagus

In a bowl, mash the tofu. Mix in most of the yeast, the salt, and the Vegecat. Add the pumpkin or other veggie and sprinkle the rest of the yeast on top. The veggie can be mixed in, used as a topping, or even omitted. Experiment.

Options: Rotate the veggie, using pureed corn, baked summer or winter squash, green beans, carrot or tomato juice, or baby food equivalents. Occasionally offer some melon, cucumber, asparagus, or corn on the cob on the side: all cat delectables. Nori flakes are nice in any of these combinations as well.

Growth Option: For the Vegecat, substitute 2 days of the daily label amount of Vegekit (compassioncircle.com).

Yield: 348 calories, about 2 days' worth, or 4 cat meals (40% protein, 41% fat)

SEA TOFU

Cat Maintenance or Growth

Another variation of an easy tofu dish, this recipe includes nori and corn, which appeal to seafood-loving kitties. This recipe is perfectly balanced with protein and fat (as a percentage of calories), which taste tests show is what finicky cats like. It is also abundant in B vitamins, good for seniors.

10 ounces super firm organic tofu (e.g., Wildwood SprouTofu)

1 tablespoon organic soy or sunflower lecithin granules

3 tablespoons nutritional yeast

¼ cup baby food creamed corn (½ jar) or any favorite pureed veggie

1 sheet crumbled nori (used to make sushi rolls)

⅛ teaspoon salt (black Himalayan salt gives an eggy flavor) or 1 teaspoon tamari soy sauce

2½ teaspoons Vegecat (2 daily cat servings)

In a bowl, mash the tofu. Mix in the lecithin and most of the yeast. Top with the creamed corn, nori, salt, Vegecat, and a sprinkle of the remaining yeast and serve.

Options: Vary the lecithin with other fats: hemp hearts, nut butter, flax or hemp oil, or ground flax-seeds. Use dulse flakes instead of nori, or leave it out. Serve with a favorite cat veggie or condiment (see end of chapter), if desired.

Growth Option: Use the daily amount of Vegekit as recommended for your mama cat and kittens (compassioncircle.com).

Yield: *614 calories, about 2 days' worth (38% protein, 38% fat)*

EGGLESS SALAD

Cat Maintenance or Growth

Pets plus People

This recipe is similar to Wild Tofu and Sea Tofu, but with an egg salad twist, and one of our favorites. After serving your cat, add some dill, pickle, green onion, and mustard if you like, and make yourself a delicious sandwich with lettuce, tomato, and cucumbers.

1 block (10 ounces) super firm Wildwood SprouTofu or 1 tub (14 ounces) Westsoy or Nasoya extra firm organic tofu

3 tablespoons nutritional yeast

1 teaspoon baco bits (optional)

1 tablespoon mayonnaise

1/2 teaspoon salt (black Himalayan salt gives an eggy flavor)

1/2 rib celery, finely minced

1 teaspoon minced parsley

1 1/4 teaspoons Vegecat (or amount per label for 1 meal)

Simple as can be. Just mash the tofu in a bowl and mix in most of the yeast plus the baco bits (if using), mayonnaise, salt, celery, parsley, and Vegecat. Sprinkle the remaining nutritional yeast on top, a great enticement. This has plenty of protein for your cat, so you can also add condiments like creamed corn or pumpkin or asparagus (see Wild Tofu on page 106).

Growth Option: Use the daily amount of Vegekit as recommended on the label for your mama cat and kittens.

Yield: 587 calories, about 2 days' worth for a cat (40% protein, 41% fat)

YUM BURGERS

Cat Maintenance or Growth

Pets plus People

A super-duper, high-protein, tasty veggie burger. This could become your cat's favorite (and yours, too). Caution: Make some for the dog as well, or he'll be unhappy! Make his with Vegedog.

1 cup dried lentils

3 cups water or broth, divided

½ cup organic textured soy protein (TSP)

2 tablespoons ground flaxseeds

2 slices whole wheat bread, crumbled

2 brown cremini mushrooms (higher protein) or white mushrooms

2 tablespoons nutritional yeast

2 tablespoons sunflower seeds

2 tablespoons pumpkin seeds

⅛ teaspoon salt, preferably black Himalayan

2 tablespoons Vegecat (or 5 days' worth)

In a medium saucepan, cook the lentils in 2 cups of the water or broth for 40 minutes or until done. Meanwhile, heat 1 cup of water or broth. Stir in the TSP and ground flaxseeds. Set aside to reconstitute. When the lentils are tender, puree them in a blender or food processor along with the bread, mushrooms, yeast, seeds, salt, and Vegecat. Add water if needed. Pour the puree into a bowl and stir in the soaked TSP and flaxseeds with a fork.

Chill a bit to make it stiffer. Preheat the oven to 350°F. Form 10 patties and place them on a baking sheet lined with parchment paper. Bake 20 minutes on each side.

When cool, serve 1 burger per cat per meal (if 2 meals a day), perhaps topped with a condiment (pages 117, 124–125). Enjoy yours in the usual people way, perhaps pan grilled, on a toasted whole wheat English muffin, with the works. Extras? Trim the parchment paper around each burger and stack with paper between them in a freezer container.

Growth Option: Use the daily amount of Vegekit as per the label for your mama cat and kittens.

Yield: 1,477 calories in 10 burgers, 5 days of cat meals at 2 a day (27% protein, 20% fat)

NEW DAY ROAST

Cats or Dogs, Maintenance or Growth
Pets plus People

Inspired by the seitan (say-tan) included in Vegepet's cat recipes for years, and some of the tasty but costly vegan roasts in the market, I (Susan) did some research and learned how to make a turkey-like plant-based roast at a fraction of the cost. Now I wish I'd learned long ago how easy it is to make seitan, an ancient Buddhist meat substitute made from wheat that became "mock duck" at Chinese restaurants. It concentrates the protein from wheat, which is the most widely consumed protein in the world. Though this is a long recipe, once you've obtained the ingredients, it goes quickly. The key is to premix 7 cups of dry mix first, enough for 3 loaves.

Hint: You could instead substitute a high-protein vegan meat, such as Field Roast's or Beyond Meat's products, plus Vegecat (per daily label).

Bulk Mix for 3 Loaves

1 package (22 ounces)—4 cups—vital wheat gluten (see Chapter 5)

1 cup garbanzo bean flour (available at natural food stores)

1¼ cups nutritional yeast

Scant ½ cup Vegecat (or 18 days' worth)

¼ cup sunflower or organic soy lecithin

1 tablespoon poultry seasoning or all-purpose herb seasoning

1 teaspoon garlic powder

1 teaspoon ground cumin

1 teaspoon paprika (optional)

1 teaspoon salt (preferably black Himalayan for hearty flavor)

In a large bowl, thoroughly mix with a fork:

To Make 1 Loaf

1½ cups water or broth

2 tablespoons sunflower butter, almond butter, or sesame butter

1 tablespoon olive oil or coconut oil

1 teaspoon organic tamari soy sauce

To make 1 loaf: Measure one-third of the dry bulk mix (2⅓ cups) into a bowl. Store the rest in a sealed container in the fridge or freezer. Copy this recipe and keep it handy. In a separate bowl, whisk the water or broth, butter, oil, and soy sauce into a froth.

Make a well in the center of the dry mix. Pour in the liquid mix and blend quickly with a fork. Add more water if it seems dry. Remove and knead for about 3 minutes. This is the fun part! Enjoy the resilient, stretchy proteins that will soon become part of your stretchy cat. Then let it rest 10 minutes to develop texture.

While it's resting, preheat the oven to 350°F, clean up, and prep the stuffing, yummy surprises that your cat will enjoy encountering. Use any of her favorites or:

2 tablespoons mashed peas (or spinach, corn, pumpkin, or butternut squash)

1 mushroom, finely minced

Perhaps some lecithin, hemp hearts, or fatty meat scraps

Lay out about 18" of parchment paper. Knead the loaf again and pull out a large square of dough. Place it on the paper. Lay the stuffing in a line on top of the dough, roll it up into a stuffed loaf, and pinch the edges to seal. Rub with olive oil and poultry seasoning. Wrap the paper around it like a burrito. Place on a baking sheet, tucking the wrap seam side down. Bake for 40 to 50 minutes, just enough to firm it up. Don't let it get too hard and dry or it will be more like bread and less like meat.

Voilà! Slice a piece, then dice it for your cat and top with a creamed corn sauce, gravy, extra yeast, or other condiments. Is the dog jealous? Add some to his Skillet Supper (page 89) or Pooch Paella (page 98) or make his own loaf using Vegedog. Save some for yourself and use like chicken or turkey in many dishes.

3-Loaf Option: Once you are familiar with the process, you may want to just triple the measurements to make 1 loaf, make all 3 loaves now, and wrap and freeze any you can't use soon.

Growth Option: Use the daily amount of Vegekit recommended on the label for your mama cat and kittens.

Yield: *5,523 calories in 3 loaves (18 days' worth, or 6 days per loaf). (47% protein, 30% fat). Can be frozen for 3 months or kept in the fridge for 1 week.*

KITTY OMELET

Cat Maintenance or Growth

Pets plus People

Here is "simple." Most cats love eggs, especially the yolks, and they make an easy meal with well-balanced and well-digested protein. Especially if you have backyard chickens or access to eggs from a humanely, healthfully raised flock of layers, this is an excellent option several times a week. As always, feed a variety of foods. The following amounts are for 1 meal for 1 cat. Multiply as needed.

Bit of olive oil, coconut oil, or water

2 small eggs

¾ teaspoon Vegecat

2 teaspoons nutritional yeast

In a skillet over medium heat, warm the oil. In a bowl, whisk the eggs lightly and pour them into the pan. Cook, stirring frequently, for 3 to 4 minutes (don't overcook them). Mix in the Vegecat. Either mix the yeast into the eggs or sprinkle it liberally on top. Perhaps offer a small piece of melon or a Toasty Tidbit (page 125) as well.

Growth Option: Use the daily amount of Vegekit as recommended on the label for your mama cat and kittens.

Yield: 143 calories, half a day's worth for a cat (38% protein, 50% fat)

BEEF AND CORN

Cat Maintenance or Growth

Another recipe with that equal mix of protein and fat that cats are known to prefer, and high in each, making it a good recipe for growth needs. It also contains corn, which cats like. A good recipe particularly for those with access to pastured beef or comparable lean red meats.

1 pound lean beef chuck

1 cup fresh or creamed corn

2 tablespoons nutritional yeast

5 teaspoons Vegecat

In a food processor, grind the raw meat and corn (if using fresh kernels), or chop in bite-size pieces. Add the yeast and Vegecat.

Substitutions: Instead of beef chuck, use venison, buffalo, elk, rabbit, mutton, or turkey or raw pet meat mixes often sold in frozen sections of pet stores. Instead of corn, use baked winter squash or yams, cooked asparagus or zucchini, or other such foods.

Growth Option: Use 3 days' worth of Vegekit instead of the Vegecat.

Yield: 1,102 calories, almost 3 days' worth of meals (39% protein, 40% fat)

TOFU MEAT LOAF FOR CATS

Cat Maintenance

Pets plus People

Enjoy this hearty comfort food yourself, along with a side of veggies or salad and some mashed potatoes and gravy (see Tahini Gravy, page 124). It is a higher-protein version of the Tofu Meat Loaf for Dogs, to meet feline needs, including the required Vegecat supplement.

1 block (10 ounces) super firm Wildwood SprouTofu or 1 tub (14 ounces) Westsoy or Nasoya extra firm organic tofu

1 slice organic whole wheat bread, finely crumbled

1 cup quick oats

2–3 teaspoons organic tamari soy sauce or black Himalayan salt to taste

¼ cup nutritional yeast

2 tablespoons ground flaxseeds

1–2 tablespoons Dijon mustard

1 teaspoon poultry seasoning

1 teaspoon dried oregano or Italian herbs (optional)

½ cup creamed corn

1 tablespoon Vegecat (or 4 days' worth, per label)

1½–2 cups water

Preheat the oven to 350°F. In a large bowl, knead together all ingredients, adding water as needed for a moist consistency. Press into a lightly oiled 9" x 5" glass loaf pan and bake for 30 to 40 minutes.

Options: Top with the creamed corn instead of incorporating it into the loaf, plus a sprinkle of nutritional yeast. Or top with Tahini Gravy (page 124). Chopped mushrooms, peas, or anything your cat likes could also be mixed into the loaf.

Yield: 1,171 calories, about 4 days' worth of cat food (28% protein, 28% fat)

TURKEY FEST

Cat Maintenance or Growth

Similar to our classic meat and grain recipes and the main recipe that our cat Ming enjoyed for some years, this has been reformulated as a 50-50 recipe—half of its calories from fat, half from protein—said to be a cat favorite. This could work well for a multicat home. Otherwise, freeze what you can't use in 3 days.

5–6 cups water

2 cups old-fashioned rolled oats

1 pound raw ground turkey

2 medium eggs

1 tablespoon nutritional yeast

¼ teaspoon salt, preferably black Himalayan

2 slightly rounded tablespoons Vegecat
(or 5 days' worth, per label)

In a medium saucepan over medium-high heat, bring the water to a boil. Add the oats and cook for about 10 minutes. Lightly scramble the turkey and eggs in a skillet. Let the oatmeal cool a bit and mix it with the turkey, eggs, yeast, salt, and Vegecat in a bowl. Serve with a condiment, whether one of the Veggie Sauces (page 117), Healthy Sprinkle (page 122), or what have you.

Growth Option: (mom and kittens): Use 5 days' worth of Vegekit, following label instructions.

Yield: *1,518 calories, 5 days' worth of cat food (33% protein, 34% fat)*

LENTILS PLUS

Cat Maintenance

Courtesy of Compassion Circle, makers of Vegepet Supplements

This recipe has been used successfully for decades to feed cats on a plant-based diet and was formulated by James Peden, founder of Vegepet supplements. We worked closely with Ashley Bass at Vegepet's new home, Compassion Circle, to update the supplements with additional amino acids and other adjustments to improve Vegecat further. Additional recipes are in the product literature that comes with the supplement or can be downloaded online. This is another recipe with equal levels of protein and fat, something cats seem to seek, and Ashley told us customers say it's a favorite.

²⁄₃ cup dried lentils

1–1¹⁄₂ cups water

³⁄₄ cup tempeh

³⁄₄ teaspoon soy sauce or ¹⁄₈ teaspoon salt, preferably black Himalayan

¹⁄₄ cup VegeYeast or nutritional yeast

1 tablespoon oil (see note)

4 teaspoons Vegecat (or 3 days' worth, per label)

In a medium saucepan over medium-high heat, cook the lentils thoroughly in the water. Coat the tempeh with the soy sauce and add it to the lentils. Then add the yeast, oil, and Vegecat. Good with a condiment (see recipes at right).

Note: For oils, the company recommends olive, safflower, sunflower, sesame, soybean, or non-GMO corn oil. You can also use flax oil once a week if you don't heat it. They also suggest that using a vegan digestive enzyme formula, such as Prozyme Plus (per label instructions), can increase absorption of some nutrients in cooked foods up to 71 percent.

Yield: 961 calories, about 3 days' worth of cat food (27% protein, 28% fat)

CONDIMENTS, TREATS, AND SPECIAL FOODS

VEGGIE SAUCES

Cats or Dogs

Pets plus People

Like people, pets love variety and tasty surprises. One way to provide that, plus hundreds of health-promoting, cancer-preventing phytonutrients, is to puree steamed or baked vegetables. You can generally use whichever they like in moderation, but consider these differences when choosing them.

1. *Asparagus, peas, tomato sauce, broccoli, lettuce, greens, tomatoes, and green beans* are surprisingly high in protein, as well as fiber, but low in calories. That makes them excellent for weight loss, but not best if your animal is active, growing, or underweight. (In those cases, minimize veggies altogether. Up the protein and fat.)

2. *Corn and carrots* have protein and fat in equal amounts, which may be part of their appeal to cats, who often like corn on the cob or carrot juice. Don't overuse them with recipes that are at the low end of the protein needs for each species (see charts on the following pages).

3. *Yams, sweet potatoes, butternut squash, potatoes, and zucchini* are lowest in protein and fat, yet starchier than other veggies. They pair well with meat, eggs, tofu, and seitan. You can use them instead of grains in most recipes.

In most cases, simply puree the cooked vegetable in a blender and pour it over your pet's food like a sauce. Then toss on a dash of Healthy Sprinkle (page 122). Freeze extras in small jars, leaving space at the top for expansion, or just make a bit at a time as you have extra veggies from your dinner.

Yield: varies

Use this chart to see the nutrients in and special features of or uses for each cat recipe, indicated by CODES. For some health conditions, a minor adjustment is suggested in the key. Veterinarians may suggest further uses based on nutrient listings. Note that vitamin C is not an AAFCO requirement, as cats make their own.

CAT MAINTENANCE RECIPES: APPROXIMATE NUTRIENTS PER 1,000 CALORIES

Calculated with tools at nutritiondata.com including custom entries.

NUTRIENTS PER 1,000 CALORIES	AAFCO ADULT CAT MINIMUM	BEEF AND CORN	CAT DAY CHICKEN AND PUMPKIN	EGGLESS SALAD	KITTY OMELET	
CODES*		C, D, F, G, M, U	A, C, D, F, G, K, M, P, V	D, F, G, P, U, V	C, D, G, P, U	
Protein (g) (2)	65.0	94.3	75.0	100.0	95.1	
Fat (g)	22.5	44.9	59.2	45.8	55.2	
Protein as % of calories	26	39	31	40	38	
Fat as % of calories	20	40	51	41	50	
Taurine (mg) (1)	500	703	667	654	811	
Methionine (1) + Cysteine (mg)	1,000	4,037	3,065	2,932	4,739	
Arachidonic acid (mg) (1)	50	77	73	72	89	
Omega 6:3 ratio (low best)		21.5	14.4	7.2	15.6	
VITAMINS						
A (IU) (1)	833	1,517	47,701	1,938	4,145	
D (IU) (1)	70	179	170	167	393	
E (IU)	10.0	29.7	30.3	30.4	38.4	

(1) A nutrient for which Vegecat is a necessary supplement in most recipes to meet AAFCO standards (do not omit)

(2) Includes amino acids in Vegecat: arginine, lysine, methionine, taurine, threonine

***Features: C** = Convenience; **E** = Economy; **M** = Meat (or can be); **P** = Pets plus People; **V** = Vegan (or can be)*

***Best choices for: A** = Allergies, GI, skin issues (no beef, lamb, seafood, corn, soy, egg, dairy, wheat gluten or can be prepared without them. Organic is best choice); **D** = Diabetes (high protein and fat, reduce fiber); **F** = Finicky eater may prefer, or it's a recipe with similar levels of protein and fat, which cats like, a 50-50 recipe; **G** = Growth or recovery from injuries; **K** = Kidney disease (reduce proteins, phosphorus, salt; increase potassium); **U** = Urinary blockage (increase protein, methionine + cysteine, vitamin C, moisture). Use Cranimals, flax, hemp. Keep a low omega ratio; **W** = Weight loss (increase squash, veggies, use less meat and dairy: hormones).*

	LENTILS PLUS	NEW DAY ROAST	SEA TOFU	TOFU MEAT LOAF FOR CATS	TURKEY FEST	WILD TOFU	YUM BURGERS
	E, F, K, V, W	D, E, F, G, P, U, V	C, D, F, G, V	F, P, V, W	A, F, G, K, M	C, D, F, G, U, V	E, F, G, K, P, V
	75.6	119.1	95.0	73.0	79.7	101.3	67.5
	33.0	34.2	42.9	31.5	38.0	46.2	24.0
	27	47	38	28	33	40	27
	28	30	38	28	34	41	20
	608	582	631	662	650	565	655
	1,812	4,713	2,853	2,641	3,870	2,767	2,346
	67	64	69	72	71	62	72
	13.2	11.5	7.5	2.7	17.5	4.3	8.0
	1,192	1,472	1,734	1,583	1,543	1,943	1,457
	155	272	161	168	186	798	167
	25.4	27.0	26.4	35.9	28.7	40.2	39.7

(continued)

NUTRIENTS PER 1,000 CALORIES	AAFCO ADULT CAT MINIMUM	BEEF AND CORN	CAT DAY CHICKEN AND PUMPKIN	EGGLESS SALAD	KITTY OMELET	
CODES*		C, D, F, G, M, U	A, C, D, F, G, K, M, P, V	D, F, G, P, U, V	C, D, G, P, U	
K (mcg)	25	32	93	108	63	
Thiamin (mg)	1.4	12.1	22.3	32.9	30.0	
Riboflavin (mg)	1.0	13.8	24.1	34.0	33.6	
Niacin (mg)	15.0	84.1	148.3	192.7	167.8	
B_6 (mg) (1)	1.0	13.3	23.3	32.1	27.9	
Folate (mcg)	200	515	795	1,051	1,111	
B_{12} (mcg) (1)	5.0	42.9	34.1	38.9	46.1	
Pantothenic acid (mg)	1.44	5.5	6.5	6.5	10.5	
Choline (mg) (1)	600	1,048	688	730	2,160	
MINERALS						
Calcium (mg) (1)	1,500	1,801	1,909	2,459	2,516	
Calcium: Phosphorus ratio		1.13	1.23	1.15	1.13	
Iron (mg)	20.0	21.8	18.9	22.0	23.1	
Iodine (mcg) (1)	150	1,922	1,823	1,793	2,222	
Magnesium (mg)	100	149	168	450	125	
Phosphorus (mg)	1,250	1,589	1,548	2,146	2,237	
Potassium (mg)	1,500	2,460	2,009	1,940	1,741	
Sodium (mg)	500	377	313	882	867	
Zinc (mg) (1)	18.8	42.7	21.0	27.4	26.6	
Copper (mg) (1)	1.25	1.4	1.4	2.2	1.4	
Manganese (mg)	1.9	0.3	0.7	5.6	0.7	
Selenium (mcg) (1)	75	242	177	250	345	

(1) A nutrient for which Vegecat is a necessary supplement in most recipes to meet AAFCO standards (do not omit)

(2) Includes amino acids in Vegecat: arginine, lysine, methionine, taurine, threonine

*Features: C = Convenience; **E** = Economy; **M** = Meat (or can be); **P** = Pets plus People; **V** = Vegan (or can be)

Best choices for: A = Allergies, GI, skin issues (no beef, lamb, seafood, corn, soy, egg, dairy, wheat gluten or can be prepared without them. Organic is best choice); **D** = Diabetes (high protein and fat, reduce fiber); **F** = Finicky eater may prefer, or it's a recipe with similar levels of protein and fat, which cats like, a 50-50 recipe; **G** = Growth or recovery from injuries; **K** = Kidney disease (reduce proteins, phosphorus, salt; increase potassium); **U** = Urinary blockage (increase protein, methionine + cysteine, vitamin C, moisture). Use Cranimals, flax, hemp. Keep a low omega ratio; **W** = Weight loss (increase squash, veggies, use less meat and dairy: hormones).

	LENTILS PLUS	NEW DAY ROAST	SEA TOFU	TOFU MEAT LOAF FOR CATS	TURKEY FEST	WILD TOFU	YUM BURGERS
	E, F, K, V, W	D, E, F, G, P, U, V	C, D, F, G, V	F, P, V, W	A, F, G, K, M	C, D, F, G, U, V	E, F, G, K, P, V
	50	43	62	54	32	255	62
	19.4	28.2	31.7	22.8	4.9	37.3	10.2
	2.0	29.0	32.8	23.4	6.1	38.2	10.4
	42.6	164.5	185.8	132.0	36.4	215.0	58.2
	12.3	28.2	30.9	22.4	5.5	37.3	9.5
	789	906	1,006	806	287	1,194	1,103
	11.1	33.7	37.5	30.1	17.0	40.8	19.1
	16.5	4.5	6.5	5.2	4.5	6.6	6.3
	725	794	1,232	729	723	698	712
	1,732	1,922	2,430	2,176	1,687	2,216	1,844
	1.13	1.14	1.01	1.15	1.11	1.08	1.00
	30.3	18.0	20.9	22.3	19.7	20.4	26.9
	1,664	1,592	1,727	1,841	1,780	1,590	1,794
	277	194	434	419	220	388	455
	1,536	1,692	2,416	1,899	1,526	2,055	1,850
	2,790	1,150	1,888	1,905	1,987	1,624	3,040
	355	581	663	1,693	832	646	454
	39.5	19.9	26.4	24.3	20.6	26.7	21.6
	3.6	1.6	2.1	2.0	1.4	2.0	3.3
	3.6	1.0	5.2	6.2	4.0	4.9	4.1
	90	191	243	220	202	238	136

HEALTHY SPRINKLE

Dogs or Cats

Pets plus People

This tasty condiment is designed with finicky felines in mind, with high and equal amounts of protein and fat, similar to levels in their prey. It's also rich in omega-3s, vitamins, and minerals as well as choline, which can be low in diets without eggs. The black Himalayan salt offers sulfur, deficient in many diets, and imparts a rich flavor comparable to that of eggs. Seafood lovers might enjoy some crumbled nori or dulse in the mix as well. Sprinkled on tofu, with the daily amount of Vegecat, this would make an easy meal for cats. But don't forget the dog. He would like some, too. Try it yourself on pasta, soups, salads, and grains.

$\frac{1}{2}$ cup nutritional yeast

3 tablespoons organic sunflower or soy lecithin

2 teaspoons hemp hearts

2 teaspoons ground flaxseeds

$\frac{1}{8}$ teaspoon black Himalayan salt (optional)

1 sheet toasted nori, crumbled (optional)

In a jar, mix together the yeast, lecithin, hemp hearts, flaxseeds, and salt and nori (if using). Store in the fridge, important for preserving the flaxseeds once they're ground. Sprinkle on the food when serving, which gives more flavor power than mixing it in.

Options: For some or all of the hemp or flax, substitute equal amounts of ground pumpkin seeds (high in zinc and good against parasites) or sesame seeds (high in methionine, which pets have greater need for than do we). If you enjoy experimentation, compare this with and without adding some powder from a capsule of glutamine, an amino acid sold for human use, which gives a good flavor. Glutamine is very high in rabbits, a natural prey for cats, and in some of their observed favorite foods. Could be something they're seeking.

Yield: 540 calories, about 15 calories/teaspoon (34% protein, 35% fat)

TOFU SOUR CREAM/YOGURT

Dogs or Cats

Pets plus People

This is an easy and satisfying plant-based substitute for yogurt or sour cream, far higher in protein than dairy products and many meats. Pour like yogurt over berries for a tasty pet or people high-protein dessert. Slather on bean dishes or burritos and wraps that dogs love (fine with lettuce and the works, except onions). Entice cats using this as a kibble sauce. This kind of tofu also keeps on the shelf, so stock up or even use it on campouts.

Still good without the teensy tad of sweetener.

1 package (12 ounces) extra firm Mori-Nu silken tofu

1 teaspoon or less lemon juice, to taste

1/2 teaspoon or less maple syrup, Sucanat, or agave nectar, to taste

1/8 teaspoon salt, or to taste

In a blender, combine the tofu, lemon juice, maple syrup, and salt. Puree until smooth. Alternatively, you can combine the ingredients in a bowl and whip for a few seconds with a fork until creamy—and you're done in less than the time it takes for a cup of tea to steep. Store in a glass jar and use within a week. Sometimes we add powdered probiotic capsules for the full yogurt effect.

Option: Pair this with 2 cups of fresh blueberries in season and your dog will love you forever, plus you will have just provided him with a nice surprise meal offering 30 percent protein, more protein than in hamburger.

Yield: 191 calories (52% protein, 30% fat)

TAHINI GRAVY

Dogs or Cats

Pets plus People

Simple, and healthier than gravies with animal fats or refined oils.

1 cup cremini mushrooms (optional)

1 cup tahini

²/₃ cup or more water

¼ cup or less tamari soy sauce

2 teaspoons nutritional yeast

Pinch of garlic powder

In a saucepan over medium heat, stir together the mushrooms (if using), tahini, water, soy sauce, yeast, and garlic powder. Use instead of the ketchup in Tofu Meat Loaf (pages 90 and 114) or over kibbles, New Day Roast (page 110), or a lean meat like turkey or venison. Refrigerate or freeze extras. Don't overuse it in starchier, lower-protein recipes or it may make the protein level too low.

Yield: 1,421 calories (12% protein, 69% fat)

SIMPLE HEALTHY TREATS

Sometimes there's nothing like a simple whole food, as grown.

FOR CATS: corn on the cob, cucumber, cantaloupe, or other melons. Nighttime: dental kibble (especially if there is tartar buildup). *No grapes, chocolate, or raisins.*

FOR DOGS: carrot sticks, broccoli stalks, sweet potato chews (sold online), or sticks to chew on. Berries, apples, bananas, cherry tomatoes, melons, papayas, avocados (peeled). *No grapes, chocolate, or raisins.*

TOASTY TIDBITS

Dogs or Cats

Pets plus People

A neighbor cat often visits us for a brief hello and sometimes a tidbit. He is pretty picky, so we were impressed when he relished some small bits of fresh whole wheat toast topped with coconut oil. To boost the protein, we add a sprinkle of nutritional yeast on this easy treat, which could also be served on a wet meal as "croutons." Pairs well with a lean meat, New Day Roast, or legumes: high-protein, low-fat foods.

½ slice organic whole wheat toast
(Food for Life is our favorite)

1 teaspoon coconut oil, flax oil, hemp oil, or any nut or seed butter

1 teaspoon nutritional yeast

Toast the bread lightly. While the toast is still warm, spread on the oil and dust with the yeast. Break into bite-size pieces for a kitty.

Yield: 65 calories (17% protein, 39% fat)

CHAPTER 7

MAKING THE SWITCH

So you're ready to do it. You cherish your animals, maybe you even "had the talk" with them, and you are ready to switch them to a new diet that's as fresh, organic, healthy, humane, and sustainable as possible. Congratulations! Looking at all of that together is the essence of a holistic way of approaching health, and life.

The first step for a happy and successful shift starts with you committing yourself to a new course. Remember why you are doing it and proceed with confidence. Let your love for your animal, for all animals, for the earth, and for future generations be your inspiration and support. And don't forget, it's also about nurturing yourself with delicious, healthy food. It's going to be tasty and it's going to be fun.

Depending on how you've been eating, you may first want to reorganize some routines and learn some new skills in the kitchen, especially if you rely on fast food and take-out. If so, that will also be a good change, for health and environmental reasons. Once you and your animal are both on your way, it should be a breeze.

If you're more of a homebody and already make special recipes just for pets, you're now going to find it much easier to team up with your animals and eat many of the same entrées. That means more time for walks, play, and puttering in the garden!

TIPS FOR FRESH FOOD DIETS

First, choose the program or approach that works best for you. If you already eat a healthy diet and are handy in the kitchen, you might prefer a broad-brush program like Fresh and Flexible. If you want more guidance and certainty that you are meeting your pet's unique nutritional needs, then definitely use recipes. In any case, you may want to have some kibble or canned foods for occasional backup, travel, or treats. In using the recipes, start with the easiest ones, such as Wild Tofu for cats (page 106) or Lentil Stew (page 88), Skillet Supper (page 89), or Pooch Paella (page 98) for dogs. After that, find three or four Pets plus People meals or programs you like. Make them often, but create variety and optimize nutrition by substituting similar ingredients. So, try quinoa instead of rice, broccoli instead of kale, pintos instead of kidney beans, lecithin instead of hemp

hearts, turkey instead of chicken, and so on.

If you have been feeding the popular "raw (meat) diet" for pets and want to continue it at least half the time, then try the Cat Day or Dog Day programs, or our Turkey Fest recipe (page 115) for cats.

Get organized and look for ways to be efficient.

- **Stock up on basic foods** so you don't run short in the middle of preparing a recipe. If you live in the boonies, order dry goods like beans, grains, and nuts online.

- **Create a good way to organize your basics.** We keep our grains and beans in reusable jars in the pantry, grouped by type and size. Frequently used condiments like nutritional yeast and spices are in a cupboard near the stove in smaller jars. It's a work of art.

- **Save money and packaging waste by cooking your own beans.** Freeze extras in wide-mouthed salsa jars, with 1 inch of space at the top for expansion. See "How to Cook Beans and Grains," on page 128.

- **Once or twice a month, make a big batch of V-Burgers, Yum Burgers, or New Day Roast.** Freeze between parchment paper and store in containers or plastic bags for future use.

- **Stock the fridge on one side with an "endless salad bar" of glass jars or containers** filled with frozen peas or corn, kidney beans or garbanzos, "eggless salad," shredded cabbage or carrots, cherry tomatoes, sliced mushrooms, roasted beets, hummus, or meaty chunks (like New Day Roast). Use these items for recipes, plus accompanying salads for you. Instead of plastic, use glass containers. They're see-through, nontoxic, and infinitely recyclable.

• **Plan and prep ahead.** Prepare one food while another is heating up. While cleaning up after breakfast, cook potatoes or quinoa, freshen the salad bar, or thaw a burger, beans, or peas for later. After dinner, soak beans or cereal for the next day.

• **Copy and post recipes to the insides of a cupboard.** An under-counter cookbook holder is really handy too, especially if counter space is tight.

• **Invest in helpful tools,** especially a good blender such as a Vitamix, digital pressure cooker (great for beans, grains, stews), and a food processor. A nut/seed grinder is useful for grinding flaxseeds and other seeds to add to pets' dishes.

HOW TO COOK BEANS AND GRAINS

For easiest cooking and digestion, lean toward lentils. Animals like them and they are tops in protein, after soy foods.

Soak garbanzos or black, red, pinto, or white beans overnight or for several hours, then rinse well until the water is clear to remove substances that inhibit digestion. Place in a pot or digital pressure cooker (one push of the "Bean" button and they're done in 30 minutes). Cover with 2 inches of water and add a piece of potato or kombu to reduce digestive gas (discard after cooking). When tender, rinse again until the water is clear. Mash or process the beans so they are easier for pets to digest or run them through a food processor. Freeze extras. This chart will help you plan.

ONE . . .	EQUALS	OR
15-oz can beans	$\frac{1}{2}$ cup dry	1.5 cups cooked
Pound dry beans	2 cups dry	6 cups cooked (four 15-oz cans)
Part dry beans/lentils	3 parts cooked	

COOKING WHOLE GRAINS

1 CUP DRY	+ CUPS WATER	COOKED FOR	YIELDS, COOKED	PROTEIN
Amaranth	2	15–20 min	2.5 cups	13%
Barley, pearled	3	45–60 min	3.5 cups	7%
Brown rice	2.5	40–45 min	3 cups	7%
Buckwheat	2	20 min	4 cups	12%

1 CUP DRY	+ CUPS WATER	COOKED FOR	YIELDS, COOKED	PROTEIN
Bulgur	2	10–12 min	2 cups	13%
Cornmeal (polenta)	4	25–30 min	2.5 cups	8%
Millet	2.5	25–35 min	4 cups	11%
Oats, steel cut	2.5	25–30 min	2.5 cups	15%
Quinoa	2	12–15 min	3 cups	15%

POSSIBLE ISSUES

Now you're geared up and ready to go. What will happen? Many animals accept a tasty, new, fresh food diet with gusto, especially dogs, who may, almost literally, wolf it down. Their health improves and it's all very encouraging. But in other cases, you may encounter a few obstacles, mainly:

• Acceptance and palatability issues (more common with cats).

• Temporary digestive disturbances as your pet's GI system adjusts to new foods.

• A brief downturn while an animal detoxes and its system "cleans house" from prior diets.

• Possible aggravation of feline urological syndrome (FUS) in cats.

Your most likely obstacle is a cat who turns up her nose, resenting that you could even consider rocking her world with something new, like the case of a client who called to say her cats on commercial foods simply would not eat their new home-prepared diet.

"What have you tried?" I asked.

"All sorts of meats, dairy, grains, and vegetables, nutritional yeast: You name it! But practically all they will touch, especially the older cat, is just canned tuna and chicken. Not only that, it has to be one particular brand!"

Sound familiar? Many cats become so habituated to certain foods that they are like addicts. Pet food manufacturers are also masters at identifying and spraying enticing smells and flavors from the innards of slaughterhouse wastes ("digest" or "paunch") onto the surface of kibbles, so that's all a cat ever really tastes. As a result, the body's natural instinct for selecting a varied, healthy, balanced diet can diminish greatly, like ours does when we are addicted to favorite junk foods.

The other main issue is a temporary downturn as their bodies adapt, as when a client reported after a new diet and remedies for a dog with some chronic problems: "At first, Henry was doing okay. But then he suddenly stopped eating and acted like he was sick, just lying around without any energy."

Or sometimes a client would report, "My dog likes the new food, and he's been on it a few weeks. But yesterday he passed a whole bunch of worms! What do I do?"

Believe it or not, I'm glad to hear responses like these last two. That's because I know from experience that they can be favorable signs in the natural process of healing. Soon after switching to a healthier, cleaner diet, it is fairly common for an animal in suboptimal health to discharge accumulated toxic material or to undergo a brief aggravation of its symptoms (often called a "healing crisis"). These apparent setbacks are normal, often necessary, bumps on the road to well-being. It is even a favorable sign that health is improving when a load of worms is passed out. Where they once found conditions that suited them, they are now no longer welcome.

FINICKY EATERS AND THE ART OF CULINARY PERSUASION

First let's address that finicky eater, nearly always of the feline sort. Remember why you want to change his diet and who makes the meals. Try not to let a finicky feeder's habits run your life or interfere with your better judgment about what's best in the big picture, just as a wise parent does not cave in to a toddler demanding candy.

That said, the first rule of thumb is to serve your feline's new food in an appealing manner. You don't need to don a chef's hat and work up a five-star presentation, just use some common sense.

- First, "seat" your prime customer in a pleasant and safe dining spot, not in the path of foot traffic or next to a litter box.
- For much better aroma and appeal, warm up cold food a bit (as in any fine restaurant) rather than "plating it" straight out of the cooler.
- Start slowly. Carefully mix a small bit of the new food into his favorite repast: To you it may be repulsive, but for him it's a great elixir. With each meal, gradually increase the new food until, a few weeks later, your cat has all but forgotten what was once the center of his daily feasts.
- To aid this process, offer some "condiments" and sauces such as Healthy Sprinkle (page 122) or nutritional yeast. Anitra Frazier, author of *The Natural Cat*, finds that nearly all cats enjoy pumpkin, winter squash, or carrots, especially baked rather than steamed, as well as zucchini and carrot juice. She's not especially keen on greens, which also could aggravate bladder sand, stones, and obstructions due to their oxalates and alkalinity, so you might scratch them off the new menu.
- If one recipe or one brand of new food doesn't appeal, try another. Some felines will tear into a new food after months of rejecting another.

- Finally, when designing the new menu, try using a recipe or food with about *half its calories from protein and half from fat.*

HALF PROTEIN, HALF FAT, THAT CAT

What? Why's that? Just last week we came across a fascinating study, "Why Cats Are Picky Eaters" (www.seeker.com/why-cats-are-picky-eaters-1860079554.html). Apparently, it stems from their evolutionary history. The aroma, taste, and texture of food matter to cats, but taste preference studies revealed that what cats really want is for about half the calories to be from protein and half from fat, according to the authors of the study, published in the journal *Royal Society Open Science*. And that's a ratio close to the diet of wild cats.

This valuable clue may explain why cats like some unexpected foods like tofu or sweet corn, and even the very uncarnivorous cantaloupe. Regardless of carbohydrate levels, all are fairly equal in protein and fat, as you can see in the table titled "Protein and Fat in Common Foods" in Chapter 5. Oats, quinoa, cornmeal, and rice have a similar balance. So we have designed some recipes with that magic ratio in mind, including Wild Tofu and the Healthy Sprinkle condiment in the previous chapter. Try them. Likewise, turkey has more promise than chicken.

We suspect there are other discoveries yet to be made that will explain why some cats will attack cucumbers, cantaloupe, corn, and asparagus. Perhaps they detect certain nutrients low in their diets. One might be choline, which stands out in those foods' nutrient profiles on nutritiondata.com. Choline is even higher in egg yolks, a cat favorite, as well as in lecithin, a good condiment to try. And it's *very* high in rabbit and chicken, more like their natural prey, whereas deer and bison don't seem to have all that much. Hmmmm.

Glutamic acid might also be a key to feline taste buds. One of the essential amino acids, it gives food that hearty "umame" flavor and is proportionally high in nutritional yeast, corn, and our tasty Yum Burger, and it's *way high* in, yes, rabbits. Hopefully, we can find some ways to spare rabbits while satisfying cats. In fact, why not open up a capsule of glutamine, as sold for people, and sprinkle it on your cat's food or add it to the Healthy Sprinkle recipe in the previous chapter? It could be a brand-new enticer. It does taste pretty good.

THE GUT BIOME: TIME FOR A NEW CREW

Here's another interesting piece of information that sheds light on why it's good to transition slowly, even if your animal isn't horribly finicky.

The virtue of a slow transition: We now know that when the diet changes, a whole complex panoply of microorganisms in the GI tract also shift in response, depending on their favorite foods. Some increase, some decrease, and there could even be some new kids on the block.

So if you were to change your animal's diet too abruptly, even from one commercial brand to another, temporary diarrhea or loss of appetite might occur, as the bacterial flora in the digestive tract die off and are replaced by new ones. It can take a week or so, but once the change is made, things should return to normal.

Probiotics: To help the flora adjust, consider using probiotics during the transition time to introduce some good tenants who might decide to take up residence in your animal's innards. Lorelei Wakefield, VMD, finds that cats especially love the taste of FortiFlora, a probiotic from Purina. So that could double as an enticing condiment as well, but any pet or human probiotic should serve.

A Little Fast?

What if all these tricks to coax a finicky eater to make the switch don't work? Then you probably have a food addict on your hands, and a more drastic measure may be needed, all for your cat's ultimate good: a fast.

We're not talking about starving him out. But a short fast is very natural to predators in the wild. It stimulates a lagging appetite, helps cleanse the body, and deconditions old taste habits, all at the same time.

For a healthy fast, your pet needs a healthful setting—plenty of fresh air, quiet, access to the outdoors, and some moderate exercise. Don't try it when installers are coming to lay new carpet, for example, and maybe

not when it's so cold your kitty just wants to stay inside and sit by the gas stove.

Here's the process.

• Start with a break-in period of 1 to 2 days. Feed a smaller quantity of the usual food, perhaps adding a bit of the new fresh food diet.

• Move to a liquid fast for the next day or two, offering your animal only pure water, vegetable juices, broths, thin soups, or perhaps some soy milk.

• Break the fast the next day by adding some solid foods to the liquid regimen, including the new diet you are introducing.

• The next day, increase the amount of the new food to a normal amount. If there is still some reluctance, a sprinkle of nutritional yeast on top (not mixed in) will likely bring him around.

In stubborn cases, it can pay to continue the fast a bit longer. One client reported worriedly that her cat wouldn't eat any of the natural foods offered as she started breaking the fast. I advised her to keep the cat on liquids for a while longer. She did, and in a few days she enthusiastically reported that her formerly finicky cat was now eating all kinds of things it would never touch before—vegetables, grains, and even soy grits!

Fasting Concerns

How long should you let your animal go hungry before you give up and offer the old diet? With dogs, 2 days should be enough. Cats are different, however, and going without food for a while seems to be no big deal for them. Some of my clients' most finicky cats do not really become hungry and willing to try a new food until 5 days of fasting have gone by. I have not seen healthy animals go longer than that before they become truly hungry.

Some dogs or (especially) cats simply do not develop a normal level of hunger even after several days of not eating. A weak appetite like this is often a symptom of chronic illness. I do not mean that these animals are necessarily ill with symptoms or a defined disease. Rather, they are in a suboptimal or low-grade state of health. In such cases I use individualized homeopathic treatment to improve the animal's overall level of health. Afterward, the animal begins to eat more normally. If your pet won't eat and you don't have access to a vet who practices homeopathy, you may want to just head straight for what I call "the compromise."

The Compromise

Say you've tried a gradual transition and your pet just won't convert to a new diet, and fasting is something you just don't want to do. Maybe it's too hard to let your friend go hungry and you can't handle the agitation she may show, asking for her familiar food, or maybe she just isn't healthy enough to fast.

In that case, simply mix the new food into the old as an ongoing compromise.

Nibbling: Not Good

The most important factor in accepting a new food is that an animal is actually hungry. Many aren't interested in trying something new because they never really get that hungry, especially if allowed to free-feed and nibble. So they lack the motivation to try something new. Cats, in particular, are so well adapted to natural cycles of feast and famine that it can take several days for them to get decently hungry.

By examining your pet regularly, you can easily monitor its overall health. No matter what you've heard, it's not normal for a dog to have a "doggy odor" or a cat to have foul breath. Pets that have an unpleasant smell about them show signs of a chronic low health level. If your animal doesn't look very healthy, then ask your local veterinarian to work with you on the diet switch. Explain what you are trying to do and why, perhaps sharing the recipes and analyses. Ask your veterinarian to examine your pet periodically to make sure that there are no health problems and to see that your pet responds to the diet as expected and does not lose weight or weaken.

If your veterinarian does not want to help as you switch your pet to a fresh foods diet, or to one that is more plant based, for example, don't hesitate to seek help elsewhere, maybe even via a phone consult, if necessary.

The Body Responds

If your animal isn't in tip-top shape, a change to a better or less toxic diet can trigger a cleansing process.

What happens? For years your animal has been eating overprocessed food that was probably loaded with the harmful ingredients discussed in Chapter 2. No doubt she has also been exposed to environmental pollutants and, perhaps, some strong drugs. So when she eats a healthier diet, strange things begin to happen. The body responds!

She usually feels better at first. Energy and nutrients are flowing through her tissues. The quality of her blood and its oxygen-carrying capacity improve, so she starts to be more active. The added exercise, in turn, helps recharge lazy tissues.

After 2 to 3 weeks, she may feel perky enough that her body will tackle some long-neglected interior housecleaning. A mass of worms that, until now, was existing comfortably inside her may be swept out, leaving behind a clean intestine.

More often, the cleansing results in a lot of discharge from the kidneys, colon, or skin, all important excretory organs. Thus, the urine might become darker and stronger-smelling, the feces dark, temporarily containing mucus or blood specks, or the skin might erupt with sores or develop a lot of dandruff. Sometimes a lot of dead hair falls out as the skin becomes more active, getting ready to grow a new crop of fresh, healthy hair (much like a plant dropping dead foliage before putting out new leaves).

THE HEALING CRISIS

Appearances can be deceiving. In spite of what you see, your pet's body *is* getting cleaner. I know that's hard to grasp. Most of us expect that when a physical problem is being treated effectively, the condition will steadily improve until the disturbance just disappears. Certainly, we don't expect it to look worse!

That's how antibiotics and other familiar drugs often work—at least for a while. Unfortunately, such drugs sometimes simply suppress the symptoms, leaving the underlying disorder that led to the illness unchanged, so the same problem or a related one may crop up again. One long-term effect of using drugs to control diseases is that the body tends to become lazy about attempting to keep itself healthy.

In bygone times, people more clearly recognized the stages of healing—one of which was a period of crisis that might show up as a fever, inflammation, or temporary exaggeration of symptoms. At such a point the patient either began to recover or died. Called a "healing crisis," it's the point at which the body's defenses are mobilized to their maximum capabilities. It's an all-out effort.

When we interfere with this process by injecting antibiotics or cortisone, however, the defense system is not utilized. That means it can't address the underlying weakness that gave rise to the disease in the first place. Like an underused muscle, the defense system gets weak. Soon resistance to any new disease is weakened, and the body needs more drugs to cope with new problems. Poor nutrition lowers disease resistance even further, which then leads to the use of still more drugs. Weakened by infections and the toxic elements of drugs, the body demands more of the available nutrition, which overtaxes the supply and creates a deficit. Before we know it, we are caught in a vicious circle.

What will break this cycle? A good diet, for one thing. By supplying optimum nutrients, we can increase disease resistance and help the body to eliminate the toxic effects of drugs.

So don't be discouraged or think you have made a mistake if you see these signs of detoxification when you improve your pet's diet. You have gotten things moving!

HERBS TO EASE THE PROCESS

Should your pet have some moderate distress in changing to a fresh diet, smooth the way (or prevent trouble at the start) with these herbs that help cleanse the body and rebuild tissue. Use only one herb, rather than a combination. Pick the one that best matches your pet's problems, using doses shown in the table on page 136.

Alfalfa (*Medicago sativa*) is an excellent tonic to stimulate digestion and appetite, help thin animals gain weight, and improve physical and mental vigor. It suits those who are underweight, nervous, or high-strung, perhaps with muscle or joint pains or urinary problems—especially with crystal formation and bladder irritation. For dogs, depending on size, add 1 teaspoon to 3 table-spoons of ground or dry-blended alfalfa to the daily ration. Or make a tea by steeping 3 tablespoons of the herb in 1 cup of boiling water for 20 minutes. Mix it with food or give orally with a bulb syringe (or turkey baster). For cats, give 1 teaspoon (dry) per day.

Burdock (*Arctium lappa*) cleanses the blood and helps the body detoxify. It's particularly good for easing skin disorders. Soak 1 teaspoon of the root in 1 cup of spring or distilled water in a glass or enamel pan for 5 hours. Then bring to a boil, remove from the heat, and let cool. Check the table on page 136 for how much to give a dog. Cats can be given ½ teaspoon per day.

Garlic (*Allium sativum*) helps to eliminate worms, strengthen digestion, and beneficially stimulate the intestinal tract. Use it to promote intestinal health. It is also indicated for animals that have been on a high-meat or high-fish diet, and those that tend to be overweight or suffer hip pain from arthritis or dysplasia. Include fresh, grated garlic with each meal, using one-half to three cloves, depending on the dog's size (see the table on page 136). Cats can be given one-quarter clove per day.

Oats (*Avena sativa*) are also a tonic, particularly for the animal whose main weakness is in the nervous system, as in epilepsy, tremors, twitching, and paralysis. Oats also counter the weakening and exhaustive effects of heavy drugging and diseases. They help to cleanse the body and nourish new tissue growth. Use oatmeal as the chief grain in the diet.

BATHING

Also, you can use oat straw to provide a healing bath: Boil 1 to 2 pounds of the straw in 3 quarts of water for 30 minutes. Add this to the bathwater or sponge it on repeatedly as an after-bath rinse by standing the animal in a tub and reusing the solution. Such treatment is useful for skin problems, muscle and joint pain, paralysis, and liver and kidney problems. Dogs enjoy it more than cats.

One of these herbs, along with the benefits of the new diet, should make the road to good health smoother and shorter. After a month or two, give your pet another exam, and I bet you'll see a difference.

Above all, don't be discouraged from trying a change of diet. Most animals that switch to natural foods do not experience the problems I have described in this chapter. The majority enjoy the new diet and digest it well. And if you follow the advice here about easing the transition period, in all probability your pet will simply be happier and healthier than ever before.

CLEANSING HERBS DOSAGE CHART

DOG SIZE	ALFALFA, DRY	ALFALFA, LIQUID	BURDOCK, LIQUID	GARLIC CLOVES
TOY (10–15 LB)	1 tsp	2 Tbsp ($1/8$ cup)	1 tsp	$1/2$
SMALL (16–35 LB)	3 tsp (1 Tbsp)	5 Tbsp ($1/3$ cup)	2 tsp	1
MEDIUM (36–60 LB)	5 tsp	8 Tbsp ($1/2$ cup)	3 tsp (1 Tbsp)	2
LARGE (61–90 LB)	7 tsp	12 Tbsp ($3/4$ cup)	5 tsp	$2 1/2$
GIANT (90+ LB)	9 tsp (3 Tbsp)	16 Tbsp (1 cup)	6 tsp (2 Tbsp)	3

tsp = teaspoons (there are 3 teaspoons in a tablespoon)
Tbsp = tablespoons (there are 16 tablespoons in a cup)

SPECIAL TIPS FOR SWITCHING CATS TO PLANT-BASED DIETS

In addition to having FFS (finicky feline syndrome), your cat may be one of those with a tendency toward FUS (feline urinary syndrome), more recently called FLUTD (feline lower urinary tract disease), especially if he's an older male or one not in top shape, or has a history of bladder issues. The alkalizing nature of a plant-based diet can encourage the formation of struvite crystals in the bladder, which can cause it to plug up and may even require surgery. Excessively acid urine, on the other hand, can cause calcium oxalate crystals.

While cats often prefer kibbles and they're better for their teeth, moist food is best to prevent urinary issues of any sort, as well as lower their stress level. FLUTD is common, and for maybe 25 percent to 35 percent of cats that people try to transition to an all-plant diet, this or other problems can arise, so you might enlist the help of your veterinarian or consult with a vegan-friendly one, such as Dr. Armaiti May (veganvet.net) or Dr. Lorelei Wakefield (vegetariancats.com), who both advised us for this section.

Both veterinarians report that they have definitely seen dogs improve on vegan diets, especially those with skin, coat, GI, and allergy issues. As for cats, Dr. Wakefield has some reservations about a completely vegan diet from her experience, but has also seen many do just fine. If in doubt, she suggests a diet that's part vegan and part conventional, but she is happy to support clients who wish to try going entirely vegan.

Dr. May's own cat is on commercial vegan kibble. For clients' cats, this is her protocol: For all males or any cat that seems at risk, measure the urinary pH before the switch (the ideal range is 6.0 to 6.5), and then again 3 weeks into it. If the pH is over 7.5 (alkaline), then add more liquid to the food, plus methionine per your veterinarian's advice (which is acidifying) or else ascorbic acid, which is easier but not as effective (10 to 30 milligrams per kilogram of body weight, three times a day). As long as they eat the food, she finds cats can do okay with these adjustments. She also recommends the use of digestive enzymes and probiotics for companion animals.

Note that methionine is an essential amino acid, important to dogs and cats for liver repair, skin and coat condition, and other functions. Levels are lower in plant foods than in meat, so a modest amount of methionine has recently been added to Vegecat, and that may make for smoother sailing. This level is safely within AAFCO limits. Any additional amount should be prescribed by a vet, as excesses overacidify the urine and could cause other issues. Intact male cats appear to require higher levels of methionine because it's involved in the production of felinine, a sulfur-containing amino acid likely important in territorial marking. This likely plays a role in greater pH and FLUTD issues for the guy cats.

Some years ago James Peden, the founder of Vegepet, developed a feline transition protocol for cats on fresh vegan foods, using his product Vegecat phi. Like Vegecat, it provides essential nutrients to supplement a home-prepared diet, but with an AAFCO-approved urinary acidifier, sodium bisulfate. Don't use sodium bisulfate in isolation, he cautions, as that could be dangerous. Peden also recommends Cranimals, a cranberry powder available online, or vitamin C. He says it's easy to test the urine at home with pH strips from a drugstore, along with a nonabsorbent litter, available along with Vegecat phi at compassioncircle.com. One

Vegepet customer likes Pretty Litter, which changes color to detect urine that is too acid or too alkaline.

Finally, in his book *Obligate Carnivore: Cats, Dogs & What It Really Means to Be Vegan,* Jed Gillen reports from years of supplying hundreds of customers with vegan pet foods and dietary supplements that most, but not all, cats thrive on the diet. After grappling with this issue, his advice is to monitor your cat's urinary pH at 2-week intervals, adjusting as needed as described above, but if the pH stays too high or a particular cat has problems (usually male), then he would incorporate some meat back into that cat's diet.

A FINAL WORD OF ENCOURAGEMENT

Making a switch in your animal friend's diet is going to do a lot of good. We realize there are some new routines and tips to learn, but it is really not that difficult. We hope this chapter has helped you try to keep it as simple as you can and proceed with confidence.

We also hope that, by trying to think of all the questions and concerns that may arise, we have not discouraged you. Most people don't have difficulty making food changes, and it is usually an enjoyable and interesting process. May it go very well for you and the animals in your life.

CHAPTER 8

SPECIAL DIETS FOR SPECIAL PETS

Our new recipes and programs in Chapter 6 are designed to meet or exceed recommended guidelines for feeding normal, healthy animals. But what about pets with special needs, such as growth and reproduction or chronic health issues? Here we will show you how to use our nutrient analysis charts in that chapter (dogs, page 100; cats, page 118), sometimes with a few adjustments, to meet those needs.

First we'll discuss how to feed normal, healthy kittens and puppies and their pregnant or nursing mothers. Then we'll take a look at diets for pets with health issues in which nutrition is especially a factor. We will refer to Chapter 6 as our foundation, and also to the Quick Reference Section, which discusses in more detail the treatment of some of these conditions.

DIETS FOR MOMS AND BABIES

(recipes coded G in the chart, or showing "Growth Options" beneath each recipe)

When kittens, puppies, or any young animals are growing, whether "in the oven" or outside of it, you need to provide extra nutrition for both babies and mom, particularly extra protein, fat, calcium, and phosphorus. The growth of new tissue uses protein as the "structure," and extra carbohydrates and fats provide the energy that drives the new growth, so they need to be ample as well, about twice the usual level. Since fat has more than twice the energy of either protein or carbohydrates, it's especially useful for this role.

These extra needs are highest in the last 3 weeks or so of a dog or cat's normal gestation period, a little over 60 days in total, and they gradually decline in young animals as they reach mature size, somewhere between 1 and 1½ years, when their growth and appetite gradually decrease. To meet their needs during these periods of growth, just use the dog or cat recipes that say "Maintenance or Growth" beneath the title and follow special supplement directions using Vegepet's growth formulas, Vegepup and Vegekit, both for the mother and her little ones.

After lactation is over, or the youngsters mature, you can move to any of the recipes in that chapter.

Giant breeds: Note that our new recipes follow the latest AAFCO recommendations limiting the amount of calcium and phosphorus in foods "for all stages of life" to account for problems that can arise in puppies of large breeds like Danes. We would also advise you to use the dog recipes with 20 to 23 percent protein, a bit less than for other moms and pups, to avoid problems that can occur with fast growth in these breeds.

ORPHANED KITTENS AND PUPPIES

Sometimes you are challenged with the care of the very young that for one reason or another don't have mom's milk available. Not easy, but doable.

KITTEN FORMULA

This formula closely replicates the constituents of cats' milk (42.2% protein, 25% fat). Give each kitten just enough at each feeding to enlarge the abdomen slightly without distending it (usually about 1½ teaspoons). Don't overfeed. Stop feeding before the kitten does.

Feed more often when they are young, about every 2 hours at first. Decrease gradually to every 3 hours, then every 4 hours, and finally to three times a day at 6 weeks.

After each feeding, gently massage the kitten's belly to stimulate a bowel movement. Swab the genital and anal areas with a tissue moistened with warm water. (Mama cats lick the same areas to stimulate proper urination and defecation.)

At 2 weeks of age, begin to add a high-protein baby cereal to the formula. At 3 to 4 weeks old, start introducing solids (cat recipes for growth in Chapter 6 or high-quality canned food). Mix with the formula to make a thin mush. Begin weaning the kittens from the bottle at about 4 to 6 weeks. By 6 weeks of age, they will likely be able to eat all food from a bowl.

2 cups whole milk (goat's milk preferred)

2 large eggs

5 teaspoons protein powder (from egg or whey)

Vegekit supplement (follow daily label directions)

In a medium saucepan, mix the milk, eggs, protein powder, and Vegekit well. Warm just to body temperature and feed with a pet nurser or doll's bottle. It is important that the milk stays warm; reheat if need be by placing it in a pan of hot water. Make sure it is body temperature—not too hot! Check it on your wrist or with a thermometer (101°F).

PUPPY FORMULA

This formula is comparable to canine milk (33.2% protein, 44.1% fat), with about 250 calories per cup.

¾ cup half-and-half

1 cup whole milk (goat's milk preferred)

2 large eggs

½ tablespoon protein powder

Vegedog Growth supplement, daily label amount

In a medium saucepan, mix the half-and-half, milk, eggs, protein powder, and Vegedog well. Warm to body temperature. Using a pet nurser or doll's bottle, feed enough to slightly enlarge the abdomen but not distend it. Amount varies according to age and breed size. If in doubt, consult recommendations for a commercial formula. Feed on the same schedule described for kittens. Clean each puppy after the feeding, as described for kittens. When the puppies are 2 to 3 weeks old, introduce solids (use the recipes for growth in Chapter 6, mixed with formula to make a gruel); wean them from the bottle at 4 to 6 weeks.

Feeding large litters can require a great deal of time, and some find it easier to tube-feed puppies when they are very small and need feeding every 2 hours. There are some excellent books on care of newborn puppies that can guide you with this technique.

Orphan Problems

The biggest challenge to health in young kittens and puppies is diarrhea that results from using the formulas or overfeeding. Be especially cautious about giving too much milk formula until you gain some experience. If diarrhea does develop, stop feeding the formula until it stops and instead give, preferably, electrolyte fluid in the nursing bottle. You can obtain it from your veterinarian.

Treatment for Diarrhea

Here's a useful herbal formula for treating diarrhea in the very young. Prepare a chamomile tea by adding 2 cups of boiling water to 2 teaspoons of dried chamomile. Let steep for 10 minutes, pour the liquid through a sieve or cheesecloth, and add ½ teaspoon of sea salt for each 2 cups of recovered liquid. You can use this as a temporary remedy to stop many forms of diarrhea. Give a dose (a couple of minutes of nursing) three times a day. In between, administer electrolyte solution by mouth (or injection if your veterinarian is helping you). If you need more help, see the Quick Reference Section for further advice on treating persistent diarrhea, including recommended homeopathic remedies.

Constipation

The other major problem is constipation. This can be a result of not enough formula or perhaps inadequate stimulation to produce a bowel movement after nursing (your job). Puppies or kittens will have rounded bellies (like they are full), but become listless. Such behavior, or if a puppy crawls away from its nest and feels cold to the touch, is a sign of illness. The easiest thing to do is to give an enema with warm water (see Chapter 18 for instructions). For kittens, use an eye dropper; for puppies that are larger, you might need a plastic syringe.

Treatment for Constipation

If this is not sufficient, the homeopathic remedy *Nux vomica* (one 6c or 30c pellet), given once, will usually suffice. With such little mouths, it is easiest administered by dissolving the pellet in some pure water and dripping a few drops into the mouth. (See more discussion of use of homeopathy in Chapter 18.)

HIGH PHYSICAL EXERTION

(recipes coded G or any with high protein and fat content)

In a similar way, there is additional need for nutrients when animals experience significant physical exertion. This will be seen mostly in dogs involved with racing, pulling sleds, or living on farms or ranches as working dogs. To some extent, as described above, additional protein can help repair the tissue worked in these activities (like muscles and tendons) and also, along with the fat, provide additional energy to make the activities possible. So, again, use the recipes designated for "growth" in Chapter 6, but use the regular maintenance supplements.

NUTRITIONAL ADVICE FOR SPECIFIC HEALTH CONDITIONS

Most of the time the recipes in Chapter 6 are fine as part of your program to restore health to your loved companion, but there are a few conditions for which some alterations or additions can be helpful.

ALLERGIES, SKIN, AND GI ISSUES

(recipes coded A and V in the nutrient charts)

The most common expressions of food allergies are skin eruptions and itching, paw licking, ear inflammation, cats suddenly attacking their skin, and digestive problems. An allergy may start out with reactions to a particular food, but then your animal may become allergic to new foods fed in its place. See Chapter 5 for lists of common allergens and further discussion. Recipes coded A in the charts are free of these foods, or can easily be made so.

When I was confronted with severe allergies in my practice, four basic pieces of advice made the most difference:

• Eliminate animal products, especially meat and dairy, the most common allergens in dogs and cats. It is surprising how much improvement occurs when this is done. See recipes marked V in the recipe analysis charts, Chapter 6.

• Use organic food sources. Though usually costlier and not always available, it's well worth the effort, especially compared to how much it costs for all the drugs and visits to the vet.

• Minimize toxic exposures, especially to genetically modified (GM) foods, chlorinated water, and antibiotics, all of which damage normal digestive microorganisms.

• Avoid yearly vaccinations not required by law. When a vaccine is given, the already overreactive immune system gets even more upset.

For more information on allergies and their treatment, see Chapter 5 and the Quick Reference Section.

ARTHRITIS

(recipes coded A and W in the nutrient charts)

Arthritis and joint issues are more common in dogs than in cats. In my practice I saw general improvement when the dogs would move to a fresh food and natural diet, but it would still be necessary for me to add in homeopathic treatment to bring them close to normal. This is a problem best *prevented:* Once there is observable discomfort and lameness, it is already fairly advanced. The best plan is therefore to start your dog on the food we are suggesting in this book, as early as possible. The excellent nutrition, coupled with minimal accumulation of toxins, will very possibly prevent joint problems. Even if arthritis does occur, it will not be as severe and will respond more readily to any additional treatment needed. Anything that causes excess inflammation, as well as obesity, seems to aggravate arthritis, so we suggest the A and W recipes, which will reduce inflammatory factors, increase phytonutrients, and aid weight loss, as will additions of richly colored vegetables like kale, broccoli, and red cabbage.

Humans who eliminate dairy and meats from their diets find substantial relief from rheumatoid arthritis. While less is known about this new way for pets to eat, anecdotal reports certainly indicate that many dogs on similar diets can get a new lease on life. It would be worth a try with your dog, along with anti-inflammatory herbs and spices like turmeric, cumin, and others.

DIABETES

(recipes coded D in the nutrient charts)

Diabetes occurs in both dogs and cats, and has been increasing over time. It is likely related to food quality, especially the toxins brought into the body. The pattern of the illness is different in dogs versus cats, so dietary advice is not the same for each. Dogs will do better on a high–complex carbohydrate and high-fiber diet, including whole grains, starchy vegetables, and legumes. Cats respond to the opposite— low-carbohydrate, low-fiber diets, emphasizing tofu, meats, and eggs.

Refer to Diabetes on page 363 for specific advice on what changes to make and what recipes to use.

GASTROINTESTINAL DISTURBANCES

(recipes coded A in the nutrient charts)

Having an upset stomach, vomiting, or diarrhea is not unusual for dogs and cats. These are usually temporary incidents. Dogs especially will enjoy less-than-healthy food variations—like garbage or compost. However, frequent symptoms often point to a disorder of the intestinal tract.

Causes can vary, but I wish to emphasize the factor of GM foods. It is likely that most pet foods contain these products (corn, canola, soy, sugar beets), and recent research has shown they are very irritating to the stomachs of animals. My advice therefore is not so much that there has to be a special diet as that the food be natural and of good quality.

The water quality is also important, as water with much chlorine will affect the bacteria important in normal intestinal functioning.

Read the topic Diarrhea and Dysentery on page 366 for more information about these conditions, including feeding specifics.

KIDNEY DISEASE

(recipes coded K in the nutrient charts)

The kidneys have the job of eliminating unwanted material through the urine, and they do that quite efficiently. Because of that, toxic substances can end up in the kidneys, so anything we can do to reduce them in the diet is wise. Our general nutritional plan should help prevent or lessen kidney disease, now very common.

If your dog or cat has an early stage of kidney disease, there is no need to pick a particular recipe. However, if the kidneys are struggling to do their job, some nutritional adjustment is appropriate. If the condition is advanced, so that toxic substances are accumulating in the blood, then it helps to reduce the protein content in the food, either by using the K recipes or by using the lower percentages of protein described in the Fresh and Flexible program (cutting down on meat or tofu, for instance). Emphasize protein foods with the best array of amino acids for dogs and cats, such as eggs, soy products, and meats. This increases the efficiency of the protein that's eaten and reduces the need to eliminate. Reducing phosphorus, increasing potassium, and reducing sodium are also helpful. If the sodium content in a recipe is high, especially if it is greater than 800 to 1,000 milligrams per 1,000 calories as shown in the charts, reduce any salt, tamari, or other salty flavorings.

Check out the topic Kidney Failure on page 397 for additional recipes helpful for treating this advanced stage.

PANCREATITIS

(recipes coded W in the nutrient charts, and others)

This is primarily seen in dogs. Use the standard recipes, while following these guidelines.

- Minimize oils and fats because the pancreas is the organ involved in digesting fats (along with the liver). Look for recipes with lower percentages of fat.
- Emphasize green leafy vegetables, which are high in vitamin A.
- Emphasize corn (raw and non-GMO) and raw cabbage.
- Avoid fruits (because of the sugar fructose).
- Feed smaller, more frequent meals.
- Feed meals at room temperature.

See Pancreatitis on page 406 for more information.

SKIN AND COAT ISSUES

(recipes coded A, V, or W in the nutrient charts, or especially with low-omega-6:3 ratio.)

Shiny, luxurious skin and fur indicate excellent health. Often, when there is even a slight decline in health, it's reflected in a lackluster coat with a greasy feel or a smell people call "doggy odor." This is a clue that adjustments are needed.

Most all the recipes in this book will really help skin and coat issues unless an allergy is involved. In any diet, increasing colorful vegetables and using high omega-3 fatty acid supplements like ground flaxseed or hemp hearts are also valuable. These fatty acids are very fragile and easily inactivated by the presence of oxygen, so keep them as fresh as you can. Hemp hearts should be refrigerated as soon as you arrive home with them; flaxseeds should either be freshly ground and added to the food right before serving or taken from a small quantity previously ground and kept in the fridge.

If you are still not seeing the best coat, try adding in additional essential fatty acids in the form of primrose, borage, or black currant oil. Add a small amount—a few drops to a teaspoon—to a meal once a day.

If you are switching from commercial foods, it may take a few weeks to see a change, as new skin and hair grow out. You may also see a period of discharge of toxins through the skin, as the body cleans house on a diet with fewer environmental or other toxins. See Chapters 7 and 18.

The primary factor to support good-looking skin and a healthy coat is that the food is really fresh and wholesome. You will see much better results using organic foods, especially vegetables and grains that have been allowed to grow to natural maturity and are thus highest in vitamins and minerals.

Other suggestions:

• Use the recipes that do not include meat or animal products. For many of my patients, this change had the most dramatic effect. See those marked V in the Chapter 6 recipe chart.

• Vegetables, grains, seeds (ground), and nuts are all tremendous sources of nutrients used by the skin.

• Vegetables with yellow and orange coloring are high in beta-carotene, a precursor to vitamin A. (Cats cannot convert this, however, so you will need to supplement them with vitamin A in the form of retinol.)

• Feed foods high in sulfur. The vegetables with the most sulfur are edamame (the highest level), sweet corn, peas, spinach, broccoli, cauliflower, cabbage, kale, asparagus, okra, lettuce, and eggplant. Among fruits, the highest sulfur levels are found in kiwifruit, bananas, pineapple, strawberries, melons, grapefruit, oranges, and peaches. Additional foods with sulfur are whole grains, sesame seeds, cashews, peanuts, pistachios, and other nuts (which need to be crumbled or ground to be digestible for dogs and cats).

URINARY ISSUES

(recipes coded U in the nutrient charts)

In addition to FFS (finicky feline syndrome), your cat may be one of those with a tendency toward FUS (feline urinary syndrome), more recently called FLUTD (feline lower urinary tract disease), especially if he is a few years old (young cats don't have it) or has a history of formation of bladder crystals. The tendency to form these crystals depends on the acidity (pH) of the urine and this, in turn, can be related to the diet.

It is generally thought that meat-based diets will produce an acidic urine and plant-based diets, alkaline urine. It appears, however, that this is not due to anything special about the protein in meat versus that in plants but rather how *much* protein is in each. The recipes for cats have been formulated to be high in protein, equivalent to primarily meat diets.

To be more certain that the new food is producing sufficient acidity, you can test the urine yourself as recommended at the end of the last chapter.

What can you do if your cat persists in having urine that is more alkaline than recommended?

- Increase the moisture content of the food (adding water or broth). More fluid flushes the bladder more frequently.
- Feed no more often than twice a day.
- Add omega-3 fatty acids to the food, which seems to help reduce this tendency.
- Incorporate meat into the diet, such as by using our Cat Day program (page 105) or Turkey Fest recipe (page 115).
- Acidify the diet, using, for example, Vegecat phi, VegeYeast, or Cranimals, or use an acidifier as prescribed and monitored by your veterinarian.

Read the topic Bladder Problems on page 339 for detailed instructions on testing urine pH and using the supplements and very helpful treatments.

If in doubt, if this seems too difficult to manage, or your cat has had issues with FLUTD but things are stable now, perhaps you should leave well enough alone and not try to change the diet presently in use.

It can also be the case that there are other health problems that might be helped with a better diet, whether using fresh foods or those with fewer toxins (lower on the food chain). In this case, we very much recommend you first establish a working relationship with a veterinarian, one who can guide you through this process.

WEIGHT PROBLEMS

(recipes coded W in the nutrient charts)

The most common problem with weight is too much rather than too little. A lot of animals are overweight these days, and this trend is on the increase. An indoor life, lying around most of the day, and nibbling on food left out all the time don't help, but I also believe that anabolic hormones high in meat and dairy products play a significant role (see Weight Problems on page 451). So, with my clients, I encourage the use of commercial foods guaranteed to be free of hormones or, better yet, home-prepared recipes using organic sources.

If your dog or cat is overweight, then choose the W recipes or Fresh and Flexible or Cat Day/Dog Day foods that are lowest in fat, with a lot of green leafy vegetables as well as winter squash and sweet potatoes, which are less calorically dense than grains or meats.

If your dog or cat is very thin, then use

the opposite tack, choosing the recipes with more fat and calories. You can also add more fat into the recipe by using coconut oil (which most animals like), hemp hearts, nut or seed butters, or tofu. Use these more than whole legumes, which do not contain as much fat.

PULLING IT TOGETHER

All of our recipes are carefully formulated to be nutritionally complete so, for most ani-mals, the wisest course is to offer a variety of recipes with a variety of ingredients. And, as we have shown in this chapter, a fresh food diet can be tweaked to emphasize or de-emphasize certain nutrients, to make it more optimal in special conditions. The principles we described can be applied to other recipes or products as well, of course.

For further nutritional understanding and treatment suggestions, read about your animal's particular condition in the Quick Reference Section.

CHAPTER 9

CHOOSING A HEALTHY ANIMAL

Selecting a pet with a very functional body is one of the most important steps you can take to increase the chances that your animal will have a healthy, happy life. Dogs have been very modified compared to their wild ancestor (cats less so), and some of these modifications can make it difficult to care for them and also cause them lifelong suffering.

It can be tempting to choose a particular breed or animal just because you like its looks—or even to pick out the most pitiful-looking pup in the litter or at the shelter because it elicits your sympathy. But it's not quite as simple as picking out the liveliest, friendliest, and most inquisitive one either.

Every type of dog or cat (pure or mixed breed) has physical characteristics—face, build, relative body proportions—that invite predictions about its potential well-being. Different breed types have different behavioral tendencies as well.

THE STICKERY POODLE

My career as a veterinarian often led me to ponder these issues. For instance, one day someone brought a lost miniature poodle into an SPCA clinic where I worked. Besides being lost, the poor dog was covered from head to foot with burrs, foxtails, and tangled hair. One eye was closed and discharging pus, and the areas between his toes were red and swollen. Clearly, he was a victim of the "foxtail season."

Foxtails and other plant awns are those stickery burrs that attach to your socks when you walk across a field. They latch onto dogs, too. Their pointed ends work their way not only into the coat but sometimes right through the skin, burrowing into eyes, ears, noses, mouths, vaginas, rectums, and between the toes.

This little guy was so badly affected that we had to give him a general anesthetic before we could begin the long process of removing stickers out of his coat, between his toes, and deep in his ear. Careful exam-ination revealed another lodged in the eye—the cause of the inflammation and discharge. As we worked, my assistant Dot-tie and I began talking about how pets get into such a state after even a short trek in the fields.

"This is why," I said, holding up some mat-ted hair we had just clipped off. "His coat is like walking Velcro. Once the stickers brush against it, there's almost no place else for them to go but deeper in."

I pondered further. "You know, really it's we who created this problem by breeding and selecting for dogs with such curly fur and floppy ears. Wild animals don't have anywhere near this issue with stickers."

A young wolf, for example, has softer or curlier hair that normally becomes more coarse, smooth, and protective when it becomes an adult, sometimes called "guard hair." We enjoy that soft feel (maybe that's why we call our animals "pets"), and so we selected for the occasional wolves that never quite grew up, just as we selected for the more docile members of most domestic species.

Through hundreds and thousands of years of selective breeding, we have created a host of other abnormal body structures as well, many that foster health problems. For example, animals with stubby legs and pushed-in faces or extra-long silky ears often face lifelong discomforts or health issues. So it's important to be mindful of what we are doing and to consider the big picture.

BREEDING FOR US, NOT THEM

When we humans began to domesticate other animals, we altered the natural pro-cess up until then, one that had always favored those best equipped to find food, reproduce, and survive on their own. It became a new kind of symbiosis, in which we called the shots. No doubt we made many good choices, often picking the strongest and the healthiest. But often we just liked a certain unusual look or something that served us, but not necessarily the animals: horses with thick, beefy legs for pulling heavy loads; toy versions of dogs for lap companions; no-tail novelty cats and the like.

Dogs have probably been more shaped by breeding than any other animal, ever since wolves first associated with us some 20,000 to 30,000 years ago (estimates vary). Over thousands of generations, we developed dogs of every size and purpose. With a social structure and instinct similar to our own, they have served us well as hunters, herders, sled dogs, watchdogs, guide dogs, religious symbols, personal companions, and even as a source of food.

Most of the traits we chose served us more than them. Yet, in some ways it was a coevolutionary process. As we took over a lot of their natural habitat, the ancestors of domestic animals adapted to a new habitat: the crops and abodes of humans. That was a version of "survival of the fittest." Those most fit to live with us were those who best survived. If we were not providing that niche, my guess is that their genetic lines would revert to their original traits pretty quickly.

In any case, cats were much less bred by us. Independent sorts, they were the last animal to share human homes. They were lured by the many mice in the granaries of ancient Egypt and became a religious symbol of that culture, their regal mannerisms no doubt suggesting that role. Their natural talent as mousers made cats welcome in households all over the world. Since they were not easily trained, the cat had few other duties except companionship.

Just page through a picture book on breeds and it's clear that dogs show much more variety in size, shape, and hair texture than cats. The difference in appearance between certain modern breeds and their wild ancestors is much more striking in dogs. This greater interference with natural selection explains why a study of birth defects in cats, cows, dogs, and horses showed that dogs had the most congenital malformations at birth and cats the fewest. That is despite the fact that cats are generally more sensitive to chemicals and other agents known to cause birth defects.

Neotony: Selecting for Immaturity

How does selective breeding lead to defects and malfunctions? One of the most significant ways we created the many kinds of dogs we have today from the gene pool of wolves was simply that we often preferred the little cute ones that never fully developed. This was made possible due to a process called "neoteny" or "juvenilization," selecting for primitive or undeveloped characteristics that occurred early in the species' existence or those common to immature puppies or kittens: short legs and muzzles, silky hair, floppy ears, and the tendency to bark (adult wolves rarely bark).

It's humbling to realize that many of the features we find appealing in purebred animals are actually the products of arrested development—either physical or psychological. In the process we often inadvertently created defects or losses of function that went along with "cuteness" or other desired traits.

For instance, breeding dogs for a short muzzle (upper jaw) has spelled trouble for breeds like bulldogs, boxers, and terriers. That's because separate genes determine related features, such as the teeth and soft palate (which separates the mouth and throat), which are still normal size. This makes the teeth so crowded that they are forced to grow in crooked and sideways. The soft palate hangs so far back into the animal's throat that it threatens constant suffocation and causes breathing problems.

Dogs with short legs (dachshunds and basset hounds) tend to have deformed spines. Tailless cats (the Manx breed) can have severe malformation of the urinary tract and genitals. The bulldog, Chihuahua, and others bred to have a small pelvis often require cesarean deliveries. Giant breeds such as Saint Bernards and Great Danes are known for their bone problems and their short lives. Generally, the largest and smallest breeds tend to suffer the most from genetic weaknesses.

Inbreeding adds to the problem. To fix a given characteristic into a breed (so that it will breed true, that is, reappear consistently), selected brothers and sisters must be mated, or a parent crossed with its offspring. Such intensive inbreeding might ensure the desired trait, but it might also perpetuate basic weaknesses in the line, such as poor resistance to disease, low stamina, low intelligence, birth defects, and inherited diseases that include hemophilia or deafness.

Breeding to meet market demand can also lead to disaster. During the 1920s, for example, the recently imported Siamese cat became so popular that breeders mated siblings as well as parents and offspring to meet the demand. The kittens born of these matings so weakened the breed that it almost died out entirely. Sobered by this experience, breeders began to make wiser selections. Many breeds of dogs—such as the collie, the cocker spaniel, the beagle, and the German shepherd—have also suffered as a result of surges in popularity.

The Ethics of Breeding

The problem of genetic disease is particularly sad. Animals undergo much unnecessary suffering because they're often bred for financial gain or for some trait considered "cute," unusual (such as squat faces, long faces, curly or silky hair, hairlessness, wrinkly skin, floppy ears, or missing tails), or useful (such as short legs for access to dens in hunting or massive size for fighting or guarding). The question of whether the animal will have a comfortable, well-adapted, potentially healthy body rarely comes up.

We also don't seem troubled by the high rate of defective pets. People rightly get alarmed at a human birth defect rate of 1 in 1,000, but many pet breeders simply accept statistics that predict 10 to 25 percent of their litters may be born defective. A related ethical issue is that breeding also produces an excess of puppies or kittens who either don't have the desired trait or are clearly defective. They must in some way be disposed of. One small thing that helps is not to get stuck on having a purebred animal. Instead one can adopt a mixed-breed animal, one that needs a home, and this gives a chance at life for the millions of mixed-breed animals that would make equally good pets that go begging. Up to 75 percent of the dogs and cats born each year face death by accidents, starvation, or euthanasia because they can't find permanent homes.

Selecting a mongrel from the local animal shelter, however, won't necessarily reduce the risk of acquiring a pet with congenital problems. Often an adopter chooses an animal that especially arouses pity, perhaps one with strangely colored eyes, or drooping ears and eyes that look sad, or a short, pushed-in, childlike face.

Or sometimes pets just find their way into our homes and hearts (such as the deaf white cat that came to us as a stray), and we accept them as is. But at least we can decide not to breed an unhealthy animal or one with characteristics that interfere with normal functioning.

Is More Breeding Necessary?

We really question the way things are now. I have worked in an animal shelter and seen the reality of the animal overpopulation situation. It is difficult to justify bringing more animals into our world when so many are not wanted. As Lorelei Wakefield, DVM, said in response to an interview question about breeding:[1]

> . . . it's unsurprising that I'm not for breeding of cats and dogs when we have this overpopulation crisis. There's not enough room in our shelters and millions are getting put down every year. It's so sad. I know that people like having certain breeds because they're lovely and certainly certain breeds are so wonderful but I just can't justify that—to breed more pets when we have too many. There are breed rescues, which is a wonderful alternative.

WHEN BREEDING GOES WRONG

In addition to selecting for a certain amount of dysfunction that often accompanies traits we like, environmental poisons and stresses also contribute to congenital problems. Some of these hazards (mutagens) cause genetic changes that are passed on to future generations. Such toxins, as discussed in Chapter 3, are very significant concerns today. The buildup of chemicals in our world is even impacting wildlife, whose young can be born with malformed eyes, thymus glands (an important part of the immune system), hearts, and lungs and even liver tumors.[2]

If you *do* want to breed a particular line of dog or cat, be aware of the concerns we brought up and do take special care to minimize risk factors suspected of damaging genes and/or fetuses. See "Protecting the Mother" on page 158.

COMMON CONGENITAL PROBLEMS IN DOGS

The parts of the dog's body most frequently affected by birth defects are:

- **The central nervous system (CNS).** For example, the German shepherd, collie, beagle, miniature poodle, and keeshond can inherit epilepsy. Other CNS issues include paralysis of the front and back legs (Irish setter), a failure of muscle coordination (fox terrier), idiocy (German shorthaired pointer and English setter), and abnormal swelling of the brain (Chihuahua, cocker spaniel, and English bulldog).

- **The eyes.** Congenital eye abnormalities, including cataracts, glaucoma, and blindness, are found in most of the common breeds.

- **The muscles.** Hernias are a typical muscular problem. The basset hound, basenji, cairn terrier, Pekinese, and Lhasa apso are at high risk for inguinal hernias (the gut protrudes into the

groin). Umbilical hernias (gut protrudes through the navel) are most common in the cocker spaniel, bull terrier, collie, basenji, Airedale terrier, Pekinese, pointer, and Weimaraner.

If you are interested in a particular breed, check out what is known about these tendencies first. Then you will know what to keep a lookout for.

COMMON CONGENITAL PROBLEMS IN CATS

While there are fewer studies of birth defects in cats, the most common affect the nervous system: the brain, spinal cord, and skeletal tissues (true of us and all domestic animals). In alphabetical order, these are common feline congenital issues.

- **Brachycephalic head** (Peke face): Marked by an unusually short and wide head, a deformity of long-haired Persians and newer strains of Burmese. Cats from these lines produce lethal birth defects involving the eyes, nasal tissue, and jaws, with an increased incidence of cleft palate in nearly 1 out of 4 kittens.

- **Brain and skull problems:** An undersize cerebellum, for example, can cause poor coordination, tremors, excess tension in the limbs, and slow reflexes. Siamese cats can inherit hydrocephalus (swelling of the brain). In some cats, the roof of the skull does not close, causing abnormal brain expansion. In others the brain degenerates even before birth (usually fatal). If a young animal has trouble moving or is uncoordinated, this could be why.

• **Cancer of the ear:** Most common in white cats due to repeated sunburn of their ears, leading to ear cancer later in life. If your cat will spend much time outdoors, consider a different color. Tabbies are a good choice and are closest to feline ancestors.

• **Cardiovascular defects:** Particularly narrowing of the aorta, the heart's main artery, or nonclosure of the aortic duct. Both can cause heart murmurs.

• **Cleft palate:** Hereditary in some Siamese, but also thought to be due to various drugs ingested during pregnancy. Causes milk to come out of the nose when nursing or drinking from a dish.

• **Cryptorchidism:** A condition in which only one testicle comes down into the scrotum. Not necessarily a problem, but makes neutering difficult.

• **Deafness:** Many blue-eyed white cats are deaf from birth and often have poor resistance to disease, reduced fertility, and impaired night vision.

• **Eye and eyelid defects:** Some Persians, Angoras, and domestic shorthairs are missing the outer half of one or both upper eyelids. Other cats have an albino or a multicolored iris (sometimes associated with deafness on that side, sensitivity to light, eye incoordination), degeneration of the retina (particularly Siamese and Persians); strabismus (an inward rotation of one eye when the other is fixed on an object, common in Siamese); or nystagmus (involuntary movements of the eye).

• **Hair abnormalities:** Some cats are born with (or even bred for) hairlessness or curly, short, plush hair, such as the "Rex" mutant, which has missing or abnormal guard hairs.

• **Hairballs:** Throwing up hairballs is common and chronic in longhairs, though not unusual for any cat, as they swallow hair while grooming. But with longhairs, it can become a more tangled ball that gets stuck.

• **Kidney missing:** More often in males, usually on the right side. Might not be a problem or noticeable, as usually the other kidney compensates and is larger.

• **Limb defects:** Kittens sometimes show missing or extra toes or legs at birth.

• **Mammary gland abnormalities:** These affect milk ducts and you are not likely to notice anything unless your female gives birth and then has difficulty with lactation.

• **Spina bifida:** The vertebrae fail to close normally around the spinal cord, leading to motor and sensory problems in areas fed by affected nerves, most common in the Manx, associated with the gene for taillessness. Symptoms include a hopping gait and incontinence.

• **Tail defects:** A missing tail is typical of the Manx but rare in others. Associated defects include spina bifida (above), a kinked tail, hindquarter deformities, and an abnormally small anus.

• **Umbilical hernias:** A common defect causing fat or part of the intestine to protrude through the navel. Can be surgically corrected, also treated homeopathically. Hernias of the diaphragm are also frequent, and more difficult to fix.

PREVENTING CONGENITAL PROBLEMS

To reduce animal suffering and the spread of these problems, avoid selecting—and especially avoid breeding:

• Animals with obvious birth defects or behavior difficulties.

• Those whose close relatives have congenital defects or inheritable behavioral or physical troubles. Try to check on the medical histories of both parents and research what percentage of related offspring have had defects. It should be less than 5 percent.

• Animals with *any* chronic health issues, as their overall systems are under par for developing healthy offspring.

• Inbred animals, particularly breeds that are currently popular in your area, which are likely weakened by intensive inbreeding.

Even if you have some healthy animals you would like to breed, it's not good to mate parents, siblings, aunts, uncles, and grandparents, which tends to "fix" latent defects into their offspring. "Kissin' cousins"

are about as close as it gets in most human cultures, and even that is frowned upon for good reason.

Look for the Most Natural Animals

The best way to avoid a lot of health problems in animals is really pretty simple. Choose breeds or mixes that best resemble canine or feline ancestors. Look for size, face shape, ear shape, color, coat length and texture, tail shape, and limb proportions that most closely match that of wolves, coyotes, and wildcats. (Try to match at least four or five of these characteristics.)

Dogs: For midsize dogs, mixed breeds are often among the healthiest. With mongrels, most likely the parents selected each other, and there's something to be said for that! Working dogs can be good choices unless overly popular or inbred. Consider retrievers, sled dog breeds, basenjis, shepherds, pointers, and spitzes. If you prefer a smaller dog, choices are more limited, as most have been intentionally bred by selecting for neoteny, characteristics in puppies (silky hair, dependence and yapping, floppy ears). Do your homework online, in books, and by asking around.

Cats: Generally most shorthairs are best, especially those with more natural colors such as tabbies, silvers, and ancient breeds such as Korats and Abyssinians. Avoid ones with curly coats, which attract stickers, or pushed-in faces, which will cause breathing problems. Long, floppy ears may harbor mites.

Occasionally, I have had the opportunity

to examine and treat injured coyotes or foxes, and never have I found one with a foxtail in its ears or anywhere else on its body! Every inch of their bodies reflects the intelligence of millions of years of natural evolution and adaptation. I have been quite impressed with how perfectly their teeth fit together and with their fine hair coats, fastidious cleanliness, natural grace, and high intelligence. (Don't try to adopt a truly wild animal: The place for them is in the wild, and they do not make good pets.)

Protecting the Mother

Protect fertile and litter-bearing females. If you plan to breed your female pet, avoid use of potentially damaging flea powders, cortisone, vaccinations, sedatives, anesthetics, and x-rays, unless natural aids fail and circumstances demand this kind of medical treatment. Feed her an optimal diet, preferably organic, and make sure she does not consume food additives, moldy foods, poisonous household chemicals, or lawn grass or other plants treated with toxic herbicides, insecticides, or fungicides. Protect her from exposure to cigarette smoke and the fumes from riding in the back of a pickup truck. Use common sense and keep the home clean before and during pregnancy and during lactation.

Also, see that she does not become overheated. Excess heat can retard fetal brain growth. Don't leave her locked in a hot car with the windows closed (a good piece of advice concerning any animal) or overexer-

cise her in hot weather (likewise). Nor should you take her on an arduous trek into high country or transport her in the baggage compartment of an airplane, because the lack of oxygen at high altitudes can induce a variety of fetal abnormalities.

SELECTING A HEALTHY ANIMAL: A CHECKUP

How can you tell if a particular animal is healthy? Here is a "checkup" you can use to pinpoint any congenital defects present. It also helps assess the likelihood of chronic health problems to come. Wait until you have some trust from the animal or help from its person, of course, before doing the more physical parts of this exam.

- **What color is the coat?** White animals, beautiful as they are, often fall victim to extra problems, such as skin cancers or deafness in white, blue-eyed cats. (Test for deafness by clapping your hands behind the animal's head.) Gray collies sometimes have a blood immune problem, with increased susceptibility to infection.

- **Check the nose and jaws.** Are they unusually long and pointed or short and pushed in? Are the upper and lower jaws the same size? Do the teeth fit together well? (This particularly applies to dogs.) Are the gums pale or inflamed? Is there a red line at the edge of the gums next to the teeth?

- **Are the eyes normal looking?** Are they both the same color? Unusually small or large? Eye discharges signal plugged tear ducts.

• **Does the animal move normally?** Or does it swing its hips from side to side as it walks—a warning sign of possible canine hip dysplasia? Are the legs normal length, and in the right proportion front and back?

• **Does the pigmentation over the nose look normal?** If not, the animal may be subject to sunburn and skin cancer.

• **Does the animal behave normally?** Observe carefully and be wary of animals that seem unusually aggressive, clinging, jealous, fearful, suspicious, hyperactive, noisy, or unaware. Whether because of inheritance or their history, such problems may be difficult to live with and even harder to correct. If you want a playful or affectionate animal, choose the one that responds to your overtures. Roll a dog on its back and hold him there. If he fights to get up, he may be difficult to train and aggressive. A dog that keeps its tail low or acts submissive will be the most devoted and easiest to train.

• **Is the coat attractive?** Does it look and smell healthy and clean, or is it slightly greasy or thin? Are there reddish patches? Is the skin light pink or off-white in color, pliant and firm, or are some areas unusually thin, thick, dry, dark, red, or crusty? Is the skin covered with fleas?

• **Does the animal breathe quietly and easily?** Raspy, heavy sounds, especially after a little exertion, are not good signs.

• **Look inside the ears.** Check for any signs of inflammation or dark, waxy discharge. This could signal a chronic tendency toward ear trouble.

• **Feel around the navel.** You're looking for a lump, which could be a sign of a hernia.

• **Check the scrotum** in an adult male for the presence of both testicles.

In spite of the many problems inappropriate breeding has caused, you can still find a genetically healthy animal or one with only minor problems. If you don't plan to breed the animal and don't mind the extra work of caring for an animal with inherited problems, you can select from a wider variety. Although you cannot always foresee or control potential congenital problems, with just a bit of common sense you can actually do a great deal to minimize the risks. In the process, you will be doing a big favor not only for your own animals and yourself, but also for those whose time is yet to come.

Choosing the Best Pet for You

When choosing a dog or cat, pick a breed that suits your lifestyle and preferences. Both dogs and cats vary widely in their temperaments and their needs, often along breed lines. Every day humane societies must euthanize healthy animals turned in because their unhappy owners did not anticipate certain issues.

For instance, a mild-mannered person would be unwise to select a large dog from a breed that tends to dominate the owner. Similarly, a family with toddlers in the house should choose a breed less likely to snap at children. Those who live in an apartment with no yard should pick an animal suited to smaller confines, such as the Korat cat.

It is also important to consider size when you are selecting a dog. Small dogs, for example, may be especially active and have a high demand for affection. Large dogs tend to be quieter and more patient with children. Dogs that are unusually large or unusually small tend to have the most genetic problems, especially structural ones.

Larger and more active dogs require the most space and food, which involves economic and ecological considerations: A 70- to 80-pound dog needs as many calories every day as an adult woman. So if you plan to feed your dog a natural diet, as we recommend, it will be easier with a smaller dog. Many people find it too expensive or time-consuming to make food for large (or multiple) dogs, so they end up on commercial food, with the accompanying lower level of health.

We realize that you do not always have a choice. Sometimes life just happens as it does, and a cat just shows up or an aunt passes away and her dog needs a home. But if you do have a choice, take the time to do a little research. It will save you a lot of vet bills, but most of all, it will make for a happier and healthier animal that will be a joy in your life.

YOUR EYES

Susan Pitcairn

With clean white cloth
I wipe your eyes I
See the ancient hunts
Of wolves who ran with men
Orphan pups who ventured by
For scraps of bread who dared to stay
To share our hearths and hearts today.
Cats who wandered deep in barns
And woke one present morn
Curled sweet and soft and still
On this my sunlit windowsill.

CHAPTER 10

CREATING A HEALTHY HOME

No matter where we have lived, we have always made sure to have a beautiful garden, filled with flowering shrubs and perennials and edibles. Caring for our piece of paradise often fills the better part of a day off. We enjoy it, of course, or we wouldn't do it.

Yet sometimes we get so busy snipping off branches or pulling up weeds that we lose touch with the slower pace of life's mysteries constantly unfolding before us. When we get too wrapped up in our activity, it helps to take a lesson from cats, who are so adept at just sitting and looking.

But often, before we know it, we find ourselves looking at what seems to be a problem to solve: Should we pull up some of those grasses before they go to seed? Are those carpenter ants? Should we destroy them so they won't destroy our home?

Yet, even weeds can have a beauty of their own, as lush and diverse as a forest floor, with tiny flowers that attract a hum of diverse beneficial insects. Ants are admirable, so energetic and so enduring. Ants crawled over this land long before we humans appeared. And despite all the wars we wage upon them, ants still thrive and will probably outlive us. Often we just let them be, humbled at how little we understand about the thousands of backyard plants and animals whose lives are affected by our actions.

When our lives get busy and we do not take the time to see and appreciate in this way, we humans seem to detach ourselves from nature and unwittingly accept the idea that we are free to tamper with the web of life. All that we have said in prior chapters about what we do to food, to animals, and to our planet, even modifying the basic code of life, DNA, is about this tampering. We think we know enough and are clever enough to step into this extraordinarily beautiful and complex web of life and remake it in our image. We humans seem to be reaching a cultural crisis, one that will require us to step back and rethink what our role on this planet truly is.

Having examined our approach to food, as well as some of the problems from creating unnatural breeds, in this chapter we now shift our focus to our homes, where we spend much of our time and where many of our dogs and cats spend their entire lives.

When you stop and think about it, our homes are often pretty far removed from nature and natural materials. We use a variety of materials such as plastics and paints that can, over time, contribute to the dust in our homes, or gas off into the air we breathe. This is particularly important for dogs and cats because they live in close contact with the ground. They sit, play, and sleep on it. Even indoors, pets are exposed to plenty of dust. A six-room urban house may accumulate as much as 40 pounds of dust in a year. And when our pets lick all this dust off their fur, they actually consume it.

That used to be fairly safe—"You'll eat a peck of dirt before you die," moms used to say.

But dirt is a lot dirtier nowadays, so we need to take special precautions to protect children and pets from possible harm. A scientific team of "dust busters" found that 25 out of 29 typical homes they studied in Seattle had rugs with excessive levels of toxins and mutagens. They also found that toddlers ingest more than twice as much dust as adults, and contaminated dust is probably more risky for pets than it is for children. Pets wear no protective clothes or shoes and, like a shag rug, their fur attracts dirt, which they then lick up during grooming.

One thing to be especially aware of in older homes is the possible presence of lead and asbestos.

LEAD

Because they settle to the ground, heavy metals are a particular hazard in dust. Lead is among the most widespread of these and enters the environment primarily from flaking layers of lead-based paint and from power plants burning coal. Because lead was used as a pigment and drying agent in "alkyd" oil-based paint, about two-thirds of the homes built before 1960 contain heavily leaded paint (as well as some homes, though fewer, built after 1960). Lead paint may be on any interior or exterior surface, but particularly on woodwork, doors, and windows. Cats, especially, will start licking walls as a symptom of digestive trouble and swallow paint flakes in this way.

In 1978, the Consumer Product Safety Commission lowered the legal maximum lead content in most kinds of paints to 0.06 percent (considered a trace amount). You can have your home tested for this common contaminant, and there are several do-it-yourself kits available at paint stores and home centers (note they are not sensitive enough to pick up low levels, which can still affect pregnant women and maybe cats and dogs). Water pipes can be another source of lead in a house, so that's another thing to check.

Symptoms from lead can be vague but often include listlessness, loss of appetite, irritability, stupor, incoordination, vomiting, constipation, and abdominal pain. Not surprisingly, lead poisoning has caused seizures in small, urban dogs.

So if your home's age falls into the range of possibility, it might be smart to check out your wall paints, floor paints, water, etc., especially if you have an animal that has shown any symptoms like the ones we listed. I often suspected lead exposure in dogs that developed epilepsy, though this is difficult to confirm with certainty. What we can do is make sure there is no ongoing exposure from someplace in the home. (Don't forget there is also lead in raw bones!)

If you are remodeling or repainting, here are some simple suggestions supported by the Seattle study.

- Be especially careful about sanding or cutting into paint layers of homes built before 1978, because most of them contain lead paints.

- Wear a dust mask while working on painted areas and keep pets and children away.

- Clean up thoroughly after each workday.

- If intact, old lead paint layers can be painted over or covered with drywall. Consider replacing old wooden doors and windows, because simply using them can create lead dust.

- Wipe the work area frequently with a solution of trisodium phosphate (sold at hardware stores). Be sure to wear gloves.

ASBESTOS

Another common ingredient in urban dust, asbestos, produces particles that have been found in the lungs of virtually every city dweller who has had an autopsy. The United States remains one of the few developed countries to not completely ban asbestos,[1] which is legal and still widely used in such common products as clothing, pipeline wraps, vinyl floor tiles, millboards, cement pipes, disc brake pads, gaskets, and roof coatings. What is usually most visible are ceiling-coating materials (what are called "popcorn ceilings"). Another source is vermiculite, used in insulation, which can contain small amounts of asbestos.

The greatest danger is inhaling the small microscopic fibers, which settle in the lungs and never come out. The body can't get rid of these fibers, and the subsequent inflammation causes serious lung disease. Some contaminated lungs develop cancer, as well.

If you think your home could have some asbestos, there are programs for safe removal and disposal. For a situation with no evidence of asbestos, best you can tell, one cautionary measure would be to install an air filter for the dust. Just in case.

INDOOR AIR POLLUTION

Besides toxic dust, air can also carry unhealthy gases and vapors, such as formaldehyde, ozone, chloroform, and radon. These waft into the atmosphere from household products, furniture, and many other common sources. A New Jersey study testing 20 common air pollutants showed that indoor levels were actually much worse than outdoor levels, in some cases 100 times greater.

This can happen because the air in the house is contained, not circulating as much, so when the furniture, carpet, paints, cleaners, and various household products give off volatile gases, they build up in the house.

A common contaminant is *formaldehyde* because it is used in so many products and is also a by-product of combustion. Formaldehyde can come from various types of gas and kerosene heaters, carpets, furniture, and the wood components used in construction (especially pressed wood or particleboard, softwood plywood, or oriented strand board).

Another common one is *radon*, an odorless, colorless, tasteless radioactive gas that occurs naturally and is found in the soil and well water in low levels everywhere. It is produced naturally by the breakdown of uranium in the soil and gradually percolates up into the atmosphere. It can be trapped in buildings with confined spaces and build up to higher levels. That it is the second leading cause of lung cancer in the United States makes this common contaminant an important issue. It gets into homes by entering through small cracks in the flooring or around the holes for pipes and wiring in the walls—and these can be plugged.

Radon is also in natural gas used for heating or cooking. Many people really like gas stoves, but it is important that the stove be well ventilated while being used (same for a heater or fireplace using natural gas).

For crawlspaces, the EPA states "An effective method to reduce radon levels in crawlspace homes involves covering the earth floor with a high-density plastic sheet. A vent pipe and fan are used to draw the radon from under the sheet and vent it to the outdoors. This form of soil suction is called submembrane suction, and when properly applied is the most effective way to reduce radon levels in crawlspace homes."[2]

For very helpful information on understanding this issue and what you can do about it, visit the EPA website https://www3 .epa.gov. Once there, if you put in the search word "radon" you will find a great resource.

WHAT CAN YOU DO?

An obvious solution is to have some ventilation of your house's air. Of course, this is easy if the weather is nice—just open some windows. But there are many times when the open window option is not the best choice— like if you live in a smoggy city, or it is too hot or too cold outside. In this case, use an air filter unit that contains a HEPA filter, which is the most efficient.

If you are building your home, or willing to remodel, a great solution is to install a whole-house fan or heat recovery ventilator (which brings in outside air but without losing the heat in the house)—very efficient. We had one installed when we lived in Oregon, for a new home we had built, and it worked great.

Outdoor Pollution

You would think that with all the available air outside, this would not be an issue, but we forget that some installations outside, like pressure-treated wood, can be a continued source of pollution. Because wood that has been sunk into the ground or exposed to water outside can quickly rot or be eaten by bugs, it is treated with a poison that does not allow any of these things to attack it. The usual substance is a combination of copper and arsenic. The wood is soaked in a liquid preservative under high pressure so that it penetrates the wood. This process allows the wood to survive 10 or 20 times longer than untreated wood, so it has a definite advantage. The drawback is that the chemicals remain on the surface as well as inside the wood and can run off with water and contaminate the soil around the post or structure built with it.

One of my clients, who had built a new screened outdoor enclosure for her cats with such wood, reported that cats going into the enclosure were having behavioral and health problems. After she covered the wood with a nontoxic sealer to prevent the fumes from reaching the animals, the cats returned to normal. It helps, therefore, to seal pressure-treated wood posts used to build a cattery or dog pen. Realize, however, that if your animal chews on this wood, it is still poisonous. Be watchful.

House and Garden Pesticides

Besides the insecticides used in flea and tick products, pets may also be exposed to high levels of other household pesticides. The National Academy of Sciences reports that homeowners use four to eight times as many chemical pesticides per acre as farmers do. Many home and garden insecticides are the same as those used on pets. Additional risks come from herbicides, fungicides, and rodent poisons. Because of their contact with the ground, pets are more likely to pick up these residues. In 1991, the National Cancer Institute found that dogs who lived where the homeowner used 2, 4-D, a common broadleaf weed killer, had twice the rate of lymphoma (a cancer of the lymph glands) of dogs who lived where it was not used.

Even if you don't use pesticides, they may drift onto your property from neighbors' yards or from heavily sprayed areas such as nearby parks, campuses, power line corridors, and orchards. Ask people to call you when they plan to spray so you can close your windows, since pesticides have a longer life span indoors.

Termite Control

Poisonous residues may persist in your house from previous occupants. The termite insecticide chlordane, for instance, has been detected in the air of some homes 14 years after application. It's also been found in soil after 30 years. I am not sure what you can do about this once it has been applied, perhaps even before you bought the house, but be aware it can be a factor. If you are planning to do termite control, then choose a less toxic option.

Automotive Products

Though we must consider the possible danger to animals from what is stored in the garage, it is easy to overlook what might drip or leak from automobiles. One is antifreeze fluid. Sometimes when cars overheat, some antifreeze runs out on the ground. Apparently it tastes good (I have never tried it), and animals will lick it up, causing serious poisoning that often ends in death. Less toxic but still harmful are transmission fluids, used oils, even batteries left out on the ground. The battery posts are lead and the insides contain acid.

Store all of these things inside the garage in sealed containers, within locked cabinets, at least 4 feet off the ground. It's not a bad idea to install childproof safety latches on the cabinet doors, either.

If you spill any of these hazardous materials, don't wash it away. Sprinkle with sawdust or cat litter to absorb the spill, then sweep it up and put it in a plastic bag to dispose of as hazardous waste (at your recycle center's hazardous waste day).

WHAT CAN YOU DO?

You might do a house survey, inventorying all the household products tucked away in your kitchen, bathroom, laundry room, and garage that contain poisonous and sensitizing chemicals. Clear out any products that are more than a few years old and that you no longer use (they may contain chemicals that have since been banned) and those with rusting or leaking containers.

For disposal, call your local trash collection service to ask about special household hazardous waste collections. Where we live, there are certain days you can take these things to the landfill, and we make an appointment to do so. If this kind of service is not available, tighten any loose containers, wrap them in several layers of newspaper, seal them in a heavy plastic bag, and put them in the trash. Do not pour such substances down the drain or on the soil.

For those products you keep, tighten lids and update fading labels. If possible, store them in a well-ventilated area away from living space. Even well-sealed containers can emit fumes, so don't confine your pet in the same space—a garage, for example.

Make sure that all gas, oil, or wood furnaces and appliances are properly serviced and ventilated. This reduces levels of carbon monoxide and other combustion by-products. You can buy carbon monoxide detection units for about $30. They plug into an electrical outlet and warn you if there is a leakage of this dangerous gas.

Seal boiler rooms from the rest of the house. When you replace units, buy electric models or choose gas furnaces with sealed combustion chambers and pilotless gas appliances.

Cleaning Strategies

What we greatly encourage you to do is begin using nontoxic products. There are very simple things you can use to clean, to control insects, to do laundry, to bathe, that are very pleasant to use and not dangerous to you or your animal.

Some clever little books I have come across list all sorts of alternative ways of cleaning things—windows, even laundry stains—using very common, readily available things like vinegar, baking soda, or salt. The ones we have are the Consumer Reports book *How to Clean Practically Anything,* and *Mary Ellen's Giant Book of Helpful Hints.*

To give you some idea of what alternatives are possible, alternatives that will not leave toxic residues for your dog or cat to walk in and later lick from its feet, here are a few ideas from the Center for Hazardous Materials Research.

All-Purpose Cleaning and Disinfecting

- Scouring powder: Use a solution of vinegar, salt, and water, or use baking soda and water. Apply with a sponge and wipe clean.
- Ceramic tile cleaner: Mix ¼ cup white vinegar into a gallon of warm water. Apply with a sponge.
- Disinfectants: Use ½ cup Borax dissolved in hot water and apply with a sponge (store Borax in a safe place; can be toxic if eaten). Use sodium carbonate (washing soda) in your washer in place of commercial detergents.

Spot Removers for Carpeting

- Set stains: Dab with white vinegar.

- Nonset stains: Sponge up or scrape off as much as possible immediately. Rub with club soda, followed by cold water.

- Butter, gravy, chocolate, or urine stains: Dab with a cloth dampened with a solution of 1 teaspoon white vinegar and 1 quart cold water.

- Grease stains: Rub with a damp cloth dipped in Borax, or apply a paste of cornstarch and water. Let it dry and brush the mixture off.

- Ink stains: Wet the fabric with cold water and apply a cream of tartar and lemon juice mix. Let it sit for an hour and then wash in the usual manner.

- Red wine stains: Clean immediately with club soda, or dab out excess moisture with an absorbent cloth and sprinkle salt on the stain. Let stand for 7 hours, then brush or vacuum away.

Floor, Rug, and Upholstery Cleaning

- Floor wax strippers and polishers: Mix laundry starch with water to make it thick, then bring it to a boil. Mix one part of this thick-boiled starch and one part soap suds; rub the mixture on the floor and polish with a dry cloth. To remove, pour a little club soda on the area, scrub well, let soak for 5 minutes, and wipe.

- Rug and upholstery cleaner: Mix ½ cup mild dishwashing detergent with 1 pint boiling water. Let cool. Whip into a paste with a mixer. Apply with a damp sponge. Wipe the suds. Rinse with 1 cup vinegar in 1 gallon of lukewarm water and let dry. Another rug cleaner is a shampoo made of 6 tablespoons soap flakes, 2 tablespoons Borax, and 1 pint of boiling water. Let cool before applying.

Alternative Pesticides

- Ants: Remove accessible food and water (removing a water source is not always easy). Pour a line of cream of tartar or chili powder where the ants enter the house. They won't cross it. A gentle discouragement that has worked for us are little electronic devices that you plug in. They give off a signal that apparently the ants don't like. I was surprised it worked when we got one, but saw a response within just a few hours, with a great decrease of ants coming in the house at that time (seasonal here, every year). Remember, however, in doing "ant control" that ants are one of the primary outside flea controls. At no charge to you they scour the yard and take the flea larvae back home for an evening snack.

- Roaches: Clean up food. Place bay leaves near cracks or caulk all cracks where accessible. Use sticky traps of boric acid powder and very little water. Set out a dish containing equal parts of oatmeal and plaster of paris.

• Fleas and ticks: Feed pets brewer's yeast and garlic (see Skin Parasites on page 419). Vacuum your pet's bedding regularly. Place eucalyptus seeds and leaves and cedar chips (cats don't like either one) near bedding.

Do you get the idea from this partial list that there are many ways in which you can use common substances instead of the array of strong chemicals we often turn to?

ELECTROMAGNETIC EFFECTS ON HEALTH

A more recent concern is the proliferation of electromagnetic transmissions through our living spaces. Signals from cell phone towers, Wi-Fi routers, home appliances, radios, televisions, computers, smart meters, and cordless phones as well as military and commercial radar have steadily multiplied the last couple of decades.

A few years ago we began to read about harmful health effects that can occur from these devices and even ordinary house wiring. So we acquired several kinds of electromagnetic field (EMF) meters to explore the levels emitted. Susan has taken particular interest in this and has tested the homes of many friends and acquaintances as well. Here is what she has found.

• Cordless (DECT) phones are the highest emitters in homes that have them, especially the main base, which emits signals 24/7.

• After that, the wireless router is highest, particularly within 10 to 15 feet of a work or sleep space.

• Cell phones are also quite high, but mostly just when in use, and especially when downloading videos. They emit higher frequencies while you are talking than while texting or listening.

• Wireless mice and keyboards can also be quite high, especially because of their proximity, and especially for those who work for hours at computers.

• Microwave ovens can be so high that she was able to detect one in the middle of the road when a neighbor turned hers on in a nearby house. They are notoriously leaky.

• Smart meters seem pretty variable, but some are quite high.

Though the proliferation of microwaves in our lives tends to be "off our radar," so to speak, some public health experts warn they can have a major impact on health. Radio frequencies can cause fast and irregular heartbeat, agitation, memory and concentration issues, infertility, and many other issues, including accelerated aging of cells and interference with neurotransmitters and hormones and increased cancers, especially of the brain. For an excellent summary of the science, visit emfwise.com and electromagnetichealth.org. Also read *Zapped: Why Your Cell Phone Shouldn't*

Be Your Alarm Clock and 1,268 Ways to Outsmart the Hazards of Electronic Pollution, by Ann Louise Gittleman.

Though our pets don't have their own devices (so far), they can be just as impacted as we are, if not more so. Cats, for example, will often sleep on a desk or shelf next to a warm router or base phone, which is very risky.

One interesting study looked at this question in dogs.[3] To understand what the researchers did, let us first describe the particular function they looked at. Our bodies (human and animal) have pretty tight control over what gets into the brain from the blood—after all, it is headquarters! This is called the "blood-brain barrier." In the study, a radioactive protein (albumin) was injected into dogs' bloodstreams and then, for the next 5 hours, a microwave signal was broadcast at their poor little heads. Researchers found that in one group of 11 dogs, measurable changes in the blood-brain barrier occurred in 4 of them, breaking down this barrier and allowing the radioactive protein to enter the brain. A similar effect has been seen in test mice exposed to 2 hours of cordless phone frequencies. If it's happening to these animals, it likely also impacts cats, not to mention ourselves. Generally, the younger and smaller seem most vulnerable.

From our extensive study of this topic, and our own observations, we suggest this exposure is a possible factor in a health problem, especially if your pet or someone else in the

HOW TO PROTECT YOUR PET FROM ENVIRONMENTAL POLLUTION: A CHECKLIST OF DOS AND DON'TS

DO

• Brush and bathe your animal often to remove toxic particles from fur.

• Use natural and less toxic methods of flea control.

• Feed a fresh diet with organic foods whenever possible.

• With a health problem, use the low-meat or vegetarian recipes to give the detoxification system a break.

• If your water is chlorinated or fluoridated, use a filter. Change the water bowl daily and keep it away from dust.

• Use natural fibers for pet bedding (organic cotton, wool, kapok, etc.).

• Vacuum and dust frequently.

• Remove shoes at the door, especially in homes by industry, traffic, or farms.

• Avoid shag and deep-pile rugs or, vacuum and steam clean often.

• Ventilate your house well to reduce indoor air pollution or install whole-house ventilation.

- Let your pet outdoors or provide sunny, open windows with screens; use a full-spectrum light for his daytime rest area.

- Close your windows and keep your pet inside on smoggy days or when pesticides are being sprayed nearby. Use air filters if you live in a polluted area.

- Remove outdated and unwanted toxic chemicals, or store in ventilated areas away from pets and living space. Use nontoxic alternatives.

- Grow houseplants that filter the air: philodendrons, spider plants, aloe vera, chrysanthemums, and gerbera daisies.

- Keep pets from chewing on poisonous plants and their fruits.

- Guard against pets encountering solvents, paints, drugs and other chemicals, and the dust from remodeling projects.

- Test your home and take recommended actions if radon gas is a risk.

- Consider a negative ion generator if you live in a large building with central heating ducts, a heavily paved city, or an area with hot, dry winds or smog.

DON'T

- Pet your animal with dirty hands.

- Confine your pet to a garage, basement, or shed that contains household chemicals or lacks natural light.

- Keep your pet outside if you live by a busy roadway.

- Exercise your pet on smoggy days or along busy streets.

- Carry your pet in the back of a pickup.

- Allow your pet to roam near a toxic dump, old landfill, industrial area, or sprayed fields.

- Let your pet drink from or play in puddles or other contaminated waters.

- Apply or dump anything in your yard that you would not want to enter the water, food, or air you consume—motor oil or paint, for example.

- Allow smoking inside your home.

- Let your pet sleep near or under house foundations that may have been treated with poison for termites.

- Use pesticides unless absolutely necessary (preferably nontoxic choices).

- Let your pet sleep on or near an operating TV, microwave, computer monitor, electric blanket or heater, clock-radio, or plug-in electric clock.

- Use medical x-rays unless needed.

family has become ill with behavioral disorders, immune problems, or anemia after a new tower has been installed close to your home, or you installed a Wi-Fi router, or the energy company put in a smart meter.

As one might expect, industry-conducted studies tend to underplay the problem, whereas independent and university studies are much more concerning. At a societal level all this "electronic smog" has become extensive and it is unlikely that it will be reduced any time soon. But there is much you can do to protect your own family, including your pets, starting today, to reduce their total exposure.

WHAT CAN YOU DO?

We have replaced the wireless devices in our own home with hardwired options, all at very little inconvenience. Using our microwave test equipment (available at lessemf.com), we found it dramatically reduced the EMF levels in our home, and we have seen some health improvements as well. Based on all this, as well as strong warnings from experts in this field, we recommend taking similar steps, especially if your animals or anyone in the family spends a lot of time near any of these devices.

• Replace all cordless phones with hardwired landlines, available online. Get a speakerphone as well as a headset if you do a lot of desk work.

• Minimize use of cell phones, especially around animals and children, who are more affected. Turn them off when not

in use and just check in as needed. Listening and texting emit fewer signals than speaking, downloading videos, and other data-intense activities. Avoid use inside cars or in areas of poor reception, conditions which really increase the phone's broadcast intensity.

• Turn off your Wi-Fi at night (use a timer) or when not in use, particularly if the device is near anyone's sleeping area. If feasible, go back to Ethernet cables instead of wireless routers, computers, and Internet television.

• Use corded mice, keyboards, and printers if at all possible. The signals from the uncorded versions are definitely significant and their convenience minimal.

• If wireless smart meters have been installed in your home, find out if you can go back to an old-fashioned analog meter.

In any case, distance is your friend, and your animal's friend, when it comes to all these devices. There is a significant dropoff in signal strength just 2 to 3 feet away. So try to locate routers and such across the room, and never near anyone's resting or working area.

OTHER HAZARDS IN THE HOME

Another potential problem, not always anticipated, is your dog or cat swallowing something that is not digestible. This happens more with dogs than cats, but is a concern for both.

HAZARDS FOR DOGS

Dogs will eat just about anything that seems like it might be a food to them. I have seen dogs that have eaten kitchen towels, metal scrubbing pads, plastic toys, clothing—whatever probably had the right smell. Recently my daughter's dog stopped eating, began vomiting, and it turned out he was plugged up with two tampons raided from a trash container. Fortunately, we were able to work though it with homeopathic treatment and avoid surgery. Try to have the dog's view on this. Anything with the smell of food or of body secretions is fair game, so take pains to put anything like that in a container that is secure. You can provide a hard vegetable or tree branch as something to chew on if the desire seems to be there.

HAZARDS FOR CATS

Cats are more particular about what they take in. They sometimes get plugged with a food piece but not often. I remember one young cat that had swallowed the end of a corncob and it had gotten stuck at the end of the stomach. More often, with cats, it's a matter of getting too involved with a thread, a piece of yarn, or a rubber band. Because their barbed tongues make it difficult to spit objects out, they may be unable to stop the swallowing process once it starts. It is hard for us to understand, but cats think nothing of grooming and swallowing hair from their coats. You can see it is a small step from that to accepting a piece of yarn or thread as well. It would not likely be a problem at all except when the piece is very long, and gets caught in the mouth. Though the signs are not specific, cats will stop eating and may have vomiting. If you think that this may be the problem (you are missing some thread or spot a yarn ball unraveled), your veterinarian may have to examine the mouth and throat under an anesthetic, as a thread caught up around the tongue is very difficult to see. A thread with a needle on it could be caught somewhere in the throat or esophagus and will show up on an x-ray. Obstructions farther down, in the intestines (sometimes from a piece of plastic), will show on an x-ray as a bunching of the intestine.

MISCELLANEOUS CONCERNS

Take care that your animal does not chew on electrical cords. Don't confine a puppy or kitten in a room with an exposed cord. Reprimand it firmly if you catch the animal chewing on or playing with one.

If you have toddlers, make sure they don't handle a small animal too roughly, because that endangers both parties. Also, the child may unintentionally cause a great stress for an animal by making a loud noise near its sensitive ears.

If a child is responsible for taking care of a pet, make sure the job gets done the same way you would do it, every day. Don't let the animal become the victim of a learning experience in "natural consequences." Teach your child the necessity of sticking to any responsibility he or she has assumed for an animal.

If you live in an upper-floor apartment (second floor and up), screen your windows. Despite their agility, cats can and do fall out of windows and off balconies. Many clients in New York City lost cats this way.

By taking these precautions and by adopting an overall attitude of watchfulness and consideration, modern life need not hold undue peril or stress for your animal or for you; instead, it can provide unique opportunities for adventure and enjoyment.

A LIFESTYLE CHANGE

What we are espousing here are things we have done ourselves that feel good. You will find that beginning to give attention to the long-range effects from cleaning or building materials starts a movement. We begin to look with different eyes at our home, our yard, the open areas that the wild creatures live and grow in. What can we do to minimize any harmful impacts? To guard our animal companions, the wildlife around our home, even the lovely trees, bushes, and flowers that grace us?

We found ourselves recycling the dishwater by pouring it onto plants, conserving water by using drip irrigation, and installing rain tanks that collect water from the roof. We installed solar panels and solar hot water. We even moved an older washing machine to the outside patio so that the "gray water" would drain off and irrigate the trees.

It comes down to a lifestyle change, a new perspective. We start with caring for our animal companions, wanting to protect them. With time, we come to feel that same caring for all creatures, and especially for Mother Earth. It's a fun trip.

THE GIFT
Susan Pitcairn

Greener than green
I clean the floor,
I spray no more
A poison mist on you.
I comb your fleas,
I wipe the dust
I earn the trust you give to me.
Your lick, your wag, your sparkling smile
Your joy, your jump:
It's all worthwhile.

CHAPTER 11

EXERCISE, REST, GROOMING, AND PLAY

GOOD HEALTH IS MORE THAN JUST DIET: IT'S A LIFESTYLE

A healthy nontoxic diet and home environment are a great foundation for a long, happy life for your dog or cat. But there are some other important things to address here and in the next few chapters, which are more about daily habits and choices, as well as attitudes and connections with nature and each other. They include regular play, exercise, exposure to sun and to nature, and taking time to savor life. In this and the next few chapters we will look at ways you can share a health-promoting, happy lifestyle with your companion animals, and why it matters.

First, we'd like to share some tips from one of the most enlightening books on health in recent years: Dan Buettner's *The Blue Zones*.[1] It's the story of how a National Geographic team discovered a cluster of key habits and practices common to *every* group of exceptionally long-lived humans in the world. Search "bluezonesproject" for some exciting programs that aim to transform cities around the world to help turn them into Blue Zones as well.

These findings are especially exciting for animal lovers. That's because a very similar cluster of lifestyle factors appears in the lives of some of the healthiest and longest-lived dogs and cats we know of as well. They are all exemplified in the life story of a Border Collie who lived to age 25,[2] plus in the lives of other long-lived dogs cared for by author Anne Heritage. We think they also explain the motivations that draw people to having a companion animal. Without a doubt, they bring daily opportunities for exercise, purpose, presence, and companionship into the lives of many.

So please keep the following keys to health and longevity in mind (and maybe tacked to your fridge!).

PETS PLUS PEOPLE:
BLUE ZONE TIPS FOR LONG, HEALTHY LIVES

Here are the Blue Zone findings about health and longevity. How much do you prioritize each of these for both yourself and your animal? What positive changes might you make?

- **Move a lot.** Blue Zone people are neither couch potatoes nor gymnasts, but they do move a lot via normal activities of work and play. In Bramble's family, the dogs went for five walks a day and could go play together in the yard otherwise. Studies find that even just one 20- to 30-minute walk a day is almost as beneficial to health as major training, and it's something that will benefit both you and your dog(s). Instead of driving somewhere, walk, and bring your dog, if possible. Just taking a short movement break every hour or two really helps, which might include short play breaks with your cat. See "The Importance of Exercise" on page 179.

- **Have a purpose.** We all need a reason to live, a purpose that gets us out of bed each day, pets included. For us it might include doing meaningful work, enjoying a hobby, volunteering for a good cause, or taking care of a family member or animal. So, what motivates your dog or cat and gets *her* excited? Exploring the world? Playing games? Socializing? Pleasing you? Love and connection? Even if you have to leave her alone to go to a job, consider ways to offer enrichment: access to the outdoors, another animal, dates with a dog walker? Perhaps a sunny windowsill by a bird feeder for an apartment cat?

• **Take time to be and see.** This means having some daily downtime, not always rushing from thing to thing, multitasking, and racing from dawn to dusk. For us, it might be listening to music, meditating, enjoying a sunset, or smelling the roses. Animals are masters at this skill and can help teach us, so enjoy time every day to be present with your animal, to look each other in the eyes and just be together. Perhaps hold, stroke, and massage your pet with mindful attention and appreciation. Greet the sunrise together. Meditate with a purring cat. You will both benefit.

• **Eat lightly.** In long-lived enclaves, it is customary to eat lightly, just enough to take the edge off hunger, not until one is stuffed. Many Blue Zoners eat a large breakfast and little or no dinner. Science has also clearly established that caloric restriction is one of the greatest predictors of longevity. So monitor your animals' weight and feed just enough so they are slightly lean, neither plump nor skinny. Take up food after they have had enough. Don't tempt them to overeat out of boredom. Make your own eating more mindful, slow, and conscious.

• **Eat mostly plants.** Blue Zone folks eat mostly just traditional plant-based staples like sweet potatoes, corn, legumes, and grains, along with home-grown fruits and veggies. Animal products are only about 5 percent of their caloric intake. Meat is only a condiment or a treat for festive occasions. California Blue Zoner Ellsworth Farnham, MD, had been vegan for more than 50 years, eating just two meals a day, when CNN interviewed him at age 100, active and sharp as a tack.[3] You might well think this particular rule would *not* apply to dogs and cats. Yet, cases like those of Joy and Bramble (Chapter 5) and many others suggest it does, at least for dogs. Consuming fewer toxins may explain longevity in vegan dogs. Reports are mixed for cats eating vegan. Many can, but it's not clear if it's better health-wise.

• **Belong to a community.** Long-lived peoples have a close-knit group of like-minded friends and family, including a faith community. Likewise, pets enjoy being part of a harmonious family of both human critters and those of their own kind. If it's just you and your dog, that's a start, and you can be each other's best friend. But also find ways to connect with others of like mind or expand your circles with other dog people, friends, a roommate, neighborhood gatherings or potlucks, or joint trips to dog parks.

Life from a Pet's Point of View

Consider what life might be like for your dog or cat. When you were very young, tall, powerful aliens came one day, picked you up, put you in a car, and took you away forever, parting you from your mother and siblings, perhaps never again to live with your own kind. They put a collar on your neck, confined you in a cage, a home, or a fenced yard. Yet they fed you and often would hold and stroke you kindly. Sometimes they scolded you in a language you could not understand. Most often, they left you alone for long periods or ignored you as they spent hours staring at small objects in their hands (phones) or light-filled boxes (computers and televisions).

Compare that to the less secure but sovereign lives of their ancestors and wild cousins. A typical dog or cat does not have to worry about getting enough to eat but is lucky to ever spend a fresh, sunny day investigating a stream, running hard through sweetly scented woods, or testing her hunting skills. Instead, most of her life is spent sleeping or pacing indoors on vinyl floors or synthetic carpets, perhaps infested with fleas. Time outdoors is limited to a small, perhaps barren yard or a wait in a stuffy parked car while people do errands.

Every week or two she may be treated to one of her great delights—a walk through the fields. But her fun may be marred by painful foxtails that lodge easily in the abnormally long, curly hairs of her coat. When she gets home, she quenches her thirst with tap water that smells of chlorine. Sometimes, largely because of these conditions, she's a bit irritable and snappish, or depressed and bored. But overall she's good-natured and takes each day as it comes.

Despite all this, most dogs and cats are forgiving, accepting, loyal, trusting, and affectionate. That's what we most love and admire about them. So, let's consider what we might do to offer them a richer and more fulfilling life and to live together as different species with needs and desires that are sometimes the same and sometimes different.

In this chapter we will address dogs' and cats' special physical needs for exercise, rest, and grooming, including flea control. In the next chapter we will consider how we can live well with another species in our care, including any necessary training or control for the good of all. Chapter 13 explores the impact of our own emotions and psyches upon the animals in our homes, and theirs upon ours. Chapter 14 offers practical tips for issues like travel and vacations. Chapter 15 covers the difficult but heart-opening process of saying goodbye, as our beloved animals usually pass long before we do. After that, we detail specific medical responses to various health conditions.

As we look at each of these issues in the next few chapters, let's bear in mind two things.

- *How can we interfere the least with natural life processes?*
- *How would I want to be treated if I were the animal?*

THE IMPORTANCE OF EXERCISE

Regular exercise is essential for optimal health. Sustained, vigorous use of the muscles stimulates all tissues and increases circulation. Blood vessels dilate and blood pressure rises. Tissues become oxygenated, which helps to clean the cells of toxins. Digestive glands secrete their fluids better and the bowels move more easily.

Exercising Dogs: As Much as You Can

Canines are strong runners because they must keep on the move in their continuous hunt for food. Wolves and coyotes can travel a hundred miles a day, and even feral dogs have been observed to travel an average of 16 miles a day through metropolitan areas.

Nearly all dogs, especially, benefit from at least half an hour or more of daily vigorous exercise. While we can't all find places to let our dogs run free outdoors on a regular basis, a walk to the food bowl is the only exercise many dogs ever get.

So think of all the ways you and your dog can both get more exercise daily together, whether it's jogging, taking a walk, playing ball, or chasing sticks and Frisbees. You may not be able to offer your dog the extraordinary schedule of at least four or five walks or runs a day, as the legendary collie Bramble enjoyed, but brainstorm ways you could offer more. Take turns with your partner. Hire a dog walker. Visit dog parks. Walk together to the store, while one of you shops and the other stays outside with the dog. Find a nearby place to play fetch.

If your dog is old, arthritic, weak, or has a bad heart, settle for slow walks around the block. If he is temporarily unable to walk because of a sore foot or a partial paralysis, encourage him to swim in place in a bathtub, large trough, swimming pool, or natural body of water to get exercise. For example, Bramble was severely injured at one point in her advanced years and was unable to walk, but even as a senior she was able to recover after therapy in a pool.

Swimming strengthens the body in the same way running does. If your pet tends to sink, place a towel or cloth as a sling under the body for support. This exercise is especially good for dogs with back problems.

Exercising their teeth and jaws is also important for dogs. Some are happy to chew on sticks and others will appreciate a rawhide chew, dried sweet potato chews, carrots, broccoli stalks, or the like. Be careful with bones, as there is the risk of splintering, especially with small ones like chicken bones. If a bone is very fresh and raw, it is reasonably safe for a dog or cat, but older bones, or ones cooked or frozen, are dangerous. Another option is Ami brand Bone Care, a bone-shaped mouth exerciser made from non-GMO vegetables.

There is no concern that this product could splinter.

Cats: Playing and Exploring

Exercise for cats is different. They are not inclined to chase balls or jog, but they do usually get enough exercise if they are allowed outside part of the time and have a suitable place to scratch.

Besides the occasional lightning-fast sprint after prey and pounce, felines love to stretch. The practice of removing claws (equivalent to cutting off the last joint of each of your own fingers) is not only cruel and painful, but it also eliminates the important feline exercise pattern of using the claws to knead and stretch, which benefits the muscles of the forelegs, backbone, and shoulders. A cat that can't perform this ritual is likely to become weaker and thus more susceptible to illness and degeneration.

So, whether it's a well-positioned log or a fancy scratching post, provide your furry feline with a satisfying way to scratch without ruining your furniture.

Most cats also love to play "thing-on-a-string," chasing and batting at a piece of string with a loop or mouse toy attached to one end. Pet stores sell many such toys for both cats and dogs, the more natural and nonplastic the better. One of our cat Ming's favorite games was to chase the beam of light from a laser pointer. He would zoom around for 5 or 10 minutes pouncing, leaping, or running in circles. (If you try this fun game, just be sure never to point the laser in anyone's eyes.)

Also, when playing games with a pet, never use your bare hand as the "bait" or the object of teasing. This can teach your animal that it's all right for her to scratch or bite your hands, a lesson you will definitely want her to unlearn in the future.

Mental Exercise

Animals also enjoy the mental exercise and stimulation of puzzles. Search "cat plays shell game" on YouTube to see how brilliantly a cat can track one fast-moving object among many. Animals can be amazingly bright. Even though we tend to consider pigs as food rather than friends, they are actually smarter than most dogs and cats and can be very sharp at playing video games. Search YouTube for "pigs playing video games." Chickens can do this also!

Dogs' favorite game is usually fetch, especially in fun outdoor locations. They love to anticipate and dash off to each new place the stick or Frisbee lands (vary it). Dogs can even master advanced skills like riding skateboards (again, see YouTube).

For a variety of fun games to entertain animals, especially cats, search the Internet or a local pet shop. As we discussed in Chapter 10, please avoid bright-colored plastic toys that may contain toxins. Search the Internet for descriptions and reviews of nontoxic, organic, or natural cat or dog toys.

When playing games with animals, please treat them as you would a person, an equal.

So don't insist they play the game if they are tired or interested in something else instead. Likewise, don't reprimand them if they fail to perform as expected. It's not about performance but about enjoyment. Keep it fun and light, encouraging their successes. Stop when they have had enough. As much as you can, learn to listen to the signals they send you and also communicate to them with simple sentences and key words like "fetch?"

Massage: Passive Exercise

Massage is another enjoyable way that both you and your animal can get some of the benefits of mild exercise (stimulation of circulation, lymph drainage, removal of toxins, stress reduction, and such). It's a relaxing, bonding thing to do of an evening, as you are sitting by the fire or in front of the television, and it's also especially helpful in recovery from stiffness and injuries.

Intuition is the best approach. Giving a skillful massage is primarily a matter of quieting down and tuning in to the animal you are rubbing. If you do it in a mindful way, it can also be a nice way of relaxing your own body. The key is to remain attentive to what you are doing, not to do it absent-mindedly, on autopilot, or in a formulaic way.

Before you start, first "ask permission" in whatever way makes sense. Rub your hands together until you feel some warmth and energy. Then gently place them on your animal's head or the back of his neck. Close your eyes and imagine his body before you. In your mind's eye, see if there are any areas

of light or darkness that draw your attention, and start there.

Or just let your hands explore slowly, gently, and yet with confidence. Search for small knots or bands and work on them much as if you were gently kneading bread. You can then proceed to stroke gently and steadily down the spine, using your fingers to explore in little circles around the vertebrae and the various muscles of the legs.

Use soothing strokes. If the animal is on the hyper side, emphasize long, slow, repetitive, soothing strokes, much like when petting him.

And stimulating circles. If he is more sluggish or tired, a more stimulating massage with gentle circular motions can help get the circulation going.

Give a good back scratch. Many animals, especially cats, really enjoy a nice rub on their rump, the back of their neck, or the top of their head, perhaps because it's hard for them to reach those spots or because they contain a lot of nerves. They let you know they love it by arching into your hands.

Pay attention for feedback, always. Watch for signs of relaxation and pleasure (sighs, eyes closing, leaning into your hand) and stay with those areas longer.

Likewise, always be ready to back off, move to a different area, or end the session at any point if your pet shrinks under your touch or moves away. It could be a signal of pain, or perhaps she is just ready to take a nap or go exploring.

Move your pet's legs. Another type of

move, especially nice when your animal fully relaxes under your hands with trust and affection, is to move her legs for her as she lets go. Extend a leg, bend it, stretch it out gently, perhaps pressing lightly around her joints as you move.

Use oppositional moves that stretch the fascia and muscles, also great for sore or aching muscles. For example, loosen the lower back or hips by pushing with one palm and pulling with the other, much the same way a nursing kitten kneads its mother with its paws. Go back and forth, alternating pushing and pulling. You might try perfecting this move on a human who can give verbal feedback. As with all moves, adjust the pressure to the size and sensitivity of the animal. Pay attention.

Provide a lymphatic massage if your animal is run-down. You can even do it on yourself at the first signs of a cold coming on. Use a light, steady, slow brushing motion to stimulate the lymph flow below the surface of the skin (instead of performing a deeper muscular or joint massage). Work from the top down. Stroke down each side of the face, down the neck, and toward the heart a few times. Then brush from the armpits toward the belly and "gather" all this energy into a clockwise circle around the belly. Now do the same thing by coming up the inner thighs to the belly, again, closing it with a clockwise circle. Finish by feeling as though you are drawing energy up and away from the belly.

If this is unfamiliar to you—either as the masseuse or as the massaged—it might help to practice with family members, which is a wonderful way to express love, relieve pain and tightness, and facilitate better circulation and health. You can find out what pressure is comfortable and how the muscles like to be handled. If you have never had a good massage yourself, ask around for recommendations and try it out. Receiving a good massage is the best training for giving one! And with people, encourage lots of feedback, especially as you are learning. Who knows? You might evolve into a professional animal masseuse!

QUIET AND REST

And that brings us to the subject of sleep. Every creature needs a clean, quiet, private, safe place to sleep and rest, warm enough in winter and cool enough in summer. It's so important for the body's work of nightly restoration and healing and in today's busy world, many people overstimulate themselves with media and electric lighting and don't allow the time or conditions for a good rest with a regular bedtime.

Even if your pet sleeps in your bed some of the time, provide a suitable place or two of its own. A lot of animals—especially big dogs—are denied these havens. Many are left out in the elements, but unlike their wild cousins who have a cozy den to hide in, they must make do with a patch of dirt next to a noisy street or perhaps a drafty slab of cement beneath a porch roof. The difference is an important one. When animals are outdoors, even just part of the time, provide a doghouse or a padded basket or cushioned patio chair under a porch overhang.

Indoors or out, cats and smaller dogs are happy with a padded basket or even just a clean folded blanket or towel in a corner or on a chair. Large dogs don't necessarily require a bed such as a basket, but they do need some kind of secure, clean place such as a carpeted corner in a room, an old chair, a special rug of its own in a quiet spot.

Cover the sleeping area with washable cotton or wool pillows, blankets or towels, preferably organic and uncolored. That way you greatly reduce their contact with harmful fire retardant chemicals, pesticide residues, and a host of chemicals used in modern synthetic fabrics. We could all stand to follow this advice (search online for organic sleepwear and underwear), but pets may be especially susceptible, since they will lick off any lint or dust from fabrics. Chances are, they also spend more time sleeping than we do.

Study your pet's preferences and offer several quiet sleeping spots. He might like one quiet, out-of-the-way place and another that's closer to the center of activity, where it's easy to keep an eye on things. Some pets like to sleep together, others apart. Cats instinctively gravitate to small, defined areas with a little elevation, "perches" that make them feel safer. Commercially made window perches or carpeted shelves affixed to windows give cats a front-row seat on all their favorite shows on "cat TV." Also consider carpeted cat houses on posts, sold at many pet stores, though we would, again, like to see you use washable towels on their resting points.

Are You Worried That Your Pet Sleeps Too Much?

It's normal for a pet that is left alone most of the day to sleep a lot. But if she does not greet you on arrival or goes back to sleep soon after you come home, it could mean she is low on energy. This is especially true with dogs. Cats naturally sleep more than dogs and often take frequent naps throughout the day and night.

The way I decide if a cat is sleeping too much is to find out if there are several active periods during the day and if she grooms herself several times a day. The healthy cat will alternate sleep with activity—looking out the window, going outside, exploring, and grooming. If this activity is rare, there may be a problem and it's time to visit the vet.

CLEANLINESS IS NEXT TO HEALTHFULNESS

A clean animal is a beautiful animal, and, more importantly, a healthy one. Every living organism is constantly breaking down and eliminating natural metabolic products and old cells. Ordinarily, about a third of the body's cells are reaching the end of their time and getting ready to be replaced. In a human being, 1 million cells are being replaced every second.

In addition, environmental pollution is

now just a fact of life, as we discussed earlier. So we need to help our animal friends handle it as best they can. Here are four natural ways to assist the hardworking eliminative organs—the skin, liver, kidneys, digestive tract, and lungs—to escort both metabolic and synthetic wastes out of your pet's body.

• **Daily exercise** stimulates waste removal through improved metabolism and circulation.

• **Fasting for a day** now and then relieves the digestive tract of its usual duties and frees the organs to break down toxins stored in the liver, fat, and other tissues. During a fast, the organs can also consume excess baggage, such as cysts, scars, and growths. The process and the therapeutic uses of fasting are described more fully in Chapter 18, How to Care for a Sick Animal.

• **Feeding lightly so your animal is lean** (but not skinny) makes it much easier for the body to eliminate toxins, rather than just store them in fat. It also likely stimulates the body to digest and turn over old, less healthy tissues.

• **Regular grooming** removes dirt and secretions directly, and also stimulates the skin's natural elimination processes. Let's take a closer look at this important aspect of pet care.

Natural Grooming and Skin Care

Nobody ever gives a wolf or a bobcat a bath, so why should we have to groom our pets? Here's why.

• A wild animal moves from place to place, which allows it to get away from a colony of parasites such as fleas. A pet, on the other hand, keeps getting reinfested with these critters from the eggs dropped in its quarters.

• Many domestic animals, especially dogs, are bred to have abnormally long, curly, or very fine hair that is too difficult to clean with just tongues, paws, and teeth.

• Dirt often contains environmental toxins: It's better if you remove debris from your pet's coat than if he licks it off and swallows it.

In short, we have changed the physical structure and environment of our animals, so it's up to us to help care for their skin and coats.

Daily brushing is important for long-haired pets. Use a special "slicker" pet brush made for picking up hair. Short-haired animals may need brushing less often. A flea comb is another excellent tool for regular grooming.

Frequent brushing and combing stimulate hair and skin health, bringing normal secretions from oil glands onto the skin and discouraging fleas. They also keep mats from building up and help to remove burrs and other plant debris.

While brushing, especially after outdoor time, check the feet, ears, eyes, and vagina or penis sheath to detect and remove fox-tails and other plant stickers before they penetrate the skin and require removal by your veterinarian.

If you live in a hot climate, have your dog's coat thinned by a professional groomer.

Bathing is one of the safest and most effective ways to immediately remove fleas, which are killed by the soap and water, but you must also attend to the living quarters (see below). Don't bathe your pets too often, however, because it can dry the skin. Unless your adult dog is unusually dirty, a bath every month or two is plenty. In the case of a bad flea infestation, skin problems, or discharges, however, you may want to bathe animals weekly. If so, use a gentle shampoo that will not strip all the natural oils from the hair.

Cats don't need frequent bathing, since they generally do a good job of it by themselves, plus most resist the process. But if your cat has problems with bad skin or fleas, you can bathe him monthly; otherwise, once or twice a year is adequate.

Shampoo with a natural shampoo bar, which will suds up quickly and work well. This will help save the planet and your pet from the toxic effects of plastic as well as the preservatives that must be added to liquid shampoos to prevent bacterial and mold growth. (Search "nontoxic" or "organic shampoo bar.") You can use human shampoos you already have on hand, but don't use hair conditioners, sulfur-tar shampoos, shampoos containing dandruff suppressors, or any other chemical medication. Think about the fact that your pet licks his fur and also has a very sensitive nose.

If fleas are a problem and you need to take action, first try a natural pet shampoo containing flea- and insect-repellent herbs. Some contain d-limonene, a natural extract from citrus fruits that will kill fleas with minimal side effects, suitable for use with dogs. Or you can make your own insect-repellent shampoo by adding a few drops of essential oil of pennyroyal or eucalyptus to a bottle of natural shampoo or Castile soap. (Do not apply these oils directly to the skin. They are too irritating.)

Use pet shampoos with synthetic insecticides only if the natural flea control program, below, fails, and they really seem necessary to reduce flea problems causing suffering for your animal or family.

Give a bath, realizing that animals often resist bathing. Be gentle and speak in soft, reassuring tones throughout the experience. Remove the collar and lower your pet into a laundry tub, bathtub, or sink as you gradually fill it with comfortably lukewarm water. Wet and lather up her neck first, to trap any fleas that might try to escape toward your pet's head.

Shampoo her entire body and rinse lightly, using either a spray attachment or a container of lukewarm water. Then shampoo a second time, working the lather well into her skin. Let it stay on for 5 minutes or as long as she will allow. This ensures the most complete treatment of fleas. Meanwhile, comb out and drown any critters making their way toward high ground.

Rinse her thoroughly. It's nice to follow

up with a vinegar-water rinse (1 tablespoon white vinegar to 1 pint warm water). It removes soap residue and helps prevent dandruff. Pour on the solution, rubbing throughout the fur. Then rinse again with plain water.

At this point you might like to try this homemade rosemary rinse used by Anitra Frazier, author of *The New Natural Cat*.[4] It's an excellent conditioner that promotes a glossy coat and helps repel fleas.

Add 1 teaspoon dried rosemary (or 1 tablespoon fresh) to 1 pint boiling water. Combine and steep for 10 minutes, covered. Strain and cool to body temperature. Pour it over your pet after the final rinse. Rub in and towel dry without further rinsing.

When you are all done, use several towels to blot off excess water. Then let her do what comes naturally, shaking and licking off more of the water. Make sure she has a warm place to dry off.

For pets that just won't put up with water baths, try this simple dry shampoo.

Spread ½ cup to 1 cup bran, oatmeal, or cornmeal on a baking sheet. Put the oven on low (200°F) for 5 minutes to warm the grain. Removing a little at a time, so that the rest stays warm but not too hot, rub the grain into the fur with a towel. Concentrate on the greasy, dirty areas. Then brush these areas thoroughly to get the grain out.

Finally, here's a spot remover that will help you get rid of grease spots in your pet's fur between baths, especially those spots that cats get on their heads from prowling under cars.

Rub a few drops of Murphy Oil Soap and a small amount of warm water onto the greasy spots. Then rinse thoroughly with warm water.

FLEA CONTROL: BEYOND TOXIC CHEMICALS

Now we come to fleas, the bane of many a beast. Fortunately, there are safe alternatives to the toxic chemicals often used for controlling these pesky little creatures on your pet and in your home. And that's important, because the worst environmental pollutants that threaten pets are surely the poisons that well-meaning owners regularly dip, spray, powder, collar, and shampoo directly onto and into their flea-bitten companions.

The labels of most flea products bear such odd cautions as "Avoid contact with skin." (I've never been able to figure out why it's all right to thoroughly drench a pet with something that's too nasty for humans to touch briefly without immediately washing it off. Skin is skin, after all.) In any case, animals and veterinary technicians alike are affected by the application of insecticides and even from the "inert" ingredients in flea-control products, both of which are absorbed through the skin and by inhalation.

In addition, pets may lick these compounds off while grooming, and we may pick them up while stroking our animals.

Some flea collars and powders are so potent that they produce extreme skin irritations and permanent hair loss on pets.

The net effect of all this poisoning is that it just makes the fleas stronger and ourselves weaker. Because fleas reproduce so rapidly, those that survive flea-control products are the ones that have developed resistance to insecticides. This is especially a problem in places like California and Florida, where warm winters facilitate year-round flea breeding.

It is a common observation among veterinarians that the animals in poorest health attract the most fleas. So the problem is not just the presence of fleas. It's that we have weakened our pets to the point where fleas can take advantage of them. After all, they are just doing what comes naturally.

A complication to the flea problem is the excessive use of vaccines, antibiotics, and cortisone-like drugs that stress the immune system and push it toward an allergy state. It is bad enough to be bitten by a flea. But it is worse to be allergic to the bite as well. You can see animals with fleas that show no evidence, or very little, of being bothered by them, yet another animal can't tolerate even one flea because of excessive reaction.

What's in all these flea-control products, anyway? Basically, they are poisons, meant to harm fleas more than pets. Most animals tolerate them fairly well, but they do add to their body's burden of toxins. Others are more sensitive to them, which can signal a health problem. So, while they have their use, I encourage you to try a safer, more natural approach first.

SAFE, EFFECTIVE FLEA CONTROL

As a part of any flea-control program, always boost your animal's health and resistance as much as possible through a healthy diet and lifestyle. It's also essential to practice thorough sanitation and cleaning of the home: understanding the life cycle of the flea makes it clear why.

Understanding the Flea Life Cycle

• Adult fleas live about 3 to 4 months. During that time, the females steadily lay tiny white eggs on your pet that look like dandruff or salt crystals. These eggs drop off and build up wherever your dog or cat spends most of its time resting or sleeping. Biologists call them "nest parasites."

• The eggs then hatch out into tiny larvae, which live in the cracks and crevices of rugs, upholstery, blankets, floors, sand, and earth. Because they can't travel much farther than an inch, these larvae feed on the black specks of dried blood ("flea dirt") that fall off along with the eggs when your animal grooms and scratches.

• After 1 to 2 weeks, the larvae go through a cocoon (pupa) stage.

- A week or two later, the pupae hatch out as small fleas, who quickly hop onto the nearest warm body (usually your pet—sometimes you!) and bite it for a meal of blood.

- Then the cycle starts all over again, taking a total of 2 to 20 weeks, depending on temperatures. During summer—flea season—the entire cycle takes only 2 weeks or so. That's why fleas increase so rapidly then.

So, no matter how many adult fleas you kill on your pet by grooming and bathing, you can figure there are another 10 or so going through development.

The good news is that these eggs, larvae, pupae, and the flea dirt they feed upon can be sucked up by a vacuum cleaner or washed away in the laundry. And because the developing fleas are so immobile until they hatch, you know where to focus your efforts: your pet's favorite spots.

That's why cleanliness is your best ally in the battle against fleas. Regular cleaning of your home and especially your animal's "nests" interrupts the life cycle of fleas and greatly cuts down their numbers, especially if you act before flea season begins.

Indoor Flea Treatment

- **Clean your carpets.** Steam clean all carpets as the first step in your program if and when fleas build up again. Though somewhat expensive, steam cleaning is very effective in killing flea eggs and it's also good for reducing accu-mulated dirt and toxins. Whenever you take this step, be sure to do all the following steps on the same day. Afterward, do them once a week or so.

- **Mop tile, vinyl, and wood floors.** Mop hard floors with very hot water, which helps kill the larvae, even if you can't get all of them up.

- **Go after fleas with the "vacuum posse."** Thoroughly vacuum all furniture and floors at least once a week to pick up flea eggs, larvae, and pupae: Focus on areas where your pet sleeps and use an attachment to reach into crevices and corners and under heavy furniture. Dispose of the bag or seal its contents in a trash bag; otherwise, it can provide a warm, moist, food-filled environment for developing eggs and larvae. If there is a heavy infestation, put an insecticidal flea collar (or part of one, if you still have some of them) into the vacuum bag to kill any adult fleas that might crawl away, or else suck some diatomaceous earth into the vacuum to dehydrate them.

- **Launder your pet's bedding** in hot, soapy water at least once a week. Dry on maximum heat. Heat kills all stages of flea life, including the eggs. Remember that flea eggs are very slippery and easily fall off bedding or blankets. Carefully roll up your pet's towels or blankets so the eggs don't fall off en route to the washer.

- **Use a fine-toothed pet flea comb** to trap and kill fleas on your animal. Start a daily, weekly, or monthly habit, depending on the degree of infestation and time of year. Cover your lap with an old towel to catch extra clumps of hair and flea dirt and to wipe the comb off as you work. Gently but thoroughly comb as many areas as your pet allows, especially around her head, neck, back, and hindquarters. As you trap the little buggers, pull them off the comb and plunge them into a container of hot, soapy water (or dip the comb and pull the flea off underwater). Afterward, flush the water and fleas down the toilet and soak or launder the towel.

• **Bathe the animal** with a natural flea-control shampoo as described on page 185. For dogs, try one with d-limonene (but not for cats—it's toxic to them).

• **Install a flea-control trap** in the room where the animal sleeps. You don't have to use one, but they are very handy and could make the difference between success and failure. They plug into an electrical outlet, creating a warmth that mimics the animal the fleas lust for. Newly hatched fleas will cross a room to jump on it, only to get stuck on a sticky membrane or drown in a liquid container. Check online.

Outdoor Flea Treatment

If your pet goes outdoors some or most of the time, follow these steps as well.

• **Mow and water your lawn regularly.** Short grass allows sunlight to penetrate and warm the soil, which kills larvae. Watering drowns the developing fleas.

• **Encourage ants.** Perhaps I should say, "Do not discourage ants." They love to eat flea eggs and larvae. So avoid outdoor insecticides.

• **"Sterilize" bare-earth sleeping spots.** If your pet hangs out in a certain bare or sandy area devoid of plants, occasionally cover it with a heavy black plastic sheet or trash bag on a hot, sunny day. The heat buildup will kill fleas, eggs, and larvae.

• **Apply agricultural lime** on grassy or moist areas to dry out fleas. Rake up and dispose of any dead leaves and grassy debris first.

Flea Repellents

Along with the above steps (are you tired by now?), here are some additional ways to repel fleas that may try to jump back on your pet, especially those harder-to-kill ones still lurking in the backyard.

• **Herbal flea powders** are available in pet and natural food stores or online, or you can make your own. (Combine one part each of as many of these powdered herbs as you can find: eucalyptus, rosemary, fennel, yellow dock, wormwood, and rue. Store in a shaker-top jar or plastic Parmesan container.) Sprinkle the powder lightly onto the base of the hair coat, especially around the neck, back, and belly, while you brush the hair backward with your hand or a comb. In severe cases, use several times a week. Afterward, put your animal in the bathroom or other easily cleaned location for an hour or so, perhaps with a towel. That way you can easily vacuum, hot-mop, and launder away the passengers who jump ship. Some herbal flea powders are not just repellents, but also contain natural pyrethrins that help kill fleas. Though not strongly lethal to fleas, they do seem to greatly discourage them.

• **Herbal flea collars** are impregnated with insect-repellent herbal oils. Some are made to be recharged with the oils and used again. Buy them at natural food or pet stores, or online.

• **A natural lemon skin tonic** recommended by animal herbalist Juliette de Bairacli Levy, which many of my clients have successfully used on animals for a general skin toner, acts as a parasite repellent and mange treatment: Thinly slice a whole lemon, including the peel. Add it to 1 pint of near-boiling water and steep overnight. The next day, sponge the solution onto the animal's skin and let it dry. Use daily for severe skin problems involving fleas. It is a source of natural flea-killing substances such as d-limonene and other healing ingredients.

Flea-Repelling Supplements

There are a couple of supplements thought to help an animal repel fleas, depending on how hungry the fleas are. In my experience their effect is not dramatic, but I have the impression they do help. There is no consensus on their effectiveness, however, especially for garlic. I suggest you give them a try, especially if you are struggling with a severe infestation.

Nutritional or brewer's yeast contains B vitamins, which are good for your pet and may also contribute to a skin odor that the fleas do not like. Cats especially like yeast. Add a teaspoon or so for a cat, and up to 2 tablespoons for a large dog, to their food. You can also rub it directly into the animal's hair if you want a more local effect.

Garlic is the other classic anti-flea supplement, sometimes combined with yeast in tablets such as those made by PetGuard. We have recommended garlic in my practice for more than 20 years, and in every edition of our book. I have never seen a problem with the use of garlic in pets, yet now many veterinarians insist that garlic harms dogs. This has become gospel, and one toxicologist claimed that even a small piece of garlic could poison a dog, though no evidence was given.

According to my research, there is only one significant garlic study in dogs, which was done in 2000. Eight dogs were given large amounts of garlic (23 garlic cloves per 30-pound dog) by stomach tube, every day for a week. They saw some blood changes but no symptoms, and considering the very large amount they were giving, this is actually reassuring.

I also checked with PetGuard, which makes products including garlic, asking if they had seen any problem with any of them. Their response was:

> *I'm very pleased to say we have not had any calls or contraindications concerning the PetGuard Yeast & Garlic Powder or Yeast & Garlic Wafers. These two PetGuard food supplements have been available since 1979. We have many generations feeding their pets these supplements.*

Considering all this, I still consider it fine to add a small amount of fresh garlic to your pet's food as part of a larger program for treating fleas (or even if they just like the taste). See Skin Parasites on page 419 for more information.

That said, if you are not comfortable with using garlic for any reason, or you locate other research that conclusively proves that our recommended, normal amounts are truly dangerous, then don't use it.

Other Treatments

Finally, if all else is insufficient in curbing fleas or your animal is ultra-allergic to them, here is one more less-toxic step you can take.

Fleabusters Rx products: There have been some developments in safe flea control. My clients have reported success with a service that applies or sells relatively nontoxic powders for treating carpets, Fleabusters (there may be others as well). Their treatment is said to safely kill fleas and their developing forms over a few weeks and to be effective for up to a year. They also have a nemotode treatment for yards.

Diatomaceous earth: Taking the precautions below, consider sprinkling natural, unrefined diatomaceous earth once or twice a year along walls, under furniture, and in cracks and crevices that you cannot access with a vacuum. This product, which resembles chalky rock, is the fossilized remains of single-celled algae. It contains silica and comprises about a quarter of the earth's crust. Though direct skin contact is harmless to pets and people, it is bad news for many insects and their larvae, including fleas. Its fine particles kill insects by attacking the waxy coating that covers their external skeletons. The insects then dry out and die. It is commonly applied to grains in storage to prevent insect damage.

Don't use diatomaceous earth frequently or directly on your animal—mostly because of the irritating dust that can be breathed in by both of you. It is also messy. Be careful about breathing it in. Wear a dust mask when applying. It is not toxic, but inhaling even the natural, unrefined form of this dust can irritate the nasal passages.

Important: Do not use the type of diatomaceous earth that is sold for swimming pool filters. It has been very finely ground, and the tiny particles can be breathed into the lungs and cause chronic inflammation.

For more information concerning both external and internal parasites, as well as skin problems in general, read further in the Quick Reference Section. Look at Skin Parasites (page 419), Skin Problems (page 425), and Worms (page 454).

CHAPTER 12

LIVING TOGETHER: RESPONSIBLE PET MANAGEMENT

Living with animals can be a wonderful experience, especially if we choose to learn the valuable lessons animals teach through their natural enthusiasm, grace, resourcefulness, affection, and forgiveness. In that same spirit, a kind person is very dear to an animal. But when it comes to living habits, the natural tendencies of people and animals often widely differ. To some of us, the joys of an animal's company are well worth the little extra mess or noise that may be part of the package. Our neighbors, however, may not be as tolerant of muddy paw prints on the car, loud barking in the early morning, dug-up flower beds, or extra "watering" of the bushes. That's why taking responsibility for the impact our dogs and cats have on the rest of the community is one of the most important aspects of our responsibility of caring for an animal.

Whether it's someone else's pet or our own, we all know the unpleasantness of dealing with animals that have not been well taught or restrained. In fact, a nationwide survey revealed that the number one citizen complaint made to city governments concerned "dog and other pet control problems."

I recall a neighborhood Doberman who used to bound into my front yard, relieve himself, then run up to my window and bark angrily at me as I sat in my own living room. And how many times have you walked through a parking lot when a big dog suddenly thrust its head through an open car window and barked ferociously, its huge jaws just inches from your face? I have had a couple of those episodes and am grateful my heart did not stop!

I think of a veterinarian friend whose hand was painfully mauled by an aggressive dog. And I remember a town I used to live in where packs of roaming dogs used to chase down joggers and bicyclists as though they were prey. I always had to keep an eye on all the "ambush" spots when I jogged and carry a stick.

A few years ago we moved into a new home. Our next-door neighbor's deck abutted our side yard and often contained several dogs excitedly barking and growling viciously inches from us as we worked in our flower beds or mowed the lawn. It is surprising to me that there is not more consideration in these situations. The neighbors couldn't possibly think we enjoyed that.

BUT CATS ARE INNOCENT!

If you have built a bird feeder in your yard only to see the neighbor's cat catch and eat the little songsters, it can be an upsetting experience. Add to that the insult of the cat finishing off its meal by urinating in the flower bed.

Such situations often pit neighbor against neighbor, with pets caught in the middle. And yet if animals could speak, they would complain about us humans—about being tied up or locked up too much, for example. Some might growl softly as they reflect on life with a rock 'n' roll fan addicted to top-volume stereo. Pets injured by cars might demand to know why we have to rush around so dangerously. And the millions of pets dropped off at animal shelters by the people who have been caring for them might tell how it feels to be abandoned. (Over half of these are given up because of unresolved behavioral problems.)

How can we, if we wish to be caring and responsible, address the inevitable conflicts between animals and people? I say start by considering the viewpoints and needs of all concerned—both humans and animals. Often a pet problem results from conflicting views on how animals should behave. For example, the person who loves his dog might think it's most natural, and therefore best, for his dog to roam freely; the neighbors, however, might think the dog should be confined because it causes problems when allowed to do so. In other cases, a person has definite ideas about how his pet should act—but the animal's ideas are different, and the expected behavior is highly unnatural.

First let's look at various ideas about how companion animals can best fit into human communities. Once we are clear on our basic standards, we can work out our differences with our pets.

WHAT IS APPROPRIATE BEHAVIOR FOR PETS?

Certain rules for pet behavior are pretty clear. That's because we apply the same standards to ourselves. We do not permit:

- Jumping on people, biting, scratching, chasing, attacking, or other aggression (except in defense against real threats).
- Excessive noise.
- Messes or destruction (especially inside the house or on someone else's property).
- Trespassing onto another's territory.

I list these because I've often seen people stand by as their dogs barked threateningly at harmless strangers or relieved themselves on a neighbor's lawn. To excuse such behavior by saying, "Well, dogs will be dogs," is not acceptable. Of course, we can't expect dogs to be just like us, but we can expect they will be controlled by those responsible for them and, at the very least, that owners will clean up after them. (Dogs love to poop at the corners of streets, and our house is on a corner.) After all, they are living in a human community—not the other way around.

Numerous towns have laws that require dogs to be on a leash when not on their own property, but many people resent such interference with their pets' freedom. Well-intended as this attitude toward animals' rights might be, it overlooks the very real problems created by large numbers of dogs and cats on the loose in an environment quite unlike a natural habitat. Completely dependent on humans, these animals exist in our communities in numbers far greater than a natural ecosystem could support. As a result, these animals endanger both the community and themselves in several ways.

- More than a million dogs and cats are killed by cars in the United States annually. Unconfined pets also cause thousands of car accidents every year when people swerve or brake to avoid hitting them.
- Every year at least a million people are bitten by dogs in the United States, making dog bites our second most commonly reported public health problem. A survey revealed that people in some areas of Pittsburgh feared being bitten by roaming packs of dogs as much as they feared being mugged. Dogs harass elderly people carrying groceries as well as young children with lunch bags.
- Free-roaming dogs kill or injure wildlife, livestock, and other pets. I've treated my share of small dogs and cats chewed up by such packs. The people responsible for the attacking dogs usually have

no idea what the family dog really does on an afternoon romp. Too many cats prowling through a neighborhood can also be a menace to birds, small wildlife, and each other.

• Pets excrete a huge amount of body waste into the environment, much of it deposited in public places and on neighbors' lawns. These wastes can transmit harmful organisms to humans through sandbox play and gardening. They can also ruin a good lawn.

• Wandering pets may fall victim to poisons, sometimes intentionally placed. More often they become victims when their scavenging instincts unavoidably collide with our toxic world—ingesting antifreeze, pesticides, decaying roadkill, and bait put out for wildlife control.

• Others may be kidnapped. Every year in the United States hundreds of thousands of dogs and cats are nabbed and sold to research labs, where they may be subjected to painful experiments and used as bait to train dogs for illegal dogfighting. Millions of other lost pets are impounded by animal control agencies. Usually, they are held for several days so that they may be claimed. But if a pet is frequently allowed to roam for long periods of time, then the absence of that pet (especially cats) may not be noticed until it is too late and the animal has been euthanized.

• On the loose, unaltered pets freely follow their mating instincts. Competing males may engage in bloody and occa-sionally fatal fights. Multiplying far beyond the carrying capacity of either the natural ecosystem or our society, only about 1 in 6 of the millions of puppies and kittens born yearly in this country will find a home.

Government attempts to cope with ani-mal control problems are a significant pub-lic expense, costing taxpayers many millions of dollars a year—in addition to untold pri-vate expenses for injuries, damaged prop-erty, and protective measures.

Let's spend some time at this point in our attempt to have some understanding of the situation examining the psychological underpinnings of both the animal and human behavior. I'll start with dogs, who are much more apt to cause problems for our neighbors than cats are.

WHY WE NEED A WIDE-ANGLE VIEW OF CANINE CULTURE

Animals are much like us in most ways. They have interests, an emotional life, memory, and desires just as we do. Yet, they have their own worldview. As an example, imagine your dominant sense was your sense of smell. Most of us rely most on our sight, and it is difficult to imagine experiencing the world through smelling it.

The Man Who Could Smell Like a Dog

A very interesting insight into what this must be like comes from a true story by neurologist Oliver Sacks in which he describes a young medical student by the name of Stephen, who had indulged in several recreational drugs and unexpectedly found his vision and sense of smell had spontaneously changed.[1]

Dr. Sacks described it like this: "Vivid dream one night, dreamt he was a dog, in a world unimaginably rich and significant in smells. ('The happy smell of water . . . the brave smell of a stone.') Waking, he found himself in just such a world. 'As if I had been totally colour-blind before, and suddenly found myself in a world full of colour.' He did, in fact, have an enhancement of colour vision ('I could distinguish dozens of browns where I'd just seen brown before. My leather-bound books, which looked similar before, now all had quite distinct and distinguishable hues.')"

The most dramatic change was his sense of smell, now extraordinarily sensitive, like that of a dog.

We know that smell is the most important sense to dogs but, of course, do not experience it like that ourselves. For this medical student, however, it became the dominant sense. As Stephen said, "All other sensations, enhanced as they were, paled before smell." As one dramatic example, he was able to identify everyone in a building by just sniffing the air. "'I went into the clinic, I sniffed like a dog, and in that sniff I recognized before seeing them, the twenty patients who were there.'"

He found that this recognition by smell

was more vivid and real than seeing the face with his usual vision. Not only his or her identity was obtained with a sniff, but also the emotions of each person. Dr. Sack adds, "He could smell their emotions—fear, contentment, sexuality—like a dog."

Another thing Dr. Sacks reports, which I thought was the most interesting, was "He experienced a certain impulse to sniff and touch everything ('It wasn't really real until I felt it and smelt it') but suppressed it, when with others, lest he seem inappropriate. Smell pleasure was intense—smell displeasure, too—but it seemed to him less a world of mere pleasure and displeasure than a whole aesthetic, a whole judgment, a whole new significance, which surrounded him. 'It was a world overwhelmingly concrete, of particulars,' he said, 'a world overwhelming in immediacy, in immediate significance.'"

Now that you have read this, try to relate to it, to see if you can get a little of the dog's perspective. I would like to emphasize how some of what the young man related points out the dog's priorities.

- Vision is much sharper, more discerning—the man was noticing shades of color not seen before.
- Vision and memory recall are very sharp and vivid, with more detail than we humans have.
- Smell is the dominant sense; all other senses "paled" before it.
- The man could identify those he knew (friends and patients) by smell.

Just opening the door and sniffing, he could identify everyone in the building immediately.

• This identification by smell was "far more vivid and evocative, more redolent (strongly communicating something to him) than any sight face."

• He could navigate through a city like New York by smell alone, recognizing every street and shop in that way.

• On encountering something or a person, there was a strong impulse to sniff and touch it or him or her.

• The experience was of a world of immediacy—the present moment was what was real, what was significant.

The dog is *immediately present*, ready for the instant to happen. This is in contrast to our everyday human experience of being half present, interacting perhaps, but while playing out a memory, thinking of future events, or evaluating/criticizing the person we are talking to. The dog is right here, ready.

It is interesting that some of the teachers of our time, like Eckhart Tolle in his book *The Power of Now*,[2] emphasize how important it is for us to come to the same state—to be completely present in the moment.

Why is it different for us humans? We differ from animals in the development and use of mental symbols. We use words, which stand for something we perceive or remember, and we have constructed the concept of time—psychological time. By this, I mean we think very much in terms of past and future. We remember the past and that memory impacts the present, and we project our ambitions, desires, fears, and anticipations into the future. Dogs and cats don't do this. They have memory, but they are not thinking of the future like we do, they are simply present, fully there for the experience. This is a significant difference for us to understand.

Your dog is also sensing subtleties of color (perhaps not color as we usually think of it, more gray tones) that we simply do not perceive. By smell alone, she knows who is in the house, in the yard, who is coming—and can determine their emotional state, if they are afraid, as well as their physical state.

Coupled with the primacy of the sense of smell is the strong, probably just about irresistible, desire to contact and sniff the person or object.

Does this give you the sense of how dogs experience the world? Do you get a sense of how completely they are engaged with the world, with what is right in front of them? Can you imagine having the ability, like your dog, to go on a walk and come to a place on the street where, by smell, you can "see" everyone who has been there that day, their emotional state, what they were eating, and so on?

If you can relate to this at all, imagine you are a dog. Now answer this question: What is the most important, interesting, and satisfying experience you can have? Obviously, it is the encounter with the new—if on a walk—

the trees, bushes, animals, insects, other dogs, cats, people.

It is these experiences, their intensity and immediacy, that give the sparkle to their lives.

Contrast that with the housebound dog. "What is new today? Oh, nothing. Might as well go lie down and sleep."

What we are coming to is a realization that life for a dog is one of adventure. This is the challenge. Often we humans want a dog in our lives for emotional reasons—for the companionship, the emotional connection, the enjoyment of caring for another. This may be the main high we get from the experience, while the dog is lying there hungering for the chance to roam!

If we understand this dichotomy, we can begin to understand some of the unpleasant dog behavior that comes from, well, let's be honest, absolute boredom. Why not bark madly at the passing person? Why not be irritable and impulsive at being asked to do something in which you have no interest?

CONTROLLING YOUR DOG

Is the answer, then, simply controlling your dog?

My parents lived for years next to a poor dog that was chained to a post in the neighbor's backyard all year round and spent most of his time barking and yowling at the top of his lungs—day after day after day. Talking to the neighbors did no good, and my dad often took food over to the dog out of pity for him. It is hard to realize that

nothing could be done about a situation like this. This was not illegal and the neighbors were not breaking any laws. Dogs are considered property and they can be treated like this with impunity. It is an attitude we need to change.

Considering what we have learned about how the dog sees the world, you begin to have a sense of what suffering it is for a dog to be confined like this. If we are going to provide a life worth living for our dog, then we need to make it interesting for him. Commit yourself to providing that. If the best you can do is go for a walk with the dog, be patient with it and make it long enough to be satisfying to him.

In my neighborhood I often see people pulling their dogs away from something obviously interesting (I should say fascinating) to the dog, sometimes admonishing them with "come on, let's go," in a hurry to finish the walk. They are probably thinking of "walk" in terms of legs moving, while the dog is using its legs to get to the next adventure! Give your dog a chance to experience things—new smells especially.

It would be nice if your dog could run off leash, and sometimes that is possible, like in a dog park or in the country. I do encourage this if at all possible; however, for many people the place they live has leash laws, and for good reason. You don't want the dog running out in front of a car, or running up to and frightening someone (not all people want to be approached by dogs).

I remember, years ago, riding my bike to

my office using a lovely bike path that went through a public park. As I breezed along, suddenly a large dog ran right in front of my wheel and I had to brake hard not to hit it and flip over the handlebars. When the fellow came up, I said (nicely), "You know there is a leash law here." His response—perhaps I should say snarl—included the F word.

You see the difficulty? I would have rejoiced in seeing the dog run free, but in the park with all the people, children, bicyclists—it was just too dangerous.

Poor dogs. It's not easy for them.

KEEPING HIM HOME

If you live in a home with a yard, your dog may be able to be free within that space. It is not the same, by any stretch, as running free through the forest, but at least he can move around and get some exercise. Most often a dog is confined by a fence, and obviously the fence a dog can see through is the most satisfactory. On the other side of the fence, for the neighborhood walker, is the unpleasant experience of being barked at, so again we have this conflict between human and dog desires. Personally, I expect the person with the dog to be sensitive to this consideration and not let the dog be out barking all the time.

Some people install what are called wireless fences that train a dog to stay within its boundaries. Aggressive dogs, however, have been known to overstep the boundary in response to strong temptations. Another limitation of invisible electric fences compared to physical ones is that they don't keep other dogs or people out, so your dog is still at risk of being stolen or attacked by another dog.

Such electronic fencing systems rely on a wire buried around the perimeter of the yard; if the dog tries to go past the wire, it triggers a mild electric shock in a special collar. It does not seriously harm the dog (I have to admit to never trying it myself), but is uncomfortable enough that they soon learn not to do it.

I knew of one dog, however, that so desired to get out that he would endure the discomfort anyway. Knowing the shock was coming, he would start making crying sounds at the point he decided he was going to go for it—well before he could feel anything. That didn't stop him from making the run and getting away, though. He would start crying as he started his run, the cry getting louder and louder as he approached the barrier, and with a final yelp would leap out of the yard and on to freedom. My client tried two electronic collars on him at the same time, to no avail.

I don't really like this option myself. Somehow it does not feel right to put a shock collar on an animal, and I have discouraged this option. I have to say, however, it might be better than the experience of the poor dog always tied to a pole that lived next to my parents.

Whatever the situation—yard-bound, pen-bound, housebound, apartment-bound, there is still a need for excursions. Remember that what the dog needs is adventure, new encounters, smells, interactions. Providing this will greatly improve your dog's behavior, will make her happy, will make her a good companion.

DEVELOPING COMMUNICATION WITH YOUR DOG

There are a lot of ideas as to how best to train your dog. I don't know much about training myself and asked my friend and colleague Dr. Lisa Melling, a specialist in animal behavior, the best way to get a dog's attention.

Dr. P: *If a dog is doing something you don't like, say barking or digging a hole, whatever, what is the best way to get her attention?*

Dr. Melling: Redirect her attention and reward her for stopping the undesirable behavior. For this to work, it is assumed that the dog has already been trained with basic commands. If not, the first step is enrolling in an obedience class that teaches positive reinforcement behavior training. With this type of training, you give the command that tells her to stop, reward her, and ask her to do something else that is a more desirable behavior.

Example: The dog is digging a hole in the yard. The person whistles, claps, or calls the dog's name to catch her attention, and when the dog looks up, he says "Leave it" (or whatever command he has trained the dog to understand). The dog leaves the hole and comes to the person, at which point she receives verbal praise or a treat or some other valuable reward, and then she is given a different job, such as playing ball toss or going for a walk. (It is also important to remind people that digging a hole or barking at another dog, while undesirable to us, is perfectly within the realm of dogginess.)

I can see Dr. Melling's answer reflecting what we discussed earlier. What one is doing by clapping or calling is bringing the dog's attention to the more interesting situation. From there you guide her to the desired outcome. Obviously the basic commands have to be established. This is necessary, as we have been discussing, for both the dog's and people's safety.

Dr. P: *What would you consider to be the basic commands (should I say agreements?) that dogs should know and respond to?*

Dr. Melling: I am a big fan of a well-trained dog, and even though I know how to teach my dog many commands, I still take each new dog I adopt to a basic obedience class. There, handler and dog learn to communicate with each other, and how to act appropriately around other dogs and people. The basic commands a dog learns in these classes include sit, come, lie down, stay, and to heel on a leash. The more advanced classes also teach dogs to "leave it," which means they do not pick up something, usually food, until the person tells them it is okay. They also learn essential greeting behaviors, such as how to sit and be petted when someone new approaches. In addition, they learn good socialization skills by interacting with other dogs. The best classes use positive training techniques, and never dominance or punishment training.

SOME SPECIFIC ISSUES

Dr. P: *Any advice on managing dogs that bark from their yards excessively (at people, etc.)?*

Dr. Melling: This is more of a person management issue—it is natural for dogs to protect their yard. Depending on the breed and the personality of the dog, as well as how much daily exercise it receives outside the fence on walks, some will tend to bark more than others. While a dog can be taught to stop barking on command, this requires the people to be attentive and present to correct the behavior. It has been my experience that the best way to manage a dog that barks excessively from the yard is for the person to not permit this behavior. There are punishment devices such as shock collars that can be triggered by the dog's bark, but I feel these are inhumane and should not be used.

Dr. P: *How would you train a dog not to jump up on visitors?*

Dr. Melling: There are three main techniques that can be used. The first is to ignore the dog when it jumps on you, and reward it when it is calm. The second technique is to have the dog on leash when visitors approach so the handler can better control, correct, and prevent jumping behavior. The third technique is my favorite—teach the dog an alternative behavior when greeting people. This is best learned in a positive training class, but the essential idea is that a dog cannot jump on a visitor if he is sitting. This is done by teaching the dog to sit and stay, using food rewards. With persistent training, the dog learns that he gets a food reward for sitting calmly for visitors.

Dr. P: *How would you describe the difference in dog behavior on leash versus off leash?*

Dr. Melling: Many dogs tend to be more reactive when they are on leash, especially when meeting new dogs or people. Sometimes this is simply because they are excited to see another dog. When they bark nervously, the theory behind this change in behavior is that a leashed dog can't escape if an approaching dog makes it uneasy, so it tends to bark and act more nervous because its ability to run from the dog is impaired. Also, most dogs that approach another dog directly would be interpreted as acting aggressively, so it is common for dogs being walked toward each other on leash to become anxious with this unnatural greeting behavior.

Our discussion so far assumes that we are dealing with normal, healthy dogs. Without learning to live in human society, they can get into trouble, so we want to find a lifestyle that allows them enjoyment but also is not dangerous or annoying to others. Another area we need to consider is special circumstances or mental/emotional problems that complicate our efforts.

Dog Bites

Dog bites can be serious business. Every year a handful of Americans, mostly small children, are killed by family pets or neighbors' dogs. US medical personnel treat at least a million dog bite cases annually, ranging from nips on the ankle to mutilation requiring stitches or reconstructive surgery. It's true that vicious bites come mostly from guard dogs and roaming dog packs; the majority of dog bites, however, come from animals known to their victims, dogs that have a reputation for being "nice." Your own child could be the victim of such a dog, perhaps even your own pet.

In my first year of practice, two of my patients were the cause of a child being killed. We knew these dogs to be trouble because of their behavior in our clinic, usually biting whoever would hold them, but the

client did not take any action that we knew of to control her dogs. One morning, while she was babysitting and carrying someone else's child, she went out to stop her dogs from digging holes in the backyard. I will spare you the details, but it was unfortunate that she was carrying the child in her arms when she went out. It was a shock to all of us and brought home to me the real dangers of the uncontrolled aggressive animal.

I ran this question by Dr. Melling.

Dr. P: *Recently in the news a 3-day-old baby was killed by the family dog. All were in bed together. Any advice on new babies?*

Dr. Melling: Never trust a dog around a baby or child. Even the best dog should be closely supervised around small children. There are many desensitization exercises that can be done to get a dog accustomed to the presence of a baby in advance, including getting the pet used to the sound of a baby crying. Dog gates or crates should be used to keep the pet from interacting with the baby without supervision.

There are many causes of canine aggression. Problems can often be traced to inconsistent leadership or an overly emotional home. Other factors that can lead a dog to bite are too little exercise, violent treatment, teasing, failure to correct dogs that nip you in play, too much confinement, physical discomfort from aging or injury, poor breeding, and minimal human contact during puppyhood (more likely for dogs from "puppy mills").

Preventing Aggression

You should prevent your dog from endangering strangers by keeping him inside or secured behind a fence, or else under your control on a leash. If your dog is left alone in a yard with a fence that a neighbor child can reach through, talk to local parents, urging them to make sure their children understand the possible dangers. (If necessary, put up a Beware of Dog sign.)

Watch for subtle warning signs of a problem and take them very seriously. Many people mistakenly deny that their dog poses a potential danger, either because they see it as an insult to the dog or to themselves or because they don't know how to solve the problem. Their dog might have actually snarled or attempted to bite someone, but they make excuses—he was startled or had his tail stepped on, for example. Such aggressive reactions tend to get worse, not better, especially in older pets. Take my word for it and correct this now before it causes some real harm. Think how you'd feel if you ignored the problem and a child was bitten.

Play it safe. The guidelines that follow should reduce the risk of dog bites from your own dog, as well as someone else's. Make sure your children understand and follow them.

First, learn these tips on how to avoid provoking a dog.

• Don't disturb a dog while it's eating or sleeping. If you learn your dog is gra-cious enough to allow this, then fine, but don't assume it.

• Do not intrude upon the private territory of a restrained or confined dog. Neutral territory, like a park, is usually much safer for any interaction.

• Never tease a dog by dangling food or toys over its head. A playful nip can easily get out of control.

• Stop hugging or holding a pet that wants to be free. He may feel he has to fight (bite) to get away.

• Teach children to avoid stray dogs completely. Also, it's dangerous to pet a strange dog on a leash unless you ask if it's safe. The dog might be a watchdog trained to attack—or just in a bad mood.

• Do not scream and wave your hands around dogs. Children who do this when scared or excited can unintentionally provoke aggressive dogs.

Once you know how to avoid provoking a dog, it's also helpful to know how to mollify a dog that approaches you in a threatening manner. You can tell from a dog's body language whether he means serious business or just wants to engage in some rough-and-tumble play.

A friendly dog avoids direct eye contact, looks to the side, perhaps exposes his throat and even grins. He keeps his ears flat, tail tucked down, and body low. If his head is lower than his tail (think of bowing), but he is crouching, pouncing, or thrusting about, he's probably just playing and is not a threat.

Be on the lookout for these signs of a potentially dangerous dog: ears raised up and forward, teeth bared in a snarl, and hair raised on the shoulders and rump. Even more threatening signs: becoming stiff-legged, raising a front leg, urinating, growling, staring you in the eye, and slowly waving a high, arched tail. An animal that bites out of fear may send mixed messages, so read the whole animal carefully and avoid threatening any dog that acts wary of you. Unfortunately, some dogs attack without any of these warning signs.

If a dog runs at you, stay calm. Turn partially sideways and speak in a soothing voice. Keep your head slightly lowered and your hands down. This conveys peaceable intentions. Do not face the dog head-on or stare it in the eye. Do not turn and run unless you are certain of reaching safety. The dog tends to see a running creature as escaping prey. Some veterinarians and animal handlers confound threatening animals they must approach by whistling softly (while turned away) or calling in a friendly tone.

If a dog chases you on your bike, slow down and speak soothingly. Get off your bike if you can, on the side away from the dog. Walk at an unhurried pace, without turning your back to the dog.

If a dog should bite you, stay calm. A scream may provoke the attacker further. Try to put an object (like a purse, newspaper, book, or jacket) near his mouth to give him something besides you to bite. Wash the wound with soap and water. Call your doctor for advice. Report the incident right away to the public health department and establish the dog's identity if you can.

When two dogs fight, get out of the way. I have seen many clients receive terrible injuries from trying to intervene in a dogfight. If you feel safe at a distance or behind a barrier, the best way to break up a fight is to turn a hose on both dogs.

The Vaccine Factor

Chronic encephalitis underlies many canine behavior problems, including aggression. This condition is an inflammation of the brain and central nervous system in reaction to vaccines or due to an autoimmune disease (see Chapter 16). Over the years, I began to associate some of this aggressive behavior with bad results from rabies vaccinations, specifically. Dogs that were formerly pleasant would become suspicious, aggressive, impulsive, and destructive, often breaking out of their yards to wander—in a word, dangerous animals. These are symptoms of rabies disease, and though these dogs did not have rabies, it did appear that the vaccine had set off some of the same behaviors as the disease. I always cautioned people with dogs like this not to vaccinate them again, but the legal requirement for rabies can make this difficult. Many veterinarians now offer to take a blood sample to test for immunity to rabies (rabies titer), but not all counties will recognize this as legitimate.

I am mentioning this because, in my experience, it is a most dangerous situation.

These dogs become impulsive, fearful, and aggressive, and what they might do is unpredictable. If you see this sort of thing happening with your dog—within a few weeks of the rabies vaccination, he changes personality, acting aggressive, fearful, withdrawing from social interaction—I strongly encourage you to get help for it. Most of my experience has been with homeopathic treatment and I know, from experience, that the behavior can be corrected with this method, but there may be other effective ways. I do not encourage using drugs to dull the brain—that is only buying time. The problem needs to be corrected at its root.

WHAT ABOUT CATS?

Cats are quite different from dogs. One of my favorite jokes is to say that recent research has shown that cats don't really say "meow." They are actually saying "me now!" (Cats never appreciate this.)

Actually, I have not felt I understood cat mentality very well and so I ran some questions by my friend and colleague Dr. Andrea Tasi, a feline-exclusive practitioner.

Dr. P: *I have always thought of cats as being loners and that when people have several cats in the same house it is unusual for them to be together like that. Is this the correct way to understand the situation?*

Dr. Tasi: That is actually not true when there are adequate food sources. Barn cat colonies, which have been extensively observed by cat behavior experts, show that many cats have "preferred associates" (the behaviorist's word for friends!), with whom they will play, rest, mutually groom. Related queens will often co-raise kittens and sometimes there is even the phenomenon where a young male from a past litter will help his mom with new kittens!

So cats are probably way more social than we give them credit for. They are, however, always solitary hunters, except for the queen teaching her kittens. *And* cats are quite xenophobic: Strange cats are not quickly accepted and are often driven away. Sociability has been shown to have a heritable component, especially from the tom. So kittens from a feral father often are less sociable than from a "tame" one. If one wants to have a multiple-cat household, the greatest chance for domestic harmony comes with adopting a mom/queen and her kittens.

Dr. P: *Where we live there are many coyotes as well as the occasional mountain lion, so this is also definitely a risk to them. Most people here keep their cats inside at night.*

Dr. Tasi: There are companies that make fences specifically for cats. Purrfect Fence is the one I am most familiar with, and it really works. If you would prefer to let your cat wander outside your property, as in some areas it is probably safe to do so, here are some guidelines.

• Spay or neuter your cat. This will reduce fights and spraying and address the pet overpopulation problem as well.

• Confine your cat at any sign of disease. It's especially important to keep your cat indoors and separate from other cats if it has a contagious disease.

• Teach your cat to come when called. Repeat her name often when you are playing together or feeding her. Ring a bell or whistle just before feeding her dinner. Call her frequently, offering a tidbit of her favorite food. Praise her and give her lots of affection when she responds. Soon she will associate pleasant things with coming when she's called, and she may begin to associate the bell or whistle with feeding time.

• Be sure your cat is wearing a collar and identification tag with your name and phone number on it. Soft leather or nylon collars are the most comfortable. To avoid the danger that she'll get her collar caught on something, fit your cat with the special quick-release type that automatically opens with sufficient pressure on the collar. Attach a bell to the collar to warn birds—the birds will thank you!

• Keep your cat in after the evening feeding. Cats are more apt to get into fights or get hit by cars at night.

• Invite your neighbors to let you know if your cat is causing problems for them. If you get such reports, take responsibility for your cat's behavior and do what's needed to rectify the situation.

• Be prepared to break up occasional cat fights. If you catch two felines staring each other down, a loud clap of the hands will usually cause one or both to back off. If the fur is already flying, splash water on the combatants.

Whether your cat gets out or not, do spend some time playing with her. You can use something on a string to yank around, a wand toy, toy mice—there are many very clever ideas people have come up with. Set time aside every day to interact with her.

Many cats also like scratching posts and seem to enjoy the ones where they can also climb up to shelves. The activity of climbing is very natural to them (see page 209, "Scratching and Biting: What to Do").

THE GREAT LITTER BOX PROBLEM

Some of the most troublesome cat problems can be resolved if you take on a feline attitude. For example, when cats urinate and defecate outside the litter box, it can mean they are unhappy about something in the environment. It's a cat's way of expressing agitation, not a personal message to you. Inappropriate elimination may mean the litter box is not clean enough or the particular litter that's used is not to their liking. Some long-haired cats get upset because the dirty litter gets in their fur. Sometimes the cat is just reacting to a change of litter box location, which is best done in a gradual manner. Certain cats just seem to want a more vertical surface, a problem that may be solved by propping a second litter box on its side, inside the main horizontal one.

One of my clients has solved this problem by setting up a piece of plastic at one side of the litter box (any rigid washable material would do). She then drapes a small terry-cloth towel over it, which her cat seems to prefer to urinate on. Of course, she washes it frequently.

Dr. Tasi: There are companies that make high-sided litter boxes for the cats who tend to stand more when they urinate. It is also very easy to make a litter box out of a high-sided plastic storage box, cut down on one side.

The other major cause of urinating or having bowel movements outside a box is that there may be something wrong physically.

Dr. Tasi: Cats who stand to urinate but didn't use to often have arthritis-related pain or some sort of hind leg weakness going on.

Cats can sense there is something not right and don't want to put the urine or stool where other cats can smell it and realize they are not well. What I mean by this is that in nature cats will use their excreta as a marker defining their territory, but if they are not well that same marker can let a rival know they are weak—so they hide it.

Once the problem is corrected, the behavior returns to normal. It is always a good idea to look closely at the urine to see if there is a hint of blood or perhaps some gritty, gravelly stuff in it. Yes, you have to use your fingers to feel it. What you do is empty the litter box, clean and dry it, then put some shredded paper strips in it. This way, when the cat urinates, there is no litter to absorb the urine, which collects on the bottom. Once the sample is there, pour it off into a jar, let it settle, then look for crystals or sediment on the bottom (and feel with your fingers if you're not sure).

To see blood in urine, put a white paper on the bottom of the litter pan and just a little litter over it. You may be able to see the pinkish tinge contrasting with the white paper by shaking the litter aside. Inappropriate elimination may signal chronic health problems, such as allergies.

If there are bowel movements outside the box, look to see if the stool is normally formed or has mucus or blood around it. Some stools are hard at the beginning and soft at the end, which is not quite normal. Any of these things can indicate intestinal irritation, possibly from worms, constipation, allergies, infection, or immune problems.

If your cat is spraying (the way cats mark territory), it can mean that he is disturbed by recent adjustments in his life and surroundings—a new person in the household, a more anxious attitude from you because of stress, or a move to a new home.

A very common cause of agitation can be the presence of a new cat, even if it's just in the neighborhood.

Once a cat has sprayed in a particular spot, he tends to keep doing it. Thoroughly cleaning the area will help, but often cats can smell the urine scent through any scrubbing you might do. It may help to finish off by applying mint tea or something that smells minty, as cats generally don't like that smell. Another thing you can do is to tape aluminum foil over the area for a while. That will prevent your cat from smelling the old urine and, if he does spray again, tends to splash the urine back at him.

HERDING CATS

There are behaviors we don't want to encourage in cats; in a sense, we need to "train" them not to do these things. It is really a process of communication but, unlike dogs, cats don't get as involved with your enthusiasm and praise, which makes cats much less interested in the training game.

It helps to remember that both cats and dogs are gamblers. Research shows that if they are positively rewarded for a behavior as little as one time in 20 tries, they may continue the behavior. They're willing to gamble on the reward despite the long odds. This is what you're up against in trying to get a cat to change its behavior. If you don't want kitty on the counter, but every once in a while when she gets up there she finds food, that jackpot will motivate her to try again at least another 15 or 20 times. On the other hand, negative consequences (being pushed away, told "no," not finding any food there) often have to be much more consistent to condition a cat than a dog.

Because of this, your training efforts are best spent in making sure your animal is never rewarded for undesirable behaviors. Don't pick your cat up to remove her from the counter, admonishing her sweetly and scratching her affectionately in the process. Avoid the temptation to say yes now and then when you really should say no.

Another effective technique is to channel your animal's behavior into a rewarding direction. Give her a treat whenever she earns it. Or consistently greet her with affection when she jumps on your lap in appropriate times and places, like when you're stretched out in your easy chair in the evening. Provide her with an appealing scratching post (see below) and some toys for pouncing. Most cats behave much better if you create suitable outlets for their energy.

Dr. Tasi: Cats in the wild need to kill about nine mice a day to meet their caloric needs. For each mouse successfully caught, there are probably two or three chase sequences that don't end with a catch. Thus, hardwired into the brain of the carnivorous predator that all cats are is the need for about 27 chase sequences per day. All cat play is modified hunting behavior, so our goal as attentive guardians should be to help the cat have somewhere near this mental/physical quotient of activity. I tell folks two 10-minute play periods per day probably get most cats up to this number of chase sequences. Play is the single thing most often missing in cats' lives.

Scratching and Biting: What to Do

A common training problem with cats is teaching them not to scratch your carpets, drapes, and furniture. If we realize that this scratching is part of normal cat behavior, then the obvious thing to do is provide a way for this to happen that is safe for our furnishings.

Dr. Tasi: Cats need a favored scratching substrate in every room of the house. Having an excellent scratching post in the living room will not prompt a cat upstairs in the bedroom, when it is thinking about scratching, to think "Hey, let me run down a flight of stairs and go scratch that thing in the living room." Nope, the cat will go to town on the end of your brand new fancy mattress and bedspread.

One of the most universally favored scratching substrates, which comes in all shape and sizes, both vertical and horizontal, is cardboard, and these products are inexpensive compared to many others. You can find many choices by searching "cardboard cat furniture" online.

If you would like to make your own post, nail an untreated four by four (2 to 3 feet tall) to a base of half-inch plywood about 16 inches square. Then wrap the post with sisal rope or a piece of carpeting turned inside out to expose the rough side (posts with soft coverings are not sufficiently attractive to most cats). For maximum stability, lean the post up against the corner of a room or tilt it on its side. Make sure the post is secure. If it falls over and frightens your kitty even once, it may be enough to make her avoid the post altogether.

If your cat needs instructions on the use of a scratching post, simply lay it sideways and place her on top of the post. Scratch the post yourself with one hand and use the other to firmly stroke her neck and back (that will stimulate the urge to scratch). Don't try to push your cat's feet against the post, as cats will resist force. If your pet is still inclined to scratch at the furniture or drapes at times, move the drapes or the chair slightly and put the post in that spot. Move the post gradually and put the furniture back when the cat is actually using the post instead. You may need to cover a corner of the couch or roll up the drapes temporarily until your cat makes the transition. It's often good to position the scratching post near the spot where your cat sleeps, since many cats like to stretch and scratch on waking from a nap.

Declawing? Ouch!

Declawing your cat is not a suitable solution to scratching problems. It is a painful and difficult operation that many veterinarians refuse to do. In fact, it's the equivalent of removing the first joint of all your fingers. It can impair a cat's balance, weaken it (from muscular disuse), and cause it to feel nervous and defenseless. The resulting stress can lower your pet's immunity to disease and make it more likely to be a biter. Obviously I am recommending against it.

As an alternative, it may be helpful to trim your cat's claws. Because they are shaped like a scythe, their very tip is the part that does the most damage. A cat will slide that curved tip behind a loop of upholstery fabric and pull its foot straight back— snapping the loop. If the cat makes a practice of this, your sofa will soon look like it needs a shave.

The nail tip is also the part that so easily punctures the skin. It can be removed with ordinary nail clippers. (Be sure to clip only the very tip, about $\frac{1}{8}$ inch, or you might hurt the cat.) Wait until your cat is relaxed, perhaps taking a nap in your lap. To extend a claw for clipping, press your index finger on the bottom of her foot while pressing with your thumb just behind the base of the nail at the top of the foot. Press gently. The claw will slide from its sheath so that you can get at it with the clippers you're holding in your other hand. You may get to cut only two or three claws in a single sitting, but you can try again later.

Here's another piece of advice about claws. Never let a cat or kitten scratch your bare hands—even in play. If you do, the animal will think it's okay to bite and scratch you and won't understand that he can hurt you. So when playing games like "pounce on the prey," use a toy or a piece of cord. Save your hands for stroking and holding.

If your cat has developed a habit of clawing or biting at you, you can break it fairly easily by consistently following a method described by Anitra Frazier in her book *The New Natural Cat*.[3] If the claws are in you, relax and calmly disengage them by first pushing the cat's feet a bit forward. To get out of a bite grip, relax and press your arm or hand toward the teeth (which confuses the cat). Then put the cat away from you with a gentle but firm message of disapproval and disappointment. To underline the message, ignore her for several minutes. Don't even look at her. A few repetitions are usually all that is needed for a cat to learn that if she wants to play with you, it's not acceptable to claw and bite. Thereafter, she will respect your wishes.

The First Vet Visit

Regardless of whether you let your cat outdoors or keep it inside, you need to teach it to accept a carrier. A few days before your cat's first visit to the veterinarian, place an open carrier out in the house. Encourage the cat to view it as a fun place to explore. To entice him further, place a tidbit inside. Without this familiarity, you could have a battle on your hands trying to shove a resistant cat into a cage on your way out the door to the vet's.

To avoid more serious contact with cat teeth and claws, which are quite sharp, never try to hold on to a cat that wants to be free (unless you are trained in handling cats properly). Teach children this point, too. If you must restrain a cat to give it medicine, wrap it firmly in a towel or blanket. To transport it, use an animal carrier. (I know of more than one serious accident caused by a frightened cat bounding loose in a moving car.)

Cat Aggression

A few cats have a more deep-seated problem with aggression. I'm talking about cats that are completely, violently intolerant of all other cats, even their own adult offspring. And once in a while, I've treated cats that are pretty nasty to their caretakers, too. Over the years I've come to the conclusion that many of these problems are more rooted in the constitutional makeup of certain cats than in situations.

Chronic disease can also play a role in such behavior problems. In many cases, careful, individualized homeopathic treatment has helped. Cats that are unusually timid or aloof for no apparent reason have also responded to this treatment.

GOOD SANITATION: A BASIC NECESSITY

Sanitation is an important issue for both dogs and cats; it's right at the top of both the animal and human lists.

For puppies, the most painless housebreaking takes advantage of two things: a pup's natural cleanliness and the regularity of his bowels. Well-socialized pups go outside of their own den to soil. It's not reasonable to expect a young puppy to understand that your whole house is his den.

When mistakes are made in the house, a pup has usually run into another room (outside the den to him) to go. So set your pup up for success.

Feed him on a regular schedule and take him outside a few minutes after each meal and nap. When you put him outside to relieve himself, go with him to make sure that he goes. Praise him when he does. Afterward, let him run around a bit indoors. For the first few weeks you may need to restrict the area he can wander in, like the uncarpeted areas of the house, for easy cleanup—just in case.

If you have to work all day, you may need to have someone else come in to let him out, or else train him to use papers when he's young and then switch to outside only as he becomes able to hold his bowels longer. Don't expect a young pup to be able to go more than 4 to 6 hours at most without a pit stop. Do keep him confined to a small area while you're gone. For a young pup, this space should be at least the size of a large dog's kennel and no bigger than a very small kitchen.

Animals instinctively seek to relieve themselves away from their own living area, which is why the neighbor's yard is often a favorite bathroom. You can wean a dog away from this habit and save a major part of your own lawn, too, by teaching him to use just a certain portion of your yard, such as behind the garage or near certain shrubs. Place some of his stool there and take him to that spot when it's time for him to answer nature's call. When he uses the spot, praise him enthusiastically. Placing some kind of low border around the area can help to make its limits clear to him and to friends and family.

When you're walking your dog on stormy days or in cold weather, you naturally want him to do his business ASAP. Some people choose to associate command words like "hurry up" with the act of defecating or urinating. This may sound funny, but it can be very useful. On cold or rainy days, this command can actually encourage your dog to go.

To discourage defecation in certain areas of the yard or garden, promptly remove droppings from areas you don't want the dog to soil. If necessary, spray those areas with a dog-repelling deodorant made with natural ingredients like citron, lemon oil, eucalyptus, geranium oil, capsicum, and oil of lavender.

A lot of dogs do their business while walking about the neighborhood, and the more conscientious people will pick up the waste with a plastic bag over their hands. Unfortunately, this then goes into the trash. You can figure that plastic bag with dog poop in it will be there in the landfill 200 years from now, when archaeologists are studying this era.

A much better solution is to compost your dog's poop. You can buy devices like the Doggie Dooley pet waste disposal system. It works like a small compost tank, reducing the waste to a safe liquid that can be put in the ground, as a nice fertilizer. Much more ecological. Yes, you will have to transfer the waste from the plastic bag to the unit. Yes, you will have to wash out the bag and let it dry to use again. But isn't this well worth the effort? I think so.

For cats, it's usually a simpler matter. Just provide a full, clean box of litter. Cats prefer litter of a sandy, granular type. Keep it clean and keep it in the same place. Too much odor could put your cat off. Keep a clean litter box in your yard as well as in your house, and the cat will have something else to use besides Mrs. Jones's flower bed. Keep the boxes out of reach of toddlers and clean them regularly. Wash your hands well afterward, because cat feces can carry potentially harmful organisms. (This is a good practice to follow after a dog cleanup, too.)

THE DISEASE PROBLEM

Given that animals and people live together, we need to consider the unpleasant topic of disease transmission. It is fortunate that people are not susceptible to most of the infectious or contagious conditions animals experience, but there are exceptions. I have seen very, very few problems like this among my clients, so I don't want to give you the idea here that this is a common problem. Still, it seems we should talk about it, don't you think?

Most diseases picked up from cats and dogs fall into three groups, depending on their means of transmission—through feces or urine, skin and hair contact, or bites and scratches.

Let's consider each group individually.

Diseases Transmitted in Wastes

Roundworms *(Toxocara canis, Toxocara cati)*: The infectious form of these worms is their eggs, which can incubate for several weeks in the ground where an animal has defecated. If a child plays there and puts his dirty hands in his mouth, he can swallow the eggs and become infected. Thus, migrating animal roundworms are most often seen in toddlers. The disease is only rarely fatal. More commonly, it is mild and hardly noticeable, especially in adults. Children are more likely to be contaminated and will have more problems than adults. When children swallow these common parasites carried by dogs and cats, the parasites often migrate through the body tissues and cause damage, including liver enlargement and fever. These symptoms may last as long as a year. In some children the larvae may enter the eye and cause inflammation. This is serious business, since surgeons have been known to mistake the eye lesions for early cancer and unnecessarily remove an eye. There is also some research that suggests that some children may become allergic to the migrating parasites, which complicates the situation.

Hookworms (Cutaneous larva migrans): These parasites are similar to roundworms, but they enter the body differently. Instead of being swallowed, the hookworm larvae directly penetrate the skin where it comes in contact with feces-contaminated soil or sand—usually the bare feet. Though the parasites try their best, they are not really suited to living in people and eventually die after moving several inches under the skin. The inflammation is called "creeping eruption" and ends after several weeks or months. In the United States, it is most often seen in the South.

Leptospirosis: Swimming in or otherwise coming in contact with water contaminated with animal urine is the way this serious bacterial disease is usually acquired. Many animals can carry it, particularly rats. Pets can catch it by drinking contaminated surface water (or licking it off their fur) or by eating food on which rats have urinated. In humans the disease is similar to flu, with fever, headache, chills, tiredness, vomiting, and muscular aches. In addition, the eyes and the membranes covering the brain and spinal cord can be inflamed. In some cases, the liver and the kidneys are damaged. Few die from this condition, but it can make you miserably sick for 2 or 3 weeks.

Tapeworms (*Dipylidium caninum*): Tapeworms are a different type of worm, in that they cannot directly infect people with their eggs. Rather, the tapeworm larvae go into some other creature first, end up in the muscle tissue, and then infest the intestines when these animals—often fleas or gophers—are eaten.

Children can get tapeworms either by ingesting fleas while nuzzling the pet's fur or by being licked on the mouth by an animal with a flea on its tongue. Human infestation is rare, however, compared with infestations of other types of tapeworms we can get from eating undercooked, infected beef or pork. Only 16 cases of tapeworm infestation coming from a dog or cat have been reported in humans within the last 20 years, including those from Europe, China, Japan, India, Sudan, Latin America, and the United States. Almost all of the cases were found in children, and fortunately, most of the infections are without symptoms.[4]

Toxoplasmosis: Many people are exposed to this infectious disease through ordinary activity and develop a natural resistance to it. On rare occasions, however, it has killed adults. More often, it causes birth deformities in children born to women who were infected during preg-

nancy and had not previously developed immunity. It can be picked up by contact with feces from an infected cat or contact with contaminated soil. Also, the disease can come from eating raw or undercooked meat. Because the fetus of a pregnant woman can be very vulnerable, Toxoplasmosis is covered in more detail on page 444.

Prevention of Diseases Transmitted in Wastes

Besides cleaning up your pet's droppings, there are a few simple precautions you should take and should teach to your children.

Wash your hands after contact with soil where an animal may have relieved itself.

Avoid going barefoot in areas where an animal may have relieved itself, especially in the warmer climates, where hookworms flourish.

Remind children to wash their hands before eating and not to put their hands in their mouths while playing with animals or on potentially contaminated ground. Teach them all other precautions as well.

Give your dog a bath if it has gone swimming or wading in a pond or creek that could be harboring leptospirosis.

Diseases from Skin and Hair Contact

Fleas: Though fleas prefer feasting on pets, they will make a meal of people if the opportunity appears. Flea infestation is often at its worst in a house that was formerly occupied by an animal and then left vacant. Many young fleas, recently hatched, will be eager to eat and though they prefer their usual meal, they will dine on you if you are the only course on the menu.

Ringworm (*Microsporum canis*): Caused by a fungus that eats skin and hair, ringworm often shows up in humans as scaly, red areas. As the organism grows, it spreads outward in a circle, much as a ripple forms when a stone is dropped into a pond. In dogs, affected areas tend to be hairless, thickened, scabby, and irritated. They are typically disk-shaped and about an inch or more in diameter. But most ringworm transmitted by pets comes from cats, who tend to show very few observable symptoms (dogs can also carry the spores without showing visible signs). An infected cat may have hairless gray areas without inflammation or scabbing. Generally, the animal doesn't itch either. Children are more susceptible to ringworm than adults, though humans can get it at any age.

Rocky Mountain Spotted Fever (*Rickettsia rickettsii*): While usually not fatal to humans (it is commonly treated with antibiotics), this infectious disease can still make a person mighty sick. Starting suddenly with fever, headache, chills, and reddening of the eyes, it may last several weeks. In the eastern and central United States, the responsible organisms are carried by the dog tick (*Dermacentor variabilis*). In the West, they are borne by the wood tick (*Dermacentor andersoni*). Incidence of the disease has risen sharply in North America in recent times.

The most common means of contracting spotted fever is from a direct bite by an infected tick. Pets can readily transport these infected ticks into a house or yard, where people can later be bitten. (All the tick's young will carry the infection, too.) It also is possible to become infected while pulling a tick off your animal if the tick's body is crushed or its feces released. So it's safest to wear gloves when you remove ticks.

Scabies (sarcoptic mange): In dogs, this form of mange is less common than the demodectic ("red") mange. It does, however, occur in both dogs and cats and causes itching, irritation, and thickening of the skin. I can't remember ever seeing a case myself, but that may be a reflection of the part of the country I lived in. People can be infected by contact—usually from holding an afflicted animal close. The result is intense itching, especially at night, and in those areas that were most in contact with the animal (like the inside of the arm, the waist, chest, hands, and wrists). Though the animal mange mite can live in human skin, it cannot reproduce there. So eventually the problem ends on its own—lasting just a few weeks at most. If, however, reinfection occurs, then of course it can keep happening. Note that we humans have our own brand of scabies mites, which can cause us prolonged aggravation and is not self-limited like the dog scabies.

Prevention of Diseases from Skin and Hair Contact

A healthy animal is less likely to harbor parasites like fleas, ringworm, and mange mites. Under natural conditions, the animals living in nature may have parasites but, believe it or not, they don't really cause a problem most of the time. Where it becomes significant is when there is diminished health. Then the parasites thrive. You can think of it like this: The role of parasites in nature is to feed on sick and dying animals. Therefore, proper nutrition and overall care are important preventive measures. In addition, frequent grooming and inspection, along with herbal repellents, will catch most of these problems early. Be especially attentive when your animal has been in contact with other pets or is under stress from disease, emotional upset, or a stay in a kennel.

If your dog or cat seems healthy, you need not worry much about this, but if you want to take special care after close contact with her, wash your hands. Also, since stray hairs can carry active ringworm spores, too, keep the house clear of hairs if your animal is infected (or keep your pet confined outside in a pen or fenced yard until the problem is cured).

Avoid or minimize bodily contact with an animal with mange and do not let it sleep on your bedding, clothes, or towels.

Diseases Caused by Bites and Scratches

Cat scratch fever: After being scratched by a cat, some people develop a fever, malaise, and enlarged lymph nodes near the area of the scratch or bite. These symptoms usually occur 1 to 2 weeks after the injury. The condition is not serious or fatal, but it is uncomfortable and may be followed by complications. Nobody knows what causes it. A cat bite infected with the *Pasteurella multocida* bacteria looks similar and should be differentiated from cat scratch fever by your doctor.

Rabies: Everyone has heard of this disease and of its high fatality rate (close to 100 percent once the clinical signs appear). Fortunately, it is not common in the United States. Only one to three cases are reported annually. Thirty-four cases of human rabies have been diagnosed in the United States since 2003, out of which 10 were found to have been contracted outside of the United States and its territories.[5]

Transmitted through the saliva of a biting animal, the rabies virus travels from the bite area to the brain in a matter of days or weeks. There it causes severe tissue inflammation, with symptoms such as convulsions, hysteria, and frothing at the mouth. The most common sources of human exposure are skunks, foxes, raccoons, bats, and dogs, though theoretically almost any warm-blooded creature can acquire the disease and transmit it.

The animal with clinical signs of rabies shows peculiar or erratic behavior. For instance, a wild animal may uncharacteristically approach humans or be sluggish and unable to dodge a speeding car. A dog may show evidence of a personality change—acting friendlier than usual or hiding in dark places. Eventually, a staggering, glazed-eyed, aggressive condition may develop—the stereotype of the rabid dog.

Prevention of Diseases Caused by Bites and Scratches

The best way to prevent cat scratch fever is to be cautious when handling cats, as suggested earlier. Cats, however, are not always predictable and might turn on you suddenly if they become frightened or are ill. After a scratch or bite, encourage the wound to bleed for a minute or two to help flush it out. Then wash the wound well with soap and water and soak it in a hot solution of Epsom salts.

Alternate the hot soak with a soak in some cold (not ice cold) tap water, going back and forth several times to stimulate bloodflow and immune response. Do your final soak in the cool water.

Stray dogs or wild animals should never be handled unless you have special training or equipment to do so safely. If you see a dog or wild animal with symptoms resembling rabies, get away from it and phone an animal control agency or the police as soon as possible. One complication is that a dog can transmit rabies through a bite (or saliva-contaminated scratch) 3 days before any clinical signs appear. So if you're bitten by any stray or wild animal, get help, and try to follow the animal to learn where it lives so it can be caught and tested. The testing procedure for dogs begins by putting a live animal in quarantine for 10 days, during which time it is observed by a veterinarian. If rabies symptoms develop, the animal is killed and the brain sent to a lab for verification. If necessary, you might try to catch a small creature that bit you, like a bat or a skunk, using a bucket, tub, or dog carrier. If you must kill it, don't injure the head.

If you are bitten by an animal that's a stranger to you or by one you suspect might be rabid, follow the same procedure as for cat scratches and bites. Also, report to your doctor as soon as possible. Your chances of getting rabies are really very low. Dog bites account for less than 5 percent of the rabies cases in North America.

THE PET POPULATION PROBLEM

Finally, one of the most important ways to be a responsible pet caretaker is to ensure that your animal does not add to the burgeoning pet overpopulation problem.

Spaying your female pet will keep packs of males from invading your property every time she comes into heat, and neutering a male will reduce his desire to roam and fight, which your neighbors will appreciate. Moreover, that one simple procedure in a male cat will spare you years of trying to remove the offensive odor of tomcat urine from your house.

Why do people allow their pets to breed when there are already too many being born? They believe:

- Their children should witness the process.
- They can find homes for the litter, or they assume the local humane society will do the job.
- A spay or neuter operation costs money, can be painful, and holds possible adverse health effects if all does not go smoothly.
- Neutering a pet is unnatural and diminishes a pet's true self.
- It's easy and fun to make a little extra cash selling purebred offspring.

Yet when you consider the vast suffering that befalls unwanted, homeless dogs and cats, these reasons have little merit. For example, it is surely more important to teach children responsibility to animals in general than it is to bring more surplus pets into the world as "an experience" for the children. Humane societies cannot find homes for most of the animals they receive. And even if you could find homes for the animals you breed, how many pets will be kept? And how many offspring will they produce? If she and her descendants are allowed to breed freely, one female dog can be the source of thousands of animals in just 5 or 6 years. Cats are even more prolific. And assuming you are able to find good, responsible people to care for each puppy or kitten, consider that these people might otherwise have adopted animals that were destroyed for want of homes.

Anyone who can afford to provide decent care for a pet can also afford a spay or neuter operation. Many towns and cities have low-cost clinics. Ask your local humane society for information about these. The operation is painless, performed under anesthesia by skilled veterinarians, and involves very little risk. It not only prevents unwanted births and discourages straying and fighting among the animals, but it prevents health problems like cancers of the reproductive organs, stress and complications from breeding, and abscesses and injuries from mating. Contrary to popular belief, neutered pets do not automatically get fat. Because they may be less active, they may burn less energy. So the solution is just to feed less.

If you are extremely conscientious, the old-fashioned methods of animal birth control, the door and the leash, may work for a female dog. Lock her up securely inside your house during the 2- to 3-week period of her heat. Be prepared for the fact that male dogs for miles around are likely to gather on your doorstep—and smiling!

Confinement does not work for cats. They come into heat more often than dogs, they can be very vocal, and they are very persistent in trying to get out. They almost inevitably succeed at some point. You should also know that an unspayed female cat prevented from mating may develop hormonal imbalances from complications, cystic ovaries, or uterine problems caused by not completing the reproductive cycle.

The idea that keeping pets reproductively intact is best because it's "more natural" is very shortsighted. We don't live in a natural world. These are not animals out in the woods hunting for their food and being hunted, falling victim to disease and hardship, living as an integral part of a balanced ecosystem and being governed by a complex interplay of hormones, social systems, and territories that regulate their breeding. These are descendants of wild animals living in close company with us and with thousands of other animals in an entirely unnatural and overpopulated environment. A male wolf in the wild is exposed to the scent of females in heat only a few weeks out of the year. An intact male dog is bombarded by the same scent much more frequently. That's a long way from being natural or fair.

As for the profit incentive behind breeding pets, not only do such ventures often yield little financial return, but repeated breeding can cost you money if the female's

health breaks down. Most puppy mills, which add 2.5 million puppies to the glut of dogs born annually in this country, are actually small home businesses run by amateurs whose ignorance and carelessness in breeding are a direct cause of much of the rise in congenital and health problems in many breeds. Surely there must be a better way to earn a buck.

I can understand and appreciate people's desire to see their pets bear young. But, unlike most people, I have had direct exposure to the scope and everyday reality of the pet overpopulation problem. I worked for several years at a humane society clinic associated with an animal shelter, where I saw firsthand the tragic results of uncontrolled breeding. One walk into the refrigerator containing barrels of euthanized animals is enough to convince anyone of the needless suffering involved in uncontrolled animal reproduction.

The sheer numbers are staggering. Estimates are that 5 million to 12 million animals are euthanized each year in US shelters. The reality—in flesh and blood and not just as abstract statistics—is devastating. Each one looks at you, and each is capable of much love and potential. And most never leave that shelter alive. When everyone takes responsibility for pet overpopulation, we'll see an end to the suffering it causes. It's best for society and best for the animals.

CHAPTER 13

CONNECTIONS: EMOTIONS AND YOUR ANIMAL'S HEALTH

Jasmine Rose Peden is the picture of a happy, healthy dog, smiling at her loving person, James, after a romp by the river. She is treated with kindness and respect and has lots of time in nature. She is so well behaved that she is welcomed wherever she goes, even in a store. Not all animals have such lives, and unraveling the complex interplay of emotions that can play into chronic health issues is often the job of a veterinarian. I think of an early case in my own career, when I came face-to-face with a big hulk of a dog. He glared at me suspiciously as I carefully examined the foul-smelling, hairless patches that oozed bloody discharges on his back, underside, legs, and muzzle. As if to demonstrate just how bad it was, he jerked around and chewed violently on the base of his tail.

"Stop that, Bandy!" my client yelled sharply. Calming down, he explained, "The biting and chewing only make things worse, so I always make a point of scolding him."

"There are some particularly bad spots under his tail," his wife noted. Slowly, I started to raise his tail to look.

Hurling around, he snapped at me angrily, barely missing my hand. Pronouncing the exam complete, I sat down with the distraught couple to find out more about how this problem began.

"It happened pretty quickly," the woman began. "He had just a slight mange on his face when I got him as a puppy 3 years ago, but the real problem—chewing and licking all over himself—has gone on for about 6 months. The vet called it a flea allergy but didn't offer much for it. We took him to several vets. One called it 'hot spots.'"

He shaved the areas and gave Bandy antibiotics and cortisone, but "nothing really helped." Finally, he advised either putting Bandy to sleep or doing a bunch of pricey treatments that still might not work.

"Do you have any idea why it got bad 6 months ago?" I inquired. "Anything special happen around that time?"

"Well, all I can think of was that our baby was born a couple of months before it started. I didn't want Bandy to be around the baby—you know, worms and all that—and he was jealous he wasn't number one anymore. So we started keeping him outside. Maybe that affected him. I've had itchy skin myself for years, and I've never known why."

As we went on to discuss his irritability, she mentioned that she preferred an aggressive dog: She felt safer living in the country. Occasionally, the man would interject something. As he did, I sensed an underlying tension between the couple.

This case first prompted me to pay closer attention to emotional factors in pet illnesses. Through the years I have repeatedly observed several patterns similar to Bandy's:

• Pets may develop health problems soon after an upsetting change in the home, usually involving a loss of attention, of a relationship, or of territory.

• An animal's health can be affected by recurrent tension, anxiety, depression, anger, and other upsets in the family.

• People's attitudes and expectations about the illness or disturbance can have a pronounced effect on its outcome.

• Pet illnesses often mirror those of the primary person with whom they bond.

I have noticed these patterns particularly in pets with emotional and behavioral issues, but often with chronic physical problems as well. By paying special attention to emotional issues in the home, you can foster a more positive atmosphere that helps restore and maintain your animal's health.

PROBLEMS THAT START AFTER LOSSES

Many animals suffer from a loss of attention and/or territory when a baby or a new pet arrives in the home or when the family moves, especially to a small apartment or to an area with unfriendly neighboring animals. It can happen when a family member dies, leaves home, takes a time-consuming job, goes on a long vacation, or just loses interest. Sometimes the house is redecorated and the animal is no longer welcome inside.

Whatever the cause of the loss, it is often followed by a decline in the pet's health. In cases like Bandy's (banished outdoors after the baby was born), boredom and frustration may then worsen any preexisting tendency for skin irritations, leading to excess licking, scratching, and chewing. That, in turn, may aggravate what was only a slight weakness, creating more inflammation and irritation. Before long, a vicious cycle is well under way.

More mild-mannered animals may respond with lethargy and apathy. This inactivity and disinterest, in turn, lowers the strength of the immune system and makes them more susceptible to illness.

Some pets may become stressed by territorial conflicts with new animals. If the disputes are not resolved, the constant stress can wreak havoc, setting up fertile ground for health problems.

Sometimes people unintentionally reinforce such problems. Say your dog feels lonely because you went back to work and you have less time for him. Soon he develops a minor symptom—a cough—that worries you. So, every time he coughs, you rush over, pet him, and murmur comforting words. (This sounds a bit like dog training, no?) Pretty soon he gets the idea that, every time he coughs, he gets your loving attention. What is his incentive to get well and stop coughing? Even if you were to scold him (as Bandy's person did for scratching), he could prefer negative attention to complete neglect.

I have to smile when I think of another unintentional reinforcement. Sometimes when we are out on a walk, a dog starts barking vigorously, and then its person comes out and yells at him. It goes like this.

Dog: "Woof!"
Person: "Stop!"
Dog: "Woof!"
Person: "Stop!"

The dog might see the person as *joining* him, yelling along in territorial defense. In any case, it rarely works.

Attention-seeking scenarios are most likely to express as coughing, limping, or scratching: actions over which the animal has some control. Veterinarian Herbert Tanzer, author of *Your Pet Isn't Sick (He Just Wants You to Think So)* found that teaching people to stop coddling pets in response to a symptom, while coddling them more at other times, would resolve many irksome cases that seemed to have no physical cause.

WHAT TO DO

- **Watch for any changes** in your pet's psyche that might be the result of new household schedules or a family crisis. Animals are individuals, just like people, and some require more attention, social bonding, territory, and routine than others.

- **Try to see altered situations** at home from your animal's perspective, and use your common sense to ease the situation. Perhaps you simply need to spend special one-on-one time with each animal. Maybe a German shepherd needs daily walks, while just holding and petting a Siamese may be all she needs.

- **Consider confining a new pet** to limited space until the "senior" one accepts the newcomer. With animals that are particularly hostile or territorial toward others (often cats), you might have to remain a one-animal family. But highly sociable animals, especially dogs that have just lost a dear companion, may respond well to a new friend, particularly an easygoing one of the opposite sex.

- Sometimes the best resolution may be to **find your animal a more suitable home** than you can now provide. That is a loving choice. Or it may just allow Rover back on his favorite chair, protecting your new upholstery with a blanket.

- **Resist the temptation to baby or fuss** over him whenever he limps, coughs, or scratches. Instead, pet and play with him more when he's behaving normally.

- And, of course, **take him to the vet** for a professional evaluation and give him whatever physical care he may need.

THE EMOTIONAL CLIMATE

Apart from these more circumstantial situations, animals are also affected by our ongoing feelings and states of mind, particularly those of the people with whom they are most bonded. Most dogs and cats form a strong emotional connection with the people they depend on for food, shelter, safety, and affection. That's why they so readily tune in to our emotional cues.

Except perhaps for a few brief verbal commands or names, animals rely completely on the emotional messages communicated by our posture, tone of voice, facial expressions, and, well, just plain feelings in the air, which are like an emotional climate that may be generally sunny or cloudy, mild or extreme. Shorter-term feelings are more like today's weather.

Smell is a primary sense for dogs and cats. Just as we might detect a subtle smell in the air when rain is on the way, they can easily detect stress chemicals your body emits when you are upset. It tells them something is wrong but they may not understand why. Say you are feeling anxious and you are broadcasting some level of fear. They sense there is something to be afraid of, but what?

Imagine yourself in that situation. The same thing happens to us as young children. Say your parents are anxious, whether or not it's warranted. It's like they are saying, "Watch out, there is something bad coming!" Wouldn't you be looking for it all the time? Get a little jumpy?

That is what happens for animals. They don't know that you were just unfriended on Facebook. They may imagine there is a dangerous predator or intruder out there. So if a random pedestrian strolls by (like me?), they run out and bark their heads off. They sense there is danger afoot and their job is to protect your home.

In the same way, dogs and cats often soak up angry, sad, or fearful feelings from family members upset over issues that have nothing to do with them. Frequent arguments are especially stressful for animals, who may react with irritability or fear. Emotional tensions can trigger issues that have a behavioral component, such as increased aggressiveness, destructiveness, or extreme restlessness. Or, they might impact the nervous system and contribute to irritated skin, ears, bladder, and the like.

Just like animals suffering from losses and changes, a chronically emotionally stressed animal who has a predisposition to skin or bladder problems, for example, might scratch or urinate still more. This in turn will further irritate the tissues and create a vicious cycle. Whatever discomfort is already there becomes more noticeable and annoying when the emotional pitch is heightened.

ANXIETY ABOUT THE ANIMAL

Sometimes the anxiety a person broadcasts is actually about the animal herself. Say you become upset on seeing something about your dog or cat that does not seem right. Whether it's a behavioral change or a physical symptom, your mind launches into a whole imagined scenario—the terrible diagnosis, the ineffective treatment, the euthanasia, the loss of your friend.

Your animal senses this anxiety, particularly when it is directed toward her. Something *must* be wrong! Your fears only increase her own anxiety, which may already be heightened by the discomfort of any developing illness. She may even begin to hide.

Not only will fear and stress from this danger signal diminish your animal's capacity to heal, but they can also impact effective treatment. Clients have often told me that, acting from fear or a sense of urgency, they made decisions that they later regretted. For example, when animals get tumors or cancers, clients often feel under tremendous pressure to have the growths immediately removed, as though every passing hour were critical. But there is no evidence to support such urgency. In fact, the stress of the surgery can make the animal even more difficult to treat using less drastic and more natural methods.

Similarly, concern about a bout of intense scratching from skin allergies can drive clients to get corticosteroids and undo several weeks of progress from nutritional and homeopathic treatment.

True healing of chronic disease requires, above all, patience. The desire for immediate relief is very seductive. That's the appeal of using strong drugs to control symptoms. But, since they don't actually cure the underlying ailment, the illness recurs, gradually worsening over time or taking a different and more difficult form.

Excessive anxiety can also push people to jump from one veterinarian or treatment to the next, whether conventional or holistic. This can overwhelm and confuse your pet's body, never allowing any one method a chance to work. On the flip side, worry and discouragement can lead people to give up on medical treatment without really trying.

I know this is a challenge. Understandably, you don't want to stay with a treatment that is not working, yet you don't want to jump ship before giving it a chance. The best advice I can give is the understanding that true healing of the body takes time. It took time to get where it is, and it will take time to undo the damage.

SHARED ILLNESSES?

Even our own illness may impact our pet's health in ways we don't quite understand.

Veterinarians often see cases in which pets develop the same problems as the people they live with, at a frequency seemingly beyond coincidence.

Why would this be? It could, of course, indicate a common toxin or other agent in the home environment. But it's also possible that the strong bond between some pets and people can create a kind of sympathetic resonance, akin to "catching" a yawn or the urge to scratch from someone nearby.

Many experiments and anecdotes attest to a mysterious, seemingly extrasensory connection between animals and people. So it is not surprising that the same health problem is often shared between a person and an animal. If you see this happening with you and your animal, it's worth contemplating, perhaps even exploring any underlying psychological beliefs and emotions that may accompany your own condition. That is often helpful in human health and could radiate out to help heal your animals as well.

There is much we still need to learn. Yet, as many now understand, the intention to be well, along with faith in the healing capacity of nature, life, the universe, God—however you conceive of that—are central to all healing.

THE POSITIVE SIDE

Conversely, your calm, positive response to a pet's first symptoms relaxes and reassures the animal, helping to strengthen its immune response. All else being equal, I have observed time and time again that the animals likeliest to recover from chronic and difficult illnesses are those that live with people who manage to be calm and maintain a positive outlook. While it may be difficult to find calm in the face of suffering, it's the best thing you can do for your animal.

How can you do this? There is not one answer. I think it must be necessary to first acknowledge the anxiety that is there. I have suggested this at times, to sit with the animal, relax as best one can, and just be open mentally to what comes up. If the thoughts of fear are there, just consider them rationally. Is that true? Is it inevitable? Are there options? Just the looking at it, working through it as something to understand or deal with, often removes much of the emotion. If it is possible to come to a calm state while sitting with the animal, I am sure it will do good.

Inner Calm

For finding that inner calm, a regular practice of meditation is very helpful. By "meditation" I mean, really, simply taking time to just sit in silence, alert and present. There are different techniques to help still the wandering mind, but, in my experience, the essence of meditation is simply to sit with the essence of what we each are: pure consciousness, the being behind all the thoughts in which we get so involved. Susan and I take time to sit quietly each day, and it's a real benefit. Animals will sense the stillness and calm as well, and have their own ways of

meditating. Cats especially enjoy sitting on the lap of someone in meditation.

Encouragement

Sometimes, in conversation with a client, I am prompted to suggest that she talk to her animal, share her feelings and thoughts with him in that calm state. I am not really thinking the dog or cat will understand all the words like we do, but I do believe it will receive a communication. I ask the client to tell the animal that he is becoming well, even to promise some special treat if he does. She can propose taking three walks a day instead of two, extra trips to the dog park, extra play time, whatever she thinks the pet might like.

When you take a pet into the family, he often ceases to be "just an animal." Instead, he becomes a distinct personality, Charlie, who likes kids but not the mailman, who loves the old chair in the corner and who always sizes up people correctly. Suddenly, your attitude toward the animal changes. He's no longer a "dumb beast," but an intelligent, unique individual. And when you begin to hold your animal friend in high regard, and sometimes see life from his point of view, a strange and wonderful form of communication can grow.

A PSYCHIC CONNECTION

Animals and humans often seem to develop a psychic or telepathic sensitivity to each other, which I've seen in my practice. Not only have I met several people who are certain their pets have this ability, but several writers have described this kind of communication in detail.

The sensitivity they describe encompasses not only a responsiveness to cues that can be picked up by the five senses, but also to those that are intangible.

Biologist Rupert Sheldrake has carefully tested this phenomenon, described in his book, *Dogs That Know When Their Owners Are Coming Home.* By using video recordings in the home and at the person's workplace, he was able to show that at the exact moment the person decided to head home, his dog would suddenly get excited, go to the window, and look out with anticipation, for example. It is quite an amazing exploration, and it was not just dogs who did this but also cats, rabbits, guinea pigs, parrots, and other domestic animals. They were obviously in tune. See his YouTube interview, "Rupert Sheldrake—Dogs Who Know When Their Owners Are Coming Home."

We first became interested in this deeper mental bond after reading books by J. Allen Boone, who made human-animal communication his lifework. He first became aware of the psychic sensitivities of animals while caring for an intelligent movie star dog named Strongheart, described in *Kinship with All Life.* Strongheart was expert at detecting dishonesty in people and at anticipating Boone's thoughts and plans—such as his intent to go for a walk, even when in another room—and many other ways of transmitting and receiving complex communications.

Boone discovered, by careful study and intent, he could create a two-way channel of communication with animals of many species. As his work developed, he concluded that animals often behave as we expect.

If you think a housefly is nothing but a pest, then it will act like a pest. But suppose you honor the housefly as an expression of the same universal source as people. Suppose you admire it—say, for its ability to fly, or for the delicacy of its body. How might a common housefly then behave? For Boone, the housefly became "Freddie," who came when silently called, and who, when requested, refrained from walking on his bare skin.

Inspired by Boone, one day while we were enjoying some ice cream with our son, Susan placed a small drop of it in front of a tiny spider crawling on the tabletop. "Here," she said, thinking of him as a welcome guest, "would you like some?" Amazingly, he sucked it dry. Further intrigued, she placed a drop of water before him: "Would you like to wash up?" To our amazement, he did just that, stroking his little legs clean. Finally, she offered him a napkin to wipe himself dry. And that he did. We were all dumbfounded. I have since developed a lifelong habit of taking house spiders outside, usually in my bare hands, and I always enjoy saying hello to "Petey," the tarantula who has lived in our irrigation box for several years, who moves aside so I can work on the valves.

One time while trying to rid a garden of a gopher that was pulling down her young broccoli plants, Susan finally resorted to flooding the gopher run with water. A minute later, she heard some rustling in the shrubbery on the border.

"I know you're there," she offered, somewhat apologetically. "How about you come out and we have a talk?" A soggy, bedraggled gopher emerged from the shadows, sat up, and looked at her. "Yes?" he seemed to say. She then explained why she had done this, as Boone had modeled in his conversations with kitchen ants. "How about you live more in that field next door" she requested respectfully, "and I won't do this again." There was no more gopher damage after that.

In recent years we live where coyotes, javelina, and other larger wildlife also dwell not far from our neighborhood on the edge of town. We see them occasionally, not every day. Quite a few times, however, they have appeared just as we were telling someone about them, and sometimes even as we were describing how they appear almost magically. Another time, a neighbor was telling us how her insurance plan was with Celestial Insurance (meaning, she trusted the universe and had none officially) and a coyote appeared out of nowhere in the hot noontime sun—seemingly confirming her choice.

Likewise, the Internet is full of amazing videos of animals befriending and helping each other in the most unlikely ways, cat and bird friendships and the like. I love to see these. A recent favorite is a Canadian goose boldly approaching a Cincinnati policeman on duty, pecking at his car, and urging him to follow her into a nearby park where one of her goslings was tangled up in a balloon string, which his associate carefully untied.

What all this teaches us is that, whatever our species, we are all connected, at our deepest level sharing one consciousness.

MY ADVICE

Learn to have faith in the power of healing. Life always seeks to right itself—to close a wound, to lift up our spirits. A big thing I had to learn, in my path from veterinary school education to the outlook I have now, was to develop a confidence in the tremendous power the body has for healing. I did not realize it, and am still amazed at some of the recoveries that happen if I just give a little support to that innate power.

CHAPTER 14

TIPS FOR SPECIAL SITUATIONS

Every now and then you read the true-life story of a remarkable pet. Perhaps it's about a cat that survives without food or water for a month after being trapped accidentally in a transcontinental delivery truck. Or a tale of the family dog that gets lost during a cross-country move and somehow tracks down its home, hundreds of miles away. Such stories of resourcefulness and devotion are both inspiring and amazing.

Everyday life poses special challenges for animals living in a human world. Let's look at some of these situations and see what we can do to make it easier for our animal friends.

VACATIONS AND TRAVEL

For many of us, travel is part of day-to-day living. Sometimes it's just an overnight business or a weekend fun trip; sometimes it's a month-long vacation. Whether your four-legged friend travels with you or stays at home, you need to give some thought to your pet's special needs at such times.

There are two options here, one being to take the animal with you, usually by car or airline, or leave him at home with someone caring for him.

If you and your pet have a close bond, the animal could grieve during an absence that lasts several days or more, unaware that you plan to return soon. A long absence can sometimes lead to such an emotional upset, and this certainly can be a stress for them.

A deeply concerned woman wrote me this letter.

My dog, Lassie, will soon be 18. We've had family troubles including several deaths in these last 2 years, and now my husband and I are planning a 10-day cruise which we believe is necessary for our own health. But we will have to leave Lassie in a kennel. I read in a book that if you leave an old dog in a kennel, it might not last until you return. This has troubled us terribly, as Lassie is so accustomed to our care. Do you have any suggestions on how to care for our wonderful mutt, who has served us so well?

I sympathize with their plight. Not only would Lassie miss her human companions at a kennel, but she would be confined in a strange and perhaps uncomfortable run or cage, surrounded by barking and whining animals that might disturb her rest. She might not accept the unfamiliar food offered her; while in that stressed and weakened state, she could be susceptible to such diseases as "kennel cough," a contagious respiratory ailment (common where groups of dogs are housed). Even some younger animals do poorly during kennel stays. On the other hand, people do need to get away sometimes, and they can't always take a pet along.

THE KENNEL OPTION

Though it would not be my first choice, many an animal may be successfully placed in a kennel, if it is responsibly run and if the stay is not too long. You should definitely check out the facility in person before committing your animal to it. Look for such things as the degree of privacy provided (each animal should have a place to rest quietly), the sanitation, the noise level, and the availability of sunlight, exercise space, fresh air, water, decent food, and medical care, should the need arise.

One of the greatest drawbacks of a kennel stay is the standard requirement that the dog or cat be vaccinated beforehand. Vaccines are often overused and can cause persistent health problems, especially in older animals. If your dog was vaccinated when young, there is no need to vaccinate again for the life of your animal (the exception is the rabies vaccination; though it is likely not necessary that it be repeated so often, it is controlled by community laws protecting people, not animals). Even though there is no scientific justification for vaccinating before going into a kennel, and some studies have even shown increased susceptibility to kennel cough in those dogs that have been vaccinated, many operators of kennels still make it a requirement. In my opinion, they should leave this decision to the veterinarian and not have a policy that applies to all. Nonetheless, this is often what you will run into.

My advice is not to vaccinate because they say so, as excessive vaccines themselves can lead to unpleasant health consequences (see Chapter 16). This is especially the case if your animal is weak, old, or sickly. If you are lucky, you can just state that you don't want your pet excessively vaccinated and the kennel owner will go along with it. The other possibility is getting a letter from your vet that your dog or cat should not be vaccinated because of existing health problems. It is interesting that vaccines come to the veterinarian with an enclosed leaflet saying the vaccine is to be used *only* in healthy animals. I know, this is often ignored, and strangely, some animals with chronic diseases like allergies or thyroid problems or arthritis will be declared healthy by veterinarians. I guess it depends on what your definition of health is. If you have a sympathetic veterinarian, however, you can get a letter that exempts your animal from vaccinations. Will it work? Sometimes. Worth a try.

THE HOME CARE OPTION

Another alternative is to try in-home care. This is also a good choice if you are planning a long absence or if you simply want to provide a better alternative to the kennel experience. We have used a house sitter— either a friend or a family member—with success. We have been fortunate in finding someone who needs a place to stay and trading the use of our home for their taking care of our pets and plants. No such person in your life? Ask a veterinarian, breeder, or local pet store staff to recommend a professional pet sitter who will stop by once or twice a day to feed, groom, pet, and exercise your animal, and bring in the mail and water the plants, too. Twice a day is better for your pet (and we have used that schedule ourselves), but I realize cost is a factor. If someone is coming to your home, make sure she is insured and bonded as well. Most are. I have had very good luck with this type of service.

If you can't get any leads from professionals, you might seek out teenagers who want a summer job, students in an animal health technician program, or humane society volunteers. A close friend, neighbor, or relative who already knows and likes the animal might even take pleasure in providing the care you want for your pet while you're away. In such cases it might also work out for a friendly and well-behaved dog to stay at the sitter's residence. In contrast to dogs, cats are generally less stressed by being left alone, as long as they're on their own turf.

Here are some pointers on how to make the whole process go smoothly.

Introduce the sitter to your pet before you leave. Professional pet sitters like to meet the pet before you leave and make sure they understand its routine. Do what you can to encourage your pet to be friendly with this new person. You could even arrange for the sitter to spend some time with your animal—perhaps going for a walk, playing, or holding it quietly for a while. Such preparations alleviate much of the stress and concern for you and are particularly good for an old or easily excitable pet.

Make certain the sitter you hire can and will provide adequate food, water, exercise, and attention. If you are using a home-prepared diet, make some food up ahead of time and, if it's a long trip, freeze it in convenient packages for the sitter to thaw and use. The feeding of your home-prepared food is very important to clarify with your sitter. The most common complaint I have heard is that the sitter, while doing a good job in most respects, does not follow directions on feeding, so that people arrive home to find all their carefully planned meals still in the freezer. I don't know why this is, but it is something you should emphasize in your instructions.

Leave money and necessary instructions for taking the animal to the vet in case of an illness or an emergency. Provide phone numbers where you or a close relative can be reached during your trip.

If you anticipate any emotional upset with your animal, the Dr. Bach Rescue Remedy formula is a nice option (see Chapter 17). Have the sitter add it to the water dish—four drops each time the bowl is filled.

When you say goodbye to your pet, do so with a calm demeanor and untroubled mind. Since animals readily pick up people's feelings, you might start things off on the wrong note if you are nervous or upset when you leave. It may even help to look the animal in the eye and visualize a happy reunion scene. Once you are gone, don't cause yourself needless worry and anxiety. You did what you could.

TIPS FOR TRAVELING TOGETHER

What about taking a pet along on a vacation?

People find that many dogs and some cats (primarily the Siamese and Siamese-related breeds) can be excellent traveling companions if they are basically well behaved and psychologically and physically healthy. However, certain precautions and considerations are basic.

Make sure your pet is wearing a current ID. Should you get parted, you need some way for the finder to reach you. The best type of ID is a waterproof identification "barrel" tag in which you can enclose a small piece of paper that says, "If lost, please call [insert your info] collect." Give your cell phone number, the phone number of a friend or relative who is willing to take messages, or the number of the place where you are staying. These tags are difficult to find, but very practical.

Use a microchip. Common these days, a microchip is a small electronic device (about the size of a couple of grains of rice) that is injected with a syringe and needle under the skin at the back of the neck. Once in, it sits there quietly until a scanner comes along that can read the information encoded in it. Microchips do not give off radiation or signals on their own. Many people have asked me about health effects, and I have not really come to an opinion about them. I have never seen a recognizable problem in the animals I have worked with, and I don't see why there would be one unless for some reason the material itself causes an irritation in the tissues (which I have not heard of). I leave it up to you. I have read that the usual tags on collars are generally more successful in connecting dogs and cats to people than are the microchips, but that may change with time.

Auto Travel

On long road trips, give your pet daily exercise. For traveling dogs, at least half an hour of a vigorous game of fetch or a jog with you is important. If you like to let your dog run loose, do so only in a safe and appropriate area and, even then, only if the dog is well trained to return on command.

Cats should wear a harness attached to a leash. Car rides and strange places are more upsetting to a cat than to a dog, and felines might bolt. Cats do well in a comfortably sized crate that can also hold a little litter pan. You can put a disposable diaper under the pan in case of any spills during the ride.

Never leave your pet in a sealed car on a hot day. Heat can build up very fast in a closed car, which acts like a solar oven, causing an animal to go into heat prostration. This may lead to serious brain injury and even death. See Handling Emergencies and Giving First Aid on page 460 for first-aid treatment, should this problem ever occur.

Take familiar items with you. A basket or piece of bedding from home can make any animal feel safer and more at ease. You could also take favorite toys to give your pet something to do.

Use commercial pet health foods for convenience, if necessary. Ease into using them a couple of days before your trip to make sure all goes smoothly.

Anticipate nature's calls. For a cat, a litter box is basic gear for a road trip. Prefilled disposable ones for traveling are now available at pet supply stores. Take a dog on a short stroll on a leash at least twice a day. Carry disposable bags and a scooper to use at public parks, cities, motel properties, and beaches.

Prepare for health problems that are common to most travelers. Constipation can plague traveling pets. It can be caused by lack of exercise or water, infrequent stops, or anxiety about strange new territories. Temporary constipation is not a serious problem and will usually clear up before long. For a dog, you can prepare a useful preventive with figs and prunes, as well as fresh berries or other fruits in season. Bran or psyllium husks are also helpful. If your animal does get constipation, the homeopathic remedy *Nux vomica 6c* is very helpful. Usually one dose is enough (see Constipation on page 355).

Nausea grips some animals when they ride in a car or plane, and they will either vomit or salivate excessively. This happens more with dogs than cats. If they are loose in the car, encourage your pet to lie down on the floor of the car as a preventive. If motion sickness does occur, give your dog some *peppermint* tea or peppermint capsules to help settle her stomach (not so well tolerated by cats).

Another useful herb is *ginger*, readily available in markets. Before your trip (if by car), you can make up a tea by cutting up about a tablespoon of fresh ginger, slicing it into small pieces, and then soaking it overnight in water. During your travel, you can give your dog or cat some for the nausea—it works well. Amount? Probably about ½ teaspoon for a cat (2 to 3 milliliters if you are using a syringe) and 1 teaspoon to 1 tablespoon for a dog, depending on size.

A third choice, again to make up ahead of time, is a formula made from the 38 flower remedy preparations discovered by Dr. Edward Bach (see Chapter 17). Mix together Aspen, Elm, *Scleranthus*, and Vervain and give two drops of this formula every 2 hours to relieve your pet's emotional upset and subsequent nausea.

It may be wise to fast a susceptible pet the day before departure or on the first day of the trip. For an animal going by public transit in a carrier, a 12- to 24-hour fast before the trip will generally prevent it from eliminating during the journey.

If you have traveled with your animal before, and you know he gets really upset and fearful, a wonderful treatment is the use of the homeopathic remedy *Aconitum napellus 30c*. It really reduces fear. You will see a noticeable difference. Give one pellet of this medicine an hour before leaving home; give another pellet just a few minutes before actually leaving the house. This usually is enough for most animals and most trips. If nervousness returns, give your pet another dose (one pellet) during the trip itself. Rarely will this remedy be needed more than three or four times; in fact, most animals travel well with just the two doses given before leaving home. This medicine is very safe to use and often functions better than a tranquilizer.

Eye irritation may occur in a dog that likes to ride with its head out the window, testing all the interesting scents it passes. Sometimes dust and debris enter the dog's eyes at high speeds, scratching the cornea and irritating sensitive membranes. For a minor irritation, I suggest washing the eyes out with this mild saline solution quite similar to tears: Add a level ¼ teaspoon of sea salt to 1 cup of pure water and stir. Keep the solution at room temperature; pour a small amount into a cup or dish and apply it by dripping it from a saturated cotton ball into the eye or by using a glass or plastic dropper. Administer the liquid until it runs out of the eye to flush out irritating substances.

For more serious irritations, use a cup of the same saline solution and add five drops only of tincture (or alcoholic extract) of the herb *Euphrasia officinalis*, or eyebright. Use this solution in the eye four times a day.

If your pet has a serious corneal injury, the animal will keep its eye shut most of the time. In such a case, seek veterinary help. (See also Corneal Ulcers on page 357.)

When you stop for the night, respect motel and campground properties. You and your pet, as well as those that come later, are much more apt to be welcome if you assure the management that you will:

• Never leave a dog alone in a motel room while you go out for an extended period (which may lead to barking and chewing).

• Have a bag and scooper with you and clean up any messes, inside or out.

• Only bring a neutered or spayed pet. This discourages wandering and territory marking.

• Keep the pet on a leash at all times, so it doesn't charge through tender flower beds or bother other guests.

These guidelines help make you welcome with your pet when visiting people's homes, too.

Airline Travel

Do not take an unhealthy pet on an airline. If you do take a pet on a flight, make sure that the animal won't be exposed to extreme temperatures or possible suffocation while in the cargo compartment. Shorter flights generally pose less of a problem.

Many airlines, however, allow you to take a small dog or cat with you in the passenger compartment. On takeoffs and landings, they must be in a small carrier put under the seat, but during the flight you can have the carrier in your lap. You can't take the animal out of the carrier, which is a little awkward, but some soft carriers allow you to sort of touch your pet through them. There is also a limit as to how many dogs can be on a flight. When you book your flight, inquire if any other animals are already boarding. This may well keep you from being bumped off at the last minute. There are online sites that can give you very detailed information on this.[1]

Similar rules apply for larger dogs. You provide the hard plastic or metal container or crate for travel in the cargo hold, and it must have at least three well-ventilated sides. Most airlines will only allow two large dogs to ride in cargo on a flight, so confirm with the airline that your dog will be traveling with you on the same airplane when you book. It is mandatory to label the crate with identification and contact information. Add a number to call if for some reason you can't be reached. Attach this identification so that it cannot be lost during travel. You can also put in feeding instructions and any medical requirements—just in case there is a delay in the two of you getting back together.

Either way, before you're allowed to board, you will need to show certification of your pet's health from a veterinarian. This is required for public transportation, interstate shipment, and foreign travel. I do not advise taking your pet if your destination is a country that has a lengthy required quarantine time or any special health hazards. Check on the destination country's requirements before making your plans.

Generally, try to use nonstop flights and avoid layovers, which require unloading and loading again. It is scary enough to be on a flight, much less to experience the hustle and bustle of being cargo. Realize, too, that there won't be the same temperature control in the cargo section, so there will be further stress for your pet. Because of possible temperature extremes, some airlines will not fly pets in cargo in certain months. Check ahead. It is also very helpful to have water available to give as soon as you arrive.

I have had clients traveling by air with their animals use the same treatment with the homeopathic remedy, *Aconitum napellus 30c*, that I mentioned above for car travel. Very useful. You will give the first treatment before leaving home, a second one before boarding the plane, and a third (if necessary) at any layovers (see Chapter 17).

THE MOVE TO A NEW HOME

Besides our round-trip vacations, every year many Americans make a significant one-way trip: moving to a new residence. This means an awful lot of animals have to pull up their roots, dealing once more with the stress of getting used to and claiming a new territory, as well as adjusting to new neighborhood challenges.

These relocations can easily disorient animals, so they run off, get lost, and can't find their way back. So make sure your pet is under your control at all times while the move is in progress. During the hustle and bustle of packing and unpacking, confine the animal to a quiet room, perhaps the bathroom, laundry room, or (for dogs only) a securely fenced yard.

During this time, provide your pet with **some familiar items for reassurance,** such as its bed, some toys, or a favorite rug. Why the excessive precautions? Because this is a time when pets get lost—people are coming and going, leaving doors open, scaring the animals with their noise. Cats will try to hide and end up inside a crate or furniture in the moving truck. One cat I know about spent 2 months inside a sofa bed before being found. It was skinny, but it lived.

Some unlucky pets are simply left behind when people move. This usually means slow and painful starvation, illness, bewilderment, or (if they're lucky) a quicker death by euthanasia in an animal shelter. Others may be foisted off onto a reluctant new caretaker. For example, friends bought a house from a woman who moved back to France. When they moved into their new house, there were two abandoned cats waiting for them and a note saying they would be cursed if they did not take care of them. I suppose this was her way of transferring responsibility!

Pets forced to switch allegiances too many times can develop insecure personalities and behavior problems that make them undesirable to anyone. For the same psychological reasons, a high turnover of family members (through such events as divorce, marriage, birth, death, and children leaving home) can also be stressful to an animal's sense of security. Try to give your pet as much attention as possible during times of change or upheaval.

REMODELING

A common problem time is remodeling the home. It is enough upset for you, living there, but it is also disorientating and confusing for your dog or cat. They can escape due to workers leaving the doors open or get trapped inside the construction. Patti Howard, a sometimes pet sitter in Washington, DC, tells me of the family that went to Hawaii for 3 weeks while construction was going on in their house (an attractive idea). Unfortunately, they did not arrange a comparable vacation for their pets. The sitter came in to feed the cats and could not find one because the bathroom contractors had walled her into the newly tiled bathroom. One of the cats' lives was saved by the diligent sitter searching and searching until he heard the muffled "meow" behind the wall. It took a hammer and screwdriver to break through the tile and rescue the cat. Another cat ended up stranded on the rooftop, having reached it through a temporary hole during the remodeling.

THE ADOPTION OPTION

Unfortunately, even the most loving people sometimes find they cannot keep a pet because of housing problems, allergies, animal incompatibility, or other situations that make dealing with animal care an impossibility. If so, follow the humane society guidelines (below) to help find your pet a good home. These guidelines also apply to placing a litter of puppies or kittens.

Begin your search for a good adoptive home by advertising through the local paper and posting notices. Run newspaper ads several times to ensure wide coverage. List the animal's qualities (such as "Loves kids, healthy, quiet, house-trained and affectionate") and state simply that it needs a home. Post photocopied notices (preferably with an appealing picture of the animal) where responsible people might see them—in community centers, health food stores, doctors' and veterinarians' offices, churches, senior citizen centers, and employee lunchrooms.

Many local rescue groups now have websites that post pictures of animals needing homes. They might help you out. There are also breed-specific rescue groups that find new home matches across state lines. E-mail is a great tool as well.

Be aware that if you advertise that you're giving away a pet "for free," you might attract people who would neglect or mistreat it or sell it to a lab. Unfortunately, such things do happen to pets given away indiscriminately.

When someone calls to express interest, take your pet to his home so you can check it out for yourself. This may ease the transition for your pet also. Ask yourself the following questions.

- Does the house have a safe, fenced yard of adequate size?
- Is there a dangerous highway nearby?
- Will the pet be left alone too much?
- Does the interested party appreciate the basics of responsible pet care?

- Does anyone in the family oppose the adoption?
- Is anyone in the family allergic to animals?
- Is the potential caretaker apt to move around a lot?
- What happened to any former pets? (Beware of people who have gone through a series of pets that were lost, hit by cars, or given away; this will likely be the fate of yours as well.)

If you find it difficult to ask these kinds of questions, remember that a responsible pet care person-to-be will appreciate your concern for your animal.

Though it may be difficult and even sad to place your old friend in a new home, you will feel best in the long run if you take the time and care to do the job well. Some time later you may return to find everyone pleased with the new relationship.

Lost Pets

The danger of losing a pet is not limited to moves and vacations. The possibility is ever present. By tagging your pet with proper ID and licenses and keeping it under your supervision, you greatly reduce its chances of being lost or stolen. Despite the most thoughtful precautions, however, animals sometimes still get lost. Here's what to do if your pet is missing.

Visit your local animal shelter. Go in person every day for a week or more after the disappearance. Most such organizations try to find you, but if a pet is unlicensed or not carrying identification, connecting that animal to you is almost impossible. In any case, the burden of responsibility is really yours. Visit all appropriate kennels, asking to see any quarantine, isolation, holding, and receiving rooms. Call out your pet's name as you go. Giving kennels or shelters a brief description over the phone is inadequate, since only you know your pet for sure. Many shelters are busy places and it is not unusual for the staff to be overworked and unable to remember all the animals there.

While at the shelters, be sure to fill out a lost pet report, providing photos, if possible, as well as noting any unique markings. Also, check out reports of found pets. To prevent possible euthanasia, people who find lost pets often keep them at their homes and just file reports with the local shelter or humane society. I once reunited a dog with a grateful person this way. Frightened by fireworks, the dog had jumped into the wrong pickup truck during a Fourth of July celebration. When this same truck accidentally rear-ended me on the way home, the driver was astonished to find a dog in the back of his pickup. I filed a "found pet" report and, fortunately, was able to make contact with the dog's person, who never would have traced this same path with his own inquiries.

Check with local police. This is particularly important if you have reason to suspect your animal was stolen.

Place an ad in a local daily paper. Put it in the lost-and-found section. Give a description of the animal, note the area where you last saw it, and, if possible, offer a reward.

Post notices in the area where the pet was lost. Post the notices on telephone poles, at laundromats, and on grocery store bulletin boards. Ask around.

Ask the mail person and neighbors who work at home in the area if they have seen your animal. Ask parents to ask their children. They are the ones who are often most aware of strays. Cats will get into garages and sheds surprisingly often. Our cat would do that occasionally, and one time it took repeated requests before a neighbor would check out his garage—but there our cat was!

Conclusion

Making moves can be a stressful time for all of us, especially for our animal friends who have no idea what is going on. I think most of us get caught up in the process and may not think how it is for them. Hopefully this chapter will give you some guidance beforehand so you can sit down and think it through ahead of time.

A little planning helps.

CHAPTER 15

SAYING GOODBYE: COPING WITH A PET'S DEATH

Lacey was a special dog, so gentle, loyal, playful, and full of life. When our veterinarian friend, Marybeth, finally had to say goodbye to her after many happy years, she sat and lay with Lacey for days, saying in her heart, in her words, and with her touch those special things we all feel about our most beloved companions in this world.

Likewise, when our dear cat, Ming, approached his end, we just held him and comforted him every moment we could until finally, with tears in our eyes, I administered euthanasia to relieve his pain. We wrapped him in gauze and sadly buried him by the back door, not too far away from his favorite look-out perch.

With older animals, these partings are always sad, yet we

know that sometimes a conscious euthanasia is what is best for all when it is clear that death is near. But with sickly young animals or those rescued from the jaws of death, we do not always know, so we give them every chance and we hope for miracles.

Such was the story of Miracle, the first cat Susan and I had together, but for a few days when we saw that the small black kitten was edging toward death. Only a week before, we had adopted her from the animal shelter clinic where I had twice saved her life—first from the ravages of parasites, and then from the institutional procedures that required unadopted strays to be put to sleep after a certain period. I had done all I knew how to do and yet Miracle, as we'd dubbed her on account of her heroic, though brief, rebound, was surely on her way out.

The signs were clear. Her small body grew steadily weaker and limper and her legs began to stiffen. Her eyes stared, dilated and motionless, fixed upon some awesome eternity. Occasionally she waved her head in small movements and feebly licked inside her mouth.

At that point, we could have struggled again to save her, violating her dignity with needles, tubes, and drugs. Or we could have injected her with euthanasia, a painless passport to a quick end. Yet somehow, in that situation and with that animal, it just seemed right to let her go naturally. She did not seem to be uncomfortable or in pain.

We would just be with her and support her, companions with her next step. Look-

ing at her, we saw how little we knew about the mystery of death or of life. Who or what is a cat, really? Yet we knew that beneath our surface differences there was a bond uniting all living creatures.

And we knew that soon this graceful, highly evolved body with its tiny, perfect eyes would return to the earth. We thought of how we would miss her innocence, her playful grace, her courage—and a wave of sadness swept over us. Yet this, too, is a part of life.

We placed her into her bed next to us with warm bottles covered with cloth and settled down to rest. Through the growing silence there came a few soft sounds—half-groans, half-meows. We reached over and felt Miracle's temperature. It was dropping.

Once, in the middle of the night, we awoke to another of the strange sounds, this one deeper, longer, with an air of finality.

The sunlight was streaming through the window when we awoke that morning, full of a fresh appreciation for the gift of living. We looked over, knowing what we would find. Her body was rigid and cold. Her eyes and mouth were open, frozen as if in surrender to some great force that had passed through her.

We found the right place to bury her, beneath a towering redwood on the edge of a nearby forest. We dug a small hole at the foot of the tree and then simply sat, silently.

The redwood was magnificent, sparkling in the morning light and surging up from the earth to the sky. Into this great tree something of our small friend would pass. From form to form, life would go on. We laid her body in the soil, covering it over with the tree's roots and the sweet-smelling forest loam. As we tamped down the last of it, we heard a small rustling in the bushes. We turned to see.

It was a cat, watching.

THE CHALLENGE OF DEATH

Often we think of death as something to fear, to put out of mind and avoid. Yet in the end it comes to all whom we love, and one day it will come to you and me.

But as the passing of Miracle and of so many we have known has taught us, death need not be feared. To be fully present with death and let its significance speak to us, you can make such an experience a thing of beauty and remind us just how mysterious and wondrous life truly is.

That is why it saddens me when I see and hear from so many who are deeply burdened and upset at the anticipation or the memory of a pet's death. Their grief is real—often as great as or greater than that felt at the loss of a human friend or relative.

For others, however, the temptation is to "stuff" their feelings and not really experience them, an understandable response. But when we are unwilling or unable to face our feelings and thus learn from them, we shut ourselves off not only from the pain of death but also from its beauty and meaning. Facing our emotions provides real opportunities for learning and flowering. The same is

true for any meaningful loss—of a job, of your health, your home, your purpose, or a long-held belief system.

In the case of a pet's death, reactions can be complex. All sorts of feelings can arise, including sadness, anger, depression, disappointment, and fear. With people for whom the relationship is especially important—such as a single person, a childless couple, or an only child for whom the animal has been a best friend—the grief may be that much greater. And, too, if the death was sudden and unexpected, or if it seemed preventable (as in an accident), the feelings of loss and disappointment can be particularly intense.

In addition to those psychological hurts, common to losing a human as well, a pet's death brings its own unique challenges. For one thing, the euthanasia option can burden the owner with a difficult decision. It is also less socially acceptable to mourn openly over an animal, although the grief may be just as real as if you had lost a child or a mate. It might be hard to find a sympathetic listener to help you work through the experience. And even sympathetic employers are unlikely to allow absence from work for mourning a faithful cat or dog.

It is socially acceptable to replace the lost pet with a new one right away. (If a woman were to remarry the day after her husband's funeral, however, eyebrows would be raised.) Simply replacing your last pet with a new one will not heal your grief. Only time and insight can do that. And parents who rush out to buy a new pet for their bereaved child before she has really said goodbye to one just lost should realize that the unspoken message can be: "Life is cheap; relationships are disposable and interchangeable."

HANDLING GRIEF

Above all else, you need to know how to cope with the grief and other emotions that may surface before, during, or after death. If you can do that, any choices or actions required of you will come much more easily.

Lynne De Spelder, a friend who teaches, counsels, and writes on the subject of death and dying, emphasizes that coping with an animal's death is much the same as coping with the loss of a human friend: "It's really important to handle the grief. Research has shown the costs of mismanaged grief can be great, [such as] illness among survivors, for example. Hiding from grief makes it worse."

How can you handle it? Start with the most important thing: Give yourself permission to grieve. Lynne observed, "Women often deal with grief better than men simply because they are allowed to cry. Also, it's good to find someone who'll listen. If your spouse won't, find someone who will. If someone makes light of your grief, it's probably his own fear of emotion."

Suppose your crying and sadness seem to go on too long? That's a signal that you are dwelling too much on your thoughts and memories. Grief counselors encourage people suffering from loss to discover and engage in nurturing activities—such as yoga, hiking, music, or sports—help us lov-

ingly let go of the past and to open to the goodness of the present.

Even so, I think we can also resist letting go of these thoughts, even though we may agree it would be the healthiest thing to do. If the relationship has been close, it can almost feel like a betrayal of that closeness to stop thinking about it. It becomes sort of an expression of loyalty that we hold on to the feelings and memories. To get beyond this, we have to realize that our lives would just come to a stop if we never got over the losses that life will undoubtedly bring us. I can still know that I loved the person or animal in my life; that will never change. It isn't a betrayal of him or her to carry on with what it is we have to do and with our own lives.

HELPING THE YOUNG CHILD

When you must help a child cope with the loss you all feel, it's important to first understand your own feelings. You must be honest and open about what happened. But don't try to console the child with an instant replacement or with explanations that can be dismissive such as "he went away" or "she was taken to Doggie Heaven." If the child wants to see the dead body before burial, understand that it is a natural curiosity and should be allowed, provided you are emotionally stable about it yourself.

Talk with the child and make sure he is not harboring misunderstandings. Don't let him blame himself, or even you, for the death. If you had the animal put to sleep because it was clear that a painful death was inevitable, say so, and give the child a chance to understand. It helps to communicate your own dilemma, that you "did not know what else to do." It is a common human situation to have to act in the face of uncertainty and there is no shame in doing so.

Research in human psychology tells us that the young child has an immense capability for understanding these things. If we look at these times as part of the education of life, they become an opportunity for learning for the child rather than only for suffering.

The Issue of Guilt

I have been on the listening end for many, many people who have lost animals. Sometimes, with people I know well, I have asked more about their feelings: "What are you feeling the most about losing them?" or "How do you feel about how things went?" referring to their choice to use alternative forms of medicine instead of the conventional approach.

I am really surprised at the answers I get. The most common response I hear is that "I should have done more." Now, of course, this is always possible, that one could have done more, but I will hear this statement even from the most devoted people you can imagine. It can be someone who cared for a dog that could not walk or control its bowels, who for months has been carrying the dog in and out, cleaning up after him all that time. These are people who have spared nothing in their nursing care. So I won-dered, "How could they feel they had not done enough?"

I think this reveals something in the human-animal relationship that has not been understood—at least, I didn't under-stand it. For some people, caring for an ani-mal is of immense importance; it represents something very basic about who they are—often, their own innocence. When that car-ing is not seen to succeed, the sense of personal failure is so great that it dominates everything else.

I don't know the answer to this pain, but my thoughts about the situation run like this: It is a noble human feeling to be responsible for another; it is appropriate, and we need more of it in the world. None-theless, we must realize our limitations as humans. It is simply the way things are that, in spite of our best efforts, all beings will die, many from diseases that are unfortu-nate. So one thing to realize is that if you have tried your best, then that is all you can do. Yes, theoretically there may have been something missed or a path not taken, but it is always that way. Hindsight is wonderful—just not available when we need it. So it may help to first reflect on that: You did your best at that time.

Let me ask you: What if you had not been there? What would have happened if you were not in the picture? I think questions like this can help to put things in perspec-tive. That you were there has meaning. Sure, you can always think of things you could have done differently, but the fact is you were the one who was there. What you were able to do for your friend could not have been done by anyone else. It was a gift.

MAKING A CHOICE

If your pet is suffering and you are forced to consider euthanasia, familiarity with the procedure and its alternatives may help you know what to expect.

Euthanasia

The idea of "putting an animal out of its misery" has long been accepted as a humane option, even though we rarely accept it as a choice for ourselves.

Veterinarians perform euthanasia in their office or sometimes on a house call by injecting an overdose of a barbiturate anesthetic into a vein or the heart. The animal loses consciousness within a few seconds, slumps over, and the vital functions cease soon thereafter. It is considered painless. However, if the animal is agitated (perhaps by its upset human companion), that can make it harder for the doctor to do the job properly. It can be very helpful, especially in a situation where there is anxiety or pain, to use a tranquilizer before giving the final injection. There is then a period of relaxation first.

Personally, I've always found the whole process rather uncomfortable, and I think most veterinarians feel the same. After all, we started in this business with the desire to return animals to a healthy state, so this is a challenge to that desire. Mercy killing can make sense, however, in cases where the animal is in great and prolonged pain and the death is slow but inevitable.

It's unwise to make a hasty decision for euthanasia in a moment of anguish, before you clearly and rationally understand the animal's chances of survival and any other alternative possibilities. Otherwise, as we have discussed above, you may be burdened with doubts and regrets, forever wondering if your pet would have survived. I have found this depends to a great extent on what the diagnosis is. The animal with itchy skin may go through much discomfort, but one would never think of euthanasia because of this. If your pet has the diagnosis of cancer, however, then slight symptoms can be interpreted as the reason to make that decision—perhaps prematurely. I have overseen cases of cancer in pets that are doing quite well with minimal discomfort, even getting better; to have them "put down" because they did not feel well one day would have been rash.

It is really best to look past the diagnosis and directly at the situation of your animal. Is she relatively free of pain? Able to function? If so, then don't come to a hasty decision. Consider one of the alternative ways of treatment we will discuss in Chapter 17. I have been blessed to be able to help many "dying" animals recover enough to live normal lives for some time.

Hospital Care

When your animal is so ill that you are considering hospitalizing it, ask the veterinarian for a realistic opinion of your pet's chances of recovery. Special care often pulls an animal through a serious crisis and enables it to live a few more years. Some conditions, however, allow for little hope for recovery. Heroic efforts to prolong a pet's life might involve extensive care and expense, as well as drawn-out suffering for the animal, only to prove futile in the end. I know it's a tough call, but here are some thoughts to consider in making the decision.

The cost of emergency treatment for an animal in a crisis can vary considerably. Typically, the cost can be several hundreds of dollars after just a few days of intensive care. Compared with human care, it's a real bargain. Still, the cost is a consideration, especially if extraordinary care is not going to make a significant difference.

Certainly there is a place for this kind of care in some situations. It may be obvious, however, that the animal can't survive and that heroic measures are not really appropriate. This can be difficult for you to judge yourself, so don't be afraid to ask your veterinarian for an assessment. Ask her to be frank with you. If it is clear that your pet can't be saved, she can still be made comfortable without having to go through all the procedures involved in trying to "rescue" her. For example, a veterinarian can administer fluids and drugs that will allow the animal to rest quietly. As soon as it becomes apparent that death is near, most doctors then put the animal "to sleep" (with your prior permission).

Home Care

In the scenario in which death is expected and a decision is made not to continue the attempts to cure the animal, it is an option to allow your pet to die at home—like a hospice situation.

Why would one consider taking this path? A chief reason is that home is familiar and comfortable, whereas being taken in a car to a strange place with strange sounds and smells creates anxiety. It seems a better thing for the dying animal not to go through this anxiety in the last hours of life. There are veterinarians who make house calls for the purpose of euthanasia, and this is also better in terms of reducing anxiety.

The other reason for allowing an animal to die at home is the chance to be with her in the last hours, to take care of her at this time, and to ensure that the suffering is minimal. Many conditions that are terminal are relatively painless. The animal is not completely free of discomfort, but not suffering greatly. It is usually a path of becoming weaker and colder, culminating in what appears to be sleep.

Over the years I have worked with a large number of clients who chose to let their animals die at home. It has very often been followed by a feeling of gratitude that the choice was made. In my practice I also used some homeopathic remedies that were very, very helpful in making the transition as painless and peaceful as possible. In a moment, I will describe their use. (I would have used homeopathic treatment to help

Miracle with the transition if I had known of it at the time.)

There are some ways of dying that are not easy, however, and my recommendation is to avoid putting pets through the suffering. Some examples of this are cats that have fluid accumulating in their chests (pleural effusion or hydrothorax), resulting in suffocation, or dogs having continual seizures. Use this guideline: If your animal is very agitated, crying in pain, restless, or struggling to breathe, then consider euthanasia rather than letting the process continue.

If it is better to take your pet to the hospital for this, you can still comfort him at the last. Ask your veterinarian if you can be there, to hold him, when the injections are given. Many veterinarians allow, even encourage, this. Talk it over with yours. In some places I have worked, the doctor would perform the euthanasia procedure, then leave the room and allow the person to be alone with his friend for final goodbyes.

WHAT CARE SHOULD BE GIVEN IN THE LAST HOURS?

In terms of physical care, don't feed a dying animal; just give it water or vegetable juices. Provide a warm, comfortable, quiet place to rest. Occasionally your pet may need your help to go outside or to the litter box to eliminate. The dying animal may welcome the gentle and calm presence of those it loves, but do protect your pet from too much noise, activity, or disturbance.

When the end is very near, the animal will grow quite weak. The body temperature will drop below normal (for dogs and cats, below 100°F, or 37.8°C), and breathing may be faster than usual. At the moment of death there is often spasmodic or gasping breathing. The pupils may dilate and the animal may stretch out or perhaps pass urine. This final dying process usually lasts for only about a minute or less.

Homeopathic Help for the Dying Animal

As I discuss in Chapter 17, homeopathy is a method of treatment with the expectation that health will be restored. But it also can be used to help the dying animal. In this instance, we understand that we have done all we can and do not expect recovery. The treatment, then, is intended to relieve pain, anxiety, and restlessness and make the process as smooth as possible.

To forestall confusion later, I will explain here that these same medicines are also used in the treatment of other diseases, and they are not drugs that cause death. In fact, homeopathic remedies are not instruments of euthanasia in the usual sense, meaning drugs that cause quick death. They are euthanasia in the original sense of the Greek word, which meant "an easy or happy death." The difference, however, is that homeopathic remedies will not cause an animal to die if it is not already doing so. They can ease the transition, but they do not *cause* death. In a sense, we are treating the "condition" of dying to relieve pain and suffering.

If the animal is close to death, it will come—perhaps not now, but soon. If the animal is not ready to go, then the remedy may actually improve his condition temporarily.

Here are the most useful remedies and their indications (to understand more about the use of homeopathy, see Chapter 17). Each one is accompanied by a brief description as to how the animal will look or act. Use this description as a guide for which remedy to use. What you are expecting to see is relief of the suffering, and if this happens after the treatment, then give nothing more. It is usual for just one remedy and one treatment to be sufficient.

How long before relief can be expected? Very quickly, in just a few minutes. If a half hour goes by without any obvious effect, then one of the other options can be chosen. However, we are speaking here of observable restlessness and discomfort, not the time of dying. If you are giving the remedy not because there seems to be pain but rather to help the dying process, I emphasize again that the remedy will not directly cause death like a drug will do. If your animal is reasonably comfortable yet showing signs that the end is coming (as described above), then let the remedy act overnight.

1. *Arsenicum album 30c* is the one most useful and most often indicated (in 95 percent of patients). The animal will be restless, have extreme weakness (such as inability to stand), increased thirst, and a cold body. If you check the temperature, it will be below normal (below 100°F or 37.8°C). Not all of these elements need to be present at the same time for this remedy to be appropriate. It often happens, however, that you will notice restlessness or weakness coupled with this low body temperature. Give one dose of 1 to 2 pellets, which can be dissolved in a small amount of water and given with a dropper or syringe.

2. *Tarentula hispanica 30c* is a remedy for similar symptoms, in that there is just as much discomfort and restlessness. What is different is the patient will roll back and forth, from side to side. There may be nervous movements of the right front and rear legs. Typically, the animal keeps in constant motion; curiously, soothing music will sometimes relieve this discomfort. I tend to use this remedy when *Arsenicum album* has no effect. Use one dose as described above for *Arsenicum*.

3. *Tarentula cubensis 30c* is a remedy that will not often be needed; however, it is suitable for the animal dying from a severe infection. It will be very weak, perhaps not completely conscious, with a condition such as an overwhelming viral infection (like parvovirus in dogs) or a bacterial infection such as blood poisoning. Another condition can be gangrene, where part of the body is dying, as may happen in some cancers. The affected areas tend to turn a purplish color. This remedy is particularly helpful in the very

last stages of dying. The medical literature states that it "soothes the last struggles," which is as good a description as any. Use one dose as described above for *Arsenicum*.

4. *Pulsatilla 30c* is appropriate for the animal that is whimpering, complaining, or wanting to be held or carried about. It is also useful for the stage right before death when breathing becomes loud and labored (usually the animal is unconscious at this point). Use one dose as described above for *Arsenicum*.

What you will see in using these remedies is a noticeable relaxation. Pain will be relieved; there will be a quieting. Often death will come almost unnoticed, it will be so easy for the animal. As to time of dying after a remedy, it very often happens in the night, especially after midnight. You may have given the medicine during the day, seen an effect, perhaps even felt hopeful the animal would recover, yet next morning find she has passed.

As was mentioned earlier in this chapter, my experience using this approach, with clients who asked for it, has been very good. It almost always makes the process much easier all the way around. Yet there can be exceptions, and if you have given a remedy, or two, and not seen any change, then it will be best to get your veterinarian involved.

WHAT HAPPENS AFTER?

Many people have raised the question, "What happens to my animal after it dies?"

What is implied in that question is the wondering whether animals have a soul that persists beyond the physical form. I don't know the answer myself, but will share with you an intriguing book on this: *Animals and the Afterlife: True Stories of Our Best Friends' Journey Beyond Death*. The author, Kim Sheridan, writes of experiences with her own animals and having connections with them beyond the physical. She also describes similar experiences of other people. I have had clients say similar things.

I especially like her quote by veterinarian James Herriot: "If having a soul means being able to feel love and loyalty and gratitude, then animals are better off than a lot of humans."

THOUGHTS TO SHARE

Over the decades I have seen this loss of a loved pet play out many times. The people for whom I feel the most are the ones who seem devastated by the loss. There is sadness, yes, which all will feel, but for some, *sadness* is too small a word. I often asked myself, "Why is it this difficult for some?" I am not saying I know the answer but will share some thoughts with you.

If we look at what is different in the relationship with an animal, some aspects stand out. It is an emotional connection, yes, but one that allows touching, hugging, stroking—actions not always available in other relationships.

Another clue might be the frequently voiced words "she is my life" or "unconditional love." The animal is simpler in a way, more immediately present, and most importantly, not judgmental. He is not voicing criticisms, holding grudges. If a person experiences the animal as the only relationship in which she does not feel judged, or the only relationship where another being is really glad to see her, you can see what a significant loss this can be.

What I want to tell this person is that the greatest gift their animal friend could give her is the lesson that such a relationship is possible again. It is possible with many forms of life. One of the most satisfying paths one can take is to learn how love can be shared with so many other beings. The experience with the animal friend can be a springboard to recognize that the same qualities of relationship they so much enjoyed can be found with so many other animals, even with the beautiful forms of nature. Mother Earth could use such an embrace.

MISSING HER

RICHARD PITCAIRN

She is gone
yet the hole is filled.

Could love leave?
Not really.

Like beauty as a flower
it comes, it goes,
yet the scent remains.

Before, I thought love
was there, contained.
Now I see it is everywhere.

I put her leash in the drawer.
I put her bowl on the shelf.
I wipe the tears from my eyes.

CHAPTER 16

VACCINES: FRIEND OR FOE?

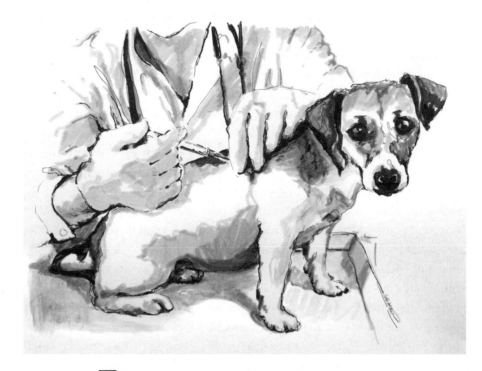

There seems to be quite a bit of controversy about the use of vaccines. There certainly are strong opinions on both sides. What I would like to do in this chapter is attempt to communicate why I began to question their use, and also give a simplified explanation of the immune system, of how it works, so you can come to a decision about this issue yourself. It is a complicated topic but not impossible to comprehend if you will roll with me on this.

MY FIRST LOOK AT VACCINES

When I graduated from veterinary school in 1965 I first went into practice for 2 years in California and after that took a position at Washington State University veterinary school, on the faculty in the microbiology department. It was during this year of teaching that I had the opportunity to enter a graduate program toward a PhD degree, and this I did with the focus on study of the immune system. I found the immune system to be a fascinating topic, so clever, so intricate, and this kept my attention for the next 5 years, until I finished my degree.

During this study we looked at vaccines in detail and I learned that the situation is much more complex than injecting a vaccine that then produces immunity. For example, many people assume that vaccines are 100 percent effective. This belief can be so strong that even a veterinarian may tell you, "Your dog can't have distemper (or parvovirus, hepatitis, or whatever) because he was vaccinated for that disease. It must be something else." But one thing I learned from my doctoral studies in immunology is that vaccines are far from 100 percent effective. It is not just the injection of the vaccine that confers immunity; the response of the individual animal is the critical and necessary factor.

Several things can interfere with an ideal response (production of antibodies and immunity). These include vaccinating when the animal is too young; vaccinating when it is sick, weak, or malnourished; using the wrong route or schedule of administration; or, most importantly, giving the vaccine to an animal whose immune system has been depressed because of a previous disease or drug therapy.

As well, the routine practice of giving vaccinations at the same time a pet is undergoing surgery (for example, a spay operation) can introduce the vaccine organism at a time when the immune system is depressed, by the anesthetic and surgery, for several weeks. It is equally unwise to use corticosteroids (to control skin itching, for instance) at the time of vaccination. The steroid acts to depress the immune response and disease resistance, at the same time the vaccine challenges the body to respond vigorously to an introduced organism.

Even if your animal does have a good vaccine response and develops antibodies, there is no guarantee the disease will not occur. The immunity may be more against the vaccine organism than the natural disease. Or it may be that a mutant germ comes along that will not be susceptible to the antibodies formed. Or if something weakens the animal's immune system later, that system may lack the ability to respond fully, and the natural disease may be able to get a foothold. Such weakening factors include the kinds of things we've been discussing throughout this book—stress, malnutrition, lack of vitamins, toxicity, drug effects, and so on. We see that the effectiveness of vaccination is a complex phenomenon depending on many factors, not the least of which is the overall level of health as determined by the total lifestyle.

Basically all of this information I learned

in graduate school was about how the vaccines were not always effective, mainly due to a dog or cat not being able to respond properly. There was nothing said about vaccines causing any health problems themselves, so the upshot was that though I heard of some possible limitations in their use, I still came out of the training with a confidence in the usefulness of vaccines and even a pride at what the medical system had accomplished. I say this so you will understand I was not at all predisposed to consider that vaccine use might be harmful or produce illness! I heard occasional statements about vaccines being a problem but disregarded them as uninformed.

This changed with time.

How I Learned More about Vaccines in Clinical Practice

I developed an interest in nutrition during my time in graduate school. While I was acquiring much information about the immune system, I wasn't really learning anything about how to make it work more effectively. Mostly we learned how it could go wrong, how the immune system could be compromised in its effectiveness. However, one time I was doing research in the library and found an article by some doctors who had been working with children in Africa and described how the use of some nutrients made a significant difference in how their immune systems responded. Up to this time I had never thought of a connection between

nutrition and immunity, so it was an "aha!" moment. I began to read more about nutrition, experimenting with it on myself and, to what extent I could, with my own animals. But it was when I reentered practice that I could begin to really work with it in a clinical setting. It was there that I saw positive results (as described in Chapter 1), which encouraged me to investigate further. As I studied nutrition, my interest expanded to consider other ways of healing, and this eventually brought me to homeopathy. All of this experience culminated in my opening a veterinary practice that offered *only* nutrition and homeopathic medicine in treatment, and this I did for more than 20 years.

I give you this story as background to what I understood about vaccine use, that I was not one of those convinced that vaccines were not a good thing. But here is what happened.

In my practice using these "alternative" methods, I worked with quite a number of challenging problems and was understandably enthusiastic when seeing a previously very ill animal gradually return to a healthy state. To be clear, these were often conditions considered incurable by conventional veterinary practice. It was like covering new ground, and it was exciting.

What I began to notice, over time, was that an animal I was seeing good progress with would receive a vaccine and take a turn for the worse. It would even happen that sometimes I could not bring the animal back to its prior improvement and we would just have to admit defeat. There were many ways in which my mind dismissed this, explaining it as due to other causes, as coincidence, etc. Eventually, I had to admit that the vaccines were causing problems in some of these animals. And I did not know why.

Once I accepted the possibility that vaccines could actually create illness in some animals, I saw it more and more. I began to note what symptoms would follow vaccines, like what happened after a distemper vaccine, a rabies vaccine. Gradually, I learned some of the patterns.

A STORY OF VACCINOSIS

Vaccinosis is the term used for illness following vaccination. The way it shows up varies, though some common forms are more easily recognized. The term *vaccinosis,* however, refers in general to any health problem following vaccine use.

Here is a typical story about a family that adopted a young dog at age 8 weeks, a puppy that seemed normal in all respects.[1] As recounted by Ruth Downing in *Dogs Monthly* magazine, they experienced the puppy as "a fast learner, very bright," and he was house-trained in 3 days.

At ages 8 and 10 weeks, they took the puppy into their veterinarian's office for examination and vaccination. After the second set of vaccines, at 10 weeks, things changed. A few days after, he became restless and, when Ruth reached down to stroke him, he snapped at her hand. This was a

marked change—unfortunately, the beginning of many more. By the time he reached 6 months of age, according to Ruth, "he'd suddenly become very vocal, hyperactive, and didn't seem to want to concentrate for any length of time. He also developed an ear infection, which was to recur throughout his life." [Note: What is here being called an "ear infection" was not really an infection, but an autoimmune condition deriving from use of the vaccine. See the topic Ear Problems on page 370.]

This behavior, stemming from the time of the second puppy vaccinations, was put down to "a behavior problem," which of course explained nothing. In an attempt to moderate his behavior, they had the puppy neutered, which had no beneficial effect on his behavior. When he was then given his first annual booster vaccinations, "he became even more hyperactive. He would grab at sleeves and mouth people's arms and refuse to sit quietly when people came over to the house."

His people turned to consulting animal behaviorists and trainers, "most of which were of the opinion that we just had a dominant dog who needed to be put in his place." Following the advice of the behaviorists, they tried dominating him, which just made things worse—"he did not understand why his family appeared to turn against him, using the 'strong arm' methods advised . . . " He became worse, "mistrusting and possessive of everything he considered his—from his toys to his bed, and even his space in the car, growling and nervously looking around if anyone came too close. This warning from him was met with disdain by us, and he was shouted at to stop it each time he did it. The end result of this was that he quickly learned that growling got him into trouble so he stopped, but then used the only self-protection open to him if he felt threatened—and that was to bite."

By this time family members were afraid of his behavior and delayed going to their veterinarian. When they finally screwed up their courage and took him, the vet said he was overdue on his vaccinations and he would have to start "the full vaccination program again. This consisted of seven vaccine viruses given twice over a 2-week period, which were duly administered."

The puppy's behavior worsened after this and continued to over the next 2 years; "two family members were bitten for being too close to 'his space,'" and they felt they did not know how to cope. Fortunately, they turned to another behaviorist with a different approach, and over several months of working with this new, more gentle, approach, they saw significant improvement—their pet became relaxed, calmer, even responding well to learning hand signals and tricks. He improved so much that they decided to take him again to the veterinarian for his booster vaccinations. Once again the veterinarian insisted on starting a "full course of inoculations as (his) booster was overdue, despite my querying the necessity of this."

A few days after his vaccinations, this poor dog developed "an itchy skin, scratching so hard that he made his hocks bleed from where he had banged them on the floor. His ears were bright red and he was sensitive all over. He snapped at me when I went to stroke him, and was terribly agitated."

It was at this point that they put two and two together and realized that the vaccines were the factor in all this. They did research, found information on vaccinosis, and began to understand what had happened all along. They turned to a veterinarian using a holistic approach, which helped some but not enough, and they finally, very reluctantly, had their dog euthanized.

This story is not an unusual one. It is sad to read and to think of all the emotional commitment, the time and money, the disappointment. It is even difficult to not be angry about what happened. Very, very often the problems following vaccination are behavioral ones such as described here, appearing as aggressive acts, though in some animals vaccinosis can express more as extreme fear. It is also very common to have skin problems, especially itchiness. You may have noticed the common ear disorder seen in dogs which, along with excessive licking of the feet, often follows the use of vaccines as well.

WHY DOES THIS HAPPEN?

In a nutshell, the problems associated with vaccination have to do with its unnatural method of preparation and use. The idea of using a mild disease to protect against a more serious one is very appealing, and it is quite understandable that people would embrace it. However, this does not mean that it should not be reevaluated.

THE MAGNIFICENT IMMUNE SYSTEM

To understand where the problems arise with vaccines, you need a basic understanding of the immune system. The immune systems of dogs, cats, and humans are pretty much the same. Evolution has developed a pattern it really likes, so why change it? It is magnificent, and I would like for you to see this as well. I will try to simplify it for you.

For purposes of our discussion we can say there are four major parts of the immune system. These are the:

- **Complement system**—about 30 proteins always circulating in the blood, found in every animal or person as naturally occurring substances. They make up about 10 percent of all the proteins in the blood.

- **Guardians**—cells that sit at the possible body entrances, just inside the tissues, that are active in recognizing and destroying any invaders. These include ones called macrophages, mast cells, dendritic cells, and eosinophils.

- **Travelers**—cells circulating in the blood, ready to move to wherever they are needed. There are several types,

called neutrophils, monocytes, eosinophils, and basophils.

- **Learners**—cells that produce specific antibody molecules that will attach to the invaders and mark them for destruction. These are called B cells and T cells (and there are several subtypes).

The complement system, guardians, and travelers together (all three) are called the *innate immune system.* The three categories of guardians, travelers, and learners are also called *white blood cells.* They originate in the bone marrow and travel through the blood to their various functions and destinations. There are over a billion of these made each day.

To take our understanding further, let's look at each of these categories in more detail.

THE COMPLEMENT SYSTEM

The first thing to realize is that the immune system inside us and our animal friends evolved over a very long time. This earliest system of immunity is a group of about 30 proteins that are always circulating in our blood. To give you some idea of how old it is, even sea urchins living 700 million years ago (about 450 million years before dinosaurs appeared) had this defense system. Immunologists call it the *complement system.*

Development of these proteins was a very early way of handling invaders. What these proteins do is attach themselves to anything foreign to destroy it. They evolved as proteins that could recognize and interact with the sort of material bacteria and parasites were usually made of.

One big advantage of this system is how fast it acts. The proteins are already there, and as soon as bacteria or other organisms get into the blood or tissues—like, immediately—this system deals with it. Sometimes the complement system, by itself, is sufficient to deal with the problem. The other great thing is that it also gives off chemical signals that alert cells of the immune system that something here may need attention.

The Guardians

A later development of the immune system were specialized cells that have the job of guarding the possible entry points of pathogens. We tend to think of the surface of our body as being the main intersection with the world, but a much larger area (about the size of two tennis courts) is made up of the mucous membrane linings of the eyes, mouth, throat, and rest of the digestive tract (stomach, intestines, colon); the respiratory tract (nose, trachea, bronchi, lungs); urinary tract (urethra, bladder); and the reproductive tract (vagina). About three-fourths of the immune system is stationed at these places. There is more than one type of cell in these tissues, as noted above. They are situated just below the surface of barrier tissues and have the basic assignment of guarding the portals and destroying anything naughty that gets in. Here is a simple list of their day jobs.

- **They eat anything foreign**, digesting it into smaller pieces.

- **They take some of the fragments they have digested,** carry them to where other types of cells are waiting to act (lymph nodes), and **present the pieces** to them, saying "lookee, lookee, see what I have found."

- **They send out signal**s that let the rest of the immune system know there is a problem, and this pulls in additional troops, through the blood, to help in the battle.

It is the guardians (the macrophages) that run the immune show, signal everyone, call in support, present pieces for identification, and alert the learners (see below) to make antibodies. This part of the innate immune system acts very quickly—within seconds or minutes.

The Travelers

There are other cells of the immune system whose job is to circulate through the blood, checking around, sampling the environs. They are on the watch, and are triggered to action by activity of the complement system, or by signals from the guardians. Once their attention is engaged, they head to the battle zone, squeeze through the blood vessels, and add additional useful weapons to the fray. (The activity of this group, migrating in response to a problem, is seen as an elevated white blood cell count in a blood analysis of your animal.) When they get to their destination (where the bacteria, virus, or splinter is), they start to eat or kill the invader or toxic material that has gotten in.

In the process of doing this, over and over, they can exhaust themselves and die (they have done their maximum). It is the accumulation of these cells, having done good work by disabling the bacteria or toxin, but now broken down, that we call *pus* (which is a good thing—a sign the system is working).

THE LEARNERS

The most recent development of the immune system is called the *adaptive system.* It came along about 200 million years ago, first in fish, and this is the system most of us think of when we hear the words "immune system." What is different about it is that it can learn how to respond to the invaders. Whereas the system we have considered until now is pretty much fixed in makeup, the learners can look at the details of the invader and adapt themselves to respond specifically to it, especially if it is something new. This is how antibodies are made—the foreign material is evaluated, and a specific protein that corresponds to it is made. This ability is so amazing that probably any new thing could be responded to, it is that flexible.

This part of the immune system works hand in hand with the older part and is really an extension of it—the new kid on the block. If you remember, I mentioned that the digested part of the invader is "presented" to other cells so they can recognize what the invader is made up of. This presentation is important to the adaptive system: It is how it learns about the invader.

Antibodies

Antibodies are proteins made by the adaptive immune system (the learners), which are released into the blood in large numbers. When they encounter what they were sent out to recognize (the bacteria or virus), they combine with it, and this marks the invader to be taken up by other cells, the guardians and the travelers. It is a way to identify, for destruction, various microorganisms that the other part of the immune system has not been able to handle. The older part of the immune system may never have encountered this microorganism or toxin before and may not be quite sure how to recognize it. It is the learners that figure it out and send the signal out that marks the invader as foreign.

As an interesting side note, there is a class of antibody that actually goes into the intestines, where the food is, to neutralize any potential pathogens. This antibody is resistant to acids and enzymes so it can do its work in such a challenging environment— for example, disabling bacteria that come along with food.

Another thing that is important to know is that if the older (innate) immune system (complement system, guardians, travelers) is able to handle whatever the problem is, then this adaptive system is not called into action. It is not necessary. The adaptive immune system is like the last resort. Keep this in mind, as it is important to our discussion about the vaccine issue.

Even from this rather simple presentation, you can see that the immune system is a complex and orchestrated movement.

WHO RUNS THE SHOW?

Here I want to emphasize, again, something important to know—it is the guardians in the tissues (cells called *macrophages*) that direct the whole defense movement. They attack and eat the invaders, they digest them and present their parts to other cells for further action (as we discussed above), they send out signals calling for support troops, they tell the body to increase the bloodflow to bring fluid into the tissues (thus causing swelling and redness), and they alert the adaptive system that makes the antibodies. It is these cells already present in the tissues that respond very quickly to a threat, while the learners, important as they are, work much more slowly, taking a week or 10 days to produce their contribution.

THE INFECTION SEQUENCE

There is one more aspect of the immune system to understand before we look at how some of the problems with vaccines can arise. We will do this by looking at how natural infection occurs. We will use, as an example, a viral infection, like canine distemper, parvovirus, or panleukopenia.

Infectious viruses come in through the eyes, nose, or mouth (if swallowed, moving to the throat, stomach, or intestines). There are a few exceptions, like viruses carried by mosquitoes (yellow fever) or introduced through a bite (rabies), but most viral infec-

tions enter by being breathed in or swallowed. What the virus then encounters is a series of barriers.

- First is the lining of the eyes, nose, mouth, throat, or intestines, which is covered by mucus and traps any little critters trying to get in.
- If they do get through, then there are the cells waiting on the other side to gobble them up (the guardians).
- The lucky virus that makes it farther still has to navigate the lymph nodes (which drain the fluids of any area of the body), where immune cells congregate, just looking for a job.
- If it gets as far as the blood (after traveling up the lymph channels), then it could be engulfed by the cells in the blood, or during its passage through the liver or spleen—which filter the blood and take out the bad guys—or neutralized by the complement system.

Most viruses have preferred parts of the body where they can reproduce themselves. Their intent is to get there. Obviously, the healthy and vigorous individual will make that very difficult, as we have just explained. If the viruses manage anyway to get to their target cells, then we finally have the observed infection (a sick dog or cat).

I am presenting this process to you simply, but the point here is that a number of barriers in place work really rather well in preventing infection. It is the *natural process* of the pathogen surmounting these barriers, and the extensive resistance the body puts up, that pull in the learners (adaptive immune system) and get it set up to produce antibodies against the infection and "killer cells" that attack the virus-infected cells. This brings us to consideration of how this process compares with what happens when a vaccine is injected.

WHY VACCINES ARE DIFFERENT FROM A NORMAL INFECTION

Several aspects of vaccine use make the process unnatural. Now that we have seen how the immune system works, how it evolved over literally millions of years to very efficiently handle invaders, we can recognize how the vaccine violates that arrangement.

MULTIPLE VIRUSES

These days, vaccines are combined pathogens—several viruses mixed together. A vaccine may include distemper, hepatitis, leptospirosis, parvovirus, parainfluenza, *Bordetella*, rabies, Lyme disease, brucellosis, and more (which may be given all at the same time to dogs), or panleukopenia, rhinotracheitis, calicivirus, feline leukemia, rabies, chlamydia, feline infectious peritonitis, etc. (often given simultaneously to cats).

In nature, it is highly unusual for more than one virus to come into the body at one time. Yes, there can be epidemics, but one at a time. In our cleverness, we humans thought,

"Why not combine several viruses together to save time?" but again, this is unnatural and the body does not do well with it. If you think how, to a great extent, the immune system focuses on recognition—what is normal and safe versus a potential threat—you can see how throwing too much information at it can result in confusion.

THE VACCINE PATHWAY

Vaccines also take a different entry route. They are usually injected into the leg or back—into muscle or under the skin. Compared with a natural infection, which will be just a few virus particles, this involves a pretty large load of organisms coming in the back door. So, instead of encountering the sequence of barriers described above, they arrive all at once and skip these steps.

The immune system has evolved over inconceivable eons, honing itself to be ready for the way infections are established, and it is the *working of this mechanism* that sets up long-term immunity. Remember that it is the guardian cells in the tissues that are in charge, that run the show. Once alerted, they orchestrate things, even among the part of the immune system that makes antibodies. The vaccine will certainly engage these cells, but the unnaturalness of its entry (the injection) can allow the virus to be in the bloodstream within minutes, moving fast and without fully engaging this normal evolutionary process. Does this make sense? I have tried to think how I could communicate how much of a shock this is to the immune system so you could get a sense of the disorder that follows. Here is an analogy that may do that.

Imagine a young woman, living alone, wanting to have a home that feels completely safe. She sets it up for maximum security. At the edge of the property is a strong and high fence, one that will be very difficult to get over. The front gate is locked and inside the fence, in the yard, are several guard dogs prowling the property. They are formidable, and not much will get past them. As well, the front door of the house is locked, there are alarms on the doors and windows, and running about inside the house are smaller (but equally effective) sentry dogs. Just to make sure, the woman retires for the night, locking her bedroom door, and crawls into bed. After relaxing a bit, she rolls over and finds herself face to face with a guy who says "hi."

You can imagine the shock, the frenzy—how could someone get in without going through all the barriers and alarms? It is unthinkable.

This is the way it is for the immune system when a vaccine is injected. Bypassing the barriers, suddenly here is the virus going throughout the body. Where did it come from? Why wasn't there any reaction before now? The immune system is startled, shaken, tries to cope and, in the chaos, mistakes are made.

ADJUVANTS

In the development of vaccines, it was learned that injecting just the virus by itself might not result in adequate immunity. Someone, by experimentation, found that adding in certain substances like mercury or aluminum made it seem much more a threat and thus increased antibody production. These additional substances are called *adjuvants,* from the Latin, meaning "helping toward." Immunologists don't really know why using adjuvants makes such a difference, but it does. There is some suggestion that the metals do this by altering normal body proteins, which causes the immune system to react against them as well (thus leading to allergies). A number of studies also suggest that these adjuvants are a major factor in causing postvaccine illness. You may have heard of a movement to have mercury removed from vaccines, for example. This might help but, as I am saying here, the problem is more complex.

CONTAMINANTS

The picture just painted, of pathogens being injected, is too simple in that it implies that only the vaccine virus is put in. This is the way it would be in a natural infection. The virus comes in, goes through the process we have described, getting through the barriers if possible—but it is just the virus, no other garbage.

Realize, however, the vaccine virus was grown in a laboratory using a tissue culture of cells from a kidney or some other part of the body. In this culture, the viruses infect the cells, which then make hundreds more viruses that are then released out into the fluid. This is how the many viruses in the vaccine are made. When the vaccine fluid is being prepared, it is not possible to extract just the virus. The fluid contains cell debris, DNA, and various components of the growth medium used to feed the cells (which will contain animal protein). When this mix is injected into your animal, it is all seen as dangerous. The tricky part is that when the immune system reacts against the tissue fragments, it can make antibodies that then attack its own body's normal cells. This is called *autoimmunity,* an immunity against normal body tissues.

Several studies of this phenomenon were done at Purdue University School of Veterinary Medicine, comparing vaccinated with nonvaccinated dogs, and they found the vaccinated dogs did make autoantibodies—to several of their own important body constituents important to normal function, including DNA and even collagen, which is what holds the body tissues and joints together.[2]

The same thing has been shown to happen to cats. A study of administering vaccines grown on cat kidney cells resulted in the animals making antibodies against their own kidney cells.[3]

SO WHAT HAPPENS?

We could go on with details of how the immune system gets screwed up by the injection of many different foreign materials coming into the body by an abnormal pathway, but those details are not really necessary to understand what we are looking at here.

Let's list the main considerations.

• More than one virus or microorganism is injected at one time, which confuses and overwhelms the recognition function of the immune system, causing errors to happen.

• Toxic substances like mercury and aluminum in the mix cause the formation of abnormal proteins, and the metals themselves even have effects in the rest of the body (like getting stored in the brain).

• The vaccine mix contains many cellular components that the viruses were grown on, and the immune system gets them confused with its own normal body tissues. This results in the formation of chronic immune disorders and allergies.

• Vaccines have been shown to often contain other viruses they aren't supposed to, ones that were in the cells the vaccine viruses were grown on, unbeknownst to their manufacturers (this is what happened with the polio vaccine, which was later found to contain SV40, a monkey virus that has been shown to cause cancer[4]). It is possible that these can cause further illness on their own.

• It has been observed in clinical experience that for a time after vaccine administration the immune system is weakened and the animal more susceptible to other diseases. I don't think it is very well understood why this happens. It may have to do with the unnatural process itself.

So What Do We Do?

Ah, that is the question. What makes sense depends to a great extent on what options are available to you. In my practice, I did no vaccinations for more than 20 years. I did this because I was confident that, if there were illnesses, I could successfully treat them with homeopathy. I also had the use of homeopathic remedies that could prevent the diseases, called *nosodes*, which are made from natural disease products.

Homeopathic Nosodes

Distemperinum, for example, is made from the secretions of a dog ill from canine distemper. It is sterilized, diluted, and carefully prepared in accredited pharmacies. When properly used, this medicine can protect a dog from distemper even better than the vaccine can. In fact, this method of disease protection, first developed by a veterinarian in the 1920s, showed impressive results even before vaccines were developed,[5] though it was never adopted by the profession.

Nosodes are also available for kennel cough, parvovirus, panleukopenia, and other common dog and cat diseases. We homeopathic veterinarians have been using this method of protection for a long time with very satisfactory results and without the side effects and illness associated with vaccine use.

Are homeopathic nosodes simply a replacement for vaccines? No. They are not the same. They are used only temporarily and only during times of likely exposure.

For example, I was able to stop an epidemic of parvovirus in a dog-breeding colony by using the nosode for parvovirus for only the week when the disease was likely to occur in the puppies. Once through that "window," they were all right and remained healthy. You will need guidance from a homeopathic veterinarian to use nosodes properly.

Modified Vaccination Schedule

What if you cannot find this service or you are afraid to not vaccinate? Let me suggest a modified plan that will at least minimize the chance of vaccine problems.

- Use single or simple virus vaccines instead of complex vaccines. Ideally, this means vaccinating for one disease at a time. As of this writing, it is still possible to obtain just distemper vaccine for dogs and panleukopenia for cats. However, most practitioners will balk at such a request because they will have to buy each single-disease vaccine in quantity (an entire box) to serve only one client, suffering financial loss and wasting the unused vaccine. You could offer to pay the difference or go in with some friends who want to follow the same method and perhaps your veterinarian will go along with that. Other than this, having only a multivirus vaccine choice, go for the ones with the fewest. For example, for dogs this will be a DH (distemper-hepatitis) and for cats a "3-in-1" (panleukopenia, rhinotracheitis, and calicivirus) vaccine.

• Don't vaccinate an animal too early. Avoid the temptation to vaccinate before 16 weeks of age. Remember that the earlier your animal begins vaccinations, the more harm may be done to the immune system, and also the more vaccines received, the greater the chance for vaccine-induced illness. It is during these early months that the immune system is maturing and deciding what is normal for that body.

• Use a reduced vaccination schedule for young animals. You do not have to give a lot of vaccinations to have as much protection as possible. In most instances, immunization of puppies or kittens is enough for several years or a lifetime of protection.

Puppies

If you really want to play it safe, keep your new puppy isolated from contact with other dogs and just vaccinate once—at age 22 weeks or older. In my opinion, the only essential vaccines are distemper and parvo. Get the distemper vaccine at 22 weeks of age and the parvo a month later. (As I noted above, however, you might have to get distemper and hepatitis together.) This should be very safe if your puppy is not exposed to other sick animals during this time.

If this plan of giving vaccines at a later age and as single doses seems too risky to you, and you are getting a lot of pressure to do the usual, here is a compromise plan your veterinarian may go along with. Get two vaccinations (for each disease), starting at 16 weeks, using this schedule.

First distemper (hepatitis): 16 weeks
First parvo: 20 weeks
Second distemper (hepatitis): 24 weeks
Second parvo: 28 weeks

I prefer the first plan, obviously, as it waits until the immune system is more mature, but this second plan will probably work all right. We have had it in all previous editions of our book and have not heard of any problems with it.

Kittens

Using the same plan as above, you have your kitten receive the distemper (feline panleukopenia) vaccine once at age 22 weeks, and this is sufficient for the life of the cat. I do not recommend the rhinotracheitis and calicivirus vaccines, as I have the impression they are not very effective.

Again, as with puppies, if you have a lot of pressure from family or your veterinarian, you could get the vaccine at age 16 weeks and it will probably go all right. Well over half of the animals, probably three-fourths, will have a mature immune system by them.

As regards other vaccines, a warning about the feline leukemia vaccine. It is the most harmful of all the cat vaccines available. I have seen many cats become ill with feline infectious peritonitis after receiving this vaccine, and this is because the leukemia vaccine depresses the immune system. Be careful of this.

Also, avoid annual boosters. There has

never been scientific justification for the yearly booster shots recommended by veterinarians, even though they have become a popular practice. I advise against any further vaccinations after the initial series, as they are not necessary. Also, the latest official veterinary opinion states that annual revaccinations are neither required nor effective. Your veterinarian may not know of this or even agree with it. Rest assured, however, that experts in the field of veterinary immunology have taken this position and support your decision not to have your animal vaccinated every year. This is not new information, just ignored information. An exception could be the older adopted dog or cat that comes without any historical information so you don't know if it was vaccinated or not. There are two options.

- Have a titer run. This is a blood test that determines if there are antibodies already present in the blood. If so, a vaccine is not necessary.
- Have just one vaccination, not more. One vaccination (preferably with a single-virus vaccine) is sufficient for lifelong protection.

THE RABIES PROBLEM

What about rabies vaccination? This is a difficult problem for many people to face. From my own experience, I am convinced that some animals are made ill by this vaccine. Yet rabies is the only vaccine required by law for dogs (and for cats in some states).

This requirement is really for the protection of human beings, regardless of its benefit or harm to pets, so few exemptions are allowed.

I do not suggest using the homeopathic nosode for rabies instead of the vaccine. We don't have enough clinical evidence as to how effective the nosode is, and it is a legal risk to you.

Dogs

The most common disturbances following rabies vaccination are aggressiveness, suspicion, unfriendly behavior, hysteria, destructiveness (of blankets, towels), fear of being alone, and howling or barking at imaginary objects. These can be treated with homeopathic medicine, but sometimes with difficulty. One of the saddest things in our practice is to restore a dog's health (sometimes after prolonged and careful work), only to have the animal suffer a relapse and go into a decline after we acquiesce to a required rabies vaccine. It would be far better if we didn't have to vaccinate these animals again, but our present legal situation requires it.

We homeopathic veterinarians find that the best we can do is to treat the dog for any symptoms that come up. I would have clients monitor their dog very closely the first month after the vaccination, and if there was a change of personality or appearance of physical symptoms, then we would use the indicated remedy as treatment. This was quite practical in my hands. There are about 35 useful remedies, so it is best to let the

KVCC KALAMAZOO VALLEY COMMUNITY COLLEGE LIBRARY

dog's condition point to which is appropriate (of course, you must work with a homeopathic veterinarian to determine this). This is the safest way.

If you don't have this option, look at the Rabies topic on page 414 for another suggestion.

Other Options

• If you have a dog that has had an unfortunate reaction to prior vaccines, sometimes a letter from your veterinarian that your animal is not healthy enough to receive a rabies vaccine will be accepted, especially if the animal is older and previously vaccinated.

• Another possibility is that blood can be taken from your animal and tested for protection (antibodies) against rabies. We discussed this above; it is called determining the "rabies titer." Some counties, here and there, are accepting this in place of a booster vaccine (but not for the first vaccination). Check out this option with your veterinarian. It may be necessary for you to find out yourself by contacting your local department of health and persisting with questions about this option.

At this point you have no other legal alternatives to getting rabies vaccinations for your dog. Many states require that you vaccinate your puppy at age 4 months (check your specific state requirements).

How can we fit this into our recommended schedule? The best scenario is to have the rabies vaccine last, at least a month after completing all the others. However, this may mean waiting what is considered too long to get the rabies vaccine. If this is not possible (that is, legal), then get the rabies vaccination first at age 4 months (16 weeks), wait until age 22 weeks, and then carry on with the schedule I gave you above for the other vaccines.

Cats

The same discussion applies to cats, though I have not seen as many behavioral changes in cats as I have in dogs. They can be affected by the vaccine, however. It may be possible to have a titer run as suggested for dogs, especially if you are being asked to get a booster. As discussed above, whether or not this would be accepted really varies by county, so check first.

If you feel you must have your cat vaccinated, the best timing is 1 month after the distemper vaccine is received (age 5 months or older).

AN EXPERIMENTAL ALTERNATIVE

Those of us who are on the front lines, dealing with the social demand for vaccination protection and also finding ourselves treating dogs and cats that are ill from the vaccines, have looked for other ways that these animals could be protected, ways more natural. We know that newly born

animals living in nature have protection from their mothers. During their development, antibodies that the mother has made herself are transferred to the fetus, and after birth the antibodies come through the breast milk the first couple of days. These antibodies coat the intestines and protect against the common diseases, and they also circulate in the blood in case needed there. This is called "passive immunity." How long it lasts depends of course on how many antibodies the newborn got, but for many puppies, this immunity can last as long as 18 weeks.

During this time of protection from the mother, under usual conditions, there would be some exposure to the viruses that are around, yet the young animal would be protected from illness. As this immunity gradually wears off, it would be partially protected and yet be able to react and develop its own immunity. This is how it happens in the wild, in animals never vaccinated yet that remain healthy.

During my annual meeting with vets practicing veterinary homeopathy, we discussed this at some length. A paper had been just presented by a veterinarian who had kept careful records, and he was able to show that the pups vaccinated for parvo had less chance of surviving the disease than the ones not vaccinated. This prompted homeopathic veterinarian Rosemary Manziano of New Jersey to share her experience in "natural immunization." Where she lived, there was a place in the country where distemper was commonly seen in raccoons. For those of her clients willing to try it, she had them take their puppy there, let it out for 5 minutes, and then bring it home. They did this twice. When the puppies were tested a week later, they were found to have antibodies to distemper and were immune—and this without being vaccinated. She had done this for 11 years with more than a hundred puppies.[6]

This is an interesting idea, the mimicking of Mother Nature. I find it very appealing, but obviously more experience is needed to know how reliable it is as an alternative.

FUTURE FEARS

If we don't vaccinate most animals, do we run the risk of bringing back diseases? This is a legitimate concern, and if we did nothing but just stop vaccinating, it would be a risk. That is not what I am suggesting here.

If I could summarize the message in this chapter, it would be that vaccines, though they have had beneficial effects on frequency of diseases, have problems of their own. As I described in relating my learning process, a variety of illnesses follow the indiscriminate use of vaccines for the whole population. Vaccines are not 100 percent safe, and not anything like 100 percent effective. If we are to seriously consider the question, don't we have to factor in the many animals made ill by vaccine use? We may reduce the frequency of infectious diseases, but the poor dog that has seizures every day would rather have taken its chances with the disease.

What I am espousing here is giving more emphasis to establishing a high state of health, with natural resistance to disease. With such a population, if an infectious disease appears, few will be susceptible. If we couple that with alternative ways of dealing with disease—use of homeopathic nosodes, establishing natural immunity in the young (as described above), even using vaccines only when there are epidemics—we would manage much better.

I find the perspective of the veterinary profession to be that vaccines work well and are "a final solution." This is not true. The first step in acknowledging that we need a better way is to see that our present vaccine program is *not* a final solution.

CONCLUSION

Vaccination, while it seemed a good idea at the time of its invention, is an unnatural way of establishing immunity. It bypasses the elegant system of immunity honed by evolution, introduces toxic substances, and results in reactions against one's own body (allergies). It sometimes makes the recipient more prone to get the disease vaccinated against.

I very much recommend that it be used minimally, only for life-threatening conditions, and not repeated routinely. There are alternatives: homeopathy and, if you feel experimental, even natural exposure plans. If you decide to be wary of the excessive vaccinations used in today's world, it will be best for you to work with a veterinarian who can advise and monitor the process, and give you options.

CHAPTER 17

HOLISTIC AND ALTERNATIVE THERAPIES

"My dog has arthritis. Can you tell me what vitamin or mineral will help him?"

Here is a very common question. It's not hard to understand. This person is asking if there is a nutrient that will act much like a miracle drug—without realizing the answer is not that simple. If it were, then problems like arthritis would not plague us.

The truth is that a health problem is rarely caused by just one factor, as we have been exploring in the previous chapters. Even when it seems that it is, like an infection caused by bacteria or a virus, we come to realize that the hidden factor of the animal's level of health is as important as how virulent the bug is. In a group of animals exposed to an infectious disease, there are always some that do not become ill—and that is the key to understanding how to protect your animal. It comes down to how much resistance she has to becoming ill. This is the critical factor. It is never just the one thing—the bad bug, the nasty virus, the toxic chemical—there are always two factors involved, the other one being the health of the animal that is threatened. If the state of health provides a good environment to grow in, then the germs will take advantage of that. If the "soil" is not suitable, then they can't grow there, no matter how much they want to. In the same way, if the means of dealing with toxins is not compromised, the effect of that exposure may not even be significant.

Let me put this differently. We have given a lot of attention, in the previous chapters, to the effect of food quality on health. Now you will understand if I say that what very good food does is maintain a high level of health, so that there is optimal resistance to infections and toxins. What we are considering in this chapter is the other side of the issue, that of resistance. How does this individual animal handle those challenges? The food may be deficient, or of low nutritional value, or contaminated, let us say. Yet the effect will vary. Some animals are very healthy and deal with the situation quite well. Others are not so healthy, and what can seem like a minor stressor has big effects.

For example, one person might say how well his dog is doing on one of the recipes in this book, while another responds that her dog cannot tolerate it, gets diarrhea or something. The difference here is the state of health of that animal. The one that seems sensitive, allergic, easily upset, is expressing a low level of health, while the other dog is responding quite nicely.

If a person tries a different food with his animal and sees it not going so well, he may object to using this food item, such as corn, or soy, or vegetables. He may make the generalization that this food is not good for all dogs or all cats. This is not a correct assumption. This difficulty, when it arises, can be corrected: It is indicative of a lower level of health, and it is important that this be acknowledged and addressed.

In my practice, I had the advantage that if I put the animal on a recipe and there were any problems (which was not common), I could then treat the symptoms that appeared with alternative medicine, specifically homeopathy. This would correct them, bring health up to the optimal level, and the animal would then do fine.

So in this chapter I want to present this option to you—the use of alternative therapies.

There are many reasons why our pets' resistance can be low, and, if we put aside the food concerns, which we have already covered, then these are also worthy of consideration.

- Sickness from household or environmental exposures; flea sprays or dips or collars; medicines frequently given such as for intestinal worms or heartworm

- Emotional stress
- Infectious disease, perhaps treated, but not eliminated
- Poor health since a vaccine reaction (vaccinosis)
- An immune disorder—allergies, thyroid disorder, arthritis, chronic ear problems

AN UNDERLYING ILLNESS

Many of the animals brought to me in my practice were suffering from one of these problems—showing up already sick, often vigorously treated using the conventional approach without bringing back good health, and having reached the point where the illness was advanced. You may do all that you can to improve environmental conditions, provide the best nutrition you can find, and yet your animal still is not doing well.

Nothing saps our energy more than suffering from the pain and discomfort of illness. If there is already something wrong—arthritis, stomach pain, back pain—then this weakened area will more easily break down with time. Many, many of the difficult, long-term problems that plague our animals are of this type. Though antibiotics and vaccines have made infectious diseases much less frequent, the

teeter-totter has dipped down on the side of chronic diseases. The common problems of today—the hyperthyroid cats, the dogs with hip dysplasia, the cats with inflammatory bowel disease or chronic bladder inflammation, the dogs with diabetes—were extremely rare when I first entered practice. It was not because I was unable to recognize them. They did not exist then.

By far the majority of today's common and chronic problems have appeared in the last 30 years or so, and many are caused by the immune system going haywire. By this I mean these are "autoimmune diseases," which means some part of the body is being attacked by the very system of defense meant to protect it from outer danger. The other most common conditions are the results of toxic chemical accumulation in the tissues and then the subsequent, inadequate, treatments that have compounded the problem.

When we have situations like this, it may not be enough to improve food quality and living conditions. The body will need help in coming back to a condition of health. The option then is to have additional treatment, and what I am recommending to you is the system of treatment we call "holistic" or "alternative."

These terms are now known to most people but not always understood. I would say what I hear most often is something like, "My veterinarian does holistic treatment. She gives my cat vitamins." In other words, many understand the terms to mean using some approach other than drugs. So let me clarify for you what is meant by these terms and share my experience.

THE LIMITATIONS OF A PARTIAL APPROACH

Like all veterinarians, I learned the conventional approach of diagnosis and treatment in school and practiced it for years. And it has certainly had some remarkable successes, particularly with acute infections and trauma. Yet when we approach health problems from a symptom-centered perspective, our thinking tends to get so specialized and materialistic that we lose sight of the larger biological patterns and processes. Instead, we tend to rely heavily on the use of drugs and surgery, often to the exclusion of a broader program of health building and prevention.

As a result, contemporary medicine generally is geared toward controlling and counteracting symptoms and disturbances. It virtually ignores the body's innate ability to heal itself, given the right supports. Instead of strengthening the patient, the methods largely put down the body's healing attempts.

Understandably, we are so eager for quick and easy solutions that we turn rather indiscriminately to some drug or vitamin, like the questioner at the beginning of this chapter. As a result, we get pulled into this method of covering up symptoms. Unfortunately, some modern drugs are especially good at such suppression. As an example, the various forms of synthetic cortisone are so powerful that they can stop a great many widely varying symptoms in their tracks, but the disturbance continues in the body, now hidden from view.

Time and again, when my associates and I take medical histories, we observe that animals vigorously treated with such drugs (apparently successfully) have gone on to develop another condition a few weeks or months down the line. Usually, it is more serious. For instance, a dog with a skin problem that is continually suppressed with a cortisone-like drug may later develop calcification of the spine, pancreatitis, or breakdown of the joints. Or a cat with a chronically inflamed bladder that is treated with drugs will often later show a deeper problem like kidney failure, diabetes, or hyperthyroidism.

Though we tend to regard the new conditions as being unrelated to the prior ones, I suggest they are not. The suppressed disorder has simply made a more serious inroad into the body, now involving internal and more critical organs. We must remember that symptoms are there for a reason, that they are part of the body's defense mechanism, and that to suppress them over and over again will only weaken the animal.

PROBLEMS CAUSED BY DRUGS

A related problem associated with such dependence on powerful drugs is the production of side effects or even iatrogenic ("doctor-caused") diseases. Although iatrogenic disturbances are considered to be a serious problem in human medicine, veterinary researchers have made little study of them. In my own opinion and experience, however, they are common in animal medicine as well. I have seen many pets improve considerably when prolonged drug treatment is simply stopped.

Some examples of common drug-related complications are loss of appetite or diarrhea (from the use of oral antibiotics), as well as skin rashes, convulsions, hearing loss (from the use of tranquilizers or antibiotics), severe life-threatening anemia (decreased number of red blood cells, most often from antibiotics), and behavioral changes— usually toward irritability and aggressiveness, but sometimes anxiety manifesting as fear of noise, thunder, strangers, and even unusual objects (from using psychoactive medications).

If symptoms like this appear soon after therapy begins, they are probably related to the drug. It may not be that the drug is directly toxic so much as that the animal is experiencing an overall energy-depleting effect of such suppressive medicine. The most common effect of long-term drug use is the animal becoming sluggish and inactive.

In many situations, drugs are not even called for, yet they are used to appease the client and to justify the expense of the office call. As an example, antibiotics are often prescribed to treat viral diseases. Yet, antibiotics are only effective against bacteria, not viruses. It is not just the veterinarian (or MD) who is to blame. Many people insist on a shot or some pills to take home, and if the doctor doesn't comply, they will go to another who will. Unfortunately, we have all been sold on the necessity for these drugs. I question that assumption, both on the basis of my own success and that of many other people who use more natural methods that work with the body's healing forces. Is it so difficult to think there may be other ways of healing disease besides using drugs? Why have we come to rely so heavily on drugs and surgery?

DIVERGENT VIEWS IN MEDICINE

The historical development of Western medicine is a complex subject, but I think a lot of it boils down to several culturally shared ways of thinking that most of us hold, whether doctor or client. One of these is that we want a "quick fix." We don't want to change our lives or habits that much. It's easier to just continue on the main pathway of our culture, even if it is limited by certain assumptions. We often settle for just adapting ourselves to live with a problem that we assume we can't change.

For example, we learn to avoid certain foods that cause allergic reactions. Yet if we took the time and care to work a little harder at understanding and treating the disorder, we might be able to do away with the allergic state altogether. In fact, I expect my patients to actually recover from problems like food allergies during nutritional and homeopathic treatment.

THE FORCE OF LIFE

An even more fundamental stumbling block comes from the materialistic view that has long dominated Western science, with profound effects on modern thought and culture. Because scientists cannot see or measure such slippery phenomena as consciousness, thoughts, feelings, life energies, or whole systems, most of them have only studied the physical, material aspects of life. Accordingly, our current science, medicine, and culture regard the body as though it were a mere physical object, much like a machine, a collection of chemical and mechanical processes, basically reducing the patient to a "meat bag."

As a result, while virtually all cultures and systems of healing in the history of the world, including ours, have alluded to the presence of a unifying life force, most of our scientists no longer do.

The Chinese call this life force *chi.* The Polynesians knew it as *mana.* The Sioux referred to it as *wakonda.* To the Egyptians it was *ka,* and to the Hindus it is still *prana.* In the Middle East, the word is *baraka.* In Africa, the Bushmen speak of *n/um.* The Aborigines, the most ancient culture on Earth, call it *arungquiltha.*

In our own history of Western medicine and philosophy, it was called the "vital force." What do we mean when we use a term like this? The words themselves are not important. We could use *chi* or "the energy that makes us live"—it doesn't matter as long as we understand the concept, that a controlling, directing field of energy (an information field) is behind our physical and psychological manifestation. It is this which grows the body in its perfect order, which keeps it regenerating, and, especially important for our purposes, repairs anything that is broken or damaged. I would love to explore this with you in more detail, but entire books could be (and have been) written about it. Let me give you just one small example of the amazing organizational ability of the force of life.

Ocean sponges are relatively simple creatures, in that there are a limited number of cells that live on top of a supporting skeleton that gives the sponge shape (similar to how our bones give our bodies shape). The sponge creatures, of which there are many types, are consistent enough in their form and characteristics that we can recognize them under different names, as different species. You can take one of these sponges, cut it up into little pieces, and squeeze them through a silk cloth so that all the little cells are separated from each other, resulting in a "porridge" that has no recognizable shape or resemblance to what you started with. Here is the interesting part: If you let this gruel stand for a while, it will gather and reorganize itself, resulting in a completely normal sponge identical to the one that was separated, a sponge that goes on living like nothing has happened.

As if this is not amazing enough, in one experiment, two different types of sponges—a red and a yellow species, not related to each other—were put through this process and mixed together. Nonetheless, over the next 24 hours the red and yellow cells managed to separate themselves and reorganize back into the original sponges that they were at the beginning. As Lyall Watson puts it in his remarkable book, *Supernature*, describing these experiments, "This ability to instill order is the most vital and peculiar characteristic of living beings."

However, as modern science was taking shape, a philosophical split occurred between the vitalists, who asserted the existence of such a force that animated and governed physical organisms, and the materialists, who denied it and said that all life could be explained in terms of chemical and physical processes. The materialists predominated, and their views became the underpinning of our contemporary science, medicine, and culture. Because this perspective mostly discounts the organism's guiding intelligence, it is not surprising that mainstream medicine generally treats symptoms like an enemy that must be controlled and suppressed.

Understandably, this turning point in the history of science explains why most of us today look almost exclusively to physical explanations for disease. We look first for germs, parasites, genetic defects, or just plain wear and tear from old age. In addition, our bias is to focus our research money on those physical factors that best tie in with marketable solutions, such as a new drug, rather than those that would require a change of diet or lifestyle or a cleanup of the environment. Just think of the 82,000 chemicals now introduced into our Earth's environment, many of which are toxic or carcinogenic, and how little attention is given to stopping this or cleaning it up.

EMOTIONAL STRESS

Another example of the disconnect between our commonsense views and those of contemporary medicine has to do with emotions causing disease. Although doctors may pay some lip service to avoiding emotional stress or may notice how often patients get sick after suffering a psychological upset, the usual fix for a health problem still involves drugs or surgery. While we may personally acknowledge the importance of thoughts and feelings and perhaps even a unifying intelligence responsible for our living form, as a society we do not seriously take this perspective into account in the prevention and treatment of most diseases.

THE REEMERGENCE OF HOLISTIC THERAPIES

In recent times many practitioners and laypeople alike have felt constrained by the limits of this approach and have begun to explore and revitalize a number of holistic therapies, both for humans and for animals. What do we mean by the word *holistic*? I have to laugh at some of the definitions I have come across. I already gave you the example of confusing holistic medicine with giving vitamins. Considering what we have been talking about in this chapter so far, it will not be a surprise for me to say that *holistic* implies a different perspective on health. Let's start with what is familiar to us—the usual—and then contrast it with what we are calling the holistic view.

Allopathic Medicine

Shall we call the medicine of our common experience contemporary medicine? Such contemporary medicine is also called allopathic medicine, the word *allopathic* meaning that treatments are intended to control, stop, or inhibit the expressions of disease. This is the approach most of us are used to: the doctor and the veterinarian who offer antibiotics, shots for allergies, vaccinations, surgery, and so on. The basic principle with a drug or surgery is to control or to block what is seen to be the symptoms of illness. For example, an anti-inflammatory drug (aspirin, steroids) is used in allopathic approaches to stop the expression of inflammation.

You will often hear, in reference to inflammation, that inflammation is "bad" and should be eliminated. What is not appreciated is that inflammation is the way the body heals and repairs itself. If it goes on too long, chronically, then there is underlying disorder the body is trying to correct. To suppress inflammation leaves that disorder unchanged and the patient weakened overall.

Another example is a drug that stops epileptic seizures by inhibiting some brain functions. Yes, I know—it seems self-evident, common sense, to do whatever you can to stop the seizures. If a drug will "quiet" the brain, why not? Yet we do have to acknowledge that if contemporary medicine were completely successful, I wouldn't be writing about this and you wouldn't be interested in reading it.

My path in searching for other ways of healing started, and continued, precisely because I came to see the limitations of this approach. Yes, the drug could stop the symptoms—for a while. But it did not seem to really cure the patients. They would still not feel really well or would have fewer but now chronic, persistent symptoms. Sometimes they would later develop other problems as bad as or worse than the first ones.

The Fragmented Approach

Another characteristic of allopathic medicine is the technique of looking at the patient "in pieces." Take Benny, for example. Benny was a cute little fox terrier with an excitable nature. When he had his first seizure, it was thought he may have been poisoned. When they recurred, he was put on an antiepileptic drug by his usual veterinarian. This did make the seizures go away, but Benny spent more time lying about and sleeping. As the months went by, he began losing hair in patches and getting an oily feel to his coat. Another diagnosis was made, of hypothyroidism, meaning that his thyroid gland was underactive. He began to take a drug that replaced the thyroid hormone that was not being produced, and Benny did become perkier and his coat got somewhat better. But now he was on two drugs—the antiepileptic drug and the thyroid hormone—and he was expected to stay on these the rest of his life.

Things went along fairly well for a couple of years, until he started having trouble with the stairs. Instead of taking them like a bouncy little guy, he came up the stairs slowly and carefully. He was clearly stiff. Further evaluation with x-rays resulted in the diagnosis of spondylitis, meaning, basically, an arthritis-like condition of the spinal vertebrae. So he went on an anti-inflammatory drug and a painkiller. Now he was on four drugs, and though Nancy, Benny's person, did not exactly ask her veterinarian about the expected outcome, it was assumed he would be on these four drugs the rest of his life.

This little story brings out two points. One is that these health problems were being dealt with one by one, as if they were not connected to each other. After all, how could a problem with Benny's brain (seizures) have anything to do with the thyroid gland? How could having hypothyroidism make him have arthritis of his spine? I think it's fair to say that most veterinarians would tell their client that these were unrelated problems.

This is an example of seeing the patient in fragments. It is part of allopathic medicine to have this view. It makes dealing with things easier if you can just handle them one piece at a time.

The second point is that with this perspective in medicine, there is an increase in the number of drugs used over time. As new symptom patterns appear, an additional diagnosis is made, with the resultant "appropriate" medication added to the program. It can get complicated.

THE HOLISTIC PERSPECTIVE

How would a case like Benny's be handled with the holistic approach? I can speak from the way I would do a homeopathic workup (and the methods can vary depending on the form of holistic medicine used—Chinese medicine will emphasize the pulse or tongue appearance, for example). What I want to know are the details of the condition to start with. What is of the most importance is how the seizure condition began, what it looked like when it was first seen and before any treatment was done. For example, these are the types of questions I would ask.

• When was the first seizure seen? Was it during the day? At night? During sleep?

• What position did he take when he had the seizure? Falling down? Thrashing about? Just standing rigidly?

• Did he remain conscious throughout?

• How long did the seizure last?

• Did he pass stool or urine during the seizure?

• How did he act afterward? Hungry? Thirsty? Disoriented? Aggressive?

- As time went on, how often did the seizures happen? Did they change in pattern or remain pretty much the same?
- Did there seem to be anything that set them off? Stress? Emotional upset? Being startled? Eating?

You can see that we want to get a very clear view of what this seizure pattern is like and we want to know how it was *before* any treatment was done by Benny's veterinarian. Why does this matter? Because at the outset we are seeing the disease condition as it occurs naturally, and this is the pattern we have to understand. Later, after treatments, the pattern will be different. If it is not cured by whatever treatment has been done, then the way the seizure pattern continues to show itself will have been modified by the treatment, creating a mixture of both natural disease and medicinal effect. This mixture can mislead us and make it harder to understand the condition and how to treat it. You see, the homeopathic approach will not use the same remedy for every pattern of seizures in dogs. There is a remedy for seizures occurring during sleep, another for seizures during which there is loss of urine, and so on.

But there is yet more to this holistic approach. We will want to know how the health was *prior* to the seizure condition. There may have been other diagnoses of conditions that were also an expression of the health problems of this poor dog, and we need to know about them. We take the entire historical sequence, from puppyhood all the way up to the present day, learn all we can about that, and consider all of this information in making our treatment plan.

Going back to Benny's case, once we have all the seizure info, we add to it how the condition evolved over time. It was seen that his skin and coat changed, that the thyroid acted up, and finally that arthritis occurred in his spine. If I took his case, I would be getting details about his seizures and other conditions. Finally, all of this information in place, the treatment I came up with would address the entire pattern—seizures, hair loss, oily coat, thyroid malfunction, and spinal arthritis. The homeopathic remedy prescribed would address *all* of these problems. The perspective is that instead of seeing the problems as separate things, we see it as the *health condition* of Benny over time. This health condition showed disorder and malfunction in several different ways.

Can you see now why the term *holistic*, in the sense of looking at the whole animal, is used? The holistic view has this different assumption—that successive health problems are connected to each other. Why? Because only one individual is affected by these symptoms. This animal is *one individual* intimately connected at all levels and, as with any complicated process, if one aspect is out of balance, this can throw off another seemingly unrelated area.

So, in Benny's case, I would see that what began as a seizure was an expression of a deeper disorder that was not cured by using a sleepy drug that made his brain run slower. With time, another expression of this disorder showed itself—the thyroid problem—which was also not cured by using a replacement drug. It did not fix the thyroid, just provided a synthetic form of the natural hormone. That he developed arthritis in some form was a further development of this same trouble. The seizures, the underactive thyroid, the patchy hair loss and greasy coat, and the arthritis of the spine are all the same disease condition from beginning to end. The holistic perspective will not divide these up into different diagnostic categories separate from each other. Again, this becomes even clearer if instead of *holistic* we spell the word *wholistic*.

"So," you say, "my vet is holistic, yet gives me a diagnosis for each health problem, just like you describe." Yes, this is common. Many veterinarians who are holistic in their perspective will still talk this way because they think you, as the client, are expecting this kind of language. Nonetheless, the truly holistic practitioner will understand the connection between these conditions in the linked way we are discussing here. That this is significant will be made clearer when we talk about holistic therapies.

The Meaning of Symptoms

Earlier we talked about how, from the allopathic perspective, symptoms were to be countered with treatment. Holistic medicine is different here as well. Most practitioners with a holistic perspective, including myself, take the view that symptoms represent the action of the individual's life force, that energy or influence that maintains the body. In creating symptoms, the life force is doing its best to throw off the disturbance through, say, diarrhea, vomiting, coughing, sneezing, pus formation, and the like. That is, the symptoms are there for a reason, are the mechanisms of the body restoring its balance. Diarrhea is used to eliminate toxic material from the intestines, vomiting to do the same from the stomach. Coughing and sneezing are ways of discharge as is, also, the flow of pus from an abscess. Accordingly, we as practitioners try to work with the action of the symptoms, gently helping the body in its attempt to restore harmony. We do not attempt to suppress the symptom, but rather to help the body complete what it is trying to do. We also consider emotional and mental factors in health, carefully observing fluctuations at these levels and often advising changes that will promote greater internal harmony.

We are not denying the importance of physical factors. Certainly there are virulent microorganisms and environmental assaults of all kinds to consider. But it is important to realize that individuals who are exposed equally to these factors vary tremendously in their resistance.

Let me recap it like this: The individual animal is a whole organism, not parts patched together. When healthy and balanced, everything moves along smoothly and there are no symptoms. However, when injured or exposed to an infectious organism, the whole patient responds, and this response includes the production of symptoms. These symptoms (even inflammation or pain) are expressions of the healing process the body is going through.

Does this make any sense to you? It did to me, years ago, and both transformed my thinking about health and disease and enabled me to be much more effective in restoring health than I had ever been before.

A Contrasting Example

Let's use an example that will make the difference between the two medical perspectives' understanding of symptoms more clear. Imagine, if you will, that you cut your arm and it bled for a while. Wouldn't you fully expect the wound to heal? Wouldn't you also know that the healing will take a while?

The usual stages are (1) bleeding, (2) clotting, (3) the wound contracting, (4) a scab forming, (5) new skin growing in under the scab, (6) the scab coming off, revealing fresh, more fragile healed skin underneath, and (7) the new skin becoming tougher, until it is like your other skin. Typically, this whole process will take a number of days, possibly a couple of weeks. Isn't it obvious that all of these stages are necessary for healing to occur?

Now consider this alternative. You start with the same cut but now take a drug that in a few short hours results in the wound becoming completely healed, just like new.

Possible? No, of course not. Yes, there are drugs that stop bleeding, take away pain, and prevent infection—yet to truly heal, the tissues still have to go through all the healing stages. If the wound is interfered with very much—using antibiotic ointments, picking off the scab, taking painkillers—it will actually take longer to heal, as these interventions work against the natural healing process.

Realize that we are talking about the healing of a fresh wound in a (presumably) healthy individual. Compare this now to a more chronic condition. Let's say your dog has arthritis in his rear legs, and he is given a prescription that reduces inflammation and pain. Amazingly, in just a few hours, he is markedly improved—running around like a puppy again. Wouldn't most people tell their friends about the wonderful cure? But think about it. Arthritis is a much slower and more gradual process than a wound. It comes on over months, maybe years, and there is considerable change in the body—thickening of tissues around joints, change in the joint fluid, even distortion of the cartilage and bones. Is it even possible for something like this to heal in a few hours? Or even in the 2 weeks it takes a wound to heal? Of course not. It takes considerably longer for arthritis like this to naturally heal to as close to normal as possible—literally months, maybe a year.

So what is happening with this fast response brought on by the drug that seems so miraculous? The drug is *suppressing the symptoms* that the body is producing in its attempts to heal the condition. It is an artificial effect. By blocking the process, it looks like everything is better, but nothing has been healed. We have come to expect this kind of rapid response as one of the miracles of modern allopathic medicine, and it does seem a miracle. The problem is that by blocking symptoms, yet not providing a way for the condition to be healed, the result is a superficial effect that allows the deeper disease to progress over time. This is why you may have had the experience of your pet getting sicker over time rather than better.

Does this perspective seem novel to you? You may be wondering, "Did you just make all this up?" Actually, science has come up with many ideas that now support this approach.

Support from Modern Physics

Interestingly, developments in modern physics have offered support for the holistic and vitalist (that there is a life force) perspectives. When the materialist doctrine became the prevailing view, physicists held the now-outdated Newtonian idea that the world is ultimately composed of minute particles, discrete "basic building blocks" of matter, such as electrons, photons, and neutrons. Yet, as modern physicists have searched for increasingly smaller particles in hopes of finding The One Basic Building Block from which the rest are formed, they have not found it. Instead, they arrived at a wholly different view. Matter is not really so solid. In fact, according to Fritjof Capra in *The Tao of Physics,* "Particles are merely local condensations of the field; concentrations of energy which come and go, thereby losing their individual character and dissolving into the underlying field." To put it differently, it is an illusion to try to analyze things as though they were separate entities or parts, for all phenomena are manifestations of a whole field of energy that underlies their manifestation.

One of the important implications of this fundamental breakthrough of understanding in physics is that the fragmented, specialized, particulate approach to knowledge that typifies most of science (including medicine) is erroneous at its very root. We must learn to see problems in relation to the whole and not become lost in the divisions of our artificial labels and definitions.

Evolving into this new way of perceiving is not easy. It has taken me years to get where I am now, but I have worked with the method of homeopathy for almost 40 years and it has been, other than nutrition, my method of treatment in a very successful practice. I feel that I have confirmed the correctness of this understanding and this approach in a very practical way.

HOW TO PUT THIS INTO PRACTICE

It would require many volumes to thoroughly describe all of the possible therapies that could help your animal. However, let's look at the general philosophy and methods of some of the more common holistic therapies that veterinarians and others have used to heal animals. Then I'll describe in greater detail the approach that I favor, homeopathic medicine, as this is the system I most understand and with which I have the most experience.

Bear in mind that these therapies are not as separate as they may appear. Most of them share the basic philosophy that I've been talking about here, and many include more than one alternative therapy. For instance, herbal medicine and dietary changes are often used along with acupuncture. As we discuss these treatments, I will suggest which methods will work best together.

NATUROPATHY

Defined by a medical dictionary as a "drugless system of therapy by the use of physical forces, such as air, light, water, heat, massage, etc.," naturopathy entails a comprehensive approach that emphasizes supporting the whole body's physical attempts to eliminate disease; that is, it assists the discharge of disease products.

Naturopaths consider the major physical cause of disease to be an excessive buildup of toxic materials, often due to improper eating and lack of exercise. They consider that these clog the usual avenues of waste disposal.

Naturopaths employ a number of techniques to clean out the body, including some used by various cultures throughout recorded history. One is fasting, a way to rest the digestive system and allow the body to do some internal housecleaning. Patients who are fasting are often advised to drink a lot of pure water or juices to flush out the kidneys, and to take enemas or colonic irrigations to clean out the lower intestines.

Hot and cold treatments may be used to stimulate the circulation or encourage sweating (in people, of course). They may include baths, saunas, packs, compresses, fomentations, steaming, and the like. Other naturopathic methods include exercise, sunbathing, good hygiene, and various massage techniques and brushing of the skin and coat. Besides the cleansing processes, patients are put on supportive programs of good nutrition (often emphasizing raw, organic foods and juices), proper food combining (to aid digestion), and judicious use of specific food supplements, vitamins, minerals, and herbs.

Some of these methods are rather difficult or awkward to apply to animals, but others lend themselves easily—particularly fasting, exercise, good nutrition, sunbathing, and grooming (a form of massage). I encourage their use in many cases.

Donald Ogden, DVM, who made extensive and successful use of naturopathic methods for years in animal medicine, reported that 9 out of 10 of his skin irritation cases would improve within only 2 weeks. He has attributed his success to thoroughly bathing the animal, then fasting her for 7 days on vegetable broths, and then for 7 additional days on vegetable solids and soups. He has advised breaking the fast with raw meat and raw or steamed leafy vegetables, followed by a balanced natural foods diet (like we have described in this book).

Dr. Ogden has also found that quiet rest and fasts of 3 to 10 days (until the pet's temperature is normal and symptoms disappear) are very beneficial for many inflammatory conditions, including obesity, rheumatism and arthritis, constipation, chronic cardiac insufficiency, bronchial diseases, heartworm, kidney and bladder stones, gastritis, kidney disease, pyorrhea, diabetes, liver disorders (unless cirrhosis has developed), open sores, and the fever stage of distemper.

However, he has advised against fasting an animal with a wasting disease such as cancer, advanced uremia, tuberculosis, prolonged malnutrition, hookworm disease, or distemper.

Naturopathic medicine works well in combination with other holistic approaches, including herbal medicine, chiropractic and other manual therapies, acupuncture, Chinese medicine, and homeopathic medicine. In my practice, I use fasting and enemas occasionally but rely more on nutrition (as emphasized in this book) and the body cleanliness and grooming aspects of naturopathic medicine to supplement my treatments.

HERBAL MEDICINE

It has been long observed by those who study animals in nature that they will seek out specific plants to eat when they are not well. They apparently know that it will help them. You can see the same thing with a horse or cow in a pasture—they will eat some of the plants not normally consumed when there is a problem with parasites or digestion. Those of us with dogs and cats have seen them gobble grasses or specific plants in the same way.

Herbalists have carried this further, into a system of treatment using various parts of plants—leaves, roots, berries, seeds, flowers—to stimulate healing. Basic to folk medicine in every culture since ancient times, herb use is probably the most fundamental system of using plants for treatment.

In fact, many of our modern pharmaceutical drugs are actually compounds originally isolated from herbs and considered to be their active elements. For instance, digitalis, used for treatment of the heart, derives from foxglove; atropine (an important drug to treat poisonings as well as other conditions) from belladonna (called deadly nightshade); caffeine from coffee; theophylline (used to ease breathing in lung diseases) from tea; and reserpine (used for high blood pressure) from *Rauwolfia serpentina*.

Herbalists contend that the pharmaceutical derivatives and the whole plants from which they come are not the same, however, and I agree with this from my experience.

The strength of herbs is in the unique and complex properties of the original natural plant, which contains literally hundreds of substances. As was said above in the description of the holistic perspective, the whole is more than the sum of its parts.

As compared to their pharmaceutical counterparts, herbs generally exhibit a slower and deeper action. They assist the healing process by helping the body to eliminate and detoxify, thus taking care of the problem the symptoms are expressing. For instance, they may stimulate physiological processes like emptying of the bowels or urination. In addition, they can serve as tonics and builders that resonate with and strengthen tissues in specific parts of the body (or the whole body, depending on the herb in question). They can also be highly nutritious, containing large amounts of various vitamins and minerals and other nutrients. And there are some herbal practitioners who believe that plant medicines, particularly those found locally, bring the healing energy of the environment to the user.

Herbal remedies have been successfully used to treat many illnesses in animals throughout the centuries. Animal herbalist Juliette de Bairacli Levy popularized their use for this purpose through her detailed writings (which also emphasized the importance of a natural diet and fasting). She reported good results in using herbs to treat dogs with worms, fleas, skin problems, mange, distemper, kidney and bladder trouble, arthritis, anemia, diabetes, leptospirosis, obesity, wounds and fractures, constipation, diarrhea, jaundice, heart disorders, warts, and cataracts. De Bairacli Levy recommended using the freshly gathered herb whenever possible and replacing dried herbs yearly. I concur with this advice. In Chapter 18, I will describe the standard methods of preparing infusions, decoctions, and tinctures from herbs. In the Quick Reference Section, I'll suggest specific herbs for various illnesses.

Besides the difficulty of finding fresh herbs, one disadvantage of using internal herbal therapy for companion animals is that the remedies are usually administered in sizable quantities at frequent intervals over long periods of time (weeks to months). Since they rarely taste appealing, you need to give them to a pet in capsules or else disguised in food (and that can be tough to do—they have really good taste buds). As every animal lover knows, it's not easy to force medication down a pet's throat, much less over a long period.

For that reason and others, I prefer to emphasize homeopathic medications, which taste good and are given less often. Many of these are also derived from plants. Though my experience using herbs by mouth is limited, my impression is that homeopathy acts more decisively even when prepared from the same plant.

I find herbal preparations most useful for external treatments on animals (as in flea powders and rinses and for mite control, skin problems, and wounds) or for minor upsets (such as diarrhea, indigestion, and the like) that do not require prolonged treatment.

In summary, herbal medicines will act physically by providing nutrients and substances that promote more normal functioning. They also can stimulate the natural healing processes of the body. In this way they serve as a sort of bridge between drug use and the more subtle effects of homeopathy and Bach flower essences.

Herbal medicine works well with naturopathy, chiropractic and other manual therapies, acupuncture and Chinese medicine, and, when restricted to the milder herbs used externally, homeopathic medicine.

CHIROPRACTIC AND OTHER MANUAL THERAPIES

Since the time of Hippocrates, manipulative therapies have been in use throughout the world. Some of these, like chiropractic and osteopathy, both founded in the 19th century, view disease conditions as the result of misaligned or abnormal bodily structures (especially in the spine) that interfere with the normal flow of life force, nerve impulses, and blood circulation. Chiropractic treatment and osteopathic treatment had separate origins but are similar in the emphasis on structural manipulation as an important part of their treatment method. Of these, chiropractic has become the largest drugless healing profession in the United States. I first became interested in the potential this

therapy holds for animals when I talked with a local chiropractor, who told me that many different conditions in pets have been helped by chiropractic, including epilepsy. As time went on, and my three children matured, it happened that all three became chiropractic physicians and have their individual practices in Oregon.

The original theory of chiropractic holds that subtle vertebral misalignments can block the essential flow of nerve energy passing through the spinal column. This irregularity, known as a subluxation, puts excessive pressure on the spinal nerves, thus interfering with various body functions. I have read that this "energy" is considered, at least by some chiropractors, to be a nonphysical force, much like the life force concept in homeopathic medicine.

Treatment consists of careful manipulation of the vertebrae to restore correct alignment and full working order. To achieve this specialized skill, practitioners usually undergo at least 4 years of medical training.

A broader way to understand how manipulative therapies may work is to, once again, view the body and mind as one whole. Each part of the body both reflects and affects the whole system. Disturbances in one local part are felt throughout the entire system and may cause "resonant" problems in a generalized way. If there is a persistent condition in one place, then the body is not unaware of it, and adjusts itself to compensate for it.

A number of advocates of diagnostic and

manipulative therapy focus on certain parts of the body with the understanding that they reflect or represent the whole organism. For instance, an iridologist "reads" disturbances in various organs by a careful examination of the iris of the eye. Practitioners of reflexology pinpoint and treat disturbances elsewhere in the body by manual pressure on certain points of the feet and hands. Some acupuncturists diagnose and treat problems solely at points on the ear, which is said to reflect the whole body. I have met one veterinary acupuncturist who says he successfully now uses only the ear to treat health problems in horses—even lameness! Polarity therapy, which involves the placing of hands on different parts of the body to channel energy flows, has also been used on pets and relies upon a method of reading and treating disturbances by a similarly holistic approach.

In the same way, it may be that body and mind disturbances are reflected in the spinal column, associated with irregular muscular tensions and vertebral displacements. If so, they should respond to corrective spinal manipulation.

Regardless of how and why it works, chiropractic manipulation has proved to be a real boon for many animal patients. For example, a reader of our column in *Prevention* magazine wrote me to describe the amazing response of her 18-year-old cat to chiropractic therapy. Twelve years prior, her cat began developing severe attacks of vomiting, loss of appetite, and intense itching of the face and shoulders. The poor cat licked and scratched until its skin was bloody. This person consulted several different veterinarians, but their drug therapy offered only temporary help, at best.

By chance, this woman mentioned the situation to her chiropractor and he offered to try to help. Just one adjustment brought startling results: The cat stopped vomiting and began to eat well. Four adjustments were done, and the condition has not reappeared in the 2 years since.

Another case reported in a veterinary publication concerned a silky terrier diagnosed by his veterinarian as having a "protruding disc," with pain and loss of function. X-rays revealed calcium deposits in the area and a misaligned vertebral joint. Surgery was rejected because of the high cost. After 2 weeks of unproductive drug therapy and confinement, chiropractic treatment was suggested. Though the dog had to be carried into the office, a couple of minutes after the adjustment, he walked out painlessly. The improvement was lasting.

The use of chiropractic manipulation by veterinarians has developed rapidly in the last decade, and it is more common now to find a veterinarian who can offer this treatment. The American Veterinary Chiropractic Association trains veterinarians and can guide you to available practitioners.

Chiropractic works well in conjunction with herbal medicine, naturopathic medicine, acupuncture and Oriental medicine, and homeopathic medicine.

Acupuncture and Oriental Medicine

One traditional holistic approach that has made fairly significant inroads into the modern veterinary profession is acupuncture and other aspects of Oriental medicine. There are texts on the subject, as well as organizations for the training of veterinarians—the International Veterinary Acupuncture Society, the American Academy of Veterinary Acupuncture, and the Chi Institute of Traditional Veterinary Medicine. In response to growing interest among students, some veterinary schools are also offering an elective course in acupuncture and Chinese medicine.

The basic theory behind this ancient and comprehensive system is that the fundamental energy fields (chi) that make up the body (as well as all aspects of the universe) manifest as two poles, yin and yang. They are reminiscent of the positive and negative electrical charges described by physics. They are considered to be one energy with two opposite expressions. In terms of the physical body, to have excellent health, these two polarities are to be properly balanced. Your state of health depends on this balance between these two sides of the same coin. A skilled therapist can correct excesses or deficiencies by manipulating certain critical points along the body's meridians, the channels through which energy flows. If it is seen that energy has accumulated excessively in one area, the flow can be redirected. This may be done with needles (acupuncture), finger pressure (acupressure or shiatsu), burning the herb mugwort near the point (moxibustion), or, in modern times, electrical stimulation (electroacupuncture), injection of various solutions (aquapuncture), the use of ultrasound (sonapuncture), lasers, and the implantation of small gold beads.

The American Veterinary Medical Association has taken an interest in acupuncture and has encouraged scientific documentation of its results. According to Allen Schoen, DVM, one of the pioneers in the field of holistic medicine and the one who introduced acupuncture to the well-known Animal Medical Center of New York City, the kinds of conditions that acupuncture can best help include:

- Musculoskeletal problems, such as arthritis, slipped disc, and hip dysplasia (malformed and dislocated hip joint)
- Skin diseases and allergic dermatitis
- Chronic gastrointestinal diseases, such as chronic diarrhea or vomiting, equine colic, and prolapsed rectum
- A variety of other problems such as chronic pain syndrome, breeding problems, respiratory arrest, and coma

Dr. Schoen notes that acupuncture, like other alternative healing methods, may take time and repetition to produce results. He asks new clients to commit themselves to at least eight treatments in chronic cases. "If someone has six treatments without seeing any results, and then stops, it doesn't mean that acupuncture doesn't work. It can take a while to stimulate the body to heal itself," he emphasizes. I have found the same thing in working with homeopathy—that it takes more time to observe the healing process happening than we expect from our experience with suppressive drugs, especially in the cases of chronic disease.

Like any system of medicine, acupuncture has its "miracles." Sheldon Altman, DVM, of Burbank, California, an active teacher, writer, and practitioner of veterinary acupuncture, tells of a Doberman suffering from panosteitis (a painful bone disease). With only one treatment, he walked out pain-free after 6 months of limping. The pain did not return. Don't we all wish such results for our own animals?

One of the most wonderful things about a holistic system like this is how such apparently hopeless cases can be so helped. Dr. Schoen recalls the case of a golden retriever with a paralyzed esophagus who had vomited about 16 times a day for the previous year and a half. All conventional therapies had failed, and the owners had to use special feeding techniques to keep the food down. After four acupuncture treatments, her vomiting finally ceased. Treatments were tapered off and she has remained well since.

As you might guess, such an approach can also be used to prevent disease, much like getting a "tune-up" for the body. In fact, the ancient Chinese, who developed acupuncture over thousands of years of practice and observation, emphasized prevention above all else. They resorted to acupuncture or herbs only when the preferred methods (meditation, exercise, massage) were insufficient. Most contemporary acupuncturists emphasize a total approach to health and include advice on the use of food, herbs, and lifestyle recommendations, as well.

Acupuncture and Chinese medicine, like homeopathy, is a complete system that stands on its own. For that reason, it is best not to combine it with homeopathy, because, in my experience, the two can interfere with each other. Some practitioners use it along with naturopathic and manipulative therapies, and an experienced practitioner can best determine the suitability of this.

FLOWER ESSENCES

This treatment is a little like herbal medicine, a little like homeopathy, in that small doses of plant "influences" are used. Originally called the Bach flower essences or remedies, they were developed in England by Dr. Edward Bach and used to treat emotional states. This system differs from herbal medicine in how the remedies are prepared. The dilute infusions of flowers and tree buds are made by immersing the plant in a bowl of water while bathing it in sunlight for an hour. After preserving the fluid with added brandy, it is further diluted to make the bottle of extract used in treatment. These extracts are given orally several times a day, often for several weeks.

The flower essences are said to act primarily upon the mental/emotional state, although a psychological improvement often brings a physical one as well, not surprisingly. They are not the same as homeopathy, however, and act in a different way. I used these early on, for a few years, but as time went on used them less because I came to prefer the homeopathic method.

One case in which I used a flower essence involved a dog, Jamie, with a host of distressing symptoms. These included a loss of appetite, lack of energy, withdrawing and acting frightened, vomiting, collapse, fever, a moist coat, a tense abdomen, and enlarged spleen. In addition, laboratory tests showed that she was anemic, with abnormally shaped red blood cells, an above-normal number of white blood cells, elevated liver enzymes (indicating liver damage), elevated cholesterol and bile pigments, high blood sugar, and so on. The x-rays taken were normal.

Because I knew the family was under stress, I suspected that emotional disturbance was playing an important role. Accordingly, I prescribed one of the Bach flower essences, Larch, to be given four times a day for a week. For the first few hours after starting the treatment, Jamie's symptoms became exaggerated, but she was markedly better by the next day. A week later, her symptoms were gone and have not returned for over a year. In addition, her personality changed. For the first time, she became more playful and outgoing with the other animals in the family. This change has persisted even though the original treatment was for only a week.

I've also found the Bach flowers useful in some conditions that developed shortly after a traumatic or upsetting experience. For instance, a woman brought in a cat a couple of weeks after he had been violently shaken by a large dog. He was uncomfortable, irritable, and constipated, with a fever, weight loss, fluid accumulation in the lungs, and a painful abdomen. The most severe injury was a displaced vertebra in the lower back, which I could feel was out of place. It hurt the cat very much when I touched it.

I prescribed the Bach flower Star of Bethlehem (indicated for fright after trauma), two drops every 2 hours. Three days later, the cat's person called to say that her cat was quite recovered. The drops had noticeably relaxed him. After a couple of days of treatment, he began stretching by hooking his claws in a piece of firewood and pulling from side to side. Apparently the stretching corrected the back problem. Soon it was difficult to medicate the cat—he was too busy leaping tall fences in a single bound!

The 38 flower preparations discovered by Dr. Bach are compatible with any other system of treatment. They are quite useful for emotional upsets, after injuries, and where there is a great fear. They are mild in their effect and cannot cause problems even when "overused." I generally do not use them with homeopathy, preferring one method at a time so I don't get confused interpreting what the treatments are doing. If you are not using homeopathy, a handy and easy treatment for common stresses is the formula Rescue Remedy. Great name, isn't it? Who would not want to be rescued? This is a combination of some of the flower essences that addresses the usual emotional state of upset, fear, and stress. It is readily available, already formulated, in places that sell the flower essences.

Since Dr. Bach's original work, people have collected other plants and made them into medicines in the same way. I have no experience with any other than the Bach originals so cannot advise you in their use.

HOMEOPATHY

We now come to my own particular love, the science of homeopathy. In my search for effective holistic therapies, I started out using nutrition and herbs. I still do to a limited extent, along with naturopathic methods. But, by themselves, they didn't always address every circumstance. Excellent as the nutritional approach is, there are instances when the animal simply will not eat or will reject all but the most specific foods, a limiting factor. Also, some severe illnesses, like bacterial or viral infections, simply progress too fast for nutrition to make a difference. One wants a treatment method that will act decisively in these situations, restoring appetite and enhancing resistance against the infection, yet work with the body's healing process.

So I kept my eyes and ears open for a more effective system. I kept hearing praise for homeopathy. Finally, I decided to examine it for myself. That decision was a turning point that expanded my horizons to embrace a medical approach of unique elegance, order, and effectiveness.

Homeopathy is practiced on both people and animals in most of the world and has been for more than 200 years. Because it is so powerfully effective, it deserves far more attention than it presently receives in the United States. The contributions of homeopathy to our general understanding of health and disease have been enormous. Because of its many virtues, I hope it will become a prominent medical art of the future.

To further this goal, in 1992 I began a postgraduate course for veterinarians, and it has continued every year since. In 1995, some of us who were practicing veterinary homeopathy started a professional organization, the Academy of Veterinary Homeopathy, which accredits training programs, holds an annual conference, publishes a journal, and certifies veterinarians as qualified to practice. As of 2015, almost 500 veterinarians have participated in this training and incorporated homeopathy in their practices.

The real beauty of the homeopathic system lies in the simplicity of its basic principles, combined with richly researched detail to guide the practitioner in choosing the most suitable remedy. *The Science of Homeopathy*, by George Vithoulkas, is an important modern discussion of the principles involved and is invaluable for a person interested in any form of holistic therapy.

Homeopathy was founded on one basic unifying principle, "Like is cured by like" (*Similia similibus curentur*), known as the Law of Similars and recognized by Hippocrates and many others. This principle has remained the foundation of homeopathy ever since the early 1800s when the German physician Samuel Hahnemann originated the system.

What does this phrase "like is cured by like" mean? Remember that earlier in this chapter we talked about the allopathic method of countering symptoms. Homeopathy is just the opposite in its approach. Medicines are used that stimulate similar symptoms in the body. "Whoa," you may think, "this doesn't make any sense. My cat is already sick; he doesn't need more of this."

Allow me to explain.

Dr. Samuel Hahnemann noted that some herbs that were really, really helpful in curing some diseases would produce similar but milder symptoms of the illness if given to a healthy person. In other words, it is one thing to treat a sick person, but what does this herb really do in the body? He tested this theory by testing herbs in healthy people to see what changes would occur. What he found is that an herb (or other substance—we will get to that) that could produce mild but similar symptoms to the disease condition being treated acted to stimulate the body's healing mechanism. He had actually found a way to enhance recovery from disease by using the body's own natural processes.

How does it act? Let me give you an example. Before I go into this I want to make clear that very small doses of homeopathic medicines are used. One of the fortuitous discoveries that Dr. Hahnemann made was that it took quite tiny amounts of this similar medicine to do the trick. Keep this in mind when we look at my example.

Let's say that you have an allergy—certain foods will set off a painful skin eruption of raised red welts, bumps that itch and sting. These bumps appear all over your body, along with a bad headache and a feeling of sleepiness and sluggishness. The only thing that gives relief (short of powerful pain-killers) is to put a cold cloth over the worst places. The headache is slightly better from pressing on the head with the hands. What a terrible condition to have!

To treat this homeopathically, we can use a different substance (it is important that it be different from the food that set it off) that will result in similar symptoms. Is there such a homeopathic medicine? Yes, made from honeybee venom. It was discovered by carefully studying the effects of this venom, that it can result (in people stung, for example) in a skin eruption just like this—raised welts like nettle rash, relieved only by cold applications. Not only that, but some people will get a headache that is relieved by pressure and also feel sleepy and out of sorts. A good match, wouldn't you say?

To treat this, the person will be given a

tiny dose of bee venom by mouth. How small? Much smaller than a drop—perhaps a millionth of a drop. This is when the miracle occurs. No sooner are the homeopathic pills put in their mouth than symptoms start to clear up, often in just a few minutes. It is like a miracle—indeed, it *is* one when you are the one suffering.

An example you may be more familiar with is the use of the drug Ritalin in children who are hyperactive. Ritalin causes nervous, excitable activity when taken by normal, healthy children but when given to children already in this condition it has the opposite effect, just like the bee venom on the food allergy. As long as the children are kept on the drug, their behavior becomes calmer and more normal. It is the ability of the drug to cause "hyperactive" behavior that makes it useful in treating the similar symptom in those naturally affected.

So this is the basic principle: The medicine used has been studied as to its effects in various dosages and has been found to cause similar symptoms to your patient's expression of his natural (untreated) disease. When this medicine (usually called "remedy" in homeopathy) is given in very small doses, too small to have the usual physical/chemical dose effect, it will trigger a reaction that allows the body to heal itself. I want to emphasize this—homeopathic treatment never opposes or blocks symptoms but only works with the natural healing mechanism the body already has going.

A good practitioner can read a whole set of signals flashed by a disease. Rather than prescribing one medication for a headache, another for an upset stomach, and a third for depression, the homeopathic doctor will offer a single remedy for the whole set of symptoms present in the patient. She will choose the one medication that would produce all three symptoms if given repeatedly to a healthy person.

The specially prepared remedies used in homeopathy contain minute doses of botanicals, minerals, or animal products, such as bee venom and cuttlefish ink. These substances are diluted and repeatedly agitated many times, so that only minuscule amounts actually remain. Sometimes dilution is so extreme that it goes far beyond the point where the substance could act on a molecular level. While there is much debate about how such diluted materials can work, many homeopaths (myself included) believe what Dr. Hahnemann originally said about it—that the specially prepared medicine carries a healing energy derived from the original material, what he referred to as "potency." One of the nice things about using these products is that because the physical amount of the substance is so small, even undetectable, we do not have to be concerned about side effects.

Let me tell you about a few animal cases that demonstrate homeopathic treatment.

Acute Cases

When I was first learning homeopathy, I encountered Misty, a cat suffering with septicemia, a rare postsurgical reaction following a routine spay. It involves bacterial spread in the bloodstream and a general breakdown of the blood-clotting mechanism. She was in pitiable condition, with a high fever and vomiting. Dark blood leaked from her back, stomach, legs, feet, mouth, and vagina. I also detected bleeding under the skin (dark blue swellings under the eyelids and ears). Though antibiotics might help, I was not sure they would act quickly enough in this crisis situation—they usually are not effective when the condition so advanced. She seemed to get worse even while I was examining her!

As a temporary measure, I decided to administer fluids under her skin, to help counter her moderate dehydration. While doing so, I immediately noticed that she was very hypersensitive to pain, far more than I would expect. She could not bear being touched at all! At this point, I recognized the similarity between Misty's condition and the known effects of the remedy *Arnica montana* (from the herb leopard's bane). Among the characteristics of Arnica, when tested in healthy people, are fever, hemorrhage, black and blue spots under the skin from bleeding, septic conditions, hypersensitivity to pain, and an aversion to touch.

So I immediately gave Misty a tablet of Arnica and repeated it in a few hours. Later in the day she was much improved. By the next morning, her temperature had dropped and she was no longer bleeding. She was obviously calmer—eating for the first time since becoming ill. Within 48 hours, the only remaining evidence of what had so recently been a life-threatening condition were a few dry scabs where the hemorrhages had been, and she was discharged. She remained in good health. I was quite impressed that such results had occurred without any necessity to use antibiotics or other drugs.

I'm often amazed to see how rapidly homeopathic medications can work. I find that in acute problems, they restore health much more quickly than drugs, and I have used them to treat a gamut of acute problems from severe infections like parvovirus or distemper to bites, punctures, abscesses, even gunshot wounds! One dog I remember had been shot through the shoulder and was in a great deal of pain. He received only one dose of a homeopathic remedy, *Hypericum*, and walked out the next morning, using the leg normally and without evidence of any discomfort. It is cases like this that make you a believer.

Homeopathic treatment also excels in chronic conditions, which are the bulk of my practice—allergies, autoimmune diseases, hyperthyroidism, urinary disorders, appetite problems, behavioral abnormalities, paralysis, skin problems, gum disease, and so on—in short, the whole gamut of animal diseases.

A Case of Severe Spinal Arthritis

A recent example of a more advanced chronic condition is a dog I treated with severe advanced spinal arthritis. Wilkie was an old Lab cross with arthritis of the spinal bones, weakness of the rear legs, and gradual wasting away of his muscles. As often happens with this condition, he exerted himself too much on an adventure and was unable to rise to his feet the next morning. The weakened spine will be easily injured, or there will be a small break in the calcium deposits around the bones. In any case, he couldn't use his legs anymore because of the paralysis and extreme pain. With homeopathic treatment, he improved to where he could take fairly long walks—even running along at times. The difference in these chronic, advanced cases is that progress is slower, in this case taking several weeks to achieve this much recovery.

A Case of Chronic Infectious Disease

Homeopathy works very well with nutritional therapy. An example case that comes to mind is Toby, an older cat whose lab tests had confirmed that he had feline infectious peritonitis—an often terminal condition, not curable with drugs. His symptoms included repeated vomiting, diarrhea, loss of appetite, and swelling of the abdomen with fluid. Over a period of several days, my client and I gradually changed his diet to a home-prepared one (as outlined in this book) and increased his vitality through the use of vitamins and other nutritional supplements. I then recognized an appropriate homeopathic remedy, which for this particu-

lar fellow was *Arsenicum album* (white oxide of arsenic). (Lest this alarm you, let me assure you that, once again, the amount of arsenic in a homeopathic remedy is much, much less than is found in the food you eat, where it is present as a trace mineral.)

So I gave him one dose, which was followed by a short aggravation of symptoms for a couple of days and then a continued improvement for a long period. Two months later the vomiting began to recur and I gave one more dose. He quickly returned to normal health and has remained stable ever since. On top of it all, his personality improved, so that he is now considerably calmer and steadier, and his weight increased from 6 to 11 pounds!

Treating Emotional Problems

Favorable personality changes often accompany successful physical treatment. Indeed, homeopathic remedies can be used to treat behavior problems. For instance, one client's cat had spontaneously developed a drastic personality change for the worse. Where she had once been friendly, she was now irritable, resistant to being held, and generally standoffish. Homeopathic treatment with *Nux vomica* (poison nut, a plant naturally growing in India and China) restored her normal, affectionate self.

This improvement of emotional or personality disorders is one of the most exciting aspects of working with homeopathy. Before I was knowledgeable about homeopathy, behavior problems in animals were frustrating and seemed hopeless to deal with. Usually, the best advice available was using drugs like tranquilizers or elaborate training that was time-consuming and not very effective. With homeopathy, that whole picture has changed.

Another example is that of a dog who underwent a Jekyll-Hyde transformation not long after getting a rabies shot. Formerly happy and friendly, he became suspicious, aggressive, and "barky." Worse yet, he began biting people—hard! Fortunately, I was able to restore this dog to his normal, happy self with one dose of a remedy called *Stramonium* (thorn apple, a plant also called *Datura*). This remedy is used for disturbances of the brain with the above symptoms of suspicion, aggressive behavior, and biting. (It's used in people who are mentally disturbed and who, believe it or not, exhibit this same behavior.) Unfortunately, we see these behavior disorders coming on after rabies vaccination much too often. Apparently, it causes a low-grade inflammation of the brain in some animals.

A Cat and Snake Story

Let me share one more story with you, one close to my heart, as it is about my own cat. After he survived this threatening condition, I was prompted to write it up as a dramatic story, so I will put it here as I wrote it (with the name of the other cat changed to protect the guilty).

The fight started under the forsythia bush, which is probably what saved his life.

The low-hanging branches allowed an escape and a quick, limping run to the house.

It had been coming on for some time now. Ming was quite aware of the new cat who had moved in next door, into what had been Ming's territory for the last 2 years. It was soon clear that the new cat was not going to leave. It was time to take a stand.

Very early in the morning, at first light, Ming took his position at the border of the yard, in front of the forsythia. Sitting erect and staring intently at the other yard, he put forth his challenge. It did not take long for Blackie to respond, and soon the two cats were in a face-off, staring intently at each other. It took about 20 minutes to go through the stages of escalating conflict— the posturing, the slow movements, the yowling. When the fight started, it was fast. In a blur of rolling, twisting movement, the two cats came together, the fast blows punctuated by startling screams. And much too fast for me to do anything more than look startled.

It is not possible for us human beings to see what is happening at these times. It would be interesting to have a slow-motion viewing of a cat fight, like the slow-motion films showing a horse running or water dropping. To us, it is a blur. To the cats, with their fast nervous systems, it is a dance of blows and counterblows.

Ming was actually the first to make a significant strike. With a sharp twist and parry, he turned to come down with his mouth on the neck of Blackie—a good, sharp hit that would have inflicted serious damage. Unfortunately, Ming had been born without hearing (white cat with blue eyes) and he missed an audio clue that would have told him that Blackie was making his move at the same instant. His bite was a very good strategic move, but it had little effect on his enemy. Indeed, it gave time for Blackie to clamp down on Ming's elbow with a deep, penetrating bite that went into the muscles and tendons around his joint.

The intense burning pain shot up Ming's arm and was so intense it was almost completely debilitating. It took all his forces to gather himself into a roll away from the engagement into the arms of the forsythia bush. In the heat of the moment, in spite of the severe wound, he was able to thread his way through the branches and use the injured leg for his getaway.

Many cat bites do not result in a serious problem. If a cat is healthy and strong, recovery will occur in a couple of days without resultant infection. Bacteria and other foreign material are often introduced into the wound, but a healthy body has the capacity to neutralize them, or to localize them as an abscess that will open and discharge to the outside.

Unfortunately for Ming, the injury was too much for him to handle. He ran off and hid for 2 days and simply could not be found. When he finally showed up, the bite wound was discharging a very bad-smelling pus and the tissues around the bite area had

died and turned dark—what is called gangrene. This is the most serious kind of injury a cat can sustain.

There is a difference between a cat bite that happens in the heat of battle when a cat is angry and intends to inflict harm and the bite that happens "accidentally" or with a little annoyance. It has been shown that the saliva of a cat becomes more toxic when it is angry, containing a form of cyanide. Perhaps it is the emotional state behind the intent that makes it a more serious bite. The bite of an angry cat is much like the bite of a venomous animal and will cause very serious harm, not just at the bite area but to the whole animal. Veterinarians know this and, though dog bites can cause more immediate destruction, cat bites are especially feared. Many vets have ended up in the hospital with what would seem an insignificant wound.

Ming was the unfortunate victim of the bite of an angry cat and was suffering for it. When he finally showed up, and I saw the problem, I had to decide how it best could be treated. My experience as a veterinarian had long ago shown me that antibiotic treatment of these injuries is only partially successful, if at all, so I considered using homeopathy as the best choice. I could see this was a more serious wound than most. For one thing, there was no evidence of a strong inflammatory reaction, which the body usually uses as a defense (swelling and fever). For another, the pus that had formed was very bad smelling, actually a rotten smell of something decaying. Lastly, the tissue and skin around the wound had died, turning dark and hard, and the hair had come off, showing the full extent of the problem. All in all, probably 25 percent of the lower arm was affected.

In conventional veterinary medicine, this would be seen as life-threatening, and if not improving with vigorous antibiotic treatment, amputation would be suggested. Instead I gave one single dose of the homeopathic remedy *Lachesis muta*, the venom of the bushmaster snake of South America.

"What?" you say. "What kind of voodoo medicine is this? Giving snake venom to a sick cat is not my idea of proper treatment." Let me explain, and you will see how this makes very good sense.

Remember at the start of this discussion we talked about using a substance that would produce a similar condition? Ming had, in a sense, been poisoned by Blackie, and we needed a remedy that would do a similar thing. You may not know a lot about snakebites except that they are not desirable. The bite of the bushmaster snake is very poisonous. Snakes hiss and strike quickly, burying their fangs into their victim and injecting a poisonous substance. (Sound familiar so far? Are you getting the picture of that angry cat hissing and striking with his fangs?) The poison many snakes inject causes the tissue around the wound to die and become gangrenous, and eventually a discharge of blood and decomposed flesh comes out of the wound. Not only that, but the whole animal is made sick, unwilling or unable to eat, and sitting huddled and miserable from the effects of the poison. People bitten by poisonous snakes have described it as a feeling of "being very toxic or poisoned."

Those of you who have had cats made sick from a cat bite will immediately relate to this picture and realize how similar the cat bite effect and the snakebite effect are. It is this similarity that makes *Lachesis muta*, the bushmaster snake poison, such a wonderful homeopathic remedy to use in these cases.

Of course, it would not work to have a poisonous snake bite Ming as a treatment! It would just make things worse. What is actually done is that a homeopathic pharmacy processes the poison to make it nonharmful in a chemical way; in other words, there is no directly poisonous effect left in the medicine. The venom is processed, sterilized, and diluted so that one gives just a little tiny bit of it by mouth—just enough to jolt the body into responding to the wound and to healing it.

And that is what happened with Ming. As soon as the medicine was given, the pus decreased, the bad smell went away, and the tissue began to heal. By the next day, he was able to use the leg and, within a short time, the hair grew back over the new skin and you cannot even see that there was ever an injury there. This is actually a remarkable response, as any veterinarian will attest.

Advantages of Homeopathy

From these examples, I think you can get a sense of the usefulness of homeopathic treatment. See how easy it is to give a single dose of medicine by mouth? How advantageous to avoid the side effects of antibiotics, the stress of anesthesia and surgery? And how elegant to use the body's own healing ability to resolve the problem? We can use substances that would ordinarily be quite harmful (like the venoms), yet in homeopathic form, they are entirely safe and effective.

Dr. Hahnemann's discovery caused a revolution in medicine that continues to this day. Though many people today have never heard of him, his methods of treatment were so successful that an appreciative public did him a rare honor. On June 21, 1900, with the attendance of President William McKinley, a large granite platform surrounded by four columns and containing a bronze statue of Dr. Hahnemann was unveiled at Scott Circle in Washington, DC. This monument still stands today.

Veterinarians can be trained in the use of classical homeopathy for animals by attending the Professional Course offered by the Pitcairn Institute of Veterinary Homeopathy. Information on the course and the current scheduling is available on the Pitcairn Institute Web site, pivh.org.

THE HOLISTIC ALTERNATIVE

As you can see, some pretty remarkable things can happen when we adopt a new view of the wholeness of the body and mind and treat from there. The success of the holistic therapies described in this chapter depends on the skill of the practitioner, the strength and will of the patient, the degree of support in the environment, the appropriateness of the selected method, and the cooperation of you, your animal's friend and companion.

This brief survey was meant to introduce you to the many exciting approaches that can help to relieve the suffering of animals. And if we are but willing to extend our mental horizons, how much more is possible?

LOVE HEALS, MAGIC HAPPENS

RICHARD AND SUSAN PITCAIRN

I am here she says she
Turns a bit her tattered ear to see.
It hurts, she cries yet wags her tail
Her heart is weak her tongue is pale.
I look beneath this outer shell:
The Love We Are shall make her well.

CHAPTER 18

HOW TO CARE FOR
A SICK ANIMAL

If your animal gets sick, there are several advantages to caring for it at home. First, home is familiar and safe, free of the stress a pet is likely to feel trying to recuperate in a busy veterinary hospital filled with unfamiliar animals and people. Second, you can provide some really useful nursing care at home. Fasting, special nutrition, or meticulous cleaning might not be provided in a hospital, either because these things take too much time or because the philosophy of disease treatment is different. Third, at home you are in charge; alternative or natural forms of treatment can be used without conflict.

On the other hand, a veterinarian is a skilled professional. Years of training and experience enable him or her to assess the seriousness of a condition and use the proper diagnostic techniques. For conditions that are either very messy to take care of (like severe vomiting and diarrhea) or life-threatening (such as a car accident or severe infection), the veterinary hospital offers support that is impossible to provide at home, including such treatments as anti-shock therapy, intravenous fluids, and surgery.

Both at home and in the hospital, your pet can recover faster and more completely if you utilize the general health care principles in this book and some of the nursing care methods outlined in this chapter. If, however, you are giving your animal a prescription drug recommended by your veterinarian, do not use the homeopathic remedies suggested in the Quick Reference Section of this book, since they tend to work against each other and it is not pleasant for your dog or cat. You can, however, use some of the herbal recommendations, particularly those suggested for external use or whose primary purpose is to help rebuild the tissues.

A seriously ill animal has certain basic needs. When wild animals are sick or injured, they go off by themselves to rest in a secure, peaceful place and to allow nature to heal the condition. We need to provide our pets with a comparable opportunity. Most sick animals want to be quiet, safe, and warm and to have access to fresh air and sunlight. Also, they often will fast instinctively. The loss of appetite seen in many diseases, especially acute infectious ones, is part of the healing response, rather than a symptom to be forcibly overridden.

So provide comfortable bedding in a cozy spot that is free of drafts, disturbances, and loud noise, where your dog or cat can rest peacefully and feel protected. Keep the area clean, changing the blankets or towels as necessary. If your pet desires it, allow some access to fresh air and sunlight (but don't impose it).

DETOXIFICATION

An idea that pops up right away for many people is that of detoxifying the body. When something gets in that needs to be eliminated, there are mechanisms in place that do that.

THE LIVER— THE MAIN PLAYER

In the human body (as an example, as I don't know the figures for a dog or cat), 2 quarts of blood go through the liver every minute. All the stuff coming in from the intestines—bacteria, bacterial endotoxins, even antigen-antibody complexes, as well as anything eaten that is not used for nutrition—all of this goes directly to the liver for processing. The liver is the main organ that has this function of neutralizing and removing these unwanted substances.

It does this in two ways. The first is a chemical process, utilizing enzymes, which will either neutralize a toxin (changing its structure) or modify it by breaking it apart and then neutralizing the parts. This very efficient activity evolved over many, many thousands of years, based on exposure to a very wide array of bacterial, plant, and animal toxins. The liver is poised and ready to recognize and dispatch the unwanted.

The second way it does this is by putting toxins into the bile that it manufactures for use in digestion. Bile is made by the liver and stored until needed, and its release is triggered by the presence of fats in the intestine after food is eaten. Bile then flows into the intestines and breaks the fat down into smaller units so they can be absorbed and used. The liver takes advantage of this opportunity by putting some of the toxins into this bile fluid that will be pooped out eventually. Clever. This second process using the bile works best when there is adequate fiber in the diet, as it is the fiber that absorbs these toxins.

But here's the rub. Even though the liver has had so much experience in recognizing and dealing with toxic materials, in these modern times we have created new substances that the liver cannot recognize. We have made many synthetic chemicals that simply have never existed on the earth before. So what is the liver to do? What would you do? Okay, what I would do is put the stuff I could not handle up on a closet shelf—out of sight, out of mind. The liver does something like this. If it does not have the enzymes to process something, or can't grab it (with other molecules) to get it into the bile, then it just stores it

in other tissues—usually the fatty ones.

This is why chemical toxicity and the subsequent poisoning of our bodies, and those of our animal friends, has become such a critical issue. Think about it for a moment. There are so many poisons used now. When we put out bait or spray something, where do we think it is going to go? After its use, will it just disappear?

How Can We Help?

Let's make this assumption: Much of what comes through, the liver can deal with. Not everything, as we have discussed. Some will have to be stored, but we can support the liver's work by making sure it is healthy. How? There is no simple answer, no single nutrient or herb that will do this. It is much too complex. Each liver cell contains millions of proteins, and there is no way we can cover the liver's needs with just a few foods or herbs.

The very best way to support the liver in its detoxification is to provide a very healthy, nutritious diet, one that will likely provide everything it needs. To go the extra yard, if you can do so, grow wheatgrass, sprouts, and fresh greens in your garden or yard. Add these—freshly picked, cut off, or shredded— to food. Unbelievably nutritious.

Another nice thing to do is to plant a variety of herbs in your garden that your dog or cat can go munch if that is his choice. Animals in nature will do this. When they don't feel well, they seek out a certain plant (who knows why that one!) and scarf it down. We can promote this natural response by making a variety of plants available.

Jan Allegretti, author of *The Complete Holistic Dog Book*, who has worked quite a bit with herbs, assists us in understanding the detox function, with this advice: Dandelion root is a wonderful ally in supporting the liver's detoxifying function. It's gentle, provides valuable minerals and other nutrients that aid in digestion, and has the added benefit of supporting kidney function. Use the dried herb, or make a strong decoction to add to meals. Most dogs and cats enjoy the earthy flavor. Burdock root and milk thistle are also widely used for liver support, and can also be administered as a dried herb or decoction."

FASTING

Fasting is one of the oldest and most natural methods of healing and greatly reduces the body's usual assimilation and elimination load, allowing it to break down and expel older wastes that may have accumulated in the liver and fatty tissues. The body also gets a chance to unload the products of inflammation, tumors, and abscesses. Once the body has cleansed itself, the overworked glands, organs, and cells have a chance to repair and restore themselves.

See Naturopathy on page 282 of Chapter 17 for conditions that generally benefit from fasting, as well as for those for which fasting should not be used.

FASTING CONCERNS

Some people are frightened by the idea of fasting their pet. Somehow we have convinced ourselves that a day or two without food will take a cat or dog close to death's door. Not true.

Your veterinarian may have told you that cats must eat every day, or else they run the risk of liver disease and jaundice. This does happen apparently, but only in cats who are already not well. I have never seen it myself. Animals at risk of liver problems will often be overweight and have a finicky appetite and a history of other problems.

Cats, being true carnivores, actually prefer a 28-hour eating cycle. In fact, healthy cats trapped in moving vans and such have been known to survive without any food or water for periods of up to 6 weeks. Because they live with people, they have actually had to adapt to eating two or three times a day. But that's not natural to them, or even desirable.

If you have a young, vigorous cat of normal weight, however, it should be fine to fast her for a while. Obese dogs have been known to fast on just water and vitamins for as long as 6 to 8 weeks without ill effect. Wild carnivores fast naturally, since prey may elude them for days.

So don't worry about fasting your pet for a few days. But if this concerns you, or your cat is aging and has a history of health problems, run it by your veterinarian first. Many holistically minded veterinarians have experience with fasting animals and can guide you.

Using Fasting to Aid Detoxing

It can be helpful to encourage fasting the first day or two of an illness, especially if there is a fever. A good rule of thumb is to fast your pet until its temperature returns to normal—1 to 2 days, or as long as 4 to 5, if necessary, provided that the animal is in reasonably healthy condition to start with. Remember that a normal body temperature for a dog and cat is less than 101.5°F (38.6°C).

The following program is a good basic guideline for fasting your animal. It can be used during illnesses, but it also can help your pet switch from its old eating habits to a new natural foods diet.

It is smart to get professional guidance in doing a fast, especially if this is new to you. A veterinarian can monitor your pet's basic functions, making sure nothing is too stressed.

The Break-In Period

Begin by easing the animal into the fast for 1 to 2 days. Feed it a lighter, simpler diet that includes a moderate or small amount of lean meat or tofu (crumbled, flavored with nutritional yeast),[1] along with some vegetables and cooked oatmeal. (Of course, if your animal is suddenly ill and loses its appetite, this step is not an option as she has already begun fasting, so to speak.)

Use vegetables considered beneficial to the kidneys and the liver—organs that will play major roles during the fast. They include broccoli, kale, cauliflower, cabbage, beets and turnips (with tops), dandelion greens, squash, spinach, corn, potatoes, cucumbers, parsley, carrots, and tomatoes. Serve them either raw and finely grated (which is preferable), or lightly steamed. Cats especially like nutritional yeast sprinkled on them for flavor.

The Liquid Fast

Next, proceed with the main part of the fast, a liquid diet. In acute problems, continue the fast until the temperature is normal and the animal is well on its way to recovery. In more chronic or degenerative conditions, the length of the fast may vary from 3 to 7 days—until there is substantial improvement and a hearty appetite returns. If you begin reintroducing solids and your animal doesn't seem hungry, stay with the liquid fast a little longer.

During this period, offer plenty of the following:

- **Water:** Use a pure source, such as spring, filtered, or distilled water. Do not use tap water, which may contain unwholesome chemicals.

- **Vegetable juices:** Use fresh juices only. Don't use juice more than 48 hours old (assuming it has been refrigerated). If you can't give your pet fresh juice, offer chopped or grated raw vegetables (especially greens and juicy ones) blended with pure water and strained through a sieve. If you can't do either, feed water and the broth recipe that follows.

• **Vegetable broth:** Using the vegetables listed for the break-in period, make a soup stock by chopping and then simmering them for 20 to 30 minutes. Pour off the liquid for the animal and save the solids for a soup or casserole for yourself. If your animal is young or run-down and seems to need a little extra energy, vegetable broth is very helpful in replenishing minerals and vitamins.

If your pet is having strained or constipated bowel movements early in the liquid fast stage, you can help get things going by slowly (over 1 to 2 minutes) administering an enema (see instructions under "Special Care," opposite). Though an enema is seldom needed during a short fast if your pet is in fairly good shape, the animal with a chronic disease or an acute infection may benefit from one or more enemas during a longer fast. If, after one or two enemas nothing more comes out, that is enough.

Breaking the Fast

When it's time to end the fast, give your pet a simple diet for several days. This transition diet should last 2 to 3 days for every 7 days the animal was on liquids. Offer water, juice, vegetable broth, or a moderate amount of raw or steamed vegetables (from the same group used before). After this period, begin adding other natural foods, starting with oatmeal or flaked barley cereal (cooked), soy milk, and figs or prunes. Then, after a day or two, offer the usual recipe from this book that you have been using. Many dogs and cats recovering from an illness will not eat large amounts at first, so you may find a half portion is all that is consumed the first day.

It is very important to break the animal out of the fast gradually and avoid any temptation to feed commercial foods or highly processed tidbits at this point, or else you may undo the beneficial effects of the fast and cause serious digestive upsets by overtaxing the system before it has fully reestablished peristalsis, the contractions that aid in digestion.

Animal foods (meat, milk products, cheese, eggs) are more difficult to digest and produce more toxins, so I prefer to avoid them until appetite and normal elimination (bowel movements) are established.

Carried out properly, a fast of this sort can be a great boon for your animal's health. I hope that you understand the spirit of the fasting instructions and do not misinterpret them. I am not saying that you can just put a sick dog on the back porch with no food and a little water to drink! I am not suggesting neglect by any means, but rather an attitude of support, which includes doing the right things at the right time. Though outwardly the two approaches may appear similar, your inner intent and concern make the difference. If you are not sure what to do or how long to keep the fast going, consult with a holistically oriented veterinarian before proceeding.

If Your Pet Won't Eat

Sometimes an animal (usually a cat) starts fasting on its own but does not regain its appetite at the end of the fast. This can happen as a result of stomach upset, inflammation of the digestive organs, or as a reaction to toxic chemicals in the body or the environment (from pollution or kidney failure, for example). In cats, it is a very common symptom of chronic disease.

Fasting becomes a problem if there is rapid weight loss and developing weakness that robs the body of the energy to heal. So it may be necessary to force-feed (put food in the animal's mouth) to keep a pet alive or to get it started eating again. This is not pleasant and I don't strongly encourage it, but I have seen situations where it has kept a cat alive long enough for homeopathic or other treatment to turn things around.

SPECIAL CARE

Depending on the animal's condition and symptoms, you may also need to provide other kinds of nursing care.

ENEMAS

Animals can benefit from enemas in some conditions, particularly in fasting, constipation, bowel irritation caused by bone fragments or toxic material (like garbage or spoiled food), dehydration, or vomiting.

Use pure water that is warm but not hot (test it on your wrist)—only about 2 tablespoons for a cat and up to a pint for a large dog. (Even a small amount of fluid will stimulate the bowel to empty itself.) Add a few drops of freshly squeezed lemon juice to the water and administer the solution with a plastic or rubber syringe (or enema bag and nozzle with larger animals) over a 2- to 3-minute period.

Here's how: First, lubricate the end of the syringe with vegetable oil and, while someone else calmly and gently holds the animal while it stands on the ground or in a tub, insert the nozzle carefully, slowly, into the rectum. With gentle, consistent pressure against the anus (so the fluid does not leak out), slowly fill the colon. If the solution does not flow in readily, it's probably because the syringe is up against a fecal mass, in which case you'll need to pull back on the nozzle or syringe and adjust the angle a bit. A bowel movement is usually stimulated within just a few minutes.

Administer an enema in this fashion once or twice a day for a couple of days. That's usually enough.

Dehydrated animals may simply retain the fluid. I have seen this many times. What happens is that the colon absorbs the fluid, which the body desperately needs. Thus, enemas are an excellent way to administer fluid therapy at home! Give them about every 4 hours under these circumstances, or until fluid is no longer retained.

If your animal has been vomiting a lot and can't keep water in its stomach, an enema can introduce fluid as well as salts needed to replace those lost through vomiting. Add a pinch of sea salt to the enema water, plus a pinch of potassium chloride (KCl, a salt substitute for people on low-sodium diets that is sold in supermarkets). This same salt-replacement fluid therapy will help a dog or cat with prolonged diarrhea. Again, administer every 4 hours or until fluid is no longer retained.

BATHING AND CLEANING

In some cases an animal is so fouled by vomiting, diarrhea, or skin discharges that a bath is definitely in order. You should, however, take on this task only at the end of an illness, when the animal is well on the way to recovery and its temperature is normal. Otherwise, rely upon the cleaning methods described below. Even then, be sure the animal does not become chilled. Dry him quickly by giving him a good toweling, followed by a warm sun bath or blow-dry, with the dryer set on low and held not too close to the fur. The only exception to the rule of waiting until toward the end of an illness is when the dog or cat, particularly a young one, is so heavily parasitized with fleas and lice that its strength is being sapped. Then a soapy bath that will remove and drown these parasites is in order. The Dr. Bronner's soaps, which are organic, are very nice for this use. One of their formulas made with lavender will be especially effective against fleas and ticks, as the lavender herb has been known for some time to be effective against these parasites.

Care of the Body Openings

Very often, a disease will cause discharges from various body orifices, especially the nose, eyes, ears, and anus. Sick animals, particularly cats, are made miserable by accumulations they cannot remove and that can irritate underlying tissues. Here are a few simple cleansing techniques that offer great relief.

The nose: If plugs and secretions have formed, carefully clean the nose with a soft cloth or gauze saturated with warm water. Sometimes patience is needed to soften the material so you can gradually remove it. Two or three short sessions may be better than a single long one.

Once the nose is clean and dry, smear the area with *almond oil*, perhaps mixed with vitamin E oil from a capsule, or *calendulated oil* (available from homeopathic pharmacies). Apply two or three times a day.

The eyes: To clean crusts and secretions from the eyes and eyelids, make up a soothing, nonirritating saline solution by mixing ¼ teaspoon of sea salt into a cup of distilled or filtered water. Stir well and use it to clean the eyes as described above for the nose. Then put one drop of one of the following soothing treatments in each eye: *almond oil* (for mild irritation) or *castor oil* (for more irritated and inflamed eyes).

Or, instead of the above treatment, bathe the eyes frequently with one of the following two herbal infusions.

An infusion of *eyebright* (*Euphrasia officina-*

lis) is useful where there are injuries or irritation of the eyes. To make it, bring 1 cup of pure water to a boil; pour over 1 teaspoon of the herb. Let it steep, covered, for 15 minutes. Then pour off the liquid through a sieve or through cheesecloth, leaving the solid herb pieces behind. For every cup of the infusion, add ¼ teaspoon of sea salt. This makes the solution mild and soothing (like natural tears).

Goldenseal root is helpful when the eyes are infected or discharging thick, yellow material. To make a treatment solution, pour 1 cup of boiling water over ¼ teaspoon of goldenseal powder. Let it steep for 15 minutes; then filter off the liquid part. To this liquid, add ¼ teaspoon sea salt.

When the solution you are preparing has cooled down, gently clean and treat the eyes three times a day, or as needed. Keep these solutions covered at room temperature on your countertop for 2 days. To avoid contamination, always pour off a little into a dish or cup to use for treatment, and then put the cover back on the main batch. Discard this treatment fluid rather than return it to the stock you made.

The ears: If the ears contain much oily or waxy secretion, trickle about ½ teaspoon of *almond oil* into the ear hole, using a dropper or squeeze bottle. First, warm the oil in a cup or glass that is partly immersed in a sink or bowl of hot water. Firmly lift the ear flap or tip. You may need someone to hold the animal's head in place, because if you let go

or the animal pulls away before you finish the job, he will shake oil all over you. Let the almond oil run down into the ear for a few seconds.

Then, while still holding the ear flap, reach down with your other hand and massage the ear canal from the outside at the bottom of the ear opening. It feels like a firm plastic tube that you can compress as you massage. If you do it right, you'll hear a squishy sound. This treatment loosens up and dissolves the lodged wax. Use a tissue to remove any excess oil and materials that work their way out. Don't use a cotton swab except around the opening. When you let go of the ear, it will be vigorously shaken, so be prepared.

My experience has been mostly using almond oil and olive oil for dissolving waxy substances. Another suggestion comes from Jan Allegretti.

> *I've had great success using coconut oil in the ears, for cleaning and for infections. Since it's naturally antibacterial and antifungal, it works well on its own. Coconut oil has the added advantage that it's easy to administer in its solid form. It's liquid at body temperature, but it solidifies when it's 76 degrees or cooler. I keep it in a cool cabinet so it's solid when I need it. A small piece of the solid oil is easy to place in the animal's ear, then as the ear is massaged the oil very quickly melts and fills the ear canal.*

If the ear is very red and inflamed, use *calendula oil* or *aloe vera juice*. This can be obtained from health food stores or as fresh juice from a plant. It's usually adequate to treat the ear this way once every day or two.

Another treatment for irritated ears is *green tea infusion*. Put a tea bag (or a teaspoon of the loose herb) in a mug and fill with boiling water. Steep for 10 minutes and take the bags out (or pour the mixture through a sieve). When cooled down, use to flush out the ears.

On the other hand, if the ear is painful when touched at the massage point but shows no discharge, some foreign body, such as plant material or a tick, may be inside the ear canal. It is best to have your veterinarian examine the ear. If there is no obvious cause for the ear pain, a good treatment to use is *arnica oil* (available at a homeopathic pharmacy or a health food store). Gently treat the ear (as described previously) once a day until the discomfort is gone.

The anus: Often the anus will get very inflamed as a result of excessive diarrhea, causing the surrounding tissue to get irritated and sometimes infected with bacteria. To keep this area clean during the diarrhea stage of an illness, sponge it gently with a damp cloth (rubbing can further irritate it). Pat (don't rub) it dry and then apply some *calendula ointment* two or three times a day or as needed.

HEALING HERBS

Herbal treatment is very helpful in many illnesses. Herbs gently assist the body in various ways—to support discharge, enhance digestion, cleanse the blood, and so on.

Here is a listing of some of the most useful herbs in my experience. Use only one herb rather than a combination. Pick the one that best matches the problems described, using doses shown in the chart on page 136.

- **Alfalfa** (*Medicago sativa*) is an excellent tonic to stimulate digestion and appetite, help thin animals gain weight, and improve physical and mental vigor. It suits those who are underweight, nervous, or high-strung, perhaps with muscle or joint pains or urinary problems— especially with crystal formation and bladder irritation. For dogs, depending on size, add 1 teaspoon to 3 tablespoons of ground or dry-blended alfalfa to the daily ration. Or make a tea by steeping 3 tablespoons of the herb in 1 cup of water for 20 minutes. Mix it with food or give orally with a bulb syringe. For cats, give 1 teaspoon (dry) per day.

- **Burdock** (*Arctium lappa*) cleanses the blood and helps the body detoxify. It's particularly good for easing skin disorders. Soak 1 teaspoon of the root in 1 cup of spring or distilled water in a glass or enamel pan for 5 hours. Then bring to a boil, remove from the heat, and let cool. Check the table on page 136 for how much to give to dogs. Cats can be given ½ teaspoon per day.

• **Oats** (*Avena sativa*) are also a tonic, particularly for the animal whose main weakness is in the nervous system, as in epilepsy, tremors, twitching, and paralysis. Oats also counter the weakening and exhaustive effects of heavy drugging and diseases. They help to cleanse the body and nourish new tissue growth. Use oatmeal as the chief grain in the diet.

BATHING

Sometimes an oat straw bath can help the skin to discharge. Boil 1 to 2 pounds of the straw in 3 quarts of water for 30 minutes. Add this to the bathwater or sponge on repeatedly as an after-bath rinse by standing the animal in a tub and reusing the solution. Such treatment is useful for skin problems, muscle and joint pain, paralysis, and liver and kidney problems. Dogs enjoy it more than cats.

HOW TO PREPARE AND GIVE MEDICINES

Using herbal and homeopathic medicines is not familiar to many people. Here is detailed information on acquiring, preparing, and administering these medicines.

USING HERBAL PREPARATIONS

Three basic forms of herbs can be used in preparing treatments: fresh, dried, or tinctures.

Fresh Herbs

When possible, use an herb that has been freshly harvested right before use. If you have some knowledge of herb use already and know how to identify them, it can be fun to harvest them yourself in vacant lots, along roadsides (avoid heavily traveled areas because of car exhaust contamination), in country fields or woods, or perhaps in your own herb garden.

For optimal effectiveness, pick an herb when its essential oils (the most active ingredients) are at their peak. In general, that means you should collect any above-ground parts in the morning, after the dew has dried but before the hot sun has evaporated some of the oils. Ideally, leaves should be harvested just before the plant is about to begin its flowering stage. Gather flowers just before they reach full bloom (they have much less value after that).

If you're going for the whole above-ground part (leaves, stems, and all), pick it just before the flowering stage. Roots and rhizomes are best collected in the fall, when the sap returns to the ground, the leaves are just beginning to change their color, and the berries or seeds are mature.

Because many people are unfamiliar with using fresh herbs, the instructions in this book usually refer to dried herbs. But if the fresh plant is available, use about three times the volume indicated for dried herbs in the listings.

Dried Herbs

In most cases you will probably just buy the herb dried, either loosely cut or powdered and perhaps packaged in gelatin capsules. Dried herbs can be administered either in these capsules or mixed with water in an infusion, decoction, or slurry. You can save some money on capsuled herbs by buying empty capsules from a pharmacy and packing your own. One "00" capsule holds about ½ teaspoon of powdered herb. I like the cellulose caps made from plant ingredients (called "veggie caps" or "vege-caps") rather than cow hooves. I think they are more easily digested and healthier. If you need to powder the herb, use a coffee grinder or mortar and pestle to grind it to a fine dust.

If you gather or grow your own herbs, you can dry them for later use. Collect them after the morning dew on the leaves has dried. Tie in bunches and hang them upside down in a well-ventilated, dry, shaded area. Enclosed attics are good. If you gather roots and barks, scrub them well, then chop them up and dry them on screening in direct sunlight. Once they are thoroughly dried, store them in opaque or capped brown jars in a cool, dark place. Properly cured and stored, herbs retain most of their medicinal qualities for some time. Since these properties are destroyed by heat, sunlight, and exposure to air, however, it is best to keep them no more than a year.

Herbal Tinctures

Another way to obtain and use herbs is in a tincture (extracted in alcohol and water) form. The easiest way to get tinctures is to buy them from herbal supply houses or homeopathic pharmacies. But if you have access to the fresh plant, the best form of tincture is one made from freshly collected, organically grown material.

To make your own tincture, macerate and grind the fresh herb (or use a blender). Add 1 rounded tablespoon of herb to ½ cup vodka or brandy (at least 80 proof). Store the mixture out of the sun in a clean, tightly capped jar. Shake it once or twice a day over 2 weeks. Then strain off the solids through a fine cloth or paper filter, collecting the liquid, which is your tincture. Store it in tightly capped glass bottles in a cool, dark area. (If you use dried herbs instead of fresh, use 1 rounded teaspoon of the cut or powdered herb for each ½ cup of alcohol.)

Herbal tinctures are a very potent form of medicine. Use carefully at low dosages, as the specific instructions in the Quick Reference Section will indicate. Tightly capped, they keep for 3 years.

Preparing Herbal Medicines

Either the fresh or dried forms of herbs can be used to make infusions, in which boiling water is added and they are steeped (like making tea). To make a less strong-tasting, more palatable version of an infusion, double the amount of herb used and just soak it in cold water overnight. This is called a cold extract. If the herb comes as a root or a bark, simmer it in boiling water for 15 to 20 minutes (called a decoction).

Infusions or cold extracts should be prepared in a covered, nonmetallic container such as (nonlead) pottery or glass (to retain the volatile substances). Simmer decoctions in an open, nonmetallic pan (to concentrate the product). Always use purified water (distilled or filtered) for these preparations. Specific amounts to use are given on pages 470–471.

Tinctures should always be diluted, three drops per teaspoon of water, just before administering.

ADMINISTRATION OF THE MEDICINES

Sometimes giving a recommended herb or plant can be simple—like putting it on a plate, setting it on the floor, and watching your dog devour it. But other times it is not so easy, so here is some advice.

How to Give Liquid Medication

There are two techniques I recommend for getting any form of liquid medication (conventional medicine or a diluted tincture, decoction, infusion, or cold extract) down an animal's throat.

Pry the mouth open. Lightly grasp the animal's upper jaw with one hand and insert your thumb and fingers in the gaps just behind the fangs. (For a cat or tiny dog, just one finger is needed in addition to the thumb.) Most animals will then relax their mouths slightly so that you can pour the liquid with a spoon or dropper between the front teeth. Tilt the head back when you

do this so the liquid runs down the throat.

Alternatively, make a pouch out of the animal's lip. Use one hand to pull out the corner of the animal's lower lip to make a little pouch and, keeping the head tilted back, pour the liquid into it with the other hand.

In either instance, if the liquid doesn't go in, it's because the teeth are clenched too tightly. If so, pry them open slightly with your fingers. If your animal backs away, put its rear end in a corner so it can't move away from you during the process, or get someone to help hold your pet. Another way to do this is to sit on the floor or a bed with your pet between your legs. With her rear end toward you and the head facing away,

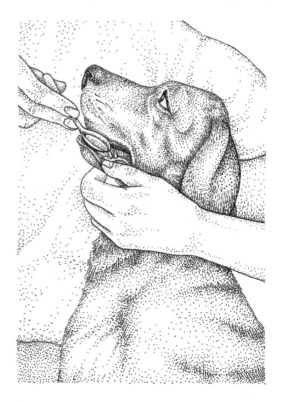

you can keep her positioned more easily for the administration.

For a cat, you may need someone to help by gently but firmly holding its front feet, or you can do the job alone by wrapping the cat quickly and snugly in a towel. Be gentle and positive so your animal doesn't have reason to feel afraid and put up a struggle. You don't have to make a big prying effort. Just firmly and persistently work at putting your fingers between the teeth to open the mouth until the teeth separate a little.

After the medicine is in, induce swallowing by gently holding the mouth almost closed and massaging the throat. Swallowing is signaled by the tongue's emerging briefly from between the front teeth. Alternatively, you can briefly put your thumb over the nostrils to achieve the same purpose.

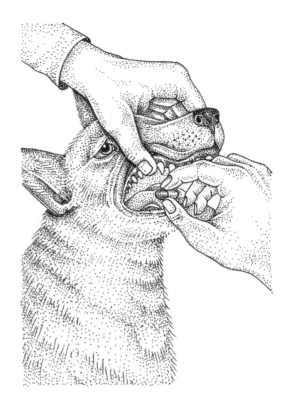

How to Give Pills and Capsules

To give most solid medications like herbal capsules or vitamin pills, open the animal's mouth by grasping around the upper jaw, as described for liquids. Hold the capsule or pill between your thumb and the first finger or else between the first and second fingers. Use the remaining fingers to press down the lower front teeth and thus pry the jaw open.

Insert the medication into the throat, pushing it as far back as you can. Then induce swallowing as described above. At first this will seem difficult and awkward. After a few tries, however, you will become more experienced and find it much easier.

Another way is to put capsules or pills in some tasty food. Dogs like peanut butter, for example. Oftentimes, if they don't taste bad, you can open capsules, or grind up pills, and mix the contents with some liquid food that they like. For example, many cats will take something mixed in with milk or half-and-half (but maybe not if they can taste it!).

How to Prepare and Use Flower Essences

Dr. Bach's flower essences are available in 38 individual "stock" bottles. The specific preparations are made by combining them and diluting them into a formula. Here is how it is done: If you wanted to make a formula of Chicory, Heather, and Clematis (three of the flowers out of the available 38), for example, you would first put two drops from the stock bottle for each of these flowers into a clean, 1-ounce dropper bottle. Then you would fill the bottle with spring water (not distilled) to make the dilution. This is your "treatment" bottle; a standard dosage is to give two drops four times a day. The drops can be put on the tongue, inside the lips, or added to food or water. Usually, this treatment is done for several days or weeks, depending on need.

USING HOMEOPATHIC MEDICATIONS

To give a homeopathic medicine, use one of four methods.

1. Give the tablets or pellets whole. Administer them from the cap of the vial or from a clean spoon directly into the mouth (it's best not to touch them). For dogs, putting them in a clean bowl or dish will often work as well, as they like to eat them.

2. Crush pellets to a powder (use three pellets). To do the crushing, make a crisp fold in a heavy paper, folding it in half. (A small index card is very good for this.) Pour the tablets from the bottle into the open fold. Fold the paper flat, in half, with the pellets inside against the crease, and put the folded paper on a hard countertop. Tap against the pellets (in the paper) with something heavy like a glass or other object. You don't have to hit hard, just tap, and you will hear them break up. The pellets from some pharmacies and other suppliers can be very hard, so don't try to do this on your antique wooden table.

With a word of encouragement, invite your animal to lick the powder off the paper (it tastes sweet). If he is not interested, use the same holding and prying technique described for other pills to get the medicine in. Prepare by pushing the powder down to the edge of the paper with your fingernail, then open the mouth and flick the powder from the paper onto the animal's tongue.

3. Alternatively, you can dissolve the powder (as made above) in a small amount of water and administer with a spoon or syringe. All the animal needs is to taste it, so not all of the liquid need be given. Sometimes with cats you can put the liquid on their nose or front paws and they will lick it off.

4. For animals more difficult to medicate, when putting the pellets or powder into the mouth is not an option, add the remedy to a small amount of milk and invite them to drink it.

One of the nice things about working with the homeopathic medicines is that they do not have to be given for long periods, sometimes even just once, so that makes treatment much easier.

The homeopathic remedies mentioned in

the Quick Reference Section can be either ordered online or purchased in natural food stores.

Your Home Remedy Kit

Don't wait until your animal needs treatment to track down basic supplies. Like a Boy Scout, be prepared. In Handling Emergencies and Giving First Aid (page 460), some of the most useful remedies for injuries will be listed and these are useful, of course, to obtain before they are needed.

HOW TO USE THE QUICK REFERENCE SECTION

In this book we are emphasizing prevention as much as we can—good food, healthy lifestyle, fun living—yet we know there are certain health issues for which additional advice would be welcome. We will address them in this section. These recommendations are treatments that, from my experience, have a reasonable chance of working. It is, of course, far better to work with a veterinarian who offers the holistic choice (as described in prior chapters), is trained in one of the alternative forms of therapy (and I especially emphasize homeopathy), and is knowledgeable about nutrition. This is what I recommend if at all possible. However, the reality is that I regularly get requests from people to help them find such a veterinarian and it is often the case that there is no one in their area. (A list of veterinarians I have trained in homeopathic practice through the Pitcairn Institute of Veterinary Homeopathy is available on our website, http://pivh.org).

This section is done with the intention of giving some guidance on what you could try yourself. I try to make the instructions clear and the method safe to use, but, please, if you feel at all hesitant or uncertain, find a veterinarian to work with along these lines. Sometimes a conventional veterinarian, not necessarily trained in these other methods, will still help you assess what you are doing by examining your animal and confirming that she is healthy.

As much as possible, select from the treatment choices the

one that best fits your pet's particular situation and most accurately corresponds to what you see as the problem. This will require careful observation on your part. You will find an emphasis on using homeopathic medicine because that is what I have the most experience with.

Some of these treatments can be used in conjunction with conventional veterinary treatment, if necessary. Others, particularly homeopathic medicines, should not be used with drugs or other treatment methods like acupuncture, so read the instructions carefully.

Nutrition and Lifestyle

You may recall from the first part of the book that we believe optimal health requires a total approach. At the start, it's important to consider and address any causative or contributing factors in the lifestyle, environment, or diet so that there are no external obstacles to your animal's recovery. Because we are emphasizing the importance of nutrition in this edition and in the instructions that follow, it is assumed that you will be incorporating the nutritional guidance given here as the start of any health program.

In past editions of our book there were specific vitamin supplements mentioned as part of the treatment, but since that time, this has become more questionable. There have been some reports that the total balance of nutrients can be off when doing this, and also the quality of some products is uncertain. It has always appealed to us to try

to use whole foods, organically produced, rather than isolated nutrients, and this is the approach we are taking in this edition as much as we can.

The instructions that follow are focused on treatments using herbs, naturopathic methods, and homeopathy. We are assuming the foundational part of your program is the nutritional advice we are giving you and that the treatments will be built *on that foundation*. In the recipe charts for both dogs and cats in Chapter 6, Recipes for Today, at the top of each chart is a row of codes that will direct you to the recipes best for some specific conditions. For example, the code A tells you that this recipe is particularly useful for animals with allergies and gastrointestinal problems. The code D identifies the recommended recipes for diabetes.

How to Look Up a Particular Disease

To find an elusive topic, check under a larger grouping. For example, canine distemper and also chorea, which is a common aftereffect of distemper, are both listed under Canine Distemper and Chorea. Many conditions are grouped according to the body part or organ they affect: Stomach Problems, Skin Problems, or Ear Problems, for example.

What You Can Expect

Except in some acute conditions that may clear up rapidly, healing generally takes time. It took a while for the body to get out of balance, and it takes time to restore it. Of course, if we give a painkiller or a suppressive drug such as cortisone, we may see some rapid relief, but this is not a true cure. Take away the drug and the symptoms are likely to return eventually, often worse than before.

Since our aim is to address the underlying weakness and restore health permanently, it's important to recognize the progressive stages and understand the gradually changing picture of symptoms in healing. That way we can tell if our treatment is really helping or whether another approach should be tried.

When a treatment is working, in the sense of health being recovered, an acute illness (sudden, self-limited) generally responds quickly (often within a few minutes, or sometimes in a few hours). Chronic illness, on the other hand, changes slowly. It often takes several days to see the signs of a change for the better, and this becomes more apparent over a couple of weeks. In terms of complete recovery, it can take months or even a year or more if it is an advanced condition.

The chance of complete recovery depends on several significant factors, including the age, level of vitality, and extent of illness in your pet. Though a disease that has progressed far enough to do extensive damage to the body may not be completely reversed, it can be alleviated, sometimes very significantly. Of course, it isn't reasonable to expect organs or tissues to always return to their previous undamaged state, but we may be able to stop the progression of the

chronic disease permanently and enhance healing to the limit of the body's abilities.

For example, an old cat with kidney failure can be brought from a state of debilitating illness to one of relative normality. The treatment, however, may have to continue for the rest of his life with occasional use of homeopathic medicines, a restricted protein diet, and fluid therapy as needed. Internally, our treatment may only have improved the kidneys' functioning from a level of 25 percent to 35 percent effective use. That 10 percent, however, can make all the difference.

On the other hand, if your animal is younger and has been ill only a relatively short time (not years), with little physical damage in the organs or tissues, there is a real chance of restoring the animal to its original healthy state. Actually, one will often see the level of health better than before when these natural methods are used.

Another consideration is the extent of previous drug treatment or surgery. The long-term action of drugs such as cortisone, for example, can damage the glands and organs of an animal so that a healing response cannot be aroused, or if it can, not right away (that is, it may be delayed, sometimes for weeks).

Surgery is the most irreversible of all treatments. Obviously, if an organ is removed (a common example is the removal of thyroid glands in cats with hyperthyroidism), it cannot be healed. If a client brings such an animal to me, I know at the outset that a complete cure is not possible. This is because we have to restore the thyroid glands to normal functioning to return this animal to true health. But if there are no thyroid glands . . .

I can say that, in general, improved nutrition and use of healing methods like homeopathy, herbal medicine, and nutrition will surely improve the quality of your animal's life—often dramatically.

Signs of Progress

Many natural therapies include the notion of the "aggravation," a brief increase of symptoms that occurs just before the patient really starts to recover. You need to understand the significance of this favorable sign. Otherwise, you might jump to the conclusion that things are getting worse and load the animal down with a host of heavy-duty drugs that could actually interfere with the cure.

How can you tell whether your pet is going through a healing process or is actually getting worse? Here is a good general rule: If your animal has an increase of (usually) one symptom (diarrhea, for example) but, at the same time, seems to feel better overall, then the change is favorable. Equally important, a temporary healing increase in a symptom is almost always over quickly. Typically, in my work with homeopathy, this reaction to effective treatment will be gone quickly, often in an hour or two, perhaps up to 12 hours. In my work, if my assessment was that the medicine was working all right, I would have the client check in with me the next day and by then things would be improving.

So the idea here is that with a healing ther-apy, some of the symptoms may temporarily worsen, but this period will be brief and followed by definite improvement. If your pet goes through a period of increased symptoms that lasts for days and she still seems sick, it is probably not a healing crisis and the situation should be reevaluated. It is important here to understand that the animal that is getting worse in general, or has several symptoms, is not being healed—the disease is getting worse. What is different with a healing process is that one or two symptoms may be mildly increased for a brief period, during which time your pet feels better and acts more normal. (See Chapter 18 for more discussion of this topic.)

Many physicians and healers have noticed certain patterns that the body expresses in its attempt to cope with health imbalances. Homeopaths have formalized these patterns as "Hering's Law of Cure," named after a famous American homeopathic physician, Constantine Hering. Here is the way to understand the process.

There is an underlying intelligence in the body (in homeopathy, it's called the vital force) that is in charge of maintenance and repair. To do this, the body utilizes a few basic strategies to limit the problem and protect its most vital and important functions. Specifically, it attempts to:

• Prevent disturbances from spreading (for example, creating a local abscess instead of allowing the infection to spread throughout the body).

• Keep the disease on the surface of the body rather than let it get to the vital organs.

• Focus disease around the limbs, rather than on the trunk (the main part of the body).

• Confine disease to the lower end of the body, away from the head, and therefore away from the brain and sensory organs.

• Maintain the problem at the physical level rather than the emotional or mental level, which would interfere more seriously with the overall functioning of the individual.

Therefore, a patient's health is taking a wrong turn if symptoms start to spread or begin to involve deep-seated organs. Common sense tells us that the more the condition disturbs the functioning of parts of the body that are most crucial to its survival and governing capacities, the worse it is.

Hering's Law can also help you to recognize a turn in the right direction, toward greater health, which can initially require a careful reading of more subtle indications. It is a favorable sign, for instance, if an animal with a chronic degenerative disease affecting vital organs begins to develop a skin rash or discharge, thus shifting symptoms away from organs toward the surface. Overall improvement will take place during this process, and, gradually, the surface problem will lessen as the internal disorder is healed. The vital force of the body focuses on this surface lesion as a way to rid itself of the disturbance.

Some cases can be more difficult to interpret, especially those in which the animal begins to reexperience old symptoms that were previously treated by a process that did not really cure them, but simply suppressed them for a time. In such situations it is best to work with a skilled holistic veterinarian.

If you study the principles outlined above, however, you will have an excellent guide for determining whether, as a whole individual, your animal is actually getting better or worse. Much of it is really common sense if you think about it.

Let's look at some examples. Suppose your dog tends to get fungus infections around the feet and lower legs. After months of strenuous drug treatment, the feet have cleared up. Recently, however, little bald patches and irritations have begun to appear on the skin of the abdomen, chest, and near the head. Though this new problem may be diagnosed differently, it is really just another expression of the original problem that was suppressed but not really cured. It is the same disease, but it has changed form and location. And it has progressed from a less important, peripheral location (the feet) closer to a more important area (the head).

Here's a more subtle example of a condition getting worse. After repeated treatments and even surgery, your dog's chronically inflamed ears have finally cleared up. But now, several weeks later, you notice that he isn't as friendly as he used to be. He prefers to go off by himself and may even growl or bite. The seat of the disturbance has moved inward, from the physical to the emotional level. Though various drugs may be tried in an effort to control the personality changes, the overall problem will only get worse. Tranquilizers may make him easier to live with, more subdued and passive. But over time, he may weaken at the mental level, perhaps acting sluggish and disoriented. He may have spells of confusion. At this point the disturbance will interfere with the basic mental processes that help him process information and orient himself. (I have observed many dogs treated in this way develop seizures.)

Though this may sound like a far-fetched example, I assure you it is not. Cases like this happen all too often. If this same dog were treated in a curative way at the point when his problem became emotional, you would see a return of the earlier physical symptoms after his moods improved. Most likely, it would be a reemergence of the ear inflammation. Then the ear or any other surface problem could be treated with the methods we discuss in this book. Once you have stimulated the body to move in a curative direction, it is also possible that the ear condition will go away on its own, without further treatment.

As another example, let's say you have a cat with an abscess. She also has been showing emotional signs of trouble—depression and lethargy. After treatment, however, she has begun to run around and act frisky. Even though there may still be a discharge from the abscess, the psychological improvement is a very favorable sign, and it will be followed by physical healing. It is indeed the first sign that healing is under way.

In general, these signs during therapy also indicate good progress.

- An increase in energy and overall playfulness
- Return of a calm, good-natured manner
- Self-grooming (especially true of cats)
- A return of normal appetite
- Reestablishment of normal bowel movements and urination
- Ability to have sound and restful sleep

Healing Discharges

Let's also look carefully at some of the methods the body uses to heal itself. Generally, when a disease is being eliminated, you will see signs of discharge. It signals that buildups of toxic materials are leaving the body. This is not always seen—it depends on the condition as well as how far along it is. However, if it does occur, the most common ways this elimination occurs are through:

- Formation of a pus pocket and drainage out of the body
- Development of skin eruptions (a very common route)
- A strong body odor ("doggy odor"), which is temporary

- Darker or strong-smelling urine
- Dark, smelly feces or diarrhea
- Vomiting (especially during acute conditions)
- Shedding of the nails or of skin from the bottoms of the paws

When using the holistic methods discussed in this book, you may see one or more of these forms of discharge, to a mild degree. This will particularly happen if the problem has been well established in the body.

Sometimes the discharge can be fairly dramatic. For example, I'm reminded of a dog whose owner used herbs and fasting to successfully help her pet recover from a severe attack of distemper. Soon afterward, however, the animal was covered with red, itchy skin that oozed sticky fluid—clearly a discharge phenomenon. A few more days of supportive treatments were followed by full recovery. Once such a recovery is complete, an animal will be much stronger and better able to withstand future diseases.

Let's summarize the ways to evaluate progress. Supportive, nonsuppressive therapies exhibit two processes: (1) movement of symptoms in a favorable direction (away from the head toward the feet; away from vital organs to surface tissue; from mental and emotional to physical) and (2) some form of discharge. If you see these signs, chances are very strong that the animal is getting better, regardless of which form of therapy you are using.

I should add as a cautionary note, however, that treatment with some drugs, particularly with cortisone, can create a false sense of well-being that disappears when the drug is discontinued. So keep in mind that you are looking for a response that comes from the natural processes of the animal, assisted by the treatment. Such a response will lead to recovery and permanent healing, not a dependence on a drug.

In this Quick Reference Section there are several references to small, medium, and large dogs, related to diet and kinds of treatments. Here is a general guide for sizes of dogs.

- Toy dogs—up to 15 pounds
- Small dogs—16 to 35 pounds
- Medium dogs—36 to 60 pounds
- Large dogs—61 to 90 pounds
- Giant dogs—over 90 pounds

COMMON PET AILMENTS
AND THEIR TREATMENTS

ABSCESSES

Abscesses are a common complication of puncture wounds from fights. They plague cats much more than dogs, because cats' needlelike teeth and sharp, penetrating claws inflict narrow but deep wounds. Feline skin seals over very quickly, trapping bacteria, hair, or other contaminated material inside. Sometimes, even a broken-off claw or tooth is retained under the skin.

Cat abscesses usually occur around the head and front legs or at the base of the tail. Wounds around the head indicate that your cat was either the aggressor or bravely facing the enemy. Wounds at the tail area or on the rear legs mean that your cat was trying to get away.

In dogs, abscesses are usually caused by foxtails or plant awns that get trapped in the hair and work their way through the skin (especially between the toes, around or in the ears, and between the hind legs). An abscess that keeps draining and does not heal (called a fistula) may indicate the presence of a foreign object somewhere in the tissue, sometimes several inches from the place of drainage.

Treatment: Cats

I have had several very healthy, well-fed cats that seldom, if ever, developed abscesses after injuries. My experience is that excellent nutrition is the best preventive in the sense that even with a bite they can handle it early on and there is no need for an abscess to form.

Neutering also greatly reduces the problem. When several intact male cats live in close proximity, there will be frequent warfare as each tries to establish a territory and compete for females. In such circumstances, abscesses can be a recurrent problem.

Warm Compress

If the injury is recent it helps to apply a warm compress to the area to bring more blood supply in. If your cat will allow you to do it, use a washcloth or small towel that has been in comfortably warm, not hot, water. Fold and squeeze out excess water and hold against the injured area. You may rewarm the cloth every few minutes. If possible, do this for 15 minutes and a couple of times a day.

Medicinal Treatment

Often, you can prevent an infection or abscess by giving the homeopathic remedy *Ledum 30c* within a few hours of the fight. Use Homeopathic Schedule 2. Very often this will result in the bite healing very quickly and without an abscess forming.

If you can't treat it quickly, however, or an infection (or abscess) is already established, further symptoms will usually occur, such as swelling, pain, and fever (locally or of the whole body). In this case, the cat should fast for 24 hours, taking only liquids—see Chapter 18 for how to do this.

Instead of the recommended *Ledum 30c* (above), use one remedy from the following list, whichever best fits the situation.

Homeopathic—*Hepar Sulph Calcareum 30c*: The abscess has formed but not yet opened and drained. It will be extremely painful when touched. The cat will often become angry and try to bite or scratch. (It is normal that cats don't like to be touched where it hurts, but this reaction is excessive.) Using this remedy will open the abscess so it drains out and begins to heal. Use Homeopathic Schedule 2.

Homeopathic—*Silicea 30c*: Best for a developed abscess that has opened and is already draining pus. It will not be so excessively painful as the ones needing the remedy above. Use Homeopathic Schedule 2.

Homeopathic—*Lachesis muta 30c*: If the tissues near the abscess are turning bluish or blackish or the skin is dying (it becomes very hard and starts to come off) and the pus smells just terrible. This will be a later stage, usually a few days after the bite. Use Homeopathic Schedule 2.

Herbal—*Purple coneflower* (*Echinacea angustifolia*): This remedy is indicated for the animal that is in poor condition, thin, very weak, and develops recurrent abscesses. It functions primarily to purify the system, especially the blood, and also restores health to the skin. Use Herbal Schedule 1.

If an abscess has actually opened and drained, prevent the drainage hole from closing prematurely by cleaning away any discharge or scab once or twice a day either with *hydrogen peroxide* or with the herb *Echinacea* used according to Herbal Schedule 4 or 6.

Later, when the abscess is healing and there is no longer any drainage, use the herb *Calendula* (marigold) for external treatment, according to the same method as described for Echinacea above (Herbal Schedule 4 or 6). Don't use this before the last healing stage or it may stimulate the drainage to close too early, before all the discharge is out.

If the abscess has been present for a long time and has been draining pus for several weeks, administer the homeopathic remedy *Silicea 30c*, using Homeopathic Schedule 3. If there is no improvement after 1 week, then give *Sulphur 30c* with the same schedule.

TREATMENT: DOGS

If the abscess is the result of an animal bite, treat it the same way you would for a cat (above). As described for the cat, applying a warm compress is a very helpful thing to do and may go easier with your dog.

However, if the abscess has been caused by plant material, porcupine quills, splinters, or other embedded foreign matter, the discharge will not stop until the object is eliminated. Since the tissues cannot "digest" the object, it must either be expelled or removed surgically.

The natural expelling process can be aided by using the homeopathic remedy *Silicea 30c* according to Homeopathic Schedule 5. A beneficial adjunct, though not absolutely necessary, is to apply hot compresses of a solution made up of *oat straw* (*Avena sativa*). Use Herbal Schedule 4. If the affected area is a paw, soak the whole foot in a jar of the hot solution. Use Herbal Schedule 6.

In natural healing, the tendency is for pus or fluid to drain out at a place lower than the site of the foreign body, allowing gravity to assist. Therefore, apply the poultice not only at the opening, but also several inches higher, so you cover the probable location of the foreign body. The hot solution will promote the flow of blood into the affected area and keep the process moving. When enough pus has formed around the foreign body to loosen it, it may flow out, right along with the pus, so watch for it. At that point, drainage will soon stop.

Note: Because of their structure, foxtails and plant awns tend to migrate deeply into the tissues. If you don't get results within a short time, you may have to resort to surgery. It is worth trying these methods first, however, as surgery is not always effective in locating these little intruders. (See Foxtails.)

ACCIDENTS

See Handling Emergencies and Giving First Aid, the section that follows this.

ADDISON'S DISEASE

This is a disorder of the adrenal glands, which secrete natural cortisone (cortisol) as well as hormones that regulate the different salts of the body. The adrenals are small glands, one above each kidney. This condition is seen more often in dogs than cats and is not very common. With this disease, the problem is that the glands no longer produce the steroid hormones that are critical for being able to adapt to changes. Without this function, the animal cannot live.

One cause is thought to be a type of auto-immune disorder, in which the body attacks the glands and damages them—though more often this results from prolonged use of cortisone-like drugs (prednisone being a common one) to control symptoms of other illnesses, like skin allergies. Because the synthetic drugs are several times more powerful than the natural hormone, the adrenal glands get the message that they don't have to work anymore and just shut down.

How do you recognize it? Signs are vague and even veterinarians may have trouble figuring it out. It is certainly a clue if your pet has been on steroids for a long time and then becomes ill, but to confirm diagnosis requires some testing. Most commonly, the affected animals (usually dogs) have recurrent periods of appetite loss, vomiting, diarrhea, and weakness—which are not very specific symptoms. In serious situations, vomiting and diarrhea can be accompanied by a life-threatening weakness and low body temperature.

The Addison cases I have worked with have come to me already on drug treatment—usually replacement adrenal hormones, including cortisone-type drugs, as well as others that help regulate sodium and potassium. It is possible to cure these animals, but it takes patience along with a plan to gradually taper off the drugs being used. You can see that making the decision to reduce drugs and determining when the health has improved enough to do this is challenging, so working with your vet for periodic assessment is really necessary.

Start with the recommended nutrition and, after using a natural diet for a few weeks (with added sprinkles of salt to compensate for elevated potassium), have the blood test done again and see if adjustments need to be made. The vitamin pantothenic acid (vitamin B_5) has been found to be especially important in adrenal function. It is high in meats, and also whole grains, legumes, sweet potatoes, broccoli, cauliflower, oranges, and strawberries.

Homeopathic treatment can bring back adrenal function. It is possible, but this being one of the more serious and life-threatening diseases, I am not encouraging you to do this on your own. However, I will share with you my experience and a plan you can suggest to your veterinarian that will often work.

Homeopathic—Start by giving the remedy

Thuja occidentalis 30c. Use Schedule 4, giving it only once.

Homeopathic—A month later, give the remedy *Phosphorus 30c*, Schedule 4.

Finally, a month after this second dose, have your animal evaluated again. This is the point that if improvement is seen (going by your observations, and also the blood tests) you can begin to taper off the drugs.

This may not be enough to finish the treatment, but if improvement is seen, then continue work with a homeopathic veterinarian to carry on.

AGGRESSION

See the section entitled Behavior Problems on page 335; also Chapter 12, Living Together: Responsible Pet Management.

ALLERGIES

An allergy is an abnormal immune reaction to something that is actually harmless to the body—like plant pollen, for example. What has become more common are abnormal reactions against some part of the body itself, like the skin, pancreas, or thyroid. We call these autoimmune diseases, the "auto" part meaning the reaction is directed against very innocent, normal tissues.

The function of the immune system is to protect against infections or foreign material finding its way into the body. This is the way it works in a healthy animal. Modern conditions, especially the excessive use of vaccines, have confused the immune system (see Chapter 16, Vaccines: Friend or Foe?). It can think that some normal part of the body (the adrenals, thyroid, ears) are a threat and react against them.

Another cause, as it has been learned in people, is that the presence of some chemicals in foods, especially the herbicides and pesticides, can cause abnormal gut conditions, what is called "leaky gut." The leaky part has to do with things getting into the blood that are not supposed to be there, and the immune system again makes the error of seeing these as invaders to be eliminated. This problem has greatly increased since I first entered practice 50 years ago. Now these immune disorders are among the most common conditions we are asked to treat—involving arthritis, cystitis, dog ear "yeast infections," thyroid disorders, epilepsy, skin itching, and so on.

Allergies present themselves differently in dogs than they do in cats. Dogs typically begin with itchy skin and eruptions, especially on the lower back near the base of the tail. However, these eruptions can occur anywhere and everywhere on the body. Other commonly associated symptoms are inflamed ears, excessive licking of the front feet, digestive upsets (gurgling, gas, and a tendency toward diarrhea), inflammation of the toes, and an irritated rear end (anus, genitals), with licking and dragging of the rear on the floor. Though other symptoms can also occur, this is a typical picture.

Like dogs, cats can also have skin eruptions, often called miliary dermatitis. Cats are also more prone to cystitis (bladder inflammation) and digestive problems. They can sometimes have a condition in which they suddenly attack some skin area, licking and chewing until there is a raw area or ulcer. There is no visible eruption on the skin, but cats will be greatly annoyed by stinging or biting sensations of the skin so that they are always jumping around, frantically licking themselves and pulling hair out in clumps. They act as though fleas were causing the problem (which of course can sometimes be the case). Veterinarians will call this feline hyperesthesia syndrome.

Two similar immune disorders that occur—hyperthyroidism and inflammatory bowel disease—are chronic and serious conditions that require careful treatment. It can happen that some animals are born with a tendency to immune problems like this because of the accumulated effect of the things we have been discussing—like excessive vaccinations and unhealthy food—over several generations. You can see it takes patience in working with these problems, yet much can be done to improve things.

In my practice, one of the most important things I did was to put the dog (and if possible, the cat) on a diet not using animal products. It is surprising, almost shocking, how much improvement can follow from this. In dogs, for example, meat is the chief thing they react to. This is why many veterinarians will advise changing the food from beef or chicken to lamb, or duck, or some "new"

meat. This is done because the immune system will not react so much to this new item. Unfortunately, after a while, it learns to do so and this recipe change to another meat is not a long-term solution. Read more about the allergy problem and things you can do in Chapters 5 and 8.

TREATMENT

Nutritional

Many dogs and cats are benefited by the supplement quercetin. This is a naturally occurring bioflavonoid, a plant pigment that plays an essential role in attracting pollinators to plants. It has an antiallergy action that is quite helpful. The amount that can be given is important to determine carefully, so see your veterinarian about setting up a dosage regimen. Also, it should not be used in dogs or cats that have kidney disease.

Coupled with glutamine, it is especially helpful in repairing the damage to the intestinal tract, what we called "leaky gut." Research in people has shown that using these two supplements along with probiotics is very healing for this problem.

Look at the recipe charts in Chapter 6, Recipes for Today, for the code A in the second row. This will identify for you the recommendations for this condition.

Homeopathic

I used homeopathic remedies to relieve symptoms while we worked with the dietary changes. Here are suggestions.

Rhus toxicodendron 30c: Especially useful for the dog that itches most of the time, and gets worse from getting warm. Itching seems irresistible, the skin becomes red and thickened, and the dog is restless with the discomfort. Use Schedule 5.

Calcarea carbonica 30c: If the remedy above, *Rhus toxicodendron*, has apparently helped to some degree but not eliminated the problem (allowing at least a couple of weeks to see how much improvement can occur), then this one will often follow and result in even more improvement. Use Schedule 4.

Phosphorus 30c: For cats that tend to have appetite issues as well, or a tendency to vomit food or water, especially a few minutes after drinking. Use Schedule 4.

Sulphur 30c: For cats or dogs that have a poor-looking coat, one that is smelly and dirty, especially if they are no longer grooming themselves. Use Schedule 4.

Thuja occidentalis 30c: For both dogs and cats that have not responded to any of the suggestions above. Use Schedule 4 and find a homeopathic veterinarian to work with.

ANAL GLAND PROBLEMS

Difficulties with the anal glands are primarily canine problems. Dogs have a pair of small scent glands on either side of the anus, under the tail. Similar in structure to the scent gland of the skunk, they contain a strong-smelling material that is used to mark territory. The glands are emptied during the bowel movement and they leave a "calling card" that identifies which dog has made the deposit. The glands also can empty during extreme fear.

Problems manifest either as abscesses that form within the glands themselves or as what is called *impaction*, in which the glands become inactive (don't empty) and overfilled with secretion. In the latter case, the dog will often scoot along the floor or ground in an attempt to empty these glands, which have exceeded their normal capacity. Some of the factors that may play a role in the development of these problems are:

- **Frustration in trying to establish a territory,** perhaps from being crowded with other animals or from having inadequate space for exercise and exploration.
- **Constipation or infrequent bowel movements,** especially as a result of not being allowed outside frequently. Many an indoor animal will hold its urine or feces to the very limit rather than soil the house and displease its people.
- **Toxicity because of poor food and inadequate exercise.** In such a case a disorder of the skin or ears frequently occurs as well (also see Allergies).

PREVENTION

Make sure your animal has adequate exercise, the opportunity to go outside and have frequent bowel movements (at which time the glands empty), and psychological "space."

If this is a chronic, recurrent problem give serious attention to the quality of the food as this may be what is sustaining the problem. The glands are squeezed empty when the stool is large enough to stretch the anus on coming out. It may help to increase the fiber content in the diet, as in the recipes we recommend, which will make the stool larger and more effective.

TREATMENT

Anal Gland Abscess

Homeopathic—First use the remedy *Belladonna 6c*, using Homeopathic Schedule 2. See if the abscess looks better the next day. If not clearly healing, then give *Silicea 30c* using Homeopathic Schedule 3. Belladonna helps with the initial inflammation and Silicea promotes the discharge of pus and encourages healing. Also apply warm or hot *Calendula* (marigold) solution twice a day for at least 5 minutes each time. Continue the Calendula treatment about 3 days, though a longer period is fine, if necessary. Use the method described in what follows.

Impacted Anal Glands

Since this condition is associated with sluggishness of the tissues, regular vigorous exercise is an important part of the treatment. It is also helpful to emphasize foods high in fiber (vegetables) to increase the amount of stool that is passed. Copious evacuation will stimulate the natural emptying of the glands.

In addition, a hot fomentation of either *Calendula* (marigold flower) solution or *Red Clover* (*Trifolium pratense*) blossoms will stimulate the glands and soften their contents. Make a tea with these herbs, adding boiling water to the herb. A good ratio is a heaping tablespoon of the herb over which you pour a quart of boiling water. Let sit for 15 minutes or so, until cool enough to handle. Then pour off the liquid into a bowl and immerse a washcloth or small towel into the warm solution. Wring it out and apply to the body. As necessary, warm up the compress every couple of minutes by putting it back in the bowl and wringing it out again.

The idea is to warm the affected area, increasing bloodflow and softening the tissues. You can also make up this solution by using herbal tinctures—add 1 teaspoon of the tincture to 1 quart of warm water.

Immediately after the application, use gentle pressure with a "milking" action (fingers on either side of anus and pulled toward center) to help to empty the glands manually. Consider the manual emptying as a temporary measure, not something to do regularly. It's much better (I'm sure you would agree!) if the glands empty naturally.

Homeopathic—A useful adjunct to the above measures is to give one dose of the remedy *Sulphur 30c*. Use Homeopathic Schedule 3.

ANEMIA

Anemia is often caused by blood loss from wounds, or parasites such as fleas and worms, especially hookworm. The problem is characterized by white (or pale) gums, weakness, and a fast pulse. Occasionally, it indicates more serious diseases like feline leukemia or a toxicity resulting from drug exposure. Here, however, we'll consider only the more common and simple anemia caused by blood loss, with an emphasis toward promoting the growth of new red blood cells.

TREATMENT

If the blood was lost from the body (actually leaked out or sucked out by parasites) then it is helpful to provide foods that have a higher content of iron. These are especially beans, dark green leafy vegetables, wheat germ, whole grains, and tofu. Meats, especially organ meats, have iron in them but have the disadvantage, as we have discussed, of bringing along a lot of other things we don't really want. Surprisingly, the nonmeat foods have as much or more iron as animal tissue. One-half cup of tofu (3.5 milligrams), for example, has more iron than 3 ounces of lean beef (3.2 milligrams). Iron is especially high in brewer's yeast, wheat bran, pumpkin seeds (which need to be ground), wheat germ, and molasses. Vitamin B_{12} is also very important in the formation of new red blood cells. It is present in many animal products and you can also buy it as a liquid spray bottle that can be added to the food.

Look at the recipe charts in Chapter 6, Recipes for Today, for the code G in the second row. This will identify for you the recommendations for this condition.

In addition to the nutritional supports, give one of these remedies (whichever seems best indicated) for 10 days.

Homeopathic—*China officinalis 6c*: Strongly indicated following blood loss that has resulted in marked weakness and loss of strength. Use Homeopathic Schedule 6(a).

Homeopathic—*Nux vomica 6c*: This remedy is appropriate when your pet has become withdrawn and irritable after the blood loss. Use Homeopathic Schedule 6(a).

If anemia is caused by parasites, these must be controlled (see Skin Parasites or Worms in this section). Flea infestations are most safely controlled by a combination of frequent bathing with a nontoxic soap (there are several types available, some with herbal constituents; some contain d-limonene from citrus, which can be used on dogs but not cats), controlling fleas in the environment, and using the lemon skin tonic described in Chapter 11. When the animal is stronger, you can use more strenuous flea-control methods if required, but I do discourage the use of poisonous chemicals, because they are not really effective in a long-term way and are very toxic to both humans and animals.

Sometimes very young kittens or puppies are so besieged by fleas that they are almost drained of their blood. In such cases, it is essential not to use flea powders or sprays, even though the temptation is great. The young animals are much too small and weak to handle such an assault. Instead, bathe them often and use the lemon tonic rinse. To prevent them from getting chilled, dry them thoroughly afterward. Towel them off and then use a hair dryer set on low or place them in a warm, sunny spot. Keep them warm and quiet in general and, if the weather allows, give them some fresh air and sunlight. Also use a flea comb to remove fleas not killed by the baths. Feed only natural foods—no commercial fare—and follow the treatment program suggested for anemia. You will be amazed at how quickly these little creatures can respond.

APPETITE PROBLEMS

CATS

Changes in normal appetite often show up as an aspect of an illness. This is a problem more commonly seen in cats than in dogs, probably because cats have such stringent nutritional requirements. The thing to understand is how gradually an inadequate appetite can creep up with a cat. Usually the first indication is what most people would call a finicky cat, one who rejects many different foods and prefers just one or two brands. Most people just give in to this

demand and don't think much about it. However, especially if it is coupled with regular water drinking, you have the beginnings of a more serious condition.

The next stage is a fluctuation in preferences. Maybe your cat no longer relishes what it once did. Or perhaps you find it necessary to open a different brand of food at each meal. Even this variation is not always totally acceptable, and your cat may pester you frequently for more food, only to reject what you offer. It is no wonder that some people end up feeding their cat tuna or liver exclusively!

If this deterioration continues, the next stage is inadequate eating with a gradual loss of weight. You may see a skeletal cat that eats just barely enough (with coaxing and indulgence) to maintain life. Cats like this do not eat enthusiastically. They just lick at their food or eat around the edges, leaving the less desirable parts in the bowl. Over time, these cats will waste away until they are finally diagnosed with some disease that is the end product of this long decline.

How will you know if your cat has started into this pattern? Ask yourself some questions: Is your cat addicted to a particular brand of food? Will she eat only dry food? Must you open a new can at every feeding (can't use any leftovers)? Do you find yourself adding irresistible foods like tuna or liver to get your cat to eat? Are you required to sit there with your cat while she eats (perhaps petting her the whole time) lest she will leave her food?

If the answer to any of these questions is yes, you probably have a problem. Another test is to begin modifying the diet. Begin to utilize the nutritional advice given in this book, adding in a small amount of the new recipe to the usual diet. It may take a few days for acceptance but once that happens then you can begin to add, gradually, a greater quantity of the new food over time (see Chapter 7, Making the Switch). However, if you work at this without success, or your cat will go several days without eating at all, then you definitely have a problem.

This is a difficult challenge to deal with. It seems that it has to do with taste or smell not seeming right. If the food is not somehow appealing enough, it simply will not be accepted. I think a big part of this lack of appeal is how unnatural these foods are to cats. In nature, they eat only freshly killed animals. They do not scavenge like a dog, or eat an animal killed yesterday. They have adapted to the domestic lifestyle to a great extent, but this issue will still come up for some cats. You might think "but I feed fresh meat," but what you are referring to is the meat from the local market, which is anything but fresh. The meat purchased there is a couple of weeks old or more, having been hanging in a locker to "age" (which means partly decay) as this is how we human beings like it. Cats do not like it.

What I have had success with is using homeopathic treatment. If the underlying disorder can be corrected, then appetite returns and the option of a better diet, especially as recommended in this book, becomes a possibility. You might try one of these remedies.

Homeopathic—*Phosphorus 30c*: Indicated when the cat will look at the food, perhaps sniff it, then turn away and not eat. Use Homeopathic Schedule 4.

Homeopathic—*Lycopodium 30c*: When there seems to be interest in the food at first. The cat may even eat a few bites but then turn away, as if satisfied. This is the pattern most of the time, regardless of the food offered. Use Homeopathic Schedule 4.

Homeopathic—*Sulphur 30c*: If appetite is reduced but thirst increased. Usually cats do not drink much at all, but when they begin to do so, noticeably, it is a symptom. Use Homeopathic Schedule 4.

DOGS

Have I forgotten dogs? Not really, but their situation is different. Most often if there is a problem with appetite in dogs it has to do with the stomach. They don't want to eat if it causes stomach pain; instead, they try to eat grass (or if grass is not available, then fabrics in the house or other objects). By eating more indigestible material, they are hoping to push through whatever is upsetting them in the stomach. If this problem is new, not a recurrent chronic problem, then this remedy will often resolve it.

Homeopathic—*Nux vomica 30c*: Use Homeopathic Schedule 2.

Also look at the topic Stomach Problems for more information on what could be going on.

ARTHRITIS

Arthritis and bone disease are much more common in dogs than in cats and usually take one of several forms.

Hip dysplasia: a malformation of the hip sockets that allows excessive movement in the joint, causing chronic inflammation, calcium deposits, and further breakdown. This can be seen in any dog size but is more noticeable in the larger dogs because of the weight they carry. Chiefly the effect of repeated vaccinations; see the topic Hip Dysplasia for more information.

Dislocation of the kneecap: a malformation of the leg bones that causes the kneecap to repeatedly pull out of position, slip back and forth, and set up a continuous low-grade inflammation (patellar luxation). Mostly seen in small breeds, it is fostered by poor breeding practices and low-quality food.

Deterioration of the knee joint structure: the ligaments that hold the knee joint together gradually weaken, eventually break, and the knee moves about abnormally. This is called anterior cruciate ligament (ACL) tear or rupture.

Degeneration of the shoulder joint: the breakdown of cartilage in the shoulder, leading to inflammation and pain on movement. Mostly found in medium to large breeds, it is always an aspect of an overall chronic disease condition that affects other parts of the body as well.

Arthritis of the elbow: the joint of the front leg, more or less where a human elbow would be, becomes inflamed and painful. Like shoulder joint problems, it is part of a larger chronic disease condition.

PREVENTION

Many of these conditions could be prevented if the female were properly fed throughout her pregnancy—though with all the various body sizes and shapes of dogs these days it can also be a hereditary influence. The time of growth in the uterus is critical in terms of the formation of essential structural tissues. Inadequate nutrition is most detrimental at this time (see Pregnancy, Birth, and Care of Newborns in this chapter). Avoiding commercial foods and feeding a natural, wholesome diet is an important part of a preventive program.

Homeopathic treatment *during pregnancy* is also an excellent means of minimizing the likelihood of this problem in the next generation. Of course, the mother should not be vaccinated while she is pregnant and, unfortunately, the excessive vaccination of the young animals also contributes especially to these bone and joint problems (see Chapter 16, Vaccines: Friend or Foe?). Prevention is very important in arthritic conditions, because once the joints are distorted, the damage has been done.

TREATMENT

Even in the face of an already-established condition, there are several things you can do to minimize your animal's arthritic discomfort.

Nutritional—*Glucosamine* is made by the body from sugar (glucose) and is found in high concentration in cartilage of the joint. It helps in the production of lubricating fluid that keeps the joint movable and also removes free radicals, reducing damage to the tissues. When there is joint damage, it can be helpful to add additional amounts as a supplement. It is derived from the shells of crustaceans, such as crabs, lobsters, crayfish, shrimp, krill, barnacles, and also the cartilage of sharks. The crustaceans and sharks are so heavily contaminated now I do not recommend them being used as a food or as a nutrient. Instead, I recommend looking for vegan formulas from plant-based sources like soybeans or vegetables. Start with a dose of 10 milligrams/pound of body weight, and see if there is an effect. If necessary, you can increase it as overdosing is not really a problem. If you see a beneficial effect after a few weeks, you can reduce the amount and see if it holds (or perhaps other treatments here have brought about stable improvement).

Also look at the recipe charts in Chapter 6, Recipes for Today, for the code W in the second row. These recipes are anti-inflammatory and helpful if obesity is adding strain to the joints.

Herbal—*Alfalfa* (*Medicago sativa*) is indicated for the thin, nervous animal with a tendency toward digestive problems as well as arthritis. Depending on its size, add 1 teaspoon to 3 tablespoons of ground or dry blended alfalfa to the daily ration. Or you can administer alfalfa as an infusion using Herbal Schedule 3. A third choice is to give your pet two to six alfalfa tablets a day. *Turmeric* is also a proven anti-inflammatory that can be added to food.

Homeopathic—*Rhus toxicodendron 6c*: Indicated for a dog or cat with chronic arthritis, pain, or stiffness that is most apparent when the animal gets up after a long rest (for example, overnight). When it first starts to move, the animal shows discomfort or stiffness, but after a few minutes it seems to loosen up and feel better. If the pet also has a tendency toward red, swollen, itchy skin, Rhus tox will work on both problems (see Skin Problems). Use Homeopathic Schedule 6(a).

Homeopathic—*Bryonia 6c*: A treatment helpful when the arthritis is worse from *any* movement. The dog or cat just does not want to move for if she lies quietly, she is reasonably comfortable. Use Homeopathic Schedule 6(a).

Homeopathic—*Belladonna 6c*: Especially useful when there is quite a bit of inflammation. There may be a fever (temperature over 101°F or 38.6°C) or palpable heat over the affected joint (felt with the hand). Use Homeopathic Schedule 6(a).

Homeopathic—_Nux vomica 6c_: Indicated if the painful condition, when it flares up, results in the animal becoming irritable, withdrawing from company, finding a place by himself until it is over. Use Homeopathic Schedule 6(a).

Homeopathic—_Pulsatilla 6c_: The choice if the dog or cat wants more attention than usual, to be close or held. He will seem needy. Sometimes he will seek out cool places to lie. Use Homeopathic Schedule 6(a).

BEHAVIOR PROBLEMS

Behavioral abnormalities can be complex and difficult to change, but often you can help considerably. Poor breeding practices, especially in purebred dogs, have fostered the development of many such disturbances, including viciousness, epilepsy, repetitive habits, and other signs of nervous system imbalances. It is also my impression that many behavior problems have their roots in one or more of the following: poor nutrition and associated toxicity, chronic encephalitis (brain inflammation) following vaccination, inadequate exercise, insufficient psychological stimulation and attention, and the influence of the owner's personality patterns, expectations, or conditioning. For instance, family conflict, excessive attachment to a pet as an attempt to escape loneliness, or the desire to have

an aggressive animal to feel safer from other people can all have a strong adverse influence on an animal's personality (see Chapter 13, Connections: Emotions and Your Animal's Health).

TREATMENT

In this discussion we'll focus on general measures that can be very helpful and, in some cases, may be sufficient to treat the disturbance, provided that the contributing environmental factors are understood and eliminated. It really makes no sense to try to fix this while the underlying causes continue.

Start with nutrition. As we have emphasized throughout, our modern condition of so many chemicals accumulating in our bodies can certainly be a factor. Mercury and aluminum, for instance, are known to get into the brain and certainly must have effects. For example, it has been shown that under the influence of mercury, people can have the sudden urge to kill.

Many dogs, especially, will greatly improve if put on a diet devoid of any animal products. It can actually be quite remarkable.

As well, minimize exposure to toxic substances. Make sure your animal is protected from accidental poisoning by various household chemicals. Just as important, minimize its exposure to such pollutants as cigarette smoke, car exhaust, and antiflea chemicals (which affect the nervous system).

In addition to these measures, one or more of the following treatments may be useful.

Homeopathic—*Belladonna 30c*: Indicated for a hyperactive, excitable animal, especially if there is a tendency to bite. He may be prone to spasms and convulsions or see things that are not there, like flies in the air or bugs crawling on the carpet (hallucinations). Use Homeopathic Schedule 5. If this remedy is effective, then work with a homeopathic veterinarian for continued treatment with other medicines, as there are others than can follow this for a deeper effect.

Herbal—*Common oat (Avena sativa)*: Oats are well suited as a general nerve tonic and are particularly useful where nerve weakness or irritability may have appeared after other stressful diseases. This herb is good for animals that have received a lot of drugs, are old, or have a tendency to epilepsy. It is also helpful for the animal with weak legs, muscle twitching, or a trembling associated with weakness. All of this, of course, will be in addition to any particular behavior problems exhibited (this applies to all of the herbs to be described).

Though feeding rolled oats as a cooked grain in the diet is helpful, a more potent preparation is the tincture. Use Herbal Schedule 1.

Herbal—*Blue vervain (Verbena)*: Vervain is suited for animals that are depressed and have weak nervous systems. It's also for those with irritated nerves and muscle spasms and is especially appropriate for those whose abnormal behavior is associated with epilepsy; in such cases it will strengthen the brain function. Use Herbal Schedule 1.

Herbal—*Skullcap (Scutellaria lateriflora)*: This herb is useful for behavior disturbances that center around nervous fear. The animal may also show one or more of the following signs: intestinal gas, colic, diarrhea, muscle twitching, and restless sleep. Use Herbal Schedule 1.

Herbal—*Valerian (Valeriana officinalis)*: Valerian suits the animal that tends to get hysterical, associated with a hypersensitivity. The animal shows a changeable mental disposition and an irritable temperament. Like skullcap, valerian may be most successfully used for animals that have digestive disturbances like gas and diarrhea when the nerves supplying the abdominal organs are overactive and those that may also have a history of leg pains or joint inflammation.

Since valerian is one of those herbs that can cause a toxic reaction if given in large doses over a long period of time, I advise that you try Herbal Schedule 1 for no more than a week. If you don't see beneficial results by then, discontinue use and try one of the other suggested remedies, such as the oat tincture.

Herbal—*German chamomile (Matricaria)*: Animals that will benefit from this herb are noisy, whining, moaning, and complaining. They will let you know about their pains or discomforts. They are sensitive, irritable, and thirsty and may snap or try to bite. Such animals don't like to be hot and are often mollified or quiet only when being carried or constantly petted. Use Herbal Schedule 1.

General Herbal Advice

Use the suggested schedule for the herb you have chosen for 2 to 3 weeks (except for valerian, which should not be used for more than a week). If you see an improvement in that time, even a slight one, continue the treatment as long as the improvement goes on, up to a maximum of 6 weeks. Then discontinue the regular use of the herb, but give a few more doses of it whenever symptoms return or worsen.

Also, the herb can be used preventively. Give it to your pet before an event you know will trigger the problem behavior, for example, before leaving him alone for long periods. In this way it can be used occasionally, as needed, over several weeks or months.

What if you don't see a good response over the trial period? Then discontinue the selected herb and either try it again after a few weeks on a better diet or use one of the alternative herbs suggested.

Bach Flower Remedies

I would like to suggest another alternative for those who are willing to go a little further. An easy-to-use herbal system for behavior problems with psychological roots is the use of the 38 flower preparations, known as Flower Remedies, discovered by Dr. Edward Bach.

These were originally developed for human use by Dr. Bach in England in the 1930s. See Chapter 17, Holistic and Alternative Therapies, the Flower Essences topic, page 288.

I have found them to be effective for animals. They are dilute extracts of selected flowers given orally over a long period (from weeks to months), often resulting in remarkable improvements.

These 38 preparations are supplied in a small bottle from which you make a dilution to use in treatment.

- *Chicory,* for the overly attached, possessive animal
- *Holly,* for the vicious, aggressive, suspicious, or jealous animal
- *Impatiens,* for the uptight, impatient, or irritable pet
- *Mimulus,* for the animal afraid of specific things, like the dog afraid of men or of thunder
- *Rock rose,* for use where attacks of terror or panic are part of the disturbance
- *Star of Bethlehem,* for use where physical or emotional shock seems to have initiated the imbalance
- *Walnut,* for the animal that is overly influenced by a strong personality (human or animal) or apparently under the influence of bad heredity

Select up to four (no more) of the best-suited essences. Add two drops from the stock bottle of each of these essences to a clean 1-ounce dropper bottle. Then fill the bottle with spring (not distilled) water.

Store it at room temperature. If the solution clouds up in a few days, make a fresh batch.

Regardless of the size of your animal, give two drops of this diluted medicine orally four times a day until the desired results are obtained. If you can, drop it directly in the mouth. If not, mix it with a little food or milk. There is no unfavorable side effect or possible toxicity with this system.

The Vaccination Factor

In my experience it is not unusual that, especially in dogs, these behavior problems arise after being vaccinated. This is not surprising as the natural diseases of rabies and distemper both affect the brain. The vaccine made from these diseases does not produce the entire disease, of course, but can still affect the brain and thus alter behavior. Some dogs will have seizures after vaccinations, but here we are considering behavior changes.

When this occurs people will notice that what was before a happy puppy will, within a short time after receiving the vaccines, become withdrawn, irritable, aggressive, or anxious. Withdrawing from social interaction is common, but most scary is when the animal becomes aggressive and begins to bite. (For a detailed example of this, read Chapter 16 on vaccines.) There are several possible patterns, of course, but I will give you here some of the most common ones and how to address them with homeopathy.

Homeopathic—*Belladonna 30c*: For the dog or cat that becomes aggressive and will bite if annoyed or even touched sometimes. This remedy is especially indicated if the pupils of the eyes tend to be overly dilated. Use Homeopathic Schedule 4.

Homeopathic—*Lachesis 30c*: The pattern seen is similar to that for Belladonna (above) but there is no response to Belladonna or this behavior appeared after receiving the rabies vaccination. Use Homeopathic Schedule 4.

Homeopathic—*Stramonium 30c*: If the behavior is now unpredictable, including sudden violence, biting, and a tendency to vocalize (whining, howling), especially if there are very persistent impulses to escape and run away. Use Homeopathic Schedule 4.

Note: These behavior issues can be very serious. If an animal is aggressive, it can be dangerous. I have seen nasty injuries in people in this type of situation. I tell clients not to let any aggressive dog or cat near children until this is clearly resolved. I strongly encourage you to seek help in dealing with this. Behavioral training can be useful but not always enough in itself. These guidelines are to give you things you might try when you have no other options. Be careful.

BIRTH

See Pregnancy, Birth, and Care of Newborns.

BLADDER PROBLEMS

Inflammation of your pet's bladder lining and urethra or the formation of urinary mineral deposits and stones is not unusual, particularly for a cat. Symptoms show up as increased frequency of urination, the appearance of blood in the urine, and, in severe cases, extreme discomfort, with straining and partial or complete blockage of the bladder due to accumulation of mucus and swelling of the internal parts.

POSSIBLE CAUSES

Even though this is a common problem of cats, the causes are not completely understood. It may be there are several factors rather than just one. Let's discuss some of these ideas.

Though conventional veterinary treatment almost always includes antibiotics, research shows that these bladder problems in cats are not caused by bacteria (though sometimes they are in dogs). In my own practice I have not found it necessary to use antibiotics for this problem for over 35 years.

Another common idea is that because gritty material accumulates in the bladder, ash (minerals) in the food is responsible for urinary tract trouble. However, research shows that ash doesn't cause the problem; rather, grit forms because the urine becomes too alkaline. This can happen in cats if the diet is not high enough in protein, and when it is not, the urine becomes alkaline (above

pH 7) for some hours after a meal. You can test the pH yourself at home as the strips are readily available at a pharmacy. Just stick the test strip in the freshly made wet litter "ball" just made by your cat. The target range for cats is a pH of 6.2 to 6.6. There can be fluctuation, but it should not be much higher.

An easier way to monitor the urine is the use of Pretty Litter, a product made expressly to show how acid or alkaline the urine is. It doesn't give you the pH number but shows by color whether the urine is too acid or too alkaline.

Another very possible factor, as we have mentioned elsewhere, is toxic effects of mercury. This happens especially with cats because they are so often fed fish. It is estimated, that per pound weight, a cat eats 30 times the amount of fish that people do. Mercury has accumulated in sea life to very high levels, which is why people are warned not to eat fish very often (like once a month). The cat eating fish on a regular basis will store large amounts of mercury, and one of its known effects is inflammation of the bladder and increased tendency to formation of bladder sand and stones.

Lastly, we have to consider if vaccines are pushing this. We know that illness following vaccines tends to localize in the urinary and reproductive tract, so we have to keep our minds open to this possibility. (See the topic Kidney Failure for more information on vaccines and kidney disease.)

Fortunately, I've found that, once through

the crisis, the condition is very responsive to diet changes and natural therapies, resulting in a stable cure rather than temporary relief.

TREATMENT

Fasting is especially useful here, as it has been observed that continued eating aggravates and prolongs the problem. Therefore, during the acute phase of the condition (opposite), put the animal on a liquid fast, offering a broth.

After improvement or recovery, as a continuation of the treatment program, you are encouraged to improve the diet as we have suggested in earlier parts of this book. Look at the cat recipe chart in Chapter 6, Recipes for Today, for the code U in the second row. This will identify for you the recipes we think will be most beneficial for you to use.

It is also helpful to feed your cat only twice a day—morning and evening. Don't leave the food out for more than 30 minutes. If she does not want to eat at these times, let a natural hunger develop until the next feeding time. This is very important. Frequent feeding alkalizes the urine, leading to formation of sand and stones (as we discussed above). Wildcats like bobcats and mountain lions do not eat often, sometimes not for several days. The ancestor of the domestic cat, most likely eating mice and other rodents, might have eaten more often but there was never food constantly available. It is the period of fasting between meals that allows the urine to return to its normally acid state.

An additional nutritional supplement that is helpful for this condition is omega-3 fatty acids, as shown in a yearlong study in cats.[1] Adding this to the food will greatly lower the recurrence of this condition. Most readily available sources are ground flaxseeds and hemp hearts. If you have a seed grinder, buy whole flaxseeds, which can be kept at room temperature, and grind just enough to use in a week, as they do not keep well once ground. You could also use flax oil, but it is even more susceptible to breakdown from oxygen, so again, buy small quantities and keep it tightly capped in the fridge.

As to quantities to use, ½ to 1 teaspoon of ground flax or hemp hearts can be added to the food, mixed in well. If easier, or if cats object to the solids, then add a few drops of flax oil to each meal instead, again mixed in well.

James Peden, the founder of Vegepet, has also developed a protocol, using Vegecat phi, a supplement that's the same as Vegecat but with an AAFCO-approved urinary acidifier, sodium bisulfate, which must be used carefully in combination with the product, not in isolation, which could be dangerous. He also recommends Cranimals, a cranberry powder, or vitamin C.

Methionine is an essential amino acid, important to dogs and cats for liver repair, skin and coat condition, and other functions. It is lower in plant foods than meat, so Vegecat has recently added a modest amount of methionine to Vegecat. Levels are safely within the AAFCO limits, and any additional amount should be prescribed by a DVM, as excesses overacidify the urine and could cause other issues. Intact male cats appear to require higher levels because it's involved in the production of felinine, a sulfur-containing amino acid likely important in territorial marking.

Acute Cases

If the urethra has become thoroughly plugged up, the cat cannot pass urine, and the bladder will become enlarged and hard from urine accumulation. It feels like a large stone in the back part of the abdomen. This is a special problem for male cats, because they tend to have long and narrow urethras. (A female cat may have bladder problems, but she isn't likely to get plugged.) The condition is quite serious, since urine and poisonous waste products are backing up into the bloodstream. Make an emergency run to your veterinarian to have a catheter put in, a plastic tube that relieves the obstruction and allows urine to pass. If you are too far from a veterinarian or can't reach one right away, however, try one of these treatments while you are waiting for help.

Homeopathic—*Nux vomica 30c*: A remedy best for the cat that, before the bladder trouble came on, has become irritable, doesn't want to be touched, and withdraws from company, preferring to be by himself. Use Homeopathic Schedule 2.

Homeopathic—*Pulsatilla 30c*: Indicated for the cat that becomes quiet and unusually affectionate, wanting to be held as the attack comes on. Use Homeopathic Schedule 2.

Homeopathic—*Cantharis 30c*: The cat that needs this medicine will be very upset, angry, and growl, with almost constant and intense attempts to urinate. Often the anger and growling are directed against the inflamed penis as he licks it intensely. Use Homeopathic Schedule 2.

Homeopathic—*Coccus cacti 30c*: Choose this remedy if one or more of the previous ones listed here are not effective and it appears there is complete blockage and no urine coming out (due to stones or mucus plugging the urethra). Use Homeopathic Schedule 2.

Homeopathic—*Thuja occidentalis 30c*: A remedy to use after the crisis is over. It often corrects the tendency that has come on after excessive vaccine use. Use Homeopathic Schedule 4.

With any of these treatments, improvement will mean a sudden passing of a large quantity of urine with considerable relief for your cat. Often the cat will now drink a large amount of water and begin to be more comfortable, even grooming himself for the first time. If this happens, you may be through the crisis and catheterization will be unnecessary. Watch closely for the next several days to make sure that urination continues unimpeded. Follow the crisis with the nutritional changes already discussed above.

If your cat needs to be catheterized, an additional treatment that will assist recovery from this procedure is:

Homeopathic—*Staphysagria 30c*: Helps relieve the pain associated with passing a plastic catheter up the urethra (the narrow passage to the bladder). Realize the urethra will be inflamed when this happens and the catheter will be rubbing on sensitive and inflamed tissue. Use Homeopathic Schedule 2.

Subacute Cases

Here, the problem is not obstruction but inflammation. The cat feels a frequent urge to urinate, but the flow is scanty or blood-tinged. This misery can go on for days, perhaps with temporary improvement (especially with antibiotics). However, the problem may continue or recur every few weeks. The remedies that follow are often useful for this stage of the problem. From the four remedies below, choose the one that best suits the condition. Don't mix them.

Homeopathic—*Belladonna 30c*: If the symptoms are intense pain, agitation, frequent urges to urinate, even some traces of blood in the urine. Pupils of the eyes will be very dilated even in good light. Cat very excitable and nervous. Use Homeopathic Schedule 2.

Homeopathic—*Pulsatilla 30c*: Very useful for the cat that does not like heat in any form. Here is how you can tell. Put out a hot water bottle or heating pad wrapped with a towel. If your cat is not interested in huddling next to it and prefers to lie on something cool like cement, tile, linoleum, or even the bathtub or sink, then you will know it prefers coolness to heat. Usually the urine is passed in small amounts and contains blood. Use Homeopathic Schedule 2.

Homeopathic—*Cantharis 30c*: This remedy will have the same indications as given above, especially the anger and growling at the condition. Symptoms intense. Use Homeopathic Schedule 2.

Homeopathic—*Mercurius vivus (or solubilis) 30c*: The cat needing this remedy will act very annoyed with his rear end, doing a lot of licking after urinating, thrashing the tail around, and straining to produce small quantities of urine. Sometimes the straining is associated with passing stool, with continued efforts even after some has been passed. These cats will have prior or concurrent mouth problems, with red, inflamed gums and loose teeth. If the cat also has become unusually thirsty before the attack, this is probably the remedy to use. Use Homeopathic Schedule 2.

Note: If you do not see any improvement after 24 hours of using one of these homeopathic preparations, discontinue the treatment and reassess the situation. If antibiotics and other drugs were used at any time, they may have altered the symptom picture. Think back to the symptoms that were present before treatment was started. Use these as your guidelines in choosing a remedy.

Chronic Cases

If one of the treatments above has been successful or if your cat has needed catheterization and is now recovered, then it is time to think of giving a homeopathic treatment that will stop the tendency for formation of sand and sludge in the bladder. You will unfortunately find that this is a problem that tends to return, and when that has happened a couple of times, then you are alerted to this being a chronic condition (that is, long-lasting, recurrent).

Bladder problems can also be related to the diet, as we discussed in the first part of this topic, so it may help to do periodic pH checks of the urine after trying different foods or recipes.

Here are some remedies that are most frequently effective in removing this chronic tendency.

Homeopathic—*Phosphorus 30c*: Indicated for the cat that has developed what are called struvite crystals. If you can see them, they tend to look like white sandy material. These crystals form in the bladder and, along with the inflammation, tend to plug things up, requiring a catheter. Use Homeopathic Schedule 4.

Homeopathic—*Lycopodium 30c*: For the animal that has had appetite issues, not eating all its food, and losing weight. When urinary trouble occurs, the animal will cry out before urinating. If you can see it, the urinary crystal sediment tends to be made of larger pieces. Use Homeopathic Schedule 4.

Homeopathic—*Thuja occidentalis 30c*: This remedy is especially useful when other ones have been tried and have not been completely successful. Use Homeopathic Schedule 4.

Continued Treatment

Further treatment can be needed, perhaps not right away, but in a few months' time. How will you know if there are mineral deposits in the urine? The easiest way is to feel it with your fingers. Yuck! I know, an unpleasant thought, but it is surprising how easy it is to detect that way. Prepare the litter pan like this: Wash it out and, when dry, instead of putting litter in it, just tear up some strips of paper about ½ inch wide and several inches long. Put these in the pan instead of litter. It sort of looks to the cat that there is something there and he will scratch around in it and urinate just the same as with litter. Where the urine has settled on the bottom, feel it for grittiness. It will feel like small sand grains. Another way to check this is to pour the urine into a glass jar and let it sit for an hour. Any sandy material will settle to the bottom and you might be able to see it.

If you (understandably) don't want to do this, then collect the urine in a clean container and take it to your veterinarian right away (or refrigerate it until you can), to be analyzed under the microscope. She will let you know if there is a problem.

Note: If you take some urine in a jar to a veterinarian, she may say to you that it will do no good to analyze it because it is not sterile. The veterinarian is thinking of looking for bacteria. Ask her to do it anyway. What we want is not a bacterial evaluation (that's not the cause anyway), but a "microscopic examination" to see if crystals are being formed.

What if indications are too vague to fit any of the remedies listed above? Try the following herbal treatment, helpful for a cat that never has a severe bladder problem, just a weakness in that area, such as a tendency toward urinary frequency or urinating outside the litter box.

Herbal—Use *Shavegrass*, also known as horsetail grass or scouring rush (*Equisetum*). To use the medication, use Herbal Schedule 2, for 2 to 3 weeks.

Dogs

Though bladder problems are more common in cats, dogs do get them, too. Their most common disturbances are either cystitis (as in cats) or stone formation.

If your dog has a case of acute cystitis resembling the symptoms described above for cats (increased frequency of urination, discomfort, blood in the urine), you can use the same feline treatment program. I usually start with *Nux vomica 30c* or *Pulsatilla 30c*, using Homeopathic Schedule 2. They seem suitable for many dogs with this condition.

What if it's a stone problem? They occur in two forms—small, pellet-size stones that form in the bladder but move down and block the urethra, and very large stones that fill the bladder.

Small stones are most troublesome to the male dog. They pass down into the urethra and get caught at the point where it passes through the bone in the penis (a hard opening that cannot become larger). When this happens, the unfortunate fellow will attempt to urinate frequently, without success, or will give off little spurts of urine instead of a full flow. In such cases immediately use:

Homeopathic—*Pulsatilla 30c*: Will often relieve the spasms of the muscles of the urethra where the stone is caught, allowing it to move out. Your dog will want to be close, comforted. First one to try. Use Homeopathic Schedule 2.

Homeopathic—*Nux vomica 30c*: Helpful for the dog that is irritable, withdrawn from others, goes off by himself, and doesn't want to be handled. Homeopathic Schedule 2.

Homeopathic—*Coccus cacti 30c*: Especially a treatment for obstruction of the urethra with a stone. The urging to urinate is not always successful, or urine is slow to come out. There is considerable straining and perhaps apparent painful spasms. Some dogs will do a lot of licking of the opening of the urethra. Use Homeopathic Schedule 2.

Homeopathic—*Urtica urens 6c*: Very helpful when there are *large stones* in the bladder with subsequent bleeding from irritation of the bladder wall. Can be used until surgery can be done to remove them. Use Homeopathic Schedule 6(a).

Herbal—*Shepherd's purse (Thlaspi bursa pastoris* or *Capsella)*: Like *Coccus cacti*, this is a treatment for presence of stones. Use Herbal Schedule 1.

Herbal—*Barberry (Berberis vulgaris)*: This herb is good for an animal with arthritic or rheumatic tendencies (muscle and joint soreness) in addition to bladder or kidney stones. Use Herbal Schedule 1 for a month to give it an adequate try.

Herbal—*Sarsaparilla (Smilax officinalis)*: Useful in cases where "gravel" and small stones are in the urine, accompanied by bladder inflammation and pain. Urination may be painful and blood may be passed. Often the animal suited to this herb will also have dry, itchy skin that flares up most in the springtime. Use Herbal Schedule 1 for a month to give it an adequate try.

Expectations

Sometimes the stone will pass through when these treatments are used. The remedy will not make the stone dissolve, of course, but it may reduce the spasms and inflammation from the presence of the stone. If it is small enough, the stone may then pass through.

Large stones are another matter. Numerous large stones can grow to fill the bladder and eventually irritate the lining, causing bleeding and recurrent bacterial infections. This form of large stone formation is more common in dogs than in cats. Such stones usually need to be surgically removed, though I have sometimes seen stones diminish in time in dogs that were too ill for surgery.

The animals I have worked with have done well on a natural diet program with appropriate homeopathic treatment.

Do not restrict calcium in the diet. Sometimes people are advised to follow a low-calcium diet with the idea that restricting calcium will reduce the formation of stones. However, there is no evidence that this is effective; in fact, insufficient calcium actually makes the problem worse by increasing the amount of oxalate (a common component of bladder and kidney stones) in the urine.

Considering the many kinds of stones that can form and the many clinical problems that they can be associated with, however, I can give only this general advice that may be helpful regardless of the type of stone involved. More specific, individualized treatment to prevent recurrence will be needed for persistent and recurrent problems.

Correcting the Tendency

Homeopathic—The treatment most likely to be effective, in my experience, is this sequential homeopathic treatment: First give the remedy *Thuja occidentalis 30c* (arborvitae), using Homeopathic Schedule 4. Wait for 1 month and then do the same treatment (Schedule 4) with *Silicea 30c*. This treatment program will not be effective in every case, but will with many and is worth trying. It is important not to give the remedies more than once.

Postsurgery

If your dog does have surgery to remove bladder stones, here's a treatment to relieve pain and assist recovery afterward. Start it the day after (not before) surgery, if possible.

Homeopathic—*Staphysagria 30c*: Use Homeopathic Schedule 2.

BREAST TUMORS

There is more of a tendency for tumors to appear in dogs and cats than when I started in veterinary practice in the 1960s. As with any problem involving growths or tumors, it is best to avoid unnecessary vaccinations and to emphasize the purest foods. A pure diet is especially important because the hormones that stimulate cancer growth are often in meat products. The people raising livestock routinely give them hormones to make them grow faster or fatter, and these

hormone residues are in the meat coming from these animals. In my practice, for cases like this, I strongly advised a diet without any animal products at all.

TREATMENT

Sometimes breast tumors are malignant, and radical surgery involving removal of associated lymph nodes is usually recommended. My experience, however, is that this is not always the best approach. Surgery will result in a weakened immune system and can result in a decline in health, especially in animals not in the best of health to begin with. I prefer starting with a natural, less invasive approach, to see how much it can do. One is often surprised how much progress can be made with nutrition and the approaches we are discussing here. The advantage of starting this way is that you still have a functional immune system to work with. If you try it the other way—surgery, perhaps chemotherapy or radiation—then the approaches described here will not later have much effect, as the immune system is so damaged by these other treatments that it cannot respond to the measures that would usually work.

I know it is difficult to decide what to do. This is definitely a situation where you will be most comfortable working with a veterinarian who guides you through the process.

Here are some of the treatments I have used.

Homeopathic—First give the remedy *Thuja occidentalis 30c*. Use Homeopathic

Schedule 4. If nothing is getting worse, the tumor is not growing, then wait the month and use one of these other treatments. (Of course, if the tumor is going away, leave well enough alone.)

Homeopathic—*Arsenicum album 30c*: For the animal that has rapidly lost weight, become thirsty and restless. Use Homeopathic Schedule 4.

Homeopathic—*Conium 30c*: Tumor very hard, painful to touch, or prevents sleeping at night. Use Homeopathic Schedule 4.

Homeopathic—*Phosphorus 30c*: If the tumor tends to bleed easily. Use Homeopathic Schedule 4.

Homeopathic—*Lachesis muta 30c*: This is suitable for a tumor that is in a left breast, when the skin over the tumor is dark, bluish, or blackish. Use Homeopathic Schedule 4.

Homeopathic—*Silica 30c*: If any tendency for the tumor to ulcerate or develop pus. Use Homeopathic Schedule 4.

Herbal—*Poke root (Phytolacca)*: A very important herb for treating inflammation, infection, and drainage from the breast. It is indicated for tumors or hardening of this tissue with discharge of pus or bad-smelling fluid. Use Herbal Schedule 3 (internal) and 4 (external), for as long as is necessary.

Herbal—*Goldenseal (Hydrastis canadensis)*: Generally useful in treating any kind of cancer, especially if it is associated with a loss of weight. Another indication is if the tumor has appeared on the surface of the body as a large sore or ulcer. Use Schedule 1 for as long as it seems helpful. When using this herb for long periods, supplement the diet with extra B-complex vitamins, as goldenseal tends to deplete the body of these vitamins.

Nutritional—*Curcumin* (turmeric): An herb that is a member of the ginger family and known to be an effective antioxidant, so it is useful for many conditions where there is excessive inflammation. There are reports also of its effectiveness in cancer treatment, so it will be a useful part of your program. See dosage schedule under the Cancer topic below.

BRONCHITIS

See Upper Respiratory Infections (Colds).

CANCER

Cancer is the most frightening disease we will be discussing. When we hear this word, it evokes such fear and hopelessness. I hope in this discussion to encourage you to have more confidence in what can be accomplished with natural methods. In my practice I have been surprised at how much can be done with nutrition and homeopathic treatment and want to share that with you.

A great part of the discouragement about treating cancer is that, deep down, we know the conventional methods in use are not really curing the disease. It has been long enough now that a number of doctors have come out with the conclusion that cancer treatments are not really effective. An example is the communication by John C. Bailar III, MD, PhD, a professor in the Department of Epidemiology and Biostatistics at McGill University and a statistical consultant to the *New England Journal of Medicine*. He is a former staff member of the National Cancer Institute (for over 20 years), where he served, among other assignments, as acting director of the Cancer Control Program and editor of the *Journal of the National Cancer Institute.*

His statistical analysis of breast cancer treatment and mortality led to a 1986 publication in which he showed that there had been no significant improvement in effectiveness of treatment over the last 35 years. This was not welcomed by the medical community, yet the numbers, the patient records, supported that conclusion. Since that time, he has stated again that there has been no significant progress in later years, since this first publication.

Let's look at why this might be so. The conventional allopathic view of cancer is that it is a disease, different from the patient's body, that is to be vigorously attacked. Surgery is done to physically remove the tumor, then drugs are used to kill off any remaining cancer cells. The problem with this is twofold. Doctors know that when a tumor is removed, this stimulates the growth of tumors in the same or another location. As well, chemicals are used with the idea that the cancer cells are growing quickly (which is not always the case) and the growing cells will be killed by the drugs. However, many other growing cells in the body are also damaged—the ones that make blood, that line the intestines, that grow skin and hair, and especially that are part of the all-important immune system. To give you some idea of this, the average human makes around 50 billion to 70 billion new cells each day. When anticancer drugs are used, these new cells are killed instead of taking on their intended functions. So the strategy is to use the drugs for a while, hoping the cancer will be killed and that the rest of the body can recover. Of course, this is exactly the problem: The treatment has very long-lasting and damaging effects. Sometimes there is no recovery.

Radiation is similar in that the anatomical area where the tumor is located is focused on and killed with radiation. But the other, normal tissues around the tumor are also killed. And, of course, the use of radiation makes the chance of cancer occurring later much more likely.

The natural approach we are considering here has a different view. We see the body as highly intelligent and very capable of dealing with cancer, given the proper support.

The first thing is to remove any influences that are promoting the cancer. These include chronic exposure to cigarette smoke; inhaling exhaust from riding in the back of a pickup truck; resting on or close to a color TV set; drinking water from street puddles (which can contain hydrocarbons and asbestos dust from brakes); frequent diagnostic work with x-rays (all radiation effects are cumulative in the body); use of strong toxic chemicals over long periods (as with flea and tick control); and consuming pet foods high in organ meats and meat meal (concentrators of pesticides and growth hormones used to fatten cattle, which can promote cancer growth), as well as preservatives and artificial colors, known to cause cancer in lab animals. In my practice, when faced with a cancer case, I put a dog on a diet that did not use any animal products at all; if a cat, I prescribed minimal use of animal products and only organic sources. It is also very helpful to use nutrient-rich foods as they enhance the cell repair mechanisms.[2] Then my approach was to use homeopathic treatment, tailored to the pattern that the animal was showing.

This approach I am describing is working with, assisting, the body mechanisms already in place—the functions of natural healing, the activity of the immune system and ways of eliminating toxins that are inherent and necessary if health is to be restored.

What can we expect with this approach? There are three possibilities: maintaining good-quality life during the time remaining, extending life beyond what is usually expected, or curing the condition with diminution or disappearance of the tumors.

The majority of my cases fall into the first two groups, because most of the animals brought to me in this condition are older and not particularly healthy to start with. But even then the animal's quality of life usually remains good, much better than expected, during nutritional and homeopathic treatment. However, the animal may not live much longer than was expected when diagnosed. This outcome is true of about a third of my cancer cases. A very positive aspect of this, though, is that during this time they feel rather well, remain active, and free of suffering.

Another third of my patients live longer than expected, sometimes considerably longer, especially if they are younger and have not had prior surgery, chemotherapy, or radiation. Eventually, they do succumb to the disease. This is more likely to happen with some types of cancers than others, of course.

The remaining third do better than this, with the tumors no longer growing—perhaps even regressing and disappearing. As you would expect, this improvement is more likely to occur in a younger animal with more vitality. It seems to be very important that there be no prior use of corticosteroids or surgery if I am to obtain results like this.

Let's look at treatments. You will understand that there are many natural ways of helping the body, and I will list just some of the more frequently useful ones from my experience. It is highly recommended that you set in place a relationship with a holistic veterinarian who can guide you in this process.

TREATMENT

Homeopathic—*Thuja occidentalis 30c*: This treatment should be done at the outset of any cancer case, as it removes the influence of prior vaccinations that may stimulate the growth of tumors. Use Homeopathic Schedule 4. After allowing this remedy to act for the month, then move to one of these others.

Homeopathic—*Arsenicum album 6c*: These animals will show a rapid weight loss. This may be due to not eating well, but also can be seen even where there seems to be enough food intake. They become anxious, thirsty, restless, and as time goes on, increasingly weak. There is also a seeking out of warm places. There is a tendency to the development of ulcers on the surface of the body, which smell bad and bleed easily. Pains are felt especially at night, after midnight. Use Homeopathic Schedule 6(a).

Homeopathic—*Carbo animalis 6c*: Indicated if the glands are affected, becoming hard and enlarged, in several parts of the body—neck, armpits, groins, breasts. These are painful. As the condition develops there can be a bad-smelling discharge from the affected area. It is associated with developing weakness and desire to be alone. Use Homeopathic Schedule 6(a).

Homeopathic—*Conium 6c*: Tumor very hard, like a stone, painful to touch, or prevents sleeping at night. The animal has a tendency for tumors of the breast and inside the abdomen; also useful when cancer has metastasized to the glands of the body. This type of tumor is more likely to arise after injury to a part of the body. Use Homeopathic Schedule 6(a).

Homeopathic—*Lycopodium 6c*: For tumors affecting the right side of the body, animal thin, tends toward gassiness, worse in the mornings. There can be a history of urinary problems. Tumors containing a lot of blood vessels. Use Homeopathic Schedule 6(a).

Homeopathic—*Nitric acid 6c*: Areas of the body affected are mouth, anus, or bones. Tendency to warts. Pain after having a bowel movement, pain that lasts a long time. Use Homeopathic Schedule 6(a).

Homeopathic—*Phosphorus 6c*: For dogs or cats that have a tendency toward vomiting or diarrhea. They are often excitable, may be afraid of noises (thunder, for example), are quick to react. Developed tumors have a tendency to bleed, or the location of the cancer may be affecting the blood (as in bone marrow or spleen). Use Homeopathic Schedule 6(a).

Homeopathic—*Phytolacca 6c*: Especially affects mammary glands and testicles. Also useful for lipomas (fatty tumors). Use Homeopathic Schedule 6(a).

Homeopathic—*Silica 6c*: For hard tumors affecting face or lips, or bones. Tendency to formation of pus. Use Homeopathic Schedule 6(a).

Herbal—*Goldenseal (Hydrastis canadensis)* is generally useful in treating any kind of cancer, especially if it is associated with a loss of weight. Another indication is if the tumor has appeared on the surface of the body as a large sore or ulcer. Use Schedule 1 for as long as it seems helpful. When using this herb for long periods, supplement the diet with extra vitamin B complex, as goldenseal tends to deplete the body of these vitamins.

This is a useful list, but realize there are another 30 or so homeopathic remedies that can also be applicable in some cases. If you see some progress with one of these remedies, you can of course continue to use it as seems indicated, but will do best to work with a veterinarian to interpret the response.

Nutritional—*Curcumin* (turmeric) is an herb member of the ginger family known to be an effective antioxidant, so it is useful for many conditions where there is excessive inflammation. There are reports also of its effectiveness in cancer treatment, so it will be a useful part of your program. The suggested dosage is approximately 15 to 20 milligrams per pound of body weight in dogs, 150 to 200 milligrams total for cats. A simpler way of looking at it is $\frac{1}{8}$ to $\frac{1}{4}$ teaspoon per day for every 10 pounds of dog weight.[3]

CANINE DISTEMPER AND CHOREA

We will consider both of these conditions together, since they are related. Chorea (uncontrollable twitching or jerking) is a possible result of distemper. Let's discuss each in turn.

CANINE DISTEMPER

Distemper used to be common, but it is not seen so much in its natural form now because of vaccinations. Earlier in my practice I would now and then see a case, and more often would be asked to treat an outbreak in a litter or a kennel.

Distemper progresses in stages. After a 6- to 9-day incubation (usually not noticeable), the dog contracts a brief initial fever and malaise. Afterward, the dog is apparently normal for a few days or a week, and then he will suddenly show the typical distemper symptoms: fever, loss of appetite and energy, and perhaps a clear discharge from the nose. Within a short time the condition advances and he now develops one or more of the additional symptoms: severe conjunctivitis (eye inflammation) with a thick discharge that sticks the lids together, heavy mucus or yellow discharge from the nose, very bad-smelling diarrhea, and skin eruption on the belly or between the hind legs.

Though early in my career I treated many distemper cases with the orthodox approach of antibiotics, fluids, and other drugs, I did not see it do much good. Indeed, sometimes it seems to increase the likelihood of encephalitis, a severe inflammation of the brain (or smaller areas in the spinal cord) that often arises after apparent improvement or recovery. At this point dogs are usually put to sleep because medical treatment is almost always ineffective. I am convinced that the use of drugs increases the likelihood of encephalitis, while natural methods make it less probable. I have witnessed many successful recoveries in distemper cases treated with homeopathy and nutritional therapy. The suggestions that follow are gleaned from this experience.

TREATMENT

In order to prevent complications like encephalitis, it is crucial to withhold solid food while the dog is in the acute phase of distemper with a fever. The normal rectal temperature is 100.5°F to 101.5°F (38°C to 38.6°C). It might be a little higher at a veterinarian's office because of excitement. Fast the dog on vegetable broth and pure water, until at least a day after the temperature becomes normal. If the fever returns, fast again. Because fevers tend to rise in the evening, record temperatures both morning and night to get a better overview.

In case you are wondering how long dogs can go without solid food before starving, the normal healthy animal can get along all right for several weeks. A dog that is sick with distemper can profitably fast for 7 days, provided it is an adult of normal weight and general condition. However, few will need to fast this long. Make sure you have fresh, pure water available at all times.

Vitamin C is an important aid. Many distemper cases can recover without ill effects by using vitamin C along with fasting. (However, I always used homeopathic treatment as well in my practice.) Dose as follows: 250 milligrams every 2 hours for puppies and small dogs, 500 milligrams every 2 hours for medium dogs, 1,000 milligrams every 3 hours for large or giant dogs. Don't continue the dosing through the night, because rest is also important. Once the acute phase and fever have passed, double the interval between doses. Continue until recovery is complete.

Special eye care may be necessary, because the lids can get severely inflamed. Bathe the eyes in a saline solution (see Chapter 18). Then put a drop of *sweet almond oil* (also simply called almond oil), or *olive oil*, in each eye to help heal and provide protection. Use of oil is especially helpful when there are ulcers.

During the early stages of distemper, use of one of the following remedies should help considerably.

Homeopathic—*Distemperinum 30c*: Specially prepared from the distemper-diseased animal, this is the most effective remedy for the early stages. I've seen it produce recoveries in just a day or two. The dog needing this will have been ill just a short time with symptoms like a cold and a runny nose with fever. Give one pellet morning and evening until improvement is evident and the temperature has returned to normal. Then give only if symptoms flare up again.

Note: Some pharmacies may restrict this remedy to veterinarians. Check with more than one.

Homeopathic—*Natrum muriaticum 30c* is another choice and is appropriate for the early stage, with a lot of sneezing as the indication. Use Homeopathic Schedule 2.

Homeopathic—*Pulsatilla 30c*: This remedy is suitable for the stage of conjunctivitis with thick, yellow, or greenish eye discharge. Use Homeopathic Schedule 2.

Homeopathic—*Arsenicum album 30c*: This remedy is indicated for the dog that is very ill, with rapid weight loss, loss of appetite, weakness, restlessness, frequent thirst, and a slight clear discharge from the eyes that causes irritation of the eyelids and surrounding areas. Use Homeopathic Schedule 2.

If none of these works, consult with a homeopathic veterinarian if you are able to—there are many other remedies worth trying.

Later Stages

During the later stages of distemper, with bronchitis and coughing, select one of the following treatments (in case you did not treat earlier or it has gotten worse despite treatment).

Homeopathic—*Hydrastis canadensis 6c*: Indicated for advanced distemper, with a thick, yellow discharge of mucus from the nose or down the back of the throat. Often there will be loss of appetite and emaciation. Use Homeopathic Schedule 6(c).

Homeopathic—*Psorinum 30c*: This is most useful for the dog that has survived distemper but cannot completely recover. Often there is a poor appetite, skin eruptions or irritated skin, and a bad body smell. Use Homeopathic Schedule 4.

Recovery

With proper treatment, distemper is not too severe, and you can generally expect recovery in a few days to a week. The initial state of health of the animal and the degree of immunity acquired from the mother (in the case of puppies) seem to be important factors in the severity of individual cases.

If recovery is not easy or complete or leaves the animal in a weakened condition, the following measures should help.

In the healthy diet you will be using,

emphasize the use of oats, which strengthen the nervous system. It also helps to give B vitamins (give a natural B-complex tablet in the 5- to 10-milligram range, once a day, for a week or so). You can use "human" formulas; just cut down the dose accordingly.

For the dog weakened with distemper, give a tincture of the *common oat (Avena sativa)*, a beneficial nerve tonic available from herb stores, natural food stores, or homeopathic pharmacies. Twice daily, give two to four drops for small dogs or puppies, four to eight drops for medium dogs, or eight to twelve drops for large ones.

If the animal is left with a weakened digestive system, residual diarrhea, or chest complications, give fresh grated *garlic (Allium sativum)* three times daily. Use half a small clove for small dogs or puppies, half a large clove for medium dogs, and one whole clove for large ones. Add the grated garlic to the food or mix it with honey and flour to make pills.

There is controversy about using garlic in dogs, some saying that it is toxic. I have never seen a problem with using it myself, but if this worries you, then do not use it. It might be the amount given that is the factor, as the study I read gave very large amounts to dogs and reported some blood changes. (See Chapter 11, Exercise, Rest, Grooming, and Play, for more discussion of the use of garlic.)

CHOREA

Usually an aftereffect of the distemper virus infection, chorea is a condition in which some muscle in the body (usually a leg, hip, or shoulder) twitches every few seconds, sometimes even during sleep. It results from damage to part of the spinal cord or brain. Most pets with chorea are put to sleep because it is not considered curable; however, once in a rare while a spontaneous recovery occurs. I think it is worth giving alternative therapy a try, as it will improve the odds. You can try these remedies.

Homeopathic—*Nux vomica 30c*: After this treatment, wait and observe for a week. If there is no change for the better, then use the next treatment.

Homeopathic—*Belladonna 30c*: Again, give one dose, then watch and wait for a week. If this noticeably helps but does not completely eliminate the problem, then use . . .

Homeopathic—*Calcarea carbonica 30c*: Use Homeopathic Schedule 4.

Homeopathic—Another remedy to consider is *Silicea 30c*, especially if these other medicines have had no effect. Give one dose and allow it to act for several weeks.

If this has still not solved the problem, there are other medicines that can be used, but you will need guidance from a homeopathic veterinarian.

CATARACTS

See Eye Problems.

CHOREA

See Canine Distemper and Chorea.

CONSTIPATION

Constipation sometimes occurs when animals don't get enough bulk in their diet or don't get enough exercise. If a dog or cat is not allowed to evacuate when the urge is there, the animal may develop the habit of holding its stool. A dog that is not let out often enough or a housebound cat with a dirty litter box is most likely to develop this habit. In relatively simple cases like this, the following treatments will generally suffice.

TREATMENT

A natural diet that includes fresh vegetables for adequate bulk is really helpful. If the animal's stools seem dry, add ½ teaspoon to 1 tablespoon of bran to each meal (depending on the animal's weight). It will help the stools retain additional moisture. A similar treatment is to use ¼ teaspoon to 2 teaspoons of powdered psyllium seed, which is available in health food stores.

Many cats will accept pumpkin added to their food and in the same way this will help to increase the size of the stool and increase moisture in it.

You can use mineral oil temporarily where there is a large buildup of hard stools. Depending on the animal's size, add ½ teaspoon to 2 teaspoons to the food once a day, until a bowel movement occurs, but for no

more than a week. Continued use is inadvisable because the oil will draw reserves of vitamin A from the animal's body and may also create a dependency on its use for normal evacuation. We could use a vegetable oil like olive oil, for example, but mineral oil has the advantage of remaining undigested as it passes through, while the vegetable oil is usually absorbed into the body and never makes it to the rectum.

Give the animal plenty of opportunity to relieve itself. Make sure your cat has a clean, accessible litter box. A suggestion I have seen is to provide a litter box for each cat in the house plus one extra. Let your dog out several times a day to make sure he gets plenty of exercise. This is very important for massaging the internal organs and increasing bloodflow throughout the body, often stimulating a sluggish metabolism. Long walks or runs or a game of fetch are excellent. For a cat, try games involving pouncing, such as "thing-on-a-string."

Dogs

If your dog has a constipation problem, try one of these remedies in addition to the advice just given. Pick the one that most closely matches your pet's situation.

Homeopathic—*Nux vomica 6c*: This is an effective treatment for constipation caused by poor-quality food in the diet, eating too many bones, or emotional upset (frustration, grief, reaction to scolding). It is best suited to a dog that has repeated but ineffectual straining and may show irritability, pain, and a tendency to hide or be alone. Use Homeopathic Schedule 6(a).

Homeopathic—*Silicea 6c*: Silicea is best for the constipated animal that seems to have a weak rectum. With this weakness, the stool, though partly expelled from the anus, slips back in again. It's also good for a dog that has trouble getting the whole bowel movement out and for the poorly nourished animal. Use Homeopathic Schedule 6(a).

Homeopathic—*Natrum muriaticum 6c*: Useful when constipation is a continuing problem but there is no desire to have a bowel movement (or little concern about it). Use Homeopathic Schedule 6(a).

Homeopathic—*Sulphur 6c*: There is a recurrent tendency to constipation, though sometimes the desire is for a stool during the night, or early in the morning. Stools tend to be hard; the desire to pass them frequent, without result. Can be red around the anus. Use Homeopathic Schedule 6(a).

Homeopathic—*Calcarea carbonica 30c*: Stool won't come out, has to be dug out with an instrument or enemas. Sometimes there is the alternation of constipation with soft stools coming out on their own, without control. Use Homeopathic Schedule 4.

Where the rectum is weak, you should also consider the possibility of aluminum poisoning. Signs include chronic constipation with straining, and stools that are sticky and messy rather than hard. Even though the stool is soft, weak rectal muscles make passage difficult. Consider the possibility of aluminum poisoning in all recurrent cases, even though the symptoms may be different from those given. If you suspect this problem, stop using aluminum cooking pots or dishes for your animal's food. Avoid pet food sold in aluminum cans. Also, do not feed processed cheeses (which may contain sodium aluminum phosphate as an emulsifier), table salt (which often contains sodium silicoaluminate or aluminum calcium silicate to prevent caking), white flour (which may be bleached with an aluminum compound, potassium alum), and tap water (aluminum sulfate may be used as a precipitant to remove water impurities).

Please understand that not all animals are adversely affected by aluminum; however, there are some individuals that are very sensitive to it.

Cats

For the cat with constipation, use the basic treatment described above. In addition, choose the one remedy below that best suits your cat's condition.

Homeopathic—*Nux vomica 6c*: Use for the cat that strains ineffectually or passes only small amounts of stool without relief. It may act irritable, withdraw to be alone in another room, or avoid your touch. Constipation may follow emotional upset, stress, or too much rich food. There may be a history of nausea and vomiting. Use Schedule 6(a).

Homeopathic—*Calcarea carbonica 30c*: This is indicated for one of the more severe and persistent forms of constipation in cats, what is often called *obstipation*. Some cats never empty their bowels adequately, going 2 or 3 days between inadequate bowel movements. Use Schedule 4. Do not repeat the medicine.

Homeopathic—*Phosphorus 30c*: Recurrent constipation, every couple of weeks; stools are thin and narrow instead of normal size. Use Homeopathic Schedule 4.

Homeopathic—*Lycopodium 30c*: Like *Calcarea carbonica* (above) this is used for very severe and persistent problems of constipation. Typically the cat will feel the urge, suddenly hunch up as if cramping, then make many and fruitless attempts to pass the stool. He becomes oversensitive, not wanting to be touched or messed with. This can be coupled with a ravenous appetite and yet weight loss. Use Homeopathic Schedule 4.

Herbal—*Common garlic (Allium sativum)*: For the cat with a big appetite that likes a lot of meat and tends to constipation, add one-half clove of freshly grated raw garlic to the daily food. Many animals like the taste.

Herbal—*Olive oil (Olea europaea)*: This oil serves as a tonic for the intestinal tract and stimulates the flow of liver bile and the contraction of intestinal muscles. Any excess oil will also lubricate the fecal mass and soothe the mucous membrane linings of the intestine and rectum. Give ½ to 1 teaspoon twice daily, mixed with food, until the movements are regular. (You also can give it once a week as a tonic or to prevent hair balls.)

Note: Also consider the possibility of aluminum sensitivity, as described for dogs.

CORNEAL ULCERS

See Eye Problems.

CUSHING'S DISEASE

This disorder is a dysfunction of the adrenal glands, much like Addison's disease. With Addison's, the adrenal glands are not producing enough hormone; with Cushing's, the opposite is true—the glands are *overproducing* corticosteroids (principally cortisol). Of course, what we want is "just enough and not too much," so this overproduction can be a real problem.

Why does this happen? It's not really understood very well, but we do know that many dogs and cats develop Cushing's because the pituitary gland (a hormonal "master gland" in the brain) is pushing the adrenal glands to do so. This accounts for about 85 to 90 percent of cases. The situation is further complicated because the pituitary gland is influenced, in turn, by the brain, and it's entirely possible that the whole cascade of problems occurs because of psychological or physical stress—at least as contributing factors. Chances are that if your pet has this diagnosis, it is a dysfunction of the pituitary gland (and thus adrenal glands) that is the problem.

The remaining 10 to 15 percent have tumors in the adrenal glands themselves, which causes the excessive production (the pituitary gland is not involved). These tumors are often benign (not malignant).

What happens as a result of this condition? The usual and most common symptoms are excessive drinking and urinating (that precede the condition by weeks or months); enlargement of the abdomen due to weakness of the muscles, production of excessive abdominal fat, and enlargement of the liver; loss of body hair (on both sides equally), which comes out very easily. This latter is associated with developing thinness of the skin and a color change to dark brown or black (most often on the undersides). Though these symptoms are common, there are many other changes that can occur—changes in reproductive cycles, symptoms of diabetes, excessive weight gain (obesity), and so on. It is a very complicated condition and mimics many other disorders, so it takes considerable skill to determine that this is the problem.

A further complication is that Cushing's disease may occur along with other chronic problems, almost as if it's a further deterioration of health in a pattern of decline. For example, your dog may have had years of skin allergies, arthritis due to hip dysplasia, or cruciate ligament breakdown (knee joint deterioration), and now Cushing's disease pops up. It seems to me that it is a fundamental breakdown in the body's ability to regulate inflammation and repair of tissues (in which the adrenal glands are intimately involved).

Recognizing this problem and treating it requires the skill of a veterinarian. There are blood tests of various types that can be done—both for testing hormone levels and for testing the functions of the adrenal glands. I have treated many of these cases over the years and, though surgery or drugs are the conventional approach, I still prefer to use homeopathy and nutrition as my first tools in resolving it.

Because there can be multiple problems, how to treat this is very individual. I suggest you work with a homeopathically trained veterinarian who can set up a treatment schedule to address all the problems your animal has. As you might anticipate, excellent nutrition and reduction of stress are necessary adjuncts.

TREATMENT

In cases I have seen, there does not seem to be a very definite pattern to symptoms so it's difficult to suggest much that is specific. Really, the treatment has to be individualized, based on the details of the history as well as the current symptoms. Here is one remedy I have frequently used (but there are many more possible).

Homeopathic—*Calcarea carbonica 30c*: Many dogs will respond favorably to this remedy. Worth a try. Use Homeopathic Schedule 4.

CYSTITIS

See Bladder Problems.

DEMODECTIC MANGE

See Skin Parasites.

DENTAL PROBLEMS

The mouth and its associated structures are especially important to animals, not only for eating but also for grooming and manipulating things. This part of the body contains many nerves and is served by a plentiful blood supply, making dental problems more serious than you might expect. Mouth pain can keep an animal from eating enough or grooming properly.

Four problems are most common: accidents that damage the teeth or gums, congenital or developmental disorders, periodontitis (calculus on the teeth and associated gum disease), and tooth decay. Let's look at each in turn.

ACCIDENTS

If a pet is hit by a car, it's not unusual that teeth are broken off or knocked out. In most cases, after the initial inflammation has subsided, the animal feels no real discomfort.

Generally, a broken tooth can be left in place (if still firmly attached), at least until a convenient occasion for removal occurs, such as another need for surgical anesthesia. Sometimes, however, the root will become abscessed and require removal.

As for injured gums, an excellent immediate treatment to stop bleeding and promote rapid healing is:

Herbal—*Calendula tincture (Calendula officinalis)*: Apply it directly to the bleeding gum with a saturated cotton swab, or dilute the tincture with 10 parts water and use it as a flushing mouthwash, applied with a syringe or turkey baster.

An excellent treatment for mouth pain from injuries is:

Homeopathic—*Arnica 30c*. The next day, give *Hypericum 30c*. Use Homeopathic Schedule 2.

CONGENITAL OR DEVELOPMENTAL DISORDERS

Problems of this sort are so common in some breeds of dogs that they seem to be standard equipment. Cats, in contrast, have very few congenital mouth problems, probably because they've been less modified by intentional breeding.

Some dogs, especially toy breeds, have teeth that are simply too crowded, often overlapping in position. Sometimes the jaw is too long or too short. Worst of all is the fate of breeds like the bulldog and Boston bull terrier, who have very short jaws with teeth that are crammed together, turned sideways, and completely out of position. They really have a mouthful of problems.

What can you do about it? I recommend extracting some of the permanent teeth as they develop, preferably while the dog is still young. Left untreated, the crowding and poor fit may lead to gum disease and loose teeth.

Some dogs have relatively straight, uncrowded teeth, but one jaw is longer or shorter than the other. As a result the teeth don't meet properly, causing discomfort and premature breakdown of both teeth and gums. If the difference between the jaws is ¼ inch or less, removal of some of the deciduous (baby) teeth before the arrival of the permanent set may restore proper alignment. But if the difference is greater, little can be done preventively. The treatment with the greatest chance of restoring normal mouth anatomy is to give:

Homeopathic—*Calcarea carbonica 30c*: Helpful when growth seems delayed or incomplete. In some animals you will see further development after using it. Use Homeopathic Schedule 5.

Other structural problems include supernumerary (extra) teeth, which should be removed to prevent accumulation of food and debris, and retained baby teeth, which force the permanent teeth to grow beside or in front of them (trapping debris and per-

haps distorting the jaw formation). They, too, should be removed by a veterinarian.

PERIODONTAL DISEASE

This is the most common tooth and gum problem. There is a tendency for the gums to be inflamed, red, and swollen and for the saliva to change, which creates a buildup of calcium salts, food, hair, and bacteria on the animal's teeth. These deposits put pressure on the gums, causing inflammation, swelling, pulling away, and receding gums. A pocket opens up between the gums and teeth, which collects still more debris and further worsens the problem. Eventually, the process can loosen the teeth and cause them to fall out. A serious complication is the development of an abscess, which destroys the root of the tooth.

You can detect this in dogs by examining the back teeth to see if there are brownish deposits over the teeth, especially at the bottom. In cats, an early sign is a red line that is seen along the line of teeth, right where the teeth and gums meet. With time, this extends, and more of the gum becomes involved. You may also see the animal dropping food while eating or turning its head to the side to chew only on one side.

It is not surprising that nutrition is important here, but also a very significant factor to keep in mind, especially for cats, is mercury poisoning from eating fish. Many cat foods (and some dog foods) include some form of fish (or fish meal), which is excessively high in mercury. A primary symptom of mercury poisoning is inflammation of the mouth and gums and looseness and decay of teeth. When I was first in practice (1965) it was very rare to see any mouth trouble in cats; they rarely needed even teeth cleaning. Now periodontal disease affects the majority of cats. I think to a great extent it is, like the canary in the coal mine, an indication of how much mercury has been accumulating in our environment.

The usual treatment is to clean and extract teeth under anesthesia, and it will certainly help for a while. Believe it or not, I have actually heard veterinarians recommend removing *all* the teeth in cats to prevent this!

Much better is to clean up the diet. Without proper nutrition the gums can't repair themselves or maintain necessary resilience. Emphasize those vegetables rich in niacin, folate, and minerals—leafy greens, broccoli, asparagus, lima beans, potatoes, and lettuce. Another good folate source is plain peanuts (which can be given as unsalted peanut butter, organic of course).

Also give your pet its own natural "toothbrush"—either bones or a hard raw vegetable like a carrot (for the dog), or cucumber (for the cat). Do this at least once a week, feeding the meal of the bone or vegetable. If you are going to use bones, again make sure they are from organic sources and both fresh and raw. Avoid cooked bones

(which splinter) and small or easily splintered bones from chickens and turkeys. These can be dangerous. Bones that have been frozen and thawed are also risky.

In dogs, for the first few weeks, limit bone chewing to 30 minutes a day and watch to make sure that large pieces are not swallowed.

Cats can be given small raw bones as well, but they do not really pick up on this practice unless they are started quite young. Somewhat more accepted is to feed part of a raw game hen once a week instead of the regular meals. However, having lost their natural instincts, many mature cats will not adapt even to this.

After any dental work at the hospital, you can do a lot with follow-up care to promote rapid healing. The gums will be very sore and inflamed. Certain herbs will be very helpful. Pick one of the following that seems best suited (or, if indicated, you may use both the goldenseal and the myrrh, ½ teaspoon of each).

Herbal—*Purple coneflower (Echinacea angustifolia)*: This is useful where teeth are found to be infected and the animal is thin and run-down. Boil 1 teaspoon of fresh-smelling rootstock in 1 cup of water for 10 minutes. Cover, remove from heat, and let steep for an hour. Strain and apply this decoction directly to the gums with a swab or use it as a mouthwash. It promotes saliva flow, so don't worry if your pet begins to drool.

Herbal—*Goldenseal (Hydrastis canadensis)*: This herb is antiseptic and helpful for new gum tissue growth. Steep 1 teaspoon of powdered rootstock in a pint of boiling-hot water until cool. Pour off the clear liquid and use it to flush out the mouth and gums.

Herbal—*Myrrh (Commiphora myrrha)*: Myrrh is indicated for loose teeth. Steep 1 teaspoon of the resin in a pint of boiling water for a few minutes. Strain it and paint the infusion on the gums, or flush them using a syringe or turkey baster.

Herbal—*Plantain (Plantago major)*: This herb helps when the condition is not serious enough to require major cleaning but when you see minor deposits on the teeth and the gums are inflamed. Bring 1 cup of water to a boil. Turn off the heat and add 1 tablespoon of the leaves. Steep for 5 minutes. Strain and use as a mouthwash.

General directions for herbs: Whichever herb you pick, use it twice a day for 10 to 14 days. Alternatively, use the herb in the morning and apply vitamin E (fresh out of the capsule) to the gums with your fingers at night. (This treatment is very soothing.)

Homeopathic treatment as an alternative to herbal:

Homeopathic—A dose of *Mercurius vivus* or *Mercurius solubilis 30c* given once, then followed in a month with one dose of *Sulphur 30c*, will often help both dogs and cats in a general way, improving the health of the mouth.

TOOTH DECAY

Tooth decay most often happens in the root of the tooth, or along the edge of the gum. There is little that can be done to reverse this once it happens and usually the teeth need to be removed. However, I have sometimes seen the process stop and go no further in animals getting an improved diet. Prevention is essential and the advice given in this book about nutrition is most important.

Homeopathic—*Thuja occidentalis 30c*: Giving this remedy once a month for 3 months can often reverse or at least stop the progression of decay that is happening at the gum edges.

POST-DENTAL TREATMENT

A very excellent treatment program to use after dentistry (don't give these *before* as it will increase the amount of anesthesia needed) is to give *Arnica 30c* on picking up the cat or dog from the veterinarian's office (or at home). This will reduce pain and swelling in the gums and pain where teeth have been removed. The next day, give *Hypericum 30c* once, to remove any residual pain, especially from extraction of teeth.

One more thing: If you're about to select a new pet, look for one with properly formed teeth and jaws (and parents with the same). See Chapter 9 for information on choosing a healthy animal.

DERMATITIS

See Skin Problems.

DIABETES

Seen in both dogs and cats, diabetes in these animals is similar in most ways to the diabetes seen in humans. Dogs develop type 1 (juvenile, insulin-dependent) diabetes, while cats overwhelmingly (more than two-thirds) get type 2 (the non–insulin dependent form).[4] Because of this difference in the type of diabetes, we will have different nutritional advice for each species. Look at the dog and cat recipe charts in Chapter 6, Recipes for Today, for the code D in the second row. This code indicates to you which recipes we think most useful for this condition.

First, let us consider the possible causes of diabetes appearing in our animal companions. There are likely many factors rather than just one. In human beings, it is correlated with obesity, though it may not be the state of obesity that causes it. The obesity could be another expression of the health problem itself.

What has struck me as a very significant factor, one that likely also plays a role in dog and cat diabetes, is the presence of environmental toxins in the body. For example, a study of over 2,000 people, done between 1999 and 2002, focused on six of the most prevalent pollutants, which were found in more than 80 percent of the participants.[5] Researchers found a strong correlation between how much of these toxins was found in the tissues and the incidence of diabetes—the higher the amount of toxins, the greater likelihood the person had diabe-

tes, up to 38 times the usual incidence. Not surprisingly, the levels of these toxins build up year by year, becoming higher as time goes on, with older people having the most. This certainly would fit with the clinical observation that diabetes is not observed so much in young animals but later in life (as the toxins accumulate). This also would fit the observation that diabetes is steadily increasing in populations. In dogs, the rate has tripled over the last 30 years.

Another possible cause for animals might be a disorder of the immune system. It has been determined that human diabetes can be an immune disorder, in which the body attacks the pancreatic cells that make insulin. It is likely this same process that destroys the insulin-producing ability of our pets, especially dogs. Most of these immune problems we see in animals are made worse by vaccination or can come on after being vaccinated, so be aware of this link and be cautious about vaccinating animals in this condition (see Chapter 16 on vaccinations).

DIABETES IN DOGS

The form that dogs get, which is called type 1, is a loss of the cells of the pancreas that make insulin. As these cells disappear, then less and less insulin is available in the blood. What does insulin do? Its function is to help the transport of blood sugar into the cells to be used for energy. Since almost all energy used in the body is from blood sugar, this is very significant. Oddly enough, there can be enough blood sugar circulating, actually more than enough, but it can't get into where it is needed. The extra blood sugar (glucose) then ends up in the urine. All this wonderful nutrition just spills onto the ground.

You can see that the condition dogs will experience is not having enough energy. They eat a lot but still get thinner and thinner and progressively weaker. The continuous presence of sugar in the urine also causes fluid loss. That's because the sugar must be dissolved in water to be eliminated, so it carries the water out with it. As a result, the dog is abnormally thirsty and passes large volumes of urine.

We have made the picture simple here, as there is apparently more to this condition than just lack of insulin. Even if insulin needs are carefully met with injections of this hormone, progressive changes and weaknesses may still persist. These sometimes include recurrent pancreatic inflammation, formation of eye cataracts, and an increased susceptibility to infection (particularly of the urinary tract).

DIABETES IN CATS

Cats develop the other form, called type 2, which is also the most common one seen in people. What is different here is that the cells that make insulin in the pancreas are still there and active but the body cells that insulin is sent to (via the blood) do not properly respond to it. Above, for the dog, we explained that insulin is needed for blood sugar to move into the cell but the amount of insulin is greatly decreased. In cats, there is plenty of insulin, even more than normal, being produced, but the body cells do not respond to it by taking in the blood sugar. Why it takes this form in cats is not understood, but research of this diabetes pattern has shown that this metabolic change (called insulin resistance) is part of a normal metabolic pattern seen during acute illnesses. Apparently, making this adjustment is a way to maintain necessary quantities of glucose for brain activity during serious infections. This, of course, does not explain why diabetes develops as a chronic form in cats (or in people) but does suggest there must be something the body is responding to in the same way it would an acute illness.

The incidence of type 2 diabetes has steadily increased in people, from around 30 million affected in 1985 to about 368 million as of 2013. This is too short a time for the cause to be genetic and, as explained above, it appears to be associated with accumulation of environmental toxins, especially PCBs and dioxin.[6]

TREATMENT FOR DOGS

The recommended treatment is a diet high in fiber and complex carbohydrates (commercial formulas) and also daily injections of insulin (derived from the glands of other animals). Dogs therefore will do best on the following recipes: Pitcairn's Malibu Special, Pooch Paella, Skillet Supper, Savory Stew, and Lentil Stew.

The conventional advice is to feed canned food once a day, about 12 hours after the insulin is given (when its activity is highest). However, the diabetic dogs I have treated have also done well eating two or three meals during the day, rather than one large one. Their insulin needs seem to stabilize, rather than going through erratic ups and downs from day to day. You may need to experiment with your animal to find the best frequency of feeding, also taking into account the advice of your veterinarian.

Above all, avoid the soft, moist dog foods that come in cellophane bags and don't need refrigeration. These products are very high in sugars that are used as preservatives, as well as artificial colors and other preservatives. What you want to feed is *complex* carbohydrates like those found in grains, beans, and vegetables.

Certain foods are particularly beneficial, so emphasize them in your selections—especially millet, rice, oats, cornmeal, and rye bread. Excellent vegetables are green beans (the pods of which contain certain hormonal substances closely related to insulin), winter squash, dandelion greens, alfalfa sprouts, corn, parsley, onion, and Jerusalem artichoke.

A supplement that is quite helpful is *glucose tolerance factor*, a natural chromium-containing substance found in yeast. It can assist the body in using blood glucose more effectively. I always recommend supplementing the natural food diet with this element. Give 1 to 3 teaspoons *brewer's yeast or nutritional yeast* with each meal to replace B vitamins that get washed out with all the urinating.

See that your animal gets lots of exercise, which has the effect of decreasing insulin needs. Erratic exercise could destabilize insulin needs, though, so a regular, sustained program of exercise is best. It is also important for your pet to maintain a normal weight. Obese animals have a much harder time with this disease.

TREATMENT FOR CATS

Cats, having the other form of diabetes (type 2), will respond best to a diet high in protein and fat and low in carbohydrates (10 to 20 percent of the recipe). It was thought for a while that feeding a high-carbohydrate diet (most commercial foods) would predispose cats to this condition, but it has turned out not to be the case.[7] However, once the disease has developed, changing the diet as described has been helpful to reduce and sometimes eliminate diabetes.[8]

Using the recipes in this book, for a low-carbohydrate diet for cats, rotate these four meals: Kitty Omelet, Wild Tofu (substituting ⅛ teaspoon salt for the tamari and reducing the yeast to 1½ tablespoons or less), Sea Tofu, or the meat dinner in Cat Day. In each case only use low-calorie veggies (asparagus, greens or lettuce, cucumber), not the starchy ones like winter squashes or tubers. For meats, favor lean ones like turkey or venison.

It may well happen that just a diet change, especially if early on, will correct the problem, but sometimes it is necessary to use a form of insulin (long-lasting) to help regulate the situation. The schedule and dosing have to be determined, so you will work with your veterinarian in this regard.

As was suggested for dogs, it might be useful to use *glucose tolerance factor*. Cats generally love brewer's or nutritional yeast, so it is easy to give to them in this form. Sprinkle about a teaspoon on top of each meal, rather than mixing it in.

HOMEOPATHIC TREATMENTS FOR DIABETES

I have found homeopathic treatment to work very well along with this nutritional change. Animals who have not had diabetes for long can become normal and not need insulin. Those on insulin for years can be helped to reduce but perhaps not eliminate it.

Homeopathic—*Thuja occidentalis 30c*: Give once when first diagnosed. Use Homeopathic Schedule 4. If after a month diabetes persists, then look at the treatments suggested next. If the problem is resolved, then no further homeopathic treatment is needed.

Homeopathic—*Natrum muriaticum 6c*: Those it is suitable for have appetite problems (usually excessive) and a marked weight loss. Sugar will be detectable in the urine, and there will be a tendency to anxiety and fearfulness. These animals do not tolerate heat well. Use Schedule 6(b).

Homeopathic—*Phosphorus 6c*: These animals have always been thin, have outgoing personalities, love attention, have ravenous appetites though they vomit easily, and a thirst for cold water. Often there is a history of pancreatitis (inflammation of the pancreas). Use Schedule 6(b).

Homeopathic—*Phosphoric acid 6c*: Useful when nothing else has worked. May not cure diabetes completely but often mitigates the problem and makes it more manageable. Start with Homeopathic Schedule 6(a), and if that has helped during the week or so that you have given it, then you can use it now and then as needed in the future. For example, give a dose every 3 or 4 days.

DIARRHEA AND DYSENTERY

Diarrhea, though common, is not very specific. Many things can cause it and have a similar clinical appearance (frequent, soft, or fluid bowel movements), including worms, bacteria, viruses, spoiled or toxic food, food sensitivities (see Allergies), bone fragments, or indigestible material like hair, cloth, or plastic.

Diarrhea and gastrointestinal upset are becoming more common lately, with emerging evidence of issues impacting important intestinal microorganisms that help with digestion, break down foods, and even produce useful nutrients. These little guys normally live in harmonious balance with the intestinal lining and its functions. But if various microorganisms change, die off, or are reduced in number, others move in that can cause problems. "Leaky gut" can result, meaning that the intestinal lining is more permeable and material gets through that is not meant to, such as proteins and sugars that have not been properly broken down. This, in turn, causes upset that the gastrointestinal tract tries to fix by vomiting or diarrhea.

Studies in animals indicate that consuming genetically modified foods as well as the herbicides used on them can play a role in such GI problems. Amazingly, it's been often observed that animals that usually readily eat grains—like cattle, pigs, chickens—will simply not eat GMO grains if given a choice. One autopsy study of pigs fed GMO corn showed significant stomach inflammation compared to those eating non-GMO feed of the same kind. And yet in countries like the United States, something like 97 percent of products containing corn on grocery shelves contain genetically modified corn, so you can be sure the same is true for pet foods containing corn, as well as soy, canola, and their derivatives.

The body's primary response to GI upset is to increase the frequency of bowel contractions (called peristalsis) in order to flush out the system. Because the intestines move contents along more quickly, the colon does not absorb the amount of water it usually does. Thus, the bowel movement is abnormally fluid.

Depending on what part of the tract is irritated, you may see certain additional symptoms. If there is inflammation and bleeding in the upper part of the small intestine, near the stomach, then the bowel movement will be very dark or black from digested blood. You also may notice a buildup of excess gas that causes belching, a bloated stomach, or flatulence. The animal in this pattern usually shows no particular straining when passing a stool.

A different picture appears when the inflammation is lower down in the colon. There is no problem with gas buildup. The diarrhea tends to shoot out of the rectum with force and obvious straining. If there has been bleeding in the colon, the blood will appear as a fresh red color mixed with the stool. The bowel movements tend to be more frequent than when the disturbance centers in the small intestine. Often you may notice excessive mucus that looks like clear jelly.

Because diarrhea can be associated with so many causes and other disorders, we must be alert to the possibility of other conditions causing this symptom. Most of the time, however, diarrhea is caused by eating the wrong kind of food or spoiled food, overeating in general, parasites (in young animals especially), or viral infections.

The following guidelines are useful for treating simple or mild conditions that fall in the above categories. If they don't resolve it, or if conditions are severe or otherwise seem to warrant it, seek professional help—sooner rather than later.

TREATMENT

Most importantly, do not feed any solid food for the first 24 to 48 hours. A liquid fast will give the intestinal tract a chance to rest and do its job of flushing things out. Make sure that plenty of pure water is available at all times and encourage drinking. A danger of excessive diarrhea is dehydration from the loss of water, sodium, and potassium. So provide these in the form of a broth made from vegetables, flavored with a little nutritional yeast. You may also add a small amount of naturally brewed soy sauce to enhance flavor and provide easily assimilated amino acids and sodium. Offer only the liquid part of the soup, serving it at room temperature several times a day during the fast period.

If the condition is mild or is a sudden attack following consumption of spoiled food, this treatment alone may suffice. In more severe cases, however, it will be wise to use one of the following as well. Some useful treatments are:

Slippery elm powder: Available in most health food stores, this material from the inner bark of the slippery elm tree is an excellent treatment for diarrhea from any cause, and I use it frequently with the animals I treat. To make it, thoroughly mix 1 slightly rounded teaspoon of slippery elm powder with 1 cup of cold water. Bring to a boil while stirring constantly. Then turn the heat down to a simmer and continue to stir for another 2 to 3 minutes while the mixture thickens slightly. Remove from the heat, add 1 tablespoon of honey (for dogs only—cats don't like sweets, so leave it out), and stir well. Cool to room temperature and give ½ to 1 teaspoon to cats and small dogs, 2 teaspoons to 2 tablespoons for medium dogs, and 3 to 4 tablespoons for large dogs. Give this dose four times a day, or about every 4 hours. Cover the mixture and store at room temperature. It will keep for a couple of days. It is easiest to buy the herb in bulk as a loose powder. It's available in capsules, but it is both less efficient and more expensive that way. You can order it in bulk through natural food stores.

Activated charcoal: Sold in drugstores as a powder or in tablets, this type of charcoal prepared from plant matter has the ability to absorb toxins, drugs, poisons, and other irritating material. It's especially useful for treating diarrhea that was caused by eating spoiled food or toxic substances. Mix it with water and give it by mouth every 3 or 4 hours for a 24-hour period (except during sleep). Because overuse of charcoal could interfere with digestive enzymes, a short course is best. Depending on the animal's size, use ½ to 1 teaspoon of powder or one to three tablets.

Roasted carob powder: Available in health food stores, this plant substance is commonly used as a chocolate substitute. However, it is also a popular and soothing aid to diarrhea. Give ½ to 2 teaspoons three times a day for 3 days. Mix it with water and perhaps a little honey, giving it by mouth.

Here are some homeopathic treatments especially useful for diarrhea.

Homeopathic—*Podophyllum 6c*: This remedy is often useful for the diarrhea with a forceful, gushing type of stool, especially if it smells unusually bad. Use Homeopathic Schedule 2.

Homeopathic—*Mercurius vivus or Mercurius solubilis 6c*: The severe diarrhea attack (frequent, bloody stools with continued straining *after* passing the stool) is suited to this medicine. This type of diarrhea can come on after eating toxic substances or from a viral infection. Use Homeopathic Schedule 2.

Homeopathic—*Arsenicum album 6c*: Use this remedy for diarrhea resulting from eating spoiled foods, especially meat. Usually there are frequent bowel movements, rather small in quantity. Also there is weakness, thirst, and chilliness. In dogs this can be because of raiding a garbage can or compost pile. Use Homeopathic Schedule 2.

Homeopathic—*Pulsatilla 6c*: This is a good remedy for dogs or cats that have overeaten or had food that is too rich or fatty. They will get diarrhea from an upset stomach, generally becoming subdued and timid. Typically, they do not have any thirst with the diarrhea (which is unusual). Use Homeopathic Schedule 2.

Homeopathic—*Phosphorus 30c*: This is appropriate for longer-lasting diarrhea in cats and dogs, especially if the above treatments have not been completely effective.

General Advice

During the treatment it is important to be watchful for the possibility that some new factor has set it off—a new flea collar? A change of food? Access to spoiled food in somebody's garbage can or a compost pile? An animal's lack of response to treatment can sometimes be traced to the persistence of such a continuing cause. Also, consider worms and infectious diseases and treat them at home or with your veterinarian's help, as is appropriate (see the topic Worms).

When you are bringing your pet out of the fast after a couple of days, start with the broth, mixed with the solid vegetables used to make it. After 24 hours, you can introduce the regular diet, especially using white rice (just for a few days, then brown rice) as the grain, because it is generally good for slowing down diarrhea.

You might also talk to your veterinarian about adding digestive enzymes and probiotics to the usual ration.

After Recovery

As part of a long-term plan, choose non-GMO food sources, or better yet, organic if you can.

Look at the dog and cat recipe charts in

Chapter 6, Recipes for Today, for the code A in the second row. This will identify for you the recipes we think will be most beneficial for you to use.

Assuming you are making the food from recipes given here, be careful about what you make the recipes with. You can find a useful document to download from the Institute for Responsible Technology, a shopping guide that identifies what foods contain GMO products. Go to http://responsibletechnology .org/take-action/action-tool-kit/. If you are buying commercial pet foods, go to this link for "Pets and GMOs" for listings of those dog and cat foods that do not contain GMO products: http://petsandgmos.com.

See also the topics Allergies and Stomach Problems in this chapter.

DYSENTERY

See Diarrhea and Dysentery.

EAR MITES

See Ear Problems.

EAR PROBLEMS

Inflammation, irritation, pain, and swelling of the ears are common problems for dogs, less so for cats, though they happen sometimes. This is part of a larger picture, reflecting allergy or skin problems that also manifest in other parts of the body. Such allergies express themselves periodically as a sudden redness or flushing of the skin, perhaps after a meal, or during specific times of the year, such as pollen season. A dog with ear problems is likely an allergy victim if it also chews its front feet excessively or scoots its rear end along the floor or ground.

Cats can develop a similar problem, with an accumulation of dark wax or oily material in the ears, causing itching and head shaking. Ear mites are another possible cause of cat ear trouble, but more often it's allergies.

This can be a very frustrating problem to deal with as it is very persistent, either not going away or coming back again and again. It appears most often as an accumulation of dark material (which is mostly wax secretion) and pawing of the ear or frequent shaking of the head. It can be smelly, the ear can be somewhat red and swollen, and in advanced cases the ear hole (the meatus) can be narrowed down and very small while the rest of the outer ear gets enlarged and hard.

What veterinarians most often will attribute this to is "yeast infection," but this is not really the right way to understand it. Yeast is found in all dogs' ears, so it is a normal inhabitant. However, when there is this allergic condition, then the excessive secretion of fluid and wax is like a free lunch for the yeast so they celebrate and grow to large numbers. They are not really the cause and it is not really an infection, so trying to kill the yeast with drops is a waste of time. If you pay attention to what a veterinarian gives for treatment you will almost always find the drops contain a corticosteroid (like prednisone), which counteracts the immune inflammation. If the steroid is not included, the drops don't do much.

It's important to understand that this larger issue of allergies usually underlies the ear problem. Otherwise, you might just focus on the ears and ignore the rest of the situation or even make the situation worse if the ear treatment is suppressive, as it usually is. For more information on the underlying problem, see Allergies.

Keeping the ears clean of discharges and secretions is very helpful in reducing the irritation. Here are some alternatives to the usual ear drops that will do this.

Herbal—If the discharge is watery, smelly, and thin, flush and massage the ear canal once or twice a day with a solution of 1 cup of pure water (distilled, spring, or filtered), 1 teaspoon of a tincture or glycerin extract of *marigold flower buds (Calendula officinalis)*, and ¼ teaspoon sea salt (see Chapter 18 for more information on treatment of the ears).

Herbal—*Aloe vera*: For ears that are painful, sensitive, and raw looking inside but have little discharge, treat in the same way as above, but use fresh juice or a liquid gel preparation made from the leaves of the aloe vera plant.

Herbal—*Sweet almond oil (almond oil)*: To soften and dissolve dark, waxy, oily ear discharge, flush and massage the ear canal with sweet almond oil (*Prunus amygdalus*), which is also soothing and healing to the skin. If the ear is painful as well, alternate with the aloe treatment on a different day (oil and water don't blend well).

Herbal—*Green tea*: For ears that are producing mostly dark, smelly material. First, clean them with the almond oil (above), then use this treatment starting the next day. Put two tea bags (or 2 teaspoons loose tea) in a mug, add boiling water, and steep for 15 minutes. Strain and use warm to flush the ears. You can do this twice a day.

Along with one of these cleaning methods, it's helpful to use:

Homeopathic—*Pulsatilla 6c*: The ear will be very swollen, red, and painful. The dog or cat will be submissive and pitiful and want to be held or comforted. Use Homeopathic Schedule 2.

Homeopathic—*Silicea 30c*: If Pulsatilla noticeably helped but did not completely clear up the problem, then give this remedy to finish the treatment. Give one dose.

Homeopathic—*Belladonna 6c*: Indicated if the ear has flared up suddenly, with much heat and redness in that area. Often there will be a slight fever. The pupils will be dilated even in a lighted room. The dog or cat will be agitated and excitable. Use Homeopathic Schedule 2.

Homeopathic—*Calcarea carbonica 30c*: If treatment with Belladonna has been strikingly effective, then wait 2 to 3 days after finishing that treatment and give one dose of this remedy to prevent the problem from returning in the future.

Homeopathic—*Hepar sulphuris calcareum 30c*: These ears are extremely painful. The animal will not allow them to be touched and will bite if you persist. Use Homeopathic Schedule 2.

Homeopathic—*Graphites 30c*: If other treatments have failed and the problem persists as itchy, sensitive ears, then try this remedy. Use Homeopathic Schedule 4.

Several other factors can complicate and aggravate allergy-related ear problems or may be problems in their own right. For many breeds of dogs, the major factor has to do with the shape of their ears. Other minor and associated causes are water in the ear canal, which predisposes the ear to infections, trapped foxtails or other plant awns, and ear mites (a parasite, more often found in cats). Let's examine each of these.

ANATOMICAL PROBLEMS

In nature, canine ears evolved to stand upright from the head—the best design both for hearing and for ear health. An upright ear like that of a wolf or coyote works well to funnel sounds directly into the ear canal. It also allows a proper exchange of air and moisture between the ear canal and the outside. If water should get in the ear, head shaking and free flow of air will soon reduce the humidity to the proper level. Throughout thousands of years of raising domestic dogs, however, people selected many with heavier, hairier ears that tended to fold over or hang down (basically a puppy trait). Maybe they seemed cute, or perhaps this type of ear just happened to accompany some other feature the people desired. In any case, floppy ears have caused a great deal of unnecessary suffering for dogs and expense for people. A hanging ear creates an effective trap. It closes off the ear canal from the free exchange of air and moisture and makes it easier for stickers and debris to get stuck inside. Some breeds, like poodles, even have hair growing inside the ear canal, making the problem worse. With this in mind, now let's look at three complicating factors in ear problems. While they may afflict any dog, all three are inevitably worse in dogs with floppy ears.

Water in the Ear Canal

Many dogs enjoy a good swim. Invariably, they get water (sometimes not so clean) down their ears. In excess, such moisture can lead to a condition much like swimmer's ear in people—a low-grade irritation that can occasionally develop into more serious infections.

If your dog has this tendency, flush out the ears after a swim with a slightly acidic solution of warm water and lemon juice (figure about half a small, fresh-squeezed lemon to a cup of water; alternatively, use about a tablespoon of white vinegar or apple cider vinegar to a cup of water). This will diminish the chance of bacterial or fungal growth and is also healing to the ear tissue. If either preparation seems to burn, dilute the mixture further with warm water. With the help of a dropper or small cup, fill and then massage the ear canal from the outside (see ear care instructions, Chapter 18). Afterward, allow the animal to shake its head well (it's hard to keep them from it!). Blot off all the excess moisture from the inside ear with a tissue and gently swab out just inside the ear opening with a cotton swab. Remember, you are just absorbing moisture; do not rub against the skin.

As an additional precaution, you can clothespin or tie the ears up behind the head to allow them to dry out further. Do not pin or tie the ear itself, only the hair at the end. Also, if hair grows inside your dog's ears, ask your vet or groomer to show you how to pull it out every so often to allow better air circulation.

Trapped Foxtails

Floppy ears are much likelier to trap foxtails and other plant stickers. The flap is like a hinged trapdoor that directs the stickers right into the ear canal. Though you can do little to prevent stickers (other than cutting down your weeds and controlling where your animal runs), here is how to deal with them if they get trapped in your dog's ears.

After the dog has an excursion in a field, immediately check the ears (and between the toes as well). If you see foxtails, pull them out. If you can't see any but think there is one deep down in the ear, don't try to remove it yourself. The ear can easily be damaged or the foxtail pushed right through the eardrum. Try pressing gently on the ear canal, which feels like a small plastic tube under the ear. If the dog cries out in pain, there is a good chance a foxtail is trapped inside.

If you can't get immediate veterinary care, put some warm oil (almond or olive) into the ear to soften the sticker and make it less irritating. There's also a slight chance that your dog can shake the foxtail out after this procedure, but don't count on it. As soon as possible, take your dog to a veterinarian, who will remove the culprit with the proper instruments (sometimes under anesthesia). Otherwise, more damage can occur by puncturing the ear drum.

Ear Mites

These parasites are more common in young cats, and when dogs get them it is usually from cats. If you have a cat with ear mites and your dog shows symptoms, there's a good chance he has them too. However, in my practice I did not see dogs getting this infestation very often.

Though the mites are not possible to see with the naked eye, the discharge that forms in the ear is. It looks much like deposits of dried coffee grounds down in the ear canals.

An affected cat will scratch like mad whenever you touch its ears.

A dog will shake its head and scratch its ears frequently. Usually, there is no bad smell or any discharge like that seen in cats, but the ear canal looks quite red and inflamed (different than in cats, who have less irritation) when your veterinarian peers in with an otoscope.

Generally, low vitality invites infestation, so an improved diet will indirectly aid in both prevention and recovery.

A mixture of ½ ounce of almond or olive oil and 400 IU vitamin E (from a capsule) makes a mild healing treatment for either cats or dogs. Blend them in a dropper bottle and warm the mixture to body temperature by immersing it in hot water. Holding the ear flap up, put about one-half dropperful in the ear. Massage the ear canal well so that you hear a fluid sound. After a minute of this, let the animal shake its head. Then gently clean out the opening (not deep into the ear) with cotton swabs to remove debris and excess oil. The oil mixture will smother many of the mites and start a healing process that will make the ear less hospitable for them. Apply the oil every other day for 6 days (three treatments in total). Between treatments, cap the mixture tightly and store at room temperature. After the last oil treatment, let the ear rest for 3 more days. Meanwhile, prepare the next medicine, an herbal extract that is used to directly inhibit or kill the mites.

Herbal—Once the ears are cleaned out, one of the simplest ways to kill mites is with the herb *Yellow dock (Rumex crispus)*. Prepare it as described in Herbal Schedule 1, and apply it in the same way as the oil, above. Treat the ears once every 3 days for 3 to 4 weeks. Usually, this is enough to clear up the problem. If you observe irritation or inflammation during the treatment process, then also use the treatment for allergy ears, in the Allergies topic.

In a very stubborn case, you may need to thoroughly shampoo the head and ears as well. The mites can hang out around the outside of the ears and crawl back in later. Also shampoo the tip of the tail, which may harbor a few mites from when it is curled near the head. Use a tea infusion of yellow dock as a final rinse. Remember also that toning up the skin with a nutritious diet is absolutely necessary for the pet with a stubborn mite problem.

If there is no improvement, the problem may not be mites at all. It's just as likely to be an expression of an allergy, as we discussed at the beginning. Here's how to tell the difference: Ears with mites have a dry, crumbly, "coffee ground" accumulation observable (with a light) down in the ear canal only; allergy ears exude an oily, waxy, dark brown, fluidlike discharge that flows up out of the ear canal and is also seen around the outside of the ear.

ECLAMPSIA

See Pregnancy, Birth, and Care of Newborns.

ECZEMA

See Skin Problems.

EMERGENCIES

See Handling Emergencies and Giving First Aid, page 460.

ENCEPHALITIS

See Canine Distemper and Chorea.

EPILEPSY

Epilepsy has become fairly common in dogs, unfortunately, while it is more unusual in cats. In some cases it seems to be an inherited tendency, probably tied to intensive inbreeding. I think the biggest factor, however, stems from yearly vaccinations. I have seen many dogs that first developed epilepsy within a few weeks after their annual shots. Apparently, it is triggered by allergic encephalitis, an ongoing, low-grade inflammation of the brain caused by a reaction to proteins and organisms in the vaccine. This vaccine reaction resulting in encephalitis was discovered many years ago and has been well documented in laboratory animals. Some have even pointed to it as a significant cause of human behavior and learning problems. Fortunately, now that we know that annual vaccinations are not necessary, it will be easier to avoid this possible cause (see Chapter 16).

In general, the health of the nervous system and brain is influenced by heredity, nutrition during the mother's pregnancy, lifelong nutrition, and any toxic or irritating substances that reach the brain. Also, certain brain diseases (for example, distemper) or a severe head injury can result in epilepsy.

For most animals, however, it's hard to point to an obvious cause. The convulsions may start without warning and continue with increasing frequency. An epileptic animal may be either young or old at the time of the first attack. The diagnosis of epilepsy is usually made only after other possibilities—like worms, hypoglycemia (low blood sugar), tumors, and poisons—have been eliminated. Thus, it is a sort of diagnosis by default, and the epilepsy may actually be caused by a mixed bag of things.

The appearance of a seizure can vary. It can be relatively mild, with the animal just "freezing up" and not moving for a couple of minutes. He may be able to move his eyes and look pitifully at you, asking for help! The more severe forms are convulsions with falling down and flopping about, usually just for a minute or less.

After a seizure, the animal may return to normal. Sometimes he will be dazed, and a few will be extraordinarily hungry (probably needing blood sugar).

TREATMENT

In my practice I gave a lot of attention to providing excellent nutrition and avoiding exposure to possible toxins in the environment. As we have been emphasizing, we must give careful attention to the food quality. When possible, I would put the animal on a diet that did not include animal products, as they are the chief source of these substances that irritate the brain. If this is difficult for you to do, at least make the attempt for a 3-month period as a trial. It is very likely you will see the benefit and it will be easier for you to justify the extra work to continue this.

Use special supplements. Since the B vitamins are very important to nerve tissue, use a natural, complete B complex in the 10- to 50-milligram range, depending on your pet's size. Niacin or niacinamide should be given, a minimum of 5 to 25 milligrams. Also supplement with ¼ to 2 teaspoons of lecithin and 10 to 30 milligrams of zinc (the chelated form is best). Give about 250 to 1,000 milligrams of vitamin C daily to assist detoxification. Again, use the level best suited to your pet's size.

Protect your animal's environment. Avoid exposing your epileptic pet to cigarette smoke, car exhaust (rides in the back of pickup trucks are particularly harmful), chemicals (especially flea sprays, dips, and collars, which affect the nervous system), and excessive stress or exertion (but moderate regular exercise is beneficial). Don't let your animal lie right near an operating color TV or close to an operating microwave oven.

Use treatments that strengthen the nervous system. See the herbs suggested under Behavior Problems, giving special attention to common oat, blue vervain, and skullcap.

As an alternative to herbal treatment, specific homeopathic remedies are often quite useful in this condition.

Homeopathic—_Belladonna 30c:_ Start with this treatment and observe for a month. Use Homeopathic Schedule 4. If the problem is no better, go to the next remedy (if the animal is better, do not give further remedies, but continue with the nutrition and other supportive methods discussed above). If the seizures come back after another month or so, then give one more dose of Belladonna 30c to see if that once again improves the situation.

Homeopathic—_Calcarea carbonica 30c:_ If Belladonna (above) has helped but the seizures, though less frequent, still continue, then follow with this remedy. Use Homeopathic Schedule 4. It is very possible that this will resolve the problem.

Homeopathic—_Thuja occidentalis 30c:_ In many dogs, epilepsy comes on after being vaccinated, especially for distemper or rabies, as these diseases have a tendency to affect the brain. If the treatment already suggested above has not eliminated the problem, then give a dose of _Thuja 30c,_ using Homeopathic Schedule 4. Let it act the month. If the problem is not completely eliminated, then follow this with one dose of _Silica 30c,_ again using Homeopathic Schedule 4. Be aware that if either Thuja or Silica has solved the problem, the epilepsy is likely to return if your dog is vaccinated again.

Homeopathic—*Arnica montana 30c*: This remedy is indicated for the animal that has developed seizures after a head injury. It is an alternative to the remedies just discussed and is appropriate only if you know that the cause of the problem is an injury to the head. Give one dose and allow a week or so to assess if the seizures have stopped. If the problem continues, then give one dose of *Natrum sulphuricum 30c*. This treatment protocol will resolve many seizures from concussion to the head, but if the problem still persists, there are other medicines that can be used in this way. Consult a homeopathic veterinarian.

Homeopathic—*Aconitum napellus 30c*: This remedy has a very special use, for prolonged seizures that will not stop. When this happens it is called "status epilepticus," and it is very difficult to manage. If you can give this remedy, Aconitum, every 5 minutes for two or three doses, most animals will stop seizing. You have to be very careful giving a remedy to a seizing animal, as you could be hurt trying to put it in the mouth. The safest way is to dissolve the remedy in some water and pour it over the mouth so that some of it gets in. Another way is to use a syringe with a large needle and, from a distance, to spray the liquid into the mouth or between the lips as best you can. This treatment is not a final cure, and is not likely to prevent the seizures from eventually return-ing, but it is very valuable for this emergency situation.

EYE PROBLEMS

Five major problems can affect animals' eyes: cataracts, corneal ulcers, inflammation (infection), ingrowing eyelids (called *entropion*), and injuries. We will consider each of these in turn.

CATARACTS

This condition is just like what happens with people. The round, clear lens in the interior of the eye (behind the pupil) that transmits and focuses light becomes cloudy or white (milky). Sometimes this happens as a result of injury to the eye. It is not common, but sometimes will be an accompaniment of chronic disease and immune disorders in dogs. Some of the dogs with chronic skin allergies, hip dysplasia, and ear problems will develop this as they get older. Cataracts are also more common in animals that have diabetes mellitus, even with insulin treatment.

Veterinarians sometimes remove the lens surgically, and this may help. Unless the underlying condition is satisfactorily addressed, however, the eye is never really healthy. Prevention, by treatment of the chronic illness, is really the only effective method.

Treatment

See Allergies and Skin Problems for treatment suggestions, even though these do not deal directly with the eyes. You must take the approach of healing from the inside out.

If the cataract is the result of an injury of the eyes, however, use this treatment.

Homeopathic—*Conium maculatum 6c*: Indicated when there is much pain and inflammation of the eye. Use Homeopathic Schedule 4.

Homeopathic—*Symphytum 30c*: Most useful when the eyeball has been bruised by being hit by a solid object. It may not show a lot of inflammation but is very painful. Use Homeopathic Schedule 4.

There are other remedies that can be used for eye problems that are the result of injury. If this one is not effective, contact a homeopathic veterinarian.

CORNEAL ULCERS

Ulcers of the cornea are also usually the result of an injury, such as a cat scratch. When the surface of the eye is broken, it hurts, and tears will form. The injury itself can be so small it's invisible unless a light is shone upon it from the side or a special dye is used. Bacteria may infect the scratch, but in the healthy animal a rapid, uncomplicated recovery is common, often in a day.

Treatment

If the injury is deep or there is debris or a splinter stuck there, it will need careful professional removal under anesthesia. Superficial injuries do not bleed. If you see blood, suspect penetration into and damage of delicate internal structures. This kind of injury can be very serious. The following recommendations are for treating slight irritations, shallow ulcers, or noninfected scratches only.

Topical—Put a drop or two of *almond oil* on the eye, two or three times a day. It's usually more easily administered if it is slightly warmed before using. It is protective and allows faster healing of the cornea. You can add a drop or two of liquid vitamin A to the mix if you like. The eye likes vitamin A.

Nutritional—*Vitamin A* is always helpful to the eyes. Use the typical 10,000 IU vitamin A capsule people would take. Puncture and squeeze a couple of drops onto each meal. Do this for 2 to 3 days.

Herbal—*Eyebright (Euphrasia officinalis)*: Use the extract (which is available as either tincture or glycerin), five drops to 1 cup pure water. To this mixture also add ¼ teaspoon of sea salt. Mix well and store at room temperature. Put two or three drops in the affected eye three times a day to stimulate healing.

An immediately useful homeopathic treatment for the pain and inflammation is:

Homeopathic—*Aconitum napellus 30c*: This is a remedy suitable for the condition of pain and inflammation that follows the injury. Often very relieving. Use Homeopathic Schedule 2.

INFLAMMATION

This is often part of a viral or bacterial infection. Use the eye-cleansing treatment methods discussed in Chapter 18 (with saline washes).

INGROWING EYELIDS (ENTROPION)

In this condition, the lids turn in and press the eyelashes against the corneal surface. The constant rubbing of the hairs causes a large (sometimes white), long-lasting ulcer to appear. This problem is not as easy to observe as you might suppose. Gently pull the lids away from the eye and let them fall back. Repeat several times. If the animal has ingrowing eyelids, you should be able to see the turning in of the lids as they are released. Some dogs are born with this condition, so you can see it when they are quite young. Others develop it after a long period of low-grade conjunctivitis (inner eyelid inflammation). The repeated inflammation and contraction cause the lids to turn in. Ingrowing eyelids are more common in dogs than cats.

Treatment

The usual correction is surgery, which is quite easy to perform and usually successful. I have also had very good results in young animals with this condition using:

Homeopathic—*Calcarea carbonica 30c*: Especially useful in the young, growing animal. Use Homeopathic Schedule 5.

Homeopathic—*Silicea 30c*: Helpful for the eye that has been inflamed for some time, especially if there is any scarring or hardening of the eyelids. Another indication is the tendency for tears to run down beside the nose. Use Homeopathic Schedule 5. The inflammation may subside but if the eyelid is not corrected, surgery will still be needed.

Herbal—It will help, temporarily, to put a drop of *almond oil* in the affected eye three times a day.

Of course, if the underlying cause is chronic inflammation, then you must deal with that. A helpful treatment is:

Herbal—*Goldenseal (Hydrastis canadensis)*: Use the extract (tincture or glycerin) and add five drops to 1 cup of pure water. To this mixture also add ¼ teaspoon of sea salt. Mix well and store at room temperature. Put two or three drops in the affected eye three times a day to stimulate healing.

INJURIES

Other eye injuries include scratches, abrasions, and bruising of the eyeball itself. In these cases, use one of the following homeopathic treatments.

Homeopathic—*Euphrasia officinalis 30c*: This is also especially useful for scratches and abrasions of areas other than the cornea (eye surface). Use Homeopathic Schedule 2.

Homeopathic—*Symphytum (comfrey) 30c*: This remedy is indicated for blows or contusions to the eyeball (the whole eye, not just the cornea in front—for example, from being hit by a rock, a car, or a club). Use Homeopathic Schedule 2.

FELINE IMMUNODEFICIENCY VIRUS (FIV)

This disease was discovered in California in 1986 and found to be quite widespread in the United States and in other countries as well. It has this name because the virus affects the immune system, resulting in lowered resistance to diseases or parasites. It is somewhat an unusual condition in that, while infectious, a cat that picks it up may not show symptoms at all, or for some years. I think this tells us that the general state of health is critical as to susceptibility to actually exhibiting this illness. Another way of putting it is to say that the healthy cat can handle it, keep the virus in check. In my practice I saw many cats that were diagnosed as being positive for the disease, therefore infected, but didn't show any observable signs of being sick.

If there are early signs of an infection, they are usually fever, enlarged lymph nodes, lethargy, sluggishness. There can be anemia, loss of weight, poor appetite (a common symptom in cats with any health problem). One of the challenges in making the diagnosis is there is such a wide range of other symptoms that can develop. Not surprisingly, if the general immunity is diminished, then what stresses the cat experiences in its life determine where the weakness will be manifested.

We can say, generally, that cats with the more advanced form tend to have eye and mouth problems, inflammation of the eye (conjunctivitis), and inflammation of the gums and mouth (gingivitis, stomatitis). But there can be many other changes one would not necessarily relate to this disease. Examples of other problems include blood disorders, anemia, bacterial infections, skin eruptions and infection, persistent mange (skin parasites), chronic diarrhea (and wasting away), inflammation of the interior of the eye, fevers, lymph gland enlargements, chronic abscesses, recurrent urinary tract infections (cystitis), and loss of appetite and weight. In addition, there can be other persistent infections, like fungal diseases or toxoplasmosis (see Toxoplasmosis). One of the most alarming expressions of the disease affects the brain. Cats will act demented, have convulsions, or attack people or other animals.

You can see how, with such a number of ways that cats can become ill with FIV, it is difficult to make this diagnosis on the basis of symptoms. Usually what happens is that a blood test shows there are antibodies against the virus and, on that basis, it is assumed there is an infection with the virus. What complicates this is that having antibodies against a virus also indicates immunity, so in any particular case one has to do a careful examination and evaluation of the cat to confirm the likelihood that the infection is present and active.

PREVENTION

The best prevention, not surprisingly, is a very healthy diet. If the immune system can be kept strong, even exposure to the virus is not necessarily going to be a problem because the immune system will prevent it from getting established. It makes sense, too, that preventing your cat from roaming and fighting significantly reduces the chance of infection. This is not always easy to accomplish, as cats tend to do what they want (in case you haven't noticed!).

If a new cat is coming into your home, isolate him or her from the other cats for at least 3 weeks. During this time, have a test done for FIV (and feline leukemia at the same time). This involves taking a blood sample at the veterinarian's office and is quite useful in determining if this new cat is carrying either virus. (Of course, if the test is positive, the cat will have to be kept isolated from the others to prevent transmission of the disease.)

Another important point is that any cat suspected of having FIV (or feline leukemia or other chronic viruses) should never be vaccinated. That's because the vaccine viruses stress the body (possibly triggering the latent state and making the virus active) or, alternatively, can depress the immune sys-

tem in many cats. The principle is to avoid anything that will disturb or weaken the immune system. I know this advice runs counter to that of many veterinarians, who encourage vaccination as a way to protect a weakened cat. My clinical experience and background in immunology, however, convince me that this is the worst thing to do.

TREATMENT

It is possible to greatly help cats with this problem. Success depends on how much damage has already occurred and the age of the cat. Some will need treatment the rest of their lives and never regain their health. Others, younger and less advanced in the disease, may recover—at least in the sense that the disease goes into remission and they lead normal, healthy lives.

Because of the tremendous variability of symptoms, I cannot offer many specific treatments here. You can apply the different treatments described in other parts of this Quick Reference Section as appropriate to the symptoms your cat has. It will be best, however, if you can work with an alternative veterinarian.

If nothing else is available to you, this treatment can sometimes clearly help, at least to a degree.

Homeopathic—*Sulphur 30c*: Use Homeopathic Schedule 5. If after a month you can conclude that it did help, the remedy can be used in the future when it seems there is a decline in general condition. It should not be given often and most doses will last a month.

FELINE INFECTIOUS PERITONITIS (FIP)

This serious infection can be fatal for cats that develop symptoms. It seems to come on after something depresses the immune system. For example, I have seen many cases occur within a few weeks of the cat receiving a vaccine against feline leukemia—probably from a temporary immunosuppressive action of the vaccine (an effect known to occur with several vaccines). It is not that the vaccine causes the disease directly, but rather that the cat was already carrying the FIP virus and the vaccine gave it an opportunity to rear its little head.

FIP is caused by a coronavirus, a group of viruses that also cause disease in pigs, dogs, and humans. As far as is known, however, the FIP virus does not spread to humans or other animals.

It is thought that cats become infected through the mouth and throat, the upper respiratory tract, or, perhaps, the intestinal tract. People often don't realize when their cats begin to get FIP because they may show no particular symptoms or may run just a mild fever and seem like they're not feeling well for a few days. During this period (1 to 10 days after initial infection), the virus can be shed from the throat, lungs, stomach, and intestines and spread to other cats. After this the virus incubates anywhere from a few weeks to several years before symptoms appear.

Once symptoms appear and the disease progresses, the cat gradually loses its appetite (and weight), develops a persistent fever, and becomes depressed (inactive, subdued). Meanwhile, the virus spreads throughout the body tissues, especially affecting blood vessels. It is interesting to note that by this time (when symptoms are so evident) the cat is no longer shedding the virus and is not contagious.

This points up one of the real problems in control. When the cat is the most contagious, you don't realize anything is wrong, but once symptoms appear it does no good to isolate the cat. However, sanitation can be very helpful in limiting the spread of disease from one cat to another, because the virus can persist in the environment (soiled floors, food or water bowls) for a long time—up to 3 weeks in home conditions. It is no surprise that this disease primarily impacts multiple-cat households or catteries and is not as likely with cats isolated from others.

Along with the common symptoms mentioned above, some cats will develop an accumulation of fluid in the chest or abdomen, which is a more serious form, as it will interfere with breathing or digestion.

Early symptoms can also resemble those of a common cold, with sneezing and watery discharges from the eyes and nose. (Some of the chronic upper respiratory problems in multiple-cat households can be caused by this virus.) In other cats, the first symptoms may involve the gastrointestinal tract (vomiting, diarrhea); this is a serious form that can rapidly become fatal.

FIP can also affect the eyes, causing one pupil to be larger than the other or causing fluid or blood to accumulate in the eyeball. Like the other serious cat virus diseases in this section, FIP can sometimes affect the brain or interfere with reproduction.

PREVENTION

See the prevention advice for Feline Immunodeficiency Virus (FIV) on page 380.

Unfortunately, the diagnostic test to see if a cat is carrying the virus is extremely inaccurate. There are too many other mild and insignificant related viruses that will give false positives on the test, indicating a problem where there is none. Many veterinarians no longer even test for this virus.

TREATMENT

Since FIP takes many forms, I can give only some general guidelines for its most common manifestations. The more severe forms require very careful and persistent treatment under the guidance of a veterinarian. I strongly suggest not using antibiotics or corticosteroids, however, as these drugs do not help at all and only further weaken the cat, almost certainly leading to eventual decline and death from the disease.

As severe as the disease can be, I have had very satisfying results in the majority of cases I have treated with homeopathy and nutri-tion. Inevitably, I will be asked if the cat is completely cured and free of the virus. Clinically and by their appearance, many cats can become normal. Because there is no way to be sure that the body is free of the virus (by testing or other means), however, this aspect of the question cannot be answered. But most people are satisfied when their cat begins to act normally and look well.

Here are some guidelines for treatment.

In the early stages of FIP (which are characterized by fever and loss of appetite), try the treatments for feline leukemia (the next topic).

If the symptoms are primarily upper respiratory symptoms, then refer to the Upper Respiratory Infections section.

In the intestinal form with vomiting and diarrhea, use the treatments under the corresponding sections for Vomiting and Diarrhea.

If your cat has the very unfortunate form of FIP with accumulation of fluid in the chest and abdomen (hydrothorax or pleural effusion in the chest, ascites in the abdomen), the following treatments may help.

Homeopathic—*Arsenicum album 6c*: Indicated for the anxious, chilly, thirsty, and restless cat. This is the most likely remedy to help. Use Schedule 6(a).

Homeopathic—*Mercurius sulphuricus 6c*: Tremendous difficulty with breathing. The cat has to sit up all the time because of the fluid in the chest. Use Schedule 6(a).

Homeopathic—*Apis mellifica 6c*: Very difficult breathing (as described above), but there is an aversion to heat and the cat seeks out the coolest places to sit (tile floor, bathtub, next to the toilet). The cat will also cry out occasionally, sometimes even while asleep. Use Schedule 6(a).

These remedies all have usefulness in treatment of this condition. Try one, and if it doesn't help after a few days, try one of the others.

VACCINATION

There is a vaccine for this disease, but research has shown it to be useless or even harmful if the cat already has the virus in its body. Not recommended.

FELINE LEUKEMIA (FELV)

This is a viral disease, similar to feline immunodeficiency virus (FIV), found around the world. The incidence in the United States is about 2 to 3 percent of cats. The virus is spread from one cat to another through body fluids (saliva, urine, blood, feces). For the same reason, mother cats can give it to their young during pregnancy or nursing. Fortunately, it takes close or prolonged contact between cats for the virus to spread. Most contagion occurs from bites, grooming, or sharing water and food bowls. It is not transmitted through the air or via human handlers.

Many cats will come in contact with this virus but, fortunately, nearly all of them recover spontaneously—showing little or no illness. Those that are weak, however, are affected more severely. The incidence of serious illness is also much higher in multi-cat households. It can happen that the virus persists and becomes more active when the cat is weak from other causes, so it might appear as an observable illness even years after exposure.

There are several types of feline leukemia virus, which cause slightly different symptoms. The most common signs of illness, especially early on, are weight loss, fever, and dehydration (lack of water in the tissues). Other possible symptoms include enlargement of lymph glands, pale gums, tendency to diarrhea, and inflammation of the mouth and gums.

The symptoms can appear in many other forms, as is typical with these chronic virus infections. Sometimes persistent bladder inflammation is seen; another odd finding is one eye pupil smaller or larger than the other. Many affected cats cannot reproduce properly, having spontaneous abortions, stillbirths, or what is known as fading kittens—kittens that waste away in spite of the best care. As if this were not enough, many affected cats develop tumors or cancer. It is estimated that 30 percent of all cat tumors are a result of this virus.

The infection starts in the mouth and throat (from contact with the virus) and will not go further than this in healthy cats. If it can, it will spread throughout the body, especially settling in the tear glands, salivary glands, and urinary bladder. At this stage, the affected cats are now shedding the virus and are infectious to other cats.

PREVENTION

Follow the same preventive guidelines given for feline immunodeficiency virus (FIV), including testing and isolation of new cats coming into the home.

TREATMENT

Vitamin C can be very helpful to cats showing the active symptoms of this disease; give about 100 to 250 milligrams (depending on the size of the cat) twice a day. Vitamin C has some antiviral effect and though it won't eliminate the infection, it can help along with the treatments to follow. Often sodium ascorbate, the salt form of vitamin C (ascorbic acid), is best tolerated. Add the powder to food or, if necessary, dissolve it in water or broth and give it with a syringe.

Other useful treatments include:

Homeopathic—*Nux vomica 30c*: This is especially indicated for the cat that becomes irritable and withdraws to a quiet part of the house or apartment. Use Homeopathic Schedule 2.

Homeopathic—*Pulsatilla 30c*: Most useful for the cat that becomes clingy, wanting a lot of attention and to be held. She will act sleepy and sluggish and perhaps vomit easily if the food is too rich. There may be a tendency to lie in the bathtub or other cool places. Use Homeopathic Schedule 2.

Homeopathic—*Phosphorus 30c*: This remedy is indicated for the cat that is extremely lethargic, acting like a wet washrag when picked up or handled. Another indication is the cat that vomits about 10 to 20 minutes after drinking water (but not after eating food). Use Homeopathic Schedule 2.

Homeopathic—*Arsenicum album 30c*: This cat will be very chilly, restless, and thirsty. What is most noticeable is how weak the cat is, barely able to walk, but weaving as he does so. The body temperature may be low, below 100°F (37.8°C) and the coat very dry and sticking up. Use Homeopathic Schedule 3.

Homeopathic—*Nitricum acidum 30c*: This medicine is a good choice for a cat with a very painful, inflamed mouth. If she is also very irritable or angry when ill, then this medicine may be especially helpful. It is also suitable for lesions on the lips, anus, or eyelids. (The lesions look like ulcers or painful, raw areas.) Use Homeopathic Schedule 4.

Homeopathic—*Belladonna 30c*: Use this if the mouth becomes extremely painful, the cat almost hysterical with the pain, the pupils dilated, perhaps even some fever. Use Homeopathic Schedule 2. If this helps, wait about 5 days and give one dose of *Calcarea carbonica 30c* (one dose only, using Homeopathic Schedule 4).

There are many other remedies that can be used. Consult a trained homeopathic veterinarian to continue this treatment if you see some response to what is listed here and want to continue with it.

VACCINATION

Only partially effective. In my experience, vaccination makes cats more likely to become ill with other diseases such as FIP (see page 382). Not recommended.

FELINE PANLEUKOPENIA (FELINE DISTEMPER; INFECTIOUS ENTERITIS)

This disease of cats comes on suddenly and severely, without apparent warning, commonly killing young kittens within 24 to 48 hours. The associated virus is thought to be spread through urine, feces, saliva, or the vomit of an infected cat. Epidemics can happen.

After an incubation period of 2 to 9 days (usually 6), the first signs are a high fever (up to 105°F or 40.6°C), severe depression, and severe dehydration. Vomiting often follows soon afterward. Initially, it is a clear fluid; later, it's tinged yellow with bile. Typically, the cat will lie with its head hanging over the edge of its water dish, not moving except to lap water or vomit.

Apparently, it's not just the panleukopenia virus itself that produces these severe symptoms, but a secondary infection that results from the destruction of various tissues, including the white cells (which protect the body against infections). In many cases they are almost eliminated, which opens the door to the growth of other bacteria or viruses. In many ways this disease is very similar to the parvovirus infection of dogs.

TREATMENT

The most crucial factor in successful treatment is to catch the disorder in its earliest stages. Since young animals can die very quickly, there often isn't enough time to get a home treatment under way. Clinical methods like whole-blood transfusion, fluid therapy, and antibiotics can be successful if started early, so get professional care if possible.

If you aren't able to get such care right away and you are prepared with supplies, here is a regimen I suggest: As long as there is fever or vomiting, fast the animal on liquids (Chapter 18). Administer high doses of vitamin C, about 100 milligrams per hour to very small kittens and 250 milligrams per hour to young and adult cats. It's easier to give it as sodium ascorbate powder. Use a pinch to make a 100-milligram solution or $\frac{1}{16}$ teaspoon for a 250-milligram solution. Mix the sodium ascorbate with water and give orally.

If vomiting causes both the loss of essential fluids and the vitamin C you have administered (characterized by a rough hair coat, dry-looking eyes, and skin that is stiff when pulled up), focus on using the following homeopathic treatment alone until symptoms are improved. Then go back to giving vitamin C along with the homeopathic treatment.

Homeopathic—*Veratrum album 6c*: Use this if the cat is weak, depressed, and cold, with vomiting (aggravated by drinking water) and diarrhea. Use Homeopathic Schedule 1. If there is improvement, gradually decrease how often you give it over the next couple of days. Eventually, give one tablet at a time when there is any recurring nausea or lethargy.

Homeopathic—*Phosphorus 6c*: This is the best choice for a cat that is limp, with extreme lethargy and apathy. If you pick the cat up, it will hang over your hand like a damp rag. If alert enough, it will also be thirsty for cold water, yet vomit about 10 to 20 minutes after drinking. The cat that should be treated with phosphorus has less coldness but more listlessness than the cat treated with *Veratrum album*. Use Homeopathic Schedule 1.

If you find that despite either treatment, the vomiting is very severe and life-threatening, then follow the advice under the topic Vomiting in this section.

Herbal—If you have the ingredients in stock, consider this alternative herbal treatment: Mix 1 teaspoon of the tincture or decoction of *purple coneflower (Echinacea angustifolia)* with 1 teaspoon of the tincture or decoction of *Boneset (Eupatorium perfoliatum)* in ½ cup pure water. Give one drop of the mixture every hour until you see improvement, then reduce to every 2 hours until recovery.

If the cat is already very ill and close to death, you'll need a different approach. Such a cat will lie in a comatose state, hardly moving. Its ears and feet will feel very cold to the touch. Its nose may have a bluish look. As an emergency measure, administer camphor. Use an ointment containing camphor, such as Tiger Balm. Hold a small dab in front of the cat's nose so that a few breaths will carry in the odor. Repeat every 15 minutes until there is a response.

Once you see improvement, you can go to one of the other treatments outlined. Be sure to discontinue the camphor and remove it from the vicinity when homeopathic or herbal remedies are used, or it will counter their effects.

RECOVERY

Once the cat is obviously getting well and the fever is gone (a temperature less than 101.5°F or 38.6°C), give solid food again. Small meals given more frequently is a good plan. Supplementing with a B-complex formula, in the 2.5- to 5-milligram range, for a week or so will help replenish the loss of the water-soluble vitamins from the illness. Take care to minimize stress and avoid chilling for several days after the initial recovery, as a relapse is possible.

FELINE UROLOGICAL SYNDROME

See Bladder Problems.

FLEAS

See Skin Parasites.

FOXTAILS

See also Ear Problems.

The number one enemy of dogs and cats could well be the numerous foxtails, plant awns, and wild oat seeds (or any other local name for these prickly plants) that get caught in the hair and crevices of their bodies. Because of the way these stickers are constructed, they will not easily dislodge. Instead, they tend to migrate through the skin or into body openings (eyes, ears, nose, mouth, anus, vagina, sheath), where they cause tremendous problems. If a foxtail works through the skin, the body cannot digest it; even years later it will look fresh on removal.

Thus, although the body makes every effort to eliminate the sticker, it clings tenaciously to the tissue. The result is a constantly inflamed tract that drains pus and never heals completely. The plant material can migrate a foot or more into the body, making it difficult, if not impossible, to find. Toes are a favorite lodging place, as are the ears and eyes, where they can get behind the "third eyelid" and cause a lot of irritation.

PREVENTION

Always check over your animal after it has run in fields, vacant lots, or other weedy places. Check all the body openings, and run a comb or brush through the hair. Be sure to check between the toes, too. If you clip the hair between the toes during foxtail season, your job will be much easier and your animal's life much more comfortable. Also, have the hair coat trimmed to a short length, an inch or less, and trim away any hair growing around the ear hole or inside the ear flap. Stickers are much likelier to get into the ears of dogs with hanging ears. See Ear Problems for treating foxtails in the ears. Also, see Abscesses.

TREATMENT

If your animal already has a foxtail under the skin, with chronic discharge from a small opening, and your veterinarian is not able to find and remove it, the following treatment may help as a last resort, only if surgery fails.

Homeopathic—*Silicea 6c*: This treatment can result in the body rejecting the foxtail through an opening in the skin. If you see that, you will know the problem is solved. It also helps to use hot compresses above the draining hole. The increased warmth will bring more blood into the area and more cells to participate in the healing process. Use Homeopathic Schedule 6(b).

If the sticker does not work its way out, your veterinarian must keep trying to remove it surgically. Remember, in the case of foxtails, an ounce of prevention is worth at least a pound of cure.

HAIR LOSS

See also Skin Problems.

Hair loss is often the result of skin allergies and excessive licking and chewing. Sometimes, however, the hair falls out without any sign of skin irritation. This can signal inadequate protein intake, as in cats that eat poorly, or it can mean that the protein is not very digestible even when appetite is good. Other deficiencies, particularly of trace minerals, will slow hair growth.

There are two remedies that are especially useful for simple hair loss unaccompanied by other symptoms.

Homeopathic—*Calcarea carbonica 30c*: If this treatment is successful, you will see signs of hair growth within a month. Do not repeat this remedy without supervision. Use Homeopathic Schedule 4.

Homeopathic—*Thuja occidentalis 30c*: This remedy is indicated when hair growth is very, very slow. Most often this is seen when some of the hair has been clipped off, like for treating a part of the body, or for surgery. It seems like it takes forever for the hair to grow back, maybe months. Use Homeopathic Schedule 4.

HEART PROBLEMS

Disorders of the heart are sometimes seen in aging pets, both dogs and cats. They do not have atherosclerosis and the type of heart attacks that afflict humans, however. Rather, the problem is usually a weak heart muscle, with enlargement of one or both sides of the heart. Sometimes there is inadequate heart valve action or a rhythm that is too quick or too slow.

Typical signs of a heart problem include one or more of the following: becoming easily tired by exercise, bluish discoloration of the tongue and gums upon exercise, sudden collapse or prostration, difficult breathing or wheezing, a persistent dry cough that produces little expectoration, and an accumulation of fluid in the legs or abdomen (a potbellied look).

TREATMENT

Conventional veterinary treatment includes the use of a digitalis-type drug, a diuretic, and a low-sodium diet. The assumption is that the condition is progressive, and so treatment aims to control symptoms rather than to cure.

I prefer an alternative approach, emphasizing nutrition and homeopathic or herbal remedies. Though complete recovery may not be possible, these measures do more than just counteract symptoms; they can actually strengthen the affected tissues. Of course, the chance of help from any treatment depends upon the degree of tissue damage and the age of the animal.

The best route of all is prevention, in the form of a healthy lifestyle, with nutritious food and regular exercise. If symptoms have already developed, however, here is what I suggest.

Use spring water or other water that is nonchlorinated and not fluoridated. If the animal is overweight, slim it down. Weight reduction is important, because the extra weight increases both the effort to pump the blood about and to physically move around.

Cats need to have adequate amounts of the amino acid taurine, and you can obtain this at a health food store as a supplement. Give your cat about 200 milligrams a day. This supplement can be especially helpful for the cat or dog that is overweight as taurine deficiency contributes to that condition and supplementing with taurine will reduce the weight.[9]

The nutrient coenzyme Q10 is very helpful as well, as it increases oxygen flow coming into the heart. You can give 30 to 40 milligrams/day to dogs and 10 milligrams/day to cats. It is even better absorbed if nutritional yeast is included in the diet.

Other important measures are regular, daily exercise that is not too strenuous or exciting (a walk is ideal) and the avoidance of cigarette smoke. In the sensitive animal, many of the symptoms of heart disease can be caused by exposure to secondary cigarette smoke—including irregular pulse, pain in the heart region, difficult breathing, cough, dizziness, and prostration.

Specific remedies may be helpful. If the condition is not very advanced and has been recently diagnosed, try these remedies.

Homeopathic—*Calcarea carbonica 30c*: Helps to restore strength to the heart muscle, especially if dilated and the action is weak. Cats or dogs needing this have had ravenous appetites in the past (though this may have changed since the heart problem), tend to be overweight, and prefer to be where it is warm, like on top of a radiator, heat vent, or equivalent. Use Homeopathic Schedule 4. Do not repeat this remedy without supervision.

Homeopathic—*Natrum muriaticum 30c*: Helpful for the animal that in the past has had a strong appetite but kept losing weight anyway. It will tend to have a strong thirst and an aversion to heat, avoiding warm rooms and disliking warm weather. Pulse tends to be irregular. When ill, the animal does not want much attention and gets irritated if you try to hold it or make it feel better. Use Homeopathic Schedule 4.

Homeopathic—*Phosphorus 30c*: Those needing this remedy vomit easily and crave very cold water (like from a faucet), which may be vomited up 10 to 20 minutes after drinking. Very sensitive to noise and odors. Easily frightened, especially by loud noises, like from thunderstorms or fireworks. Use Homeopathic Schedule 4.

For more severe or persistent symptoms in advanced illness if not controlled by nutrition and other measures (above), pick one of the following treatments, whichever seems best indicated. (Don't skip the other measures and expect good results, however!)

Homeopathic—*Crataegus oxyacantha 3c*: Indicated for the animal with a dilated heart, weak heart muscle, difficult breathing, fluid retention, and (often) a nervous or irritable temperament. Use Homeopathic Schedule 6(c).

Homeopathic—*Strophanthus hispidus 3c*: For the weak heart with valvular problems. The pulse is weak, frequent, and irregular, and breathing is difficult. There may also be fluid retention, loss of appetite, and vomiting. Obesity and chronic itching of the skin also point to this medicine. Use Homeopathic Schedule 6(c).

Homeopathic—*Digitalis purpurea 6c*: Give one pellet after each attack in which the animal collapses or faints after exertion, with the tongue turning blue. Often the pulse or heart rate is abnormally slow. There may be heart dilation and fluid retention. Liver disturbances may be evidenced by a white, pasty stool. If this treatment is helping, the attacks will become less frequent.

Homeopathic—*Spongia tosta 6c*: For the animal whose crises are characterized by a rapid pulse, difficult breathing, and fearfulness. It may have difficulty lying down and may breathe easier sitting up. A dry, persistent cough is an indication for this medicine. Use Homeopathic Schedule 6(b).

General directions for the homeopathic remedies are to use the medicine that seems best suited to the situation. If it helps for a while, use it as long as it does. If it stops helping or the symptoms change, then reevaluate and use another of the medicines listed. Many animals with this problem need ongoing treatment, especially if they are quite old. Some will gradually get better, however, and you will be able to discontinue treatment. It is strongly recommended that you get professional help for this condition, even in using the remedies listed here. It is a complex illness and needs frequent evaluation.

HEARTWORMS

The heartworm parasite actually lives in the heart of a dog (and, rarely, a cat), where it can grow as long as 11 inches and, in a minority of infestations, cause persistent coughing, difficulty breathing, weakness, fainting, and sometimes even heart failure. Adult heartworms produce young ones (called microfilaria), which circulate through the dog's bloodstream in greatest numbers when hungry mosquitoes are most likely to come a-biting (especially summer evenings). When a mosquito bites the dog, it can ingest these microfilaria and later infect another dog when that one is fed on.

When a mosquito carries them to a new dog, the microfilaria progress through two more developmental stages under the skin, after which they enter the bloodstream via nearby veins. After reaching the heart, they settle into their new home, where they mature and reproduce, renewing the cycle about 6 months after the original mosquito bite.

A heartworm diagnosis is made when a veterinarian finds microfilaria (baby worms) in the blood, but not necessarily any symptoms of illness. Only a small percentage of dogs in an area actually become noticeably sick from heartworm, which usually requires infestation with a considerable number of worms. Just a few worms are insignificant and may not require treatment, as they induce a natural immunity that keeps the worm numbers low. Once a dog does show clinical symptoms, however, treatment can be very involved and almost always requires hospitalization. The drugs used in treatment are very toxic and hard on the animal, so it is understandable much emphasis is given to *prevention* by regularly giving drugs to dogs that are in regions where heartworm is known to occur.

Heartworm-Preventive Drugs

These preventive drugs kill baby worms that are under the skin, those that have been picked up in the month or so before the dose. Usually the drug is started before mosquito season and continued until a month or two after mosquito season is over. In some areas this means all year.

Are there side effects? Sure. After all, these are drugs. Quite a range of symptoms have been attributed to the use of these drugs, including vomiting, diarrhea, seizures, paralysis, jaundice and other liver problems, coughing, nosebleeds, high fevers, weakness, dizziness, nerve damage, bleeding disorders, loss of appetite, breathing difficulty, pneumonia, depression, lethargy, sudden aggressive behavior, skin eruptions, tremors, and even sudden death.

Though a minority of dogs experiences these reactions, they are seen in many breeds. Veterinarians also report that many dogs get stomach and intestinal upsets, irritability, stiffness, and seem to just feel "rotten" for the first 1 or 2 weeks after each monthly dose of heartworm protection.

An American Veterinary Medical Association report on adverse drug reactions showed that 65 percent of all drug reactions reported and 48 percent of all reported deaths caused by drug reactions were from heartworm-preventive medicine.

I am reluctant, however, to tell people to stop the use of heartworm preventives, particularly in highly infested areas, partly because I cannot guarantee that their dogs will not get heartworm. Still, I dislike the use of these drugs, and I think they cause much more illness than we realize.

What other choice do we have? Unfortunately, almost all heartworm research is directed toward finding new drugs to kill the microfilaria. Very little attention goes to enhancing the dog's natural resistance to the parasite. However, we do know of several facts that make that a promising direction to pursue: One is that wild animals are quite resistant to the parasite. That is, they get very light infestations and then become immune. Another factor is that an estimated 25 to 50 percent of dogs in high-heartworm areas become immune to the microfilaria after being infested and cannot pass heartworms to other dogs via mosquitoes. Finally, after being infested by a few heartworms, most dogs do not get more of them, even though they are continually bitten by mosquitoes carrying the parasite. In other words, they are able to limit the extent of infestation.

All this points to the importance of the health and resistance mounted by the dog itself. Studies in biology have shown us that the role of parasites in nature is to grow in larger numbers in the animals that are unhealthy and weak. That takes us back to the central thesis of this book: If we care for our pets so as to maximize their health, their resistance to parasites (and disease) will be much higher. Isn't this a much more attractive way to go than to continually poison them with drugs? Clearly, we need more research in this direction.

Another overlooked factor arises when we ask why there has been such an extensive spread of heartworm in dogs all over the United States in the last 30 years. I agree with the authorities who say that the incidence of heartworm increases whenever we upset the natural balance in a way that increases the mosquito population. For example, it is happening more now because climate change is opening up new areas to mosquito reproduction that were too cold before.

So it is likely the combination of environmental upset coupled with a deteriorating level of health through several dozen generations of dogs fed on commercial foods and poisoned with drugs and insecticides that has created this unnatural explosion of parasitism. It is particularly frustrating that recent research shows the incidence of heartworm infestation in dogs in any particular geographic area is the same now as it was in 1982, even after all these years of preventive treatment. It doesn't take too much contemplation to realize that the path of continued drug use is a dead-end road.

Some veterinarians who practice holistic medicine have been experimenting with a homeopathic preventive made from microfilaria-infected blood, called a heartworm nosode. Though we have only been able to do small clinical studies, early results are encouraging. This may eventually provide a true alternative to drug use, but more research is needed.

PREVENTION

For those committed to a natural, nonchemical approach, here are some suggestions to help prevent heartworm. Use the optimal nutritional advice recommended in this book. Adding brewer's or nutritional yeast to the food provides an attractive flavor for both dogs and cats and may help repel mosquitoes from the skin. To further minimize exposure to mosquitoes, you can keep your dog indoors in the evenings and at night. Use a natural insect repellent when she does go outside: Rub one drop of eucalyptus oil, diluted in 1 cup of warm water, over the muzzle and the area between the anus and genitals (favorite mosquito-biting areas). Be careful to avoid rubbing the oil on the sensitive tissues of the eyes and mucous membranes.

TREATMENT

Remember that the presence of a few heartworms is not serious in itself. The veterinarian may report a positive blood test but, if there are no symptoms, in my practice, I had my clients work with nutrition rather than do drug treatment, and that went very well.

If your dog tests positive and has symptoms, usually a soft, dry cough and reduced tolerance for physical exertion, you might want to try this treatment before the usual drug therapy. If your dog responds well, then emphasizing nutrition from that point on may be enough.

Homeopathic—*Sulphur 30c*: Use of this remedy will strengthen the resistance to parasites in general. Use Homeopathic Schedule 5.

HEPATITIS

See Liver Problems.

HIP DYSPLASIA

This term describes a poorly formed hip joint. The veterinary profession generally regards hip dysplasia as a genetic problem complicated by a variety of environmental influences. The cause, however, is not really explained satisfactorily. Unfortunately, it is common among dogs.

Hip dysplasia is not present at birth. It develops during puppyhood, as the hip joint forms in a loose or "sloppy" way that allows too much movement of the leg bone in the hip socket. Irritation and scarring occur because the weak ligaments and surrounding joint tissues aren't able to stabilize the joint adequately. In addition, there is a rheumatic tendency—inflammation and pain in the muscles and connective tissue of the legs and hips. If untreated, gradual loss of function will result. Some older dogs actually lose use of their rear legs.

PREVENTION

Prevention is the best place to start. Generations of poor feeding practices have likely contributed greatly to the development of hip dysplasia, the effects magnifying with each generation. Starting a young dog on very good nutrition is a very smart thing to do. There is evidence that too much calcium increases the development of hip dysplasia, so best not to give more than is recommended. Just provide a wide array of very nutritious foods as we have advised here.

Another odd idea is that hip dysplasia is caused by dogs growing too fast. Some people actually advocate restricting food or protein to prevent the puppy from developing normally. They think that keeping it small will somehow prevent the problem. It does not.

There is some good evidence that hip dysplasia is in part caused by chronic subclinical scurvy (a lack of adequate vitamin C). In this view, the hip forms incorrectly as a result of weak ligaments and muscles around the joints. Vitamin C is essential to these tissues.

Wendell Belfield, DVM, reported in *Veterinary Medicine/Small Animal Clinician* journal that high amounts of vitamin C provided 100 percent prevention of hip dysplasia in eight litters of German shepherd pups coming from parents that either had the condition themselves or had previously produced offspring with it.

He used the following program.

- The pregnant female is given 2 to 4 grams of sodium ascorbate crystals in the daily ration (½ to 1 teaspoon of the pure powder; ascorbic acid could also be used).
- At birth, the puppies are given 50 to 100 milligrams of vitamin C orally each day (using a liquid form).
- At 3 weeks of age, the dose is increased to 500 milligrams daily of sodium ascorbate (given in the feed) until the puppies are 4 months old.
- At 4 months, the dose is increased to 1 to 2 grams a day and maintained there until the puppies are 18 months to 2 years of age.

VACCINATION

The other important factor in prevention is that of vaccination. Looseness of the hips is one of the possible outcomes of vaccination of young developing animals, so an important part of a preventive program is to minimize these effects by using the smallest number of vaccines possible (see Chapter 16) and using them as infrequently as you can. Many breeders very much overvaccinate puppies, a practice not necessary for or conducive to good health. If you are obtaining a puppy from a breeder, work out an arrangement with him or her beforehand to use a modified schedule such as I recommend. This is very important, as the hip dysplasia problem does not appear right away, and by the time it does it is too late to take preventive measures.

PREVENTIVE HOMEOPATHIC TREATMENT

This program can be very useful in the young dog to remove the influences of vaccination and poor heredity. You can start it as soon as you acquire the young dog, but it can be used in the older animal as well. The young dog, still forming its body, will respond the most favorably.

Homeopathic—*Thuja occidentalis 30c*: Give one dose to start the program, using Homeopathic Schedule 4. Then after the month has passed, use next:

Homeopathic—*Calcarea carbonica 30c*: Use Homeopathic Schedule 4.

Coupled with use of vitamin C, as recommended above and started as soon as you can, it is very likely to sidestep this whole problem.

TREATMENT

If the condition is already obvious, orthodox treatment centers on a number of surgical procedures that involve cutting certain muscles, repositioning the joint, removing the head of the leg bone, or completely replacing the hip joint with an artificial device. If you would like to see if you can avoid going in this direction, try this treatment.

Homeopathic—*Rhus toxicodendron 30c*: This is especially helpful for the dogs that show the most discomfort when first starting to move but after getting started seem to loosen up. Use Homeopathic Schedule 5.

Homeopathic—*Calcarea carbonica 30c*: If this first remedy (above) has noticeably helped for a while, wait a month for its full effect and then follow it with this one, which will go deeper and act longer. Use Homeopathic Schedule 4.

The other choice is to start working with a homeopathic veterinarian to move to addi-tional remedies individualized for your animal. Most often dogs with this condition can be greatly helped so that surgery is not necessary.

Chiropractic treatment can also be quite helpful and might be sufficient to manage the situation for some time.

INFECTIOUS PERITONITIS

See Feline Infectious Peritonitis.

INJURIES

See Handling Emergencies and Giving First Aid (page 460).

INTERVERTEBRAL DISC DISEASE

See Paralysis.

JAUNDICE

Jaundice, which can be caused by many factors, creates a visible yellowing of the tissues. We usually think of it as a liver disease, but it occurs for other reasons as well. If there is a rapid breakdown of red blood cells (due to, for instance, blood parasites, certain chemicals or drugs, various infections, or poisonous snakebites), the liver can't process all the released hemoglobin quickly enough. The result is a release of yellow pigment (which makes up part of hemoglobin), which backs up and stains the tissues yellow.

Your veterinarian will have to distinguish between jaundice caused by such factors and the type associated with liver disease. If the liver is ailing, the stool often looks pale in color. If the jaundice is from red blood cell breakdown, however, the stool is typically very dark from extra bile flow.

The type of jaundice caused by a sudden loss of intact red blood cells also leads to a form of anemia, even if no blood was visibly lost. To help the body form new red blood cells, follow the advice under Anemia. Apart from dealing with any of those underlying causes of red blood cell breakdown, you can treat this type of noninflammatory jaundice simply by exposing your animal to direct sunlight (or indirect if it's too hot) for several hours daily for a few days. Sunlight stimulates the elimination of the pigments responsible for the jaundice. In addition, it may help to use:

> **Homeopathic**—*Nux vomica 30c*: To enhance flow of liver bile and assist elimination of toxic material accumulated in the liver. This is especially useful if it seems likely that the problem was brought on by something toxic, like a chemical or venomous bite. Use Homeopathic Schedule 5.
>
> **Homeopathic**—*China officinalis 30c*: Most useful if the condition is brought on by extensive blood loss and the animal seems very weak. Use Homeopathic Schedule 5.

KENNEL COUGH

See Upper Respiratory Infections (Colds).

KIDNEY FAILURE

The kidneys have the function of filtering the blood and eliminating all the materials not needed or not healthy if they stay in the tissues. Considering what we have found about the accumulation of many chemicals in the food, including toxic metals like mercury, arsenic, lead, and cadmium, it is no surprise that deterioration of the kidneys is a common problem of old age for both dogs and cats. It is a leading cause of death in cats.

It starts in most cats when they are younger, with increased thirst and recurrent cystitis (bladder inflammation). After many years, usually past middle age, it becomes apparent something is wrong with the kidneys. In other words, cats that will have kidney failure will, when young, have bladder trouble first.

Often, cats with bladder trouble will be put on special diets with acid added (to prevent the cystitis symptoms by making the urine acidic), but while it helps, this simply covers up what is happening while the kidneys are deteriorating "behind the scenes."

Why cats have this problem so often is not really understood. Sometimes a bacterial infection is blamed, and many of the kidney failure cases that come to me are on antibiotic treatment. However, this condition is almost never due to a bacterial infection, so the antibiotics do not help and, if anything, make the cat sicker.

My clinical experience suggests to me, as mentioned at the outset, that toxicity is very important. As one example, consider that mercury has been building up in our environment for decades, is highest in ocean fish, and that many cats are fed foods containing these fish. This may be a factor. Mercury poisoning has a direct influence on the kidneys, and it doesn't make them happy.

I also have thought that vaccines play a role, as it has been found that vaccines will induce antibodies against one's own normal tissues. Considering that vaccine viruses are often grown on kidney cells and kidney cell material would also be in the vaccine, it seems possible that this could result in such abnormal immune function. This was confirmed in a study done at the veterinary school in Colorado.[10] Cats given vaccines grown on kidney cells (for panleukopenia, calicivirus, herpesvirus) developed antibodies against their own kidneys. This resulted in the kidneys becoming inflamed in the same way that the natural condition occurs (interstitial nephritis). All the more reason to be careful about overdoing vaccines (see Chapter 16).

The cleansing function of the kidneys is also related to that of the skin, which is another important eliminative organ. Skin irritations and eruptions often precede eventual kidney failure in old age. This process is accelerated if the skin discharge is repeatedly suppressed with corticosteroids.

SIGNS OF THE PROBLEM

It is very difficult even to be aware that this kidney condition is happening because of the tremendous capacity of the kidneys to compensate for loss of tissue. As long as one-third of the kidney tissue is functional, there are no obvious signs of sickness. Past this point, however, illness gradually develops. When only 15 to 20 percent of the kidney tissue is still functional, death comes from the buildup of toxins and dehydration.

Early Signs

The early signs of kidney failure typically are increased thirst, frequent urination with large quantities of pale urine, inability to hold urine all night, and occasional periods of low energy and lack of appetite.

How much thirst is too much thirst? For dogs, who have a thirst like humans do, use your common sense and notice any increases not attributable to hot weather or exercise.

For cats, drinking water every day (or even less often) is suspicious, even if it's a young cat of 2 or 3 years. Because they evolved in dry regions, healthy cats drink little or no water by nature. The only exception to this rule is if your cat is eating only dry food (which I don't recommend). Dry food is so low in water (about 10 percent compared to the 80 to 85 percent of a natural diet) that some cats are forced to drink even though it is not natural to them. If your cat is on a canned food or home-prepared diet (or you switch over to that) and is still drinking, however, you have a problem.

If you are observant, you can detect these signs of kidney failure early. That way you stand a much better chance of prolonging your animal's life with an optimal diet and other natural treatments than if you wait until an emergency. Certainly if you have a cat that has repeated bladder inflammations, this is a clue that health needs to be restored in this area.

Later Signs

As this condition develops, there will be nausea or vomiting that lasts for a few days at a time. Even later are changes in the mouth—foul breath, ulcers.

At this point the animal needs an emergency intravenous infusion of large quantities of fluids to save its life. Afterward, things return to a relative normal, but it's a fragile normality, for in many cases 60 to 70 percent of the kidney tissue has been destroyed and cannot be regained.

The kidneys can cope with this by moving everything along faster. The fluids are pushed through much more rapidly (up to 20 times faster), resulting in a loss of essential salts, water, and other nutrients. Think of it like this: If a major freeway were blocked and everyone had to drive on surface streets to get around it, one way to keep traffic moving would be for the police to stand at intersections waving everyone on at higher than normal speeds. Imagine them yelling "Let's go! Move it along. We've got to get the job done!" This is what the kidneys do to compensate.

This speedup gradually increases, and it gets to where too much fluid is lost and the body becomes dry, dehydrated. This adds to the problem because insufficient fluid interferes with circulation and digestion. So by this time, most animals have to be given fluids by injection, often daily, for the rest of their lives.

KIDNEY FAILURE AND UREMIA

If you are dealing with an animal that is at the stage of having uremia (backup of protein waste), seen in the advanced disease, then it is helpful to alter the diet. This is not necessary for the early stage, as it does not prevent further development of the problem. Rather, it is a way of *coping with the toxicity buildup*—making less of it to begin with.

The nutrition issue is that, compared to carbohydrates and fat, protein is not as "clean" a food. The digestion of protein discards the nitrogen extracted from it, which is carried in the blood to the kidneys to be eliminated. When the kidneys are no longer working at full capacity, this nitrogen builds up in the blood, causing symptoms—what is called *uremia*. The way to compensate is to feed less protein and more carbohydrates and fats. Ideal recipes will have enough protein, but the minimum that is needed, and shift the emphasis to the nutrients that don't have this waste product. Look at the dog and cat recipe charts in Chapter 6, Recipes for Today, for the code K in the second row. This will identify for you the recipes we think will be most beneficial for you to use for this problem.

As said above, this diet change is not needed except at the late stage of toxic buildup. Try the diet for about a month, monitoring the general condition, weight, and thirst. After this month get another blood test and see if the values have dropped. The important ones are BUN (blood urea nitrogen) and creatinine. If the diet is helping, the amounts of these two values in the blood will go down closer to the normal range.

Additional things you can do are to replace water-soluble vitamins that get flushed out of the body easily, especially vitamins B and C, and to supply plenty of vitamin A, which is good for the kidneys. This can be done with a pet vitamin, or you can use a human product, cutting down the amount to your animal's size (figure the average human is about 140 pounds).

Many cats with kidney disease will develop a state of *low potassium* levels in the body, which further complicates the situation and makes the kidney condition worse. If your cat does not respond adequately to the treatments suggested here (and below), consult your veterinarian about adding a potassium gluconate supplement to this diet. Potassium, if needed, makes a big difference in how these cats do. The usual maintenance dose for a cat is 80 to 160 milligrams of potassium a day, and it usually has to be continued indefinitely.

In the same way, the element phosphorus can become *too high* and add to the problem in its own way. Your veterinarian can determine from the blood test if this is an issue, and a substance that inhibits phosphorus from being absorbed from the digestive tract can be dispensed to you as well.

TREATMENT

You can see that the sooner we intervene in this process, the better. Obviously we want to lighten the load on the kidneys, so all the more reason to use the least contaminated food you can, and to minimize exposure to environmental toxins. You might want to again read Chapter 10, which goes into some detail about the things to be careful of in the average home.

Other Care

Vigorously brush the coat and skin regularly and give a weekly bath, especially with dogs, with a natural, mild, nondrying shampoo. Provide regular, mild outdoor exercise and exposure to fresh air and sun. Always allow easy access to a place for urination and defecation. Make lots of pure water available for drinking at all times and feed the daily rations as two meals instead of one (if that has been your practice).

Medical Treatment

Herbs and remedies that may strengthen your animal's kidney tissue are listed below. Pick one of them to try.

Herbal—*Alfalfa (Medicago sativa)*: Using the tincture, three times daily give one or two drops to cats or small dogs (it can be diluted), two to four drops to medium dogs, and four to six drops to large dogs. Continue until you see an improvement, then reduce to once a day or as needed. Alternatively, you may use alfalfa tablets, giving one to four twice a day (depending on the animal's size). Crush and mix with the food.

Herbal—*Marsh mallow (Althaea officinalis)*: Prepare an infusion by adding 2 tablespoons of the flowers or leaves to 1 cup of boiling water. Let steep 5 minutes. Or make a decoction (which is more potent) by simmering 1 teaspoon of the root in a cup of boiling water for 20 to 30 minutes. Twice a day, give ½ teaspoon to cats or small dogs, 1 teaspoon to medium dogs, and 1 tablespoon to large dogs. Try mixing it in the food. Continue for several weeks and then taper off to twice a week.

Homeopathic—*Nux vomica 30c*: This remedy is useful as an occasional treatment for uremia. Often, it will help with the symptoms of toxicity, especially nausea, vomiting, and feeling generally ill. Use Homeopathic Schedule 4.

Homeopathic—*Natrum muriaticum 6c*: This treatment will help with the body's use of water. It is indicated for the cat or dog that is very thirsty and prefers cool surfaces to lie on. Use Homeopathic Schedule 6(a).

Homeopathic—*Phosphorus 6c*: This is helpful to the cat or dog that has strong thirst for cold water and frequent vomiting after drinking or eating. Usually there is a decreased appetite, with weight loss. Use Homeopathic Schedule 6(a).

Homeopathic—*Mercurius vivus or Mercurius solubilis 6c*: The indicative condition is the development of ulcers in the mouth or on the tongue. Breath very foul, saliva increased, often sticky. These are symptoms of uremia and can be helped by using this remedy. To maintain improvement, the diet must be adjusted to reduce protein or it will recur. Use Homeopathic Schedule 4.

CRISIS THERAPY

A severe crisis in an animal with weak or failed kidneys is best handled by your veterinarian. Often the technique of intravenous fluid administration is critical to survival because anything given by mouth is immediately vomited. Your veterinarian may show you how to give daily fluid injections under the skin, which can help many cats to survive for additional months or years—often much longer than dogs survive with similar treatment.

An additional supportive treatment is that adapted from herbalist Juliette de Bairacli Levy, who advises that you withhold all solid food until the crisis passes. Instead, give:

Cool parsley tea: Steep a tablespoon of fresh parsley in a cup of hot water for 20 minutes. Give 1 teaspoon to 2 tablespoons, three times a day.

Barley water: To make this, pour 3 cups of boiling water over a cup of whole barley. Cover and let steep overnight. In the morning, strain and squeeze out the liquid through muslin or cloth. Add 2 teaspoons each of honey and pure lemon juice. Feed your animal ¼ to 2 cups of this liquid twice a day. (Make a bigger batch if necessary.)

Parsnip balls: Combine raw, grated parsnips (which help to detoxify the kidneys) with thick honey (an energy source). Roll into balls and give as desired. This combination is more likely to be accepted by dogs than cats—who are notoriously difficult to give anything unusual to by mouth.

Enemas: Make pure water available at all times. If your pet has trouble keeping fluids down, however, give one to three enemas per day until vomiting stops. For every 20 pounds of weight, make a solution combining ½ teaspoon sea salt, ½ teaspoon potassium chloride (a salt substitute available in many groceries), 1 teaspoon lemon juice, and 500 milligrams vitamin C, well dissolved in a pint of lukewarm water. (See instructions for administration in Chapter 18.) When an animal is dehydrated, it will *retain* the enema solution rather than discharging it, and this will help replenish the blood.

Remember, the single most important thing is to give large volumes of fluids to rehydrate the tissues and to flush the kidneys. Without adequate fluid, treatment will not be successful. If vomiting is severe and continuous, use the suggestions under Vomiting in this section. Particularly, try the homeopathic remedy *Ipecac*, as described there.

LIVER PROBLEMS

The liver is a most important organ of the body. It is involved in innumerable processes, including the manufacture of blood proteins, fats, and the proteins responsible for blood clotting; storage of energy (as glycogen, which is animal starch) for production of blood sugar as needed by the body; storage of the fat-soluble vitamins and iron; the detoxification of drugs, chemicals, and other unusable substances; the inactivation of hormones no longer needed; and the secretion of bile and other factors necessary for proper digestion. As if these tasks were not enough to keep it busy, the liver also must filter blood coming from the digestive tract to keep potentially harmful bacteria from reaching other parts of the body. It is the organ that prepares toxic material and waste products for subsequent elimination by the kidneys (see also Chapter 18, How to Care for a Sick Animal).

Therefore, as you can imagine, inflammation of the liver (hepatitis) and other disturbances of this vital organ are very serious conditions. Symptoms of liver trouble include nausea, vomiting, loss of appetite, jaundice (yellowing of the tissues, best observed in the whites of the eyes or inside the ears in animals), perhaps the passing of light-colored or "fatty-looking" bowel movements (from insufficient bile and poor digestion), and the swelling of the abdomen from fluid accumulation.

Liver malfunction is caused by many conditions. Viral infections or the swallowing of poisonous substances are factors, but in most cases, it's hard to tell just what initiated the problem.

TREATMENT

Because the liver is so central to the whole process of breaking down and using food, treatment includes minimizing the work it must do either by fasting for a while or feeding small, frequent, easily digested meals. In the early, acute stage of liver inflammation, fasting is best, especially if a fever is present. Follow the directions for fasting given in Chapter 18. Keep your dog or cat on a liquid diet for a few days until his or her temperature returns to normal or there is some improvement. During this period, give the following treatments.

Vitamin C: 500 to 2,000 milligrams four times a day, depending on size of the animal. This is most easily given as sodium ascorbate powder dissolved in a small amount of water (¼ teaspoon is about 1,000 milligrams).

One of the following remedies can also be helpful.

Homeopathic—*Belladonna 30c*: This is most useful for the stage of fever, restless agitation, hot head, and dilated pupils, and is often the first remedy to use. Use Homeopathic Schedule 2.

Homeopathic—*Nux vomica 6c*: Use Homeopathic Schedule 6(a). If this does not help within a few days, try this next remedy.

Homeopathic—*Phosphorus 6c*: These animals are usually thirsty, vomit easily, and have diarrhea or very narrow, hard stools. Use Homeopathic Schedule 6(a).

As the animal improves and the symptoms subside, ease into the recommended recipes but minimize fat, perhaps reducing the amount of fat temporarily. The liver may not be able to produce enough bile to digest the fat at this point. Grains are usually tolerated well, being primarily carbohydrates. After a month or two of recovery, you can gradually and carefully move to using the standard recipes.

During this time of healing, emphasize fresh and whole foods as much as possible. Some foods, of course, must be well cooked for digestion (like grains and beans). Combine the foods only after the cooked ingredients have cooled. This precaution will provide optimal amounts of unaltered nutrients needed for the quickest possible recovery. If these foods are accepted, try including raw grated beets (about 1 to 3 tablespoons) every day as a liver stimulant. One to 2 tablespoons of fresh minced parsley is also useful.

During recovery, also continue the vitamin C, though you can decrease the dose as you go along. If, after some improvement, there is a relapse, go back to using the last remedy that was most beneficial. The vitamin C can be discontinued after all symptoms are gone.

LYME DISEASE

This disease was first recognized (in people) in Europe in the early 1900s and has since been reported throughout Europe, Australia, Russia, China, Japan, and Africa. It has been called Lyme disease in this country since 1975, when it was first found to cause arthritis in children in Old Lyme, Connecticut. Considerable research revealed that the condition was caused by a spirochete (a microbe related to syphilis, though not spread by sexual contact) and transmitted by tick bites. In people, Lyme disease causes a skin rash, tiredness, fever and chills, headache, backache, arthritis, and other symptoms.

The situation is very different for animals, however. What I am going to say here you won't likely hear anywhere else. The short explanation is that this is not really a defined disease in dogs, like other infectious diseases (e.g., distemper or parvo). The long explanation will take some patience on your part. Let's start with some background.

How do we know that a germ causes a disease? Let's say that people start becoming sick with something new and we don't know what it is. If we check carefully and find some sort of bug in the blood—maybe that is what is causing it. So how do we know if that is right? After all, there are hundreds of species of bacteria, viruses, and fungi that normally live in and on our bodies and don't cause any disease at all. In terms of numbers, there are more microorganisms in the healthy, normal body than there are cells.

The obvious test is that we give the "new" bug to someone and see if they get sick—not only sick but with the same symptoms as seen before. (Well, if a human disease, we give it to a poor animal.) Logical, right? This has always been the method of determining if a microorganism is the cause of a disease. You will have to take my word for it that medical history is littered with supposed causes of disease that turned out to be quite harmless.

So, here is the story with Lyme disease in dogs. Though scientists have put the organism into dogs many, many times, they cannot reproduce the disease—they cannot cause Lyme disease by injecting the bug into dogs. Well, one way they can make dogs sick with some mild symptoms is to give them a cortisone-like drug first (which suppresses the immune system). The general conclusion is that dogs are indeed exposed via ticks, *but they are naturally resistant to it* and only those very few animals that have disturbed immune systems may show some mild symptoms. It seems that a fraction of dogs, those that already have some health issues, will have an excessive reaction, more like an allergy.

Okay, I know this is not what your veterinarian told you and that there are all these dire warnings about Lyme disease and the need for antibiotics and how you should use the vaccine, right? So how do we reconcile this? I have treated many dogs over the years that have been diagnosed as having this disease, and my experience also is that it is an insignificant disease. "Wait," you say, "dogs actually do get symptoms and veterinarians say this is what it is. How can this be?"

What veterinarians are calling Lyme disease in dogs is signs of arthritis, painful joints, and lameness (usually). Sometimes there is a fever, but just as often there is not. Because dogs in some parts of the country are frequently bitten by ticks that can leave red areas on the skin, the thinking goes like this: This dog is lame, there is evidence of a tick bite, so it must be Lyme disease. Usually antibiotics are prescribed, and most dogs get better. What is not understood is that these dogs will get better anyway. Studies of dogs with these symptoms indicate that 85 percent of them recover without any antibiotic treatment at all. The other 15 percent will continue to have symptoms whether or not antibiotics are used.

How often will tick-exposed dogs have any signs of illness? According to Dr. Meryl Littman of the University of Pennsylvania, even in areas of the country where the disease is most common and 90 percent of the dogs are exposed to the organism, only 4 percent show symptoms of lameness, decreased appetite, or fever. They appear to have a natural immunity. "Well," you say "isn't this 4 percent evidence of the disease?" One can make that argument, but the research suggests that the few that show some symptoms have weakened immune systems for some other reason. This is not an infectious disease in the usual sense.

So, what are we to make of all this? I think some insight is given by the observation of Dr. Shelly Epstein of Wilmington, Delaware. Since she greatly decreased the use of vaccines in her practice (to three or four total for an animal, using single, not combined, vaccines that are spaced out), her practice sees only one or two dogs a year with Lyme disease–like symptoms. This is in contrast to her prior experience and that of the other practitioners in her area (who give 30 to 40 vaccinations to a dog, combination vaccines), who see a case of Lyme disease every week. It is likely that the overuse of vaccines is causing a disturbed immune reaction to the Lyme organism in animals that otherwise would have been resistant.

If you think your dog (or cat, though this is rare) is showing these symptoms, it can be treated with homeopathy very easily. Here is what you can do.

TREATMENT

Homeopathic—*Aconitum napellus 30c*: This remedy is often suitable for the very earliest stage of illness with high fever, especially if it is accompanied by a restless anxiety. Use Homeopathic Schedule 1. This is the first treatment, in an early case. The remedies that follow are suitable for any remaining symptoms not cleared by this treatment.

Homeopathic—*Bryonia alba 30c*: Often dogs will lie very quietly, crying out at the slightest motion. Give this medicine to the dog that is reluctant to move because of the pain. Use Homeopathic Schedule 1.

Homeopathic—*Rhus toxicodendron 30c*: This is indicated for the dog that is stiff and sore, especially on first moving after lying for a while. As she moves around, however, the joints seem to limber up and the stiffness is not so noticeable. Use Homeopathic Schedule 1.

Homeopathic—*Pulsatilla 30c*: Give this medicine to the dog that becomes submissive or very clingy when ill and does not want to drink water. Use Homeopathic Schedule 1.

Homeopathic—*Mercurius vivus or Mercurius solubilis 30c* is helpful to the sick dog that has, along with the other symptoms, red and inflamed gums, bad breath, and a tendency to drool or salivate. Use Homeopathic Schedule 1.

Remember that any time there is an acute illness with fever, it is also helpful to fast your dog for several days (see Chapter 18).

If the above treatments are not effective, it is very likely that what you are dealing with requires the skill of a homeopathically trained veterinarian.

VACCINATION

There are several vaccines on the market, and they are aggressively pushed by many veterinarians. Dr. Littman says that the susceptible dogs (the 4 percent that may show some symptoms) may not be protected by the vaccines that are available. In fact, there is concern that the vaccines may actually make the susceptible dog have a more severe disease if it is ever infected by a tick. My advice? Save your money.

MANGE

See Skin Parasites.

MITES

See Ear Problems and Skin Parasites.

NEUTERING

See Spaying and Neutering.

NOSE PROBLEMS

See Foxtails and Upper Respiratory Infections.

OBESITY

See Weight Problems.

PANCREATITIS

This condition, usually seen in overweight, middle-aged dogs, often first appears as a sudden, severe illness. Symptoms can include a complete loss of appetite, severe and frequent vomiting, diarrhea that may contain blood, reluctance to walk, weakness, and abdominal pain (crying and restlessness). The severity of the attack can vary from a mild, almost unnoticeable condition to a severe shocklike collapse that can end in death.

The problem centers in the digestive tract, with a focus in the pancreas. The underlying cause is not known, but I think it will soon be apparent that pancreatitis is another of the immune diseases (like hyperthyroidism in cats). As an immediate trigger, attacks can come on after overindulgence in rich or fatty foods, especially after a raid on a garbage can or compost pile. Frequent attacks of pancreatitis can finally result in a lack of insulin, leading to diabetes (see Diabetes).

PREVENTION

Prevention consists partly of a properly balanced natural diet, coupled with regular and adequate exercise. Exercise is important because it improves digestion and peristaltic movements of the intestinal tract, thus regularizing the bowels and keeping this part of the body preventively more healthy. It also keeps weight under control.

Do not overfeed your dog, because obesity is a predisposing factor to pancreatitis (no one knows why). Many people end up with fat dogs because they enjoy watching the animal eat heartily. For more information, see Weight Problems.

Realize that this condition can also be chronic in nature, persisting in a low-grade form for months or years unless corrected. If you have a dog with a tendency toward pancreatitis, be especially careful about setting off an attack through a change of diet. I also advise using vaccines minimally in these animals because the immune system becomes much more active after vaccination, possibly precipitating an immune-mediated crisis.

TREATMENT

Treatment often requires hospitalization, with fluid replacement therapy in the case of extreme vomiting and diarrhea. If the condition is mild but recurrent, the following measures should help to restore a balance of health.

Feed the basic natural diet, except minimize vegetable oils, butter, as well as other fatty foods that may irritate the pancreas. Leafy green vegetables are especially helpful as they are high in vitamin A. Use vitamin E to help prevent pancreatic scarring (50 to 200 IU, depending on size of animal). For vegetables, emphasize corn (preferably raw, and of course non-GMO, and also ground or crushed kernels) and raw grated cabbage, but include a variety of others as well. Avoid fruits.

Look at the dog recipe chart in Chapter 6, Recipes for Today, for the code A in the second row. This will identify for you the recipes most useful to use for this condition.

Feed small, frequent meals instead of one large one. Offer all food at room temperature for best digestive action. Sometimes adding pancreatic enzymes to each meal will help as well, assisting the digestive process. They can be obtained in health food stores. Use the human products, giving one-half capsule to small dogs, up to two capsules for the larger dogs.

Use vitamin C and bioflavonoids regularly. Depending on the dog's size, give 250 to 1,000 milligrams of vitamin C three times a day, if possible. Sodium ascorbate powder may be better tolerated than ascorbic acid. (A teaspoon of sodium ascorbate powder has about 4,000 milligrams of C.) Give 25 to 50 milligrams of bioflavonoids (vitamin P) to enhance the action of the ascorbate.

Eliminate any food or supplement that seems to upset the digestive tract or aggravate the symptoms. Find a substitute form for any supplement you need to discontinue, for instance, a B complex instead of nutritional yeast.

In addition to these nutritional steps, try one of the following as a supportive treatment. To start treatment, work with one of these two remedies.

Homeopathic—*Nux vomica 30c*: Indicated for the dog that becomes very irritable, withdraws to another room (away from company), and is chilly. Use Homeopathic Schedule 2.

Homeopathic—*Belladonna 30c*: Use when the problem has come on very suddenly, there is considerable fever, the body feels hot to the touch, and the dog is very sen-

sitive to sound and touch, with pupils dilated and evident excitability and agitation. Use Homeopathic Schedule 2.

If neither of these remedies proves satisfactory, then work with these that follow.

Homeopathic—*Iris versicolor 6c*: This remedy is particularly suited to the pancreas. It is very useful when the dog vomits repeatedly, with much drooling of saliva. Use Homeopathic Schedule 1.

Homeopathic—*Spongia tosta 6c*: Indicated if the pancreatitis is associated with coughing or breathing difficulties. Use Homeopathic Schedule 1.

Homeopathic—*Pulsatilla 30c*: Very helpful if the dog shows no sign of thirst, seeks cool surfaces to lie on, and becomes clingy (wanting to be close all the time) and whiny. Use Homeopathic Schedule 2.

Herbal—*Yarrow (Achillea millefolium)*: Yarrow strengthens the pancreas and helps to control internal hemorrhages. It is indicated if there is dark, chocolate-colored, or black diarrhea (perhaps containing blood) that is foul smelling. Use Herbal Schedule 1.

Realize that after an attack is over, there is still susceptibility to further episodes. Be especially careful in this regard.

- Keep the diet simple and low in fat.
- Don't allow indulgences in junk food.
- Avoid vaccinations as much as possible.
- Keep the weight within normal limits.

PARALYSIS

Causes of paralysis can range from accidents that damage the spine, to blood clots that form in brain arteries, to intervertebral disc disease ("slipped disc"), as well as others. Here we will consider the two most common causes, which are intervertebral disc disease and spondylitis (a buildup of calcium on the spine from arthritis). To some extent we can regard these two conditions similarly because both are degenerative processes involving the spine.

In intervertebral disc disease, the fibrous capsule that holds the soft, gelatinous material between the vertebrae in place breaks down, and the gel leaks out. The apparent cause is a breakdown of the ligaments that keep this material in place, and this puts pressure on the spinal cord. The condition is worst in breeds that have long backs in relation to their legs, such as dachshunds.

Spondylitis is more noticeable in large dogs like German shepherds. It involves a long-term inflammation of the vertebrae, which the body attempts to alleviate by immobilizing spinal movements with calcium deposits (like a form of arthritis). Eventually, these deposits encroach on the nerves that branch out from the spinal cord, interfering with their functions. Symptoms are not obvious to the untrained eye. Be on the lookout for some rigidity of the back and some difficulty or pain on getting up. As it advances, a wasting away of the back and rear legs becomes evident, as well as difficulty using them on steps or slippery floors. Usually a diagnosis is made only after an x-ray is taken. Spondylitis is often associated with hip dysplasia, so also read about that topic.

PREVENTION

My opinion is that both intervertebral disc disease and spondylitis are expressions of the same problem—a deterioration of the spine brought on after years of poor nutrition, inadequate exercise, and stress. They are better prevented than treated. Your best insurance is to follow the natural diet recommendations we have advised. Also, avoid selecting a breed that is prone to intervertebral disc disease (long-backed dogs) and breeds that are prone to hip dysplasia (such as German shepherds).

TREATMENT

Intervertebral disc problems, once they have developed, may be alleviated by this program.

Good nutrition is especially helpful. Avoid commercial foods and treats, using only the natural diet and supplements advised in this book. If available to you, add ¼ to 1 teaspoon lecithin granules to the daily ration. In addition, give 250 to 500 milligrams of vitamin C twice a day to strengthen the connective tissue involved and to counteract stress.

For specific treatment, use:

Homeopathic—*Nux vomica 30c*: This is most effective for animals with recent pain in the back, muscle tightness or spasms along the lower back, and weakness or paralysis of the rear legs. Use Homeopathic Schedule 2.

This remedy is appropriate for the more acute phase of the problem, but other medicines are needed for the underlying arthritis. This necessitates what is called constitutional treatment in homeopathy and is based on understanding the pattern of weakness over the lifetime of your animal. Work with a homeopathic veterinarian for this.

A paralyzed animal will benefit from massage of the back and legs and passive movement of the limbs to keep the muscles from shrinking away. If there is slight voluntary movement of the legs, exercise the animal by helping it to "swim" in a bathtub or pool. Support most of its weight with a towel or harness. Acupuncture and chiropractic have also been helpful for intervertebral disc problems.

Spondylitis, on the other hand, can be more difficult to treat once it has developed. The chance of improvement is much less for a dog already paralyzed than for one that is only weakened. A short fast (see Chapter 18) may be appropriate in an early case, followed by the basic natural diet given in this book. The further instructions given under Arthritis will be very helpful.

Besides exercise and massage, use this remedy.

Homeopathic—*Belladonna 30c*: Use Homeopathic Schedule 2 and note how much improvement follows. If there is a clear benefit from its use, wait 1 week and give one dose of *Calcarea carbonica 30c* remedy.

Homeopathic—*Phosphorus 30c*: If the above suggestions have not helped, give this remedy a try. It often is helpful in this condition, but be patient as you may not be able to determine that until 3 or 4 weeks have gone by. Use Homeopathic Schedule 4.

For other treatment choices or to continue beyond this point, consult a homeopathic veterinarian for constitutional treatment.

POISONING

See Handling Emergencies and Giving First Aid (page 460).

PREGNANCY, BIRTH, AND CARE OF NEWBORNS

Also see Reproductive Organ Problems.

The key to a successful and easy pregnancy and delivery is good nutrition. During gestation (63 to 65 days for cats, 58 to 63 days for dogs), tremendous demands are made on the mother's tissues to supply all the nutrients needed to build several new bodies. The general rule is that kittens or puppies come first. That is, they get whatever is available nutritionally, and the mother gets what's left. If she doesn't consume enough food to supply complete nutrition, her body provides whatever is lacking.

A female that is not adequately fed, or that is bred again and again, accumulates a nutritional deficiency that becomes greater with each pregnancy. Eventually, the mother will become diseased or the young will be weak and susceptible to disease—perhaps during their entire lives. Therefore, if possible, allow a period of time on the nutritional program we give you in this book to build her up before the pregnancy starts. A period of 3 months would be good.

Let's look at the two most common problems—eclampsia and dystocia (difficult delivery).

ECLAMPSIA

Eclampsia is a severe disturbance that appears most often at the end of a pregnancy, right after birth, or during nursing. That's because it stems from calcium depletion. As new skeletons are formed or milk is produced, the calcium demand from the mother's body is great. Symptoms include loss of appetite, a high fever (sometimes dangerously so), rapid panting, and convulsions. During convulsions the muscles become rigid, and the animal falls over with its head back. More typically, you may see a series of rapid contractions and relaxations of the muscles that looks like uncontrollable shaking.

Strenuous treatment is necessary, including intravenous injections of calcium by your veterinarian and cool baths (to bring down the temperature if dangerously high). Such treatment is usually successful, but the condition can recur if the young continue to nurse.

The treatment most likely to help during the crisis is:

Homeopathic—*Belladonna 30c*: Give one pellet every 15 minutes until the symptoms are alleviated. Then use Schedule 1 until all is well. This treatment can be used whenever symptoms reappear.

Once your dog (this is usually seen in dogs rather than cats) has recovered, add calcium carbonate to the diet to make sure the amount is adequate. As an example, a 30-pound dog would use about ⅔ teaspoon of calcium carbonate per day (which equals about 3,500 milligrams of calcium) if on a high-meat diet. If the dog has been on a low-meat diet or plant-based diet, then the need for calcium is reduced, so you could reduce this probably to a rounded ¼ teaspoon as an additional supplement.

DYSTOCIA (DIFFICULT DELIVERY)

Cats and dogs with normal anatomy rarely have problems giving birth, particularly if they are adequately fed during pregnancy. Understandably, nutrition is important during this time, with all the young ones growing new bodies.

The most severe birthing problems occur

in dogs with an abnormal anatomy, usually from breeding trends in which the pelvis becomes too small for the size of the puppies. Other than the use of cesarean sections, little can be done about this problem except the obvious: Avoid breeding such animals and don't select them as pets (which creates a market for them).

Let's first review how delivery usually goes when all is normal. Two or 3 days before giving birth, the mother may lose her appetite and show nesting behavior (carrying toys or other things to a particular area, tearing up paper to make a nest). There will be swelling of the vulva and a slight discharge. Twenty-four to 48 hours before birth, there will be a sudden drop in body temperature to below normal (usually below 101°F or 38.3°C), but this varies according to the individual and is best determined by checking the temperature twice a day for several days before.

The next thing is for labor to begin.

Stage One is characterized by restlessness, panting, and shivering (perhaps also vomiting food once). This lasts 6 to 12 hours (but can be longer with the first birth).

Stage Two is visible contractions, with delivery of the puppy. Some mothers will start this stage by wanting to go outside to urinate. They will lie on the side as contractions become stronger, straining and licking the genitals. Some dogs will groan or even scream. Between contractions there is rapid panting. This stage lasts from 15 minutes to an hour.

Stage Three is the passing of the afterbirth(s), usually promptly eaten. It is important that all the afterbirths be passed, so each (one to a puppy) must be accounted for.

Problems can begin to occur at Stage Two, when contractions are not producing results. You will know that this is happening because straining goes on too long. If the mother labors more than 4 or 5 hours with the first puppy or 3 hours with subsequent puppies, then it has indeed been too long. In this case, use:

Homeopathic—*Pulsatilla 30c*: Give one pellet and repeat in 30 minutes. As soon as labor proceeds, stop using the remedy, even if you've only given one or two doses. Remember that the mother will often naturally rest between deliveries, even napping for an hour or two. So don't rush things too much. If there is no delivery after two doses (1 hour), then the remedy will not help. In which case, switch to:

Homeopathic—*Caulophyllum 30c*: Use the same schedule as given above. One of these remedies is usually effective.

If a puppy or kitten is partway out and seems stuck (is not immediately slipping out), pulling on it very gently may help. Hold the body, not the legs or head; note that any pressure more vigorous than an extremely gentle touch can cause damage to either the mother or the unborn. Get professional help if the baby has been trapped in the birth canal for more than a half hour (it will be dead by then). A cesarean section will probably be needed. This is a good time for your dog to be spayed, which will prevent this from happening again. Check with your veterinarian about this option.

If all goes well at home and the delivery is complete, use:

Homeopathic—*Arnica montana 30c*: This is most helpful to strengthen the mother and prevent infection. Use Homeopathic Schedule 2.

If an afterbirth remains inside, serious problems can result. If one is retained and there is fever or infection, use the following treatment along with what your veterinarian prescribes.

Homeopathic—*Secale cornutum 30c*: This remedy will often prevent or successfully treat infection following a retained afterbirth and result in the afterbirth being discharged. Use Homeopathic Schedule 2.

CARE OF THE NEWBORN

Fortunately for you, the mother will generally do everything needed to care for the newborn, and it's best not to interfere unless there's a problem. Right after birth she will clean the little ones, and, as long as necessary, she will also lick up all the urine and feces voided by her growing young. This is nature's way of keeping a clean nest. It's convenient for you, but if the infants should develop diarrhea, you may miss the evidence.

Diarrhea is one of the more common problems at this stage of life, and it's usually caused by consuming too much milk (sometimes a problem with hand-raised puppies or kittens), infection in the mother's uterus or mammary glands (check if her temperature is above 102°F, 38.9°C), or giving antibiotics to the mother (they can get into the milk).

A puppy or kitten with diarrhea will get cold and dehydrated (the skin will be wrinkled and look too big for the body). It may crawl away from the nest and usually cries, even when returned to the mother.

If the problem is with the mother's milk, you'll need to feed the babies by hand with a pet nurser bottle sold at pet stores. Use the nursing formulas in Chapter 8 or a commercial kitten or puppy formula. Dilute the formula half and half with pure water until the diarrhea is under control. The problem should correct itself after a few feedings. If not, try one of these two methods.

Herbal—Use a mixture consisting of half formula (regular strength) and half warm *Chamomile tea* (1 teaspoon herb to a cup of boiling water). Feed on a regular schedule until the problem is controlled, usually by two or three feedings.

Homeopathic—Use the half-formula/half-water mixture, but add to it a crushed pellet of the homeopathic preparation *Podophyllum 6c*. Mix well. One such therapeutic feeding should be enough, but repeat this formula every 4 hours if necessary.

Examine the mother's breasts to see if there are hard lumps, hot areas, or painful places (on pressure). If so, there may be an infection (mastitis) that will need treatment before the milk is safe for the puppies (see Reproductive Organ Problems).

After the diarrhea is under control and if there is no problem with the mother, you can return the puppy or kitten to the nest, but be watchful in case the diarrhea returns.

If, as sometimes happens, the mother does not care for the young—letting them cry and avoiding contact and not nursing—you have a potentially serious problem, as the young ones cannot go long without eating. It is possible that there is something physically wrong with the mother, like an infection or a retained puppy or kitten, so you will need to have your veterinarian check out this possibility. If the problem is emotional, however, then here is a treatment that is quite helpful.

Homeopathic—*Sepia 30c*: If the mother does not accept the young within a few hours of using this remedy, then the puppies or kittens will have to be raised with a bottle. See Chapter 8 for guidance on this. Use Homeopathic Schedule 2.

RABIES

Okay, you knew we were going to get to the big guy, didn't you? This is a scary disease both because of its violent and aggressive symptoms and because you expect every-one who gets it to die. Rabies is, indeed, a serious disease that affects many different types of animals, as well as human beings. These symptoms often include very aggressive behavior and biting, which is how the disease gets spread (via saliva). Yet, surprisingly, many people or pets bitten by a rabid animal do not develop the disease, even if untreated. Some years ago I was surprised to find that there is a form of rabies in Africa, in dogs, that does not show symptoms and from which they can recover on their own. However, the form we are more familiar with in much of the world is one that is expected to end in death, with no effective treatment. But some time ago, I heard of the amazing case of a young girl with rabies who survived after being given an anesthetic that saved her brain until her immune system could catch up. I have also heard or read of occasional reports of recovery by a variety of alternative methods, including homeopathy—fortunately, I have never treated rabies myself.

One of the most exciting and promising new treatments is the use of vitamin C. It sounds unbelievable, but as far back as 36 years ago, research studies were finding that vitamin C injections into guinea pigs infected with rabies decreased the death rate by 50 percent.[11] Considering how few treatments are available for rabies, this is a dramatic finding. One can only hope that such research continues.

Most of the danger to humans is not actually from dogs and cats, but from wild animals such as skunks and raccoons that are captured for sale and/or adopted as pets. Unfortunately, rabies vaccines developed for dogs and cats may not be completely safe or effective in these species. (For example, it is not recommended that wolf hybrids be vaccinated with rabies vaccine because of the risk of infection from the vaccine.) Since the chance of getting rabies from wild animals is so high—in addition to the ethical and ecological considerations of wild-animal adoption—it is not wise to keep them as pets.

RABIES VACCINE

Because of rabies' well-known fatality rate, local governments have adopted precautions, including a legal requirement for a periodic rabies vaccination for dogs (cats are still optional in some states, but not all). The way most of us have a relationship with this problem is from use of the vaccine.

DOGS

Many times I have seen behavior changes in dogs after the vaccine is given. The natural disease of rabies has a focus on affecting the brain, and the vaccine seems to do the same thing. It does not *cause* the disease of rabies, but seems to push the dog toward being suspicious, jumpy, tending to bite, aggressive. Sometimes the dog becomes almost impossible to keep in a yard, as it will spend all of its time digging out or finding a way to escape and travel long distances. One of the most useful treatments, if these are the changes seen, is this remedy.

Homeopathic—*Lachesis 30c*: Use Homeopathic Schedule 4. Allow a month or so to evaluate. If no improvement with behavior, there are some other remedies that may be applicable and you will need to work with the homeopathic veterinarian to determine them.

CATS

Cats are not vaccinated for rabies quite as much as dogs. They are susceptible, so it is a concern. In my practice, I did not seem to experience many cats having behavioral changes after this vaccine, though physical conditions would come up at times. A remedy that can be quite helpful is the one called Sulphur.

Homeopathic—*Sulphur 30c*: Use Homeopathic Schedule 4. Allow a month or so to evaluate. If no improvement, there are some other remedies that may be applicable and you will need to work with the homeopathic veterinarian to determine them.

RADIATION TOXICITY

The most common sources of radiation exposure for the average animal are diagnostic x-rays, especially CT scans, and radiation therapy (I do not recommend the latter). Other possibilities are less obvious—such as leakage from a nuclear power plant or storage area. Sometimes it is the water. Strange to say, there are some parts of the country where drinking water is contaminated with radiation leaking out of storage containers. (Hanford Nuclear Site in Washington, near where I used to live, has had several reported leaks over the years, and since it is next to the Columbia River, these leaks end up in the drinking water for Portland, Oregon.)

Unfortunately, the more recent nuclear reactor meltdowns in Japan have greatly increased exposure all over the world. Huge quantities of radioactive water got into the oceans. As of June 2015, the radiation in the Pacific Ocean reached the US West Coast; any seafood eaten from the Pacific Ocean is loaded with cesium-137 and strontium-90, both radioactive. This radiation in the fish is so terrible that wild-caught Alaskan salmon, Pacific herring, and Canadian white fish are being found bloody, with cancerous tumors throughout their bodies. What this means, in practical terms, is that you should not feed your cat or dog any food that has fish in it, and it will have to be this way for many decades, if not centuries, to come.

TREATMENT

If your animal has been exposed in some way, there are things you can do to assist repair of damage as much as is possible.

Nutrition is the main aid. Emphasize rolled oats as your choice of grains for several weeks. It helps counteract nausea and other side effects. Be sure to include the supplements of nutritional yeast and cold-pressed unsaturated organic vegetable oil (for vitamin F). In addition, give rutin (bioflavonoids), which has reduced the death rate in irradiated animals by 800 percent; vitamin C, which works with rutin to strengthen the circulatory system and counteract stress; and pantothenic acid, which helps to prevent radiation injuries and has increased the survival rate in irradiated animals by 200 percent. Depending on size, give daily: 100 to 400 milligrams rutin, 250 to 2,000 milligrams vitamin C, and 5 to 20 milligrams pantothenic acid.

There are a number of homeopathic remedies that have been used in people to counteract (at least to some degree) the effects of radiation. Here are a couple that are useful.

Homeopathic—*Radium bromatum 30c*: This is made from naturally occurring radioactive radium but as a remedy it has *no radiation* coming from it as it is so very much diluted. Helps in a general way for the effects of exposure. The main symptoms it addresses are increases in the white blood cells (as happens in leukemia) and overall weakness. A behavior change can be the desire to be with people all the time. Use Homeopathic Schedule 5.

Homeopathic—*Phosphorus 30c*: Helpful if a chief effect is excessive bleeding from anywhere in the body. Use Homeopathic Schedule 5.

To go beyond these suggestions, you really need to work closely with a homeopathic veterinarian who can be specific with remedy application as often a series is needed as changes come up. Not all effects from radiation are seen right away, so one has to think of monitoring and treating over a period of months.

REPRODUCTIVE ORGAN PROBLEMS

The two most common reproductive problems affect female animals—pyometra and metritis. In both cases the uterus (womb) is the seat of the disorder, and prompt treatment is needed before the condition progresses too far. We'll look at each of these, and then at mastitis (mammary gland infection).

PYOMETRA

Coming on slowly over weeks or months, pyometra first appears as irregular heat periods and a discharge of reddish mucus from the vagina between heats. If unrecognized and untreated, it progresses to the point of severe depression, loss of appetite, vomiting, diarrhea, discolored vaginal discharge (not always present), excessive water consumption, and excessive urination. The large water intake mimics kidney failure, but the other symptoms help you tell the difference, particularly if there is a vaginal discharge and the animal is an unspayed dog or cat several years old that had many heats without being bred. A probable secondary cause is a high-hormone diet (from glandular meats or meat containing hormones used to fatten cattle). Concentrated in meat meal and other commercial pet food, hormones may predispose the uterus to malfunction.

TREATMENT

Dogs (and sometimes cats, but rarely) with pyometra can suddenly develop a crisis that may require surgical removal of the uterus, which often has become quite large and distended with fluid. The process is much more serious and difficult yet basically the same as the spay operation.

Those animals not so severely affected may be helped by:

Homeopathic—*Pulsatilla 30*: This remedy is best for animals that are not very thirsty (which is unusual) and want to be comforted (petted or held). If there is a vaginal discharge, it is usually thick and yellowish or greenish. This remedy has resolved the problem in the majority of dogs I have treated. Use Homeopathic Schedule 2.

Homeopathic—*Sepia 30c*: If there has been no improvement within 5 days of completing the Pulsatilla treatment above, then use this remedy. It is often sufficient. Use Homeopathic Schedule 2.

METRITIS

Right after giving birth and occasionally right after breeding, the uterus is susceptible to bacterial infection. Should infection occur, symptoms can be severe. They include fever, depression, not caring for the young, and a foul-smelling vaginal discharge.

Normal vaginal discharge following an uncomplicated delivery is dark green to brown and odorless. If all the young and all the afterbirths have come out properly, within 12 hours it becomes more like clear mucus (though possibly tinged with blood). But if a dark green to reddish brown, thick, and unusually foul-smelling discharge continues for 12 to 24 hours after the delivery, the uterus is probably infected.

TREATMENT

Once metritis has developed, it can become severe, so you should seek professional help. However, these remedies may also help.

Homeopathic—*Aconitum napellus 30c*: This remedy is indicated for the animal that has a fever and is acting very frightened or anxious. It will startle easily and be very agitated. Use Homeopathic Schedule 2.

Homeopathic—*Belladonna 30c*: This remedy is an alternative to Aconitum and is needed by the animal that has a fever and feels hot (especially the head) and has dilated pupils. Sometimes there is also an excitability similar to delirium, with a tendency to bite or act aggressively. Use Homeopathic Schedule 2.

See the section on Pregnancy, Birth, and Care of Newborns for information on infection from retained afterbirths.

MASTITIS

The mammary glands are most susceptible to infection when they are actively secreting milk. An infected breast will be hard, sensitive, painful, and discolored (reddish purple). There may be abscesses and drainage as well. Your veterinarian will usually prescribe antibiotics. Here are some of the successful homeopathic treatments I have used.

Homeopathic—*Aconitum napellus 30c*: For the very first signs of infection, with fever, restlessness, and anxiety. Use Homeopathic Schedule 2.

Homeopathic—*Belladonna 30c*: For the dog with fever, dilated pupils, and excitability. Use Homeopathic Schedule 2.

Homeopathic—*Phytolacca 30c*: For mastitis where the breast is very hard to the touch and extremely painful. Use Homeopathic Schedule 2.

Homeopathic—*Lachesis muta 30c*: Use when a left breast is affected, especially if the skin over the area has turned bluish or black. Use Homeopathic Schedule 2.

Homeopathic—*Pulsatilla 30c*: For the dog that is whining, shows no sign of thirst, and wants comfort. Use Homeopathic Schedule 2.

RINGWORM

See Skin Parasites.

SINUSITIS

See Upper Respiratory Infections.

SKIN PARASITES

See Ear Problems for a discussion of ear mites.

External parasites (such as ticks and fleas) seem to be most attracted to animals in poor health. I have seen many pets with fleas on the outside, worms on the inside, and some other problem like a chronic skin disease. I've also observed that when an animal is placed on the recommended natural diet and other recommended lifestyle changes are made, the number of fleas and other parasites often decreases markedly without any special treatment. They don't completely disappear, but they no longer constitute a problem. Other measures of control, if needed, are then much easier and more effective.

When I'm trying to evaluate an animal's overall health, I find it useful to judge the seriousness of any skin parasites that may be present. From least serious to most serious, I rank them in this order: ticks, fleas, lice, and, finally, mange mites or ringworm. By this scale, I consider a cat with lice to be more seriously ill than one with fleas and a dog with mange worse off than one with ticks, and so on.

Let's discuss each of these parasites in turn and consider ways to control them with-out poisonous chemicals. You must realize, however, that by themselves, neither these suggested measures nor chemical insecticides are effective in the long run. The best results occur when an animal is on a natural diet, lives in a good environment, gets enough sunlight, and is exercised and groomed regularly, as discussed elsewhere in the book (see Chapter 11).

TICKS

Ticks are not permanent residents. Rather, they attach themselves, suck some blood, and later fall off to lay eggs. The young ticks that hatch out crawl up to the ends of branches and grasses and patiently wait (for weeks, if necessary) for something warm-blooded and good tasting to come along and brush against the vegetation. Then they drop on and find a nice, cozy place to attach.

Groom your pet thoroughly before you let it run in an area likely to contain ticks, such as woods or fields. Remove loose hair and mats so access to the skin is easier, and dust or rub on the coat an herbal tick repellent. (Commercial formulas containing eucalyptus and lavender are particularly useful.) Work the repellent through the hair and into the skin. These can work quite well.

When you return home after the adventure, check for any stalwart ticks that may have made it aboard your pet despite precautions. A fine-toothed flea comb may help to locate them or even capture any that are not yet attached. This also is a good time to remove foxtails (see Foxtails). Look especially closely around the neck and head and under the ears.

If you find a tick already attached, remove it like this: With the nails of your thumb and forefinger (or a pair of tweezers—some are now available just for this purpose), reach around the tick and grasp it as close to the skin as possible; don't worry, it won't bite! You want to remove the whole thing, not just pull off the tick's body and leave the head still embedded. Use a slow, steady pull (10 to 20 seconds) and, with a slight twist, pull out the little bugger—head, body, and all. You will have to pull strongly but not quickly. Look closely to see if you got the tick's tiny head; it will probably have a little shred of tissue still attached to it. Wash your hands when you are done with removal.

If the head is left behind despite your care, the area may fester for a while, much like a splinter under the skin. But this is minor and can be treated with the herbs echinacea or calendula as described under Abscesses.

Sometimes small ticks crawl down inside the ear. If your dog is shaking its head a lot after a trip through tick land, have your veterinarian look down the ear canal with an instrument to check for this or for a possible foxtail. If you can't do that, then put some almond oil in the ear and the tick will likely be shaken out later.

What about really bad infestations? I am not exaggerating to say that I have seen dogs covered with hundreds, maybe thousands, of ticks. In such situations you may have to turn to chemical treatment to control them, but in the future try working with the herbal repellents before heading out again.

FLEAS

Ah! The bane of dog and cat alike. Once again, I have found that a healthy lifestyle is the best defense. Following are some additional specific measures that can also help.

Add plenty of *nutritional yeast* to the daily ration. Use anywhere from 1 teaspoon to 2 tablespoons of yeast (depending on your pet's size) for each meal.

Mix *fresh garlic*, one-quarter to one raw clove, grated or minced, into each feeding. I used this advice for decades in my practice without ever seeing a problem with health effects in either dogs or cats. However, of late, there have been warnings from veterinarians about using garlic in dogs and cats, so there is controversy about it. I still recommend it, but read the detailed explanation in Chapter 11, Exercise, Rest, Grooming, and Play.

Wash the skin daily, if necessary, with a lemon rinse (see Chapter 11 again). This makes it less attractive to fleas.

Have your carpets treated with a borax-like powder that dramatically reduces flea populations (Chapter 11).

It's also good to know that fleas are what are called "nest parasites" in that they are found in largest numbers where the animal sleeps or rests. If there are particular areas of the house, couch, or rug where the animal hangs out, then give careful attention to vacuuming there frequently. You will suck up eggs and baby fleas and thus break the cycle.

The last suggestion I have, when the fleas persist in spite of your most vigorous efforts, is to try using flea traps. These are devices that plug into an electrical outlet and attract the fleas to the lights and warmth. They jump in, thinking they'll get dinner and instead get caught on sticky paper or something like that. They have worked well for my clients.

Do consider that the overall health of your dog or cat is critical, as the less healthy animal is very attractive to fleas. If there are other parasites like worms, these may have to be addressed as well.

Also, you might try a specific homeopathic remedy to help strengthen the body so that it isn't so attractive to fleas. One that usually works best is:

Homeopathic—*Sulphur 30c*: This is the treatment to try first; however, you must still continue all the flea-control measures suggested in Chapter 11. The remedy will only make your pet better able to resist flea infestation; it will not kill fleas directly. Use Homeopathic Schedule 4. If after a month this has not improved the situation, give next:

Homeopathic—*Mercurius vivus* or *Mercurius solubilis 30c*: Use Homeopathic Schedule 4.

Flea Collars

A note about flea collars: They don't work very well. They are toxic. Some cats even hang themselves on them or get the collars caught between their jaws, causing serious damage. Others get permanent hair loss around the neck from allergic reactions, particularly when the collar is too tight.

LICE

These little varmints are rather uncommon, but occasionally infest a run-down dog or cat. You have to look very carefully to see them on the skin or to see their eggs, which are attached to the animal hairs. Lice are slightly smaller than fleas and a lighter color—more tan or beige, rather than dark brown. Also, they don't jump like fleas. Fortunately, dog and cat lice do not infest people.

For some reason, I rarely encountered this problem in my practice so I don't have much experience with treating it. I had read in an herbal book about using lavender oil for lice infestation and I have seen reports of using it for head lice in children successfully. In my practice I advised adding a few drops of lavender oil to a natural shampoo for dogs and this went all right. Cats are said to have an aversion to lavender, so go light with it and provide plenty of fresh air afterward.

Shampooing is an obvious treatment, and I suggest leaving the lather on for 10 minutes before rinsing, if possible. Then follow with the lemon skin tonic described in

Chapter 11 (under the Flea Repellents topic). The eggs are not killed by this, only the adults. The eggs continue to hatch out over a period of time, so continued baths are necessary until all the eggs are gone.

The most difficult part of lice control is getting the nits (the eggs attached to the hairs) off. They are glued to individual hairs and, short of cutting off all the hairs, you have to in some way remove them. The least toxic, though messy, way to do it is to apply mayonnaise and work it carefully into the hairs, then wash it out. Whew!

What else to do? Without delay, build up the animal's health with a natural diet. Start right off with some home-prepared food and emphasize nutritional yeast and garlic as previously prescribed for fleas.

Use the same basic steps outlined in the flea program in Chapter 11 (including grooming) to eliminate the young lice as they hatch. Building up your pet's health will make its skin less desirable to lice.

Homeopathic—*Sulphur 30c*: Usually helps raise resistance in general and to parasites in particular. Use Homeopathic Schedule 4.

Note: We are used to quick results like those we get with chemicals that kill the lice almost immediately. They will not do anything for the animal's run-down health, however, which engendered the problem in the first place. Indeed, the toxic effect may weaken the animal even further. To work with nature is to be patient.

MANGE

The most common form is *demodectic mange,* which occurs most often in dogs (though it is also seen in rare instances in cats). It is diagnosed by finding the mites on skin scrapings (which is done by rubbing a scalpel or knife across the skin to gather the surface material and putting it on a slide to view under the microscope). The other type is called *sarcoptic mange,* caused by a scabies mite that burrows into the skin, making pets itch quite a bit.

DEMODECTIC MANGE

The mite associated with demodectic mange is very widespread and is actually found on most healthy dogs and also on people's faces (around the eyebrows and nose) without any sign of its presence. When it becomes a problem for your dog this means there is a disorder of the immune system so that the usual control of these mites (as occurs in healthy dogs) is changed. It might be the skin now is more favorable to the mites, encouraging them to grow—maybe there is more food for them. In any case, they greatly increase in numbers. Demodectic mange usually appears first as a small, hairless patch near the eye or chin. It doesn't itch much and may pass unnoticed.

Demodectic mange causes a minor problem for some young dogs, but usually clears up spontaneously without treatment by the age of 12 to 14 months. In a small percentage of those affected, however, the mite continues to spread. For some unlucky dogs, it can cover much of the body and result in hair loss and skin irritation and thickening. Bacteria (staph) can also get established, causing further complications such as "pimples" and a pustular discharge, particularly around the feet. This form of the disease is called generalized demodectic mange.

Animals that have generalized mange are susceptible to other serious illnesses and must be treated very carefully for their health to be restored. It is also very important that they not be vaccinated, as their immune system cannot react properly to the vaccine and only becomes more disordered.

It is helpful to understand that problems with this parasite depend on a weak immune system, and this is what must be addressed. Unfortunately what is almost always done is the worst possible thing. The orthodox treatment is harsh, poisonous, and generally futile. (Mild cases clear up on their own anyway.) The hair is clipped off the whole animal. Then strong insecticides are "painted" on the skin or the dog is completely immersed in them. They are sometimes so toxic that only a part of the body can be done at a time. Unfortunately, antitoxic nutrition or vitamin supplements are seldom recommended, so the dog's underlying health goes from bad to worse. Even those dogs that apparently recover after weeks or months of treatment can have recurrences, or another, more serious, "unrelated" problem will develop. Cortisone-type drugs should not be used under any circumstances. They depress the immune system further and, therefore,

just about guarantee nonrecovery (in the true sense) by any method.

Instead, I have had good results using just nutrition and homeopathic remedies, though treatment must be individualized and requires close attention to progress. Here are some general guidelines for a natural approach.

- Fast the dog (if its weight and health are good) for 5 to 7 days, as outlined in Chapter 18. Afterward, use the natural diet we have advised in this book.
- Rub fresh lemon juice on the affected spot every day, or use the lemon rinse recipe in Chapter 11.

Nutrition is especially important here. As we have discussed in earlier chapters, there can be an accumulation of toxic substances, creating a stress to the immune system that is trying its best to keep up with the changes in the tissues. The more you can emphasize a natural diet, and avoid the exposure to environmental chemicals, the quicker your dog will heal from this.

A homeopathic preparation that suits many cases of mange (either demodectic or sarcoptic) is:

Homeopathic—*Sulphur 6c*: Use Homeopathic Schedule 6(b). When the condition is obviously clearing, use the Sulphur less frequently on a tapering-off program.

The dog with a staph infection of the skin occurring along with the mange will benefit from the use of:

Herbal—*Purple coneflower (Echinacea angustifolia):* Use Herbal Schedule 1, for internal treatment, and Herbal Schedule 4 for treatment of the skin (both at the same time). You can use both this and the homeopathic Sulphur treatment if necessary, giving the Sulphur about 10 minutes before the echinacea dose.

SARCOPTIC MANGE

The dog or cat with sarcoptic mange (more irritating than other kinds of mange) responds best to this treatment.

Herbal—*Lavender (Lavandula vera or L. officinalis):* Applying a base of almond oil with some added lavender oil (a small amount, not more than 10 percent) to the affected skin areas is known to kill sarcoptic mange mites and destroy the eggs. This is suitable for treating dogs. For cats, who don't like lavender, use less of it and if they resist too much, try it with just the almond oil.

You can apply once a day, as needed.

RINGWORM

Though this disease sounds like it's caused by some kind of curly worm, it is actually the result of a fungus that's similar to athlete's foot. The growth starts at a central point and spreads out in a ring shape, much like an expanding ripple forms around a stone tossed in a pond. As the fungus grows in the skin cells and hair, the skin may become irritated, thickened, and reddened, and the hairs may break off and leave a coarse stubble behind.

In cats, which are more commonly affected, the condition often looks like circular gray patches of broken, short, thin hair, without much evidence of itching or irritation. Ringworm is contagious to people (especially children) and other animals; see the precautions in Chapter 12. Like mange, widespread ringworm indicates the animal's health is not up to snuff, as it usually is the stressed, sick, or weakened ones that get severe infestations. Like generalized mange, ringworm that covers most of the body is a very serious problem indicating a severely compromised immune system.

Nutrition

Start with a fast of 2 or 3 days (see Chapter 18); then follow with the basic natural diet program in this book. Essential fatty acids are very important for the health of skin and hair. If you have a seed grinder, prepare and add freshly ground flaxseeds to the food each day. Use ½ teaspoon to 1 teaspoon. (Flax oil, if organic and fresh, is all right to use, but tends to spoil quickly so buy small amounts at a time and keep capped and refrigerated. Grinding the seeds yourself is much preferred.)

Direct Treatment

First, clip the hair around the bare spot and about ½ inch beyond it, being careful not to injure the skin. If you clip the hair, ringworm is less likely to spread and the topical treatment is easier to apply. Burn or carefully dispose of the infected hair that you remove, as it is contagious on contact. (In order to catch loose hairs, always be sure to vacuum carefully and frequently if you have a pet with ringworm. Also wash bedding and utensils often with hot water and soap.) Be sure to wash your hands.

Treating the sore spot will speed healing and help protect others from getting ringworm. Choose one of the following two herbs plus the homeopathic remedy.

Herbal—*Plantain (Plantago major)*: Make a decoction of the whole plant by putting about ¼ cup of the plant (a common weed) per every cup of spring or distilled water into a glass or enameled pot. Boil about 5 minutes, then let the brew steep 3 minutes, covered. Strain and cool. Massage onto the skin once or twice a day until the condition clears.

Herbal—*Goldenseal (Hydrastis canadensis)*: Make a strong infusion by adding 1 rounded teaspoon of the powdered rootstock to a cup of boiling water. Let stand till cold. Then carefully pour off the clear fluid and massage it onto the skin once or twice a day.

Homeopathic—*Sulphur 6c*: Very helpful in raising resistance to skin parasites. Use Homeopathic Schedule 6(a).

SKIN PROBLEMS

Mange and ringworm are discussed under Skin Parasites.

The skin gets dumped on from two sides. The rest of the body uses it to eliminate toxic material, especially if the kidneys aren't able to handle the job; at the same time, environmental pollutants or applied chemical products assault it from the outside. One thing is for sure—skin troubles are the number one problem in dogs and cats.

On the positive side, if your animal's only health problem is a skin disorder, consider yourself lucky. It's much worse if a surface condition (such as a skin problem) has been suppressed with repeated drug use; a more serious condition would be likelier to arise in that case. If a skin condition is the only problem your pet has, you can help prevent deeper problems by addressing it in a more curative manner. (The problem of suppression is discussed in Chapter 17, under "The Limitations of a Partial Approach.")

The symptoms of skin disorder are among the easiest to detect. They usually include one or more of the following: very dry skin; flakiness or white scales resembling dandruff; large brown flakes, redness, and irritation; itching (ranging from slight to so severe that blood is drawn); greasy hair and a foul odor to the skin and its secretions (which many people mistake as normal, or even as a pleasant "doggy odor"); pimples and blisters that form between the toes and discharge blood and pus; brown, black, or gray skin discoloration; formation of scabs or crusts; and hair loss. I also include chronic inflammation inside the ear canal (and under the ear flap), anal gland problems, and underactive (hypoactive) thyroid glands as related to skin disease.

Modern medicine tends to divide these many symptoms and regard them as separate diseases. I think this only confuses the picture, so that we don't perceive the problem as a whole. From a wider view, these symptoms appear as one basic problem that manifests a little differently in individual animals depending on heredity, environment, nutrition, parasites, and so on. Thus, one dog may have severely inflamed, moist, itchy areas ("hot spots") near the base of its tail, while another may have thick, itchy skin along its back, with greasy, smelly secretions—but they are really the same health problem.

What are the causes of this overall disorder?

Toxicity: I think that the chief cause for these many manifestations of skin disease are the many contaminants from food and environment that pile up in the body. As we have discussed many times through the book, there are so many toxins these days that it becomes an unresolvable burden for many animals even though they use kidneys and skin as much as they can to eliminate the toxins.

Nutritional deficiency: Sometimes the skin can reflect the lack of a nutrient, especially certain vitamins and essential fatty acids. If you suspect this, read over the diet advice in Chapter 8, "Skin and Coat Issues" (page 146).

Vaccinations: As we discussed in Chapter 16, vaccinations can induce immune disorders in susceptible animals, and the most common form of these disorders is what we call skin allergies.

Suppressed disease: This refers to a prior health condition that was treated by making the symptoms go away but without really curing the condition and restoring health. It lurks "underground," every now and then coming out as irritated skin that itches or has a discharge.

Psychological factors: These include boredom, frustration, anger, and irritability. As I see it, however, these are nearly always secondary issues that simply aggravate an already-existing problem.

TREATMENT

It is possible to alleviate or even eliminate skin problems through proper nutrition and the total health plan suggested in this book. What has often surprised me is how much improvement there is when the diet eliminates any animal products. You would not expect this, but allergies to meat and dairy are said to be the most common triggers, so maybe this is the factor. To work with the diet does take patience as it might be a couple of weeks before you can see definite progress, but it does come along reasonably quickly. You have to bring health back to optimum, cleanse the body as much as possible, and then keep it from being contaminated again.

Check out the dog and cat recipe charts in Chapter 6, Recipes for Today, for the code A (meaning "allergies") in the second row. This will identify for you the recipes we think will be most helpful here.

Additional treatments I have used are primarily homeopathic remedies. The ones listed below can provide a real boost to healing. However, severe cases often require individualized treatment beyond the scope of this discussion; seek out a veterinarian who is skillful in the use of homeopathy, acupuncture, or other alternative therapies.

The Chief Obstacle

The most difficult conditions to treat are those previously dosed with lots of cortisone or its synthetic forms (azium, depo, flucort, prednisone, or prednisolone). Corticosteroids effectively suppress symptoms like inflammation and itching, but are in no sense curative. You may not know if your animal has received cortisone, because your veterinarian may have used terms like "anti-itch" shots or "flea allergy" pills. They usually look like clear or milky-white injections or little pink or white tablets. If you have good communication with your veterinarian, ask if he or she is giving your pet steroids. A natural approach will not work well if you also continue cortisone therapy.

Another typical treatment is a series of allergy desensitization injections with solutions made from the common flea or other suspected allergens. Sometimes they help, but often as not the relief is partial and not as satisfactory as eliminating the problem entirely.

Treatment for the Intense, Sudden Condition

For an animal with acutely inflamed, irritated skin ("hot spots") that is otherwise in good condition, start with a fast. Use the directions in Chapter 18, breaking the fast after 5 to 7 days for a dog and after 3 to 5 days for a cat. This fast mimics natural conditions in which wild predators' bodies have a chance to clean out between hunts. It also removes the demand on the system to both digest food and deal with the disorder at the same time.

Afterward, carefully introduce the natural food program we have advised in earlier chapters. As was mentioned above, in my practice I found that, for some dogs and cats, it was necessary to get completely off animal products to make significant progress. The optimal diet is an essential ingredient in really bringing your dog or cat back to being healthy.

It helps to clip away the hair on severely inflamed areas and give a bath with nonirritating soap (not a medicated flea soap; use a natural organic soap as described in Chapter 11). After drying the skin, apply a poultice or wash the area frequently with a preparation of black or green tea. It supplies tannic acid, which helps to dry up the moist places. Two to three times a day, or as needed, you also can smear on some vitamin E oil or fresh aloe vera gel (from the living plant or in a liquid preparation found in health food stores).

These homeopathic remedies are helpful for the times when symptoms flare up. (Other medicines are required to completely cure the tendency. It takes working with a skillful veterinarian for several months.)

Homeopathic—*Nux vomica 6c*: This remedy is commonly needed. The skin condition is associated with frequent itching, all over the body, even involving the head. It is worse in the evening, and often associated with something going on with the stomach (upset, loss of appetite, vomiting). Use Homeopathic Schedule 2.

Homeopathic—*Pulsatilla 6c*: Again, itching all over, worse when getting warm. Scratching actually makes it worse. The animal's scratching during the night often will wake people up. This remedy indicated especially when the skin condition comes on after eating meat. Use Homeopathic Schedule 2.

Homeopathic—*Rhus toxicodendron 6c*: Suitable as a temporary medicine when itching flares up and is very intense. There tends to be swelling of the skin and relief from applying warm compresses. Some animals will also show stiffness, trouble moving. Use Homeopathic Schedule 2.

Homeopathic—*Graphites 6c*: This remedy is indicated when the "hot spots" ooze a sticky, thick discharge, about the consistency of honey. Use Homeopathic Schedule 2.

Homeopathic—*Mercurius vivus or Mercurius solubilis 6c*: Use this one if there's a puslike yellowish or greenish discharge. Also, the hair will tend to fall out around the eruptions, leaving raw, bleeding areas. The condition is usually worse in hot weather or in very warm living quarters. Frequently these animals will have red gums, problems with the teeth, and very bad-smelling breath. Use Homeopathic Schedule 2.

Homeopathic—*Arsenicum album 6c*: This remedy suits dogs with skin eruptions that cause a great deal of restlessness and discomfort. They seem to be driven almost insane—constantly chewing, licking, and scratching. The skin lesions are very red and dry with loss of hair and an "eating away" of the skin, leaving angry red sores. Especially indicated if the dog becomes very thirsty and chilly as well. Use Homeopathic Schedule 2.

THE LONG-LASTING, CHRONIC CONDITION

For the animal with a long-term, low-grade condition of itchy, greasy, or dry and scaly skin (who may also have an underactive thyroid), start by fasting it 1 day every week, offering only broth (see Chapter 18). The rest of the time feed only the natural foods we are recommending. Change will be gradual, over weeks, so again, patience required.

If the skin is greasy and foul-smelling, bathe your pet as often as once a week, as described in Chapter 11. If the skin is dry, bathe less often. Also, be sure to control fleas (see Skin Parasites in this section), using the lemon skin rinse described in Chapter 11.

Constipation or sluggish bowels may also be contributing to the problem. If they are, address that first. Use one of the following two remedies.

Herbal—*Garlic (Allium sativum)*: Give daily ¼ to 1 whole clove (fresh grated or minced) or one to three small garlic capsules (depending on size of animal). Garlic also has the advantage of discouraging fleas (see Chapter 11).

Homeopathic—*Nux vomica 6*: Give one pellet before each meal, as needed, until bowels are regular (see also Constipation). If it is going to help, you will notice improvement within a few days.

If constipation or "hot spots" are not the present problem, then try working with one of these treatments.

Homeopathic—*Sulphur 6c*: This remedy is very helpful for the average case of dry, itchy skin, especially if your dog tends to be thin, "lazy," and not very clean, with red-looking eyes, nose, or lips. These animals generally don't like a lot of heat, but sometimes will seek out a warm stove in cooler weather. Use Homeopathic Schedule 6(a).

Homeopathic—*Pulsatilla 6c*: Those animals needing this medicine will be easygoing, good natured, and affectionate. Their symptoms tend to be worse when eating rich or fatty food, and it is noticed that they rarely drink water. Often there is a preference for lying on cool surfaces as well. Use Homeopathic Schedule 6(a).

Homeopathic—*Graphites 6c*: These dogs tend to be overweight, constipated, and easily overheated. Eruptions ooze sticky fluid. The skin is easily inflamed, even by slight injuries like scratches, and it does not heal easily. The ears can be plagued with irritation, a bad smell, and waxy discharge. Use Homeopathic Schedule 6(a).

Homeopathic—*Thuja occidentalis 30c*: This remedy is an antidote to illness following vaccinations. Many of the animals I treat developed their skin problems within a few weeks after being vaccinated. I find that giving this remedy occasionally during treatment really helps such dogs recover. Another time to consider Thuja is when other medicines have not done much good. If so, giving Thuja and then going back to one of the above remedies will sometimes result in progress. Use Homeopathic Schedule 4.

Homeopathic—*Silicea 30c*: If the problem persists in spite of the advice given so far, especially if there is an excessive appetite, stealing food, scavenging—even leading to being overweight—then this medicine will be of use. Use Homeopathic Schedule 4. Do not repeat this medicine.

Note: In general, these deeply ingrained skin conditions require patience and persistence. You will usually see clear, beneficial effects from the program within 6 to 8 weeks.

Because vaccines tend to aggravate the condition, it is very important to avoid them during the treatment period. Sometimes medicines like those used for heartworm prevention will set off an attack. In this case it is best to use the monthly type of heartworm medication and give it only every 6 weeks (or stop using it altogether in severe cases—work out a plan with your veterinarian).

Some obstinate cases will not completely recover no matter how long you treat them (though they will generally improve). These need more individualized treatment with other homeopathic remedies or one of the holistic approaches described in Chapter 17. If you can, find a skilled professional to help.

JUST HAIR LOSS

For the animal suffering hair loss, try a slightly different program. Sometimes a pet will just begin to lose hair without any other apparent problem. Or the hair loss could be the result of poisoning—not necessarily the intentional kind, but rather the accumulation of toxic substances that may affect sensitive individuals. Common agents to consider include fluoride (in some drinking water and commercial pet foods) and aluminum (from use of aluminum bowls or cooking utensils). Sensitivity to aluminum seems to vary, and not all animals show this reaction. Those that are poisoned by aluminum tend to have constipation problems as well.

It is also possible for hair loss to reflect a disturbance in the endocrine glands (especially hypothyroidism) or a deficiency of a certain nutrient. If your veterinarian has diagnosed either of these problems, then feed only the natural diet with added kelp powder. This is particularly important, because the powder's iodine content will help to stimulate the thyroid.

Discontinue use of aluminum utensils and fluoridated water (call your water company to find out if your tap water is so treated; if it is, find another source of water to bring in).

If you have addressed all these things—nutrition, toxicity, water pollution—and your animal still has hair loss (not caused by scratching or chewing)—then try these homeopathic remedies.

Homeopathic—*Thuja occidentalis 30c*: Try Thuja first because it is an antidote to the effects of vaccination, which can be a primary reason for a persistently poor hair coat or for poor hair growth. Use Homeopathic Schedule 4. (Sometimes hair loss is at a normal rate, but the issue is that no new hair grows in to replace it; in such a case this remedy is especially suitable.)

Homeopathic—*Selenium 30c*: Indicated for excessive hair loss with no new growth, especially if there are no other symptoms of illness. Use it after trying Thuja (see above), if that remedy has not been sufficient to resolve the problem. Use Homeopathic Schedule 4.

If an animal develops the hair loss soon after giving birth, then:

Homeopathic—*Sepia 30c*: Indicated for those animals for which the hair loss is associated with going through pregnancy or giving birth or nursing. Use Homeopathic Schedule 4.

SPAYING AND NEUTERING

Spaying is a surgery to remove a female's ovaries and uterus to prevent pregnancy and to eliminate her heats (periods of sexual receptivity). Neutering, or castration, removes a male's testes (leaving the scrotum, or sac) to prevent reproduction and to reduce aggression, wandering, and territorial behaviors. Both operations are performed painlessly under anesthesia, and recovery is usually rapid and uneventful. Natural treatments can help ease the process.

If your pet is slow to wake up, groggy, or nauseous after surgery, give:

Homeopathic—*Phosphorus 30c*: Response is usually fast—from a few minutes to an hour. Stop treatment as soon as there is apparent improvement. Use Homeopathic Schedule 2.

If your pet has discomfort, pain, or restless behavior on returning home, try:

Homeopathic—*Arnica 30c*: This addresses any soreness of the tissues that were cut into. Usually there is not much pain, but if the animal is uncomfortable, especially sensitive to being touched in the surgery area, then give this remedy. Use Homeopathic Schedule 2.

For any red irritation or a discharge of fluid or pus around the skin sutures (if there are any; sometimes clips under the skin are used instead), give:

Homeopathic—*Apis mellifica 6c*: Also bathe the incision site in a mixture of 10 drops of *Calendula* tincture, ¼ teaspoon sea salt, and 1 cup of pure water. Dip a warm washcloth in the solution and hold it against the incision for a few minutes three or four times a day. Use Homeopathic Schedule 1.

Flower Essences—Dr. Bach's *Rescue Remedy formula*, two drops four times a day for 2 to 3 days, is often helpful and easy to use if you don't know what else to do.

Extra vitamins A, E, and C are also useful after any surgery to help detoxify anesthetics and drugs. My standard regimen, regardless of animal size, is 10,000 IU of A, 100 IU of E, and 250 milligrams of C, all given once a day for 3 days both before and after surgery.

Does This Surgery Do Harm?

Some people are concerned about the health effects of such a major surgical alteration. Although it is surely a major intervention, the best I can say at this point in time is that neutering does not seem to cause major health problems or increase incidence of such common problems as skin allergies or cystitis. Most neutered dogs and cats live long and healthy lives. Some do tend to become less active, to act less aggressively (a benefit), and perhaps to gain weight. Obesity more often follows indulgent feeding and lack of regular exercise.

On the other hand, I have seen more obvious harmful effects when neutering is used as a medical treatment for prolonged heats, cystic ovaries, infertility problems, spontaneous abortions, vaginitis, infections, and the like. These reproductive problems are the result of chronic ill health. Simply removing the affected organs will not really cure the underlying state. So the animal later develops other symptoms—really the same disease with a different focus.

When pets have reproductive health problems, I first recommend nutritional therapy and homeopathy, assuming that it's not an emergency and we still have some time. If this is not effective, surgery is still an option. However, if we are successful, as we often are, the chronic disease is cured. Then the animal can be neutered for the usual reasons without any long-term problem.

What are the reasons to neuter a healthy animal? A female dog or cat comes into heat two or more times a year. Preventing her from breeding is demanding, frustrating to your animal, and a potential source of health problems (see "Pyometra," page 417). Allowing her to breed adds to the tremendous animal overpopulation problem. Repeated breeding can also drain her health.

Neutering reduces the havoc wreaked by intact males—property damage, fights, the smell and stain of territorial marking, accidents caused when they wander onto public roadways, and packs that attack or threaten other animals or even people. By contrast, a neutered male is typically more affectionate and gentle, making a better companion.

The best time for surgery is after a pet reaches sexual maturity, which ensures the least effect on the neuroendocrine system and allows full development of a normal adult body shape. Most females reach this point at age 6 to 8 months, most males at 9 to 12 months.

Some animals mature later, however, so you may want to wait until the signs are clear. For a female this means after her first heat (keep her carefully confined to prevent pregnancy).

A male cat matures when his urine develops an odor and he begins to show signs of territorial spraying of urine. The male dog will begin to lift one leg to urinate (and mark territory), mount other dogs, fight, roam, and become more aggressive. The risk of waiting, however, is that through inadvertent pregnancy we contribute to the overwhelming surplus of puppies and kittens. In most cases, plan to neuter females at 6 to 7 months and males at 9 to 10 months.

There are really no safe alternatives to surgical neutering. Over the years, various hormones and drugs have been used to prevent females from coming into heat or to stimulate abortion if necessary. These drugs always cause some problems, however, and they are soon pulled off the market. Perhaps a safe alternative to neutering will be found someday, but there is nothing out there now that I can recommend.

Some people, of late, are having surgeries like "tying off the tubes" that do not remove the reproductive organs but do make the animal sterile. I am not sure how well this works out. They still will have the same behavior as before, so that advantage is lost. I think it will take more experience to assess this approach.

If you're worried about money, contact a nearby low-cost spay/neuter clinic or call your local humane society for information about special reduced-fee programs arranged with area veterinarians.

STOMACH PROBLEMS

The stomach has its share of upsets, usually from eating the wrong kind of food (spoiled, tainted, indigestible) or too much food (beware the greedy eater!). However, stomach problems can also indicate a wide variety of other disorders—such as infectious diseases, kidney failure, hepatitis, pancreatitis, colitis (inflammation of the lower bowel), a foreign substance that doesn't belong in the stomach (swallowed toys, string, hair), and parasites, like worms.

Be aware that problems in other areas of the body can also cause symptoms like vomiting, nausea, and lack of appetite, fooling you into thinking that only the stomach is involved. Especially if vomiting is persistent or severe, it may indicate a serious, even life-threatening, problem—especially in dogs. Have your veterinarian make a diagnosis.

Here we will discuss three common problems that are centered in the stomach itself: acute gastritis (sudden upset), chronic gastritis (low-grade, persistent upset), and gastric dilation (swelling with gas, sometimes causing the stomach to twist shut). The suggestions offered are alternative treatments for those animals newly diagnosed with these problems or animals that have them repeatedly so that ways to deal with this other than the usual drugs are needed.

ACUTE GASTRITIS

Gastritis is a term that means inflammation (not infection) of the stomach. *Acute* signifies that the attack is sudden, appearing in a few minutes or hours. The most common sufferer is the dog that likes to raid garbage cans or to eat dead animals found on roads or in the woods (cats, being more finicky, rarely have this as a cause). Compost piles are another common source of spoiled treasures. As partial scavengers, dogs often scrounge about in garbage cans and consume an extraordinary mixture of foods (often spoiled) that just don't sit well in the stomach.

The vomiting (and usually diarrhea) that follows is the body's attempt to right the wrong by getting rid of the noxious material. Some dogs instinctively try to remedy things by eating grass, which stimulates vomiting. This behavior also occurs in animals with low-grade stomach irritation.

Another cause of acute gastritis is consuming indigestible material, like large bone fragments. This is mostly a problem for dogs not used to eating bones. It's also the likely result of their consuming cooked bones (which are more apt to splinter) or inedible materials such as cloth, plastic, metal, rubber toys, golf balls, and the like. If bones are causing the problem, give your pet only large raw bones and give extra B vitamins to dogs to ensure adequate stomach acid. Supervise carefully. If your dog keeps trying to swallow large pieces, it's best not to trust him with bones.

Indigestible foreign objects in the stomach often require surgical removal, though sometimes they can be retrieved by passing a tube into the stomach.

Cats may swallow sewing thread or yarn; if there is a needle attached, it can get caught up in the mouth or tongue while the thread passes down into the intestine. The unpleasant result can be a "crawling" of the intestine up along the thread, which is often fatal unless corrected quickly.

Though the signs are not specific, cats having this problem will stop eating and may have vomiting. A thread caught up around the tongue is very difficult to see. Just opening the mouth may not show it; a needle caught somewhere in the throat or esophagus will show up on an x-ray, as will bunching of the intestine (see Chapter 10 for more on this).

To help prevent pets from swallowing such objects, don't let them play by themselves with any toy or object that could cause problems.

TREATMENT

If you suspect that your animal has swallowed something dangerous, get professional help as soon as you can, or serious complications can arise. If you aren't sure what was swallowed, do not encourage vomiting. It would be too traumatic and dangerous for the object to come up if it is sharp, pointed, or very large. Irregular or pointy objects usually have to be surgically removed.

If you know what was swallowed, and it is small and not sharp or irregular, vomiting may expel the object, so you can allow the vomiting to proceed while you are waiting to see the vet.

The homeopathic remedy that is most useful for this problem and often resolves it before surgery is needed (the object passes on through and comes out) is:

Homeopathic—*Phosphorus 30c*: If there is vomiting, it happens after taking in water, occurring about 10 to 15 minutes after drinking. If it is possible for the object to be passed (and surprisingly it often is), that usually happens by the next day. Check every bowel movement carefully to see what is there.

The following treatments will help for a simple, acute gastritis not caused by foreign bodies. The symptoms are pain in the abdomen (it hurts the animal when you press its stomach, the animal doubles up with cramps, sits hunched, and acts depressed), vomiting or attempts to vomit, vomiting after eating or drinking, salivation, excessive drinking of water, and eating grass.

First, withhold all food for at least 24 hours and then reintroduce it slowly in small quantities. See the fasting instructions in Chapter 18. Make fresh, pure water available at all times or, if vomiting is part of the problem, offer one or more ice cubes to lick every couple of hours. (You don't want to aggravate vomiting and stomach irritation by encouraging too much drinking.)

Many dogs and cats will also eat grass to make themselves vomit when the stomach is upset. This is a natural response and is appropriate behavior at the beginning of a stomach upset. If the problem is not quickly resolved, however, eating grass only makes the situation worse.

As a supplementary treatment, make *chamomile tea*. This treatment will suffice for mild upsets. Pour a cup of boiling water over a tablespoon of the flowers, steep 15 minutes, strain, and dilute with an equal quantity of water. If the tea isn't accepted, just make the ice available.

For more serious upsets, one of the following is useful.

Herbal—*Peppermint (Mentha piperira)*: This is a good herbal treatment for dogs (cats don't like mint) and is often readily available. Use Herbal Schedule 1.

Herbal—*Goldenseal (Hydrastis canadensis)*: This very useful herb is indicated when what is vomited up is thick, yellowish, and "ropy" (for example, thick strands). Use Herbal Schedule 1.

Homeopathic—*Nux vomica 6c*: Especially indicated for the dog or cat that acts ill with the vomiting and wants to go off by itself rather than seek company. This remedy also suits the animal sick from overeating or eating garbage. Use Homeopathic Schedule 1.

Homeopathic—*Pulsatilla 6c*: Indicated for the dog or cat that wants attention and comfort, especially if it is not interested in drinking. Often animals requiring this remedy are made ill by eating food that is rich or fatty. Use Homeopathic Schedule 1.

Homeopathic—*Ipecac 6c*: Useful where there is almost constant nausea and vomiting, especially if the problem was brought on by indigestible food or if there is blood in the vomit. Use Homeopathic Schedule 1.

Homeopathic—*Arsenicum album 6c*: This remedy is par excellence for gastritis brought on by spoiled meat, or spoiled food in general. Use Homeopathic Schedule 2.

Homeopathic—*Belladonna 6c*: This is good for the animal that is primarily feverish, with dilated pupils and excitability. Use Homeopathic Schedule 1.

CHRONIC GASTRITIS

Some animals develop a long-term tendency for digestive upsets, often after eating and sometimes once every few days. This can follow inadequate recovery from a previous severe attack of acute gastritis or may result from emotional stress, poor-quality or disagreeable food, drug toxicity, or infections like feline infectious peritonitis or hepatitis. It can also be a part of an allergy problem, and many dogs and cats with skin eruptions will also have inflammation of the stomach and intestines. Sometimes there is no apparent cause.

Symptoms are poor digestion, a tendency to vomit, pain, depression or hiding (either immediately after eating or an hour or so later), loss of appetite, and gas. Many animals with chronic gastritis eat grass in an attempt to stimulate vomiting and cleansing of the stomach.

TREATMENT

The first and foremost treatment I recommend is to put the animal on a natural diet. I can't overemphasize the importance of a good diet, because the illness may be the result of the very food your pet has been eating. Research in animals, forcing them to eat GMO foods, has shown that a common outcome is inflammation of the stomach, and the GMO corn, soy, canola oil, or other substances that cause this are now common in pet foods. Look at the dog and cat recipe charts in Chapter 6, Recipes for Today, for the code A in the second row. This will identify for you the recipes we think will be most beneficial for you to use with this problem.

A further treatment might include one of the following, as indicated.

Herbal—*Goldenseal (Hydrastis canadensis)*: Good for weak digestion, poor appetite, and weight loss. Use Herbal Schedule 2.

Herbal—*Slippery elm*: To make it, thoroughly mix 1 slightly rounded teaspoon of slippery elm powder with 1 cup of cold water. Bring to a boil while stirring constantly. Then turn the heat down to simmer and continue to stir for another 2 to 3 minutes while the mixture thickens slightly. Remove from the heat, add 1 tablespoon of honey (for dogs only— cats don't like sweets, so leave it out), and stir well. Cool to room temperature and give ½ to 1 teaspoon to cats and small dogs, 2 teaspoons to 2 tablespoons for medium dogs, and 3 to 4 tablespoons for large dogs. This will often give relief and can be used once or twice a day as needed.

Homeopathic Treatment

There are several homeopathic medicines that are helpful for acute gastritis (discussed above) that are also helpful for the chronic condition. Sometimes the acute episode is the beginning of an illness that will turn out to be long lasting, though, of course, you can't know that at the beginning. Look over the remedies for acute gastritis, as any of them can be useful when the animal has the same indications as given there.

The main difference to understand is that with the chronic form of illness, the symptoms are often not as marked or as intense as in the acute stage, though the indications for the remedy are still there. For example, Pulsatilla is a frequently needed medicine. As with the acute condition, you may notice that your pet has become more clingy, wanting attention. In addition, he may drink a lesser amount of water, but still some. None of these symptoms, however, will stand out as strongly as when they are seen in the acute form.

An additional remedy that was not mentioned before is:

Homeopathic—*Natrum muriaticum 30c*: Useful for the cat that has excessive hunger, is thirsty, and has discomfort after eating. Also good for stomach problems associated with worms. Use Homeopathic Schedule 4.

GASTRIC DILATION (BLOAT)

This serious problem is seen mostly in the larger dog breeds (especially the Great Dane, Saint Bernard, and borzoi). Its cause is unknown, though veterinarians have found it sometimes linked with the feeding of large meals of dry kibble. It occurs most often in dogs between the ages of 2 and 10 years, and most often at night.

The symptoms of the condition are that approximately 2 to 6 hours after eating, the stomach (upper abdominal area) gets enlarged with liquid and gas and sometimes feels like a tight drum. Most often, you will see excessive salivation, drooling, unsuccessful attempts to vomit, extreme restlessness and discomfort, desperate attempts to eat grass (or carpeting), and, eventually, weakness and collapse.

This is an emergency situation because the increased pressure on the walls of the stomach causes fluids to leak in from the blood, with consequent dehydration, shock, and possible death in a few hours. Another complication is that the stomach can rotate on itself—a condition called volvulus—and the twisting can completely block entry into or exit from the organ. Immediate surgery is required in this instance.

PREVENTION

Feeding a natural, home-prepared diet seems to be the best way to avert such problems. If this has happened before or you think you have seen hints of it, then feed two or three small meals a day instead of a single one.

Especially avoid feeding dry food or concentrated foods that will absorb water after being eaten. The dog will eat more than its capacity, and when the food becomes distended with water, the total weight of the food is greatly increased. This can prevent the stomach from its natural emptying and also increase the chance of the stomach twisting around and blocking the movement of food out of it.

Regular exercise, which strengthens the muscles and "massages" the stomach and bowels, is extremely helpful.

TREATMENT

When gastric dilation first occurs, it is rather sudden and can be shocking. Sometimes the only thing noticed is that the dog is restless and desperately eating grass. If you look closely, you may see that the animal's belly is larger than normal, distended with gas.

Get to your veterinarian as soon as possible. If the condition is one of simple stomach dilation, it can be temporarily relieved at the hospital by passing a tube into the stomach. However, the condition tends to recur. Each time, the attack comes on sooner and with more severity. Eventually, the animal is put to sleep because of the apparent hopelessness of the situation and the high cost of repeated medical measures.

If there is also volvulus (twisting of the stomach), then surgery must be done to straighten out the twisted stomach and allow open passages in and out. The stomach wall is also "tacked down" by suturing it to the inside of the abdominal wall to prevent it from twisting in the future.

Even though you must see your veterinarian immediately, it may still be appropriate for me to give you some treatment suggestions, because there will be times when you cannot get veterinary service immediately; further, the condition tends to recur, and you will become aware of the early signs. If you can intervene with treatment soon enough, it is possible to head off an attack.

One of the easiest and most available herbal treatments is one discovered by one of my clients, Betty Lewis of Amherst, New Hampshire. She breeds Great Danes and has found that freshly made raw cabbage juice is an effective treatment at the beginning of bloat and has used it successfully many times.

Herbal—*Cabbage (Brassica oleracea)*: This plant is a member of the mustard family. Reduce fresh cabbage leaves to a liquid (with a juicer); do not add water. Give 1 to 2 ounces of this as a dose (to large breeds, less to smaller animals), repeating the treatment if symptoms return later.

Because of vomiting and the pressure closing off the opening to the stomach, I primarily use homeopathic preparations.

The pellets or tablets will act especially quickly, even if not swallowed, if they are first crushed to a powder (between folded heavy paper) and placed on the tongue.

Of course, you will need to plan ahead and order these in advance since you will need them immediately.

Homeopathic—*Pulsatilla 30c*: This is the first remedy I use in these cases. It resolves the majority of them. Give a dose of three crushed pellets every 30 minutes for a total of three treatments.

Homeopathic—*Belladonna 30c*: This remedy is indicated when the problem has come on very suddenly, with severe and intense symptoms. There is agitation, desperate attempts to eat anything: grass, rags, even carpet. Pupils are dilated and the head may be hot. Give a dose of three crushed pellets every 30 minutes for a total of three treatments.

Homeopathic—*Nux vomica 30c*: Best for the dog that becomes withdrawn, irritable, and chilly. This is the best treatment when the stomach has become twisted. Give a dose of three crushed pellets every 30 minutes for a total of three treatments.

Homeopathic—*Colchicum autumnale 30c*: The abdomen will be tremendously distended, apparently by gas. It can be accompanied by belching. This is one of the remedies that can be used for obstruction of the intestines (ileus). Give a dose of three crushed pellets every 30 minutes for a total of three treatments.

Homeopathic—*Carbo vegetabilis 30c*: Dogs needing this remedy will be greatly distended with gas and look very ill, with cold legs and ears and bluish color to the tongue and gums. It is suitable for the state of shock that accompanies this condition. Give a dose of three crushed pellets every 15 minutes for a total of three treatments. If this treatment improves the general condition, one of the other remedies may be needed to complete the treatment. Wait a bit and see if recovery ensues. If not, then try one of those already discussed.

Dogs that have had this problem before, perhaps one serious episode from which they have not fully recovered, may benefit from homeopathic treatment to resolve this and prevent future attacks. What you will see in these dogs is a pattern of recurring indigestion and gas, with periodic swelling of the animal's stomach, which causes breathing difficulty. This state of chronic ill health will produce progressive weakening, low energy, and a cold body.

Give the following treatment at a time when there is no crisis.

Homeopathic—*Hepar sulph 30c*: This is a treatment to use *between* crises, with the idea of preventing further attacks. It is indicated for the dog that has a history of skin or ear eruptions with itching and discomfort. Sometimes this history is vague; the original skin problem may have been suppressed in the past and no longer be remembered. If this treatment is successful, the stomach will improve and the skin eruption will come back for a while. Further treatment may then be necessary to resolve this condition. (See Skin Problems.) Use Homeopathic Schedule 4.

Homeopathic—*Graphites 30c*: Dogs needing this will have also had skin and ear problems in the past. Typically the eruptions tend to be worse at the base of the tail. They will be overweight, tend to be chilly (and like warmth), and be constipated. Use Homeopathic Schedule 4.

Homeopathic—*Silicea 30c*: Stomach problems are recurrent as indigestion or discomfort after eating. This can lead to frequent vomiting of food and nausea. These dogs often have accompanying rear leg trouble—stiffness, weakness, pain—that will be diagnosed as hip dysplasia, spondylitis, spondylosis, or degenerative myelopathy (all different manifestations of the same disorder). Use Homeopathic Schedule 4.

Note: If you achieve favorable results with one of these treatments, bear in mind that using drugs like tranquilizers, antibiotics, stimulants, or depressants immediately after a positive homeopathic response will very likely cancel out the favorable response and lead to a return of the original condition. For this reason, minimize or eliminate such treatment if the homeopathic remedies are doing the job.

STONES

See Bladder Problems.

TEETH

See Dental Problems.

THYROID DISORDERS

The thyroid is an extremely important gland that regulates the use of food, body weight, body temperature, heart rate, hair growth, activity level (low-thyroid individuals tend to be sluggish), and other more subtle functions. The thyroid is an endocrine gland, one of the group of body-regulating glands that includes the pituitary (linked directly to the brain, the "master gland" that regulates the other glands, controls total body size, milk production after birth, skin color, and several other functions); the pancreas (certain cells involved in insulin production); the adrenals (see Addison's disease and Cushing's disease); the parathyroid glands (which regulate calcium); and the reproductive glands, the testicles and ovaries. The endocrine glands control most of the functions of the body. When they have problems, it almost always is because they are either overactive or underactive.

HYPOTHYROIDISM

Hypothyroid (underactive thyroid) conditions affect dogs (not cats, except very rarely) and are actually quite commonly diagnosed. In the majority of dogs this disorder is part of an immune problem. In the same way that there will be allergies affecting the skin, the thyroid will be underactive because the immune system is affecting it, blocking normal function. In fact, these animals with immune problems will have several areas of the body affected at the same time—skin, ears, thyroid, and bowels being the most frequent.

Reduced thyroid function can also happen (rarely) due to inadequate iodine, and much more commonly from use of certain drugs. For example, a common treatment of skin allergies is to use corticosteroids (anti-inflammatory drugs), and these will interfere with thyroid hormone production. So, the young dog may start out with a skin problem but because of drug treatment for it, develops thyroid dysfunction secondarily. Phenobarbital, used to control epilepsy in dogs, also will block thyroid hormone production.

The signs of this problem are variable and often mimic the symptoms of other diseases. Most often one will see lethargy, mental dullness, slow heart rate, weight gain leading to obesity, recurrent infections, and intolerance of cold (seeking out warm places or the sun).

Changes in the skin are usually what alert people that something is wrong. There is a dry, dull hair coat and the hair comes out very easily. The outer coat comes off, leaving a very thick, wooly undercoat (from failure of the hair to be replaced properly so it sort of "piles up"). There may be patches of hair loss (equally on both sides, which distinguishes it from conditions where an animal scratches hair out from itchy spots, which tend not to be symmetrical), and the skin will be dry yet the hair greasy feeling, leaving a "doggy smell" on your fingers. As with Cushing's disease (an adrenal gland dysfunction), the skin can become darker than normal and be prone to infections and subsequent itchiness.

The conventional, allopathic, treatment is giving an artificial hormone every day for the life of the dog. The disadvantage of this is that the underlying cause (the immune-mediated disease or the drugs being used) is not addressed. As an additional side effect, the artificial thyroid hormone causes the thyroid gland to shrink and produce even less natural hormone than before. If this is done long enough, the poor glands will never work again.

My cases have done very well with homeopathic and nutritional therapy, and I always advise trying alternative treatments before considering complicating the problem with a replacement hormone. If the dog is young enough and has not been on hormone treatment very long, he can be brought back to normal thyroid function and have his health restored. The dogs already on hormones for long periods may not be completely curable (because of the drug effect), but usually their health can be significantly improved and the hormone dosage considerably lowered.

PREVENTION

In my practice I most often would see dogs that developed this problem after some suppressive treatment for other conditions. The prevention I can recommend is to turn more to the nutritional and alternative medical treatments we are encouraging here. Restoring health without use of suppressive drugs will prevent this from happening downstream.

TREATMENT

The endocrine disorders are very deep and serious problems because they often involve a disorder of the immune system and thus are more difficult to manage than many of those we are discussing in this section. Improved nutrition can be very helpful, but in my practice I have usually included homeopathic treatment as well to make the significant difference. Hypothyroidism needs individualized treatment by an experienced veterinarian, but here are some suggestions.

> **Homeopathic**—*Calcarea carbonica 30c*: A commonly needed remedy for this condition. Dogs needing this tend to be stocky, tend to overweight, and often have a history of skin itching and ear problems. Use Homeopathic Schedule 4.

> **Homeopathic**—*Iodium 30c*: These dogs have really big appetites but even so continue to lose weight. They can become very thin, even though eating often and large quantities of food. They tend to be restless, and sometimes have arthritis. Use Homeopathic Schedule 4.

> **Homeopathic**—*Lycopodium 30c*: These animals have yet a different appetite— they act like they are full, eating a small amount and quitting. They may have lost normal thirst as well. Diarrhea problems may be in the history, as well as skin eruptions associated with a strong smell from the body, and a tendency to attract fleas. Use Homeopathic Schedule 4.

HYPERTHYROIDISM

Hyperthyroidism (overactive thyroid) is the bane of cats. It is the opposite of what happens with dogs (as explained above). Here the thyroid gland *overproduces* hormone. Again, there is considerable evidence that it is caused by the immune system attacking the gland (and therefore part of a larger problem) but, in the case of cats, it causes the gland to become too active instead of less so, as in dogs. It is not known why there is this difference.

It is encountered in mature cats, more frequently as they get older. When I first was in practice (1965 on) we did not see this disease. Now it is extremely common, so something is responsible for this dramatic increase in incidence. There is some suggestion that vaccines are a factor resulting in an autoimmune condition; also contaminants in the food, like mercury, may be a cause, as it is known that mercury poisoning does affect the thyroid.

Because of the excessive hormone released,

we get the opposite signs seen in dogs, so rather than becoming overweight cats become thin, wasting away gradually in spite of a good, or even excessive, appetite. Some cats, however, lose their appetite and stop eating. Often they will have larger formed stools, yet some will have diarrhea. These contradictions are confusing but it is typical of these complicated endocrine disorders that there can be a variety of manifestations.

The most common signs are excessive appetite, hyperactivity, fast and more forceful heart rate (sometimes visible at the chest), excessive thirst (with subsequent increased urine output), voluminous stools or diarrhea, panting, and fever.

It is not unusual for the thyroid gland to swell up or develop bumps on it. Some veterinarians will conclude that these are malignant tumors, but they are almost never so, rather just from the overactivity of the gland.

PREVENTION

Avoid excessive vaccinations (see Chapter 16, on vaccinations), provide wholesome foods, and especially avoid feeding any fish to cats because of the high mercury content.

TREATMENT

The conventional treatment plan is to basically block the thyroid function. This is done in one of three ways: use of a drug to stop thyroid activity; use of (injectable) radioactive iodine to destroy the thyroid tissues; surgical removal of the thyroid gland.

While these measures will eliminate symptoms, there can be serious side effects, with the further disadvantage that they in no way cure the underlying problem. The thyroid is acting the way it is because the immune system is not right. Removing the thyroid does not address that and often other symptoms, part of the disease, continue on after the conventional treatment.

I have treated these cases with considerable success using nutrition and homeopathy alone. Though it can take many months to restore health, it is possible to do so with the added advantage that the overall health is much better than before. I always advise my clients to try this approach first. Once the thyroid glands have been destroyed or removed, you can't go back and expect to restore their function with other methods.

This again is one of the more complex conditions that requires the skill of an experienced homeopathic veterinarian.

Homeopathic—*Iodium 30c*: Like the dogs, these cats have really big appetites but even so continue to lose weight. They can become very thin, even though eating often and large quantities of food. They tend to be restless, thin, jumpy. It's not unusual that this condition is coupled with a kidney problem or chronic diarrhea. Use Homeopathic Schedule 4.

Homeopathic—*Lycopodium 30c*: These cats refuse to eat much food, or are quickly satisfied. They may have a tendency to bladder trouble, especially the formation of bladder stones or sand. They are weak in the morning, are thin and dry—hair sticking up—and want to be warm. Use Homeopathic Schedule 4.

Homeopathic—*Phosphorus 30c*: Before the illness has come on, these cats tend to be thin and nervous. As they become ill, they become more laid back, sleeping, not showing much interest. There is a tendency to vomiting. It is not unusual for them to become very jumpy, more frightened by things. Sometimes they lose their hearing. Use Homeopathic Schedule 4.

TICKS

See Skin Parasites.

TOXOPLASMOSIS

This disease deserves to be discussed in some detail, not so much because of its importance to cats (which usually recover from it without treatment, very often without any symptoms), but because of its importance to unborn children. If a woman is infected for the first time during pregnancy, the fetus may be born prematurely; born with serious damage to the brain, eyes, or other parts of the body; or stillborn.

Before we consider this disease further, first let's put things in perspective. The toxoplasma protozoa are found in almost all species of mammals and birds in the world. Their presence ranges from 20 to 80 percent

of all domestic animals, depending on geographical area. In the United States, about 50 percent of the human population is also exposed. But, despite the widespread occurrence of this little parasite, few infected individuals actually get sick from it. People who do get clinically ill are those whose immune systems have been suppressed as a response to drugs used with organ grafts, to cancer chemotherapy, or to x-ray therapy. People who have an immunosuppressive disease like AIDS may also become clinically ill with toxoplasmosis.

Cats are unique in that they are natural hosts for the parasite—toxoplasmosis grows better in cats than in any other animal. Those who do show symptoms will have mucus- or blood-tinged diarrhea, fever, hepatitis (liver inflammation), or pneumonia (difficult breathing). They usually get over it on their own, developing a strong immunity that protects against further infection.

Commonly, both cat and human can acquire the parasite and have no symptoms whatsoever. Here is where the danger lies: About 1 to 3 weeks after infection, the cat will often start passing oocysts, egglike structures that can infect other individuals after a day or so of further development in the warm feces or soil. The cat passes these oocysts until it develops immunity—in about 2 weeks. (If its immune system is depressed with cortisone-like drugs, however, the process can start up again.) These eggs can then be picked up by a pregnant woman who has not already had a chance to develop her own immunity. Thus, the disease spreads to the fetus, where it can cause the serious problems already mentioned.

It is thought that the risks for a pregnant woman are cleaning the litter box (cat exposure) and preparing meat in the kitchen (this is not related to cats; rather, the organism is often found in meat).

This information is not meant to scare you. Almost everyone, women included, who comes in contact with toxo does not become ill and develops an immunity to it. For a woman who has become immune, there is then no risk of infection during pregnancy. Your doctor can perform a serum test to find out if you're in this group. If you are not sure about it, just be careful about the litter box especially (isn't that the husband's job anyway?).

I have never had a case of toxoplasmosis in a cat in my practice so have no experience treating it, but if I did see one I would treat according to the symptoms that cat showed, so you could go to the section of this Quick Reference guide that discusses the symptoms you see (for example, Diarrhea and Dysentery) and follow those instructions.

UPPER RESPIRATORY INFECTIONS (COLDS)

The upper respiratory tract, which includes the nose, throat, larynx (voice box), and trachea (windpipe), is one of the favorite highways for germs traveling inside the body. Many microorganisms and viruses dry out and masquerade as dust. Others are embedded in dried secretions and scabs, which break into small particles and get stirred up into inhaled air.

In animals, these coldlike illnesses often start and remain in the upper respiratory tract, causing such symptoms as a runny nose or eyes, sneezing, a sore throat, coughing, and, sometimes, inflammation of the mouth. These infections resemble the human cold in many ways but have some unique aspects for pets.

The three most common upper respiratory diseases found in companion animals are canine infectious tracheobronchitis (often called "kennel cough"), feline viral rhinotracheitis (FVR—a viral attack on the cat's eyes and upper respiratory tract), and feline calicivirus (similar to FVR, but generally less involved with the eyes and nose). (Distemper is covered as a separate entry in this Quick Reference guide.)

KENNEL COUGH

Kennel cough, or canine respiratory disease complex, or canine infectious tracheobronchitis, is thought to be caused by a variety of viruses, sometimes complicated by bacterial infection as well. It's common where many stressed dogs, especially young ones, are in close contact. It crops up in boarding kennels, animal shelters, grooming establishments, veterinary hospitals, dog shows, and pet shops.

Symptoms, which usually appear about 8 to 10 days after exposure, are typically a dry, hacking, awful-sounding cough that ends with gagging or retching, and perhaps a clear, watery discharge from the eyes and nose or a partial loss of appetite. Though it sounds awful, it's not a serious condition. A minimal number of dogs may have complications because of their weak immune systems.

TREATMENT

I do not use antibiotics in most cases, because the disease is viral. Often cough suppressants are used, but they do not help much and can have unpleasant side effects. The most effective thing to do is to place the affected dog in a steam-filled room (such as a bathroom with a tub full of hot water or after running a hot shower) or in a room with a cool-mist vaporizer. Veterinarians recognize this as a disease that just has to "run its course" (2 or 3 weeks) before recovery. If possible, isolate your dog, since some of these viruses may also affect cats and people.

My experience has been that the whole episode can be cut much shorter by these treatments.

A liquid fast can be useful when the symptoms first appear and should be continued for 3 days. Follow the directions for fasting in Chapter 18, taking care to reintroduce solid foods carefully and slowly.

Vitamins help in several ways. *Vitamin C* is a good antiviral agent. Depending on his size, you can give your dog 500 to 1,000 milligrams three times a day. Vitamin E stimulates the immune response. Give 50 to 100 IU of fresh d-alpha tocopherol from a capsule three times a day. Puncture the capsule and squeeze the oil right into the dog's mouth. Taper off frequency at recovery. *Vitamin A* also boosts immunity, helps counteract stress, and strengthens the mucous membranes of the respiratory tract. A gelatin capsule that contains 10,000 IU of vitamin A can be punctured and two or three drops of the contents given three times a day.

All of these can be added to food if that is most convenient.

An herbal cough treatment is often helpful.

Herbal—*Peppermint (Mentha piperita)*: This is best suited for the dog with a hoarse "voice" and with coughing made worse by barking. Touching his throat is irritating and may bring on the cough. Use Herbal Schedule 1.

Herbal—*Mullein (Verbascum thapsus)*: Especially indicated when the cough is deep and hoarse and worse at night. It's also useful when the throat seems sore to the touch or there is trouble swallowing. Use Herbal Schedule 1.

A couple of homeopathic remedies useful for this are:

Homeopathic—*Lachesis 30c*: When the cough is brought on by touching the throat or by the pressure of a leash. Use Homeopathic Schedule 2.

Homeopathic—*Pulsatilla 30c*: Dog wants attention, to be held, seeks out cool areas, no desire to drink water. Use Homeopathic Schedule 2.

After recovery, your dog should be relatively immune for some time, perhaps a year or two. However, a different but similar virus could re-create the "same" condition. Remember, stress seems to be the necessary factor to allow the virus to get established.

FELINE VIRAL RHINOTRACHEITIS (FVR)

This viral disease primarily affects the eyes and upper respiratory tract of cats. Symptoms include sneezing attacks, coughing, drooling of thick saliva, fever, and a watery discharge from the eyes. The condition ranges from mild and barely noticeable to severe and persistent. In the latter, the nose becomes plugged up with a thick discharge, ulcers form on the eye surface (cornea), and the eyelids stick together with heavy discharges. The cat becomes thoroughly miserable, refusing to eat and unable to care for itself.

There is no allopathic treatment that shortens the duration of the disease, but usually antibiotics, fluid therapy, forced feeding, eye ointments, and other measures are used to provide the best possible support for the ailing body. These cats are so out of sorts, however, that they often resist handling and treatments. It can be a real challenge to provide adequate care.

TREATMENT

If you catch the condition early, this regimen may avert the more serious stage: Give no solid food the first 2 to 3 days, or until the temperature is back to normal (less than 101.5°F). The cat usually will not eat anyway. Instead, provide liquids as described in the section on fasting in Chapter 18.

It is more difficult to give nutritional supplements to sick cats that are not eating, but if you can do it, prepare some vitamin C by dissolving ⅛ teaspoon of sodium ascorbate powder (which has less taste than the usual vitamin C) in a small amount of pure water and give it three times a day.

Homeopathic—*Aconitum napellus 30c*: This remedy corresponds to the early stages of illness, which are marked by fever and a general sense of not feeling well. If given when these symptoms first appear, it may avert any further development of the illness. Use Homeopathic Schedule 2.

If the cold condition is already established, one of these remedies may help.

Homeopathic—*Nux vomica 30c*: A remedy commonly suited to this condition, *Nux vomica* is a good choice for the cat that is grouchy and averse to being held or touched. Often it will retire to a quiet room so as not to be disturbed. Use Homeopathic Schedule 2.

Homeopathic—*Natrum muriaticum 6c*: This remedy is most helpful when the cold starts with much sneezing. As it develops, there may be thirstiness and a white discharge from the nose. Use Homeopathic Schedule 1.

Homeopathic—*Pulsatilla 30c*: Cats needing this medicine are sleepy, sluggish, and have a thick discharge from the nose or eyes. Often the discharge is yellow or greenish in color. Such a cat may want to be held or comforted. Use Homeopathic Schedule 2.

Generally, at this stage it helps to clean the eyes and nose with a saline solution, which is similar to natural tears. Stir ¼ teaspoon of sea salt into 1 cup of pure water (without chlorine). Warm this to body temperature. Using a cotton ball, drip several drops into each nostril to stimulate sneezing and flushing of the nose. Also put some into each eye and carefully clean the discharge away with a tissue.

If the condition is very advanced when you start treatment, it will take more attention on your part.

Clean the eyes and nose with a warm saline solution (as described above). If necessary, saturate a cloth with the solution and hold it against the nostrils briefly to soften and loosen the dried nasal discharge. Then carefully remove the discharge and continue with the saline nose flush. Put a drop of almond oil in each eye; apply some to the nose, too (twice a day).

When cats get very sick like this, they often become dehydrated, and giving some fluid can be quite helpful. This can be done by injection (at the veterinarian's, or on a house call) or you can give fluid with a syringe or dropper into the mouth (this is where patience comes in). You can use pure water or the same fluid that is injected under the skin (if you have it).

Useful treatments are:

Homeopathic—*Pulsatilla 6c*: This is useful for the cat with thick greenish or yellow discharge, an obstructed nose, loss of appetite, bad breath, and a sleepy, sluggish demeanor. Often these cats will be attacked by other cats in the family when they are ill. Somehow the other cats sense a weakness. Use Homeopathic Schedule 6(c).

Homeopathic—*Silicea 30c*: This remedy often follows Pulsatilla to complete a treatment. These cats will be chilly (seeking out warm places) and lose their appetites (but may drink more water than usual). The eyes will be very inflamed, the lids stuck together with discharge and even ulcers of the cornea (surface of the eye). Use Homeopathic Schedule 2.

Homeopathic—*Thuja occidentalis 30c*: This remedy is sometimes needed if there is no response to other treatments or if the cold symptoms have come on within 3 to 4 weeks after receiving a vaccination. The nasal discharge can look very much like that described for Pulsatilla (above). Use Homeopathic Schedule 3.

Homeopathic—*Sulphur 30c*: If nothing else has helped, give this remedy. Use Homeopathic Schedule 3.

Herbal—*Goldenseal (Hydrastis canadensis)*: This herb is very helpful if the nasal discharge (or discharge at the back of the throat) is very yellow and stringy. There may also be considerable loss of weight, even if the cat is still eating sufficiently. Use Herbal Schedule 2.

Once the cat is eating, encourage a variety of fresh and raw foods, as we have advised in this book. A very helpful nutrient that is generally liked by cats is nutritional or brewer's yeast, which can be sprinkled on the food to encourage eating.

FELINE CALICIVIRUS (FCV)

Sometimes FCV cannot be distinguished from FVR (above), but generally the nose and the eyes are not as involved. Typical signs include pneumonia and ulcers of the tongue, the roof of the mouth, and the end of the nose (above the lip). This condition is very difficult to treat because the mouth is so sore that the cat resists having anything put in it. You may need to wrap the cat up in a towel during treatment to keep from getting scratched.

TREATMENT

Use the same early treatment as described above for FVR. In practical terms, at this stage you may not really know which of these viruses your cat has, so don't worry about making any distinction; the treatments we are discussing are suitable for either disease.

If it is clear from the presence of the pneumonia or ulcers that you are dealing with feline calicivirus, a couple of other remedies may be more suitable for this problem.

Homeopathic—*Phosphorus 30c*: Use this remedy if there is pneumonia (fever, rapid breathing, gasping, perhaps coughing). It's especially indicated if your cat desires cold water and vomits about 15 minutes after drinking or, with the pneumonia, prefers to lie on her right side. Use Homeopathic Schedule 2.

Homeopathic—*Nitricum acidum 30c*: This remedy is indicated if the focus of the illness is ulcers in the mouth. The mouth odor is very bad, the saliva blood-tinged, and the tongue red and "clean" looking (instead of heavily coated). These cats usually become very cranky and are difficult to handle or medicate. Use Homeopathic Schedule 3.

Homeopathic—*Mercurius vivus or Mercurius solubilis 30c*: Cats needing this medicine are very similar to those described above for *Nitricum acidum*. The difference is that they are not so irritable, they produce more saliva, and their tongues are coated with a yellow film and are often swollen, so that you can see indentations of the teeth on the edges. Use Homeopathic Schedule 3.

Your cat is recovering from this illness once her appetite returns and she is eating well. This is the major turning point.

UREMIA

See Kidney Failure.

VACCINATIONS

The prevention of communicable diseases by administering "weakened" forms of the germs that cause them is a very popular and strongly supported method of disease prevention. If a "live" vaccine is injected into the body, the organism will grow in the tissues and produce a sort of mini-disease that stimulates the immune response. This response is intended to protect the body against the real thing for a variable period of time—months or years. Sounds wonderful, doesn't it?

I must point out, however, that there are some very significant problems with vaccinations that should be understood by anyone interested in a holistic health approach. Vaccines are not always effective, and they may cause long-lasting health disturbances.

This question about vaccine use has become controversial and deserves some explanation, so in this edition we have devoted a chapter to it. See Chapter 16, Vaccines: Friend or Foe?

VOMITING

Vomiting is one of those symptoms of underlying illness that rarely occurs by itself. Most often it is associated with an upset stomach, but it also can occur in response to poisoning, failed kidneys, side effects of drugs, pain or inflammation in some other area (like the peritoneum, pancreas, or brain), surgery, severe constipation, and many other conditions. Therefore, it's always necessary to look beyond the vomiting to understand what the underlying situation is and to treat that.

Occasional vomiting is not unusual for either dogs or cats, though the latter do it more easily, so it does not always signal a serious problem. However, any time there is *prolonged* vomiting, seek the help of your veterinarian to determine the underlying cause. If not controlled, prolonged vomiting can lead to severe dehydration and the loss of certain vital salts, particularly sodium chloride and potassium chloride.

TREATMENT

If nothing else seems to be wrong, here is a remedy that often resolves vomiting.

Homeopathic—*Ipecac 6c*: Useful for persistent nausea and constant vomiting where much saliva is generated because of the nausea. Use Homeopathic Schedule 1.

Homeopathic—*Nux vomica 6c*: Indicated when the vomiting has come on after eating a different food, overeating, or having raided a garbage pail. Use Homeopathic Schedule 1.

In addition, withhold all food and water during the vomiting period, allowing the animal to lick ice cubes occasionally. To replace fluids and salts (if there is dehydration), give a small enema every couple of hours as described in Chapter 18. To each pint of enema water, add ¼ teaspoon of sea salt (or table salt as a second choice) and ¼ teaspoon potassium chloride (sold as a salt substitute in many markets). Given as an enema, this fluid will be retained and absorbed in a dehydrated animal.

WARTS

Dogs and older animals are the pets most likely to develop troublesome warts, which sometimes itch and bleed. Quite often, these warts (and similar growths) are an expression of vaccinosis (see Chapter 16). Such animals may also tend to develop more serious types of growths in the future if the problem is not corrected at this point.

There is no simple formula for treating warts, as it is most necessary to address the underlying tendency with individualized treatment (called "constitutional prescribing" in homeopathy). Here are, however, a few remedies that may be quite helpful.

Homeopathic—*Thuja occidentalis 30c*: This is often an effective remedy for the tendency toward wart formation. Give Thuja first, using Schedule 4. Let the stimulus of this medicine act for a month (though you may also be doing the local treatment described below). If the warts are not gone (or diminishing), then use one of the next two remedies.

Homeopathic—*Causticum 30c*: This remedy is indicated for warts that tend to bleed easily. Use Homeopathic Schedule 4.

Homeopathic—*Silicea 30c*: Useful when the wart is very large, especially if it occurs over the site of a prior vaccination. Use Homeopathic Schedule 4.

During the time that these remedies are being used, you may do one of these local skin treatments.

Nutrition—*Vitamin E*: Regular application of vitamin E from a punctured capsule can sometimes greatly reduce the size of a wart. It must be continued for several weeks to be effective.

Herbal—*Castor oil*: This oil is quite helpful when applied directly to warts and growths to soften them and to reduce irritation. Apply it when the wart is itchy or in some way troublesome. Castor oil can be obtained at most pharmacies.

WEIGHT PROBLEMS

Who would have thought that problems with weight would be such a common concern? Just as there is an epidemic of obesity in people and children especially, dogs and cats can have this problem as well.

OBESITY

I would think that one important factor is the lifestyle of not being active and yet eating a lot of meat and fat. In nature, the wolf-type animal eats a diet high in fat, worked off by its vigorous lifestyle. The poor domestic dog, getting maybe one walk on a leash, hardly matches that. I think it is like the couch potato, TV remote in hand, feasting on the diet the professional athlete would be eating.

Weight problems can also be an outcome of almost uncontrollable hunger that is very difficult to manage. I have seen this in quite a few dogs that have allergies and various skin diseases, so assume that the hunger is from this underlying disorder.

The biggest factor I suspect is the use of growth hormones to raise livestock. Those who produce cattle, sheep, pigs, and other animals want them to grow as quickly as possible and get very heavy so that they make more money when they sell them for slaughter. Accordingly, it is standard practice to use hormones, like the ones athletes use illegally to promote muscle, to make these animals become unnaturally large. There are six anabolic steroids used with beef cattle, for example, and measurements of the organs and meats from these animals show that the hormones are in meat and therefore in the food eaten. Would it be surprising that eating hormones that make you gain weight would make you gain weight?

Once the animal is overweight, it can complicate other problems. If she has a joint problem, like hip dysplasia or a cruciate ligament tear in the knee, the extra weight is only going to exacerbate the discomfort and work the joint harder.

Here are some suggestions.

Look at the dog and cat recipe charts in Chapter 6, Recipes for Today, for the code W in the second row. These are the ones that will most help with weight reduction. They emphasize grains, legumes, and vegetables as the nutrient sources. I have often heard the statement that eating carbohydrates (which is usually translated into meaning grains) is responsible for weight gain, but I have never seen this in my patients. After all, fat, which is high in animal products, has 2½ times the calories of grains, so obviously it is more of a contributor.

Use organic or hormone-free meats if you are including meat in the feeding plan.

Increase activity levels. Take your dog for daily walks and runs. Encourage your cat to play. Increased activity raises the metabolic rate and burns calories faster. (See Chapters 11 and 12.)

If what is suggested here is not sufficient, there may be a health imbalance that needs correction as well. One good indicator in dogs is that they will scavenge on walks—eating just about anything they can find, like gum on sidewalks or thrown-away food scraps. It can be that the underlying problem is the thyroid not working right, called hypothyroidism (see Thyroid Disorders).

Homeopathic—_Calcarea carbonica 30c_: This is one of the important remedies for treating obesity, especially if due to a hormonal imbalance. Might be worth a try, but if not sufficient, then start working with a holistic veterinarian to figure it out. Use Homeopathic Schedule 4.

UNDERWEIGHT

If your animal has the opposite problem and is underweight, obviously a different approach is needed. If the weight loss is sudden, it may be from an infection or some other problem that needs to be taken care of first. Have your veterinarian check out this possibility. It is uncommon for dogs and cats to be really thin unless there is something not right about their appetite or health condition.

As we have discussed earlier, this might be an effect of accumulated toxins in the body, so using food lower on the food chain can gradually help with that (see Chapters 2 and 3).

This might help if there is no other problem detected.

Herbal—*Alfalfa (Medicago sativa)*: Use Herbal Schedule 3. Continue treatment until the desired effect is achieved—increased hunger and weight gain.

Another treatment suitable for older, run-down animals is:

Homeopathic—*Calcarea phosphorica 6c*: Especially good where there apparently is poor digestion or poor utilization of nutrients, as evidenced by lack of weight gain in spite of good nutrition and adequate appetite. Use Homeopathic Schedule 6(a).

Homeopathic—*Oleum Jecoris Aselli 6c*: This remedy, made from cod liver oil, is amazingly effective in correcting emaciation and weakness. This state may have no obvious cause or may be from poor nutrition over a time. Give a trial of one treatment a day for 2 weeks. If you see a noticeable improvement you can continue it longer (but not indefinitely).

WEST NILE VIRUS

This disease is transmitted by mosquitoes and primarily affects people and horses. In human beings, only about 1 in 5 become ill with mild symptoms, much like the flu. Occasionally some people (less than 1 percent bitten by infected mosquitoes) develop encephalitis (inflammation of the brain) with severe symptoms, convulsions, even death. It is known that other animals can be infected, most noticeably horses, which can also become seriously ill on occasion. There is no evidence that the virus is passed from one person to another or from horses to people. It seems to require the bite of an infected mosquito.

What about dogs and cats? Research has shown that they can become infected, but are unlikely to have symptoms, so it appears to be basically a "nondisease" in these animals. A few cats that were deliberately infected with the virus showed some mild symptoms—slight decrease in appetite, lethargy (they were more quiet or sleepy), and some fever for a time—but likely not anything that would be noticed by most people.

If you want to prevent exposure to the virus for your pets, use a mosquito repellent if they go outside when mosquitoes are likely to be out. There are some safe herbal repellents you can use.

WORMS

Worms are internal parasites that live in the intestines of animals. They are commonly found in most animals (especially when the animals are young) and are usually not a serious problem.

It gives some perspective to realize that intestinal worms are pretty much the norm under natural conditions. There are a lot of organisms that share life with us. For example, the average human being has 2 to 4 pounds of microorganisms living in or on him, the actual number being greater than the number of cells in the body. I am saying this not to suggest that everyone is sick but to give a better idea of how things are. These organisms living with us, and with all the animals, don't cause illness and actually (as in the intestines) do some real good for us. Did you know that the reason that cows can eat grass is because they have these huge stomachs that are big fermentation vats where bacteria and fungi break down the grass into nutrients? The cows then live off the bacteria and would not survive without them.

In nature, worms can be present in most animals in very low numbers, and it is their very presence that induces the body to produce an immunity that keeps them from increasing in number. It is the little worms living in the intestines, having a little snack and causing no problems, that actually protect the animal from acquiring more of them. This kind of immunity *depends on the presence of the worms* and if they are eliminated, that immunity is lost and the animal can pick up worms again.

Having said this, I realize that most people still just don't want worms around, so let's explore this a little more.

ROUNDWORMS

Very young animals can get roundworms before birth from the mother. If the mother is not healthy, these worms take advantage of the situation and migrate in larger numbers than usual. Puppies or kittens born from these weak mothers can be heavily parasitized and never thrive. However, this is not the most common outcome. Usually it is not a serious problem, and as the puppy or kitten develops the immunity mentioned above, the worms gradually decrease. It is usual that the mature (several-months-old) animal doesn't appear to have any worms when the stool is checked, and this has happened on its own, without treatment.

As there are usually no symptoms of worm infestation, the problem is often picked up on by your veterinarian when checking a stool sample and looking for worm eggs. If you get this diagnosis, it might be helpful to ask if the infestation is light or heavy. It will give you a better idea of how significant this is.

If the infestation is heavy, you can usually spot outer signs such as an enlarged belly, poor weight gain, and, perhaps, diarrhea or vomiting. Sometimes whole worms are actually vomited or passed with the feces. They resemble white spaghetti, are several inches long, and will often wiggle when first voided. Usually, only young animals a few weeks to a few months of age will vomit roundworms.

Cats, once they get over their initial worms, become immune for life and are never again reinfested. In both dogs and cats, a few of the original worms may persist in a dormant (sort of sleeping) state until pregnancy occurs (thus spreading to the next generation), but they do not cause any problem and are not detectable in stool tests.

One important factor in the continued resistance of mature animals to roundworms is that they receive sufficient vitamin A. Long-term deficiency of vitamin A will allow worms to reinfest and grow in otherwise resistant animals.

TREATMENT OF ROUNDWORMS

What if you do need to treat young animals? I suggest the following measures (use all of them, if possible).

Homeopathic—*Cina 3c*: Use Homeopathic Schedule 6(c). Have the stool checked again in a microscopic evaluation at a lab to make sure the worms are gone.

Nutrition—Add ½ to 2 teaspoons (depending on the animal's size) of *wheat* or *oat bran* to the daily fare. This roughage will help to carry out the worms. Also, feed the same quantity of one of these vegetables—grated raw carrots, turnips, or beets.

Herbal—*Garlic (Allium sativum)*: Depending on the pet's size, mix ¼ to 1 clove of fresh, chopped, or grated garlic into the daily ration (see Chapter 11 for discussion on the controversy of using garlic in dogs and cats).

Mineral—*Diatomaceous earth* (skeletal remains of diatoms, very small sea creatures): Can be purchased at natural food stores and some pet stores. This substance, which is sometimes used for the control of fleas, is also effective against roundworms. The action is the same— the shell remnants of the diatoms are irritating to the outsides of worms (as they are to the fleas) and cause them to loosen their hold and be flushed out. Add ¼ to 1 teaspoon of natural diatomaceous earth to each meal. Don't use the kind made for swimming pool filters—just the natural, unrefined product available (usually) through herbal or garden suppliers.

Alternatively, there are several herbal wormers available now that are quite useful in treatment. If you purchase one at a health food store, follow the directions on the label.

I suggest that you give this nontoxic treatment a 3-week trial and then check again for worms. If the worms are still there in significant numbers, then it is best for your pet to get the conventional drug treatment. If a young animal has gone through this program, even if the program was not completely effective, I find that it seems to withstand the drug treatment better.

TAPEWORMS

Tapeworms can be acquired from swallowing fleas or eating gophers (usually). Pets don't get tapeworms directly from the little segments passed out in the stool. The segments, which contain the tapeworm eggs, have to go through another animal first to develop into the infective state that ends up in the muscle of that animal. It is the eating of this other animal (like a gopher) that transfers the infestation. Once the young tapeworm gets into your dog or cat, it grows in the small intestine. Each worm has a "head" that stays attached to the intestine, as well as dozens of egg-filled segments that break off and pass out with the feces when ripe. These passed segments look like cream-colored maggots, about ¼ to ½ inch long, that are visible in the fresh stool or around the anus. They do not really crawl, but move by forming a sort of "point" on one end. After drying out, they look a lot like a piece of white rice stuck to a hair near the anus.

Tapeworms are not usually a problem in young animals. They're more likely to appear after the animal is old enough to go hunting.

Though chemical worming treatment can kill the worm, sometimes it just causes the sudden loss of most of the segments, leaving the head still attached. Unfortunately, the head that remains behind soon grows a new body that begins passing segments again.

Tapeworm parasites do not usually cause any detectable health problems and are not serious (though they are disgusting to see). There's no reason to panic, thinking they must be eradicated immediately. If you follow the natural health program in this book, you will find that parasite problems lessen as your pet's general health improves. As your animal detoxifies and builds up strength, many parasites will be sloughed off naturally.

TREATMENT OF TAPEWORMS

The idea in treating tapeworms is to use substances that annoy or irritate the worms over a period of time. Eventually, the worms will give up and loosen their hold, passing on out.

Herbal—*Pumpkin seeds (Cucurbita pepo)*: These seeds are a wonderfully safe treatment against tapeworms. Obtain the whole, raw seeds and keep them in a sealed container at room temperature. Grind them to a fine meal and give them to your pet to consume immediately. If, for some reason, you must grind the seeds ahead of time, store the ground seeds in a sealed container in your freezer. Take out the needed portion quickly each day and reseal the container before much moisture enters it. It's best, however, to grind the seeds fresh before use. An electric seed grinder (sold in health food stores) or a food processor can do the job. Add ¼ to 1 teaspoon (depending on the size of your animal) to each meal.

Nutritional—*Wheat germ oil*: Buy a very good-quality wheat germ oil at a health food store, and you have an excellent natural tapeworm discourager as well as a good adjunct to other treatments. Add ¼ to 1 teaspoon, depending on the animal's size, to each meal. Feed a small amount of food so the enzymes work better.

Nutritional—*Vegetable enzymes*: The enzymes of many plant foods, especially those from figs and papaya, eat away at the outer coating of the worm. Dried figs can be chopped or ground and added to food (more accepted by dogs than cats). Use ¼ to 1 teaspoon, depending on your animal's size, at each meal. Feed a small amount of food so the enzymes work better.

Nutritional—*Papaya* is an excellent enzyme source, but it's not readily available everywhere. You can use enzyme supplements that contain papain (the papaya enzyme) and other digestive enzymes. Follow the instructions on the label.

Homeopathic—*Filix mas 3c*: A time-honored herb used against tapeworms, this remedy can be given as one tablet three times a day for 2 to 3 weeks, less time if the segments go away sooner. (The remedy discussed under roundworm treatment, *Cina 3c*, can also be used if *Filix mas* is not available.)

Fasting once a week, allowing just a vegetable broth for its enzyme content, is an excellent practice generally. It's especially useful because it weakens the worms and makes them more vulnerable to the treatments being used. Since the worms get their food from what the animal eats, they don't get to eat either.

If your pet has a stubborn problem in getting rid of any type of intestinal worm, also try an occasional dose of castor oil. Giving this after a day of fasting will flush out all the weakened worms. Use ½ teaspoon for puppies less than 3 months old and for all young cats; 1 teaspoon for puppies 3 to 6 months old and adult cats; 1½ tablespoons for medium-size dogs, and 2 tablespoons for large dogs.

WHIPWORMS

Whipworms are fairly common in dogs, less so in cats. They do not usually cause any noticeable symptoms and are not considered a threat to human health. They often lie dormant for long periods. If there are symptoms—usually persistent, watery diarrhea—I believe it means something is wrong with the animal's immune system.

I have rarely come across this as an issue in my practice. Maybe I was just lucky, but my impression is that it is not much of a problem. I would even go so far as to say that if your animal seems rather ill and these worms are blamed for it, you might look to see if there is anything else going on.

TREATMENT OF WHIPWORMS

As I mentioned, I don't have much experience with this condition, but I assume that the treatment given above for roundworms would work here as well.

HOOKWORMS

Hookworms are generally less common than tapeworms and roundworms in this country, but they are still significant and are the most serious of those worm parasites we are considering. They are more of a problem in the southern parts of the United States and in areas where crowded and unsanitary conditions prevail. They get in through the skin, from being swallowed, even in mother's milk sometimes. They can cause damage as they are bloodsuckers as compared to the other worms we have discussed that are just sharing the food in the intestines. Some species can also infect people, so if this is what you are dealing with you should try to eliminate them.

In young animals with severe infestation, the loss of blood into the intestine causes the stool to look black and tarlike. It may also become fluid and foul smelling. The gums will become pale, reflecting the developing anemia, and the youngster will appear weak and thin.

TREATMENT OF HOOKWORMS

It is probably best to have your veterinarian treat this since it is a health risk. The treatments given for roundworm might work, but I have not much experience using them in this condition myself. They would certainly be better than nothing if you have no other choice.

Note: Your parasitized animal can be a source of health problems for other animals or for children. Especially with roundworms and hookworms, people can become exposed by contact with contaminated soil. Though these parasites do not really grow well in people and do not usually cause serious problems, they can be troublesome and annoying (primarily causing skin irritation as the worms try to travel to their preferred destinations in the body). Until the problem is cleared up, it makes sense to take special care to prevent contamination of the environment. Collect all fecal material to bury (deeply) in one place, flush down the toilet, or package carefully to dispose of through your sanitary service.

HERE'S TO HEALTH

We have covered a lot of ground. I tried to address the main problems that come up. If we were to look at every possible thing that could happen, this book would be too heavy to lift. Hopefully, reading through some of these recommendations will give you an idea of the approach I am recommending to you—an approach that can be used with any health problem. We can summarize this by saying: Try to make very good nutrition the foundation of establishing health and then using some excellent tools, as described here, to build on that foundation. Another way to put this is that I have learned, over my years of clinical work, to work with the body and spirit of the animal with respect and confidence. Good health is our default, what happens when we don't interfere with it. Good health to you and your animal companions. May you be filled with light and love.

HANDLING EMERGENCIES AND GIVING FIRST AID

Important: Read this first! The care you give an animal in the first few minutes of an emergency can make the difference between life and death. The first-aid remedies I suggest definitely work and will be tremendously helpful in that time between the beginning of the emergency and arrival at your veterinarian's office. But they are meant as temporary lifesaving procedures to use while you contact the doctor and ready transportation. Do not use these methods as a way of delaying needed professional help. Instructions for more prolonged treatment apply only if you cannot reach medical care.

For this information to serve you, plan ahead and have supplies on hand in a convenient place. An emergency is not the time to begin assembling these tools and remedies or to start reading this chapter. The information that follows is provided in brief outline form, alphabetically, for ready reference when needed. But please study all the categories ahead of time so you can find the right heading in a hurry during a time of crisis.

Here is a list of supplies you should have on hand in order to make full use of my suggestions. Dr. Bach's stress-relieving rescue formula is available at natural food stores, and the other supplies are found in drugstores. Homeopathic remedies are available in natural food stores and from homeopathic pharmacies.

HOMEOPATHIC REMEDIES

From a homeopathic pharmacy, you can order 2 drams of the remedy as #10 pellets (little tiny ones, like grains of sand, which are easiest to give), approximately 10 or so as a dose given from the cap of the vial.

- *Aconitum 30c*
- *Arnica 30c*
- *Arsenicum album 30c*
- *Belladonna 30c*
- *Calendula 30c*
- *Calendula* tincture—1-ounce dropper bottle
- *Calendula* ointment—can be purchased from homeopathic pharmacies
- *Carbo vegetabilis 30c*
- *Glonoine 30c*
- *Hypericum 30c*
- *Ledum 30c*
- *Nux vomica 30c*
- *Phosphorus 30c*
- *Ruta 30c*
- *Symphytum 30c*
- *Urtica urens* tincture—1-ounce dropper bottle

OTHER REMEDIES

- Activated charcoal granules
- Ammonia water
- Fresh warm coffee (caffeinated)
- Raw onion
- Dr. Bach's stress-relieving rescue formula. Prepare a solution from a purchased small stock bottle in this manner: Add four drops of stock to a 1-ounce dropper bottle filled a third of the way with brandy, as a preservative. Add enough spring water to fill the bottle and shake well. Make this diluted solution in advance and use it

as recommended for treatment. It will keep for at least a year if kept out of the sun and away from heat.

MATERIALS

- Blankets, two—thick and strong
- Adhesive tape—1-inch-wide roll
- Elastic bandage—3 inches wide
- Enema bag
- Gauze pads—one package
- Natural soap—like Dr. Bronner's natural soap
- Plastic bowl—for preparing dilutions
- Sea salt—for making saline solution (¼ teaspoon per cup of water)
- Water—for dilution (spring or distilled water is best; tap water is okay)
- Empty plastic syringe—for administering remedies
- Empty dropper bottle(s)—for preparing remedies

WHAT TO DO IN AN EMERGENCY

BREATHING STOPPED

Follow these steps to apply this *Artificial Respiration Technique.*

1. Open the mouth, pull out the tongue, check back into the throat to make sure no obstructions are present. Clear away mucus and blood if necessary. Replace the tongue.

2. Give one dose of *Carbo vegetabilis 30c.* Place a few pellets on the tongue. Drip

water on the tongue to dissolve the pellets.

3. Close the mouth and place your mouth over the nostrils. Exhale as you fill the animal's lungs, allowing it to exhale after. Do this six times a minute for dogs, 12 times a minute for cats. Inflate the chest until you can see it rise.

4. Administer Dr. Bach's *Rescue Formula*, starting after 5 minutes. Place two drops on the gums or tongue and continue every 5 minutes until breathing is restored, then every 30 minutes (if you can't reach help) for four treatments.

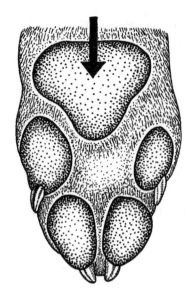

BREATHING AND HEART BOTH STOPPED

(Listen at chest.)

Follow these steps.

1. Use the Artificial Respiration Technique (above) including use of one dose of *Carbo vegetabilis 30c* (see "Breathing Stopped," above) and the External Heart Massage Technique (see "Heart Stopped," page 465), step 1, at the same time. This is easiest for two people.

2. Apply acupressure. Use the edge of your thumbnail or the pointed cap of a pen to put strong pressure over the center of the large pad of each rear foot. If there's no response at first, try reaching the same point by coming in from under the back edge of the pad. After a few seconds, release and apply

pressure to the point on the nose shown in the diagram. Alternate between acupressure and cardiopulmonary resuscitation. If two people are working, have each one apply one of the techniques continuously.

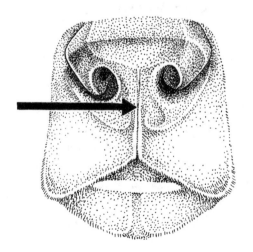

3. After 5 minutes, give one dose of *Arnica montana 30c.* Place a few pellets on the tongue.

4. After 5 more minutes, administer Dr. Bach's *Rescue Formula.* Place two drops on the gums or tongue and continue every 5 minutes until breathing is restored. Repeat every 30 minutes (if you can't reach help) for four treatments.

BURNS

(white skin or scorched hair)
Use one technique.

1. Apply *Urtica urens* tincture. Add six drops of the tincture to 1 ounce (2 full tablespoons) water. Saturate gauze with the solution and place over the burn. Do not remove the gauze, but keep it moistened by adding more of the solution. If necessary, hold in place with a bandage.

2. Give one dose of *Arsenicum album 30c.*

3. After 5 more minutes, administer Dr. Bach's *Rescue Formula.* Place two drops on the tongue every 30 minutes for a total of three treatments. Repeat every 4 hours until relief is evident.

CAR ACCIDENTS

(obvious injury; greasy or very dirty coat)
Follow these steps.

1. Move the animal to a safe place. If the animal is found on the road, without bending its spine or changing its position, slide it onto a board or taut blanket and transport it to a safer location. You may need to tie a strip of cloth or wrap a pressure bandage around the mouth temporarily (as a muzzle) or put a blanket over the animal's head, to keep it from biting someone.

2. Give a dose of *Arnica montana 30c.* Place a few pellets on the tongue every 15 minutes, for a total of three doses. Do this only if it is safe to do so. An injured animal will bite without restraint and can cause very serious injury. If it seems unsafe to administer a medicine, dissolve two pellets in some water and drip it onto the lips from a safe distance above. If you happen to have a syringe with a needle on it, you can squirt the diluted medicine, fairly accurately from a distance, between the lips and into the mouth.

3. Keep the animal warm and watch for shock (see "Shock" on page 468).

CARDIOPULMONARY RESUSCITATION

See "Breathing and Heart Both Stopped," opposite page.

CONVULSIONS

(stiffening or alternate rapid contraction/relaxation of muscles; thrashing about; frothing at the mouth)
Follow these steps.

1. Do not interfere with or try to restrain the animal during the

convulsion. It is too dangerous to you and does not help the animal.

2. If breathing stops after the convulsion, use artificial respiration (see "Breathing Stopped," page 461). If the heart stops too, use cardiopulmonary resuscitation (see "Breathing and Heart Both Stopped," page 462).

3. Give *Aconitum 30c*. If possible, put a few pellets on the tongue (see warning about being bitten in "Car Accidents").

4. If convulsions continue, after 5 minutes give *Belladonna 30c*.

5. After 5 more minutes, administer Dr. Bach's *Rescue Formula*, two drops every 15 minutes, if the animal is frightened or disoriented, up to three doses or until relief is evident.

6. Consider poisoning as a possible cause (see "Poisoning," page 467).

CUTS

(lacerations, tears)
Follow these steps.

1. Flush out the cut with clean water. Remove obvious debris like sticks, hair, and gravel.

2. Apply *Calendula* lotion. Add six drops *Calendula* tincture to 1 ounce (2 full tablespoons) water; saturate gauze pads and tape them in place. If this is irritating, flush with saline and bandage with dry pads.

3. Wash minor wounds that do not need

professional care with soap and water and dry carefully. Clip hair from the edges of the wound. Apply *Calendula* ointment twice a day until healed. Leave unbandaged if possible.

Also give one dose of *Calendula 30c*.

FRACTURES

(Leg bends at sharp angle; animal won't use leg.)
Follow these steps.

- If the lower leg is obviously broken, very carefully wrap a roll of clean newspaper or magazine around it and tape it to prevent unrolling. Do not try to set the leg yourself; just keep the lower end from swinging back and forth.

- If a wound is present at the fracture site, cover it with clean gauze before applying a temporary splint, as above.

- If the fracture is not apparent or is high up, do not attempt to splint. Let the animal assume the most comfortable posture. A padded box may be best for transporting small animals to the veterinarian. Walking on three legs may be best for a larger dog.

1. Give *Arnica 30c*. One dose is usually enough, but repeat again in 4 hours if there is still much pain.

2. Next day, give *Ruta 30c*, which will remove residual pain from having torn the membrane that covers the bones (or give after surgery to reduce pain).

3. Wait another 3 days and give *Symphytum 30c* to accelerate healing of the bones.

GUNSHOT WOUNDS

(Look for two holes opposite each other on the body, great pain and anxiety.)
Follow these steps.

1. Give *Arnica 30c*, a few pellets every 15 minutes, for a total of three doses.

2. Apply hand pressure with dry gauze over the wound, if necessary, until bleeding stops. Or temporarily use pressure over the opening (see "Pressure Bandage Technique" on page 466).

3. Give *Hypericum 30c* if there is no relief from the three doses of Arnica. Give a few pellets every 15 minutes for a total of three doses.

4. Continue treatment with *Arnica 30c* or *Hypericum 30c*, whichever was most useful. Give a dose every 4 hours, as long as it seems needed to control pain. Typically, three doses will do all the good that can be accomplished with this medicine.

5. If there is still apparent pain, give *Calendula 30c*, one dose.

HEART STOPPED

(No heartbeat felt or heard at chest.)
Follow these steps.

1. Apply this *External Heart Massage Technique.* Place the animal with its right side

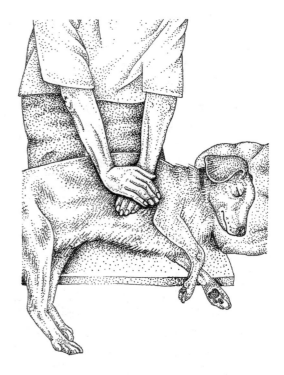

down on a firm surface. Place one or both hands (depending on animal's size) over the lower chest directly behind the elbow. Press firmly and release at the rate of once every second (see the illustration, above). Caution: Excessive pressure can fracture ribs.

2. Give one dose of *Carbo vegetabilis 30c.* As soon as you can, place a few pellets on the tongue, then drop some water on the pellets to dissolve them in the mouth.

3. Administer Dr. Bach's *Rescue Formula.* Put two drops in the side of the mouth, repeating every 5 minutes until there is a response. Then give every 30 minutes (if no help is available) for four doses.

4. Apply artificial respiration if the heart does not start within a minute (see "Breathing Stopped," page 461).

5. Successful heart massage (and respiration) can be recognized by the return of normal pink color to the gums.

HEATSTROKE

(Animal found unconscious in hot car.) Follow these steps.

1. Remove the animal immediately to a cool, shady area. Use the car's shadow if necessary.

2. Wet the animal with water. Apply continuously to cool the body as much as possible. Place ice packs or cold, wet towels around the body and head during transport to the veterinarian.

3. Give one dose of *Belladonna 30c.*

4. If no improvement within 30 minutes, give one dose of *Glonoine 30c.*

5. Administer Dr. Bach's *Rescue Formula.* Put two drops in the mouth every 10 minutes until you arrive at the veterinarian's.

6. If breathing has stopped, follow instructions for "Breathing Stopped," page 461.

HEMORRHAGE

(bleeding from a wound or body opening) For *skin wounds,* use these treatments.

1. Give one dose *Arnica 30c.* Wait for 30 minutes. If bleeding has not stopped, give the next remedy.

2. Give one dose *Phosphorus 30c.*

3. Locally apply a *Calendula* lotion (six drops of *Calendula* tincture in 1 ounce of water).

4. If necessary, use the "Pressure Bandage Technique" (see below).

For *internal bleeding* (pale tongue, gums, and insides of eyelids, with weakness), use these treatments.

1. Give one dose *Arnica 30c* and repeat it every 30 minutes for three treatments.

2. Give *Phosphorus 30c* in three doses (as above), if Arnica is not sufficient.

3. Keep the animal calm. If hysteria is a problem, begin treatment by placing two drops of Dr. Bach's *Rescue Formula* in the mouth every 5 minutes for three treatments. Then follow with *Arnica 30c* as described in step 1.

Pressure Bandage Technique

(to control hemorrhage, excessive bleeding; to keep gauze and medication in place) Follow these steps.

1. Place dry or medicated gauze (*Calendula* ointment is a good choice) over the wound and wrap an overlapping elastic bandage around it. Apply only slight tension to the wrap because excessive pressure (especially on a leg) can cut off bloodflow like a tourniquet. If the wound is on the lower half of the leg, wrap all the way to and including the foot (to prevent swelling).

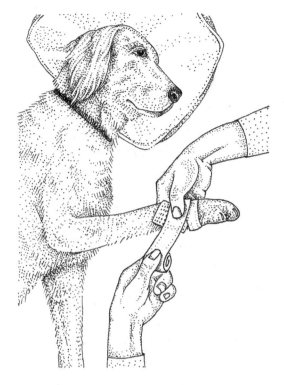

Local use: For bee, hornet, or wasp stings, apply a freshly sliced *onion*. Alternatively, rub in one drop of *ammonia water* (can be purchased for cleaning floors and windows—in a pinch, you can use ammonia detergent or an ammonia-based window cleaner).

An effective herbal treatment is to rub in a drop of nettle extract (*Urtica urens* tincture or *glycerine* extract) directly on the sting.

Hold a dull knife perpendicular to the skin and scrape across the area of the sting a few times. This will grab the stinger and pull it out without pain. Do not try to grab a stinger with your fingers or with tweezers, as it will squeeze more poison into the wound.

Internally, for all insect bites give *Ledum 30c*, a few pellets every 15 minutes for a total of three treatments.

POISONING

(Symptoms appear in three major forms: excess salivation, tears, and frequent urination and defecation; muscle twitching, trembling, and convulsions; severe vomiting.) Follow these steps.

1. Give granular *activated charcoal*. Mix 5 heaping teaspoons of granules in 1 cup of water. Depending on the animal's size, give about ¼ cup to 1 cup by spoonfuls in the cheek pouch. If this causes excess struggle or worsens symptoms, discontinue. Your veterinarian will be able to apply treatment under sedation or anesthesia.

2. Secure the end of the bandage with adhesive tape to prevent unwinding.

3. Remove the bandage at once if swelling occurs below the wrap (as on a leg). If you can reach the foot pads, periodically check that they remain warm; if they're cold, then the bandage is too tight. Remember, bandaging is a temporary measure; use it until bleeding stops or you can reach the veterinarian.

INSECT BITES

(bee, hornet, and wasp stings; centipede, scorpion, and spider bites; red, painful swellings)
Follow these steps.

2. Give *Nux vomica 30c*, a few pellets on the tongue every 15 minutes for a total of three doses. Do not continue treatment if the symptoms worsen.

3. Keep the animal warm and as quiet as possible. Stress has a very negative influence.

4. Call the ASPCA Animal Poison Control Center (APCC) if you know where the poison came from. Call 888-426-4435 (there may be a $65 credit card charge per case) for specific advice on treatment or antidotes. They are available 24 hours a day, 365 days a year.

Otherwise, bring the suspected poisons and container (if known), as well as any vomited material, to the doctor for possible identification of the poison.

PUNCTURES

(from teeth, claws, sharp objects)
Follow these steps.

1. Wash the wound with soap and water. Use a natural soap, not a strong detergent.

2. Extract any embedded hair you see in the hole.

3. Apply direct pressure over the wound with gauze only if bleeding is excessive (see "Pressure Bandage Technique," page 466). Moderate bleeding is appropriate to flush out the wound.

4. Give *Ledum 30c*, a few pellets every 2 hours, for three doses.

SHOCK

(accompanies serious injuries; symptoms are unconsciousness, white gums, rapid breathing)
Follow these steps.

- If much bruising or trauma is evident or internal hemorrhage is suspected, use *Arnica 30c*, one dose every 10 minutes until a response is seen. Then treat every 2 hours until the gums are once again pink and your pet seems to be normally alert.

- If the animal is unconscious, give *Aconitum 30c*, one dose every 10 minutes until consciousness returns. If there is no response within four doses, switch over to *Arnica 30c* and use the same schedule as you would for Aconitum.

- If the animal appears to be dying (cold, blue, lifeless), give *Carbo vegetabilis 30c*, one dose every 5 minutes for three treatments. If he rallies, follow with *Arnica 30c* as described in the first step of this section.

Note: Keep the animal warm with a blanket and placed in a horizontal position.

SUDDEN COLLAPSE

(sudden unconsciousness without warning; fainting)
Follow these steps.

1. First check to see if breathing or the heart has stopped. If so, use the treatment described under "Breathing

Stopped" (page 461) or "Breathing and Heart Both Stopped" (page 462).

2. Use Dr. Bach's *Rescue Formula*, two drops every 5 minutes until a response, and then every 30 minutes.

3. Give a warm *coffee enema* (for caffeine). Use ¼ cup for small dogs, ½ cup for medium dogs, and 1 cup for large dogs. Press gauze against the anus for 15 minutes to prevent the fluid from coming out.

4. Count out the heart rate for a minute, if possible, by listening to the lower left chest (near where left elbow touches the chest). This will be useful information for your veterinarian, as an abnormal heart rate (too fast or too slow) is a frequent cause of fainting.

If none of this has helped, give one dose of *Arsenicum album* and cross fingers.

SCHEDULE FOR HERBAL TREATMENT

General directions: Use freshly harvested and dried herbs if possible, preferably this year's crop. After a few years, herbs lose potency from exposure to air. Alcoholic extracts of herbs, called *tinctures,* are an especially useful form because they are more stable, maintaining potency for at least 2 years and sometimes longer. Available in 1-ounce dropper bottles, they are easily added to water for dilution. Gelatin capsules are also useful for preserving powdered herbs. They help the herbs stay fresh by excluding the oxygen, which degrades them.

SCHEDULE 1: INTERNAL

In this schedule, give the herbs three times a day until there are no more symptoms, or for a maximum of 7 days. The form of herb you use determines its preparation (see Chapter 18 for more information on herbs and on techniques for giving medications to pets). Here are the options.

(a) **Infusions.** Make an infusion by first bringing 1 cup of pure water (filtered or distilled) to a boil. Pour it over 1 rounded teaspoon of dried herb or 1 rounded tablespoon of fresh herb. Cover and steep for 15 minutes. Then extract the liquid by straining it through a cheesecloth or sieve.

Here's how much to give your pet three times a day (morning, midafternoon, and at night before bed): ½ teaspoon for cats or small dogs (less than 30 pounds); 1 teaspoon for medium dogs (30 to 60 pounds); or 1 tablespoon for large dogs (60 pounds and over).

(b) **Cold extracts.** Add 2 rounded teaspoons of dried herb or 2 rounded tablespoons of fresh herb to 1 cup of cold, pure water. Cover and let sit for 12 hours. Strain out the solids and administer the liquid extract three times a day, in the same quantities listed for infusions (a).

(c) **Decoctions.** In some cases the instructions specify that you should prepare a decoction, the method to prepare certain dried roots, rhizomes, and barks. To do so, add 1 rounded teaspoon of the herb to 1 cup of pure water. Bring to a boil and simmer uncovered for 15 to 20 minutes. Strain out the solids and administer the liquid three times a day, in the same quantities listed for infusions (a).

(d) **Tinctures.** If you have the tincture form of the herb (see Chapter 18 for preparation instructions, or purchase in natural food stores), dilute it, three drops to 1 teaspoon (nine drops to 1 tablespoon) of pure water. Administer this solution three times a day in the same quantities listed for infusions (a).

(e) **Gelatin capsules.** Herb capsules that are prepared for human consumption can also be given to animals, but in smaller doses. Small dogs and cats will get half of a capsule as a dose; medium dogs will get one as a dose; large dogs will receive two capsules each dose. Remember that one dose is given three times a day with this schedule.

SCHEDULE 2: INTERNAL

On this schedule, give the herbs twice a day, on approximately a 12-hour schedule. Use the same procedures and quantities as described in Schedule 1. Likewise, continue treating until symptoms are gone or a week has passed.

SCHEDULE 3: INTERNAL

With this program, you'll give the herbs only once a day (every 24 hours). Again, follow the same procedures and quantities outlined in Schedule 1, treating until the symptoms are gone, or for a maximum of 1 week.

SCHEDULE 4: EXTERNAL

This program calls for an herbal compress. First make a hot infusion, decoction, or tincture dilution of the herb (or herbs), as in Schedule 1. Let it cool a bit so that it's warm, but not so hot that it will burn or cause discomfort. If it feels good to you, then it's likely your pet will think so also. Next, immerse a washcloth or small hand towel in the solution, wring it out, and apply it to the affected area on your pet's body. Put a dry towel over this moist compress to keep the heat in. After 5 minutes, refresh the compress: Dip it back in the warm solution, wring it out again, and reapply.

If you can, treat for 15 minutes, though your pet may only allow you 5 minutes or so.

You can use this compress twice a day for up to 2 weeks.

SCHEDULE 5: EXTERNAL

Prepare a hot compress, as in Schedule 4, but alternate it a couple of times with a cold compress (a second cloth dipped in tap water). This method is more stimulating, encouraging a strong blood supply to the area. First use the hot herbal compress for 5 minutes, and then follow it with 2 minutes of the cold water compress. Repeat one more time, using the same sequence. The whole treatment lasts about 15 minutes. This

can be performed twice daily for a period of up to 2 weeks.

SCHEDULE 6: EXTERNAL

In this approach, you make a warm-to-hot infusion, decoction, or tincture dilution of the herb (or herbs), as in Schedule 1. When the temperature is acceptable, immerse your animal's foot, leg, or tail (the affected part) directly into the solution. If your pet will put up with it, soak the area for at least 5 minutes and then towel dry. Soak twice a day, as needed, for up to 2 weeks.

SCHEDULE FOR HOMEOPATHIC TREATMENT

General directions: Give the remedy by first dispensing one or two pellets into the vial cap or a clean spoon, or by crushing three of them in a small, folded paper. (Pellets come in different sizes; we are assuming the standard size, which is round pellets, about the size of the little metal beads on a pull chain. If the pellets are smaller, like poppy seeds, use more of them, about 10 or so.) The idea is for our patient to taste them and swallow at least one. Then pour them directly into your pet's mouth or throat—do not touch them yourself (see Chapter 18 for more detailed instructions and various methods that can be used).

Homeopathic remedies may not work as effectively if they are added to food. Each of the schedules below indicates how long you should withhold food before and after giving the remedy. However, I have had clients add remedies to a small amount of food to treat a difficult animal, like a wounded raccoon that comes by to steal the dog's food. You are not going to put the remedy into this patient's mouth! When we have done this, it seems as if it has worked all right, and we see good responses. Still, it's probably safer to avoid any possible interference with your animal companion and keep her away from the food for a bit.

Water is less of a problem, but it is a good practice to prevent your pet from drinking for 5 minutes before and after giving the medicine.

SCHEDULE 1: ACUTE DISEASE TREATMENT

Give one pellet or tablet every 4 hours until the symptoms are gone. Provide no food for 10 minutes before and after treatment.

If your animal shows signs of improvement, you can stop using the medicine. If there is a fever, however, then continue treatment until the temperature is below 101.5°F (38.6°C).

If you do not see improvement within 24 hours, however, you should try one of the other suggested remedies.

SCHEDULE 2: ACUTE DISEASE TREATMENT

Give one or two pellets every 4 hours for a total of three treatments. Provide no food for 10 minutes before and after treatment. No further homeopathic treatment will be needed for the next 24 hours. If your animal is not noticeably improved by then, try another remedy or go to one of the other treatment choices.

SCHEDULE 3: ACUTE DISEASE TREATMENT

In this method you give only one treatment. Provide no food for 30 minutes before and after treatment. If there is no improvement within 24 hours, then choose another remedy to use. If a definite improvement has occurred, then no further homeopathic treatment will be needed.

SCHEDULE 4: CHRONIC DISEASE TREATMENT

In this method you give only one treatment. Provide no food for 30 minutes before and after treatment. Wait for a full month before any further treatment; it would be a mistake to repeat the remedy in a few days. If at the end of that month no improvement is evident, then you will need to choose a new medicine.

SCHEDULE 5: CHRONIC DISEASE TREATMENT

Here you will give just three doses, 24 hours apart, and then wait for a month. For each of the three treatments, give two whole pellets or three pellets crushed to a powder. Place on the tongue. Provide no food for 30 minutes before and after each treatment. Do not give any further treatment for a month. If you have not seen any improvement by then, choose a new treatment.

SCHEDULE 6: CHRONIC DISEASE TREATMENT

Here you will repeat doses over a longer period. Depending on the recommended option, you will give a dose (a) once every day (b) twice a day—approximately every 12 hours, or (c) three times a day—morning, midday, and evening before bed. Provide no food for 5 minutes before and after giving the medicine.

The treatment period is usually a week or 10 days. If treatment has helped some but not enough, this can be an indication that either a better medicine should be used or there is something else slowing down the recovery. It is best to get advice from a holistic veterinarian at this point.

EVALUATING RESPONSE TO MEDICATION

Deciding whether a given treatment has helped so far is an important part of your overall success with homeopathic medicines. It determines your next move: whether to continue, stop, or try another treatment.

The first and best sign that a treatment is helping is that your animal appears to feel better overall, with improved energy, spirits, activity level, and moods. Secondarily, you will see specific improvements in his physical condition, though these will occur more slowly.

Another good sign, one that you could easily misinterpret, is that the body may produce a temporary discharge as part of the healing process. Depending on the illness, this may take the form of brief diarrhea (1 day), vomiting (once), or eruption and discharge from the skin. Or in the case of a viral infection, for instance, the body may produce a fever for a few days as it mobilizes its defenses. None of these reactions, however, should be severe or long-lasting. And, again, if the program is working, your animal will be feeling better in an overall sense.

Read the introduction to the Quick Reference Section for more detail on evaluating treatment.

Many health problems are complex and difficult to treat, and you will greatly benefit if you can work with a skilled homeopathic veterinarian. If you are in doubt or your animal is getting worse, it is best to consult such a veterinarian. You can find a list of veterinarians trained by Dr. Pitcairn in the use of homeopathy on the website for the veterinary homeopathy course, pivh.org.

ENDNOTES

CHAPTER 2

1   Ann Martin, *Protect Your Pet* (Troutdale, OR: NewSage Press, 2001), 11.

2   Donald Strombeck, *Home-Prepared Diets for Dogs and Cats* (Ames, IA: Iowa State Press, 2010), Appendix section on commercial pet food contamination. Dr. Strombeck, DVM, PhD, is professor emeritus, University of California, Davis, School of Veterinary Medicine.

3   Martin, *Protect Your Pet,* 21.

4   Ibid., 12.

5   Ibid., 22.

6   www.organic-center.org.

7   Marc Gunther, "I'm Sorry to Inform You That Your Pet is Bad for the Planet," blog post, July 31, 2015. http://www.marcgunther.com/im-sorry-to -inform-you-that-your-pet-is-bad-for-the-planet/. Gunther cites sources stating that the average cat eats about 30 pounds of fish a year, twice what Americans eat. So, if a 10-pound cat eats 30 pounds of seafood a year, that's 3 pounds per pound of cat. If a 150-pound person eats 15 pounds, that's $\frac{1}{10}$ pound of fish eaten per pound of person—thus, cats are actually eating more like 30 times the amount of seafood per pound of body weight as humans.

8   Poisoned Pets (website). http://poisonedpets. com/toxic-metals-found-in-pet-food/. Also see Mike Adams, "Pet Treats Found Contaminated with Heavy Metals," *Natural News,* April 21, 2014. http://www.naturalnews.com/.

9   Patrick Mahaney, DVM, "Pet Food: The Good, the Bad, and the Healthy," The Paw Print Blog.

http://www.petsafe.net/learn/pet-food-the-good -the-bad-and-the-healthy.

10   Martin, 41.

11   Ibid., 42.

12   FDA, "Subchapter E—Animal Drugs, Feeds, and Related Products; §582. 1666. Propylene Glycol," Code of Federal Regulations, 21 C.F.R. 582.1666.

13   Banfield Veterinary Hospital, *State of Pet Health™ 2015 Report.* www.banfield.com/state-of-pet-health.

14   According to Susan Wynn, DVM, in an interview by Sandy Eckstein, WebMD Pet Health Feature. http://pets.webmd.com/dogs/guide /caring-for-a-dog-that-has-food-allergies.

15   Joel Furhman, MD, *Eat to Live* (New York: Little, Brown and Co., 2011), describes various studies indicating that the vast majority of the major chronic diseases are preventable via healthy diet and weight, exercise, and not smoking.

CHAPTER 3

1   Bruce Ames, cited in "The Declining Nutrient Value of Food," *Mother Earth News,* January 23, 2012.

2   Ibid.

3   Virginia Worthington, "Nutritional Quality of Organic versus Conventional Fruits, Vegetables and Grains," *Journal of Alternative and Complementary Medicine* 7 (July 2004): 161–73.

4   "Organic Foods vs. Supermarket Foods: Element Levels," *Journal of Applied Nutrition* 45 (1993): 35–39. Cited in John Robbins, *The Food Revolution* (San Francisco: Conari Press, 2011), 370.

5   Joseph Mercola, "Analysis Identifies Shocking Problems with Monsanto's Genetically Engineered Corn." http://articles.mercola.com/sites/articles /archive/2013/04/30/monsanto-GM-corn.aspx, April 30, 2013.

6   Claire Robinson of GM Watch, United Kingdom, and author of *GM Myths and Truths*, in an interview with Jeffrey Smith in John Robbins's GMO MiniSummit, http://gmosummit.org /empowerment, 2015.

7   Michael Greger, "Why Do Vegan Women Have 5x Fewer Twins?" *Nutrition Facts* 22 (December 26, 2014). http://nutritionfacts.org/video/why-do -vegan-women-have-5x-fewer-twins/.

8   Brenda Davis, "Paleo Diet: Myths and Realities," YouTube talk, May 1, 2014: https://www .youtube.com/watch?v=QUXTzbjGakg.

9   Joel Fuhrman, *Eat to Live: The Amazing Nutrient-Rich Program for Fast and Sustained Weight Loss* (New York: Little, Brown and Company, 2011); T. Colin Campbell with Howard Jacobson, *Whole: Rethinking the Science of Nutrition* (Dallas: BenBella Books, 2013).

10   Ibid., 75.

11   Banfield Veterinary Hospital, *State of Pet Health™ 2015 Report*. www.banfield.com/state-of -pet-health.

12   Fuhrman, 75.

13   Garth Davis with Howard Jacobson, *Protein-aholic: How Our Obsession with Meat Is Killing Us and What We Can Do about It* (New York: Harper One, 2015).

14   Randall Fitzgerald, *The Hundred-Year Lie* (New York: Dutton/Penguin, 2006), 5.

15   US Centers for Disease Control and Prevention, "CDC's Third National Report on Human Exposure to Environmental Chemicals," July 2005. www.npr.org/documents/2005/jul/factsheet.pdf.

16   John McDougall, "Parkinson's Disease and Other Diet-Induced Tremors," *McDougall Newsletter*, November 2010. https://www.drmcdougall .com/misc/2010nl/nov/parkinsons.htm.

17   "Toxic Cats and Dogs," *New York Times*, April 18, 2008. http://well.blogs.nytimes.com/2008/04 /18/toxic-cats-and-dogs/?_r=1.

18   Mike Adams, "Pet Treats Found Contaminated with Heavy Metals," *Natural News*, April 21, 2014. http://www.naturalnews.com/044795_pet _treats_toxic_heavy_metals_Made_in_China.html.

19   "The Dirty Dozen," United Nations Industrial Development Organization. Retrieved March 27, 2014.

20   L. Ritter, K. R. Solomon, J. Forget, M. Stemer-off, and C. O'Leary, "Persistent Organic Pollutants: An Assessment Report on: DDT, Aldrin, Dieldrin, Endrin, Chlordane, Heptachlor, Hexachloroben-zene, Mirex, Toxaphene, Polychlorinated Biphenyls, Dioxins and Furans." Prepared for The International Programme on Chemical Safety (IPCS), within the framework of the Inter-Organization Programme for the Sound Management of Chemicals (IOMC). Retrieved on September 16, 2007.

21   John Robbins, *Diet for a New America*, from excerpts online at http://michaelbluejay.com /veg/books/dietamerica.html.

22   Robbins, *The Food Revolution*, Conari Press, 2011, 42, citing "FDA Launches Study on Dioxin Levels in Fish, Dairy Foods," *Food Chemical News*, February 27, 1995.

23   Michael Greger, "Dioxins in the Food Supply," *Nutrition Facts* 4 (November 26, 2010). http://nutritionfacts.org/video/dioxins-in-the -food-supply, citing several scientific studies.

24   "Analysis of Toxic Trace Metals in Pet Foods Using Cryogenic Grinding and Quantitation by ICP-MS," Part 1, *Spectroscopy* (January 2011). Cited at http://truthaboutpetfood.com/heavy-metal-pet -food-testing-paper-published/.

25   Deva Khalsa, *Animal Wellness Magazine*. http://animalwellnessmagazine.com /mercury-in-fish/.

26   Keeve E. Nachman et al., "Roxarsone, Inorganic Arsenic, and Other Arsenic Species in Chicken: A U.S.-Based Market Basket Sample," *Environmental Health Perspectives* 121 (July 2013). Available at http://dx.doi.org/10.1289/ehp.1206245.

27   Kushik Jaga and Chanddrabhan Dharmani, "Global Surveillance of DDT and DDE Levels in Human Tissues," *International Journal of Occupational Medicine and Environmental Health* 16 (1) (2003): 7–20. www.imp.lodz.pl/upload/oficyna /artykuly/pdf/full/jaga1-01-03.pdf.

28   Jeffrey Smith, director of the Institute for Responsible Technology, citing studies discovered via the Freedom of Information Act, bonus lecture with the DVD, *Genetic Roulette*.

29   Nancy Swanson et al., "Genetically Engineered Crops, Glyphosate and the Deterioration of Health in the United States of America," *Journal of Organic Systems* 9 (2) (2014). http://www.organic -systems.org/journal/92/JOS_Volume-9 _Number-2_Nov_2014-Swanson-et-al.pdf.

30   Joseph Mercola, "Monsanto Decimates Their Credibility." http://articles.mercola.com/sites /articles/archive/2013/09/10/monsanto-bt -corn.aspx, September 10, 2013.

31   Judy A. Carman et al., "A Long-Term Toxicology Study on Pigs Fed a Combined Genetically Modified (GM) Soy and GM Maize Diet," *Journal of Organic Systems* 8 (1) (2013).

32   Anthony Samsell and Stephanie Seneff, "Glyphosate, Pathways to Modern Diseases II: Celiac Sprue and Gluten Intolerance," *Interdisciplinary Toxicology* 6 (4) (December 2013): 159–84. http:// www.ncbi.nlm.nih.gov/pmc/articles /PMC3945755/.

33   Leah Zerbe, "The Crazy New Research on Roundup," *Rodale's Organic Life,* April 23, 2014: http://www.rodalesorganiclife.com/food /glyphosate-research.

34   http://www.nongmoproject.org/learn-more /gmos-and-your-family/.

35   Smith, Lecture on GMOs, Unity of Sedona, December 1, 2015.

CHAPTER 4

1   Statistics drawn from many sources online and also *Cowspiracy: The Sustainability Secret* (AUM Films, 2014) and the companion book by Keegan Kuhn and Kip Andersen, *The Sustainability Secret: Rethinking Our Diet to Transform the World* (San Rafael, CA: Earth Aware Editions, 2015).

2   Hal Herzog, *Some We Love, Some We Hate, Some We Eat* (New York: Harper Collins, 2010), 6.

3   Our calculations are based on "Crop Yields and Calorie Density," *Mother Earth News.* news.com, http://www.motherearthnews.com/organic -gardening/garden-planning/~/media /295A54F778854C39B455F7B7DB4F4C82.ashx. Information on grain-fed versus grass-fed beef yields and calories from quick Google searches and USDA figures on ground beef, using fattiest choices.

4   United Nations General Assembly Session 60, Resolution 191. International Year of the Potato, 2008 A/RES/60/191, page 1. December 22, 2005.

5   Kuhn and Andersen, *The Sustainability Secret.*

6   Michael Pollan interview in *Cowspiracy.*

7   Oliver Milman and Stuart Leavenworth, "China's Plan to Cut Meat Consumption by 50% Cheered by Climate Campaigners," *The Guardian,* June 20, 2016. https://www.theguardian.com /world/2016/jun/20/chinas-meat-consumption -climate-change.

8   Johnny Braz, *Saving Mookie (and Penny!),* Indraloka Animal Sanctuary, YouTube, https://www.youtube.com/watch?v=Fb0-iZ1XgkY.

9   Gail Eisnitz, *Slaughterhouse: The Shocking Story of Greed, Neglect, and Inhumane Treatment inside the U.S. Meat Industry* (Amherst, NY: Prometheus, 2006). Excerpts available online.

CHAPTER 5

1   Anne Heritage, *Bramble: The Dog Who Wanted to Live Forever: The Somerset Notes* (CreateSpace Independent Publishing, April 24, 2013). Also see Wikipedia, "List of oldest dogs."

2   Dan Buettner, *The Blue Zones: Lessons for Living Longer from the People Who've Lived the Longest* (Washington, DC: National Geographic, 2008).

3   Erik Axelsson, Abhirami Ratnakumar, et al., "The Genomic Signature of Dog Domestication Reveals Adaptation to a Starch-Rich Diet," *Nature* 495 (March 21, 2013), 360–64.

4   Debra L. Zoran, "The Carnivore Connection to Nutrition in Cats," Vet Med Today: Timely Topics in Nutrition, *Journal of the American Veterinary Medical Association* 221, no. 11 (December 1, 2002).

5   "Nutrient Requirements of Domestic Animals: Nutrient Requirements of Cats," revised edition, 1986, Subcommittee on Cat Nutrition. Committee on Animal Nutrition. Board on Agriculture, National Research Council (Washington, DC: National Academy Press, 1986).

6   Dottie P. Laflamme, "Cats and Carbohydrates: Implications for Health and Disease," Nestlé Purina PetCare Company, Floyd, Virginia, Vetlearn.com, January 2010. Compendium: Continuing Education for Veterinarians.

7   Lorie Huston, "What Is Grain-Free Pet Food, Really?" http://www.petmd.com/dog/centers /nutrition/evr_multi_what_is_grain_free_pet _food_really.

8   Donna Solomon, "Grain-Free Pet Food Trend a Hoax?" http://www.huffingtonpost.com /donna-solomon-dvm/grainfree-pet-food -trend-_b_5429538.html.

CHAPTER 9

1   Lorelei Wakefield, "Vegetarian Diets for Companion Animals," April 7, 2015, http://responsible eatingandliving.com/lorelei-wakefield/.

2   Judy Hoy, Nancy Swanson, and Stephanie Seneff, "The High Cost of Pesticides: Human and Animal Diseases," *Poultry, Fisheries and Wildlife Sciences* 3(1), 2015, http://dx.doi.org/10.4172/2375 -446X.1000132.

CHAPTER 10

1   Ben Leer, "Why Isn't Asbestos Banned in the United States?," September 2013. http://www .asbestos.com/blog/2012/09/17/why-isnt -asbestos-banned-in-the-united-states/.

2   EPA402/K-10/005 |March2013|www.epa.gov /radon. A downloadable PDF with excellent information on constructing or remodeling your home to minimize this problem.

3   Barbara K. Chang, Andrew T. Huang, William T. Joines, and Richard S. Kramer, "The Effect of Microwave Radiation (1.0 GHz) on the Blood-Brain Barrier in Dogs," *Radio Science* 17 (5S), published online December 2012.

CHAPTER 11

1   Dan Buettner, *The Blue Zones: Lessons for Living Longer from the People Who've Lived the Longest* (Washington, DC: National Geographic, 2008), 233.

2   Anne Heritage, *Bramble: The Dog Who Wanted to Live Forever: The Somerset Notes*, November 20, 2012.

3   CNN, "100-Year-Old Shares Secrets to a Long Life," http://www.cnn.com/videos/health/2015 /04/08/exp-human-factor-dr-ellsworth-wareham .cnn.

4   Anitra Frazier with Norma Eckroate, *The New Natural Cat,* revised, updated edition (New York: Plume, 2008).

CHAPTER 12

1   Oliver Sacks, *The Man Who Mistook His Wife for a Hat* (New York: Harper and Row, 1985), 156–58.

2 Eckhart Tolle, *The Power of Now* (Novato, CA: New World Library, 1999).

3 Anitra Frazier, with Norma Eckroate, *The New Natural Cat* (New York: Penguin, 2008).

4 Lidia García-Agudo, Pedro García-Martos, and Manuel Rodríguez-Iglesias, "Dipylidium caninum Infection in an Infant: A Rare Case Report and Literature Review," *Asian Pacific Journal of Tropical Biomedicine* 4 (July 2014).

5 Centers for Disease Control, "Human Rabies." http://www.cdc.gov/rabies/location/usa/surveillance/index.html.

CHAPTER 14

1 "Airline Pet Policies," http://www.pettravel.com/airline_rules.cfm.

CHAPTER 16

1 Ruth Downing, "We Thought We Were Protecting Him," *Dogs Monthly,* November 2013, 18–20. www.dogsmonthly.co.uk.

2 Purdue University, "Effects of Vaccination on the Endocrine and Immune Systems of Dogs, Phase II," November 1,1999, http://www.homestead.com/vonhapsburg/.

3 Michael R. Lappin, Randall J. Basaraba, and Wayne A. Jensen, "Interstitial Nephritis in Cats Inoculated with Crandell Rees Feline Kidney Cell Lysates," *Journal of Feline Medicine and Surgery* 8 (2006), 353–56.

4 Michael E. Horwin, "Simian Virus 40 (SV40): A Cancer Causing Monkey Virus from FDA-Approved Vaccines," *Albany Law Journal of Science & Technology* 13 (3) (2003): 721.

5 Horace B. F. Jervis, "Treatment of Canine Distemper with the Potentized Virus," *Journal of the American Veterinary Medical Association* LXXV (1929): 778.

6 Will Falconer, "Prevent Parvo and Distemper without Vaccination," March 17, 2014, http://vitalanimal.com/prevent-parvo-distemper/.

CHAPTER 18

1 I have had reports from some readers that they have difficulty obtaining nutritional yeast, so if that is your experience you can use brewer's yeast instead. It is still available.

QUICK REFERENCE SECTION

1 J. M. Kruger, J. P. Lulich, J. Merrills, et al., "Comparison of Foods with Differing Nutritional Profiles for Long-Term Management of Acute Nonobstructive Idiopathic Cystitis in Cats." *Journal of the American Veterinary Medical Association* 247(5) (2015): 508–17.

2 Joel Fuhrman, *Eat to Live* (New York: Little, Brown and Company, 2011), 121–22.

3 Rodney Habib, "Turmeric for Dogs," *Dogs Naturally* magazine, http://www.dogsnaturallymagazine.com/turmeric-dogs/.

4 Debra L. Zoran, "The Carnivore Connection to Nutrition in Cats," *Journal of the American Veterinary Medical Association* 221(11) (December 1, 2002).

5 Duk-Hee Lee, In-Kyu Lee, et al., "A Strong Dose-Response Relation between Serum Concentrations of Persistent Organic Pollutants and Diabetes," Results from the National Health and Examination Survey 1999–2002, *Diabetes Care* 29 (2006): 1638–44.

6 Shu-Li Wang, Pei-Chien Tsal, et al., "Increased Risk of Diabetes and Polychlorinated Biphenyls and Dioxins," A 24-Year Follow-up Study of the Yucheng Cohort, *Diabetes Care* 31 (2008): 1574–79.

7 Dottie P. Laflamme, "Cats and Carbohydrates: Implications for Health and Disease," Vetlearn.com, January 2010, Compendium: Continuing Education for Veterinarians.

8   Zoran, "The Carnivore Connection to Nutrition in Cats."

9   N. Tsuboyama-Kasaoka, C. Shozawa, K. Sano, et al., "Taurine (2-Aminoethanesulfonic Acid) Deficiency Creates a Vicious Circle Promoting Obesity," *Endocrinology* 147(7) (July 2006): 3276–84.

10   Michael R. Lappin, Randall J. Basaraba, and Wayne A. Jensen, "Interstitial Nephritis in Cats Inoculated with Crandell Rees Feline Kidney Cell Lysates," *Journal of Feline Medicine and Surgery* 8 (2006): 353–56.

11   S. Banic, "Prevention of Rabies by Vitamin C," *Nature Journal* (November 13, 1975): 53.

FURTHER READING

Jan Allegretti, DVetHom, *The Complete Holistic Dog Book: Home Health Care for Our Canine Companions* (2nd ed. in process, 2017).

Don Hamilton, DVM, *Homeopathic Care for Cats and Dogs: Small Doses for Small Animals* (Berkeley, CA: North Atlantic Books, rev. ed., 2010).

Wendy Jensen, DVM, *Practical Handbook of Veterinary Homeopathy* (Castroville, TX: Black Rose Writing, 2015).

Ann N. Martin, *Food Pets Die For* (Troutdale, OR: New Sage Press, 1997).

Allen Schoen, DVM, *Kindred Spirits: How the Remarkable Bond Between Humans and Animals Can Change the Way We Live* (New York: Broadway Books, 2002).

VIDEOS TO WATCH

Conspiracy: The Sustainability Secret (AUM Films, 2014).

"vshvideo" on YouTube, dozens of expert lectures on plant based nutrition and related eco and humane issues.

Food Inc. (Dogwoof Pictures et.al, 2009).

INDEX

Glaucoma, 155

Glonoine 30c, use for
emergencies, 461
heatstroke, 466

Glucosamine, for arthritis, 334

Glutamic acid, 131

Glutamine, 327

Gluten, 37, 70–71, 73, <u>75</u>

Glycerine extract, for insect
bites, 467

Glyphosate, 22, 35–38

GMOs, 17, 27–28, 34–39
avoiding, <u>76</u>, <u>80</u>, 144
facts about, <u>39</u>
GI problems, 145, 367
glyphosate and, 22, 35–37
GM-free diet, 38–39, <u>40</u>, 41,
63, <u>64</u>, 70
nutrient reduction and, 21–22
shopping guide, 370

Goldenseal (*Hydrastis
canadensis*), use for
acute gastritis, 435
breast tumors, 347
cancer, 351
chronic gastritis, 436
entropion, 379
eye care, 307
feline viral rhinotracheitis, 449
periodontal disease, 362
ringworm, 425

Grains
author recommendations, <u>76</u>
as enemy in diet, 57
feeding to animals in
feedlots, 23
how to cook, 128, <u>128–29</u>
pets' adaptation to eating,
66–67
rancid or moldy in pet food, 13
whole grains, 13, 67, <u>76</u>, 84,
145

Grapes, avoiding, <u>80</u>

Graphites, use for
ear problems, 372
gastric dilation, 440
skin problems, 428, 429

Green tea, for ear problems,
308, 371

Grief, 242–43

Grooming, 184–86, 188–89

Growth hormone
residues in food, 14, 22
use for fast growth, 22

Guard hair, 151, 156

Gunshot wounds, 465

Gut biome, 68, 131–32

H

Hair abnormalities, congenital,
156

Hairballs, 156

Hair loss, 187, 389, 430

Harness, 233

Hazardous waste, 168–69

Healing
discharges, 320–21
signs of progress, 318–20
time needed for, 316–17
what to expect, 316–18

Healing crisis, 130, 134–35

Health certificate, 236

Healthy lives, Blue Zones tips
for, <u>176–77</u>

Heart problems, 389–91

Heart stopped, treatment for,
462–63, 465–66

Heartworm nosode, 393

Heartworms, 391–94

Heat prostration, 233

Heavy metals, 32–34
health effects, 32–34
in pet food, 14, 29, 32
sources of, 27

Hemp hearts
in diet, <u>64</u>, <u>77</u>, 127, 148, 340
protein and fat content, <u>72</u>
in recipes, 89, 92, 97–99, 107,
111, 122
storage, 246

HEPA filter, 165

Hepar sulphuris calcareum 30c,
use for
abscesses, 323
ear problems, 372
gastric dilation, 439–40

Herbal flea collars, 190

Herbal flea powders, 189–90

Herbal medicine, 283–85

Herbal treatment, 308–9. *See
also specific ailments;
specific herbs*
difficulties with, 284
pharmaceutical derivatives
compared, 283–84
preparing treatments, 309–11
cold extracts, 310–11
dried herbs, 310
fresh herbs, 309–10
infusions, 310–11
tinctures, 310
schedules, 470–72
Schedule 1: internal,
470–71
Schedule 2: internal, 471
Schedule 3: internal, 471
Schedule 4: external,
471–72
Schedule 5: external, 472
Schedule 6: external, 472
switching diets, 135, <u>136</u>

Herbicides, 22, 27, 35–38, 166,
326

Herbivorous animals, in food
chain, 30–31

Hering's Law of Cure, 318–19

Hernia
examining for, 159
inguinal, 155
umbilical, 155, 157

Hip dysplasia, 159, 271, 333,
394–96, 440, 452

Holistic therapies, 269–98
acupuncture, 287–88
allopathic medicine
compared, 276–77
Chinese medicine, 287–88
flower essences, 288–90
herbal medicine, 283–85
homeopathy, 290–98
manipulative therapies,
285–86
meaning of symptoms,
279–81
naturopathy, 282–83

I

Sepia 30c, use for
    care of newborn, 414
    hair loss, 431
    pyometra, 417
Shampoo, 185
Shavegrass (*Equisetum*), for
    bladder problems, 344
Shepherd's purse (*Thlaspi bursa pastoris* or *Capsella*), for
    bladder problems, 345
Shock, 468
Shock collar, 199, 201
Shoulder joint degeneration, 333
Sick animal, caring for, 299–314
Silicea, use for
    abscesses, 323–24
    anal gland problems, 329
    bladder problems, 346
    breast tumors, 347
    cancer, 351
    chorea, 354
    constipation, 356
    ear problems, 371
    entropion, 379
    feline viral rhinotracheitis, 448
    foxtails, 388–89
    gastric dilation, 440
    skin problems, 429–30
    warts, 451
Sitter, 231–32
Sizes of dogs, guide for, 321
Skin care, 184–86
Skin parasites, 419–25
    demodectic mange, 422–24
    fleas, 184–91, 214, 330–31, 420–12
    lice, 421–22
    sarcoptic mange, 215–16, 424
    ticks, 419–20
Skin problems, 425–31. *See also* Skin parasites
    cancer, 158–59
    causes, 426
    diet for, 144, 146–47
    with flea-control products, 187

ringworm, 215, 424–25
    treatment, 426–31
        for chronic condition, 428–30
        for hair loss, 430–31
        obstacle to, 427
        for sudden condition, 427–28
Skullcap (*Scutellaria lateriflora*), for behavior problems, 336
Slaughterhouses, 11–14, 16, 20, 29, 51–52, 129
Sleep, 182–83
Slippery elm, use for
    chronic gastritis, 436–37
    diarrhea, 368
Smart meters, wireless, 169, 172
Smell, sense of, 195–97, 224
Snacks, 80, 85
Sociability, of cats, 205
Sodium, 146
Sodium ascorbate. *See* Vitamin C
Soil
    loss, 45
    sterile *versus* living, 21
Soy, 17, 22, 39, 70, 73
Spaying, 206–8, 218, 431–33
Species loss, 44
Spina bifida, 156
Spinach, 80
Spondylitis, 409–10
Sponges, 274–75
Spongia tosta 6c, use for
    heart problems, 391
    pancreatitis, 408
Standard American Diet (SAD), 5
Staphysagria 30c, for bladder problems, 342, 346
Star of Bethlehem, 289, 337
Starvation, 45
Stomach problems, 433–40
    acute gastritis, 433–36
    chronic gastritis, 436–37
    gastric dilation, 437–40
Strabismus, 156
Stramonium, for behavior problems, 295, 338

Stress
    after declawing, 210
    in agricultural animals, 51
    of cortisone on immune system, 187
    emotional, 271, 275, 436
    in home environment, 173–74, 222, 224, 237
    lowering, 40, 83, 137, 181, 289–90
    on puppies and kittens, 69
    spraying cats and, 208
    travel- or move-associated, 230–32, 236, 239
Strophanthus hispidus 3c, for heart problems, 391
Subluxation, 285
Submembrane suction, 165
Submissive behavior, 159
Sudden collapse, 468–69
Sugary snacks, avoiding, 80
Sulfur, 147
Sulphur 6c, use for
    constipation, 356
    demodectic mange, 423
    ringworm, 425
    skin problems, 429
Sulphur 30c, use for
    abscesses, 324
    allergies, 328
    anal gland problems, 329
    appetite problems in cats, 332
    feline immunodeficiency virus, 381–82
    feline viral rhinotracheitis, 449
    fleas, 421
    heartworm, 394
    lice, 422
    rabies, 415
Supplements. *See also specific supplements*
    author recommendations, 77, 82–85
    flea-repelling, 190–91
    vegan diet, 63, 65, 74, 84–85
Surgery, 317